Frommer's®

Costa Rica

Here's what the critics say about Frommer's:

"Pay attention to these recommendations; this has not been prepared by someone who whirled through the country in three weeks, but by a resident who knows these locations inside-out. It's the one I'll keep around the house to give visitors. I'll just hand them this book and point them in the right direction."

—*Tico Times, San José, Costa Rica*

♦

"Amazingly easy to use. Very portable, very complete."

—*Booklist*

♦

"The only mainstream guide to list specific prices. The Walter Cronkite of guidebooks—with all that implies"

—*Travel & Leisure*

♦

"Complete, concise, and filled wih useful information."

—*New York Daily News*

♦

"Hotel information is close to encyclopedic."

—*Des Moines Sunday Register*

Frommer's® 99

Costa Rica

by Eliot Greenspan

MACMILLAN • USA

About the Author

Eliot Greenspan is a poet, journalist, and travel writer who took his backpack and typewriter the length of Mesoamerica before settling in Costa Rica in 1992. Since then he has worked for the *Tico Times, La Nación* and other media, while continuing his travels in the region. He is also the author of *Frommer's Costa Rica and Belize from $35 a Day.*

MACMILLAN TRAVEL

A Simon & Schuster Macmillan Company
1633 Broadway
New York, NY 10019

Find us online at **www.frommers.com.**

ISBN 0-02862274-X
ISSN 1077-890X

Editor: Vanessa Rosen
Production Editor: Mark Enochs
Design by Michele Laseau
Digital Cartography by Ortelius Design
Page Creation by Troy Barnes, John Bitter, Jerry Cole, Toi Davis, David Faust, Deb Kincaid, and Angel Perez

SPECIAL SALES

Bulk purchases (10+ copies) of Frommer's and selected Macmillan travel guides are available to corporations, organizations, mail-order catalogs, institutions, and charities at special discounts, and can be customized to suit individual needs. For more information write to Special Sales, Macmillan General Reference, 1633 Broadway, New York, NY 10019.

Acknowledgments

Once again, I'd like to thank Anne Becher and Joe Richey, for helping Frommer's find me. Big thanks this year to Ana Domb, who helped out on the phone and on the road. And finally, I'd like to thank my parents, Marilyn and Warren Greenspan, who showed unwavering love, support, and encouragement (well, one out of three ain't bad) as I pursued words and world wandering over a more stable and lucrative career.

Contents

List of Maps viii

1 The Best of Costa Rica 1

1 The Best of Natural Costa Rica 2
2 The Best Beaches 3
3 The Best Active Vacations 4
4 The Best Day Hikes & Nature Walks 5
5 The Best Bird Watching 7
6 The Best Family Vacation Experiences 8
7 The Best Views 8
8 The Best Drives 9
9 The Most Scenic Towns & Villages 10
10 The Best Places to Shop 11
11 The Best Luxury Hotels & Resorts 11
12 The Best Moderately Priced Hotels 12
13 The Best Ecolodges & Wilderness Resorts 13
14 The Best Bed-and-Breakfasts & Small Inns 14
15 The Best Restaurants 15
16 The Best After-Dark Fun 16

2 Getting to Know Costa Rica 17

1 The Natural Environment 18
2 The Regions in Brief 20
3 Costa Rica Today 22
4 History 101 24
★ Dateline 24
5 Gallo Pinto, Ceviche & Frescos: Costa Rican Food & Drink 27
6 Recommended Books 29

3 Planning a Trip to Costa Rica 31

1 Preparing for Your Trip 31
★ The Colón, the U.S. Dollar & the British Pound 33
★ What Things Cost in San José 34
2 When to Go 38
★ Costa Rica Calendar of Events 40
3 Tips for Travelers with Special Needs 41
4 Getting There 43
5 Getting Around 46
★ Suggested Itineraries 49
6 Tips on Accommodations 49
7 Tips on Dining 51
8 Tips on Shopping 52
★ Fast Facts: Costa Rica 53

4 The Active Vacation Planner 57

1 Organized Adventure Trips 58
2 Activities A to Z 60
★ Where to See the Resplendent Quetzal 61
★ T'ai Chi in Paradise 67
3 Costa Rica's National Parks & Bioreserves 69
★ Monkey Business 74
4 Tips on Health, Safety & Etiquette in the Wilderness 76
5 Ecologically Oriented Volunteer & Study Programs 76

5 San José 78

1 Orientation 79
★ "I know there's got to be a number here somewhere . . .": The Arcane Art of Finding an Address in San José 83
★ Neighborhoods in Brief 83
2 Getting Around 84
★ Fast Facts: San José 86
3 Accommodations 89
★ Family-Friendly Hotels 96
4 Dining 105
★ Only in the Central Valley: Dining Under the Stars on a Mountain's Edge 109
5 Seeing the Sights 113
★ Suggested Itineraries 113
★ Walking Tour—Downtown San José 118
6 Outdoor Activities 120
7 Spectator Sports 121
8 Shopping 122
9 San José After Dark 126
10 Side Trips from San José 131

6 Guanacaste & the Nicoya Peninsula 140

1 Liberia 142
2 La Cruz 148
3 Playa Hermosa & Playa Panamá 150
4 Playa del Coco & Playa Ocotal 154
5 Playas Flamingo, Potrero, Brasilito & Conchal 158
6 Playa Tamarindo & Playa Grande 164
7 Playa Junquillal 174
8 Playa Sámara 177
9 Playa Nosara 181
10 Playa Tambor 184
11 Playa Montezuma 188
12 Malpais & Santa Teresa 194

7 The Northern Zone 196

1 Puerto Viejo de Sarapiquí 196
2 Arenal Volcano & La Fortuna 202
★ Taking a Soothing Soak in Tabacón Hot Springs 204
3 Tilarán & Lake Arenal 211
4 Monteverde 215

8 The Central Pacific Coast 227

1 Puntarenas 227
2 Playa de Jacó 233
3 Manuel Antonio National Park 244
4 Dominical 261
5 San Isidro de El General: A Base for Exploring Chirripó National Park 267

9 The Southern Zone 273

1 Drake Bay 273
★ Those Mysterious Stone Spheres 277
2 Puerto Jiménez: Gateway to Corcovado National Park 281
★ Trail Distances in Corcovado National Park 283
3 Golfito: A Place for Sportfishing & Touring Botanical Gardens 288
4 Playa Zancudo 293
5 Playa Pavones: A Surfer's Mecca 296

10 The Caribbean Coast 298

1 Barra del Colorado 300
2 Tortuguero National Park 303
3 Limón: Gateway to Tortuguero National Park & Southern Coastal Beaches 308
4 Cahuita 311
5 Puerto Viejo 318

Appendix 329

A Basic Spanish Phrases & Vocabulary 329
B Some Typically Tico Words & Phrases 330
C Menu Terms 330

Index 333

List of Maps

Regions in Brief 21
Costa Rica's National Parks & Bioreserves 70
San José 80
Walking Tour—San José 119
The Central Valley: Side Trips from San José 133
Guanacaste & The Nicoya Peninsula 141
The Northern Zone 197
Monteverde 217
The Central Pacific Coast 235
Manuel Antonio 246
The Southern Zone 275
The Caribbean Coast 299

An Invitation to the Reader

In researching this book, we discovered many wonderful places—hotels, restaurants, shops, and more. We're sure you'll find others. Please tell us about them, so we can share the information with your fellow travelers in upcoming editions. If you were disappointed with a recommendation, we'd love to know that, too. Please write to:

Frommer's Costa Rica '99
Macmillan Travel
1633 Broadway
New York, NY 10019

An Additional Note

Please be advised that travel information is subject to change at any time—and this is especially true of prices. We therefore suggest that you write or call ahead for confirmation when making your travel plans. The authors, editors, and publisher cannot be held responsible for the experiences of readers while traveling. Your safety is important to us, however, so we encourage you to stay alert and be aware of your surroundings. Keep a close eye on cameras, purses, and wallets, all favorite targets of thieves and pickpockets.

What the Symbols Mean

✪ Frommer's Favorites

Hotels, restaurants, attractions, and entertainment you should not miss.

The following abbreviations are used for credit cards:

- AE American Express
- DC Diners Club
- DISC Discover
- MC MasterCard
- V Visa

Find Frommer's Online

Arthur Frommer's Outspoken Encyclopedia of Travel (www.frommers.com) offers more than 6,000 pages of up-to-the-minute travel information—including the latest bargains and candid, personal articles updated daily by Arthur Frommer himself. No other Web site offers such comprehensive and timely coverage of the world of travel.

1

The Best of Costa Rica

For years, Costa Rica was the well-kept secret of a few biologists, backpackers, and beachcombers, but that's all changed. Today, the country is a major international holiday destination. The transformation happened somewhat gradually over the last 10 to 15 years, with a conspicuous boom in the early 1990s. This leveled off somewhat, but a more moderate second boom is taking place right now.

Despite this newfound popularity, Costa Rica remains a place rich in natural wonders and biodiversity but relatively poor in infrastructure and luxurious beach resorts and hotels. Nature enthusiasts still make up the majority of visitors, but snowbirds seeking a change of scenery for their annual winter escape, tour groups and charters riding around in huge air-conditioned buses, and independent adventure travelers toting fancy mountain bikes, a wide array of surfboards and, sometimes, even their own kayaks and paddles are slowly sneaking up on them. Still, Costa Rica is a great gateway to Central America and a good choice, when the Caribbean and Mexico have become old hat. Here, you can still find unsullied beaches that stretch on for miles, small lodgings that haven't attracted hordes of tourists, jungle rivers for rafting and kayaking, and spectacular cloud and rain forests with ample opportunities for bird watching and hiking.

This is my third year putting this book together, and the "best of" experiences keep racking up. Some of my personal highlights included watching the sun rise on the first day of a new year from the top of the Irazú Volcano, camping alone on a deserted beach in Guanacaste, battling a feisty snook in the Golfo Dulce, soaking in some newly discovered hot springs set alongside a jungle river as a sun bittern majestically stalked its dinner, conducting a half-hour-long photo session with a remarkably calm eyelash viper, swooping from treetop platform to treetop platform on a canopy tour, and finally learning how to surf. You might not immediately recognize an eyelash viper, a snook, or a sun bittern. Read on, and I'll show you where to find my favorite things in Costa Rica, as well as how to discover one-on-one what these species are.

The list below should point you toward some personal bests of your own. I've selected the very best of what this unique country has to offer—the places and experiences you won't want to miss. Most are covered in greater detail elsewhere in the book; this chapter is merely meant to give you an overview of the highlights so you can start planning your own adventure.

1 The Best of Natural Costa Rica

- **Rincón de la Vieja National Park** (northeast of Liberia, in Guanacaste): This is an area of rugged beauty and high volcanic activity. The Rincón de la Vieja Volcano rises to 6,159 feet, but the thermal activity is spread out along its flanks where numerous geysers, vents, and fumaroles let off its heat and steam. This is a great place to hire a guide and a horse for a day of rugged exploration. There are waterfalls, hot springs, mud baths, and cool jungle swimming holes. You'll pass through pastureland, scrub savannah, and moist secondary forest, and the bird watching is excellent. See chapter 6.
- **Arenal Volcano/Tabacón Hot Springs** (near La Fortuna, northwest of San José): When the skies are clear and the lava is flowing, **Arenal Volcano** provides a thrilling light show accompanied by an earthshaking rumble that defies description. All this can be more than a bit exciting, which is why it's nice to have a natural hot spring to soak in immediately afterward. To really get that one-two punch working, you can sit in the large pool at the **Tabacón Hot Springs Resort** (☎ **506/256-1500**) and watch the fireworks at the same time. See chapter 7.
- **The Rio Sarapiquí Region** (north of San José between Guanacaste in the west and the Caribbean coast in the east): This is perhaps the best place for an ecolodge experience. You'll be able to visit a plethora of life zones and ecosystems as protected tropical forests climb from the Caribbean coastal lowlands up into the central mountain range. **Braulio Carrillo National Park** borders several other private reserves here, and there are several ecolodges in a range of price categories from which to choose. See chapter 7.
- **Monteverde Cloud Forest Reserve Preserve** (in the mountains northwest of San José): Sure, the golden toad has disappeared and it's getting harder to spot quetzals here, but this is still a prime patch of virgin cloud forest. There's something both eerie and majestic about walking around in the early morning mist with the sound of bird calls all around and the towering trees hung heavy in broad bromeliads, flowering orchids, and hanging moss and vines. The preserve itself has a well-maintained network of trails, and the community is truly involved in conservation. Not only that, but in and around Monteverde and Santa Elena you'll find a whole slew of related activities and attractions. See chapter 7.
- **Manuel Antonio** (near Quepos on the central Pacific coast): There's a reason this place is so popular and renowned. The road leading into Manuel Antonio provides numerous lookouts that consistently produce postcard-perfect snapshots—even with a throwaway Instamatic. Steep jungle hills meet the sea. Uninhabited islands lie just off the coast. The beaches here are perfect crescents of white sand, and the national park is home to abundant tropical flora and fauna. You'll definitely be sharing it with other visitors, but there's enough beauty here to go around. See chapter 8.
- **Osa Peninsula** (in southern Costa Rica): This is Costa Rica's most remote and biologically rich region. Much of the Osa Peninsula is taken up with Corcovado National Park, the largest remaining patch of virgin lowland tropical rain forest in Central America. Jaguars, crocodiles, and scarlet macaws all call this place home. Whether you stay in a luxury nature lodge in Drake Bay or outside of Puerto Jiménez, or camp in the park itself, you will be surrounded by some of the lushest and most intense jungle this country has to offer. See chapter 9.

- **Tortuguero Village and Jungle Canals** (on the Caribbean coast, north of Limón): Tortuguero Village is a small collection of rustic wood shacks on a narrow spit of land between the Caribbean Sea and a dense maze of jungle canals. It's been called Costa Rica's Venice, but it actually has more in common with the South American Amazon. You can fly into the small airstrip, but it's better to take one of the slow boats that ply the river and canal route. On the way you'll see a wide variety of herons and other waterbirds, three types of monkeys, three-toed sloths, and huge American crocodiles. If you come between June and October, you may be treated to the awe-inspiring spectacle of a green turtle nesting—the small stretch of Tortuguero beach is the last major remaining nesting site of this endangered animal. See chapter 10.

2 The Best Beaches

With more than 750 combined miles of shoreline on its Pacific and Caribbean coasts, Costa Rica offers beachgoers an embarrassment of riches. Whether you want a broad stretch of sand all your own, a lively beach town with all-night discos, or just a quiet place to hunt leisurely for shells, there's a beach here just for you.

- **Playa Conchal:** Located smack-dab in the center of Guanacaste's Gold Coast and about 5 hours from San José, Playa Conchal is a short section of beach made entirely of small polished and crushed shells. It isn't that great for swimming, but it's a beachcomber's delight. You should have no problem filling your pockets (and a few plastic bags) with a wide range of colorful shells and fragments. Better bathing beaches are just a short walk away in either direction. The recent opening of the 310-room Meliá Conchal resort hasn't killed the charm of this once-quiet beach. So far the hotel guests seem to prefer its massive pool. See chapter 6.
- **Playa Montezuma:** This tiny beach town at the tip of the Nicoya Peninsula has weathered fame and infamy and yet retains a funky sense of individuality. European backpackers, vegetarian yoga enthusiasts, and UFO seekers choose Montezuma's beach over any other in Costa Rica. The waterfalls are what set it apart from the competition, but the beach stretches for miles, with plenty of isolated spots to plop down your towel or mat. Nearby are the Cabo Blanco and Curu Wildlife preserves. See chapter 6.
- **Playa Tamarindo:** While not overdeveloped, Tamarindo provides ample lodgings to suit every budget and excellent restaurants at almost every turn. The beach here is long and broad, with sections calm enough for swimmers and others just right for surfers. Located about midway along the beaches of Guanacaste province, Tamarindo makes a good base for exploring other nearby stretches of sand. There are plenty of surfers here, as well as one of the most lively nightlife scenes on this coast. See chapter 6.
- **Santa Rosa National Park:** If you really want to get away from it all, the beaches here are a good bet. Located in the northwest corner of Costa Rica, you will either have to four-wheel drive or hike 8 miles (13km) from the central ranger station to reach the beach. Once there, you'll find only the most basic of camping facilities: outhouse latrines and cold-water showers. But you will probably have the place almost to yourself. In fact, the only time it gets crowded is in October, when thousands of olive Ridley sea turtles nest in one of their yearly *arribadas* (arrivals). See chapter 6.
- **Manuel Antonio:** The first beach destination to become popular in Costa Rica, it still retains its charms, despite burgeoning crowds and mushrooming hotels.

The beaches inside the park are idyllic, and the views from the hills approaching the park are enchanting. This is one of the few remaining habitats for the endangered squirrel monkey. Rooms with views tend to be a bit expensive, but many a satisfied guest will tell you they're worth it. See chapter 8.

- **Punta Uvita:** Part of the Ballena Maritime National Park, this is a wide beach with calm water and plenty of trees for shade. At low tide a sandbar connects the mainland to a small offshore island. Most people visit for the day and stay in nearby Dominical, although small hotels and *cabinas* are starting to pop up closer by. Heading south from Punta Uvita, yet still part of the national park, are several more glorious and practically undiscovered beaches. See chapter 8.
- **Punta Uva & Manzanillo:** Below Puerto Viejo, the beaches of Costa Rica's Atlantic coast take on true Caribbean splendor, with turquoise waters, coral reefs, and palm-lined stretches of nearly deserted white-sand beach. Punta Uva and Manzanillo are the two most sparkling gems of this coastline. Tall coconut palms line the shore, providing shady respite for those who like to spend a full day on the sand, and the water is usually quite calm and good for swimming. See chapter 10.

3 The Best Active Vacations

- **Diving off the Shores of Isla del Coco** (off Guanacaste in the Pacific): Legendary among treasure seekers, pirate buffs, and scuba divers, this small island is considered one of the 10 best dive sites in the world. A protected national park, its surrounding Pacific waters are clear, and its reefs are teeming with life. (Divers regularly encounter schools of hammerhead sharks and docile whale sharks.) Since the island is so remote, and has no overnight facilities for visitors, the most popular way to visit is on weeklong excursions on a live-aboard boat. (On a live-aboard boat, guests live, eat, and sleep on board—with nights spent anchored in the harbor.) **U.S. Dive Travel** (☎ and fax **206/937-7484;** e-mail: divetrav@aa.net) and **Aggressor Fleet Limited** (☎ **800/348-2628** or 504/385-2628; e-mail: 103261.1275@compuserve.com) regularly run dive trips to Coco Island. See chapter 4.
- **Hooking a Billfish off the Pacific Coast:** Billfish are plentiful all along Costa Rica's Pacific coast, and boats operate from Playas del Coco to Playa Zancudo. Costa Rican anglers hold world records for both blue marlin and pacific sailfish. Go to Quepos for the best après-fish scene or head down to Drake Bay if you want some isolation. **Americana Fishing Services** (☎ **506/223-4331**) or **Costa Rica Outdoors** (☎ **506/282-6743**) can help you find a good charter skipper or specialized fishing lodge. See chapters 4, 6, and 9.
- **Rafting the Upper Reventazon River** (near Turrialba): The Class V "Guayabo" section of this popular river is serious white water. Only experienced and gutsy river runners need apply. If you're not quite up to that, try a 2-day Pacuare River trip, which passes through primary and secondary forests and a beautiful steep gorge that, sadly, may be dammed soon. Get there quick! **Aventuras Naturales** (☎ **800/514-0411** in the U.S., or 506/225-3939 in Costa Rica) or **Rios Tropicales** (☎ **506/233-6455**) can arrange either of the above tours. See chapter 4.
- **Riding a Horse from Playa Montezuma to a Waterfall** (on the Nicoya Peninsula): This is one of the most popular tours in Montezuma and justifiably so. The 5-mile (8km) ride to the waterfall is a mixture of beach riding and short sections of jungle trails. Once there you can swim in the perfect swimming hole formed

at the meeting place of a 50-foot waterfall and the sea. Leave Montezuma about midday, and you should return as the sun is setting. See chapter 6.

- **Surfing and Four-Wheeling Guanacaste Province:** This northwestern province has dozens of respectable beach and reef breaks from Witch's Rock at Playa Naranjo near the Nicaraguan border to Playa Nosara more than 62 miles (100km) away. Rent a 4 × 4 with a roof rack, pile on the boards, and explore. See chapter 6.
- **Mountain Biking Around Lake Arenal** (near Tilarán and Arenal Volcano): This huge artificial lake, with the majestic Arenal Volcano as a backdrop, has trails all around its shores and into neighboring forests and pasturelands. There are a variety of rides of all difficulty levels. The setting is spectacular, and there are hot springs nearby for sore muscles. Contact **Rio Escondido Mountain Bikes** (☎ **800/678-2252** in the U.S., or 506/695-5644 in Costa Rica) or **Aguas Bravas** (☎ **506/292-2072**). See chapter 7.
- **Windsurfing Lake Arenal:** With steady gale-force winds and stunning scenery, the northern end of Lake Arenal (see above) has become a major international windsurfing hot spot. If you're an avid boardsailor, be sure to check in with Norm at **Rock River Lodge** (☎ **506/695-5644**). See chapter 7.
- **Hiking Mount Chirripó** (near San Isidro de El General on the central Pacific coast): The highest mountain in Costa Rica, Mount Chirripó is one of the few places in the world where (on a clear day) you can see both the Atlantic and the Pacific oceans at the same time. Hiking to Chirripó's 12,412-foot summit will take you through a number of distinct bioregions, ranging from lowland pastures and a cloud forest to a high-altitude *páramo,* a tundralike landscape with stunted trees and morning frosts. See chapter 8.
- **Kayaking Around the Golfo Dulce:** Slipping through the waters of the Golfo Dulce by kayak gets you intimately in touch with the raw beauty of this underdeveloped region. Spend several days poking around in mangrove swamps, fishing in estuaries, and watching dolphins frolic in the bay. **Escondido Trex** (☎ **506/735-5210;** e-mail: osatrex@sol.racsa.co.cr) provides multiday custom kayaking trips out of Puerto Jiménez on the Osa Peninsula. See chapter 9.
- **Surfing Pavones** (on the south Pacific coast): Just 8 miles (13km) from the Panamanian border at the southern reaches of Costa Rica's Pacific coast, Pavones is reputed to have one of the longest ridable waves in the world. When this left-point break is working, surfers enjoy rides of almost a mile in length. Much more can be said about this experience, but if you're a surfer, you've heard it all before. **Tico Travel** (☎ **800/493-8426;** e-mail: tico@gate.net) specializes in surf tours to Costa Rica and will give current wave reports. See chapter 9.

4 The Best Day Hikes & Nature Walks

- **Lankester Botanical Garden:** If you want a really pleasant but not overly challenging day hike, consider a walk among the hundreds of distinct species of flora on display here. Lankester Garden (☎ **506/552-3247** or 506/552-3151) is just 17 miles (27.4km) from San José and makes a wonderful day's expedition. The trails meander from areas of well-tended open garden to shady natural forest. See chapter 5.
- **Rincón de la Vieja National Park:** This park has a number of wonderful trails through a variety of ecosystems and natural wonders. My favorite hike is down to the Blue Lake and Cangrejo Falls. It's 3.2 miles (5.1km) each way, and you'll

want to spend some time at the base of this amazing lake, so plan on spending at least 5 hours on the outing, and bring along lunch and plenty of water. There's also the Las Pailas Loop for those seeking a less strenuous hike. This remote volcanic national park is located about an hour north of Liberia (it's not far as the crow flies, but the road is rough), or it's about 5 hours from San José. See chapter 6.

- **La Selva Biological Station:** This combination research facility and rustic nature lodge has an extensive and well-marked network of trails. My favorite hike starts off with the Cantarana ("singing frog") trail, which includes a section of low bridges over a rain-forest swamp. From here you can join up with either the near or far circular loop trails—**CCC** and **CCL.** Most days there are guided hikes led by very informed naturalists. You'll need a reservation in advance (☎ **506/766-6565**). The Biological Station is located north-northeast on the Caribbean slope of Costa Rica's central mountain range. It'll take you about 1 to 1½ hours to drive from San José via the Guapiles highway. See chapter 7.
- **Monteverde Biological Cloud Forest Preserve:** In the morning rush of high season, when groups and tours line up to enter the preserve, you'd think the sign says "crowd forest." Still, the guides here are some of the most professional and knowledgeable in the country. Take a tour in the morning to familiarize yourself with the forest, then spend the late morning or afternoon (your entrance ticket is good for the whole day) exploring the preserve. Once you get off the main thoroughfares, Monteverde reveals its rich mysteries with stunning regularity. Walk through the gray mist and look up at the dense tangle of epiphytes and vines. The only noises you'll hear are the rustlings of birds or monkeys and the occasional distant rumble of Arenal Volcano. The trails are well marked and regularly tended. It's about 3½ hours by bus or car to Monteverde from San José. See chapter 7.
- **La Fortuna to the Río Fortuna Waterfall:** The hike that leads to this waterfall, about 3½ miles (5.6km) outside La Fortuna, is one of my favorites, but it's not for everyone. It used to be more of a scramble than a hike, but recent improvements have made it a bit less strenuous. Nevertheless, it's still steep, and you'll have to brave a makeshift ladder carved into a tree trunk, which is not for the faint of heart. Follow the signs out of town along dirt roads and pastureland. Once you reach the waterfall lookout, you've got another 20 minutes navigating down a sometimes slippery and muddy path to the base of the falls. The roar of the crashing water is almost deafening. If you want to swim, go just slightly downstream. It's a refreshing rinse, but expect to get muddy and sweaty again on the way back. See chapter 7.
- **Corcovado National Park:** This large swath of dense lowland rain forest is home to Costa Rica's second-largest population of scarlet macaws. The park has a well-designed network of trails, ranger stations, and camping facilities. Most of the lodges in Drake Bay and Puerto Jiménez have day hikes through the park, but if you really want to experience it, you should hike in and stay at one or more of the campgrounds. This is strenuous hiking, and you will have to pack in some gear and food, but the reward is some of Costa Rica's most spectacular and unspoiled scenery. Because strict limits are placed on the number of visitors allowed into the park, you'll always feel far from the madding crowd. See chapter 9.
- **Cahuita National Park:** The trails here are flat, well-maintained paths through thick lowland forest. Most of the way they parallel the beach, which is usually no

more than 100 yards away, so you can hike out on the trail and back along the beach, or vice versa. White-faced and howler monkeys are quite common here, as are brightly colored land crabs. See chapter 10.

5 The Best Bird Watching

- **Observing Oropendula and Blue-Crowned Motmot at Parque del Este:** A boon for city bird-watchers, this San José park rambles through a collection of lawns, planted gardens, and harvested forest, but it also includes second-growth scrub and dense woodland. Oropendula and blue-crowned motmot are common species here. Take the San Ramón/Parque del Este bus from Calles 9 between Avenida Central and Avenida 2. See chapter 5
- **Spotting Hundreds of Marsh and Stream Birds Along the Rio Tempisque Basin:** Hike around the Palo Verde Biological Station, or take a boat trip down the Bebedero River with **TAM Travel** (☎ **506/670-0098**) or **Safaris Corobici** (☎ and fax **506/669-1091**; e-mail: safaris@sol.racsa.co.cr). This area is an important breeding ground for gallinules, jacanas, and limpkins, as well as a common habitat for numerous heron and kingfisher species. Palo Verde is about a 3½-hour drive from San José. See chapter 6.
- **Looking for More Than 300 Species of Birds in La Selva Biological Station:** With an excellent trail system through a variety of habitats, from dense primary rain forest to open pasturelands and cacao plantations, this is one of the finest places for bird watching in Costa Rica. With such a variety of habitats, the number of species spotted runs to well over 300. Contact the Organization for Tropical Studies (☎ **506/240-6696;** e-mail: reservas@ns.ots.ac.cr), or see chapter 7.
- **Sizing up a Jabiru Stork at Caño Negro Wildlife Refuge:** Caño Negro Lake and the Río Frío that feeds it are incredibly rich in wildlife and a major nesting and gathering site for aquatic bird species. These massive birds are getting less and less common in Costa Rica, but this is still one of the best places to see one. **Tilajari Hotel Resort** (☎ **506/469-9091**) makes a good base for exploring this spot. The Caño Negro Refuge is way up north near the Nicaraguan border. The most popular entry point is by boat from Los Chiles, which is about 4 hours from San José. See chapter 7.
- **Catching a Scarlet Macaw in Flight Over Carara Biological Reserve:** Home to Costa Rica's largest population of scarlet macaws, Carara Biological Reserve is a special place for devoted bird-watchers and recent converts. Macaws are noisy and colorful birds that spend their days in the park but choose to roost in the evenings near the coast. They arrive like clockwork every morning and then head for the coastal mangroves around dusk. These daily migrations give birders a great chance to see these magnificent birds in flight. The reserve is located about 2 hours from San José along the central Pacific coast. See chapter 8.
- **Looking for a Resplendent Quetzal in the Cerro de la Muerte:** The ancient Aztec and Maya revered this spectacular bird. Serious bird-watchers won't want to leave Costa Rica without crossing this bird off their life lists, and neophytes may be hooked for life after seeing one of these iridescent green wonders fly overhead, flashing its brilliant red breast and trailing 2-foot-long tail feathers. **Albergue Mirador de Quetzales** (☎ **506/534-4415**) can almost guarantee a sighting. The Cerro de la Muerte is a high mountain pass located along the way to San Isidro de El General about 1½ hours from San José. See chapter 8.

- **Taking Advantage of the Caribbean's Best Birding at Aviarios del Caribe:** In just a few short years, Aviarios del Caribe (☎ **506/382-1335**) has established itself as the prime bird-watching resort on the Caribbean. If it flies along this coast, chances are good you'll spot it here; more than 300 species of birds have been spotted so far. Located on the Caribbean coast, Aviaros del Caribe is about a 3-hour drive from San José. See chapter 10.

6 The Best Family Vacation Experiences

- **San José:** If your family is like mine, you'll want to spend your nights in San José far away from the traffic and street chaos of downtown. The best place for all of you to experience Costa Rica's capital city (and still get a decent night's sleep) is the Meliá Cariari Conference Center and Golf Resort (☎ **800/336-3542** in the U.S., or 506/239-0022 in Costa Rica). With facilities that include several large pools, an 18-hole golf course, 11 tennis courts, and a game room (not to mention baby-sitting service), there's something here for everyone. If you're traveling with teens, they'll feel right at home at the new Mall Cariari, which has a multiplex theater, indoor skating rink and, of course, a food court. Located just 15 minutes from downtown, it's well situated for exploring all of the city's sights and attractions. See chapter 5.
- **Hotel Hacienda La Pacifica** (north of Cañas; ☎ **506/669-0266**): This hotel is set on expansive grounds with marked trails. There's a neighboring zoo, and a variety of tours and activities are close at hand. The gentle Corobici River is a good river float for all ages, and there are bicycles for rent, bird-watching guides, and educational tours to a nearby historic ranch. See chapter 6.
- **Playa Hermosa, Guanacaste.** The protected waters of this Pacific beach make it a family favorite. However, just because the waters are calm doesn't mean it's boring here. Check in at **Aqua Sport** (☎ **506/670-0450;** fax 506/672-0060), where you can rent sea kayaks, sailboards, paddleboats, beach umbrellas, and bicycles. See chapter 6.
- **Monteverde:** Located about 100 miles (16km) northwest of San José, this area hosts not only the country's most famous cloud forest, but it also sports a wide variety of related attractions and activities. After hiking through the preserve, you should be able to keep most kids happy and occupied riding horses, squirming at the local serpentarium, or visiting the butterfly farm and hummingbird gallery. See chapter 7.
- **Playa de Jacó:** On the central Pacific coast, this is Costa Rica's liveliest and most developed beach town. The streets are lined with souvenir shops, ice cream stands, and inexpensive eateries; there's even a miniature golf course. This is a good place for a family to rent a few mopeds for an afternoon cruise. Older children can rent a boogie board, though everyone should be careful with the rough surf here. **Hotel Club del Mar** (☎ and fax **506/643-3194**) is situated at the calm southern end of the beach. The hotel has a small pool and some shady grounds and is accommodating to families traveling with small children. See chapter 8.

7 The Best Views

- **The Summit of Irazú Volcano** (near San José): On a very clear day you can see both the Pacific Ocean and the Caribbean Sea from this vantage point. Even if visibility is low and this experience eludes you, you will have a view of the volcano's spectacular landscape, the Meseta Central, and the Orosi Valley. See chapter 5.

- **Iguanazul Hotel** (☎ and fax **506/653-0123**): Located on a high bluff above Playa Junquillal, this hotel has a wonderful view of the Pacific and the windswept coastline in either direction. It gets best around sunset, and better yet if you can commandeer one of the hammocks set in a little palapa on the hillside itself. It takes about 5 hours to drive here from San José. See chapter 6.
- **Arenal Observatory Lodge** (near Arenal Volcano; ☎ **506/257-9489;** fax 506/257-4220; e-mail: arenalob@sol.racsa.co.cr): It seems so close, you'll think you can reach out and touch the volcano. Unlike on Irazú Volcano (above), when *this* volcano rumbles and spews you may have the urge to run for cover. Make sure you ask for a room with a view. See chapter 7.
- **La Mariposa** (Quepos; ☎ **506/777-0456**): Couples who choose to dine here arguably have the best view in Manuel Antonio, and that's saying a lot. Come for breakfast or a sunset drink, because unfortunately I've had bad luck with dinner here. See chapter 8.
- **The Outdoor Restaurant at Villa Caletas** (Playa Hermosa de Jacó; ☎ **506/257-3653**): You'll have a view over the Golfo de Nicoya and the Pacific Ocean beyond. Sunsets here are legendary, but it's beautiful during the day as well. See chapter 8.
- **The Summit of Mount Chirripó** (near San Isidro): What more can one say, at 12,412 feet, this is the highest spot in Costa Rica. As on the top of Volcano Irazú, on a clear day you can see both the Pacific Ocean and Caribbean Sea from here. Still, even when it's not *that* clear, you can catch some pretty amazing views and scenery. See chapter 8.
- **La Paloma Lodge** (Drake Bay; ☎ **506/239-0954**): Instead of breakfast in bed, in the open-air A-frame cabins you can enjoy a view from your bed—flowering hibiscus and swaying palm fronds to the Pacific Ocean and Caño Island just beyond. You may never want to get out of bed. See chapter 9.

8 The Best Drives

Driving in Costa Rica can be unpleasant, to say the least. Routes are rarely marked, roads resemble bombing ranges, and the famously peaceful Ticos become downright homicidal once they climb behind the wheel of a car. Nevertheless, renting a car provides freedom and independence, and there are some drives that are noteworthy for their scenery.

- **Irazú Volcano and the Orosi Valley:** This makes an excellent day tour and drive from San José. Start out early to reach the peak of the volcano while the skies are clearest, then spend the afternoon touring the Orosi Valley, with scenic lookouts at both Orosi and Ujarrás. See chapter 5.
- **Braulio Carrillo National Park:** Any trip to the Caribbean coast will take you through this vast national park of mountainous cloud and rain forests. Giant elephant-ear plants line the steep jungle roadside. Broad vistas open up to reveal a number of waterfalls cascading out of the forested mountains. A bridge crosses over the juncture of the clear General River and the sulfuric yellow Río Sucio (Dirty River). Be careful about stopping, and don't leave your car parked here for long: Robberies have been reported along this stretch of highway. Alternatively, you can make a loop heading out of San José and through Braulio Carillo, then up to Puerto Viejo de Sarapiqui, returning via La Virgen and passing by the La Paz waterfall and Poas Volcano. See chapter 7.

- **La Fortuna–Tiláran–Monteverde:** This route connects two of the country's prime visitors' destinations: Arenal Volcano and Monteverde Cloud Forest. Along the way you can marvel at the beauty of Lake Arenal and stop at the wonderful Arenal Botanical Gardens. A four-wheel-drive vehicle is highly recommended for this route, as the section between Tiláran and Monteverde is, to put it mildly, rugged. See chapter 7.
- **The Rocky Coast South of Dominical:** This has often been compared to Big Sur, California. For years this stretch of road was the definition of rugged, but recent improvements have made it into an enjoyable ride. All along the way there are informal lookouts where you can pull over and watch the waves crash on the rocks below. On the inland side of the road are dense lowland rain forests with side roads that lead to hiking trails and mountain waterfalls. Be sure to stop for a break at Playa Piñuelas. See chapter 8.

9 The Most Scenic Towns & Villages

Earthquakes and isolation have deprived Costa Rica of the architectural splendor found in neighboring nations. San José is an unremarkable city, rapidly becoming a textbook example of what a hectic pace of poorly planned urban development can do to a Third World city. Most of the towns and villages in the country are very simple farming communities, with few attractions for traditional tourists. Still, there are towns and villages both on and off the beaten track that are worth the trip.

- **Cartago:** Located 15 miles (24km) southeast of San José, Cartago was the country's first capital and contains the most traces of the country's Spanish Catholic colonial past. Churches—some still standing, others in ruins—dominate this small city. The Basilica de Nuestra Señora de los Angeles is the most striking example of an active church and is the site of a massive annual pilgrimage. A public park now occupies what was once the site of a large unfinished church, destroyed in the wake of the 1910 earthquake. Just outside the city are the ruins of the Ujarrás church. Built in 1693, it is the country's oldest church. Cartago makes an easy and interesting day trip out of San José. See chapter 5.
- **Guayabo:** Costa Rica's oldest known city, Guayabo is nestled amid the lush forests of the mountainous Turrialba region about 45 miles (72.5km) east of San José. Today, it has the distinction of being the country's only major archaeological site. Although it lacks the ornate majesty of such Mayan cities as Tikal, Chichén Itzá, and Copán, it has a wonderfully homey, lived-in feel. Its residents were probably Olmecs fleeing Aztec persecution more than 3,000 years ago. Excavations have revealed that the ancient city had a well-designed water system, clearly defined living areas, and a stone-paved "highway" running through the city center. Today, visitors can experience this Indian past by walking among building foundations, marveling at the still-working aqueducts, viewing carved petroglyphs, and touring burial sites. Guayabo National Monument is best visited as a day trip from San José. See chapter 5.
- **Liberia:** The capital and commercial hub of the northern province of Guanacaste, Liberia still retains much of its classic Spanish colonial architecture. Walk around town and admire the plentiful adobe buildings with ornate wooden doors, heavy beams, central courtyards, and faded, sagging, red-tile roofs. Liberia is the only major city in Costa Rica not situated in the temperate Central Valley; instead, it's located on a hot and dry lowland savannah, surrounded by cattle land and distant foothills. There are plenty of lodging options, and Liberia makes a good base for exploring the beaches and national parks of Guanacaste. See chapter 6.

- **Golfito:** The hub of Costa Rica's southern Pacific zone, Golfito is 210 miles (338km) south of San José. Steep jungle hills meet the water, and you'll find the town spread out along one main road that hugs the winding coastline of the Golfo Dulce (Sweet Gulf). Golfito was once the largest base for United Fruit Company's banana operations. United Fruit pulled out but left behind their company housing, and many of these old wooden homes with gingerbread trim and manicured lawns have been turned into comfortable budget lodgings. You won't want to stay in Golfito too long, but if you'll be exploring the Osa Peninsula or the Golfo Dulce, or visiting the Wilson Botanical Gardens, it makes a good base. See chapter 9.
- **Tortuguero:** Little more than a collection of wooden shacks built on stilts and connected by footpaths, this isolated little village on the Caribbean coast is charming, laid-back, and friendly. Although the influx of tourists is having an effect, Tortuguero retains the feel of a tiny fishing and turtling village. If you tire of the town, head out into the lush jungle canals that surround it. See chapter 10.

10 The Best Places to Shop

Shopping can be difficult in Costa Rica. Coffee is the best buy and probably the most "Costa Rican" thing you can bring home with you. Costa Rica does not have a strong handcraft and artisan tradition. Most of the crafts and colorful textiles you will see for sale come from Guatemala, Panama, and Ecuador. While these may be cheap, they are obviously more expensive than they'd be in their countries of origin. The hottest new item on the market is Cuban cigars, which you'll see for sale at a variety of outlets.

- **Boutique Annemarie** (San José; ☎ **506/221-6063**): This bi-level store is actually part of the Hotel Don Carlos in San José; it sells a broad selection of crafts and clothing. Here you can buy a clay or silver reproduction of some pre-Columbian figure. Most items are similar to those you'll see on the streets or in other stores, but they're all under one roof here, and the atmosphere is friendlier and more relaxed. See chapter 5.
- **Central Market** (San José): No trip to the city is complete without a tour of this indoor labyrinth of shops, stalls, and restaurants. Everything from crafts and clothing to fresh butchered meats is sold here. The surrounding streets host a daily farmers market. This is the best place to buy fresh-roasted whole-bean coffee. See chapter 5.
- **Atmosfera** (San José; ☎ **506/222-4322**): It's a little pricey, but this three-story gallery–cum–gift shop has some very classy crafts and legitimate pieces of art. You'll find everything here, from small gifts and fine jewelry to large silk screens and oil paintings by prominent Costa Rican artists. See chapter 5
- **Sarchí** (Central Valley): This small city outside of San José has long served as the headquarters for Costa Rica's modest craft industry. Woodwork is the most developed and available craft, with traditional painted oxcarts coming in a wide range of styles and sizes. See chapter 5.

11 The Best Luxury Hotels & Resorts

Luxury is a relative term in Costa Rica. To date, no hotel I've found hits truly high standards across the board. Magnificent settings abound, but service and food can sometimes fall short. They may not be perfect, but there are a few places that try at least to treat you like a king or queen.

- **Marriott Hotel and Resort** (San Antonio de Belén, San José area; ☎ **800/228-9290** in the U.S. and Canada, or 506/298-0000 in Costa Rica): Of all the contenders in the upscale urban market, the Marriott seems to be doing the best job. It might just be that it's the newest, but everything is in great shape, the service is bend-over-backwards, the restaurants are excellent, and there are all the facilities and amenities for which one could hope. See chapter 5.
- **Meliá Playa Conchal** (on the northern Pacific coast; ☎ **800/336-3542** in the U.S., or 506/654-4123; e-mail: mconchal@sol.racsa.co.cr): If you're looking for a large and luxurious resort, with all the trappings, including an 18-hole Robert Trent Jones golf course, this is the only game in town. As a bonus, it's located on one of the nicest beaches in Costa Rica, the seashell-strewn wonder of Playa Conchal. See chapter 6.
- **Hotel Punta Islita** (on the Pacific coast in central Guanacaste; ☎ **506/231-6122;** e-mail: ptaisl@sol.racsa.co.cr): This is a great getaway. Perched on a high, flat bluff overlooking the Pacific Ocean, Punta Islita is popular with honeymooners, and rightly so. The rooms are large and comfortable, the food is excellent, and the setting is stunning. If you venture beyond your room and the hotel's inviting hillside pool, there's a long, almost always deserted beach for you to explore, as well as a wealth of activities for the more adventurous. See chapter 6.
- **Villa Caletas** (north of Jacó; ☎ **506/257-3653;** fax 506/222-2059; e-mail: caletas@ticonet.co.cr): Spread out over a steep hillside, high above the Pacific Ocean, these individual villas have a Mediterranean feel. The Greek Doric amphitheater follows the same motif. Carved into the steep hillside, the theater frequently features evening concerts of jazz or classical music. The "infinity pool" here was one of the first in Costa Rica and is still the most interesting. Sitting in a lounge chair at the pool's edge, you'll swear it joins the sea beyond. See chapter 8.

12 The Best Moderately Priced Hotels

- **Hotel Le Bergerac** (San José; ☎ **506/234-7850;** fax 506/225-9103; e-mail: bergerac@sol.racsa.co.cr): This classy little hotel has been pleasing diplomats, dignitaries, and other discerning travelers for years. Ask for one of the garden rooms, or get the old master bedroom with its small private balcony. See chapter 5.
- **Hotel Grano de Oro** (San José; ☎ **506/255-3322;** e-mail: granoro@sol.racsa.co.cr): San José boasts dozens of old homes that have been converted into hotels, but few offer the luxurious accommodations or professional service that can be found at the Grano de Oro. Throughout all the guest rooms, you'll find attractive hardwood furniture, including old-fashioned wardrobes in some rooms. When it comes time to relax, you can soak in a hot tub or have a drink in the rooftop lounge while taking in the commanding view of San José. See chapter 5.
- **Hotel Santo Tomas** (San José; ☎ **506/255-0448;** e-mail: hotelst@sol.racsa.co.cr): If you want to stay in downtown San José, this restored old mansion offers a sense of luxury at a very moderate price. There are hardwood floors and hardwood furniture throughout. Friendly service, clean and comfortable rooms, and a great location make this one of the best bets in town. See chapter 5.
- **Amor de Mar** (Playa Montezuma; ☎ **506/642-0262;** e-mail: shoebox-@sol.racsa.co.cr): This hotel has brightly varnished woodwork, immaculate rooms, hammocks strung under shady mango trees, a wide grass lawn overlooking the Pacific Ocean, and a swimming pool–sized tide pool carved into the adjoining rocky shore. They could charge much more than they do. See chapter 6.

- **El Sapo Dorado** (Monteverde; ☎ **506/645-5010;** e-mail: elsapo-@sol.racsa.co.cr): Spacious wooden cabins with fireplaces and private porches are spread across an open hillside planted with fruit trees and tropical flowers. The hotel has an excellent restaurant and is a great place to enjoy some of the best sunsets in town. See chapter 7.

13 The Best Ecolodges & Wilderness Resorts

The term *ecotourism* is fast becoming ubiquitous within the travel industry; unfortunately, it's often trumpeted by tourism operators and hotel owners who do very little in their day-to-day professional lives to combat environmental damage. (Some even contribute to it.)

Ecolodge options in Costa Rica range from tent camps with no electricity, cold-water showers, and communal buffet-style meals to some of the most luxurious accommodations in the country.

Generally, outstanding ecolodges and wilderness resorts are set apart by an ongoing commitment (financial or otherwise) to minimizing their effect on surrounding ecosystems and to supporting residents of local communities. They should also be able to provide naturalist guides and plentiful information. All of the following do.

- **Arenal Observatory Lodge** (☎ **506/257-9489;** fax 506/257-4220; e-mail: arnalob@sol.racsa.co.cr): Originally a research facility, this lodge has upgraded quite a bit over the years and now features comfortable rooms with impressive views of the Arenal Volcano. There are also excellent trails to nearby lava flows and a nice waterfall. Toucans frequent the trees near the lodge, and howler monkeys provide the wake-up calls. See chapter 7.
- **Rara Avis** (near Las Horquetas; ☎ and fax **506/253-0844;** e-mail: raraavis@sol.racsa.co.cr): A pioneer in ecotourism, this ecoresort still provides a premier natural experience in the heart of Costa Rica's central mountain rain forest. Getting to Rara Avis is no longer the kidney-splitting 4-hour ordeal it once was, but you'll still spend plenty of time in a tractor-pulled covered wagon before reaching the isolated yet comfortable Waterfall Lodge. If you're looking for a more rustic nature experience, stay at their El Plastico Lodge, a former penal colony. See chapter 7.
- **La Paloma Lodge** (Drake Bay; ☎ **506/239-0954;** e-mail: lapaloma@lapalomalodge.com): If your idea of the perfect nature lodge is one where your front porch provides some prime-time viewing of flora and fauna, this place is for you. If you decide to leave the comfort of your porch, the Osa Peninsula's lowland rain forests are just outside your door. See chapter 9.
- **Lapa Rios** (Osa Peninsula; ☎ **506/735-5130;** e-mail: laparios@sol.racsa.co.cr): Situated at the southern tip of the Osa Peninsula, this is the most luxurious ecolodge in Costa Rica. The 14 bungalow rooms all have spectacular views and are set into a lush forest. A lot of care went into the design and construction of this hotel. There are a host of tours available for guests, and the guides are usually local residents who are intimately familiar with the environment. See chapter 9.
- **Aviarios del Caribe** (Cahuita; ☎ **506/382-1335**): Avid bird-watchers cannot help but cross off a large portion of their life lists here. Walk the grounds, sit on the porch, take a boat ride through the mangroves, and check off species after species as your stay unfolds. The accommodations are modern and clean, and the rooms are always well stocked with fresh flowers. See chapter 10.

- **Selva Bananito Lodge** (in the Talamanca Mountains south of Limón; ☎ and fax **506/253-8118;** e-mail: conselva@sol.racsa.co.cr): This is one of the few lodges providing direct access to the southern Caribbean lowland rain forests. There's no electricity here, but that doesn't mean it's not plush. Outside your private cabin, the jungle is definintely lush. Hike along a riverbed, ride horses through the rain forest, climb 100 feet up a ceiba tree, or rappel down a jungle waterfall. There is fabulous bird watching here, and the Caribbean beaches are nearby. See chapter 10.
- **Cabinas Chimuri** (Puerto Viejo; ☎ **506/750-0119**): These rustic Bribri-style A-frame cabins are built out of local materials and are owned and managed by Mauricio Salazar, a local Bribri Indian. The tours, setting, and surroundings make this the perfect way really to get to know the people, customs, and ecology of the Talamanca region. Mauricio will take you to visit the nearby reservation and show you some of the secrets of jungle herbology and bush medicine. The accommodations are basic, but you'll have a mosquito net and a porch to sit on, and you can watch the Caribbean birds pass by. See chapter 10.
- **Rainbow Adventures** (☎ and fax **506/775-0220,** or ☎ 503/690-7750 in the U.S.): This was one of the first nature lodges in the remote Golfo Dulce and is still one of the nicest. Nestled on the shore of the "sweet gulf" and surrounded by miles of primary lowland rain forest, this is a great place for an escape from it all. There are plenty of trails through the jungle here, several swimming holes, and a waterfall. The rooms have only half walls, so there's nothing to separate you from the sights, sounds, and smells of the rain forest, although there are mosquito nets to keep the critters away. I've always been impressed by my guides here. See chapter 9.

14 The Best Bed-and-Breakfasts & Small Inns

- **Finca Rosa Blanca Country Inn** (Santa Bárbara de Heredia; ☎ **506/ 269-9392;** e-mail: rblanca@sol.racsa.co.cr): If the cookie-cutter rooms of international resorts leave you cold, then perhaps the unique rooms of this unusual inn will be more your style. Square corners seem to have been prohibited here in favor of turrets and curving walls of glass, arched windows, and a semicircular built-in couch. It's set into the lush hillsides just 20 minutes from San José. See chapter 5.
- **Vista del Valle Plantation Inn** (near Grecia; ☎ and fax **506/451-1165;** e-mail: mibrejo@sol.racsa.co.cr): This is a great choice for those who want something close to the airport but have no need for San José. The separate cabins are influenced by traditional Japanese architecture, with lots of polished woodwork and plenty of light. The gardens are also meticulously tended, and the chef is excellent. There's a nice tile pool and Jacuzzi, which look out over a deep river canyon. See chapter 5.
- **Almost Paradise** (Playa Nosara; fax only **506/685-5004;** e-mail: almost@ nosara.com): The name is appropriate. Sure, you could be right on the beach instead of 200 meters away, and sure, things could be fancier and more private. But at these prices, this *is* almost paradise. See chapter 6.
- **Sueño del Mar** (Playa Tamarindo; ☎ and fax **506/653-0284;** e-mail: suenodem@sol.racsa.co.cr): You may think you're dreaming here. The rooms feature African dolls on the windowsills, Kokopeli candleholders, and open-air showers with sculpted angelfish, hand-painted tiles, and lush tropical plants. The fabrics are from Bali and Guatemala. Somehow, all this works well together. Add

in the requisite hammocks under shade trees right on the beach, and you really have something. The breakfasts here are earning local renown; yours comes with the price of your room. See chapter 6.

- **Casa Verde** (Puerto Viejo; ☎ **506/750-0047**): This is my favorite budget lodging along the Caribbean coast. The rooms are clean and airy and have comfortable beds with mosquito nets. The owner is friendly and is always doing some work in the gardens or around the grounds. See chapter 10.
- **Magellan Inn** (Cahuita; ☎ and fax **506/755-0035**): This small inn is situated at the far end of Playa Negra (about 1¼ miles north of Cahuita) and is the most luxurious hotel in the area. There's a sense of elegance here that borders on tropical decadence. The pool is set into a crevice in an ancient coral reef that has been exposed with the passing of time. The bird watching is phenomenal. See chapter 10.

15 The Best Restaurants

- **Café Mundo** (San José; ☎ **506/222-6190**): This elegant little restaurant is my favorite place in downtown San José for a casual meal. The pizzas are excellent, the salads and main dishes are fresh and creative (Chef Ray Johnson prepares daily specials) and the desserts are some of the best in the country. If the weather's nice, you should grab a table in the lush patio garden, beside the small tile fountain, under large shade trees. See chapter 5.
- **La Cocina de Leña** (San José; ☎ **506/255-1360** or 506/223-3704): Located in the El Pueblo shopping, dining, and entertainment center, La Cocina de Leña (The Wood Stove) has a rustic feel to it and, slightly overpriced, takes on traditional Costa Rican cooking. The more adventurous dishes include oxtail stew served with yuca and plátano, or *chilasuilas,* tortillas filled with fried meat. See chapter 5.
- **La Luz** (Santa Ana; ☎ **506/282-4160**): Chef Sherman Johnson's fusion cooking mixes Pacific Rim, Southwestern, California, and Caribbean cuisine with a host of local ingredients. If a pan-seared veal chop stuffed with cilantro cashew pesto sounds good to you, you'll be glad to know it's just the beginning . . . and white chocolate mango cake is only one possible ending. See chapter 5.
- **La Masia de Triquel** (San José; ☎ **506/296-3528**): For years this elegant restaurant has been serving gourmet Spanish cuisine, with a level of refinement rare in Costa Rica. The paella is wonderful, of course, but so are the lamb, the rabbit, and the langostinas, large local crawfish. See chapter 5.
- **Tin Jo** (San José; ☎ **506/221-7605**): In a city with hundreds of Chinese restaurants, this place stands heads and shoulders above the competition. In addition to an extensive selection of Szechuan and Cantonese classics, there are Thai, Indian, and Malaysian dishes on the menu. Tin Jo has the most adventurous Asian cuisine in Costa Rica. See chapter 5.
- **La Meridiana** (Tamarindo; ☎ and fax **506/653-0230**): I'm not sure that a surfer town deserves such fine Italian food, but it's got it. The gnocchi here is delicate and served as small medaillons, not dumplings. If you don't want to loose sight of the fact that you're at the beach, have a fresh fillet of fish, or the homemade ravioli stuffed with lobster. This is a family-run establishment, and even the grappa is brewed by an uncle back in the homeland. See chapter 6.
- **El Gran Escape** (Quepos; ☎ **506/777-0395**): The prices are right, the portions are generous, and the fish is always fresh and expertly prepared. What more could you ask for from a seafood restaurant in a popular port town? Well, since you asked, there's an adjunct new sushi restaurant upstairs. See chapter 8.

- **The Garden Restaurant** (Puerto Viejo; ☎ **506/750-0069**): For years, travelers to the Caribbean coast have dubbed this their favorite restaurant in Costa Rica, and the reasons are as numerous as the exotic dishes on the menu. Wonderfully spiced Thai curry, local rundown (a spicy stew made with whatever ingredients the cook can "run down" that day), and Jamaican jerk chicken all coexist effortlessly and are served garnished with fresh flowers and grilled pineapple. See chapter 10.

16 The Best After-Dark Fun

- **El Cuartel de la Boca del Monte** (Avenida 1 between Calles 21 and 23, San José; ☎ **506/221-0327**): This is where San José's young, restless, and beautiful congregate. From Wednesday through Saturday the place is jam-packed. Originally a gay and bohemian hangout, it is now decidedly yuppie. There's frequently live music here. See chapter 5.
- **La Esmeralda** (Avenida 2 between Calles 5 and 7, San José; ☎ **506/221-0530**): This restaurant serves as a meeting place and central dispatch center for scores of local mariachi bands, some of which even print the restaurant's pay phone number on their business cards. Hire your own combo for a song or two, or just enjoy the cacophony as the bands battle it out through the night. See chapter 5.
- **San Pedro** (San José): This is San José's University district, and at night its streets are filled with students strolling among a variety of bars and cafes. If you'd like to join them, keep in mind that **La Villa** (☎ **506/225-9612**) and **La Maga,** 100 meters south of the Mall San Pedro (☎ **506/280-2961**), cater to artists and bohemians; **La Bodega** (no phone) and **Mosaicos** (☎ **506/280-9541**) are popular with young Tico rockers; **Omar Kahyaam** (☎ **506/253-8455**) is a great place to grab an outdoor table and watch the crowds walk by; and **Pizza Caccio** (☎ **506/283-2809**) seems to attract a good share of the U.S. students studying here. All of the spots listed above (except La Maga and La Bodega, which are across from the large Mall San Pedro) are located in a 3-block stretch that begins 200 meters east of the Church in San Pedro and heads north. See chapter 5.
- **Teatro Nacional** (San José; ☎ **506/221-1329**): This 100-year-old classical opera house has recently been restored and sits like a gem in the center of San José. Catch a show here, admire the classical ceiling mural, and then wander next door for a nightcap at the Gran Hotel's outdoor cafe. Most of the theater and popular concerts are in Spanish, but there are plenty of classical music concerts, dance performances, and other events that cross language barriers. See chapter 5.
- **El Tobogan** (San José; ☎ **506/257-3396**): There are scores of discos and dance salons in San José, but this is my favorite. The dance floor is immense, there are always live bands and the ambience is relaxed. See chapter 5.
- **Johnny's Place** (Puerto Viejo; no phone): Picture yourself sipping a cold beer at a candlelit table set in the sand with the Caribbean lapping at your feet. Could you ask for more? If so, a few steps away there's a steamy dance floor that lets loose to loud reggae. See chapter 10.

Getting to Know Costa Rica

2

In Spanish, *Costa Rica* means "Rich Coast," and when the Spanish named this region, they felt Costa Rica had great promise. In those days, Spain's quest for gold was intertwined with rhetoric about saving Indian souls—a "salvation" that usually involved being pressed into slavery. When Costa Rica yielded up little gold and few Indians, the name became somewhat of a misnomer, at least as far as the Spanish were concerned. It took nearly 500 years for the Rich Coast finally to yield its true bounty: the green gold of its natural tropical beauty. The same dense forests, volcanic peaks, and rugged coastlines that created impediments to Spanish settlement in Costa Rica are today attracting hundreds of thousands of visitors each year. They come to see some of Central America's least spoiled forests and beaches, to learn about rain forests and cloud forests, to go bird watching, white-water rafting, horseback riding, and diving, or just to sit on the veranda of one of the country's many hotels, ecolodges, or *cabinas* with a tall, cool drink in hand and contemplate chucking it all to join the more than 50,000 expatriates who already call Costa Rica home.

Costa Rica is, and has been for many years, a relative sea of tranquillity in a region that has been troubled by turmoil for centuries. For more than 100 years, it has enjoyed a stable democracy and a relatively high standard of living for Latin America. The literacy rate is high, as are medical standards and facilities. Perhaps most significant, at least for proud Costa Ricans, is that this country does not have an army. When former Costa Rican president Oscar Arias Sánchez was awarded the Nobel Peace Prize for negotiating a peace settlement in Central America in 1987, Costa Rica was able to claim credit for exporting a bit of its own political stability to the rest of the region.

Costa Rica has become acutely aware of the riches it has to offer travelers, and as a result, the country is undergoing phenomenal tourist-related growth. This is putting great strains on Costa Rica's natural resources and natural beauty. Though the nation has one of the world's best records in conservation, it's still being deforested at an alarming rate. Stretches of its coastline are being developed into massive megaresorts with little regard for the impact such developments will have on the local environment or adjacent towns and villages. However, Costa Rica should remain for many years one of the more fascinating natural destinations in the Americas, largely due to the efforts being made by international and Costa Rica–based ecological organizations.

1 The Natural Environment

Costa Rica occupies a central spot in the land bridge that joins North and South America. For millennia, this land bridge served as a migratory thoroughfare and mating ground for species native to the once-separate continents. It was also the meeting place of Mesoamerican and Andean pre-Columbian indigenous cultures.

The country comprises only 0.01% of the earth's landmass, yet it is home to 5% of the planet's biodiversity. There are more than 10,000 identified species of plants, 850 species of birds, 800 species of butterflies, and 500 species of mammals, reptiles, and amphibians found here.

The key to this biological richness lies in the many distinct life zones and ecosystems that can be found in Costa Rica. It may all seem like one big mass of green to the untrained eye, but the differences are profound.

In any one spot in Costa Rica, temperatures remain relatively constant year-round. However, they vary dramatically according to altitude, from uncomfortably hot and steamy along the coasts to below freezing at the highest elevations.

Costa Rica's lowland rain forests are true tropical jungles. Rainfall in them can be well over 200 inches per year, and their climate is hot and humid. Trees grow tall and fast, fighting for sunlight in the upper reaches. In fact, life and foliage on the forest floor are surprisingly sparse. The action is typically 100 feet above in the canopy, where long vines stream down, lianas climb up, and bromeliads grow on the branches and trunks of towering hardwood trees. You can find these lowland rain forests along the southern Pacific coast and Osa Peninsula, as well as along the Caribbean coast.

At higher altitudes you'll find Costa Rica's famed cloud forests. Here the steady flow of moist air meets the mountains and creates a nearly constant mist. Epiphytes—resourceful plants that live cooperatively on the branches and trunks of other trees—grow abundantly in the cloud forests, where they must extract moisture and nutrients from the air. Since cloud forests are found in generally steep, mountainous terrain, the canopy here is lower and less uniform than in lowland rain forests, providing better chances for viewing elusive fauna. Costa Rica's most spectacular cloud forest is the **Monteverde Biological Cloud Forest Preserve** in Guanacaste province.

At the highest reaches, the cloud forests give way to elfin forests and páramos. More commonly associated with the South American Andes, a páramo is characterized by a variety of tundralike shrubs and grasses, with a scattering of twisted, windblown trees. Reptiles, rodents, and raptors are the most common residents here.

In a few protected areas of Guanacaste, you will still find examples of the otherwise vanishing tropical dry forest. During the long and pronounced dry season (it lasts half the year, from November to March), no rain relieves the unabating heat. In an effort to conserve much-needed water, the trees drop their leaves but bloom in a riot of color: purple jacaranda, scarlet poró, and brilliant orange flame-of-the-forest are just a few examples. Then, during the rainy season, this deciduous forest is transformed into a lush and verdant landscape. Because the foliage is not so dense, the dry forests are excellent places to view a variety of wildlife species.

Along the coasts, primarily where river mouths meet the ocean, you will find extensive mangrove forests and swamps. Around these seemingly monotonous tangles of roots exists one of the most diverse and rich ecosystems in the country. All sorts of fish and crustaceans live in the brackish tidal waters. Caimans and crocodiles cruise the maze of rivers and unmarked canals, and hundreds of herons, ibises, egrets, and other marsh birds nest and feed along the silty banks. Mangrove swamps are often havens for waterbirds: cormorants, frigate birds, pelicans, and herons. The larger birds tend to nest up high in the canopy, while the smaller ones nestle in the underbrush. The Gulf of Nicoya is a particularly popular among frigate birds, whose nests sometimes rise as high as 10 feet over the mudflats.

Over the last few years, Costa Rica has taken great strides toward protecting its rich biodiversity. Whereas 30 years ago it was difficult to find a protected area anywhere, now more than 11% of the country is protected within the national park system. Another 10% to 15% of the land enjoys moderately effective preservation as part of private and public reserves, Indian reserves, and wildlife refuges and corridors. Still, Costa Rica's precious tropical hardwoods continue to be harvested at an alarming rate, often illegally, while other primary forests are clear-cut for short-term agricultural gain. Many experts predict that Costa Rica's unprotected forests will be gone by the early part of the 21st century.

This is also a land of high volcanic and seismic activity. There are three major volcanic mountain ranges in Costa Rica, and many of the volcanoes are still active, allowing visitors to experience the awe-inspiring sight of steaming fumaroles and intense lava flows during their stay. Two volcanoes near the capital—Poás and Irazú—are currently active although relatively quiet. The best places to see volcanic activity are farther north in Rincón de la Vieja National Park and at Arenal Volcano.

Costa Rica's last major earthquake shook the city of Límon on April 22, 1991. Tremors and aftershocks were felt as far away as San José. It's unlikely you will experience a major quake during your visit, but small tremors are relatively common. The first rule of thumb in an earthquake is not to panic. The best place to stand is underneath a doorway—if you can get there in time. (Most tremors will have already come and gone by the time you can get yourself into position.)

SEARCHING FOR WILDLIFE

It's hard not to enjoy Costa Rica's varied natural landscape, but keeping a few pointers in mind can make your visit even more pleasurable.

Remember, animals in the forests are predominantly nocturnal. When they are active in the daytime, they are usually elusive and on the watch for predators. Although the idea of visiting a rain forest may seem like the ultimate tropical fantasy, in reality rain forests are so dense and dark that it's extremely hard for the casual visitor to pick anything out. Birds are much easier to spot in clearings or secondary forests than they are in primary forests. Unless you have lots of experience in the tropics, your best hope for enjoying a walk through the jungle lies in employing a trained and knowledgeable guide. Also, a good pair of rubber boots (usually provided on a guided tour) is essential.

Here are a few helpful hints:

- *Listen.* Pay attention to rustling in the leaves; whether it's monkeys up above or pizotes on the ground, you're most likely to hear an animal before seeing one.
- *Keep quiet.* Noise will scare off animals and prevent you from hearing their movements and calls.
- *Don't try too hard.* Soften your focus and allow your peripheral vision to take over. This way you can catch glimpses of motion and then focus in on the prey.
- *Bring your own binoculars.* It's also a good idea to practice a little first, to get the hang of them. It would be a shame to be fiddling around and staring into space while everyone else in your group ohhs and ahhs over a quetzal.

- *Dress appropriately.* You'll have a hard time focusing your binoculars if you're busy swatting mosquitoes. Light, long-sleeved pants and shirts are your best bet. Comfortable hiking boots are a real boon, except where heavy rubber boots are necessary. Avoid loud colors; the better you blend in with your surroundings, the better your chances of spotting wildlife.
- *Be patient.* The jungle isn't on a schedule; however, you do have you best shot at seeing forest fauna in the very early morning and late afternoon hours.
- Familiarize yourself with what you're most likely to see. Most lodges and hotels have a copy of *Birds Of Costa Rica* and other wildlife field guides, although as with binoculars it's always best to have your own copy.
- Finally, remember the common refrain: "Take only photographs, leave only footprints."

2 The Regions in Brief

Costa Rica rightfully should be called Costas Ricas since it has two coasts, one on the Pacific Ocean and one on the Caribbean Sea. These two coasts are as different from each other as are the Atlantic and Pacific coasts of North America.

Costa Rica's Pacific coast, which can be divided into three distinct regions (Guanacaste and the Nicoya Peninsula, the central coast, and the southern coast), is characterized by a rugged, though mostly accessible, coastline where mountains often meet the sea. There are some truly spectacular stretches. This coast varies from the dry, sunny climate of the northwest to the hot, humid rain forests of the south.

The Caribbean coast can be divided into two roughly equal stretches, half of which is accessible only by boat or small plane. This remote coastline is a vast flat plane laced with rivers and covered with rain forest. Farther south, along the stretch of coast accessible by car, there are uncrowded beaches and even a bit of coral reef.

Bordered by Nicaragua in the north and Panama in the southeast, Costa Rica (19,530 square miles) is only slightly larger than Vermont and New Hampshire combined. Much of the country is mountainous, with three major ranges running northwest to southeast. Among these mountains are several volcanic peaks, some of which are still active. Between the mountain ranges are fertile valleys, the largest and most populated of which is the Central Valley. With the exception of the dry Guanacaste region, much of Costa Rica's coastal area is hot and humid and covered with dense rain forests.

THE CENTRAL VALLEY The Central Valley is characterized by rolling green hills that rise to heights between 3,000 and 4,000 feet above sea level. The climate here is mild and springlike year-round. It's Costa Rica's primary agricultural region, with coffee farms making up the majority of landholdings. The rich volcanic soil of this region makes it ideal for growing almost anything. The country's earliest settlements were in this area, and today the Central Valley is a densely populated area laced with decent roads and dotted with small towns. Surrounding the Central Valley are high mountains, among which are four volcanic peaks. Two of these, Poás and Irazú, are still active and have caused extensive damage during cycles of activity in the past two centuries. Many of the mountainous regions to the north and to the south of the capital of San José have been declared national parks to protect their virgin rain forests from logging. Here you can enjoy extremely easy access to the unusual experience of exploring a high-altitude cloud forest, usually shrouded in mist.

SA-0093
NICARAGUA
0
80 km
50 mi
N
CORDILLERA DE GUANACASTE
Upala
Golfo de Papagayo
Liberia
THE NORTHERN ZONE
GUANACASTE
Fortuna
Tortuguero
Caribbean Sea
Puerto Viejo
Tortuguero National Park
Tortuguero Canal
Monteverde
Monteverde Biological Cloud Forest Preserve
CARIBBEAN COAST
Nicoya
Car Ferry
Puntarenas
SAN JOSÉ
NICOYA PENINSULA
Limón
San José
Irazú Volcano
Golfo de Nicoya
Tambor
Malpais
CENTRAL PACIFIC COAST
Quepos
Manuel Antonio National Park
Río Telire
CORDILLERA DE TALAMAN
Pan American Hwy.
Pacific Ocean
SOUTHERN ZONE
Coronado Bay
Palmar Norte
PANAMA
Drake Bay
Bahia Drake
Caño Island Biological Reserve
Golfito
Golfo Dulce
Corcovado National Park
LEGEND
Airport

GUANACASTE & THE NICOYA PENINSULA With about 65 inches of rain a year, this region is by far the driest in the country and has been likened to west Texas. On the Pacific Ocean, Guanacaste province sits at the border of Nicaragua and is named after the shady trees that still shelter the herds of cattle that roam the dusty savannah here. In addition to cattle ranches, Guanacaste boasts semiactive volcanoes, several lakes, and one of the last remnants of tropical dry forest left in Central America (dry forest once stretched all the way from Costa Rica up to the Mexican state of Chiapas).

This area is the site of many of Costa Rica's sunniest and most popular beaches. Because many Americans have chosen to build beach houses and retirement homes here, Guanacaste in particular is experiencing quite a bit of new development. While Cancún-style high-rise hotels are far from the norm, condos, luxury resorts, and golf courses are springing up like gold-plated mushrooms. And when the new International Airport is up and running for real, San José will no longer be a necessary hub to the beaches of Costa Rica.

THE NORTHERN ZONE This region lies to the north of San José and includes rain forests, cloud forests, the country's two most active volcanoes (Arenal and Rincón de la Vieja), Braulio Carrillo National Park, and numerous remote lodges. Because this is one of the few regions of Costa Rica without any beaches, it primarily attracts people interested in nature and active sports. Arenal Lake boasts some of the best windsurfing in the world, and several good mountain-biking trails thread along its shores.

THE CENTRAL PACIFIC COAST Because it's the most easily accessible coastline in Costa Rica, the central Pacific coast boasts the greatest number of beach resorts and hotels. **Playa de Jacó** is the most popular destination here, attracting a large number of Canadian and German charter groups and plenty of Tico tourists, while **Manuel Antonio** caters to people seeking a bit more tranquillity and beauty. This region is also the site of the highest peak in Costa Rica: **Mount Chirripó**—where frost is common.

THE SOUTH PACIFIC COAST This is one of Costa Rica's most remote and undeveloped regions. Much of the area is protected in Corcovado and La Amistad national parks. This is a hot, humid region characterized by dense rain forests and rugged coastlines.

THE CARIBBEAN COAST Most of the Caribbean coast is a wide, steamy lowland laced with rivers and blanketed with rain forests and banana plantations. The culture here is predominantly black, with many residents speaking English or Caribbean patois. The northern section of this coast is accessible only by boat or small plane and is the site of Tortuguero National Park, which is known for its nesting sea turtles and riverboat trips. The southern half of the Caribbean coast has several beautiful beaches and, as yet, few large hotels.

3 Costa Rica Today

Costa Rica has a population of just under three million, more than half of whom live in the Central Valley and are classified as urban. The people are ethnically the most homogeneous of Central America: Nearly 96% of the population is of Spanish or otherwise European descent, and it is not at all unusual to see blond Costa Ricans. This is largely because the indigenous population in place when the first Spaniards arrived was small and thereafter was reduced to a minority by wars and disease. There are still some remnant indigenous populations, primarily on reservations around the country; the principal tribes include the Bribri, Cabécar, Boruca, and Guayamí. In addition, on the Caribbean coast there is a substantial population of English-speaking black Creoles who came over from the Antilles to work on the railroad and in the banana plantations.

In general, Costa Ricans (who call themselves Ticos, a practice that stems from their tendency to add a diminutive, either "tico" or "ito," to the ends of words to connote familiarity or affection) are a friendly and outgoing people. They believe their country to be a classless society where anyone, through hard work and intelligence, can improve his or her lot in life. While the average family is wealthy by Latin American standards, the median household income is only $3,000 per year. Nonetheless, with high levels of literacy (93%) and education, it is not uncommon to find Costa Ricans who speak English.

In conversation and interaction with visitors, Ticos are very open and helpful. In my experience, however, I've been frustrated by the fact that some Costa Ricans try so hard to be accommodating that they frequently will make promises they can't keep or tell you what they think you want to hear whether it's true or not.

In a region plagued by internal strife and civil wars, Costa Ricans are proud of their peaceful history, political stability, and relatively high level of development. This, however, can also translate into arrogance and prejudice toward immigrants from neighboring countries, who make up a large percentage of the workforce on the banana and coffee plantations.

Roman Catholicism is the official religion of Costa Rica, although freedom to practice any religion is guaranteed by the country's constitution. More than 90% of the population identifies itself as Roman Catholic, yet there are small but visible evangelical Christian, Protestant, and Jewish communities. By and large, Ticos are relatively religious. While many city dwellers lead quite secular lives, those in small villages and towns attend mass regularly. Time also has relative meaning to Ticos. While most tour companies and other establishments operate efficiently, in general, don't expect punctuality.

You will also find that modern Costa Rica is a nation of contrasts. On the one hand, it's the most technologically advanced and politically stable nation in Central America and has the largest middle class. Even the smallest towns have electricity, the water is mostly safe to drink, and the phone system is excellent. Since Costa Rica received independence from Spain in 1821, only a handful of its presidents have come from the military (which was disbanded completely in 1948), and it has had even fewer leaders who could be called dictators.

On the other hand, Costa Rica finds itself mired in economic crisis. The gap between rich and poor is widening. The government and banking institutions have been embroiled in scandal. The country's per-capita debt ranks among the world's worst. Six years ago, inflation reached a high point of 25%. In an attempt to come to terms with decades of trade deficits and pay back its debt, a more austere eco-

Impressions

We, the people of Costa Rica, believe that peace is much more than the absence of hostility among men and nations . . . . To us peace is the only ideal that, once achieved, will give us the right to call ourselves human beings.

—Oscar Arias, former Costa Rican president and Nobel Peace Prize laureate

nomic course has been taken, causing the country's vast network of social services, as well as its health care system and its educational institutions, to become overburdened and underfunded. Goaded by the World Bank and the International Monetary Fund, recent administrations have begun the process of privatizing state institutions in order to raise funds and reduce bureaucracy. This, however, has led to increased unemployment, lower wages, and more expensive goods and services.

Tourism has surpassed cattle ranching and coffee and banana exports to the point of becoming the nation's top source of income. Now Ticos whose fathers and grandfathers were farmers find themselves hotel owners, tour guides, and waiters. While most have adapted gracefully and regard the industry as a source of new jobs and opportunities for economic advancement, restaurant and hotel staff can seem gruff and disinterested at times, especially in rural areas. And, unfortunately, an increase in the number of visitors has led to an increase in crime, prostitution, and drug trafficking. Common sense and street savvy are required in San José and Limón, and it never hurts to be cautious and alert wherever you travel in the country. Only if you're reckless are you likely to have trouble.

4 History 101

Dateline

- **13,000 B.C.** Earliest record of human inhabitants in Costa Rica.
- **1,000 B.C.** Olmec people from Mexico arrive in Costa Rica searching for rare blue jade.
- **1,000 B.C.–A.D. 1400** City of Guayabo is inhabited by as many as 10,000 people.
- **1502** Columbus lands in Costa Rica in September, at what is now Limón.
- **1519–61** Spanish explore and colonize Costa Rica.
- **1563** City of Cartago is founded in Central Valley.
- **1737** San José is founded.
- **Late 1700s** Coffee is introduced as a cash crop.
- **1821** On September 15, Costa Rica, with the rest of Central America, gains independence from Spain.
- **1823** San José is named the capital. The decision is disputed, and isn't officially settled until 1835.
- **1848** Costa Rica is proclaimed an independent republic.

continued

EARLY HISTORY

Little is known of Costa Rica's history before its colonization by Spanish settlers. The pre-Columbian Indians who made their home in this region of Central America never developed the large cities or advanced culture that flowered farther north in what would become Guatemala, Belize, and Mexico. However, from scattered excavations around the country, primarily in the northwest, ancient artifacts have been unearthed that indicate a strong sense of aesthetics. Beautiful gold and jade jewelry, intricately carved grinding stones, and artistically painted terra-cotta objects point toward a highly skilled, if not large, population. The most enigmatic of these ancient relics are carved stone balls, some measuring several yards across and weighing many tons, that have been found along the southern Pacific coast. The purpose of these stone spheres remains a mystery: Some archaeologists say that they may have been boundary markers, while others speculate that they were celestial references; still others now claim that they are not human-made at all, but rather natural geological formations.

In 1502, on his fourth and last voyage to the New World, Christopher Columbus anchored just offshore from present-day Limón. Whether it was he who gave the country its name is open to discussion, but it wasn't long before the inappropriate name took hold.

The earliest Spanish settlers found that, unlike the Indians farther north, the native population of Costa Rica was unwilling to submit to slavery. Despite their small numbers, scattered villages, and tribal differences, they fought back against the Spanish until overcome by superior firepower and European diseases. But when the fighting was finished, the settlers in Costa Rica found that there were very few Indians left to force into servitude. The settlers were thus forced to till their own lands, a situation unheard of in other parts of Central America. Few pioneers headed this way because they could settle in Guatemala, where there was a large native workforce. Costa Rica was nearly forgotten, as the Spanish crown looked elsewhere for riches to plunder and souls to convert.

It didn't take long for Costa Rica's few Spanish settlers to head for the hills, where they found rich volcanic soil and a climate that was less oppressive than in the lowlands. Cartago, the colony's first capital, was founded in 1563, but it was not until the 1700s that more cities were founded in this agriculturally rich region. In the late 18th century, the first coffee plants were introduced, and because these plants thrived in the highlands, Costa Rica began to develop its first cash crop. Unfortunately, it was a long and difficult journey transporting the coffee to the Caribbean coast and then onward to Europe, where the demand for coffee was growing.

From Independence to the Present In 1821, Spain granted independence to its colonies in Central America. Costa Rica joined with its neighbors to form the Central American Federation, but in 1838 it withdrew to form a new nation and pursue its own interests, which differed considerably from those of the other Central American nations. By the mid-1800s, coffee was the country's main export. Land was given free to anyone willing to plant coffee on it, and plantation owners soon grew wealthy and powerful, creating Costa Rica's first elite class. Coffee plantation owners were powerful enough to elect their own representatives to the presidency.

This was a stormy period in Costa Rican history. In 1856, the country was invaded by William Walker, a soldier of fortune from Tennessee who, with the backing of U.S. president James Buchanan, was attempting to fulfill his grandiose dreams of presiding over a slave state in Central America. (Before his invasion of Costa Rica, he had invaded Nicaragua and Baja California.) The people of Costa Rica, led by their own president, Juan Rafael Mora, marched against Walker and

- **1856** Battle of Santa Rosa: Costa Ricans defeat the United States, which backed proslavery advocate William Walker.
- **1870s** First banana plantations are established.
- **1889** First election is won by an opposition party, establishing democratic process in Costa Rica.
- **1890** Inauguration of the railroad connecting San José with the Caribbean coast.
- **1899** The United Fruit Company is founded by railroad builder Minor Keith.
- **1941** Costa Rica's social security and health system instituted by President Rafael Angel Calderón.
- **1948** After aborted revolution, Costa Rican army is abolished.
- **1949** Women are given the right to vote.
- **1956** Costa Rica's population tops 1,000,000.
- **1963** Cabo Blanco Reserve becomes Costa Rica's first national park.
- **1987** Pres. Oscar Arias Sánchez is awarded the Nobel Peace Prize for orchestrating the Central American Peace Plan.
- **1994** Pres. Rafael Angel Calderón hands over the reigns of government to José María Figueres, in a peaceful replay of their fathers' less amenable and democratic transfer of power in 1948.
- **1996** Claudia Poll earns Costa Rica its first Olympic Gold Medal in the 200-meter freestyle swimming event at the Atlanta Summer Games.
- **1997** U.S. President Bill Clinton and the Dallas Cowboy cheerleaders visit Costa Rica.
- **1998** Costa Rica elects its first woman vice president, Astrid Fischl.

chased him back to Nicaragua. Walker eventually surrendered to a U.S. warship in 1857, but in 1860 he attacked Honduras, claiming to be the president of that country. The Hondurans, who had had enough of Walker's shenanigans, promptly executed him.

Until 1890, coffee growers had to transport their coffee either by oxcart to the Pacific port of Puntarenas or by boat down the Río Sarapiquí to the Caribbean. In the 1870s, a progressive president proposed a railway from San José to the Caribbean coast to facilitate the transport of coffee to European markets. It took nearly 20 years for this plan to reach fruition, and more than 4,000 workers lost their lives constructing the railway, which passed through dense jungles and rugged mountains on its journey from the Central Valley to the coast. Partway through the project, as funds were dwindling, the second chief engineer, Minor Keith, proposed an idea that not only enhanced his fortunes but also changed the course of Central American history. Banana plantations would be developed along the railway right-of-way (land on either side of the tracks). The export of this crop would help to finance the railway, and in exchange Keith would get a 99-year lease on 800,000 acres of land with a 20-year tax deferment. The Costa Rican government gave its consent, and in 1878 the first bananas were shipped from the country. In 1899 Keith and a partner formed the United Fruit Company, a business that would eventually become the largest landholder in Central America and cause political disputes and wars throughout the region.

In 1889 Costa Rica held what is considered the first free election in Central American history. The opposition candidate won the election, and the control of the government passed from the hands of one political party to those of another without bloodshed or hostilities. Thus Costa Rica established itself as the region's only true democracy. In 1948, this democratic process was challenged by Rafael Angel Calderón, who had served as the country's president from 1940 to 1944. After losing by a narrow margin, Calderón, who had the backing of the Communist labor unions and the Catholic church, refused to concede the country's leadership to the rightfully elected president, Otillio Ulate, and a civil war ensued. Calderón was eventually defeated by José "Pepe" Figueres. In the wake of this crisis, a new constitution was drafted; among other changes, it abolished Costa Rica's army so that such a revolution could never happen again.

Peace and democracy have become of primary importance to Costa Ricans since the civil war of 1948. When Oscar Arias Sánchez was elected president in 1986, his main goal was to seek a solution to the ongoing war in Nicaragua, and one of his first actions was to close Contra bases inside Costa Rica and enforce Costa Rica's position of neutrality. In 1987 Sánchez won the Nobel Peace Prize for initiating a Central American peace plan aimed at settling the war in Nicaragua.

In 1994, history seemed to repeat itself—peacefully this time—when José Maria Figueres took the reins of government from the son of his father's adversary, Rafael Angel Calderón.

Costa Rica's 100 years of nearly uninterrupted democracy have helped make it the most stable economy in Central America. This stability, adherence to the democratic process, and staunch position of neutrality in a region that has been torn by 200 years of nearly constant strife are a source of great pride to Costa Ricans, who like to think of their country as the "Switzerland of Central America."

5 Gallo Pinto, Ceviche & Frescos: Costa Rican Food & Drink

Very similar to other Central American cuisines, Costa Rican food is not especially memorable. Perhaps that's why there's so much international food available throughout the country. However, if you really want to save money, you'll find that Costa Rican, or *tipico,* food is always the cheapest nourishment available. It's primarily served in *sodas,* Costa Rica's equivalent of diners.

MEALS & DINING CUSTOMS

Rice and beans are the basis of Costa Rican meals. Mixed together and generally served at breakfast, they're called *gallo pinto* and come with everything from eggs to steak to seafood. At lunch or dinner, rice and beans are an integral part of a *casado* (which means "married"). A casado usually consists of cabbage-and-tomato salad, fried plantains (a starchy, bananalike fruit), and a chicken, fish, or meat dish of some sort.

Dining hours in Costa Rica are flexible, but generally follow North American customs. Some downtown restaurants in San José are open 24 hours; however, expensive restaurants tend to be open for lunch between 11am and 2pm and for dinner between 6 and 11pm.

APPETIZERS Known as *bocas* in Costa Rica, appetizers are served with drinks in most bars. Often the bocas are free, but even if they aren't, they're very inexpensive. Popular bocas include *gallos* (stuffed tortillas), ceviche (a marinated seafood salad), and *tamales* (stuffed cornmeal patties wrapped and steamed inside of banana leaves).

SOUPS Black-bean soup, *sopa negra,* is a watery soup served with a poached or boiled egg on top. It's quite popular in Costa Rica and is showing up on many menus. *Olla de carne* is a delicious soup made with large chunks of beef and several local vegetables, including chayote, ayote, yuca, and plantain, all of which have textures and flavors similar to various winter squashes. *Sopa de mondongo* is made with tripe, the stomach of a cow (I'll leave it up to you to determine if it's delicious or disgusting). *Picadillos* are vegetable purees made of potato, chayote, or plantains with a little bit of meat. They are often served as a side dish with a casado, or as bocas.

SANDWICHES & SNACKS Ticos love to snack, and there's a large variety of tasty little sandwiches and snacks available on the street, at snack bars, and in sodas. *Arreglados* are little meat-filled sandwiches, as are *tortas,* which are served on little rolls with a bit of salad tucked into them. *Gallos* are tortillas piled with meat, beans, or cheese. Tacos, tamales, and *empanadas* (meat pies) also are quite common.

MEAT Costa Rica is beef country, one of the tropical nations that have converted much of their rain-forest land to pastures for raising beef cattle. Consequently, beef is cheap and plentiful, although it may be a bit tougher than it is back home. Spit-roasted chicken is also very popular here and is surprisingly tender.

SEAFOOD Costa Rica has two coasts, and as you'd expect, there's plenty of seafood available everywhere in the country. *Corvina* (sea bass) is the most commonly served fish, and it's prepared innumerable ways, including as *ceviche,* a sort of marinated salad. Be careful: In many cheaper restaurants, particularly in San José, shark meat is often sold as corvina. You might also come across *pargo* (red snapper), *dorado* (mahimahi), and tuna on some menus, especially along the coasts. Although

Costa Rica is a major exporter of shrimp and lobster, both are very expensive here—that's why most are exported, causing them to be high-priced and in short supply at home.

VEGETABLES On the whole, you'll find vegetables surprisingly lacking in the meals you're served in Costa Rica—usually nothing more than a little pile of shredded cabbage topped with a slice or two of tomato. For a much more satisfying and filling salad, order *palmito* (hearts of palm salad). The heart (actually the stalk or trunk of these small palms) is first boiled and then chopped into circular pieces and served with other fresh vegetables, with a salad dressing on top. Hearts of palm are considered a delicacy in most places, because an entire palm tree (albeit a small one) must be cut down to extract the heart, and even in Costa Rica, where palms are plentiful, palmito is relatively expensive. If you want something more than this, you'll have to order a side dish such as *picadillo,* a stew or puree of vegetables with a bit of meat in it. Most people have a hard time thinking of *plátanos* (plantains) as vegetables, but these giant relatives of bananas require cooking before they can be eaten. Green plantains have a very starchy flavor and consistency, but become as sweet as candy as they ripen. Fried plátanos are one of my favorite dishes. *Yuca* (manioc root) is another starchy staple vegetable of Costa Rica.

One more vegetable worth mentioning is the *pejibaye,* a form of palm fruit that looks like a miniature orange coconut. Boiled pejibayes are frequently sold from carts on the streets of San José. When cut in half, a pejibaye reveals a large seed surrounded by soft, fibrous flesh. You can eat it plain, but it's usually topped with a dollop of mayonnaise.

FRUITS Costa Rica has a wealth of delicious tropical fruits. The most common are mangoes (the season begins in May), papayas, pineapples, and bananas. Other fruits include the *marañon,* which is the fruit of the cashew tree and has orange or yellow glossy skin; the *granadilla* or *maracuyá* (passion fruit); the *mamón chino,* which Asian travelers will immediately recognize as the rambutan; and the *carambola* (star fruit). When ordering *ensalada de fruita* (fruit salad) in a restaurant, make sure that it is made with fresh fruit and does not come with ice cream and Jell-O (unless that is what you want). What a shock I had when I first received a bowl of canned fruit covered with Jell-O cubes and three scoops of ice cream!

DESSERTS *Queque seco,* which literally translates as "dry cake," is the same as pound cake. *Tres leches* cake, on the other hand, is so moist you almost need to eat it with a spoon. Flan is a typical custard dessert. It often comes slightly flavored, as either *flan de caramelo* (caramel) or *flan de coco* (coconut). There are many other sweets available, many of which are made with condensed milk and raw sugar (rich and sweet). You'll find a surprising number of restaurants serve tiramisù for dessert.

BEVERAGES

Frescos, refrescos, or *jugos naturales* are my favorite drinks in Costa Rica. They are usually made with fresh fruit and milk or water. Among the more common fruits used are mangoes, papayas, blackberries (*mora*), and pineapples (*piña*). You will also come across maracuyá and carambola. Some of the more unusual frescos are *horchata* (made with rice flour and a lot of cinnamon) and *chan* (made with the seed of a plant found mostly in Guanacaste—definitely an acquired taste). The former is wonderful; the latter requires an open mind (it's reputed to be good for the digestive system). Order *un fresco con leche sin hielo* (a fresco with milk but without ice) if you are trying to avoid untreated water.

If you're a coffee drinker you may be disappointed here. Most of the best coffee has traditionally been targeted for export, and Ticos tend to prefer theirs weak and sugary. The better hotels and restaurants are starting to cater to gringo and European tastes and are serving up better blends. If you want black coffee ask for *café negro;* if you want it with milk, order *café con leche.*

If you want to try something different for your morning beverage, ask for *agua dulce,* a warm drink made from melted sugarcane and served either with milk, lemon, or straight.

WATER & SOFT DRINKS Although water in most of Costa Rica is said to be safe to drink, visitors often become ill shortly after arriving. Play it safe and stick to bottled water, which is readily available. *Agua mineral,* or simply soda, is sparkling water in Costa Rica. It's inexpensive and refreshing. If you like your water without bubbles, be sure to request *aqua mineral sin gas.* Most major brands of soft drinks are also available.

BEER, WINE & LIQUOR The German presence in Costa Rica over the years has produced several fine beers, which are fairly inexpensive. Licensed local versions of Heineken and Rock Ice are also available. Costa Rica distills a wide variety of liquors, and you'll save money by ordering these rather than imported brands. The national liquor is *guaro,* a rather crude cane liquor that's often combined with a soft drink or tonic or mineral water. Imported wines are available at reasonable prices in the better restaurants throughout the country. You can save money by ordering a South American wine rather than a Californian or European one. **Café Rica** and **Salicsa** are two coffee liqueurs made in Costa Rica; the former is very similar to Kahlúa, and the latter is a cream coffee liqueur. Both are delicious.

6 Recommended Books

Some of the books mentioned below may be difficult to track down in U.S. bookstores, but you'll find them all in abundance in Costa Rica's bookstores. Buy them during your trip to enhance your Costa Rica experience, or bring them home with you to illuminate your memories.

GENERAL *The Costa Ricans* by Richard, Karen, and Mavis Biesanz (Prentice Hall Press, 1987) is a well-written account of the politics and culture of Costa Rica. It's been out of print for more than a year now, but a new edition is allegedly in the works.

To learn more about the life and culture of Costa Rica's Talamanca Coast, an area populated by Afro-Caribbean people whose forebears emigrated from Caribbean islands in the early 19th century, pick up a copy of *What Happened: A Folk-History of Costa Rica's Talamanca Coast* by Paula Palmer (Publications in English, 1993). Or for a look at the perspective of the indigenous people of the Talamanca region, read Palmer, Sanchez, and Mayorga's *Taking Care of Sibö's Gifts: An Environmental Treatise from Costa Rica's KéköLdi Indigenous Reserve* (Editorama, 1991).

The Costa Rica Reader, edited by Marc Edelman and Joanne Kenen (Grove Press, 1989), is a collection of essays on Costa Rican topics. For insight into Costa Rican politics, economics, and culture, this weighty book is invaluable. Alternatively, you could pick up *Inside Costa Rica* by Silvia Lara (Interhemespheric Resource Center, 1995).

If you're looking for literature, *Costa Rica: A Traveler's Literary Companion,* edited by Barbara Ras and with a foreword by Oscar Arias Sánchez (Whereabouts Press, 1994), is a collection of short stories by Costa Rican writers, organized by region of the country.

For those who find the cuisine here intriguing, there's Oscar Chavarría-Aguilar's *A Bite of Costa Rica* (Gallo Pinto Press, 1994), Nelly Urbina's *My Kitchen* (self-published), and Carolina Avila and Marilyn Root's *Sabor* (self-published, 1997). Another nice new book is Ellen Sancho and Marcia Barahona's *Fruits of the Tropics* (self-published, 1997), a bilingual guide, with photos, to 52 tropical fruits grown in Costa Rica.

NATURAL HISTORY Mario A. Boza's beautiful *Costa Rica National Parks* (INCAFO, 1998) has recently been reissued in an elegant coffee-table edition. Each of the country's national parks is represented by several color photos and a short description of the park in Spanish and English. *Costa Rica's National Parks and Preserves* by Joseph Franke (The Mountaineers, 1993) is similar but with fewer photos. Other good coffee-table selections are *The Illustrated Geography of Costa Rica* (Trejos Hermanos, 1996), *Birds of the Rain Forest: Costa Rica* by Carmen Hidalgo (Trejos Hermanos, 1996), and *Portraits of the Rainforest* by Adrian Forsyth, with photos by Michael and Patricia Fogden (Firefly Books, 1995).

Dr. Donald Perry's fascinating *Life Above the Jungle Floor* (Don Perro Press, 1991) is an account of Perry's research into the life of the tropical rain-forest canopy. Perry is well known for the cable-car network he built through the rain-forest treetops at Rara Avis, as well as the new commercial Aerial Tram.

A Guide to the Birds of Costa Rica by F. Gary Stiles and Alexander Skutch (Cornell University Press, 1989) is an invaluable guide to identifying the many birds you'll see during your stay. It's often available for examination at nature lodges. Some serious bird-watchers also like to have *The Guide to the Birds of Panama, with Costa Rica, Nicaragua and Honduras* by Robert S. Ridgely and John A. Gwynne (Princeton University Press, 1992), in order to have two different illustrations for identifying some of those more subtle species variations. Bird-watchers might also enjoy Dennis Rodgers's *Site Guides: Costa Rica & Panama* (Cinclus Publications, 1996), which details each country's bird-watching bounty by site and region.

Turtle enthusiasts should read pioneering turtle researcher Archie Carr's *The Sea Turtle* (University of Texas Press, 1984). *Lessons of the Rainforest,* edited by Suzanne Head and Robert Heinzman (Sierra, 1990), is a collection of essays by leading authorities in the fields of biology, ecology, history, law, and economics who look at the issues surrounding tropical deforestation.

Other interesting natural-history books that will give you a look at the plants and animals of Costa Rica include *Sarapiquí Chronicle* by Allen Young (Smithsonian Institution Press, 1991); *Costa Rica Natural History* by Daniel Janzen (University of Chicago Press, 1983); the three-volume collection of *Butterflies of Costa Rica* by Philip DeVries (Princeton University Press, 1987 & 1997); *A Field Guide to the Mammals of Central America & Southeast Mexico* (Oxford University Press, 1998); the classic *A Neotropical Companion* by John C. Kricher (Princeton University Press, 1997), which was recently reissued in an expanded edition with color photos; and my all-time favorite book on tropical biology, *Tropical Nature* by Adrian Forsyth and Ken Miyata (Simon & Schuster, 1984). It's a well-written and lively collection of tales and adventures by two neotropical biologists.

3

Planning a Trip to Costa Rica

Costa Rica is one of the fastest-growing tourist destinations in the Americas, and as the number of visitors increases, so does the need for pretrip planning. When is the best time to go to Costa Rica? The cheapest time? Should you rent a car and what will it cost? Where should you go in Costa Rica? What are the hotels like? How much should you budget for your trip? These are just a few of the important questions that this chapter will answer so you can be prepared when you arrive in Costa Rica.

1 Preparing for Your Trip

VISITOR INFORMATION

In the United States, you can get information on Costa Rica by contacting the **Costa Rican Tourist Board** (ICT, or Instituto Costarricense de Turismo) at ☎ **800/343-6332.** They'll send you a basic packet of information, although most of it is of little help in trip planning. Much of the same information is available at their Web site, **www.tourism-costarica.com**.

If you have a computer and access to the World Wide Web, you will be able to find a wealth of information on Costa Rica just by sitting at your terminal. In this edition, we've tried to include Web site URLs for all listings, where available. In addition to these, you can try one of the following Web sites:

- **Costa Rica Homepage**
  This site at **www.cr** has a lot of useful information and good links, but be warned that most of it is in Spanish.
- **Yahoo's Costa Rica page**
  www.yahoo.com/Regional/Countries/Costa_Rica/
- **Costa Rica's Supersite**
  Despite its name, this site at **www.supersite.co.cr** is rather light on information and a bit slow.
- **Costa Rica's TravelWeb**
  www.crica.com
- **Costa Rica's TravelNet**
  www.centralamerica.com
- **Tico Net**
  www.ticonet.co.cr

- **Kitcom Costa Rica Hotel Page**
  www.hotels.co.cr
- **Arweb**
  www.arweb.com

Costa Rican Press

- The *Tico Times.* The Web site for Costa Rica's leading English-language newspaper is located at **www.ticotimes.co.cr**.
- *La Nación.* Costa Rica's leading Spanish-language daily. A large, extensive site with good links and search abilities, although mostly in Spanish. The address is **www.nacion.co.cr**.
- *Green Arrow Guide.* An on-line magazine focusing on Central America, with a lot of good information on Costa Rica. You can find the information at **www.greenarrow.com**.

ENTRY REQUIREMENTS

DOCUMENTS Citizens of the United States, Canada, Great Britain, and most European nations may visit Costa Rica for a maximum of 90 days. No visa is necessary, but you must have a valid passport. Citizens of Australia and New Zealand can enter the country without a visa and stay for 30 days. Citizens of the Republic of Ireland need a visa, valid passport, and a round-trip ticket in order to enter.

If you overstay your visa or entry stamp, you will have to pay around $45 for an exit visa and a nominal fee for each extra month you've stayed. If you need to get an exit visa, a travel agent in San José can usually get the exit visa for you for a small fee and save you the hassle of dealing with Immigration yourself. If you want to stay longer than the validity of your entry stamp or visa, the easiest thing to do is cross the border into Panama or Nicaragua for 72 hours and then reenter Costa Rica on a new entry stamp or visa. However, be careful. Periodically, the Costa Rican government has cracked down on "perpetual tourists," and if they notice a continued pattern of exits and entries designed simply to support an extended stay, they may deny you reentry.

If you need a visa or have other questions about Costa Rica, you can contact any of the following Costa Rican embassies: in the **United States,** 2112 S St. NW, Washington, DC 20008 (☎ **202/234-2945**); in **Canada,** 135 York St., Suite 208, Ottawa, Ontario K1N 5T4 (☎ **613/562-2855**); in **Great Britain,** 14 Lancaster Gate, London, England W2 3LH (☎ **71-706-8844**). In the United States, Costa Rica also maintains consulates in New York (☎ **212/425-2620**), Atlanta (☎ **404/951-7025**), New Orleans (☎ **504/887-8131**), Chicago (☎ **312/263-2772**), Denver (☎ **303/696-8211**), and Miami (☎ **305/871-7485**).

LOST DOCUMENTS If you lose your passport or need special assistance once inside Costa Rica, contact your embassy, listed in "Fast Facts: Costa Rica," below.

Most embassies can replace your passport and help you get an exit visa in about 24 hours. If your embassy won't get your exit visa for you, see a local travel agent or **OTEC Viajes,** Edificio Ferencz, 2nd floor, Calle 3 between Avenidas 1 and 3, 275 meters north of the National Theater (☎ **506/256-0633**). If you try to deal with Immigration yourself, you will face long lines, long waits, and endless frustration. Local travel agents and agencies regularly deal with Immigration and will charge you about $5 to $10 for the service (free if you ticket with them).

MONEY

CASH & CURRENCY The unit of currency in Costa Rica is the colón (¢). In early 1998, there were approximately 245 colónes to the American dollar, but because the colón has been in a constant state of devaluation, you can expect this rate to change. Because of this devaluation and accompanying inflation, this book lists prices in U.S. dollars only.

The colón is divided into 100 centimos. There are currently two types of coins in circulation. The older nickel alloy coins come in denominations of 10, 25, and 50 centimos and 1, 2, 5, 10, and 20 colónes; however, because of their evaporating value, you will rarely see or have to handle centimos. In 1997, the government introduced new gold-hued 5-, 10-, 25-, 50- and 100-colón coins. They are smaller and heavier than the older coins, and they will slowly phase out the other currency. There are paper notes in denominations of 50, 100, 500, 1,000, and 5,000 colónes. You might also encounter a special-issue 5-colón bill that is a popular gift and souvenir. It is valid currency, although it sells for much more than its face value. You may hear people refer to a *roja* or *toucan,* which are slang terms for the 1,000- and 5,000-colón bills respectively. One-hundred colón denominations are called *tejas,* so *cinco tejas* would be 500 colónes.

The Colón, the U.S. Dollar & the British Pound

Colónes	U.S. $	U.K. £
5	.002	0.012
10	.04	0.025
25	.102	0.061
50	.204	0.123
75	.306	0.186
100	.408	0.25
200	.81	0.50
300	1.22	0.74
400	1.63	0.99
500	2.04	1.24
750	3.06	1.85
1,000	4.08	2.47
5,000	20.41	12.37
10,000	40.81	24.75
25,000	102.04	61.88
50,000	204.08	123.76
75,000	306.12	185.64
100,000	408.16	247.52
200,000	816.32	495.05
300,000	1,224.48	742.57
500,000	2,040.82	1,237.62
1,000,000	4,081.63	2,475.25

In recent years forged bills have become increasingly common. When receiving change in colónes it's a good idea to check the larger denomination bills, which should have protective bands or hidden images that appear when held up to the light.

EXCHANGING MONEY You can change money at all state-owned banks. However, the service at these banks is slow and tedious. This simple transaction can often take more than an hour and cause unnecessary confusion and anxiety. I don't recommend it.

Fortunately, you don't have to rely on the state's banks. In late 1996 Costa Rica passed a law opening up the state's banking system. Accordingly, private banks have been opening up around San José and in some of the larger provincial towns and cities. So far, these private banks are kicking the state banks' butts, providing fast service at reasonable commissions, with no lines. Hotels will often exchange money and cash traveler's checks as well; there usually isn't much of a line, but they may shave a few colónes off the exchange rate.

Be very careful about exchanging money on the streets; it's extremely risky. In addition to forged bills and short counts, street money changers frequently work in teams that can leave you holding neither colónes nor dollars.

TRAVELER'S CHECKS Traveler's checks can be readily cashed at most hotels and banks. The exchange rate at banks is sometimes higher than at hotels, but bank transactions, especially at the state-run banks, can often take a very long time. If time is an issue, cash your traveler's checks at your hotel. Just be advised that the exchange rate you receive may not be as favorable.

What Things Cost in San José	U.S. $
Taxi from airport to the city center	13.00
Local telephone call	.05
Double at Radisson Europa Hotel (expensive)	140.00
Double at Hotel Grano de Oro (moderate)	72.00
Double at Hotel Bienvenido (inexpensive)	13.00
Lunch for one at Ruiseñor Café (moderate)	6.50
Lunch for one at Soda Coppelia (inexpensive)	2.75
Dinner for one, without wine, at La Cocina de Leña (moderate)	10.00
Dinner for one, without wine, at Manolo's Restaurante (inexpensive)	5.50
Bottle of beer	.90
Coca-Cola	.85
Cup of coffee	.50
Roll of ASA 100 Kodacolor film, 24 exposures	6.85
Admission to the Gold Museum	4.50
Movie ticket	3.25
Ticket at Teatro Melico Salazar	3.50–15.00

CREDIT CARDS & ATMS American Express, MasterCard, and Visa are accepted readily at most hotels, restaurants, and stores throughout Costa Rica. The less-expensive hotels and restaurants tend to operate on a cash-only basis. Before paying for a hotel with your credit card—check to see if they charge extra (from 5% to 10%) for credit card use; this is particularly common in the more remote areas of the country.

It is now possible to get money (colónes) from the various ATMs around Costa Rica, particularly in San José. This is becoming more and more common and reliable. However, success rates can still be spotty. I don't recommend using your ATM card as your primary source of financing for your trip. Check with your home bank about compatibility, but still think of your ATM card as a last resort. It's best to be prepared and come to Costa Rica with enough cash and traveler's checks. Banks can give you cash advances on your credit card, but expect to be assessed a service charge and spend a lot of time dealing with bureaucracy.

WIRING FUNDS If you need cash in a hurry, **Western Union** (☎ **0-800-777-7777**) has more than 30 offices spread around San José and several major cities in the country. Money can be electronically wired from any Western Union office in the United States to any Western Union office in Costa Rica. The process doesn't come cheap, though: A $100 wire will cost $15, and a $1,000 wire will cost $50.

HEALTH INFORMATION

Staying healthy on a trip to Costa Rica is predominantly a matter of being a little cautious about what you eat and drink, and using common sense. Know your physical limits and don't overexert yourself in the ocean, on hikes, or in athletic activities. Respect the tropical sun and protect yourself from it. Try not to eat in seedy dives where cockroaches outnumber fellow diners. I recommend buying and drinking bottled water or soft drinks, but the water in San José and in most of the heavily visited spots is safe to drink. The sections below will deal with some specific health concerns you should be aware of.

VACCINATIONS No vaccinations are required for a visit to Costa Rica, unless you're coming from an area where yellow fever exists. However, because sanitation is generally not as good as it is in developed countries, you may be exposed to diseases for which you may wish to get vaccinations: typhoid, polio, tetanus, and infectious hepatitis (a gamma globulin booster shot is often recommended). If you're planning to stick to the major cities, you stand little risk of encountering any of these diseases, but risk increases if you venture out into remote regions of the country.

TROPICAL DISEASES Your chances of contracting any serious tropical disease in Costa Rica are slim, especially if you stick to the beaches or traditional spots for visitors. However, malaria, dengue fever, and leptospirosis all exist in Costa Rica, so it's a good idea to know what they are.

Malaria is found in the lowlands on both coasts and in the northern zone. Although it's rarely found in urban areas, it's still a problem in remote wooded regions and along the Atlantic coast. Malaria prophylaxes are available, but several have side effects and others are of questionable effectiveness. Consult your doctor as to what is currently considered the best preventive treatment for malaria. Be sure to ask whether a recommended drug will cause you to be hypersensitive to the sun. It would be a shame to come down here for the beaches and then have to hide under an umbrella the whole time. Because malaria-carrying mosquitoes come out primarily at night, you should do as much as possible to avoid being bitten after dark. If you are in a malarial area, wear long pants and long sleeves, use insect repellent, and either sleep under a mosquito net or burn mosquito coils (similar to incense but with a pesticide).

Of greater concern may be **dengue fever,** which has had periodic outbreaks in Latin America since 1993. Dengue fever is similar to malaria, and is spread by an aggressive daytime mosquito. This mosquito seems to be most common in lowland urban areas, and Liberia and Limón have been the worst hit cities in Costa Rica. Dengue is also known as "bone break fever," because it is usually accompanied by severe body aches. The first infection with dengue fever will make you very sick but should cause no serious damage. However, a second infection with a different strain of the dengue virus can lead to internal hemorrhaging and may be life threatening.

Many people are convinced that taking B-complex vitamins daily will help prevent mosquitoes from biting you. I don't think the AMA has endorsed this idea yet, but I've run across it in enough places to think there may be something to it.

One final tropical fever I think you should know about (just because I got it) is **leptospirosis.** There are more than 200 strains of leptospiri, which are animal-borne bacteria transmitted to humans via contact with drinking, swimming, or bathing water. This bacterial infection is easily treated with antibiotics; however, it can quickly cause very high fever and chills, and should be treated promptly.

If you develop a high fever accompanied by severe body aches, nausea, diarrhea, or vomiting during or shortly after a visit to Costa Rica, it's a good idea to consult a physician as soon as possible.

Costa Rica has been relatively free from the cholera epidemic that has spread through much of Latin America in recent years. This is largely due to an extensive public awareness campaign that has promoted good hygiene and increased sanitation. Your chances of contracting cholera while you're here are very slight.

AMOEBAS, PARASITES, DIARRHEA & OTHER INTESTINAL WOES While the water in San José and most popular destinations is generally safe, and even though you've bought bottled water, ordered frescos en leche, and drunk your soda warm (without ice cubes—which are made from water, after all), you still may encounter some intestinal difficulties. Most of this is just due to tender northern stomachs coming into contact with slightly more aggressive Latin American intestinal flora. In extreme cases of diarrhea or intestinal discomfort it's worth taking a stool sample to a lab for analysis. The results will usually pinpoint the amoebic or parasitic culprit, which can then be readily treated with available over-the-counter medicines.

Except in the most established and hygienic of restaurants, it's also advisable to avoid ceviche, a raw seafood salad, especially if it has any shellfish in it. It could be home to any number of bacterial critters.

RIPTIDES Many of Costa Rica's beaches have riptides, strong currents that can drag swimmers out to sea. A riptide occurs when water that has been dumped on the shore by strong waves forms a channel back out to open water. These channels have strong currents. If you get caught in a riptide, you can't escape the current by swimming toward shore; it's like trying to swim upstream in a river. To break free of the current, swim parallel to shore and use the energy of the waves to help you get back to the beach.

BEES & SNAKES Although Costa Rica has Africanized bees (the notorious "killer bees" of fact and fable) and several species of venomous snakes, your chances of being bitten are minimal, especially if you refrain from sticking your hands into hives or under rocks in the forest. If you know that you're allergic to bee stings, consult your doctor before traveling. If you really want to see a fer-de-lance or eyelash viper, it might be best to visit one in San José's Serpentarium (see chapter 5).

HEALTH, ACCIDENT & LOSS INSURANCE

Before leaving on your trip, contact your health-insurance provider and find out whether your insurance will cover you while you're away. If not, contact a travel agent and ask about travel health-insurance policies. A travel agent can also tell you about trip insurance to cover cancellations or loss of baggage. If you have homeowner's or renter's insurance, you may be covered against theft and loss even while you're on vacation. Be sure to check this before taking out additional insurance. Some credit cards provide trip insurance when you charge an airline ticket, but be sure to check with your credit-card company before assuming you have it. If you decide that your current insurance is inadequate, you can contact your travel agent for information on various types of travel insurance, including insurance against cancellation of a prepaid tour.

The following companies offer various types of travel insurance: **Teletrip** (Mutual of Omaha), P.O. Box 31685, Omaha, NE 68131 (☎ **800/228-9792**); **Wallach and Co.,** P.O. Box 480, Middleburg, VA 22117-0480 (☎ **800/237-6615**); **Universal Travel Protection,** P.O. Box 1707, Monument, CO 80132-1707 (☎ **800/211-8952;** fax 800/694-4311; http://utravelpro.com; e-mail: sales@utravelpro.com); and **Access America, Inc.,** P.O. Box 90315, Richmond, VA 23286-4991 (☎ **800/284-8300**).

SPANISH LANGUAGE PROGRAMS

As more and more people travel to Costa Rica with the intention of learning Spanish, the number of options continues to increase. Courses are of varying lengths and intensiveness and often include cultural activities and day excursions. Most Spanish schools can also arrange for homestays with a middle-class Tico family for a total-immersion experience. Classes are often one-on-one and can last anywhere from 2 to 8 hours a day. Listed below are some of the larger and more-established Spanish-language schools, with approximate costs. As you'll see, most are located in San José; however, there are listings here for schools in Heredia, Monteverde, Manuel Antonio, and Playa Ballena, and all things being equal I'd certainly rather spend 2 weeks or a month in either of these spots than in San José. Contact the schools for the most current price information.

Central American Institute for International Affairs (ICAI), Apdo. 10302-1000, San José, Costa Rica (☎ **506/233-8571;** fax 506/221-5238; e-mail: icai@expreso.co.cr), offers a 4-week Spanish-language immersion program, along with a homestay, for $1,020. In the United States, contact the Language Studies Enrollment Center, 13948 Hemlock Dr., Penn Valley, CA 95946 (☎ and fax **916/432-7615**).

Centro Cultural Costarricense Norteamericano, Apdo. 1489-1000, San José, Costa Rica (☎ **506/225-9433;** fax 506/224-1480; e-mail: acccnort-@sol.racsa.co.cr), is an extension of the U.S. embassy and government programs in Costa Rica. Its facilities are the most extensive of any language school in the country. A 2-week intensive course with 4 hours of instruction per day costs $375. Homestays are also available for $250 per week.

Centro Linguístico Conversa, Apdo. 17-1007, Centro Colón, San José, Costa Rica (☎ **800/354-5036** in the U.S. and Canada, or 506/221-7649 in Costa Rica;

fax 506/233-2418; www.conversa.co.cr; e-mail: conversa@sol.racsa.co.cr), has classes in both San José and Santa Ana (a suburb of the capital city). A 2-week course here with 4 hours of classes each day, including room and board with a Costa Rican family, costs between $510 and $1,020 for one person, depending on the level of luxury you're looking for.

✪ **Centro Panamericano de Idiomas (C.P.I.),** Apdo. 151-3007, San Joaquín de Flores, Heredia (☎ and fax **506/265-6213;** www.cpi-edu.com; e-mail: anajarro@sol.racsa.co.cr). This school has two campuses: one in the quiet suburban town of Heredia and the other in Monteverde. A 4-week program, with 4 hours of classes per day and a homestay, costs $1,120.

Costa Rican Language Academy, Apdo. 336-2070, San José, Costa Rica (☎ **800/854-6057** in the U.S., or 506/233-8914; fax 506/233-8670; e-mail: crlang@sol.racsa.co.cr), has intensive programs with classes only on Monday through Thursday, to give students a chance to make longer weekend excursions. They also integrate latin dance and Costa Rican cooking classes into the program. A 2-week class with 4 hours of class per day, plus homestay, costs $510 per person.

Costa Rica Spanish Institute (COSI), Apdo. 1366-2050, San Pedro, Costa Rica (☎ **506/253-9272;** fax 506/253-2117; e-mail: cosicr@sol.racsa.co.cr), offers small classes in the San Pedro neighborhood of San José, as well as a program at the Pacific beach of Playa Ballena. The cost is $280 per week with a homestay in San José, $450 at the beach.

✪ **Forester Instituto Internacional,** Apdo. 6945-1000, San José, Costa Rica (☎ **506/225-3155,** 506/225-0135, or 506/225-1649; fax 506/225-9236; e-mail: forester@sol.racsa.co.cr), is located 75 meters south of the Automercado in the Los Yoses district of San José. The cost of a 4-week language course with a homestay and excursions is approximately $1,020.

✪ **Instituto Britanico,** Apdo. 8184-1000, San José (☎ **506/234-9054;** fax 506/253-1894). This venerable institution has installations in the Los Yoses neighborhood of San José and up in Liberia, Guanacaste. A 3-week course with 3 hours of classes per day and homestay costs $675.

Instituto Interamericano de Idiomas (Intensa), Calle 33 between Avenidas 1 and 3 (Apdo. 8110-1000), San José (☎ **506/224-6353;** fax 506/253-4337; www.intensa.com), offers 2- to 4-week programs. A 4-week, 4-hours-per-day program with a homestay costs $1,040.

✪ **La Escuela Idiomas D'Amore,** Apdo. 67, Quepos (☎ and fax **213/912-0600** in the U.S., ☎ and fax 506/777-1143 in Costa Rica; e-mail: damore@sol.racsa.co.cr), is situated in the lush surroundings of Manuel Antonio National Park. Four weeks of classes (4 hours per day) costs $1,240; with a homestay, the cost rises to $1,490. Part of your tuition is donated to the World Wildlife Fund.

Pura Vida Instituto, Avenida 3 between Calles 8 and 10 (Apdo. 890-3000), Heredia (☎ and fax **506/237-0387;** e-mail: puravida@amerisol.com). For $370, you receive 5 days of classroom instruction and 7 days lodging (room and board) with a Costa Rican family.

2 When to Go

Costa Rica's high season for tourism runs from late November to late April, which coincides almost perfectly with the northern winter and major holiday travel periods. It also coincides perfectly with the Costa Rican dry season. If you want some unadulterated time on a tropical beach and a little less rain during your rainforest experience, this is the time to come. During this period you will find tourism in full tilt—prices are higher, attractions are more crowded, and reservations need to be made in advance.

In recent years local tourism operators have begun calling the tropical rainy season (from May through mid-November) the "green season." The adjective is appropriate. At this time of year, even brown and barren Guanacaste province becomes lush and verdant. I love traveling around Costa Rica during the rainy season. It's easy to find or at least negotiate reduced rates, there are far fewer fellow travelers, and the rain is often limited to a few hours each afternoon (although you can occasionally get socked in for a week at a time).

CLIMATE

Costa Rica is a tropical country and has distinct wet and dry seasons. However, some regions are rainy all year and others are very dry and sunny for most of the year. Temperatures vary primarily with elevation, not with season: On the coasts it's hot all year, while up in the mountains it can be cool at night any time of year. At the highest elevations (10,000 to 12,000 feet), frost is common.

Average Daytime Temperatures & Rainfall in San José

	Jan	Feb	Mar	Apr	May	June	July	Aug	Sept	Oct	Nov	Dec
Temp. (°F)	66	66	69	71	71	71	70	70	71	69	68	67
Temp. (°C)	19	19	20.5	21.5	21.5	21.5	21	21	21.5	20.5	20	19.5
Days of rain	1	0	1	4	17	20	18	19	20	22	14	4

Generally speaking, the rainy season (or "green season") is from May to mid-November. Costa Ricans call this wet time of year their winter. The dry season, considered summer by Costa Ricans, is from mid-November through April. In **Guanacaste,** the dry northwestern province, the dry season lasts several weeks longer than in other places. Even in the rainy season, days often start sunny, with rain falling in the afternoon and evening. On the **Caribbean coast,** especially south of Limón, you can count on rain year-round, although this area gets less rain in September and October than the rest of the country.

In general, the best time of year to visit is in December and January, when everything is still green from the rains, but the sky is clear. However, there are advantages to traveling during the rainy season: Prices are lower, the country is greener, and there are fewer visitors. Rain doesn't usually fall all day long, and when it does, it's a good opportunity to climb into a hammock and catch up on your reading.

HOLIDAYS

Because Costa Rica is a Roman Catholic country, most of its holidays and celebrations are church related. The major celebrations of the year are Christmas, New Year, and Easter, which are all celebrated for several days. Keep in mind that Holy Week (Easter Week) is the biggest holiday time in Costa Rica and many families head for the beach (this is the last holiday before school starts). Also, there is no public transportation on Holy Thursday or Good Friday. Government offices and banks are closed on official holidays, transportation services are reduced, and stores and markets may also close.

Official holidays in Costa Rica include: **January 1** (New Year's Day), **March 19** (St. Joseph's Day), Thursday and Friday of Holy Week, **April 11** (Juan Santamaría's Day), **May 1** (Labor Day), **June 29** (Saints Peter and Paul's Day), **July 25** (annexation of the province of Guanacaste), **August 2** (Virgin of Los Angeles's Day), **August 15** (Mother's Day), **September 15** (Independence Day), **October 12**

(Discovery of America/Día de la Raza), **December 8** (Immaculate Conception of the Virgin Mary), **December 24 and 25** (Christmas), **December 31** (New Year's Eve).

COSTA RICA CALENDAR OF EVENTS

Some of the events listed here might be considered more of a *happening* than an event, so there's not, for instance, a Virgin of Los Angeles PR Committee that readily dispenses information. If I haven't listed a contact number, your best bet is to call the Costa Rica Tourist Board (ICT) at ☎ **800/343-6332** in the U.S., or 800/012-3456 or 506/223-1733 in Costa Rica.

January

- **Fiesta of Santa Cruz,** Santa Cruz, Guanacaste. A religious celebration honoring the Black Christ of Esquipulas (a famous Guatemalan statue), featuring folk dancing, marimba music, and bullfights. Mid-January.
- **Copa del Café** (The Coffee Cup), San José. An important international event on the junior tennis tour. Matches are held at the Costa Rica Country Club (☎ **506/228-9333**). First week in January.

February

✪ **Fiesta of the Diablitos,** Rey Curré village near San Isidro de El General. Boruca Indians wearing wooden devil and bull masks perform dances representative of the Spanish conquest of Central America; there are fireworks displays and an Indian handcrafts market. Date varies; call the Costa Rican Tourist Board (☎ **800/343-6332**) for current schedule.

March

✪ **Día del Boyero** (Oxcart Drivers' Day), San Antonio de Escazú. Colorfully painted oxcarts parade through this suburb of San José, and local priests bless the oxen. Second Sunday.

✪ **National Orchid Show,** San José. Orchid growers the world over gather to show their wares, trade tales and secrets, and admire the hundreds of species on display. Exact location and date change from year to year.

April

- **Holy Week** (week before Easter). Religious processions are held in cities and towns throughout the country. Dates vary from year to year (between late March and early April).
- **Juan Santamaría Day,** Alajuela. Costa Rica's national hero is honored with parades, concerts, and dances. April 11.

May

- **Carrera de San Juan.** The country's biggest marathon runs through the mountains, from the outskirts of Cartago to the outskirts of San José. May 17.

July

✪ **Fiesta of the Virgin of the Sea,** Puntarenas. A regatta of colorfully decorated boats carrying a statue of Puntarenas's patron saint marks this festival. A similar event is held at Playa de Coco. Saturday closest to July 16.

- **Annexation of Guanacaste Day,** Liberia. Tico-style bullfights, folk dancing, horseback parades, rodeos, concerts, and other events celebrate the day when this region became part of Costa Rica. July 25.

August

- **Día de San Ramon,** San Ramon. More than two dozen statues of saints from various towns are brought to San Ramon, where they are paraded through the streets. August 31.
- ✪ **Fiesta of the Virgin of Los Angeles,** Cartago. This is the annual pilgrimage day of the patron saint of Costa Rica. Many people walk from San José to the basilica in Cartago. August 2.

September

- **Costa Rica's Independence Day.** Celebrated all over the country. Most distinctive are the nighttime parades of children. September 15.
- **International Beach Clean-Up Day.** A good excuse to chip in and help clean up the beleaguered shoreline of your favorite beach. Third Saturday. For more information contact Quint Newcomer at ☎ **506/645-5053.**

October

- **Fiesta del Maiz,** Upala. A celebration of corn with local beauty queens wearing outfits made from corn plants. October 12.
- ✪ **Limón Carnival/Día de la Raza,** Limón. A smaller version of Mardi Gras complete with floats and dancing in the streets commemorates Columbus's discovery of Costa Rica. Week of October 12.

November

- **All Soul's Day/Día de los Muertos,** celebrated countrywide. Although not as elaborate or ritualized as in Mexico, most Costa Ricans take some time this day to remember the dead with flowers and trips to the cemeteries.

December

- **Día de la Polvora,** San Antonio de Belen and Jesus Maria de San Mateo. Fireworks displays to honor Our Lady of the Immaculate Conception. December 8.
- **Fiesta de la Yeguita,** Nicoya. A statue of the Virgin of Guadalupe is paraded through the streets accompanied by traditional music and dancing. December 12.
- **Fiesta de los Negritos,** Boruca. Boruca Indians celebrate the feast day of their patron saint, the Virgin of the Immaculate Conception, with costumed dances and traditional music. December 8.
- **Las Posadas.** A countrywide celebration during which children and carolers go door-to-door seeking lodging in a reenactment of Joseph and Mary's search for a place to stay. Begins December 15.
- ✪ **Festejos Populares,** San José. Bullfights, a horseback parade (El Tope), and a carnival with street dancing, floats, and a pretty impressive bunch of carnival rides all take place at the fairgrounds in Zapote. On the night of December 31, there is a dance in the Parque Central. Last week of December.

3 Tips for Travelers with Special Needs

FOR SENIORS Many airlines now offer senior-citizen discounts, so be sure to ask about these when making reservations. Due to its temperate climate, stable government, low cost of living, and friendly pensionado program, Costa Rica is popular with retirees from North America. There are excellent medical facilities in San José and plenty of community organizations to help retirees feel at home. If you would like to learn more about applying for residency and retiring in Costa Rica, contact the **Association of Residents of Costa Rica** in San José (☎ **506/233-8068;** e-mail: arcrsacc@sol.racssa.co.cr).

Elderhostel, 75 Federal St., Boston, MA 02110 (☎ **617/426-8056;** fax 617/426-8351; www.elderhostel.org; e-mail: general@elderhostel.org), offers very popular study tours and group excursions to Costa Rica. To participate in an Elderhostel program, either you or your spouse must be at least 60 years old. Great bird-watching excursions and lectures on Costa Rican culture and history are some of the more interesting aspects of these trips.

FOR SINGLES You'll pay the same penalty here that you would elsewhere: Rooms are more expensive if you aren't traveling in a pair. If you're looking for someone to travel with, you could try **Vacation Partners,** 853 Sanders Rd., Suite 272, Northbrook, IL 60062 (☎ **847/205-2008;** fax 847/205-4401; www.vacationpartners.com; e-mail: manny@vacationpartners.com), which provides a computer database matching service for a $100 annual fee.

FOR FAMILIES Hotels in Costa Rica often give discounts for children under 12 years old, and children under 3 or 4 years old are usually allowed to stay for free. However, don't expect the same type of discounts you'll find in the United States.

Many hotels, villas, and cabinas come equipped with kitchenettes or full kitchen facilities. These can be a real money-saver for those traveling with children.

FOR GAY & LESBIAN TRAVELERS Costa Rica is a conservative, macho country where public displays of same-sex affection are rare and somewhat shocking. However, gay and lesbian travelers are generally treated with respect and should not experience any harassment.

The International Gay and Lesbian Association (☎ **506/234-2411**) and **La Asociación Triangulo Rosa** (☎ **506/258-0214**) are two local organizations that may be able to provide up-to-date information and tips for gay and lesbian travelers.

FOR STUDENTS Costa Rica is the only country in Central America with a network of hostels that are affiliated with the International Youth Hostel Federation. Ask at the **Toruma Youth Hostel** (☎ **506/224-4085**), Avenida Central between Calles 29 and 31, San José, for information on hostels at Rara Avis, La Fortuna, Lake Arenal, San Isidro, Jacó Beach, Liberia, and Rincón de la Vieja National Park.

In San José, there are now two student travel agencies: **OTEC** (☎ **506/256-0633**) is located at Edificio Ferencz, 2nd floor, Calle 3 between Avenidas 1 and 3, 275 meters north of the National Theater; **Sin Límites** (☎ **506/280-5182**) is located on Calle 35 and Avenida Central, 200 meters east of the Kentucky Fried Chicken in Los Yoses. If you already have an **international student identity card,** you can use it to get discounts on airfares, hostels, national and international tours and excursions, car rentals, and store purchases. If you don't have one, stop by either the OTEC or Sin Límites office with proof of student status, two passport photos, and a passport or other identification that shows you are under 35 years old; for about $10, they'll prepare an ID card for you.

Students interested in a working vacation in Costa Rica should contact the **Council on International Educational Exchange (CIEE)** (☎ **800/226-8624;** www.ciee.org; e-mail: cts@ciee.org), which has offices around the United States, Europe, and other parts of the world. This organization has work/study programs, volunteer programs, and a network of retail outlets, which can make discounted travel arrangements and issue official student identity cards. The organization also offers a service that provides you with a work permit and basic orientation. Participants are on their own to find work. The service fee in Costa Rica is $550, but for

$650 you can also get round-trip airfare from Miami. The program is available only from June 1 to October 1 and the work permit has a 3-month time limit. CIEE also publishes *Smart Vacations: The Traveler's Guide to Learning Adventures Abroad* (St. Martin's Press, 1993), a directory of companies, organizations, and schools offering educational travel programs.

FOR TRAVELERS WITH DISABILITIES Although facilities are beginning to be adapted for those with disabilities, in general there are few handicapped-accessible buildings in Costa Rica. In San José, sidewalks are crowded and uneven. Few hotels offer handicapped-accessible accommodations, and there are neither public buses nor private vans equipped for the disabled. In short, it is difficult for a person with disabilities to get around in Costa Rica.

However, there is one agency that specializes in tours for travelers with disabilities and restricted ability. **Vaya Con Silla de Ruedas,** Apdo. 1146-2050, San Pedro Montes de Oca, Costa Rica (☎ **506/225-8561;** fax 506/225-0931; e-mail: vayacon@sol.racsa.co.cr), has a ramp and elevator-equipped van and knowledgeable bilingual guides. They charge very reasonable prices and can provide anything from simple airport transfers to complete multiday tours.

Kosta Roda Foundation, Apdo. 217-8000, San Isidro de El General, Costa Rica (☎ and fax **506/771-7482;** e-mail: chabote@ticonet.co.cr), is a nonprofit organization dedicated to helping the Costa Rican tourist industry remove barriers (architectural and societal). They can provide assistance and information for travelers with disabilities.

Mobility International USA, P.O. Box 10767, Eugene, OR 97440 (☎ **541/343-1284;** fax 541/343-6812; www.miusa.org; e-mail: info@miusa.org), is a membership organization that promotes international educational exchanges for people of all ages with disabilities. In the past they have had trips to Costa Rica and may again in the future. For a $25 membership fee, you'll receive their quarterly newsletter and access to their referral service.

AccessAbility Travel, 186 Alewife Brook Pkwy., Cambridge, MA 02138 (☎ **800/645-0001** or 617/661-9200; TTY 800/228-5378 or 617/661-9948; fax 617/661-3354; www.disabled-travel.com; e-mail: cao@fpt.com), is a travel agency specializing in handicapped-accessible travel.

4 Getting There

BY PLANE It takes between 3 and 7 hours to fly to Costa Rica from most U.S. cities, and as Costa Rica becomes more and more popular with North American travelers, more flights are available into San José's **Juan Santamaría International Airport.** There are several car-rental agencies at the airport. Consider yourself warned: Driving in Costa Rica is not for everyone. See "Getting Around" in this chapter and "Getting There" in chapter 5 for further information.

The Major Airlines There are a host of airlines flying into Costa Rica. Be warned that the smaller Latin American carriers tend to make several stops (sometimes unscheduled) en route to San José, thus increasing flying time. In fact, Aviateca, Lacsa, and Taca are actually operating under a single parent company, and they practice code-sharing, so the flight you book on one of these airlines may in fact fly under another name. The following airlines currently serve Costa Rica from the United States, using the gateway cities listed. **American Airlines** (☎ **800/433-7300**) has daily flights from Miami and Dallas/Fort Worth. **Aviateca** (Guatemalan, ☎ **800/327-9832**) flies daily from Los Angeles and Miami and three times weekly from Houston. **Continental** (☎ **800/231-0856**) offers flights daily from Houston and from Newark International. **Delta** (☎ **800/221-1212**) offers flights from Atlanta. **Lacsa** (Costa Rican, ☎ **800/225-2272**) has service from Dallas, New York, Miami, Orlando, New Orleans, Los Angeles, and San Francisco. **Mexicana** (☎ **800/531-7921**) offers flights from Montreal, Toronto, Chicago, Los Angeles, New York, Denver, Miami, Dallas/Fort Worth, San Antonio, San Jose (California), and San Francisco. **Taca** (El Salvadoran, ☎ **800/535-8780**) flies from Los Angeles, San Francisco, Houston, New Orleans, New York, Miami, and Washington. **United Airlines** (☎ **800/241-6522**) has daily flights from Los Angeles and Washington, with one stop either in Mexico or Guatemala. From Europe, you can take any major carrier to a hub city such as Miami or New York and then make connections to Costa Rica. Alternatively, **Iberia** (☎ **800/772-4642**) from Spain, **LTU International Airways** (☎ **800/888-0200**) from Germany, and **KLM** (☎ **800/447-4747**) from Holland have established routes to San José, stopping in Miami.

Regular Airfares In recent years airfares have been very unstable, and price wars have flared up unexpectedly. Fares also vary seasonally. Such instability makes it very difficult to quote an airline ticket price. **APEX** (advance-purchase excursion) fares are often similar from airline to airline, but the cost of a first-class ticket can vary greatly. At press time, an APEX or a coach ticket from New York to San José was running between $540 and $850; from Los Angeles, between $600 and $900. First class from New York starts at about $1,600; from Los Angeles, $1,450. On rare occasions, special fares may be offered at rock-bottom prices, but don't count on it. Regardless of how much the cheapest ticket costs when you decide to fly, you can bet it will have some restrictions. It will almost certainly be nonrefundable, and you may have to pay for it within 24 hours of making a reservation. You'll likely have to buy the ticket in advance (anywhere from 1 week to 30 days). You will also likely have to stay over a weekend and limit your stay to 30 days or less.

Ticket Brokers/Consolidators You can shave a little bit off the price you pay by purchasing an airline ticket from what is known as a ticket broker or consolidator. These ticketing agencies sell discounted airfares on major airlines; although the tickets have as many, and sometimes more, restrictions as an APEX ticket, they can help you save money. You'll find ticket brokers' listings—usually just a column of destinations with prices beside them—in the Sunday travel sections of major city newspapers. You'll almost never get the ticket for the advertised price, but you will probably get it for less than the airline would sell it to you. If you'd like to shop around, try **Cheap Tickets** (☎ **800/377-1000;** www.cheaptickets.com) or **Airbrokers** (☎ **800/883-3273;** www.airbrokers.com; e-mail: sales@airbrokers.com).

BY BUS Bus service runs regularly from both Panama City, Panama, and Managua, Nicaragua. From Panama City it's a 20-hour, 558-mile (900km) trip, with buses leaving daily at noon. The one-way fare is $17. It's always better to get a direct bus to Panama City rather than one that stops in David. I've heard that some of the Panama buses do have bathrooms, but they are often out of order. Call the **Tica Bus Company** (☎ **506/221-8954**) for further information. From Managua, it's 11 hours and 279 miles (450km) to San José. Buses leave Managua daily at 6 and 7am; the one-way fare is $8 to $12. For more information, call the Tica Bus Company or Sirca Company (☎ **506/222-5541**).

Neither of these bus companies will reserve a seat by telephone, so buy your ticket in advance—several days in advance if you plan to travel on weekends or holidays.

BY CAR It is possible to travel to Costa Rica by car, but it can be difficult, especially for U.S. citizens. After leaving Mexico, the Interamerican Highway (also known as the Pan American Highway) passes through Guatemala, El Salvador, Honduras, and Nicaragua before reaching Costa Rica. All of these countries can be problematic for travelers for a variety of reasons, including internal violence, crime, and visa formalities. If you do decide to undertake this adventure, take the Gulf coast route from the border crossing at Brownsville, Texas, as it involves traveling the fewest miles through Mexico. Those planning to travel this route should look through *Driving the Pan-Am Highway to Mexico and Central America* by Audrey and Raymond Pritchard, available from Costa Rica Books, Suite 1 SJO 981, P.O. Box 025216, Miami, FL 33102 (☎ **800/365-2342** or ☎ and fax 506/232-5613).

Car Documents You will need a current driver's license, as well as your vehicle's registration and a copy of its title, in order to enter the country.

Central American Auto Insurance Contact **Sanborn's Insurance Company,** 2009 S. 10th St., McAllen, TX 78505 (☎ **800/222-0158** or 210/686-0711; www.hiline.net/sanborns; e-mail: sanborns@hiline.net), located about 1½ hours from Brownsville, Texas. They can supply you with trip insurance for Mexico and Central America (you won't be able to buy insurance after you've left the United States) and an itinerary. Sanborn's also has branches at other U.S./Mexico border crossings.

Safety Along the way, it's advisable not to drive at night because of the danger of being robbed by bandits. Also, drink only bottled beverages along the way, to avoid any unpleasant microbes that might be lurking in the local tap water.

BY CRUISE SHIP More than 200 cruise ships stop each year in Costa Rica, calling at Limón on the Caribbean coast and at Puerto Caldera on the Pacific coast. Cruise lines that offer stops in Costa Rica include **Cunard** (☎ **800/5-CUNARD**), **Holland America** (☎ **800/426-0327**), **Princess** (☎ **800/421-0522**), **Royal Caribbean** (☎ **800/327-6700**), and **Royal Cruise Line** (☎ **800/872-6400**). Contact these companies directly or visit a travel agent to find out more information about cruising to Costa Rica. Most cruise travel is wholesale, and the best bargains can usually be obtained from such wholesalers and consolidators as **Cruise World** (☎ **800/588-7447**), **Cruises, Inc.** (☎ **800/596-5529**), and **Forever Cruising** (☎ **800/338-8005**).

PACKAGE TOURS It's sometimes cheaper to purchase an airfare-and-hotel package rather than just an airline ticket. This is especially true if airfares happen to be high and you plan to travel with a companion. There's a multitude of both tour operators and packagers, with various specialties, so it's best to work with a travel agent to select the tour or package that's right for you.

Companies that specialize in travel to Costa Rica include **Costa Rica Experts,** 3166 N. Lincoln Ave., Chicago, IL 60657 (☎ **800/827-9046** or 312/935-1009); **Tourtech International,** 17780 Fitch St., Suite 110, Irvine, CA 92714 (☎ **800/882-2636**); and **Holbrook Travel,** 3540 NW 13th St., Gainesville, FL 32609 (☎ **800/451-7111** or 904/377-7111). One Canadian company specializing in tours to Costa Rica is **Mony Tours,** 5540 Cote des Neiges, Montreal H3T 1V9 (☎ **514/733-5396**).

In addition, quite a few tour operators based in the United States and Costa Rica offer natural-history and "soft adventure" tours and packages that can include stays at remote nature lodges; you'll find a comprehensive listing of these organizations in chapter 4.

5 Getting Around

BY PLANE Flying is one of the best ways to get around Costa Rica. Because the country is quite small, flights are short and not too expensive. The domestic airlines of Costa Rica are **Sansa,** Calle 24 between Avenida Central and Avenida 1 (☎ **506/233-0397**, 506/233-3258, or 506/233-5330), which offers a free shuttle bus from its downtown office to the airport, and **Travelair** (☎ **506/232-7883** or 506/220-3054), which charges slightly more for flights to the same destinations, but is popular because it is more reliable. I personally highly recommend Travelair over Sansa. Sansa has an unfriendly and unwieldy reservation system, they frequently overbook flights, and they have been known to change schedules with short or little notice. Flights times are generally between 20 minutes and a little over an hour. Travelair operates from **Tobís Bolaños International Airport** in Pavas, 4 miles (6.4km) from San José. The ride from downtown to Pavas takes about 10 minutes, and a metered taxi fare should cost $6 to $8. The ride from the airport to downtown is a different story—most taxis refuse to use their meter, and the standard fee is set at double the metered rate, around $10 to $12. Sansa operates from San José's Juan Santamaría International Airport.

In the high season (December to May), be sure to book reservations well in advance. For Sansa flights, you don't have to call Costa Rica to make reservations—you can book flights through **Lacsa** (☎**800/225-2272**). But BE CAREFUL: I've heard horror stories of ticket vouchers issued in the U.S. not being accepted in Costa Rica; always reconfirm once you arrive. You can book flights on Sansa via the Web or e-mail (www.travelair-costarica.com; reservations@travelair-costarica.com).

If you plan to return to San José, buy a round-trip ticket—it's always nice to have a confirmed seat, and with Travelair you'll save a little money.

BY BUS This is by far the best way to visit most of Costa Rica. Buses are inexpensive and relatively well maintained, and they go nearly everywhere. There are three types. Local buses are the cheapest and slowest; they stop frequently and are generally a bit dilapidated. Express buses run between San José and most beach towns and major cities; they sometimes operate only on weekends and holidays. A few luxury buses and minibuses drive to destinations frequented by foreign travelers. For details on how to get to various destinations from San José, see the "Getting There" sections of the regional chapters that follow.

BY CAR Renting a car in Costa Rica is not something to be entered into lightly. The roads are in terrible shape, most rural intersections are unmarked, and for some reason, sitting behind the wheel of a car seems to turn peaceful Ticos into homicidal maniacs. In addition, although rental cars no longer bear special license plates, they are still readily identifiable to thieves and frequently targeted. (Nothing is ever safe in a car in Costa Rica, although parking in guarded parking lots helps.) Transit police also seem to target tourists. Never pay money directly to a police officer who stops you for any traffic violation. Before driving off with a rental car, be sure that you inspect the exterior and point out to the rental company representative every tiny scratch, dent, tear, or any other damage. It's a common practice with many Costa Rican car-rental companies to claim that you owe payment for minor dings and dents the company finds when you return the car. Also, if you get into an accident, be sure the rental company doesn't try to bill you for a higher amount than the deductible on your rental contract.

On the other hand, renting a car allows you much greater freedom to explore remote areas of the country. Several people have written to me to say that they feel visitors should always rent four-wheel-drive vehicles. However, unless you are going to a destination that you know requires four-wheel drive, you will probably do just fine with a standard vehicle. I have always rented a regular car during the dry season, and though there are roads I can't drive down, I have always managed to get around just fine (including to Monteverde). During the rainy season and on the Nicoya and Osa peninsulas, four-wheel-drive vehicles are recommended.

Avis Rent A Car (☎ **800/331-1212** in the U.S., 506/442-1321 at airport, 506/232-9922 in downtown San José), **Budget Car Rental** (☎ **800/527-0700** in the U.S., 506/441-4444 at airport, 506/223-3284 in downtown San José), **Hertz Rent A Car** (☎ **800/654-3131** in the U.S., 506/441-0097 at airport, 506/221-1818 in downtown San José), and **National Car Rental** (☎ **800/328-4567** in the U.S., 506/441-6533 at airport, 506/290-8787 in downtown San José) all have offices in Costa Rica. You will save somewhere between $35 and $75 per week on a car rental if you make a reservation in your home country at least 1 week before you need the car. For example, at press time, the least expensive Hertz car rents for $378 per week, including insurance in San José, but if you book this same car in advance from the United States, you can get it for $317 per week, including insurance. To rent a car in Costa Rica, you must be at least 21 years old and have a valid driver's license and a major credit card in your name. See the "Getting Around" section of chapter 5 for details on renting a car in San José. Cars can also be rented in Quepos, Jacó, Liberia, and Limón.

Gasoline Regular leaded gasoline is most readily available in Costa Rica, and most rental cars take regular. However, some of the newer models run on unleaded, which is sold as "super." Ask your rental agent what type of gas your car takes. When going off to remote places, try to leave with a full tank of gas since gas stations can be hard to find. If you need to gas up in a small town, you can sometimes get gasoline from enterprising families who sell it by the liter from their houses. Look for hand-lettered signs that say "gasolina."

Road Conditions Road conditions in San José and throughout the country became a political issue in 1995, after years of corruption and neglect in the Transportation Ministry had caused the roads to deteriorate to the point that local newspapers were running contests to find the largest potholes. There was no lack of contenders. Despite the uproar and indignation, and political promises to the contrary, little relief or repair work has been done. If possible, before you rent a vehicle, find out about the road conditions to see if it is necessary to have a four-wheel-drive vehicle to get to your destination. Even paved roads are often badly potholed, so stay alert. Road conditions get especially tricky during the rainy season, when heavy rains and runoff can destroy a stretch of pavement in the blink of an eye.

Route numbers are rarely used on road signs in Costa Rica, though there are frequent signs listing the number of kilometers to various towns or cities. In 1997, the Transportation Ministry began placing helpful markers at major intersections and turnoffs, but your best bet for on-road directions are still billboards and advertisements for hotels located at your destination.

Maps Car-rental agencies and the ICT information centers (see "Visitor Information" and "Entry Requirements" at the beginning of this chapter) at the airport and in downtown San José have adequate road maps. Other sources in San José are **Chispas Books,** Calle 7 between Avenidas Central and 1 (☎ **506/256-8251**); **Libreria Lehmann,** Avenida Central between Calles 1 and 3 (☎ **506/223-1212**); and **Jimenez and Tanzi,** Calle 3 between Avenidas 1 and 3 (☎ **506/233-8033**).

Driving Rules A current foreign driver's license is valid for the first 3 months you are in Costa Rica. Seat belts are required for the driver and front-seat passengers. Motorcyclists must wear a helmet. Highway police use radar, so keep to the speed limit (usually between 60 and 90 kilometers per hour) if you don't want to get pulled over. Maybe it just seems this way, but the police seem to target rental cars. Never give the police any money. Speeding tickets can be charged to your credit card for up to a year after you leave the country if they are not paid before departure.

Breakdowns Be warned that emergency services, both vehicular and medical, are extremely limited once you leave San José, and their availability is directly related to the remoteness of your location at the time of breakdown. You'll find service stations spread over the entire length of the Interamerican Highway, and most of these have tow trucks and mechanics. The major towns of Puntarenas, Liberia, Quepos, San Isidro, Palmar, and Golfito all have hospitals, and most other moderately sized cities and tourist destinations have some sort of clinic or health-services provider.

If you're involved in an accident, you should contact the **Transit Police** (☎ **506/222-9330** or 506/222-9245); if they have a unit close by they'll send one. An official transit police report will greatly facilitate any insurance claim. Or you can call the **Judicial Police** (☎ 117) to see if they have any units nearby. If you can't get help from any of these, try to get written statements from any witnesses.

If the police do show up, you've got a 50/50 chance of finding them helpful or downright antagonistic. Many officers are unsympathetic to the problems of what they perceive to be rich tourists running around in fancy cars with lots of expensive toys and trinkets. Success and happy endings run about equal with horror stories.

If you don't speak Spanish, expect added difficulty in any emergency or stressful situation. Don't expect that rural (or urban) police officers, hospital personnel, service station personal, or mechanics will speak English.

Last, a little tip: If your car breaks down and you're unable to get well off the road, check to see if there are reflecting triangles in the trunk. If there are, place them as a warning for approaching traffic, arranged in a wedge that starts at the shoulder about 100 feet back and nudges gradually toward your car. If your car has no triangles, try to create a similar warning marker using a pile of leaves or branches.

BY FERRY There are four different ferries operating across the Gulf of Nicoya. Three are car ferries: one across the Río Tempisque, one from Puntarenas to Playa Naranjo, and one from Puntarenas to Paquera; and one is a passenger ferry that runs from Puntarenas to Paquera. For more detailed information, see chapter 6.

HITCHHIKING Although buses go to most places in Costa Rica, they can be infrequent in the remote regions, and so local people often hitchhike to get to their destination sooner. If you're driving a car, people will frequently ask you for a ride. In rural areas, a hitchhiker carrying a machete is not necessarily a great danger, but use your judgment. Hitchhiking is not recommended on major roadways or in urban areas. In rural areas it's usually pretty safe. However, women should be extremely cautious about hitchhiking anywhere in Costa Rica. If you choose to hitchhike, keep in mind that if a bus doesn't go to your destination, there probably aren't too many cars going there, either. Good luck.

LOCATING ADDRESSES While there are some street addresses in Costa Rica, they're almost never used. Addresses are usually given as a set of coordinates, such as "Calle 3 between Avenida Central and Avenida 1." Many addresses include additional information such as the number of meters or *varas* (an old Spanish measurement roughly equal to a yard) from a specified intersection or some other well-known landmark. Often the additional information is confusing to visitors but is essential for taxi drivers. In San José, many addresses use distances from the Coca-Cola bottling plant that once stood near the market. The bottling plant is long gone, but the address description remains and is used to designate one of San José's principal bus stations. Sometimes you'll also come across the word *bis* (or just *B*) in an address, as in "Calle 3 bis" or "Calle 3B." This is used when, for instance, a street splits for a short distance, giving you Calle 3 and Calle 3 bis. In outlying neighborhoods, addresses can become long directions such as "50 meters south of the old church, then 100 meters east, then 20 meters south." Luckily for the visitor, these directions are usually pretty precise, and taxi drivers have no problem with them.

SUGGESTED ITINERARIES

Planning Your Itinerary

The following are the main travelers' destinations in Costa Rica: San José; Manuel Antonio National Park; Jacó Beach; the beaches of Guanacaste and the Nicoya Peninsula; Monteverde Cloud Forest Reserve; Tortuguero National Park; Irazú Volcano; Poás Volcano; Arenal Volcano and Arenal Lake; the Osa Peninsula; jungle lodges throughout the country; Cahuita/Puerto Viejo; and Dominical.

If You Have 1 Week

Day 1 Visit the museums and the National Theater in San José.

Day 2 Make an excursion to the Orosi Valley, Lankester Gardens, and Irazú Volcano.

Days 3 and 4 Travel to Monteverde (or another cloud-forest region) and spend a day exploring the cloud forest.

Days 5 and 6 Head to one of the many Pacific coast beaches. I'd recommend Manuel Antonio for its accessibility and range of accommodations and activities.

Day 7 Return to San José.

If You Have 2 Weeks

Day 1 Visit the museums and the National Theater in San José.

Days 2 and 3 Make an excursion to the Orosi Valley, Lankester Gardens, and Irazú Volcano one day and go river rafting on the other day.

Days 4 and 5 Travel to Lake Arenal to see the eruptions of Arenal Volcano, soak in some hot springs, and maybe go to Caño Negro National Wildlife Refuge.

Days 6 and 7 Travel to Monteverde (or another cloud-forest region) and explore the cloud forest.

Day 8 Explore Rincón de la Vieja or Santa Rosa National Park.

Days 9, 10, 11, and 12 Spend these days relaxing on a beach (I'd recommend Punta Uva) or perhaps exploring the Corcovado National Park or Osa Peninsula.

Days 13 and 14 Fly to Tortuguero National Park and spend a day there, returning the next day by boat and bus.

6 Tips on Accommodations

Tourism insiders had been predicting it for years, but 1997 was the first tough year for Costa Rican hoteliers. When the tourist boom hit Costa Rica in the late 1980s, hotels began popping up like mushrooms after a few days of rain. The past few years have seen the opening of the first megaresorts, and several more are under construction and near completion. There is a hotel glut, and this is good news for travelers and bargain hunters. A weeding-out period has apparently begun, and hotels that want to survive are being forced to reduce their rates and provide better service.

Glut notwithstanding, there are still few hotels or resorts here offering the sort of luxurious accommodations you'll find in Hawaii or the Caribbean. Sure, there are hotels that meet international standards, but Costa Rica is not yet a luxury resort destination.

The country's strong suit is its moderately priced hotels. In the $60 to $90 price range, you'll find comfortable, and sometimes outstanding, accommodations almost anywhere in the country. However, room size and quality vary quite a bit within this price range, so don't expect the kind of uniformity you find in the United States.

If you're even more budget- or bohemian-minded, there are quite a few good deals for less than $60 per double room.

Bed-and-breakfasts have also been proliferating. Though the majority of these are in the San José area, you will now find B&Bs (often gringo owned and operated) throughout the country. Another welcome hotel trend in the San José area is the renovation and conversion of old homes into small hotels. Most of these hotels are in the **Barrio Amon** district of downtown San José, which means you'll have to put up with noise and exhaust fumes, but these establishments have more character than any other hotels in the country. You'll find similar hotels in the **Paseo Colón** and **Los Yoses** districts.

Costa Rica has been riding the ecotourism wave, and there are now small nature-oriented ecolodges throughout the country. These lodges offer opportunities to see wildlife (including sloths, monkeys, and hundreds of species of birds) and learn about tropical forests. They range from spartan facilities catering primarily to scientific researchers to luxury accommodations that are among the finest in the country. Keep in mind that though the nightly room rates at these lodges are often quite moderate, the price of a visit starts to climb when you throw in transportation (often on chartered planes), guided excursions, and meals. Also, just because your travel agent can book a reservation at most of these lodges doesn't mean they're not remote. Make sure to find out how you will be getting to and from your ecolodge and just what tours and services are included in your stay. Then think long and hard about whether you really want to put up with hot, humid weather (cool and wet in the cloud forests), biting insects, rugged transportation, and strenuous hikes to see wildlife.

A couple of uniquely Costa Rican accommodation types you may encounter are the *apartotel* and the *cabina.* An apartotel is just what it sounds like: an apartment hotel, where you'll get a full kitchen and one or two bedrooms, along with daily maid service. Cabinas are Costa Rica's version of cheap vacation lodging. They're very inexpensive and very basic—often just cinder-block buildings divided into small rooms. Occasionally you'll find a cabina where the units are actually cabins, but these are a rarity. Cabinas often have clothes-washing sinks or *pilas,* and some come with kitchenettes, since they cater primarily to Tico families on vacation.

Throughout Costa Rica the more budget-oriented lodgings often feature shared bathrooms. Unless specifically noted, all the rooms I've listed in this guide have a private bath.

Please note that room rates listed in this book do not include the 16.3% room taxes. These taxes will add considerably to the cost of your room.

If you are booking direct (either by phone/fax or e-mail), remember that most hotels are accustomed to paying as much as 20% in commission to agents and wholesalers. It never hurts to ask if they'll pass some of that on to you.

I've separated hotel listings throughout into several broad categories: **Very Expensive,** $125 and up; **Expensive,** $80 to $125; **Moderate,** $40 to $80; and **Inexpensive,** under $40 double.

Please note that at the beach for under $20, you usually don't get hot water. In the mountains, you usually get what are commonly referred to as suicide showers—small heating elements that double as the showerhead.

7 Tips on Dining

Simply put, Costa Rican cuisine is unmemorable. San José remains the unquestioned gastronomic capital of the country, and here you can find the cuisines of the world served with formal service at moderate prices. At the most expensive restaurant in San José, you'll have to drink a lot of wine to spend more than $40 per person on dinner. It gets even cheaper outside of the city. There are several excellent French and Italian restaurants around the San José area, as well as Peruvian, Japanese, Swiss, and Spanish establishments. Costa Rica is a major producer and exporter of beef, and consequently, San José has plenty of steakhouses. Unfortunately quanity doesn't mean quality. Unless you go to one of the better restaurants or steakhouses, you will probably be served rather tough steaks, cut rather thin.

One recent development is worth noting, and it is slowly making my opening caveat untrue: With the increase in international tourism and the need to please a more sophisticated palate, local chefs have begun to create a "nouvelle Costa Rican cuisine," updating time-worn recipes and using traditional ingredients in creative ways. Unlike most visitors to Costa Rica however, this phenomenon hasn't traveled far outside of downtown San José.

Outside of the capital, your options get very limited, very fast. In fact, many beach resorts are so remote that you have no choice but to eat in the hotel's dining room, and on other beaches, the only choices aside from the hotel dining rooms are cheap local places or overpriced tourist traps serving indifferent meals. At remote jungle lodges, the food is usually served buffet- or family style and can range from bland to inspired, depending on who's doing the cooking at the moment, and turnover is high. Consequently, I hesitate to recommend food in such lodges—the cook I had when I visited may be long gone by the time you arrive.

If you're looking for cheap eats, you'll find them in little restaurants known as sodas, which are the equivalent of diners in the United States. At a soda you'll have lots of choices: rice and beans with steak, rice and beans with fish, rice and beans with chicken, or, for vegetarians, rice and beans. You get the picture. Rice and beans are standard Tico fare, and are served at all three meals a day. Also, though there is plenty of seafood available throughout the country, at sodas it's all too often served fried.

Costa Ricans love to eat, and they love to have a view when they eat. Almost anywhere you go in the country, if there's a view, there will be a restaurant taking advantage of it. These restaurants are often called *miradores.* If you are driving around the country, don't miss an opportunity to dine with a view at some little roadside restaurant. The food may not be fantastic, but the scenery will be.

I have separated restaurant listings throughout this book into three price categories based on the average cost per person of a meal, including tax and service charge but not including beer or wine. The categories are: **Expensive,** more than

$15; **Moderate,** $8 to $15; and **Inexpensive,** less than $8. (Note, however, that individual items in the listings—entrees, for instance—do not include the sales or service taxes.) Keep in mind that there is an additional 13% sales tax, as well as a 10% service charge. Ticos rarely tip, but that doesn't mean you shouldn't. If the service was particularly good and attentive, you should probably leave a little extra.

8 Tips on Shopping

FOOD FADS Buy coffee. Even if you're not a coffee drinker, you're bound to know someone who is, and coffee is the best buy in Costa Rica. **Café Britt** is the coffee you'll see sold in hotels and souvenir shops all over the country. Sure, it's good coffee, but it's also a little overpriced. If you go into the central market in downtown San José or a grocery store anywhere in the country, you'll find coffee at much lower prices. If you're in **Manuel Antonio,** pick up your coffee at Café Milagro (see chapter 8), and if you're in **Monteverde,** you can get some fresh roasted beans at CASEM (see chapter 7). Just be sure you're buying whole beans (*grano entero*) and not ground (*molido*). Costa Rican grinds are much finer than U.S. grinds and often have sugar mixed right in with the coffee. Costa Rica also produces its own coffee liqueur **(Café Rica),** and a creme liqueur **(Salicsa),** both of which are quite inexpensive. These are best purchased in a liquor store or a grocery store. In fact, grocery stores are where I do my best gift shopping.

If you'd like to add a little spice to your life, **Tipica Tropical Sauce** produces a line of spicy salsas made from mango, pineapple, passion fruit, and tamarind. A small bottle costs around 75¢ and makes a great gift. **Salsa Lizano,** a flavorful green sauce used the same way we use steak sauce in the U.S., is another condiment worth bringing home with you.

HANDCRAFTS Costa Rica is not known for its handcrafts, though it does have a town, **Sarchí,** that's filled with handcraft shops. Sarchí is best known as the home of the colorfully painted Costa Rican oxcart, reproductions of which are manufactured in various scaled-down sizes. These make excellent gifts. (If you want a larger oxcart, it can be easily disassembled and shipped to your home.) There's also a lot of furniture made here. So scant are the country's handcraft offerings that most tourist shops sell Guatemalan clothing, Panamanian appliquéd textiles, El Salvadoran painted wood souvenirs, and Nicaraguan rocking chairs. There's quite a bit of wood carving being done in the country, but it is, for the most part, either tourist-souvenir wooden bowls, napkin holders, and the like, or elegant and expensive art pieces. One exception is the work of **Barry Biensanz,** whose excellent hardwood creations are sold at better gift shops around the country.

COSTA RICAN SPECIALTIES A few other items worth keeping an eye out for include reproductions of pre-Columbian gold jewelry and carved-stone figurines. The former are available either in solid gold, silver, or gold plated. The latter, though interesting, are extremely heavy.

On the streets of San José you'll see a lot of hammocks for sale. I personally find the Costa Rican hammocks a little crude and unstable. The same vendors usually have single-person hanging chairs, which are strung similarly to the full-size hammocks and are a better bet.

Finally, one new item you'll see at gift shops around the country is Cuban cigars. Although these are illegal to bring into the United States, they are perfectly legal and readily available in Costa Rica.

FAST FACTS: Costa Rica

American Express **American Express** (☎ **506/257-0155**) has a counter in San José at the Banco de San José on Calle Central between Avenidas 3 and 5. It's open Monday through Friday from 8am to 7pm, and Saturday 9am to 1pm. To report lost or stolen traveler's checks within Costa Rica, call toll-free ☎ **0-800-011-0080.** To report a lost or stolen American Express card from inside Costa Rica, call ☎ **0-800-012-3211** for an English language-operator, or 0-800-001-0184

Business Hours Banks are usually open Monday through Friday from 9am to 3pm, though many have begun to offer extended hours. Offices are open Monday through Friday from 8am to 5pm (many close for an hour at lunch). Stores are generally open Monday through Saturday from 9am to 6pm (many close for an hour at lunch). Stores in modern malls generally stay open until 8 or 9pm and don't close for lunch. Most bars are open until 1 or 2am.

Cameras/Film Most types of film are available, as are developing services. However, prices are higher than in the United States, so I recommend bringing plenty of film with you and waiting until you get home for processing. For camera repair in San José, head to **Equipos Fotograficos Canon,** on Avenida 3 between Calles 3 and 5 (☎ **506/233-0176**).

Climate See "When to Go," earlier in this chapter.

Currency See "Money," earlier in this chapter.

Customs You can bring into Costa Rica half a kilo of tobacco products, 3 liters of liquor, and two cameras duty-free. You can also bring in personal electronic equipment such as laptop computers and video recorders.

Documents Required See "Visitor Information" and "Entry Requirements," earlier in this chapter.

Driving Rules See "Getting Around," earlier in this chapter.

Drug Laws Drug laws in Costa Rica are strict, so stay away from marijuana and cocaine. Many prescription drugs are sold over the counter here, but often the names are different from those in the United States and Europe. It's always best to have a prescription from a doctor.

Electricity The standard in Costa Rica is the same as in the United States: 110 volts AC (60 cycles). However, three-pronged outlets can be scarce, so it's helpful to bring along an adapter.

Embassies/Consulates The following embassies and consulates are located in San José: **United States Embassy,** in front of Centro Commercial, on the road to Pavas (☎ **506/220-3939**); **Canadian Consulate,** Oficentro Ejecutivo La Sabana, Edificio 5 (☎ **506/296-4149**); **British Embassy,** Paseo Colón between Calles 38 and 40 (☎ **506/258-2025**).

Emergencies In case of an emergency, dial ☎ **911** (which has an English-speaking operator); for an ambulance, call ☎ **128;** to report a fire, call ☎ **118;** to contact the police, call ☎ **506/295-3000** for an English-speaking operator, or 506/221-1365 or 506/221-5337 in Spanish.

Holidays See "When to Go," earlier in this chapter.

Information See "Visitor Information" and "Entry Requirements," earlier in this chapter. Also see individual city sections for local information offices.

Language Spanish is the official language of Costa Rica. *Berlitz Latin-American Spanish Phrasebook and Dictionary* (Berlitz Guides, 1992) is probably the best phrase book to bring with you.

Laundry Laundromats are few and far between in Costa Rica—more common are hotel laundry services, which can sometimes be expensive. For listings of Laundromats, see individual city and town sections.

Liquor Laws Alcoholic beverages are sold every day of the week throughout the year, with the exception of the 2 days before Easter and the 2 days before and after a presidential election. The legal drinking age is 18, though it's almost never enforced.

Lost or Stolen Credit/Charge Cards If you lose your credit or charge card, you can call the following toll-free numbers from within Costa Rica. **American Express** (☎ **0-800-012-3211**); **MasterCard** and **Visa** (☎ **0-800-011-0030**).

Mail Mail to the United States usually takes a little over 1 week to reach its destination. Postage for a postcard is 25¢; for a letter, 30¢. A post office is called a *correo* in Spanish. You can get stamps at the post office and at gift shops in large hotels. If you are sending mail to Costa Rica, it generally takes about 10 days to reach San José, although it can take as much as a month to get to the more remote corners of the country. Plan ahead. Also, note that many hotels and ecolodges have mailing addresses in the United States. Always use these addresses when writing from North America or Europe. Never send cash, checks, or valuables through the Costa Rican mail system.

Maps **The Costa Rican Tourist Board** (ICT; see "Visitor Information" and "Entry Requirements," earlier in this chapter) can usually provide you with good maps of both Costa Rica and San José. Other sources for maps in San José are **Chispas Books,** Calle 7 between Avenidas Central and 1 (☎ **506/256-8251**); **Libreria Lehmann,** Avenida Central between Calles 1 and 3 (☎ **506/223-1212**); and **Jimenez & Tanzi,** Calle 3 between Avenidas 1 and 3 (☎ **506/233-8033**).

Newspapers/Magazines There are six Spanish-language dailies in Costa Rica and one English-language weekly, the *Tico Times.* There is also a bilingual tourist weekly, *Costa Rica Today.* In addition, you can get *Time, Newsweek,* and several U.S. newspapers at some hotel gift shops and a few of the bookstores in San José. If you understand Spanish, *La Nación*'s "Viva" section lists what's going in the world of music, theater, dance, etc.

Passports See "Visitor Information" and "Entry Requirements," earlier in this chapter.

Police In most cases you should dial ☎ **117** for the police, and you should be able to get someone who speaks English on the line. Other numbers for the **Judicial Police** are ☎ **506/221-1365** and 506/221-5337. The numbers for the **Traffic Police (Policia de Transito)** are ☎ **506/222-9330** or 506/222-9245.

Radio/TV There are about 10 local TV channels; cable and satellite TV from the United States are also common. There are scores of radio stations on the AM and FM dials. 107.5 FM is my favorite English-language station, with a wide range of musical programming, as well as news and some talk shows.

Rest Rooms These are known as *sanitarios, servicios sanitarios,* or *baños.* They are marked *damas* (women) and *hombres* or *caballeros* (men). Public rest rooms are hard to come by. You will almost never find a public rest room in a city park or downtown area. There are usually public rest rooms at most national park entrances, and much less frequently inside the national park (there are usually plenty of trees and bushes). In the towns and cities it gets much trickier. One must count on the generosity of some hotel or restaurant. Same goes for most beaches. However, most restaurants, and to a lesser degree hotels, will let you use their facilities. Especially if you buy a Coke or something. Bus and gas stations often have rest rooms, but in many cases these are quite disgusting.

Safety Though most of Costa Rica is safe, crime has become much more common in recent years. San José is known for its pickpockets, so never carry a wallet in your back pocket. A woman should keep a tight grip on her purse (keep it tucked under your arm). Thieves also target gold chains, cameras and video cameras, prominent jewelry, and nice sunglasses. Be sure not to leave valuables in your hotel room. Don't park a car on the street in Costa Rica, especially in San José; there are plenty of public parking lots around the city.

Rental cars generally stick out, and they are easily spotted by thieves, who know that such cars are likely to be full of expensive camera equipment, money, and other valuables. Don't ever leave anything of value in a car parked on the street, not even for a moment. Public intercity buses are also frequent targets of stealthy thieves. Never check your bags into the hold of a bus if you can avoid it. If this can't be avoided, keep your eye on what leaves the hold. If you put your bags in an overhead rack, be sure you can see the bags at all times. Try not to fall asleep.

For safety tips while swimming, see "Riptides" under "Health Information," above.

Taxes All hotels charge 16.3% tax. Restaurants charge 13% tax and also add on a 10% service charge, for a total of 23% more on your bill. There is an airport departure tax of $17.

The departure tax is actually a separate little piece of paper that you must fill out (name, passport number, etc.) and that has a few official governmental stamps on the back. These must be purchased at the airport (either from some independent guys roaming around out front, or from one of two desks inside the airport) or in advance through a local (CR) travel agent; the tax/piece of paper is turned in to Immigration after check-in, as you enter the gate area.

Taxis Taxis are common and inexpensive in San José but harder to find and more expensive in rural areas. In San José, taxis are supposed to charge metered fares. Outside of the city and on longer rides, be sure to agree on a price beforehand. For more information on taxis in San José, see "Getting Around—By Taxi" in chapter 5.

Telegrams/Wiring Money **Western Union** (☎ **0-800-777-7777**) has numerous offices around San José and in several major towns and cities around the country. It offers a secure and rapid, although pricey, money wire service, as well as telegram service. **Radiográfica** (☎ **506/287-0087**) at Calle 1 and Avenida 5 in San José also has telegram service.

Telephones/Faxes Costa Rica has an excellent phone system, with a dial tone similar to that heard in the United States. All phone numbers in Costa Rica have seven digits. For information, dial ☎ **113.** A pay phone costs around 10 colónes (5¢) per minute. Pay phones will either take a calling card, or 5-, 10-, or 20-colón coins. Calling cards are becoming more and more prominent, and you can purchase them in a host of gift shops and pharmacies. However, pay phones are generally hard to find and frequently unreliable. It is often best to call from your hotel, although you will likely be charged around 100 colónes per call.

For making international calling-card and collect calls, you can reach an **AT&T** operator by dialing ☎ **0-800-011-4114, MCI** by dialing ☎ **0-800-012-2222, Sprint** by dialing ☎ **0-800-013-0123, Canada Bell** by dialing ☎ **0-800-015-1161, British Telephone** by dialing ☎ **0-800-044-1044,** and a **Costa Rican international operator** by dialing ☎ **116** (pay phones may sometimes require a coin deposit). The Costa Rican telephone system allows direct international dialing, but it's expensive. To get an international line, dial 00 followed by the country code (1 for the United States) and number.

To call Costa Rica from the United States, dial the international access code, 011, followed by the country code 506, then the local number.

You can make international phone calls, as well as send faxes, from the **ICE office,** Avenida 2 between Calles 1 and 3, in San José (☎ **506/255-0444**). The office is open daily from 7am to 10pm. Faxes cost around $2 per page to the United States. (Many hotels will also offer the same service for a fee.) **Radio-gráfica** (☎ **506/287-0087**) at Calle 1 and Avenida 5 in San José also has fax service.

Time Costa Rica is on central standard time, 6 hours behind Greenwich mean time.

Tipping Tipping is not necessary in restaurants, where a 10% service charge is always added to your bill (along with a 13% tax). If service was particularly good, you can leave a little at your own discretion, but it's not mandatory. Porters and bellhops get around 75¢ per bag. You don't need to tip a taxi driver unless the service has been superior—a tip is not usually expected.

Useful Telephone Numbers For directory assistance, call ☎ **113;** for international directory assistance, call ☎ **124;** for the exact time, call ☎ **112.**

Visas See "Visitor Information" and "Entry Requirements," earlier in this chapter.

Water Though the water in San José is said to be safe to drink, water quality varies outside of the city. Because many travelers do get sick within a few days of arriving in Costa Rica, I recommend playing it safe and sticking to bottled drinks as much as possible and avoiding ice.

4 The Active Vacation Planner

Although it's possible to come to Costa Rica and stay clean and dry, most visitors want to spend some time getting their hair wet, their feet muddy, and their adrenaline pumping. To many, tropical rain forests and cloud forests are the stuff of myth and legend. Those who are lucky enough to explore them come back speaking with awe and admiration about what they've experienced. Partly because evolution is a slow process, and partly because much of the country's natural landscape is protected in national parks and bioreserves, Costa Rica's primary forests are still in pretty much the same state as when early explorers such as Columbus saw them and are open to adventurous travelers. Along the coasts and just offshore, there are an equal number of options for the active traveler.

As awareness of the value of tropical forests and interest in visiting them have grown, dozens of lodges and tour companies have sprung up to cater to travelers interested in enjoying the natural beauties of Costa Rica. These lodges are usually situated in out-of-the-way locations, sometimes deep in the heart of a forest and sometimes on a farm with only a tiny bit of natural forest. However, they all have one thing in common: They cater to environmentally aware people with an interest in nature and offer such activities as bird watching, rafting, kayaking, horseback riding, and hiking. For detailed listings of these lodges, many of which offer special packages, see the "Where to Stay & Dine" sections of the regional chapters that follow (chapters 6 through 10).

There are myriad approaches to planning an active vacation in Costa Rica. This chapter lays out your options, from tour operators who run multiactivity package tours that often include stays at ecolodges, to the best places in Costa Rica to practice particular activities (with listings of tour operators, guides, and outfitters that specialize in each), to an overview of the country's national parks and bioreserves, with suggestions for how to combine a visit to one or two of these places during your stay. After a few tips on health and safety in the wilderness, the chapter closes with a list of educational and volunteer travel options for those with a little more time on their hands and a desire actively to assist Costa Rica in the maintenance and preservation of its natural wonders.

1 Organized Adventure Trips

Since many travelers have limited time and resources, organized ecotourism or adventure travel packages, arranged by tour operators in the United States or Costa Rica, are a popular way of combining several activities. Bird watching, horseback riding, rafting, and hiking can be teamed with, say, visits to Monteverde Biological Cloud Forest Preserve and Manuel Antonio National Park.

Traveling with a group has several advantages over traveling independently: Your accommodations and transportation are arranged, and most (if not all) of your meals are included in the cost of a package. If your tour operator has a reasonable amount of experience and a decent track record, you should proceed to each of your destinations quickly without the snags and long delays that those traveling on their own can face. You'll also have the opportunity to meet like-minded souls who are interested in nature and active sports.

In the best cases, group size is kept small (between 10 and 20 people), and tours are escorted by knowledgeable guides who are either naturalists or biologists. Be sure to ask about difficulty levels when you're choosing a tour. While most companies offer "soft adventure" packages that those in moderately good, but not phenomenal, shape can handle, others focus on more hard-core activities geared toward only seasoned athletes or adventure travelers.

U.S.–BASED ADVENTURE TOUR OPERATORS

These agencies and operators specialize in well-organized and coordinated tours that cover your entire stay. Many travelers prefer to have everything arranged and confirmed before arriving in Costa Rica, and this is a good idea for first-timers and during the high season. Be warned, most of these operators are not cheap, with 10-day tours generally costing a little over $2,000 per person, not including airfare to Costa Rica.

Costa Rica Connections, 975 Oso St., San Luis Obispo, CA 93401 (☎ **800/345-7422** or 805/543-8823; www.crconnect.com; e-mail: crconnec@crconnect.com), specializes in natural history tours of major national parks. There is a complete range of independent packages and scheduled group departures for fishing, ecotourism, kayaking/rafting, and dive trips, plus a special family-oriented package.

International Expeditions, One Environs Park, Helena, AL 35080 (☎ **800/633-4734** or 205/428-1700; e-mail: nature@ietravel.com; www.ietravel.com), specializes in independent programs and 10-day natural history group tours.

Journeys International, 4011 Jackson Rd., Ann Arbor, MI 48103 (☎ **800/255-8735** or 313/665-4407; www.gorp.com; e-mail: info@journeys-intl.com), offers small-group (no more than 4 to 12 people) natural history tours guided by Costa Rican naturalists. Eight-day, 10-day, and 3-week itineraries are available.

Mountain Travel–Sobek, 6420 Fairmount Ave., El Cerrito, CA 94530 (☎ **888/MTSOBEK** or 510/527-8100; fax 510/525-7718; www.mtsobek.com; e-mail: info@mtsobek.com), offers natural history tours with naturalist guides. Ten-day itineraries can include visits to Corcovado and Tortuguero national parks, Monteverde, and Arenal Volcano; activities include jungle walks, boat rides, snorkeling, and swimming. You'll spend your nights in nature lodges or out camping, with the exception of the first and last nights of each itinerary, which are spent in hotels in San José.

Overseas Adventure Travel, 625 Mount Auburn, Cambridge, MA 02138 (☎ **800/353-6262** or 617/876-0533), offers natural history and "soft adventure" 10- and 12-day itineraries, with optional 3-day add-on excursions. Tours are limited to no more than 16 people and are guided by naturalists. All accommodations are in small hotels, lodges, or tent camps. Itineraries include visits to most major national parks and private nature reserves.

Wilderness Travel, 1102 Ninth St., Berkeley, CA 94710 (☎ **800/368-2794** or 510/558-2488; www.wildernesstravel.com; e-mail: webinfo@wildernesstravel.com), specializes in 14-day natural history and bird-watching group tours that are arranged with tiered pricing, meaning that your trip's cost will vary depending on the number of people who sign up (cost increases with a smaller group). Tours include visits to Corcovado and Tortuguero national parks, Monteverde, Arenal Volcano, and Caño Negro National Wildlife Refuge, among other destinations.

In addition to these companies, many environmental organizations, including **The Sierra Club** (☎ **415/977-5500;** www.sierraclub.org; e-mail: information@sierraclub.org), **The Nature Conservancy** (☎ **800/628-6860;** www.tnc.org), and **The National Audubon Society** (☎ **800/274-4201;** www.audubon.org), regularly offer organized trips to Costa Rica.

COSTA RICAN TOUR AGENCIES

Since many U.S.–based companies subcontract portions of their tours to established Costa Rican companies, some travelers like to set up their tours directly with these companies, thereby cutting out the middleman.

There are literally scores of agencies in San José that offer a plethora of adventure options. These agencies can generally arrange everything from white-water rafting to sightseeing at one of the nearby volcanoes or a visit to a butterfly farm. Because these tours are sometimes held only when there are enough interested people or on set dates, it pays to contact a few of the companies before you leave the United States and find out what they might be doing when you arrive.

Costa Rica Expeditions, Dept. 235, P.O. Box 025216, Miami, FL 33102 (☎ **506/257-0766** or 506/222-0333; fax 506/257-1665; www.expeditions.co.cr; e-mail: costaric@expeditions.co.cr), offers 3-day/2-night and 2-day/1-night tours of Monteverde Biological Cloud Forest Preserve, Tortuguero National Park, and Corcovado National Park, as well as 1- to 2-day white-water rafting trips and other excursions. All excursions include transportation, meals, and lodging.

Costa Rica Sun Tours, Apdo. 1195-1250, Escazú (☎ **506/255-3418;** fax 506/255-3529; e-mail: suntours@sol.racsa.co.cr), specializes in multiday tours that include stays at small country lodges for nature-oriented travelers. Destinations visited include Arenal Volcano, with stays at the Arenal Observatory Lodge; Monteverde Cloud Forest, with stops in Poás and Sarchí; and Corcovado and Manuel Antonio national parks, with overnight stays at Tiskita Jungle Lodge, Corcovado Tent Camp, Lapa Rios, and Drake Bay Wilderness Lodge, among other accommodations.

Ecole Travel, Calle 7 between Avenidas Central and 1, San José, Costa Rica (☎ **506/223-2240;** fax 506/223-4128), offers tours and day trips around the country.

Fantasy Tours, Apdo. 962-1000, San José, Costa Rica (☎ **800/272-6654** in the U.S., 800/453-6654 in Canada, or 506/220-2126 in Costa Rica; fax 506/220-2393; www.fantasy.co.cr; e-mail: info@fantasy.co.cr), offers a comprehensive list of full-day tours to destinations that include Arenal Volcano and Tabacón Hot Springs, Poás and Irazú volcanoes, Manuel Antonio National Park, Carara Biological Reserve, and Bosque de Paz, a private biological reserve. White-water rafting expeditions, fishing trips, island cruises, and multiday tours are also available.

OTEC Viajes, Apdo. 323-1002, San José, Costa Rica (☎ **506/256-0633;** fax 506/233-2321; e-mail: gotec@sol.racsa.co.cr), offers a wide range of tour options and specializes in student and discount travel.

Sin Límites, Calle 35 and Avenida Central, 200 meters east of the Kentucky Fried Chicken in Los Yoses (☎ **506/280-5182;** fax 506/225-9325), specializes in student and discount travel.

Tam Tours, P.O. Box 1864-1000, San José, Costa Rica (☎ **506/256-0203;** fax 506/222-8092), offers a full gamut of San José–based day tours to such destinations as Arenal Volcano and Tabacón Hot Springs, Carara Biological Reserve, Sarchí, and local national parks. All tours include transportation, entry fees, lunch, and a guide. Prices range between $25 and $90.

2 Activities A to Z

Each listing in this section describes the best places to practice a particular sport or activity and lists tour operators and outfitters. If you want to focus on only one active sport during your Costa Rican stay, these companies are your best bets for quality equipment and knowledgeable service.

BIKING

There are several significant regional and international touring races in Costa Rica each year, but as a general rule the major roads are dangerous and inhospitable for cyclists. They're narrow, there's usually no shoulder, and most drivers show little care or consideration for those on two wheels.

The options are much more appealing for mountain bikers and off-track riders, however. Fat-tire explorations are relatively new to Costa Rica but growing fast. If you plan to do a lot of biking and are very attached to your rig, bring your own. However, several companies in San José and elsewhere rent bikes, and the quality of the equipment is improving all the time. See the regional chapters for rental listings.

The area around Lake Arenal and Arenal Volcano wins my vote as the best place for mountain biking in Costa Rica. The scenery's great, with primary forests, waterfalls, and plenty of trails. And nearby Tabacón Hot Springs is a perfect place for those with aching muscles to unwind at the end of the day. (See chapter 7.)

TOUR OPERATORS & OUTFITTERS

Aguas Bravas, P.O. Box 1504-2100, Costa Rica (☎ **506/292-2072;** fax 506/229-4837; www.aguas-bravas.co.cr; e-mail: info@aguas-bravas.co.cr), has a range of mountain-biking trips and is a particularly good bet in La Fortuna.

Coast To Coast Adventures, Apdo. 2135-1002, San José, Costa Rica (☎ and fax **506/225-6055;** www.ctocadventures.com; e-mail: info@ctocadventures.com), has its namesake 2-week trip that spans the country, traveling on horses and rafts, by mountain bikes, and on foot—with no motor vehicles involved. Custom-designed trips of shorter duration are also available.

Eco Treks Adventure Company, Dept. 262, P.O. Box 025216, Miami, FL 33102 (☎ **506/654-4578;** e-mail: ecotreks@ecotreks.com), based out of Playa Flamingo, specializes in mountain biking, among other sports and adventures.

Experience Plus/Specialty Tours, 1925 Wallenburg Dr., Ft. Collins, CO 80526 (☎ **800/685-4565**), offers self-guided and assisted bike tours across the country.

Rio Escondido Mountain Bikes, c/o Rock River Lodge, Apdo. 95, Tilarán, Costa Rica (☎ **800/678-2252** in the U.S., or 506/695-5644 in Costa Rica; e-mail: exextra@rio.com), offers rentals and tours around the Lake Arenal area.

Where to See the Resplendent Quetzal

Revered by pre-Columbian cultures throughout Central America, the resplendent quetzal has been called the most beautiful bird on earth. Ancient Aztec and Maya Indians believed that the quetzal protected them in battle, and even the bird's brilliant breast plumage has an Indian legend to explain it: When Spanish conquistador Pedro de Alvarado defeated Maya chieftain Tecun Uman in 1524 near what is today the town of Quezaltenango, Guatemala, the Maya chief was mortally wounded in the chest. Tecun Uman's protector quetzal covered the dying chieftain's body, and when, upon Tecun Uman's death, the quetzal arose, the once white-breasted bird had a blood-red breast. So integral is the quetzal to Guatemalan culture that its name is given to that country's currency.

About the size of a robin, the males of this species have brilliant red breasts; iridescent emerald green heads, backs, and wings; and white tail feathers complemented by a pair of iridescent green tail feathers that are nearly 2 feet long. The belief that these endangered birds live only in the dense cloud forests cloaking the higher slopes of Central America's mountains was instrumental in bringing many areas of cloud forest under protection as quetzal habitats, but researchers have recently discovered that the birds do not in fact spend their entire lives here. After nesting, between March and July, quetzals migrate down to lower slopes in search of food. These lower slopes have not been preserved in most cases, and now conservationists are trying to salvage enough lower elevation forests to help the quetzals survive. It is hoped that enough land will soon be set aside to assure the perpetuation of this magnificent species.

Though for many years Monteverde Biological Cloud Forest Preserve was the place to see quetzals, throngs of people crowding the preserve's trails now make the pursuit more difficult. Other places where you're more likely to see quetzals are in the Los Angeles Cloud Forest Reserve near San Ramón, on the Cerro de la Muerte between San José and San Isidro de El General, in Tapantí National Wildlife Refuge, and in Chirripó National Park.

Serendipity Adventures, Apdo. 64200, Naranjo, Costa Rica (☎ **800/635-2325** and fax 734/426-5026 in the U.S., or 506/556-2592; fax 506/556-2593; www.serendipityadventures.com; e-mail: costarica@serendipityadventures.com), offers several mountain-biking trips among its many other expeditions.

BIRD WATCHING

As one of the world's foremost ecotravel destinations, Costa Rica is visited by thousands of avid bird-watchers each year. With more than 850 species of resident and migrant birds identified, great bird-watching sites abound. Lodges with the best bird watching include: **Savegre Mountain Lodge,** in Cerro de la Muerte, off the road to San Isidro de El General (they can almost guarantee sightings of resplendent quetzals); **La Paloma Lodge** in Drake Bay (where you can sit on the porch of your cabin as the avian parade goes by); **Villa Blanca** in San Ramón (on the edge of a cloud forest reserve where quetzals are often seen); **La Selva Biological Station** in Puerto Viejo de Sarapiqui; **Aviarios del Caribe** just north of Cahuita; **Lapa Rios** and **Bosque del Cabo** on the Osa Peninsula; and **Rainbow Adventures** on Playa Cativa along the Gulfo Dulce.

Some of the best parks and preserves to visit are **Monteverde Biological Cloud Forest Preserve** (for resplendent quetzals and hummingbirds); **Corcovado**

National Park (for scarlet macaws); **Caño Negro Wildlife Refuge** (for wading birds, including jabiru storks); **Wilson Botanical Gardens** and the **Las Cruces Biological Station**, near San Vito (the thousands of flowering plants here are bird magnets); **Guayabo, Negritos, and Pájaros islands biological reserves** in the Gulf of Nicoya (for magnificent frigate birds and brown boobies); **Palo Verde National Park** (for ibises, jacanas, storks, and roseate spoonbills); **Tortuguero National Park** (for great green macaws); and **Rincón de la Vieja National Park** (for parakeets and curassows). Some good excursions to consider if bird watching is your passion are rafting trips down the Corobicí and Bebedero rivers near Liberia, boat trips to or at Tortuguero National Park, and hikes in any cloud forest.

U.S. Tour Operators

Field Guides, P.O. Box 160723, Austin, TX 78716-0723 (☎ **800/728-4953** or 512/327-4953; fax 512/327-9231; e-mail: fgileader@aol.com), is a specialty bird-watching travel operator. The 16-day tour of Costa Rica costs $2,850 not including airfare. Group size is limited to 14 participants.

Wings, 1643 N. Alvernon Way, Suite 105, Tucson, AZ 85712 (☎ **520/320-9868;** fax 520/320-9373; www.widdl.com/wings; e-mail wings@rtd.com), is also a specialty bird-watching travel operator with more than 26 years of experience in the field. The 17-day Costa Rica trip covers all the major bird-watching zones in the country and costs around $3000, not including airfare. Trip size is usually between 6 and 18 people.

Costa Rican Tour Agencies

Both **Costa Rica Expeditions,** Dept. 235, P.O. Box 025216, Miami, FL 33102 (☎ **506/257-0766** or 506/222-0333; fax 506/257-1665; www.expeditions.co.cr; e-mail: costaric@expeditions.co.cr), and **Costa Rica Sun Tours,** Apdo. 1195-1250, Escazú (☎ **506/255-3418;** fax 506/255-3529; e-mail: suntours@sol.racsa.co.cr), are well-established companies with very competent and experienced guides who offer a variety of tours to some of the better birding spots in Costa Rica. **Jungle Trails,** Apdo. 2413, San José 1000 (☎ **506/255-3486;** fax 506/255-2782), is a much smaller local company that sponsors 1-day birding excursions to Braulio Carrillo and Poás national parks, as well as more extensive multiday tours.

BUNGEE JUMPING & BALLOONING

Both of these sports are new to Costa Rica, so as yet there's only one operator who specializes in each activity. The price you'll pay is generally cheaper than in the United States, and the scenery is certainly more lush, so if you've never done either activity, this is a great place to give it a try.

Tropical Bungee (☎ **506/233-6455;** fax 506/255-4354; e-mail: galagui@sol.racsa.co.cr) will let you jump off a 265-foot bridge over the Rió Colorado for $45; if you want to do it twice, the cost is $70.

Serendipity Adventures, Apdo. 64200, Naranjo, Costa Rica (☎ **800/635-2325** and fax 734/426-5026 in the U.S., or 506/556-2592; fax 506/556-2593; www.serendipityadventures.com; e-mail: costarica@serendipityadventures.com), will take you up, up, and away in one of their hot-air balloons on a variety of single- or multiday tours, beginning around $195 per person.

CAMPING

Heavy rains, difficult access, and limited facilities make camping a real challenge in Costa Rica. Nevertheless, a backpack and tent will get you far from the crowds and into some of the most pristine and undeveloped nooks and crannies of the country.

Those who relish sleeping out on a beach but wouldn't mind a bit more luxury (beds, someone to prepare meals for you, and running water) might want to consider staying in one of the tent camps on the **Osa Peninsula** (Drake Bay Wilderness Resort or Corcovado Lodge Tent Camp) or down in **Manzanillo** (Almendros and Corales Tent Camp). See chapters 9 and 10 for details. Camping isn't allowed in all national parks, so read through the descriptions for each park carefully before you pack a tent.

If you'd like to participate in an organized camping trip, contact **Coast To Coast Adventures,** Apdo. 2135-1002, San José, Costa Rica (☎ and fax **506/225-6055;** www.ctocadventures.com; e-mail: info@ctocadventures.com), or **Serendipity Adventures,** Apdo. 64200, Naranjo, Costa Rica (☎ **800/635-2325** and fax 734/426-5026 in the U.S., or in Costa Rica at 506/556-2592; fax 506/556-2593; www.serendipityadventures.com; e-mail: costarica@serendipityadventures.com).

Another option is to hook up with a **Green Tortoise** (☎ **800/867-8647** or 415/956-7500 in the U.S.; e-mail: info@greentortoise.com) tour of Costa Rica. This bus tour/camping outfit runs around five trips each year in Costa Rica, with a 15-day tour of the country costing around $520 dollars, not including transportation to Costa Rica.

Finally, you can also rent your own Volkswagen Westfalia camper from **Siesta Campers** (☎ **310/530-3737** in the U.S.; e-mail: siesta@sol.racsa.co.cr).

In my opinion, the best place to pop up a tent on the beach is in Santa Rosa National Park, or at the Puerto Vargas campsite in Cahuita National Park. The best camping trek is, without a doubt, a hike through Corcovado National Park, or a climb up Mt. Chirripó.

CANOPY TOURS

Canopy tours are taking off in Costa Rica, largely because they are such a unique way to experience tropical rain forests. It's estimated that some two-thirds of a typical rain forest's species live in the canopy (the uppermost, branching layer of the forest). From the relative luxury of Aerial Tram's high-tech funicular to the rope-and-climbing-gear rigs of more basic operations, a trip into the canopy will give you a bird's-eye view of a neotropical forest. There are now canopy tour facilities in Monteverde, Aguas Zarcas (near San Carlos), and Rincón de la Vieja, as well as on Tortuga Island and at the Iguana Park. With the exception of the Aerial Tram, most involve strapping yourself into a climbing harness and being winched up to a platform some 100 feet above the forest floor, or doing the work yourself. Many of these operations have a series of treetop platforms connected by taut wires. Once up on the first platform, you glide to the next on a pulley, using your hand (protected by a leather glove) as a brake. My favorite canopy tour is at **Monteverde,** where the ascent goes up the inside of a strangler fig, in the space where the host tree once lived. Before you sign on to any tour, ask whether you have to hoist yourself to the top under your own steam, then make your decision accordingly.

CANOPY TOUR OPERATORS

Aerial Tram, Apdo. 1959-1002, San José, Costa Rica (☎ **506/257-5961;** fax 506/257-6053; www.rainforest.co.cr; e-mail: dosela@sol.racsa.co.cr), is located 50 minutes from San José. For $47.50 (transportation extra), this modern tram takes you on a 2-hour trip through the rain forest canopy. The entrance fee includes an additional guided hike.

Canopy Tours, Interlink 227, P.O. Box 025635, Miami, FL 33152 (☎ and fax **506/257-5149** or 506/256-7626; www.canopytour.co.cr; e-mail: canopy@sol.racsa.co.cr), is the largest canopy-tour operator, with sites in Monteverde, Aguas Zarcas, and Iguana Park.

CRUISING

Despite having extensive coastlines on both the Pacific Ocean and Caribbean Sea, cruising is still relatively underdeveloped in Costa Rica. Several of the major cruise lines pass briefly through Costa Rica, but these are generally on cruises that feature a crossing of the Panama Canal as their highlight. In terms of sailboat cruising, charter options are rather limited, and bareboat fleets are nonexistent.

Cruising options in Costa Rica range from transient cruisers setting up a quick charter business to converted fishing boats taking a few guests out to see the sunset.

Perhaps the most popular cruise in the country is a day trip from San José (the boats actually leave from Puntarenas) to Isla Tortuga in the Nicoya Gulf (see "Recreational Day Trips" in chapter 5, under the section "Side Trips from San José"). Alternatively, you can book a cruise to Tortuga from Playa Montezuma at the tip of the Nicoya Peninsula (see chapter 6 for details). It's much cheaper from here (around $25 per person), but the excursion doesn't include the gourmet lunch that's usually featured on cruises leaving from San José.

One interesting recent entry into the Costa Rican cruising scene is the **Windstar Cruise** line's (☎ **800/258-7245;** www.windstarcruises.com) 148-passenger, four-masted sail-assist cruise ship, *Wind Song,* which leaves out of Caldera on weeklong trips.

Another option is to take a cruise on the *Temptress.* This small cruise ship plies the waters off Costa Rica's Pacific coast from Santa Rosa National Park in the north to Corcovado National Park in the south. The ship has no pool or casino, but it does usually anchor in remote, isolated, and very beautiful spots. Each day you can choose between a natural-history tour or a recreational and cultural tour. For information, contact **Temptress Cruises,** 1606 NW LeJeune, Suite 301, Miami, FL 33126 (☎ **800/336-8423** or 305/871-2663 in the U.S.; 506/220-1679 in Costa Rica).

If diesel fumes and engine noise bother you, the best places to charter a sailboat are Playa del Coco, Playa Hermosa, and Playa Flamingo in Guanacaste province (see chapter 6); Quepos, along the central Pacific coast (see chapter 8); and Golfito, along the southern Pacific coast (see chapter 9). You can get information about sailboat rides at any one of the larger lodgings in these areas. If you're at Flamingo Beach, head to the marina, where you should be able to find a captain who will take you out. My favorite place to charter a sailboat is **Golfito.** From here, it's a pleasant, peaceful day's sail around the Golfo Dulce (see chapter 9).

DIVING AND SNORKELING

Many islands, reefs, caves, and rocks lie off the coast of Costa Rica, providing excellent spots for underwater exploration. Visibility varies with season and location. Generally, heavy rainfall tends to swell the rivers and muddy the waters, even well offshore. Banana plantations and their runoff have destroyed most of the Caribbean reefs, although there's still good diving at Isla Uvita, just off the coast of Limón, and in Manzanillo, down near the Panamanian border. Most divers choose Pacific dive spots like Caño Island, Bat Island, and the Catalina Islands, where you're likely to spot manta rays, moray eels, white-tipped sharks, and plenty of smaller fish and coral species. But the ultimate in Costa Rican dive experiences is a week spent on a chartered boat, diving off the coast of Coco Island.

Snorkeling is not incredibly common or rewarding in Costa Rica. The rain, runoff, and wave conditions that drive scuba divers well offshore tend to make coastal and shallow water conditions less than optimum. If the weather is calm and the water is clear, you might just get lucky. Ask at your hotel or check the different beach listings to find snorkeling options and operators up and down Costa Rica's coasts.

Scuba Diving Outfitters & Operators

In addition to the companies listed below, check the listings at specific beach and port destinations in the regional chapters.

Aggressor Fleet Limited, P.O. Box 1470, Morgan City, LA 70381-1470 (☎ **800/348-2628** or 504/385-2628; fax 504/384-0817; www.aggressor.com; e-mail: 103261.1275@compuserve.com), runs the 120-foot *Okeanos Aggressor* on regular trips out to Coco Island.

Aquamor, Manzanillo, Limón Province (☎ **506/228-9513;** e-mail: aquamor@sol.racsa.co.cr), is located just off the beach in Manzanillo and does combined kayak/dive trips as well as shore diving, boat dives, and certification classes.

Bill Beard Diving Safaris, Apdo. 121-5019, Playas del Coco, Costa Rica (☎ **800/779-0055** in the U.S., or 506/672-0012; fax 506/672-0231; www.diving-safaris.com; e-mail: billbeards@netrunner.net), is perhaps the largest, most professional, and best-established dive operation in the country. Based out of the Sol Playa Hermosa Hotel in Playa Hermosa, they are also the local pioneers in nitrox diving.

Buzos del Tropico, Apdo. 366-3100, Santo Domingo de Heredia, Costa Rica (☎ and fax **506/236-6135**), offers equipment rental, certification classes, and trips.

Eco Treks Adventure Company, Dept. 262, P.O. Box 025216, Miami, FL 33102 (☎ **506/654-4578;** e-mail: ecotreks@ecotreks.com), runs diving trips out of Playa Flamingo, in addition to mountain-biking and surfing tours.

Mundo Aquatico, Apdo. 7875-1000, San José, Costa Rica (☎ **506/224-9729;** fax 506/234-2982; e-mail: mundoac@sol.racsa.co.cr), offers equipment rental, certification classes, and tours. Tours go to Catalina and Bat Islands, as well as Isla del Caño.

Undersea Hunter (☎ **800/203-2120;** www.underseahunter.com; e-mail: cocos@underseahunter.com) offers the *Undersea Hunter* and its sister ship the *Sea Hunter,* two pioneers of the live-aboard diving excursions to Coco Island.

FISHING

Anglers in Costa Rican waters have landed more than 65 world-record catches, including blue marlin, Pacific sailfish, dolphin, wahoo, yellowfin tuna, guapote, and snook. Whether you want to head offshore looking for a big sail, wrestle a tarpon near a Caribbean river mouth, or choose a quiet spot on Arenal Lake to cast for guapote, you'll find it here. The best place to land a marlin is anywhere up or down the Pacific coast.

Fishing Lodges & Tour Operators

The lodges and operators listed below cater specifically to anglers. Many of the Pacific port and beach towns—Quepos, Puntarenas, Playas del Coco, Tamarindo, Flamingo, Golfito, Drake Bay, Zancudo—support large charter fleets; see chapters 4, 8, and 9 for recommended boats and captains. Costs for fishing trips usually range between $550 and $1,000 per day (depending on the size of the boat) for boat, captain, tackle, drinks, and lunch.

Americana Fishing Services, SJO 795, P.O. Box 025216, Miami, FL 33102. Ask for Richard Krug (☎ **506/223-4331**; fax 506/221-0096; e-mail: fishing@sol.racsa.co.cr). Richard writes a fishing column for the *Tico Times* and offers a wide body of knowledge about fishing. He can arrange and book tours, as well as provide useful advice.

Costa Rican Dreams, P.O. Box 79, Belén, Heredia, Costa Rica (☎ **506/239-3387** or 506/777-0593; fax 506/239-3383; e-mail: dreams@sol.racsa.co.cr). This is an agency/operator with its own boats.

Costa Rica Outdoors, Dept. SJO 2316, P.O. Box 025216, Miami, FL 33102 (☎ **800/308-3394** in the U.S., or 506/282-6743; fax 506/282-7241; e-mail: jruhlow@sol.racsa.co.cr).

Fresh Water Fishing Adventures, Via Alta, Bello Horizonte, Escazú, Costa Rica (☎ **800/434-6867** in the U.S., or ☎ and fax 506/228-4812 in Costa Rica).

J. P. Tours, P.O. Box 66-1100, Tibás, Costa Rica (☎ **506/257-8503;** fax 506/244/0552; e-mail: jpfishin@sol.racsa.co.cr).

Fishing Lodges

Rio Colorado Lodge, 2121 W. Juneau Ave., Tampa, FL 33604 (☎ **800/243-9777** in the U.S., or 506/232-4063; fax 815/933-3280 in the U.S., or 506/231-5987; www.sportsmansweb.com/riocolorado; e-mail: tarpon@sol.racsa.co.cr). Located at the Barra del Colorado National Wildlife Refuge.

Silver King Lodge, P.O. Box 025216, Dept. 1597, Miami, FL 33102 (☎ **800/847-3474** or 800/309-8125 toll-free from the U.S., or 506/381-1403; fax 506/381-0849; www.silverkinglodge.com; e-mail: slvrkng@sol.racsa.co.cr), is a luxury lodge at Barra del Colorado.

GOLF

Golf is still a nascent sport in Costa Rica. There are currently only three regulation 18-hole courses open to the public and/or tourists, but several others are either under construction or in the planning stages, with a potential boom shaping up in Guanacaste. Very shortly, there should be new courses in operation in playas Hermosa and Panamá, and near the port of Caldera at La Roca Resort.

The Meliá hotel chain runs two of the three courses, with the Meliá Cariari course (☎ **800/336-3542** in North America, or 506/239-0022 in Costa Rica; fax 506/239-2803; e-mail: cariari@sol.racsa.co.cr) just outside of San José. Greens fees here are $45. The hotel chain also runs the **Meliá Playa Conchal** (☎ **506/654-4123**; e-mail: mconchal@sol.racsa.co.cr) up in Guanacaste. Greens fees are $90 including cart. The Cariari course is open only to guests of the Cariari and Herradura hotels; the Playa Conchal course is brand-new and is currently accepting golfers staying at other hotels in the region. The only other course in operation is **Rancho Las Colinas** (☎ and fax **506/654-4089;** e-mail: rlc@compusource.net) near Playa Grande, also in Guanacaste. Greens fees there are $42 ($20 for a cart). This course is tentatively open to the public at the moment, but if the surrounding condominiums start selling, it may get more exclusive.

Golfers interested in a package deal or potentially playing a variety of courses should contact either the Meliá Cariari Hotel above, or **Golf Costa Rica Adventures,** Interlink 854, P.O. Box 02-5635, Miami, FL 33102 (☎ **800/477-8971** in the U.S., or ☎ and fax 506/446-6489; e-mail: golf@centralamerica.com).

HORSEBACK RIDING

Though Costa Rica is moving rapidly away from being a primarily agricultural economy, it retains its rural roots. This is perhaps most evident in the continued use of horses for real work and transportation throughout the country. What this means for travelers is that horses are easily available for riding, whether you want to take a sunset trot along the beach, ride through the cloud forest, or take a multiday trek

T'ai Chi in Paradise

For the past 9 years, tai chi master and two-time U.S. national champion Chris Luth has been leading weeklong retreats to Costa Rica, combining intensive classes in this ancient Chinese martial art with rain forest hikes, river rafting, and just enough beach time. For more information contact The Pacific School of T'ai Chi (☎ and fax **619/259-1401**).

through the northern zone. Almost anywhere outside San José is fine for climbing into a saddle.

OUTFITTERS & TOUR OPERATORS

Coast To Coast Adventures, Apdo. 2135-1002, San José, Costa Rica (☎ and fax **506/225-6055;** www.ctocadventures.com; e-mail: info@ctocadventures.com), specializes in 2-week trips spanning the country via horseback, raft, mountain bike, and on foot, with no motor vehicles involved. Other trips are also available.

Rancho Savegre Horseback Tours, Rancho Savegre, c/o Hotel Sirena, P.O. Box 02592, Miami, FL 33102 (☎ **506/777-0528;** fax 506/777-0165), offers 1-day and multiday horseback tours based out of Rancho Savegre, near Quepos.

Serendipity Adventures, Apdo. 64200, Naranjo, Costa Rica (☎ **800/635-2325** and fax 734/426-5026 in the U.S., or 506/556-2592; fax 506/556-2593; www. serendipityadventures.com; e-mail: costarica@serendipityadventures.com), offers many other activities including horseback treks and tours.

SURFING

When *Endless Summer II,* the sequel to the all-time surf classic, was filmed, the production crew brought its boards and cameras to Costa Rica. Point and beach breaks that work almost year-round are located all along Costa Rica's immense coastline. **Playas Hermosa, Jacó,** and **Dominical,** on the central Pacific coast, and **Tamarindo,** in Guanacaste, are becoming mini–surf meccas. **Salsa Brava** in Puerto Viejo has a habit of breaking boards, but the daredevils keep coming back for more. Crowds are starting to gather at the more popular breaks, but you can still stumble on to secret spots on the **Osa** and **Nicoya peninsulas** and along the northern Guanacaste coast. Costa Rica's signature wave is still found at **Playa Pavones,** which is reputed to have one of the longest lefts in the world. The cognoscenti, however, also swear by places like **Playa Grande, Playa Negra, Matapalo, Malpais,** and **Witch's Rock.** If you're looking for an organized surf vacation, contact **Tico Travel** (☎ **800/493-8426** in the U.S.; www.ticotravel.com; e-mail: tico@gate.net).

WATCHING SEA TURTLES NESTING

Few places in the world have as many sea turtle nesting sites as Costa Rica. Along both coasts, five species of these huge marine reptiles come ashore at specific times of the year to dig nests in the sand and lay their eggs. Sea turtles are endangered throughout the world due to overhunting, accidental deaths in fishing nets, development on beaches formerly used as nesting areas, and the collection and sale (often illegally) of their eggs. International trade in sea turtle products is already prohibited by most countries (including the United States), but sea turtle numbers continue to dwindle.

Among the species of sea turtles that nest on Costa Rica's beaches are olive Ridley (known for their mass egg-laying migrations, or *arribadas*), leatherback, hawksbill, green, and Pacific green turtles. Excursions to see nesting turtles have become common, and they are fascinating, but please make sure that you and/or your guide do not disturb the turtles. Any light source (other than red-tinted flashlights) can confuse female turtles and cause them to return to the sea without laying their eggs. In fact, as more and more development takes place on the Costa Rican coast, hotel lighting may cause the number of nesting turtles to drop. Luckily, many of the nesting beaches have been protected as national parks.

Here are the main places to see nesting sea turtles: **Santa Rosa National Park** (near Liberia), **Las Baulas National Marine Park** (near Tamarindo), **Ostional National Wildlife Refuge** (near Playa Nosara), and **Tortuguero National Park** (on the northern Caribbean coast).

See the regional chapters for listings of local tour operators and companies that arrange trips to see sea turtles nesting.

WHITE-WATER RAFTING & KAYAKING

Whether you're a first-time rafter or a world-class kayaker, Costa Rica's got some white water suited to your abilities. Rivers rise and fall with the rainfall, but you can get wet and wild here even in the dry season. If you're just experimenting with river rafting, stick to Class II and III rivers, like the **Reventazon, Sarapiquí,** and **Savegre.** If you already know which end of the paddle goes in the water, there are plenty of Class IV and V sections to run. Die-hard river rats should pick up a copy of *The Rivers of Costa Rica* by Michael W. Mayfield and Rafeael E. Gallo (Menasha Ridge Press, 1988), which is loaded with technical data and route tips on every rideable river in the country. The best white-water-rafting ride is still the scenic **Pacuare River,** though unfortunately it may be dammed soon.

WHITE-WATER RAFTING & KAYAKING OUTFITTERS

Aguas Bravas, P.O. Box 1504-2100, Costa Rica (☎ **506/292-2072;** fax 506/229-4837; www.aguas-bravas.co.cr; e-mail: info@aguas-bravas.co.cr), specializes in trips on the Sarapiquí and Peñas Blancas rivers.

✪ **Aventuras Naturales,** P.O. Box 107360-1000, San José, Costa Rica (☎ **800/514-0411** in the U.S., or 506/225-3939; fax 506/253-6934; www.toenjoynature.com; e-mail: avenat@sol.racsa.co.cr), is a major rafting operator running daily trips on the most popular rivers in Costa Rica. Their Pacuare Jungle Lodge is a great place to spend the night on one of their 2-day rafting trips.

✪ **Costa Rica White Water,** Dept. 235, P.O. Box 025216, Miami, FL 33102 (☎ **506/257-0766** or 506/222-0333; fax 506/257-1665; www.expeditions.com; e-mail: costaric@expeditions.com. This white-water company was the first building block in the Costa Rica Expeditions empire. It remains one of the better-run rafting operations.

Escondido Trex, Apdo. 9, Puerto Jiménez, Osa Peninsula, Costa Rica (☎ and fax **506/735-5210;** e-mail: osatrex@sol.racsa.co.cr). If you're out on the Osa Peninsula, these are the folks to see.

Iguana Tours, Apdo. 227, Quepos, Costa Rica (☎ and fax **506/777-1262;** e-mail: iguana@sol.racsa.co.cr), is based in Quepos/Manuel Antonio and specializes in the Savegre and Naranjo rivers.

Rancho Leona Kayak Tours, Rancho Leona, La Virgen de Sarapiquí, Heredia, Costa Rica (☎ **506/761-1019**). This small, hostel-like roadside hotel caters to kayakers looking to ply the Río Sarapiquí. They also run a pretty nice little stained-glass studio. See chapter 7.

✪ **Rios Tropicales,** Apdo. 472-1200, Pavas, Costa Rica (☎ **506/233-6455;** fax 506/255-4354; www.riostro.com; e-mail: info@riostro.com), is one of the major operators in Costa Rica, running most of the runnable rivers. They've got a very comfortable lodge on the banks of the Río Pacuare for their 2-day trips.

Serendipity Adventures, Apdo. 64200, Naranjo, Costa Rica (☎ **800/635-2325** and fax 734/426-5026 in the U.S., or 506/556-2592; fax 506/556-2593; www.serendipityadventures.com; e-mail: costarica@serendipityadventures.com). This adventure travel operator offers everything from ballooning to mountain biking, as well as most of the popular white-water rafting trips.

WINDSURFING

Windsurfing is still not very popular on the high seas here, where winds are fickle and rental options are limited, even at beach hotels. However, **Lake Arenal** is considered one of the top spots in the world for high-wind board sailing. During the winter months, many of the regulars from Washington's Columbia River Gorge take up residence around the town of Tilarán. Small boards, water starts, and fancy gibes are the norm. The best time for windsurfing on Lake Arenal is between December and March. The same winds that buffet Lake Arenal make their way down to **Bolaños Bay**, near Santa Cruz, Guanacaste, where you can also get some good windsurfing in. See chapters 6 and 7 for more information.

3 Costa Rica's National Parks & Bioreserves

Costa Rica has 31 national parks protecting more than 11% of the country and ranging in size from the 530-acre Guayabo National Monument to the 474,240-acre La Amistad National Park. Many of these national parks are undeveloped tropical forests, with few services or facilities available for visitors. Others, however, offer easier access to their wealth of natural wonders.

After several years of fee hikes, scaled pricing, green passes, and heated controversy, national park fees seem to have settled on a flat $6 per-person per-day fee for any foreigner. Costa Ricans and foreign residents continue to pay just $1. At parks where camping is allowed, there is an additional charge of $1.50 per person per day.

The section that follows is not a complete listing of all of Costa Rica's national parks and protected areas but rather a selective list of those parks that are of greatest interest and accessibility. They're popular, but they're also among the best. You'll find detailed information about food and lodging options near some of the individual parks in the regional chapters that follow. As you'll see from the descriptions, Costa Rica's national parks vary greatly in terms of attractions, facilities, and accessibility. If you're looking for a camping adventure or an extended stay in one of the national parks, I recommend **Santa Rosa, Rincón de la Vieja, Chirripó,** or **Corcovado.** Any of the others are better suited for day trips or in combination with your travels around the country. Since the entrance fees are rather steep, it makes sense to plan ahead and try to pick a park (or parks) that fits your needs and interests.

For more information, call the national parks office at ☎ **506/257-0922** from the United States, or by dialing ☎ **192** from Costa Rica. You can also stop by the National Parks Foundation office (☎ **506/257-2239**) in San José, which is located between Calle 23 and Avenida 15. It's open 9am to 5pm daily.

Costa Rica's National Parks & Bioreserves

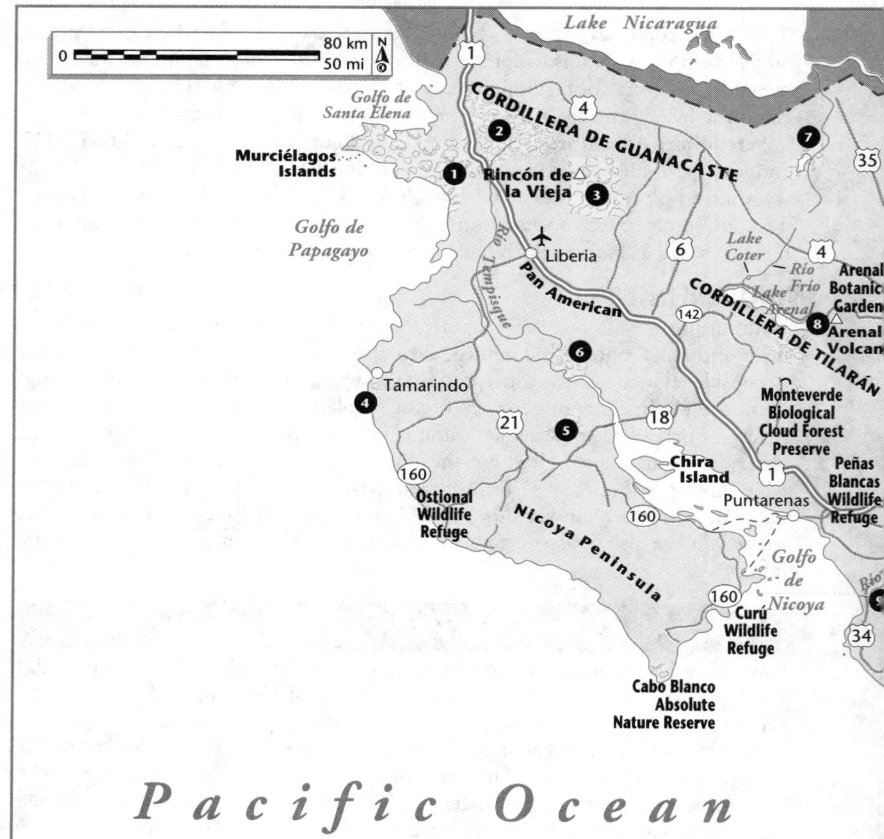

Arenal National Park 8	Irazú Volcano National Park 14
Barra Honda National Park 5	Las Baulas Marine National Park 4
Braulio Carrillo National Park 11	Manuel Antonio National Park 16
Cahuita National Park 19	Marino Ballena National Park 17
Caño Negro National Wildlife Refuge 7	Palo Verde National Park 6
Carara Biological Reserve 9	Poás Volcano National Park 10
Chirripó National Park 18	Rincón de la Vieja National Park 3
Corcovado National Park 20	Santa Rosa National Park 1
Guanacaste National Park 2	Tapantí National Wildlife Refuge 15
Guayabo National Monument 13	Tortuguero National Park 12

NICARAGUA
Río San Juan
Barra del Colorado
National Wildlife
Refuge
Caribbean
Sea
Río
Colorado
Sarapiquí
35
4
Puerto Viejo
de Sarapiquí
Río
140
12
Tortuguero Canal
4
11
141
10
Barva
Volcano
32
13
Turrialba
Volcano
CORDILLERA CENTRAL
Pacuare
Reventazón
Río
Limón
135
1
34
Parcoles/Virilla
14
SAN
JOSÉ
Cartago
Lankester
Botanical Garden
209
15
36
2
Hitoy-
Cerere
Biological
Reserve
19
Punta
Uva
Gandoca-
Manzanillo
Wildlife
Refuge
Quepos
34
Cerro de
la Muerte
Río Telire
18
Cerro
Chirripó
CORDILLERA DE TALAMANCA
16
San
Isidro
Cerro
Dúrika
Pan American Hwy.
Cerro
Kámuk
17
PANAMA
34
Coronado
Bay
San
Vito
2
Río
Sierpe
Caño Island
Biological
Reserve
Drake
Bay
Wilson
Botanical
Garden
Golfo
Dulce
Golfito
Osa Peninsula
20
Puerto
Jiménez
Pacific
Ocean

Arenal National Park

A new park, created to protect the ecosystem that surrounds Arenal Volcano, it has few services or attractions. Basically, the government has set up a toll booth on the access road leading to an up-close view of the volcano's lava flows. However, there are a few good and gentle trails into the park, which lead to some of the cooled off lava flows. I don't recommend going into the park in order to watch the volcano. Most travelers and tour operators choose to forgo the entrance fee and watch the volcano from spots along the dirt road leading to the Arenal Observatory Lodge. From there, you're only about 1 kilometer away, which is still plenty close to the volcano. **Location:** 80 miles (129km) northwest of San José. **Region:** The Northern zone. See chapter 7.

Barra Honda National Park

Costa Rica's only underground national park, Barra Honda features a series of limestone caves that were once part of a coral reef, some 60 million years ago. Today the caves are home to millions of bats and impressive stalactite and stalagmite formations. Only one cave, **Terciopelo Cave,** is open to the general public. There's a camping area, rest rooms, and an information center here, as well as trails through the surrounding tropical dry forest. **Location:** 208 miles (335km) northwest of San José. **Region:** Guanacaste and the Nicoya Peninsula. See chapter 6.

Braulio Carrillo National Park

Occupying a large area of the nation's central mountain range, this is the park you pass through on your way from San José to the Caribbean coast. A deep rain forest, Braulio Carrillo receives an average of 177 inches of rain per year. There are beautiful rivers, majestic waterfalls, and more than 6,500 species of plants and animals. The park has an information center, picnic tables, rest rooms, and hiking trails. Camping is allowed.

Be careful here. Make sure you park your car and base your explorations from the park's main entrance, not just anywhere along the highway. There have been several robberies and attacks against visitors reported at trails leading into the park from the highway. This park also seems to have the highest incidence of lost hikers. **Location:** 14 miles (22.5km) north of San José. **Region:** The Northern zone. See chapter 7.

Cahuita National Park

A combination land and marine park, Cahuita National Park protects one of the few remaining living coral reefs in the country. The topography here is lush lowland tropical rain forest. Monkeys and numerous bird species are common. Camping is permitted, and there are basic facilities at the Puerto Vargas entrance to the park. If you want to visit for only the day, however, enter from Cahuita village, because as of press time, the local community had taken over that entrance and was asking for only a voluntary donation. **Location:** On the Caribbean coast, 26 miles (42km) south of Limón. **Region:** The Caribbean coast. See chapter 10.

Caño Negro National Wildlife Refuge

A lowland swamp and drainage basin for several northern rivers, Caño Negro is excellent for bird watching. There are a few basic cabinas and lodges in this area, but the most popular way to visit is on a combined van and boat trip from the La Fortuna/Arenal area. **Location:** 12½ miles (20km) south of Los Chiles, near the Nicaraguan border. **Region:** The Southern zone. See chapter 9.

CHIRRIPÓ NATIONAL PARK

Home to Costa Rica's tallest peak, 12,536-foot Mount Chirripó, Chirripó National Park is quite a hike, but on a clear day, you can see both the Pacific Ocean and Caribbean Sea from its summit. There are a number of interesting climbing trails here, and camping is allowed. **Location:** 94 miles (151.3km) southeast of San José. **Region:** The Cental Pacific coast. See chapter 8.

COCO ISLAND NATIONAL PARK

A large, uninhabited island located 360 miles (580km) off Costa Rica's Pacific coast, Coco Island National Park is beautiful, with many native species of flora and fauna. The diving here is also world renowned. **Aggressor Fleet Limited,** P.O. Box 1470, Morgan City, LA 70381-1470 (☎ **800/348-2628** or 504/385-2628; fax 504/384-0817; www.aggressor.com; e-mail: 103261.1275@compuserve.com), runs the 120-foot *Okeanos Aggressor* on regular trips out to Coco Island from Puntarenas.

CORCOVADO NATIONAL PARK

The largest single block of virgin lowland rain forest in Central America, Corcovado National Park receives more than 200 inches of rain per year. One of Costa Rica's increasingly popular national parks, it's still largely a remote area (it has no roads, and only dirt tracks lead into it). Scarlet macaws live here, as do countless other neotropical species, including two of the country's largest cats, the endangered puma and jaguar. There are camping facilities and trails throughout the park. **Location:** 208 miles (335km) south of San José, on the Osa Peninsula. **Region:** The Southern zone. See chapter 9.

GUAYABO NATIONAL MONUMENT

The country's only significant pre-Columbian archaeological site, it's believed that Guayabo supported a population of about 10,000 people some 3,000 years ago. **Location:** 12 miles (19.3km) northeast of Turrialba, which is 33 miles (53km) east of San José. **Region:** Central Valley/San José area. See chapter 5.

IRAZÚ VOLCANO NATIONAL PARK

Irazú Volcano is one of Costa Rica's four active volcanoes and a popular day trip from San José. At 11,260 feet, it's the country's highest volcano. A paved road leads right up to the crater, and the lookout also allegedly allows you a view of both oceans on a clear day. The volcano last erupted in 1963—the same day President John F. Kennedy visited the country. There's an information center, picnic tables, rest rooms, and a parking area here. **Location:** 34 miles (54.7km) east of San José. **Region:** Central Valley/San José area. See chapter 5.

MANUEL ANTONIO NATIONAL PARK

The grande dame of Costa Rican national parks, Manuel Antonio supports the largest number of hotels and resorts of any national park. This lowland rain forest is home to a healthy monkey population, including the endangered squirrel monkey. The park is best known for its splendid beaches. However, at $6 a pop for the entrance fee, you may want to think about finding another place to sunbathe and beachcomb. **Location:** 80 miles (129km) south of San José. **Region:** The central Pacific coast. See chapter 8.

PALO VERDE NATIONAL PARK

A must for bird-watchers, Palo Verde National Park is one of Costa Rica's best-kept secrets. This part of the Tempisque River lowlands supports a population of more

Monkey Business

No trip to Costa Rica would be complete without at least one monkey sighting. Home to four distinct species of primates, inhabiting the forests along both coasts as well as those in between, Costa Rica offers the opportunity for one of the world's most gratifying wildlife-watching experiences. You'll need a good guide to see your first few families, but in no time you'll be spotting them on your own. The deep guttural call of a howler or the rustling of leaves overhead on a jungle trail will be your cues.

Costa Rica's most commonly spotted monkey is the white-faced or **capuchin monkey** (*mono cara blanca* in Spanish), which you may recognize as the infamous culprit from the film *Outbreak.* Contrary to that film's plot, however, these monkeys are native to the New World tropics and do not exist in Africa. Capuchins are agile, medium-sized monkeys that make good use of their long prehensile tails. They inhabit a diverse collection of habitats, ranging from the high-altitude cloud forests of the central region to the lowland mangroves of the Osa Peninsula. It's almost impossible not to spot capuchins at Manuel Antonio (see chapter 8), where the resident white-faced monkeys have become a little too dependent on fruit and junk-food feedings by tourists. Please do not feed wild monkeys, and boycott establishments that try to attract both monkeys and tourists with daily feedings.

Howler monkeys (*mono congo* in Spanish) are named for their distinct and eerie call. Large and mostly black, these monkeys can seem ferocious because of their physical appearance and deep, resonant howls that can carry for more than a mile, even in dense rain forest. (To make these guttural noises, the throat sacs of male howlers vibrate. When a male howler sounds, biologists believe he is marking the boundaries of his territory.) In the presence of humans, however, howlers are actually a little timid and tend to stay higher up in the canopy than their white-faced cousins. Howlers are fairly common and easy to spot in the dry tropical forests of coastal Guanacaste and the Nicoya Peninsula (see chapter 6).

Even more elusive are **spider monkeys** (*mono araña* in Spanish). These long, slender monkeys are dark brown to black and prefer the high canopies of primary rain forests. Spiders are very adept with their prehensile tails but actually travel through the canopy with a hand-over-hand motion frequently imitated by their less graceful human cousins on playground monkey bars around the world. I've had my best luck spotting spiders along the edges of Tortuguero's jungle canals (see chapter 10), where howlers are also quite common.

The rarest and most endangered of Costa Rica's monkeys is the tiny **squirrel monkey** (*mono titi* in Spanish). These small brown monkeys have dark eyes surrounded by large white rings, white ears, white chests, and very long tails. In Costa Rica, squirrel monkeys can be found only in Manuel Antonio (see chapter 8) and the Osa Peninsula (see chapter 9). These seemingly hyperactive monkeys are predominantly fruit eaters and often feed on bananas and other fruit trees near hotels in both of the above-mentioned regions. Squirrel monkeys usually travel in large bands, so if you do see them, you'll likely see quite a few.

than 50,000 waterfowl and forest bird species. Various ecosystems here include mangroves, savanna brush lands, and evergreen forests. There are camping facilities, an information center, and some nice new accommodations at the Organization for Tropical Studies research station here. **Location:** 125 miles (201.25km) northwest of San José. Be warned, the park entrance is 17½ miles (28km) off the highway down a very rugged dirt road. It is another 5½ miles (9km) to the OTS station and campsites. For more information, call the OTS (☎ **506/240-6696;** e-mail: reservas@ns.ots.ac.cr). **Region**: Guanacaste and The Nicoya Peninsula. See chapter 6.

Poás Volcano National Park

Poás is the other active volcano close to San José. The main crater is more than 1 mile wide, and it is constantly active with fumaroles and hot geysers. The area around the volcano is lush, but much of the growth is stunted due to the gasses and acid rain. The park sometimes closes when the gasses get too feisty. There are nature trails, picnic tables, rest rooms, and an information center. **Location:** 23 miles (37km) northwest of San José. **Region:** Central Valley/San José area. See chapter 5.

Rincón de la Vieja National Park

Rincón de la Vieja National Park is a large tract of parkland that experiences high volcanic activity. There are numerous fumaroles and geysers, as well as hot springs, cold pools, and mud pots. There are also excellent hikes to the upper craters, as well as to several waterfalls. You should hire a guide for any hot spring or mud bath expeditions, because inexperienced visitors have been burned. Camping is permitted at two separate sites, each of which has an information center, picnic area, and rest rooms. **Location:** 165 miles (265.6km) northwest of San José. **Region:** Guanacaste and the Nicoya Peninsula. See chapter 6.

Santa Rosa National Park

Occupying a large section of Costa Rica's northwestern Guanacaste province, Santa Rosa National Park contains the country's largest area of tropical dry forest, as well as important turtle nesting sites and the historically significant La Casona monument. There are also caves for exploring, and the beaches here are pristine and have basic camping facilities. An information center, picnic area, and rest rooms are located at the main campsite and entrance. **Location:** 160 miles (257.6km) northwest of San José. **Region:** Guanacaste and the Nicoya Peninsula. See chapter 6.

Tortuguero National Park

Tortuguero National Park has been called the Venice of Costa Rica due to its maze of jungle canals that meander through a dense lowland rain forest. Small boats, launches, and canoes carry visitors through these waterways, where caimans, manatees, and numerous bird and mammal species are common. The extremely endangered great green macaw lives here. On the beaches, green sea turtles nest here every year between June and October. Still, many visitors to Tortuguero pass through the park only on their way to and from the village, since nearby canals that are outside of the park (and hence free from entrance fees) offer many of the same sights and thrills. Nevertheless, the park does have a helpful information stand and some well-marked trails. **Location:** 160 miles (257.6km) from San José. **Region:** The Caribbean coast. See chapter 10.

4 Tips on Health, Safety & Etiquette in the Wilderness

Much of what is discussed below is common sense. For more detailed information, see "Health & Insurance," in chapter 3.

While most tours and activities are extremely safe, there are risks involved in any adventure activity. Know and respect your own physical limits before undertaking any strenuous activity. Be prepared for extremes in temperature and rainfall and for wide fluctuations in weather. A sunny morning hike can quickly become a cold and wet ordeal, so it's usually a good idea to carry along some form of rain gear when hiking in the rain forest, or to have a dry change of clothing waiting at the end of the trail. Make sure to bring along plenty of sunscreen when you're not going to be covered by the forest canopy.

If you do any backcountry packing or camping, remember that it really is a jungle out there. Don't go poking under rocks or fallen branches: Snakebites are very rare, but don't do anything to increase the odds. If you do encounter a snake, stay calm, don't make any sudden movements, and *do not* try to handle it. Also, avoid swimming in major rivers unless a guide or local operator can vouch for their safety. Though white-water sections and stretches in mountainous areas are generally pretty safe, most mangrove canals and river mouths in Costa Rica support healthy crocodile and caiman populations.

Bugs and bug bites will probably be your greatest health concern in the Costa Rican wilderness. Mostly, bugs are an inconvenience, although mosquitoes can carry malaria or dengue (see chapter 3 for more information). A strong repellent and proper clothing will minimize both the danger and inconvenience. On the beaches you will probably be bitten by sand fleas, or *pirujas.* These nearly invisible insects leave an irritating welt. Try not to scratch, as this can lead to open sores and infections. Pirujas are most active at sunrise and sunset, so you might want to cover up or avoid the beaches at these times.

And remember: Whenever you enter and enjoy nature, you should tread lightly and try not to disturb the natural environment. There's a popular slogan well-known to most campers that certainly applies here: "Leave nothing but footprints, take nothing but memories." If you must take home a souvenir, take photos. Do not cut or uproot plants or flowers. Pack out everything you pack in, and **please** do not litter.

5 Ecologically Oriented Volunteer & Study Programs

Below are some institutions and organizations that are working on ecology and sustainable development projects. Contact them if you are interested in studying or volunteering with them. Many of these projects are ongoing and ask that volunteers devote more than a week of their time.

Asociación de Voluntarios para el Servicio en las Areas Protegidas (ASVO), Apdo. 10104, San José, Costa Rica (☎ **506/222-5098;** fax 506/256-3859), organizes volunteers to work in Costa Rican national parks. A 45-day minimum commitment is required, as are several letters of recommendation and a basic ability to converse in Spanish. Housing is provided at a basic ranger station, and there is a $7 per day fee to cover food, which is basic tico fare.

Global Volunteers, 375 Little Canada Rd., St. Paul, MN 55117 (☎ **800/487-1074** or 612/482-0295; www.globalvlntrs.org; e-mail: email@globalvlntrs.org), is a U.S.–based organization that offers a unique opportunity to travelers who've always wanted a Peace Corps–like experience but felt they couldn't make a 2-year commitment. For 2 to 3 weeks, you can join one of their working vacations in Costa Rica. A certain set of skills, such as engineering or agricultural knowledge, is helpful but by no means necessary. Each trip is undertaken at a particular community's request, to complete a specific project. However, be warned, these "volunteer" experiences do not come cheap. You must pay your transportation as well as a hefty program fee, around $1,600 for a 2-week program.

Institute for Central American Development Studies (ICADS), Apdo. 3-2070 Sabanilla, San José (☎ **506/225-0508;** fax 506/234-1337; www.westnet.com/costarica/icads.html; e-mail: icads@netbox.com), offers internship and research opportunities in the areas of environment, agriculture, human rights, and women's studies. They also offer an intensive Spanish-language program, which can be combined with work-study or volunteer opportunities. Their U.S. address is Dept. 826, P.O. Box 025216, Miami, FL 33102-5216.

Monteverde Institute, Apdo. 69-5655, Monteverde de Puntarenas, Costa Rica (☎ **506/645-5053;** fax 506/645-5219; www.costarica.cea.edu/mvi.v1; e-mail: mviimv@sol.racsa.co.cr), offers study programs in Monteverde and also has a volunteer center that helps in placement and training of volunteers.

Organization for Tropical Studies, Apdo. 676, San José (☎ **506/240-6696;** e-mail: reservas@ns.ots.ac.cr), represents several Costa Rican and U.S. universities. This organization's mission is to promote research, education, and the wise use of natural resources in the tropics. Research facilities include La Selva Biological Station near Braulio Carrillo National Park and Palo Verde and the Wilson Botanical Gardens near San Vito. Housing is provided at one of the research facilities. A wide range of courses is offered, ranging from full-semester undergraduate programs (at around $11,000) to specific graduate courses (of varying durations), to their recently added straight tourist programs (these are generally being sponsored/run by established operators—Costa Rica Expeditions, Elderhostel, etc.). These range in duration from 3 to 10 days, and costs vary greatly. Entrance requirements and competition for some of these courses can be demanding. The best way to find out is to contact OTS directly or visit their Web site: **www.ots.ac.cr/**.

5 San José

At first blush, San José may seem little more than a chaotic jumble of cars, buses, buildings, and people. The central downtown section of San José is an urban planner's nightmare, where once-quiet streets are now burdened by traffic and in a near constant state of gridlock. Leaded fuels and a lack of emission controls have given San José a brown cloud. Below the cloud, the city bustles, but it is not particularly hospitable to travelers. Sidewalks are poorly maintained and claustrophobic, and street crime is a problem. Most visitors quickly seek the sanctuary of their hotel room and the first chance to escape the city.

Still, San José is the most cosmopolitan city in Central America. Costa Rica's stable government and the Central Valley's climate have, over the years, attracted people from all over the world. There's a large diplomatic and international business presence here. One result has been the amazing variety of cuisines available in the city's restaurants, and another (more recent) has been the proliferation of small, elegant hotels in renovated historic buildings. Together, these restaurants and hotels provide visitors with one of the greatest variety of options found anywhere between Mexico City and Bogotá.

If you plan on doing any terrestrial travel (by bus or car) or hope to visit several different destinations while in Costa Rica, San José will invariably serve as a default hub or transfer point (at least until the Liberia airport gets more flights). This chapter will help you plan your time in the capital and help ease your way through the pitfalls inherent in such a rough-and-tumble little city.

IT'S IN THE BEANS

San José is a city built on coffee. This is not to say that the city runs on bottomless pots of java—like, say, Seattle or New York. No, San José was built on the profits of the coffee export business. Between the airport and downtown, you still pass by working coffee farms, and glancing up from almost any street in the city you can see, on the surrounding volcanic mountains, a patchwork quilt of farm fields, most of which are planted with the *grano de oro* (golden bean), as it's known here. San José was a forgotten backwater of the Spanish empire until the first shipments of the local beans made their way to sleepy souls in Europe late in the 19th century. Soon, San José was riding high. Coffee planters, newly rich and craving culture, imposed a tax on themselves in order to build the Teatro Nacional, San José's most beautiful building. Coffee profits also built the city a university. Today, you can wake up and smell the coffee roasting as you wander the streets near the central market, and in any cafe or restaurant you can get a hot cup of sweet, milky *café con leche* to remind you of the bean that built San José.

Why does coffee grow so well around the city? It's the climate. The Central Valley, in which the city sits, has a perfect climate. At 3,750 feet above sea level, San José enjoys springlike temperatures year-round. It's this pleasant climate, and the beautiful views of lush green mountainsides, that makes San José a memorable city to visit. All you have to do is glance up at those mountains to know that this is one of the most beautifully situated capital cities in Central America. And if a glance isn't enough for you, you'll find that it's extremely easy to get out into the countryside. Within an hour or two, you can climb a volcano, go white-water rafting, hike through a cloud forest, and stroll through a butterfly garden—among many, many other activities.

1 Orientation

ARRIVING

BY PLANE Juan Santamaría International Airport (☎ **506/443-2942** for 24-hour airport information) is located near the city of Alajuela, about 20 minutes from downtown San José. A taxi into town will cost around $12.50, and a bus is only 55¢. The Alajuela–San José buses run frequently and drop you on Avenida 2 between Calles 12 and 14. At the airport you'll find the bus stop about 100 meters directly in front of the main terminal. Make sure to ask if the bus is going to San José, or you'll end up in Alajuela. If you have a lot of luggage, you should probably take a cab. There are several car-rental agencies located at the airport, although if you're planning on spending a few days in San José, a car is a liability. (If you're heading off immediately to the beach, though, it's much easier to pick up your car here than at a downtown office.) You'll find the taxi stands up the stairs and after you clear Customs. The car-rental agencies are located on a little island in front of the main terminal.

Even though the distance is negligible, it's common to have a porter carry your bags to a taxi or car-rental agency—though you're certainly welcome to do it yourself, you'll literally have to fight off the porters. Most of these porters wear a uniform identifying them as such, but sometimes "improvised" porters will try to earn a few dollars here. Either way, make sure you keep an eye on your bags. You should tip the porters about 50¢ per bag.

You have several options for exchanging money when you arrive at the airport. There's an official state bank inside the main terminal. It's open Monday through Friday from 9am to 4pm. When the bank is closed (and even when it's open), there are usually official money changers (with badges) working both inside and outside the terminal. Outside the terminal, you may be approached by unofficial money changers. Three things to note: (1) Though black-market money changing is illegal, it's quite common; (2) there's never much variance between the official bank rate and street exchange rate; (3) the airport is one of the safer places to try black-market exchange, though you should be careful wherever and whenever you decide to change money. See "Exchanging Money" in chapter 3 for more details.

If for some reason you arrive in San José via Travelair, private aircraft or another small commuter or charter airline, you may find yourself at the **Tobías Bolaños**

San José

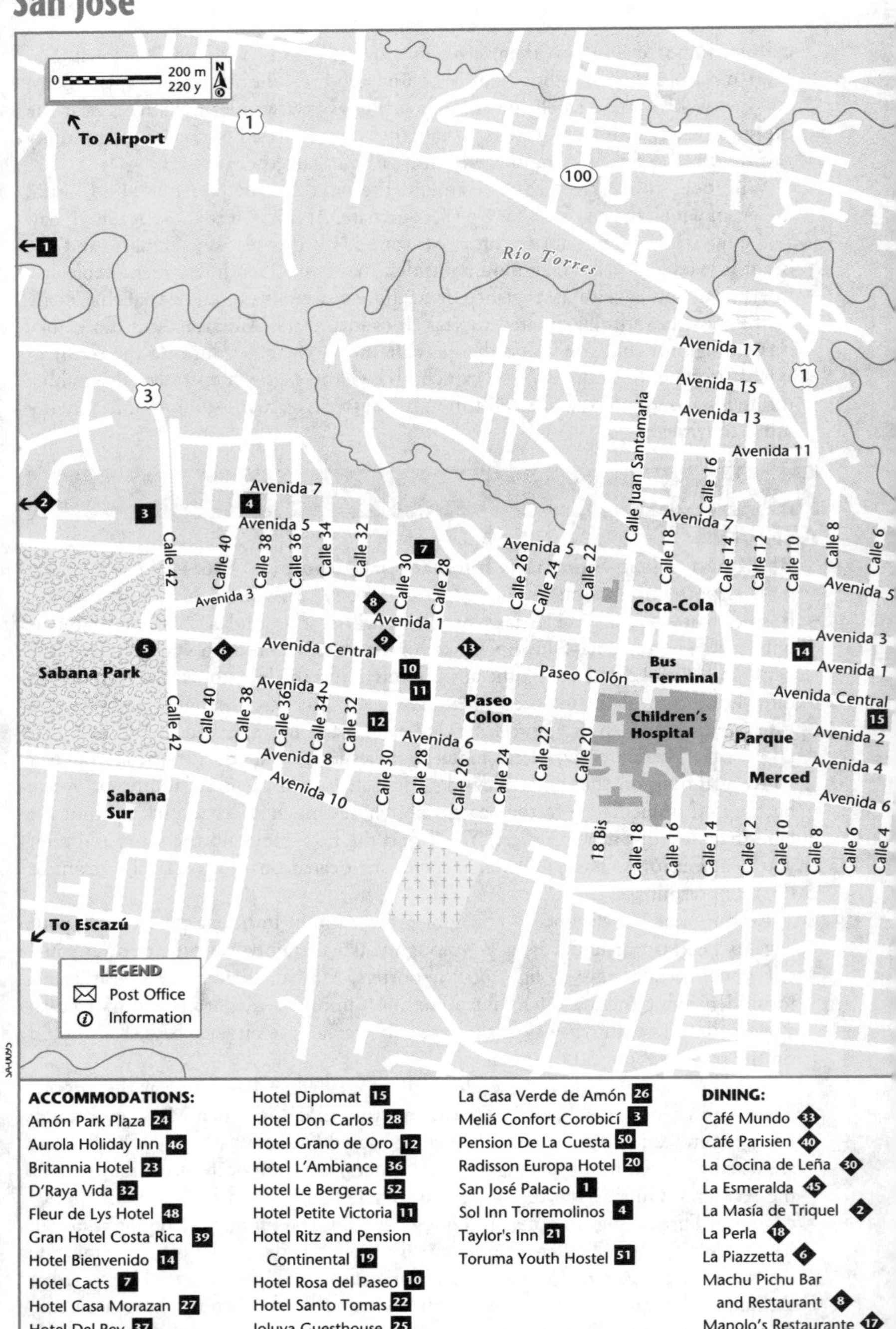

0
200 m
220 y
N
To Airport
1
100
Río Torres
3
Avenida 17
Avenida 15
Avenida 13
Avenida 11
Calle Juan Santamaria
Calle 16
Avenida 7
Avenida 5
Avenida 3
Avenida 1
Avenida Central
Avenida 2
Avenida 4
Avenida 6
Avenida 8
Avenida 10
Calle 42
Calle 40
Calle 38
Calle 36
Calle 34
Calle 32
Calle 30
Calle 28
Calle 26
Calle 24
Calle 22
Calle 20
Calle 18
Calle 14
Calle 12
Calle 10
Calle 8
Calle 6
Calle 4
18 Bis
Coca-Cola
Bus Terminal
Paseo Colón
Paseo Colon
Children's Hospital
Parque Merced
Sabana Park
Sabana Sur
To Escazú
LEGEND
Post Office
Information
ACCOMMODATIONS:
Amón Park Plaza 24
Aurola Holiday Inn 46
Britannia Hotel 23
D'Raya Vida 32
Fleur de Lys Hotel 48
Gran Hotel Costa Rica 39
Hotel Bienvenido 14
Hotel Cacts 7
Hotel Casa Morazan 27
Hotel Del Rey 37
Hotel Diplomat 15
Hotel Don Carlos 28
Hotel Grano de Oro 12
Hotel L'Ambiance 36
Hotel Le Bergerac 52
Hotel Petite Victoria 11
Hotel Ritz and Pension Continental 19
Hotel Rosa del Paseo 10
Hotel Santo Tomas 22
Joluva Guesthouse 25
La Casa Verde de Amón 26
Meliá Confort Corobicí 3
Pension De La Cuesta 50
Radisson Europa Hotel 20
San José Palacio 1
Sol Inn Torremolinos 4
Taylor's Inn 21
Toruma Youth Hostel 51
DINING:
Café Mundo 33
Café Parisien 40
La Cocina de Leña 30
La Esmeralda 45
La Masía de Triquel 2
La Perla 18
La Piazzetta 6
Machu Pichu Bar and Restaurant 8
Manolo's Restaurante 17

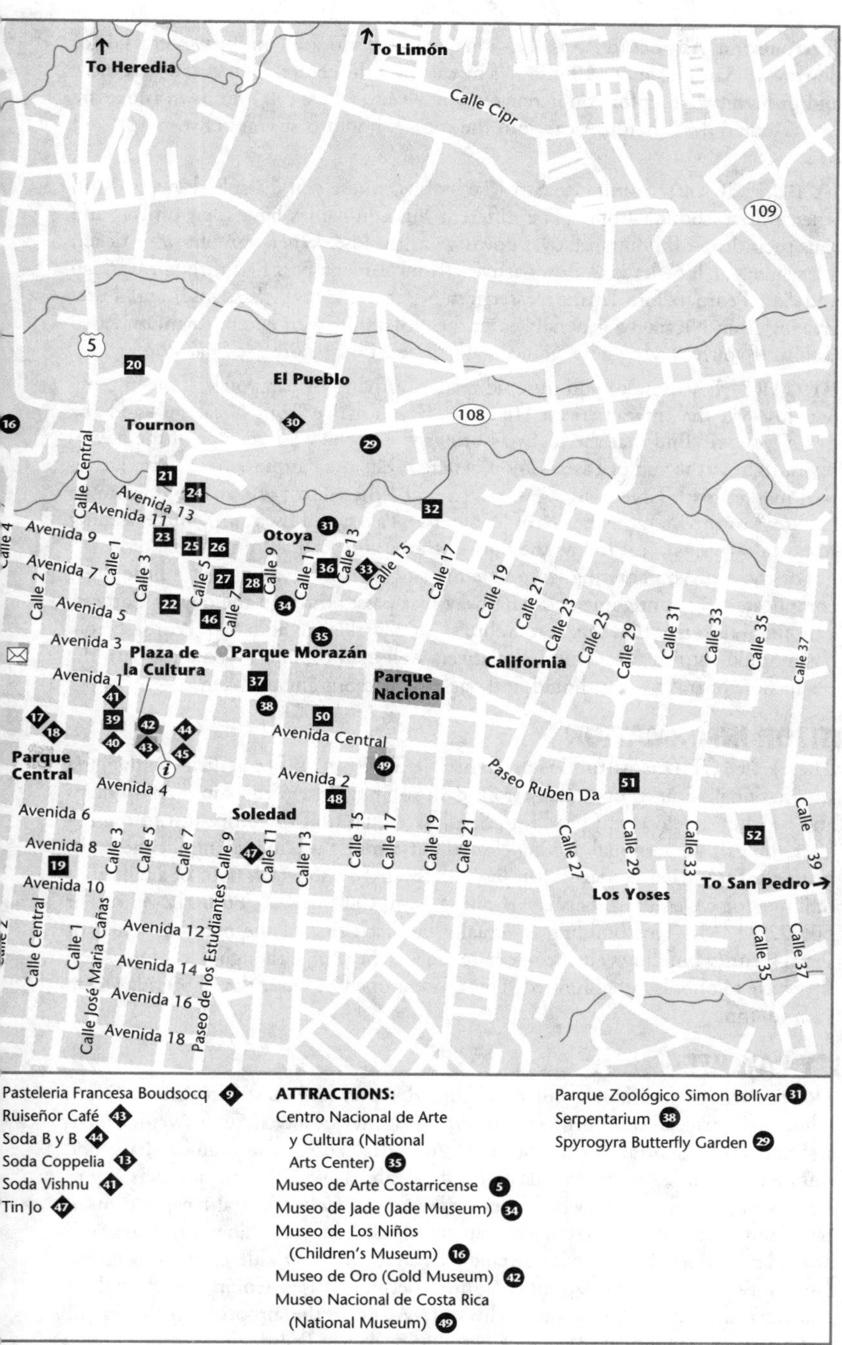
To Heredia
To Limón
Calle Cipr
109
5
108
El Pueblo
Tournon
Otoya
Parque Morazán
Plaza de la Cultura
Parque Nacional
California
Parque Central
Soledad
Los Yoses
To San Pedro
Paseo Ruben Da
Avenida Central
Avenida 1
Avenida 2
Avenida 3
Avenida 4
Avenida 5
Avenida 6
Avenida 7
Avenida 8
Avenida 9
Avenida 10
Avenida 11
Avenida 12
Avenida 13
Avenida 14
Avenida 16
Avenida 18
Calle Central
Calle 1
Calle 2
Calle 3
Calle 5
Calle 7
Calle 9
Calle 11
Calle 13
Calle 15
Calle 17
Calle 19
Calle 21
Calle 23
Calle 25
Calle 27
Calle 29
Calle 31
Calle 33
Calle 35
Calle 37
Calle 39
Calle José María Cañas
Paseo de los Estudiantes Calle 9
Pasteleria Francesa Boudsocq 9
Ruiseñor Café 43
Soda B y B 44
Soda Coppelia 13
Soda Vishnu 41
Tin Jo 47
ATTRACTIONS:
Centro Nacional de Arte y Cultura (National Arts Center) 35
Museo de Arte Costarricense 5
Museo de Jade (Jade Museum) 34
Museo de Los Niños (Children's Museum) 16
Museo de Oro (Gold Museum) 42
Museo Nacional de Costa Rica (National Museum) 49
Parque Zoológico Simon Bolívar 31
Serpentarium 38
Spyrogyra Butterfly Garden 29

International Airport in Pavas. This small airport is located on the western side of downtown San José about 10 minutes by car from the center. Unless you have a car and/or driver waiting for you here, you will have to take a cab into town (there are no car-rental desks here). A cab into the center should cost you between $10 and $12.

BY BUS If you're coming to San José by bus, where you disembark depends on where you're coming from. (The different bus companies have their offices, and thus their drop-off points, all over downtown San José. When you buy your ticket, ask where you'll be let off.) Buses arriving from Panama pass first through Cartago and San Pedro before letting passengers off in downtown San José, and buses arriving from Nicaragua generally enter the city on the west end of town, on Paseo Colón. If you're staying here, you can ask to be let off before the final stop.

BY CAR For those of you intrepid readers arriving by car, you will be entering San José via the Interamerican Highway. If you arrive from Nicaragua and the north, you will find that the highway brings you to the western edge of the downtown, right at the end of Paseo Colón, where it hits the Parque Sabana. This area is well marked with large road signs, which will either direct you to the downtown (*"centro"*) or the western suburbs of Rhomerser, Pavas, and Escazú. If you're heading toward downtown, just follow the flow of traffic and turn left on Paseo Colón.

For those of you entering from Panama and the south, things get a little more complicated. The Interamerican Highway first passes through the city of Cartago, and then through the San José suburbs of Curridabat and San Pedro, before reaching downtown. This route is relatively well marked, and if you stick with the major flow of traffic, you should find San José without any problem.

VISITOR INFORMATION

There's an **ICT (Instituto Costarricense de Turismo)** office at Juan Santamaría International Airport, open daily from 8am to 5pm, where you can pick up maps and brochures before you head into San José. You'll find the office just to the left after you exit the terminal, having cleared Customs. If you're looking for the **main visitor information center** in San José, it's located on the 11th floor of a tall office building on Avenida 4 between Calle 5 and Calle 7 (☎ **800/012-3456,** or 506/223-1733). This building is actually the back side of the popular "Caja" or social security building. The people here are very helpful, although the information they have to offer is rather limited. This office is open Monday through Friday from 9am to 4pm.

CITY LAYOUT

Downtown San José is laid out on a grid. *Avenidas* (avenues) run east and west, while *calles* (streets) run north and south. The center of the city is at Avenida Central and Calle Central. To the north of Avenida Central, the avenidas have odd numbers beginning with Avenida 1; to the south, they have even numbers beginning with Avenida 2. Likewise, calles to the east of Calle Central have odd numbers, and those to the west have even numbers. The main downtown artery is Avenida 2, which merges with Avenida Central on either side of the downtown area. West of downtown, Avenida Central becomes Paseo Colón, which ends at Sabana Park and feeds into the highway to Alajuela, the airport, and the Pacific coast. East of downtown, Avenida Central leads to San Pedro and then to Cartago and the Interamerican Highway heading south. Calle 3 will take you out of town to the north and put you on the Guapiles Highway out to the Caribbean coast.

"I know there's got to be a number here somewhere...": The Arcane Art of Finding an Address in San José

This is one of the most confusing aspects of visiting Costa Rica in general, and San José in particular. Though there are often street addresses and building numbers for locations in downtown San José, they are almost never used. Addresses are given as a set of coordinates such as "Calle 3 between Avenida Central and Avenida 1." It's then up to you to locate the building within that block, keeping in mind that the building could be on either side of the street. Many addresses include additional information, such as the number of meters or *varas* (an old Spanish measurement roughly equal to a yard) from a specified intersection or some other well-known landmark. These landmarks are what become truly confusing for visitors to the city because they are often simply restaurants, bars, and shops that would be familiar only to locals. Things get even more confusing when the landmark in question no longer exists. The classic example of this is "the Coca-Cola," one of the most common landmarks used in addresses in the blocks surrounding San José's main market. Trouble is, the Coca-Cola bottling plant it refers to is no longer there; the edifice is long gone, and one of the principal downtown bus depots stands in its place. Old habits die hard, though, and the address description remains. You may also try to find someplace near the *antiguo higuerón* ("old fig tree") in San Pedro. This tree was felled years ago. In outlying neighborhoods, addresses can become long directions such as "50 meters south of the old church, then 100 meters east, then 20 meters south." Luckily for the visitor, most downtown addresses are more straightforward.

Oh, if you're wondering how letter carriers manage, well, welcome to the club. Some folks actually get their mail delivered this way, but most people and businesses in San José use a post office box. This is called an *apartado*, and is abbreviated Apdo. or A.P. on mailing addresses.

NEIGHBORHOODS IN BRIEF

San José is sprawling. Today it's divided into dozens of neighborhoods known as barrios. Most of the listings in this chapter fall within the main downtown area, but there are a few outlying neighborhoods you will need to know about.

Downtown San José's busiest area, this is where you'll find most of the city's museums. There are also many tour companies, restaurants, and hotels downtown. Unfortunately, traffic noise and exhaust fumes make this one of the least pleasant parts of the city. Streets and avenues are usually bustling and crowded with pedestrians and vehicular traffic, and street crime is most rampant here.

Barrio Amon/Barrio Otoya These two neighborhoods, just north and east of downtown, are the site of the greatest concentration of historic buildings in San José, and in the past few years some enterprising entrepreneurs have been renovating the old buildings and turning them into hotels. If you're looking for character and don't mind the noise and exhaust fumes, this neighborhood makes a good base for exploring the city.

La Sabana/Paseo Colón Paseo Colón, a wide boulevard west of downtown, is an extension of Avenida Central and ends at La Sabana Park. It has several good, small hotels and numerous excellent restaurants. This is also where many of the city's rental-car agencies have their offices.

San Pedro/Los Yoses Located east of downtown San José, Los Yoses is an upper-middle-class neighborhood that is home to many diplomatic missions and embassies. San Pedro is a little farther east and is the site of the University of Costa Rica. There are numerous college-type bars and restaurants all around the edge of the campus and several good restaurants and small hotels in both neighborhoods.

Escazú/Santa Ana Located in the hills west of San José, Escazú and Santa Ana are suburbs with a small-town feel. Although the area is only 15 minutes from San José by taxi, it feels much farther away because of its relaxed atmosphere. This area has a large expatriate community, and many bed-and-breakfast establishments are located here.

2 Getting Around

BY BUS Bus transportation around San José is cheap—the fare is usually somewhere around 15¢ (though the Alajuela–San José buses that run in from the airport cost 55¢). The most important buses are those running east and west along Avenida 2 and Avenida 3. **The Sabana/Cementerio** bus runs from Sabana Park to downtown and is one of the most convenient buses to use. You'll find a bus stop for the outbound Sabana/Cementerio bus across the street from Costa Rica Expeditions on Avenida 3 near the corner of Calle Central, and another one near the famous Key Largo bar, across Parque Morazán from the towering Holiday Inn. San Pedro buses leave from Avenida Central between Calle 9 and Calle 11, in front of the Cine Capri, and will take you out of downtown heading east. Buses are always boarded from the front, and the bus drivers can make change, although they don't like to receive larger bills. Be especially mindful of your wallet, purse, or other valuables, since pickpockets often work the crowded buses.

BY TAXI Although taxis in San José have meters (*marías*), the drivers sometimes refuse to use them, so you'll occasionally have to negotiate the price. Always try to get them to use the meter first. The official rate at press time is around 65¢ for the first kilometer and around 30¢ for each additional kilometer. If you have a rough idea of how far it is to your destination, you can estimate how much it should cost from these figures. After 10pm, taxis are legally allowed to add a 20% surcharge. Some of the meters are programmed automatically to include the extra charge, but be careful: Some drivers will use the evening setting during the daytime, or (at night) try to charge an extra 20% on top of the higher meter setting. Tipping taxi drivers is not expected.

Depending on your location, the time of day, and the weather (rain places taxis at a premium), it's relatively easy to hail a cab downtown. You'll always find taxis in front of the Teatro Nacional (albeit at high prices) and around the Parque Central at Avenida Central and Calle Central. Taxis in front of hotels and the El Pueblo tourist complex usually charge more than others, although this is technically illegal. Most hotels will gladly call you a cab, either for a downtown excursion or for a trip back out to the airport. You can also get a cab by calling **Coopetaxi** (☎ **506/235-9966**), **Coopetico** (☎ **506/224-6969**), or **Taxicoopeguaria** (☎ **506/226-1366**).

ON FOOT Downtown San José is very compact. Nearly everyplace you might want to go is within a 15-by-4-block area. Because of the traffic congestion, you'll often find it faster to walk than to take a bus or taxi. Be careful when walking the streets, both by night and by day. Flashy jewelry, loosely held handbags or backpacks, and expensive camera equipment tend to attract thieves. You should also watch your step: Between the earthquakes, wear and tear, and negligence, the sidewalks in San José have become veritable obstacle courses and the cause of more than one sprained ankle.

Avenida Central is a pedestrian-only street for several blocks around Calle Central toward the Cultural Plaza. It has recently been redone with interesting paving stones and the occasional fountain in an attempt to create a comfortable pedestrian mall.

BY MOTORCYCLE Motorcycles rent for about the same amount as cars: $35 a day or $210 a week. Due to poor road conditions and the difficulty of driving in Costa Rica, they are not recommended unless you're an experienced rider. This is even truer in the city. If you really want to rent a motorcycle in the San José area, try **Dirt Rider Rent A Moto** (☎ **506/257-3831**), located on Paseo Colón, in front of the Mas X Menos supermarket.

Alternatively, if you want to take a guided tour on a bigger bike, check in with **Tour Harley** (☎ **506/253-3451**; e-mail: harleytr@sol.racsa.co.cr). A full-day tour with lunch costs $135 per person (you can carry a passenger on your bike for an extra $25). Half- and multiday trips are also available. The typical half- and full-day tours tool around the Orosi Valley, taking in Cartago and the Irazú Volcano. However, depending on weather conditions and client needs, they might head to the Poás Volcano, stop for bungee jumping, or go shopping in Sarchí (although it's hard to carry home an oxcart on the back of a Harley).

BY CAR It will cost you between $35 and $65 per day to rent a car in Costa Rica. Most rental car agencies will either pick you up or deliver the car to any San José hotel. If you decide to go this route and pick up your rental car in downtown San José, be prepared for some very congested streets. The following companies have desks at Juan Santamaría International Airport, as well as offices downtown: **Ada Rent a Car** (☎ **506/441-1260** at the airport, or 506/233-7733 in downtown San José); **Adobe Rent a Car** (☎ **506/442-2422** at the airport, or in downtown San José (☎**506/221-5425**); **Avis Rent A Car** (☎ **800/331-1212** in the U.S., 506/442-1321 at the airport, or 506/232-9922 in downtown San José); **Budget Rent A Car** (☎ **800/527-0700**, 506/441-4444 at the airport, or 506/223-3284 in downtown San José); **Elegante Rent A Car** (☎ **800/283-1324** in the U.S. and Canada, 506/441-9366 at the airport, or 506/221-0066 in downtown San José); **Hertz Rent A Car** (☎ **800/654-3131** and 506/441-0097 at the airport, or 506/221-1818 in downtown San José); **National Car Rental** (☎ **800/328-4567** and 506/441-6533 at the airport, or 506/290-8787 in downtown San José); and **Thrifty Car Rental** (☎ **800/367-2277** in the U.S., 506/442-8585 at the airport, or 506/255-4141 in downtown San José).

You will save somewhere between $35 and $75 per week on a car rental if you make a reservation in your home country at least 1 week before you need the car. For example, at press time, the least expensive Hertz car rents for $378 per week, including insurance, in San José, but if you book this same car in advance from the United States, you can get it for $317 per week, including insurance. The savings are even slightly greater for a four-wheel-drive vehicle. If you have American Express or another credit card insurance policy that applies if you charge the rental on its card, check carefully before you arrive in the country to determine the exact coverage it provides. Though it's possible at some car-rental agencies to waive the insurance charges, you will have to pay all damages before leaving the country if you're in an accident. Even if you do take the insurance, you can expect a deductible of between $500 and $1,250. At some agencies, you can buy additional insurance to lower the deductible.

There are dozens of other car-rental agencies in San José, and most of them will arrange for airport or hotel pickup or delivery. Some of the more dependable agencies are **American Rent A Car**, 425 meters north of the Toyota dealership on Paseo Colón (☎ **506/221-5353**); **Hola! Rent A Car**, west of Hotel Irazú, La Uruca, San José (☎ **506/231-5666**); **Prego Rent A Car**, Paseo Colón between Calles 32 and 34 (☎ **506/257-1158**); **Tico Rent A Car**, Paseo Colón between Calles 24 and 26 (☎ **506/222-8920** or 506/223-9642); **Tropical Rent A Car**, at the entrance to the Hotel San José Palacio (☎ **506/232-0077**); and **Toyota Rent A Car** (☎ **506/223-2250** or 506/223-8979).

During the high season, I highly recommend reserving your car in advance, as the car-rental fleet is often smaller than the demand.

To rent a car in Costa Rica, you must be at least 21 years old and have a valid driver's license and a major credit card in your name.

FAST FACTS: San José

Airport See "Arriving," earlier in this chapter.

American Express **American Express** (☎ **506/257-0155**) has a counter in San José at the Banco de San José on Calle Central between Avenidas 3 and 5. It's open Monday through Friday from 8am to 7pm, and Saturday 9am to 1pm. To report lost or stolen traveler's checks within Costa Rica, call toll free ☎**0-800-011-0080**. To report a lost or stolen American Express card from inside Costa Rica, call ☎**0-800-012-3211** or 0-800-001-0184 for an English-language operator.

Bookstores **Chispas Books**, Calle 7 between Avenidas 1 and Central (☎ **506/256-8251**), has a wide range of new and used books in English, with an excellent selection of tropical biology, bird, and flora books; it's open daily from 9am to 7pm. For a wide selection of new books in English and Spanish, you can also check out **Libreria Internacional** (☎ **506/283-6965**), open Monday through Saturday from 9:30am to 7pm, located 300 meters west of the Taco Bell in San Pedro. Libreria International also has a store in the Multiplaza mall in Escazú (☎ **506/288-1131**).

Camera Repair **Equipos Fotograficos Canon**, Avenida 3 between Calles 3 and 5 (☎ **506/233-0176**), specializes in Canon but may be able to repair other brands. You could also try **Dima**, Avenida Central between Calles 3 and 5 (☎ **506/222-3969**).

Car Rentals See "Getting Around," earlier in this chapter.

Climate See "When to Go," in chapter 3.

Country Code The telephone country code for Costa Rica is 506; there are no city or area codes.

Crime See "Safety," below.

Currency Exchange The best thing to do is to exchange money at your hotel. If they can't do this for you, they can direct you to a private bank where you won't have to stand in line for hours. Avoid exchanging money on the street.

Dentists If you need a dentist while in San José, your best bet is to call your embassy, which will have a list of recommended dentists. Many bilingual dentists also advertise in the *Tico Times*. Because treatments are so inexpensive in Costa

Rica, dental tourism has become a popular option for people needing extensive work.

Doctors Contact your embassy for information on doctors in San José.

Drugstores There are countless pharmacies and drugstores in San José. Many of them will deliver at little or no extra cost. **Farmacia Fischel**, Avenida 3 and Calle 2, is across from the main post office (☎ **506/257-7979**). It's open Monday through Friday from 8am to 7pm, Saturday from 8am to 5pm.

Embassies/Consulates See "Fast Facts: Costa Rica," in chapter 3.

Emergencies In case of fire, dial ☎ **118**; for the police, dial ☎ **117**; for an ambulance, dial ☎ **128**; and for general emergencies, dial ☎ **911**.

Express Mail Services Many international courier and express mail services have offices in San José, including: **DHL**, on Paseo Colón between Calles 30 and 32 (☎ **506/290-3020**); **EMS Courier**, with desks at the principal metropolitan post offices (☎ **506/233-2762**); and **United Parcel Service**, Avenida 3 between Calles 30 and 32 (☎ **506/257-7447**). *Beware:* Despite what you may be told, packages sent overnight to U.S. addresses tend to take 3 to 4 days to reach their destination.

Eyeglasses Look for the word *optica.* **Optica Jiménez** (☎ **506/257-4658** or 506/233-4475) and **Optica Vision** (☎ **506/255-2266**) are two dependable chains, with stores around San José. They can do everything from eye exams to repairs.

Faxes You can make international phone calls as well as send faxes from the **ICE office** at Avenida 2 between Calles 1 and 3 (☎**506/255-0444**). Faxes cost around $2 per page to the United States. Many hotels will offer the same service for a fee.

Holidays See "When to Go," in chapter 3.

Hospitals **Clinica Biblica**, Avenida 14 between Calle Central and Calle 1 (☎ **506/257-5252** or, for emergencies, 506/257-0466), is conveniently located close to downtown and has several English-speaking doctors.

Information See "Visitor Information," earlier in this chapter.

Laundry/Dry-Cleaning **Sixaola**, Avenida 2 between Calles 7 and 9 (☎ **506/221-2111**), open Monday through Friday from 7am to 6pm and Saturday from 8am to 1pm, is a dependable place downtown to get clothes cleaned. Unfortunately, their prices are quite high. Your best bet is to have your laundry done at your hotel—most offer a laundry service, though these, too, are usually expensive.

Luggage Storage/Lockers Most hotels will store luggage for you while you're traveling around the country. Sometimes there is a charge for this service.

Maps The Costa Rican Tourist Board (ICT) (see "Visitor Information" in this chapter) can usually provide you with good maps of both Costa Rica and San José. Other sources in San José are **Chispas Books**, Calle 7 between Avenidas Central and 1 (☎ **506/256-8251**); **Libreria Lehmann**, Avenida Central between Calles 1 and 3 (☎ **506/223-1212**); and **Jimenez and Tanzi**, Calle 3 between Avenidas 1 and 3 (☎ **506/233-8033**).

Newspapers/Magazines The *Tico Times* is Costa Rica's principal English-language weekly paper and serves both the expatriate community and visitors.

You will also see *Costa Rica Today,* a bilingual weekly geared toward visitors, which has almost no news. You can also get the *International Herald Tribune, Miami Herald, The New York Times, USA Today, Time,* and *Newsweek,* as well as other English-language publications. You'll find these publications in hotel gift shops and in bookstores that sell English-language books.

Photographic Needs Film is expensive in Costa Rica, so bring as much as you will need from home. In a pinch, you can buy film and other photographic equipment at several places around town. I recommend that you wait to have your film processed at home, but if you must develop your prints down here try **Fuji Foto**, Avenida Central between Calle 1 and Calle Central (☎ **506/222-2222**). For more serious photographic needs (equipment, repairs, etc.), try **Dima**, Avenida Central between Calles 3 and 5 (☎ **506/222-3969**).

Police Dial ☎ **117** for the police. They should have someone who speaks English.

Post Office The main post office (*correo*) is on Calle 2 between Avenidas 1 and 3. You can purchase stamps (from vending machines) Monday through Friday from 7am to 10pm and Saturday from 8am to noon. For mailing packages and buying stamps from a real person, hours are Monday through Friday from 8am to 7pm.

Radio/TV There are about 10 local TV channels, plus local cable and satellite TV from the United States. There are dozens of AM and FM radio stations in San José.

Religious Services The *Tico Times* has a listing of churches in San José. You can also ask at the tourist office for a list of the city's churches, or ask at your hotel. The following suggestions for English-language services. Call for locations. **Episcopal**: Church of the Good Shepherd (☎ **506/222-1560**); **Reform Judaism**: B'nai Israel (☎ **506/257-1785**); **Roman Catholic**: the International Chapel of St. Mary at the Hotel Herradura complex (☎ **506/293-4457**); **Nondenominational Christian**: Christian Fellowship (☎ **506/289-4096**); **Baptist**: International Baptist Church (☎ **506/225-2829**); **Quaker**: Call ☎ **506/233-6168** for information.

Rest Rooms These are known as *sanitarios* or *servicios sanitarios.* You may also see or hear them called *baños.* They are marked *damas* (women) and *hombres* or *caballeros* (men). Public rest rooms are rare to nonexistent; most big hotels and public restaurants will let you use their bathrooms. If you're downtown, there are public bathrooms at the entrance to the Gold Museum.

Safety Never carry anything you value in your pockets or purse. Pickpockets and purse slashers are rife in San José, especially on public buses, in the markets, on crowded sidewalks, and near hospitals. Leave your passport, money, and other valuables in your hotel safe and carry only as much as you really need when you go out. It's a good idea to make a photocopy of your passport's opening pages and carry that with you. If you do carry anything valuable with you, keep it in a money belt or special passport bag around your neck. Day packs are a prime target of brazen pickpockets throughout the city. Stay away from the red-light district northwest of the Central Market. Also, be advised that the Parque Nacional is not a safe place for a late-night stroll.

Other precautions include walking around corner vendors, not between the vendor and the building. The tight space between the vendor and the building is a favorite spot for pickpockets. Never park a car on the street, and never leave anything of value in a car, even if it's in a guarded parking lot. Don't even leave your car unattended by the curb in front of a hotel while you dash in to check on your reservation. With these precautions in mind, you should have a safe visit to San José. Also see "Safety" in "Fast Facts: Costa Rica," in chapter 3.

Taxes All hotels charge 16.3% tax. Restaurants charge 13% tax and also add on a 10% service charge, for a total of 23% more on your bill. There is an airport departure tax of $17.

Taxis See "Getting Around," earlier in this chapter.

Telegrams/Telexes You can send telegrams and telexes from the **ICE office** on Avenida 2 between Calles 1 and 3 (open daily from 7am to 10pm). **Radiográfica** (☎ **506/287-0087**) at Calle 1 and Avenida 5 in San José and **Western Union** (☎ **0-800-777-7777**) with numerous offices around the country also have telegram services.

Telephones Pay phones are not as common in San José as they are in most North American and European cities. When you do find one, whether on the street, in a restaurant, or hotel lobby, it may take coins of various denominations, or it may take only the old-style 5- or 10-colón coins, or it may take a calling card. Calling cards are becoming more and more prominent, and you can purchase them in a host of gift shops and pharmacies. A call within the city costs around 10 colónes per minute. Pay phones are both hard to find and notoriously unreliable, so it may be better to make calls from your hotel, though you will likely be charged around 100 colónes per call.

For making international calling card and collect calls, you can reach an **AT&T operator** by dialing ☎ **0-800-011-4114**; **MCI** by dialing ☎ **0-800-012-2222**; **Sprint** by dialing ☎ **0-800-013-0123**; **Canada Bell** by dialing ☎ **0-800-015-1161**; **British Telephone** by dialing ☎ **0-800-044-1044**; and a Costa Rican international operator by dialing 116 (pay phones may sometimes require a coin deposit). The Costa Rican telephone system allows direct international dialing, but it's expensive. To get an international line, dial 00 followed by the country code (1 for the United States) and the local number.

Time Zone San José is on central standard time, 6 hours behind Greenwich mean time.

Useful Telephone Numbers For directory assistance, call ☎ **113**; for international directory assistance, call ☎ **124**; for the exact time, call ☎ **112**.

Water The water in San José is said to be perfectly fine to drink. Residents of the city will swear to this. Nonetheless, travelers sometimes experience stomach discomfort during their first few days drinking it. If you want to be cautious, drink bottled water and *frescos* made with milk instead of water. *Sin hielo* means "no ice," and this is what you'll want to say; just because it's frozen doesn't mean it's not water.

Weather The weather in San José (including the Central Valley) is usually temperate, never getting extremely hot or cold. May to November is the rainy season, though the rain usually falls only in the afternoon and evening.

3 Accommodations

Just a few years back, hotels were popping up all over downtown San José, but in recent years the boom seems to have stopped and there is, in fact, a distinct glut of accommodations. This is good for you, the visitor, as it's created a healthy degree of competition—it pays to shop around and ask if anyone's offering special packages or promotions when you plan to visit.

Of the many hotels in San José, your choices range from luxury resorts to budget pensions charging only a few dollars a night. However, these two extremes are the exceptions, not the norm. The vast number of accommodations, and the best deals, are to be found in the $30 to $90 price range. Within this moderate bracket, you'll find restored homes that have been turned into small hotels and bed-and-breakfasts, modern hotels with swimming pools and exercise rooms, and older downtown business hotels. When considering where to stay in San José, you should take into consideration how long you plan to stay, what you expect to do while you're here, and whether you want to be in the heart of the city or out in the suburbs.

Downtown hotels, many of which are in beautifully restored homes, are convenient to museums, restaurants, and shopping but can be noisy. Many people are also bothered by the exhaust fumes that permeate downtown streets. If you want clean air and a peaceful night's sleep, consider staying out in the suburbs. **Escazú** is quiet and has great views, while **Los Yoses** is fairly close in yet still quiet. If you've rented a car, make sure your hotel provides secure parking, or you'll have to find (and pay for) a nearby lot. If you plan to take some day tours, you can just as easily arrange these from a hotel situated outside the downtown area.

If you're heading out to Guanacaste, the central Pacific, or the Northern zone, you might consider a hotel or bed-and-breakfast either near or beyond the airport. Sure, you give up proximity to downtown, but you can cut as much as an hour off your travel time to any of these destinations. Many car-rental companies will even deliver or pick up cars at these establishments.

In the past few years, dozens of bed-and-breakfast inns have opened up around the San José area. Most are in residential neighborhoods that are quieter, though less convenient, than downtown locations. You can find out about many bed-and-breakfasts by contacting the **Costa Rica Bed and Breakfast Group** (☎ **506/223-4168;** fax 506/223-4157).

If you plan to be in town for a while or are traveling with family or several friends, you may want to consider staying in an *apartotel.* As the name implies, this is a cross between an apartment and a hotel. You can rent by the day, week, or month, and you get a furnished apartment with a full kitchen, plus housekeeping and laundry service. Options to choose from include: **Apartotel El Sesteo** (☎ **506/ 296-1805**; e-mail: sesteo@sol.racsa.co.cr); **Apartotel La Sabana** (☎ **506/220-2422**; e-mail: lasabana@sol.racsa.co.cr); and **Apartotel Los Yoses** (☎ **506/225-0033**).

The price categories used below are defined as follows (for a double room): **Very Expensive**, $125 and up; **Expensive**, $80 to $125; **Moderate**, $40 to $80; **Inexpensive**, $40 and under. However, please keep in mind that the 16.3% combined sales and hotel tax, which adds quite a bit to the price of a room, is not included in the rates I've listed. If you've set $90 as your total daily room budget, you'll want to look for a hotel charging between $65 and $75 per night before tax.

DOWNTOWN SAN JOSÉ/BARRIO AMÓN

VERY EXPENSIVE

Aurola Holiday Inn. Avenida 5 and Calle 5 (Apdo. 7802-1000), San José. ☎ **506/ 233-7233.** Fax 506/222-2621. 200 units. A/C TV TEL. $120–$130 double; $150–$370 suite. AE, DC, MC, V. Free parking.

Situated directly across the street from the attractive Parque Morazán, this is San José's only high-rise deluxe hotel. The rooms are everything you might expect in this price range—but nothing more. The hotel has been around for quite a few years, and the age is starting to show. Moreover, I've found the service can be somewhat hit-or-miss. However, if you get one of the upper-floor rooms on the north side, you'll have one of the best views in the city.

Dining/Diversions: The Mirador, up on the 17th floor, is the Aurola's top restaurant and serves good continental and international fare—and the view is one of the best in San José. There's also a casino on this same floor. Just off the lobby is the more casual Tropicana, which serves an impressive, though pricey, breakfast buffet. Bar La Palma overlooks the lobby and Parque Morazán. There is also a snack bar adjacent to the pool.

Amenities: Room service, laundry service, car-rental desk, travel agency, tour desk, indoor pool, hot tub, saunas, exercise room, gift shop, executive center.

✪ **Radisson Europa Hotel.** P.O. Box 538-Calle Blancos (behind La Republica building), San José. ☎ **800/333-3333** or 506/257-3257. Fax 506/257-8191. E-mail: eurohot@sol.racsa.co.cr. 114 units. A/C MINIBAR TV TEL. $140–$160 double; $220 junior suite; $500 presidential suite. AE, DC, MC, V. Free parking.

This hotel is geared primarily to business travelers, but I think it's the best choice for anyone looking for a big, dependable, luxury hotel close to downtown San José. The rooms are all comfortable and large, and they feature either one king or two double beds. Wooden headboards and angular window nooks and other small architectural details, give these rooms a slight edge over those in the Aurola Holiday Inn. For an extra $20 you can ask for an executive room, which is basically a standard with a coffeemaker, scale, terry-cloth bathrobes, and extra telephone in the bathroom. The junior suites are called CEO Club rooms here and are in an isolated wing with it's own comfortable lounge and honor bar. They come with all the above amenities, as well as a desk and chair, in-room fax machine and small balcony.

Dining: There are two restaurants here, an informal cafe for breakfast and lunch, and the more formal Acuarelas, serving up a varied plate of international fare in a more elegant setting.

Amenities: Pool, small gym, casino, gift shop, art gallery, tour desk and car-rental agency. Business travelers will find a full-service business center, as well as ample conference facilities.

EXPENSIVE

Amón Park Plaza. Avenida 11 and Calle 3 bis (Apdo. 4192-1000), San José. ☎ **800/575-1253** in the U.S., or 506/257-0191. Fax 506/257-0284. E-mail: amonpark@sol.racsa.co.cr. 90 units. A/C TV TEL. $115 double; $130–$210 suite. AE, DC, MC, V. Free parking.

Located on the north edge of the Barrio Amón historic neighborhood, this hotel stands out in size and luxury from most of the area's smaller hotels. Moreover, in terms of service, location, and price, this hotel gets my nod over the nearby Holiday Inn. The rooms are spacious and up to international standards.

Dining: The Park Plaza restaurant is the hotel's most formal dining option, serving well-prepared international and nouvelle Costa Rican cuisine. There is also a more casual 24-hour lobby restaurant and the Tamesis Bar.

Amenities: The hotel features a casino, a small gym, tour desk, and gift shop.

✪ **Britannia Hotel.** Calle 3 and Avenida 11 (Apdo. 3742-1000), San José. ☎ **800/263-2618** in the U.S., or 506/223-6667. Fax 506/223-6411. www.centralamerica.com. E-mail: britannia@sol.racsa.co.cr. 24 units. TV TEL. $89–$117 double. AE, DC, MC, V. Parking nearby.

Of the many hotels that have been created from restored old houses in downtown San José, this is the most luxurious. The big pink building, with its wraparound veranda, is unmistakable and is certainly one of the most attractive old houses in the neighborhood. In the lobby, tile floors, stained-glass large picture windows, a brass chandelier, and reproduction Victorian decor all help set a tone of tropical luxury. Along with restoring the old home, the owners have built a four-story addition, which is separated from the original building by a narrow atrium. Rooms in the original home have hardwood floors and furniture, and high ceilings and fans help keep them cool. In the deluxe rooms and junior suites, you get air-conditioning. Though the streetside rooms have double glass, light sleepers will still want to avoid them. The quietest rooms are those toward the back of the new addition.

Dining: In what was once the wine cellar, you'll find a casual restaurant. The buffet breakfast is served in the adjacent skylit room. Afternoon tea and happy hour drinks are also served.

Amenities: There are room service and laundry services, and the hotel will store luggage and arrange tours.

✪ **Hotel L'Ambiance.** 949 Calle 13 between Avenidas 9 and 11 (Apdo. 1040-2050), San José (mailing address in the U.S.: c/o INTERLINK, 179, P.O. Box 526770, Miami, FL 33152). ☎ **506/222-6702.** Fax 506/223-0481. 7 units. TV TEL. $90 double; $140 suite. Rates include breakfast. MC, V. Parking nearby.

L'Ambiance is a beautifully restored stucco building with a central courtyard patio reminiscent of old Spain. The building is on a quiet street only a few blocks from the heart of downtown San José, so you get both the convenience of the city and the quiet of a suburban location. Tile floors in the halls and on the veranda surrounding the courtyard provide a touch of old Costa Rica, while European and North American antiques add a bit of international flavor. Guest rooms have high ceilings and either hardwood floors or carpeting. There is a mix of antique and modern furnishings, and though there is no air-conditioning, overhead fans manage to keep the rooms cool. Rooms vary in size.

Dining: The hotel's dining room/bar is a surprising contrast to the rest of the hotel. Potted plants, brightly painted tiles, and white lattice walls give it a greenhouse feel. Well-prepared continental dinners are served here by candlelight.

Amenities: Concierge service and laundry service.

MODERATE

D'raya Vida. Apdo. 2209-2100, San José (mailing address in the U.S.: P.O. Box 025216-1638, Miami, FL 33102-5216). ☎ **506/223-4168.** Fax 506/223-4157. E-mail: draya@yellowweb.co.cr. 4 units (2 with bathroom). Nov–Apr, $85 double; May–Oct, $65 double. Rates include full breakfast. AE, MC, V. Free parking.

This little bed-and-breakfast is so secluded that it seems to be in a world all its own, yet it's in downtown San José. To find the inn, go east on Avenida 9, then turn left on Calle 17. After 100 meters, turn left on Avenida 11. Follow this road to the dead end at the inn's front gate. Behind the gate, in a shady old garden, is a miniature villa. The restored old stucco home is furnished with the owners' eclectic collection of crafts from around the world, and in the living room you'll find a grand piano and fireplace. (Sounds like a B&B up north, doesn't it?) Guest rooms are all different. One of the upstairs rooms has its own private balcony, while the other has an unusual four-poster bed. My favorite rooms, however, are the two downstairs, which have private bathrooms. One is decorated with masks from around the world, and the other has Indian art and a fountain just outside. D'Raya Vida offers free airport pickup and drop-off.

Fleur de Lys Hotel. Calle 13 between Avenidas 2 and 6, 50 meters south of the Plaza de la Democracia (Apdo. 10736-1000), San José. ☎ **506/222-4391** or 506/257-2621. Fax 506/257-3637. E-mail: florlys@sol.racsa.co.cr. 19 units. TV TEL. $70 double; $80–$90 suite. Rates include breakfast. AE, DC, MC, V. Parking nearby.

Located close to the National Museum and Plaza de la Democracia, the Fleur de Lys is a restored mansion that has been painted an eye-catching pink. Inside, the historic mansion is less ostentatious. The lobby and hallways feature polished hardwoods and old tiles, while in the guest rooms, each of which is different, there are modern furnishings. The standard rooms tend to be a bit small, so if you need space, you may want to opt for a suite. All the rooms are decorated with unusual original artworks that give this hotel a character unique in San José. Carpeting and modern tiled bathrooms with contemporary fixtures assure you of the creature comforts. The most unusual room is the master suite, which has black lacquer furnishings, a cordless phone, halogen lamps, a black-tile bathroom, and a tiny sunroom off the bedroom. This room is definitely worth the extra expense. There is an elegant little restaurant off the lobby serving modern interpretations of traditional Costa Rican cuisine, and a bar in a front room with a street-side terrace.

Gran Hotel Costa Rica. Avenida 2 between Calles 1 and 3, San José. ☎ **506/221-4000.** Fax 506/221-3501. 113 units. TV TEL. $71 double; $78 triple; $81–$189 suite. AE, DC, MC, V. Free parking.

Though the Gran Hotel Costa Rica can claim the best location of any downtown hotel (bordering the National Theater and the Plaza de la Cultura), it does not, unfortunately, offer rooms to match the prestigious location or name. Though most of the guest rooms here are fairly large, they have not been well maintained over the decades, giving them an adequate but rather run-down feel, especially in the bathrooms.

The Café Parisien is the hotel's greatest attribute, and it's memorable not so much for its food as for its atmosphere. The restaurant is an open-air patio that overlooks the National Theater, street musicians, and all the activity of the Plaza de la Cultura. On the opposite side of the lobby, there's a small and very casual casino. The hotel also maintains a tour desk and gift shop, and it offers 24-hour room service and laundry service.

Hotel Casa Morazan. Calle 7 and Avenida 9 (Apdo. 10063-1000), San José. ☎ **506/257-4187.** Fax 506/257-4175. 11 units. A/C TV TEL. Nov 15–Apr 14, $65 double; Apr 15–Nov 14, $55 double. Rates include breakfast. AE, MC, V. Parking nearby.

The Barrio Amon district of downtown San José saw a rapid proliferation of hotels a few years back, and this is one of the better ones. The interior styling is very modern, with art deco accents throughout. Guest rooms are carpeted and many have king-size beds. The bathrooms are of average size but have modern fixtures. Unfortunately, most of the rooms get quite a bit of traffic noise. The hotel has a small restaurant, serving continental meals at reasonable prices. The staff here is very helpful and can help with tour and car-rental arrangements, as well as luggage storage and laundry.

Hotel Del Rey. Avenida 1 and Calle 9 (Apdo. 6241-1000), San José. ☎ **506/257-7800.** Fax 506/221-0096. E-mail: delrey@ticonet.co.cr. 106 units. A/C TV TEL. $68–$75 double; $75–$85 triple; $125 suite. AE, MC, V. Parking nearby.

You can't miss the Del Rey; it's a massive pink corner building with vaguely colonial styling. The lobby continues the facade's theme with pink-tile floors and stone columns. Inside, every guest room is marked by a carved hardwood door. Behind these impressive doors, you'll find wall-to-wall carpeting and hardwood furniture. The rooms vary in size and comfort: There are quiet interior rooms that have no windows, and larger rooms with windows (but also street noises). Try for a sixth-floor room with a balcony. The hotel's only restaurant is the Del Rey Cafe, which serves respectable U.S.-style deli sandwiches and light meals. Much of the first floor is taken up with a lively casino and the neighboring Blue Marlin Bar, which is very popular with sports fans and prostitutes. The hotel has full-service tour and sport fishing desks.

✪ **Hotel Don Carlos.** 779 Calle 9 between Avenidas 7 and 9, San José (mailing address in the U.S.: Dept. 1686, P.O. Box 025216, Miami, FL 33102-5216). ☎ **506/221-6707.** Fax 506/255-0828. www.doncarlos.co.cr. E-mail: hotel@doncarlos.co.cr. 36 units. $50–$60 double. Rates include continental breakfast. AE, MC, V. Parking nearby.

If you're looking for a small hotel that is unmistakably Costa Rican and hints at the days of the planters and coffee barons, this is the place for you. Located in an old residential neighborhood, only blocks from the business district, the Don Carlos is popular with both vacationers and businesspeople. A large reproduction of a pre-Columbian carved-stone human figure stands outside the front door of this gray inn, which was a former president's mansion. Inside, you'll find many more such reproductions, as well as orchids, ferns, palms, and parrots. After a day of exploring the capital, there's nothing like settling down in the lounge, the small courtyard, or the sunny deck, where the wicker furniture, bubbling fountain, and tropical breezes will make you think you're Hope or Crosby on the road to somewhere. The rooms are all distinct and vary greatly in size, so be specific when you reserve, or ask to see a few if possible when you check in. The gift shop here is one of the largest in the country, and the paintings hung throughout the hotel are also for sale. There's a helpful in-house tour company. The complimentary breakfast and moderately priced meals are served in the Pre-Columbian Lounge.

✪ **Hotel Santo Tomas.** Avenida 7 between Calles 3 and 5, San José. ☎ **506/255-0448.** Fax 506/222-3950. www.hotels.co.cr/santomas.html. E-mail: hotelst@sol.racsa.co.cr. 20 units. TV TEL. $60–$90 double. Rates include continental breakfast. No credit cards. Parking nearby.

Even though it's on a nondescript street, this converted mansion is a real jewel inside. Built 100 years ago by a coffee baron, the house was once slated to be bulldozed in order to expand the Aurola Holiday Inn's parking lot. Needless to say, it was not, and under the direction of American Thomas Douglas, it's been restored to its former grandeur. The first thing you see when you walk through the front door is the beautiful carved-wood desk that serves as the reception area. In the guest rooms you'll find similar pieces of exquisitely crafted antique reproductions, made here in Costa Rica from rare hardwoods. Keeping with the theme, the hardwood floors throughout most of the hotel are original and were made from a type of tree that has long since become almost impossible to find. The rooms vary in size, but most are fairly large and have a small table and chairs. Skylights in some bathrooms will brighten your morning, and queen-size beds will provide a good night's sleep. Maps of Costa Rica hang on the walls of all the guest rooms so you can get acquainted with the country. There are a couple of patio areas, as well as a TV lounge and combination breakfast room and outdoor bar. Laundry service and a baggage storage room are available. The staff and management are extremely helpful with tour arrangements and any other needs or requests.

La Casa Verde de Amón. Calle 7 and Avenida 9 no. 910, San José (mailing address in the U.S.: Dept. 1701, P.O. Box 025216, Miami, FL 33102-5216). ☎ and fax **506/223-0969.** E-mail: casaverd@sol.racsa.co.cr. 7 units. TV TEL. Dec 1–Apr 30, $72–$96 double, $96–$126 suite; May 1–Nov 30, $55–$72 double, $72–$116 suite. Rates include breakfast buffet. AE, MC, V. Parking nearby.

This tropical Victorian house was built around 1910 and was completely renovated between 1989 and 1992. There are beautiful old tile and polished hardwood floors throughout the building, which give the house a patrician air. Off the lobby, there's a small patio and open-air breakfast room. Up on the second floor, there's a large, high-ceilinged central seating area with a 110-year-old baby grand piano and stained-glass large picture windows that bathe the room in a beautiful blue light. Rooms are all different, but most are furnished with antiques. Some have their original porcelain fixtures and brass faucets; you may find a bathtub or only a shower in your bathroom. The Don Carlos suite is huge, with a high ceiling, king-size beds, and a separate seating area. All the rooms have clock radios, but unfortunately, it's likely that traffic noises will wake you in the morning if you have a room on the street side of the hotel. You shouldn't have any trouble finding this hotel, especially if you remember that *casa verde* translates as "green house," and this one is painted a prominent green.

Taylor's Inn. Avenida 13 between Calle 3 and 3 bis (Apdo. 531-1000), San José. ☎ **506/257-4333.** Fax 506/221-1475. www.catours.co.cr. E-mail: taylor@catours.co.cr. 12 units. TV. $60–$70 double; slightly lower in the off-season. Rates include continental breakfast. AE, MC, V.

This is yet another lovely converted home turned bed-and-breakfast. The rooms are all arranged around the interior courtyard, which features a small garden of heliconia and flowering ginger—a perfect place for eating breakfast. Most rooms have one single and one double bed, although a few have sleeping lofts and are good for families. All are very clean and feature artworks from prominent Costa Rican artists. The suite is a bit bigger, with a 20-inch television. Don't expect a sense of hermetic privacy here though—most of the rooms open onto the courtyard, and the old wooden construction guarantees that you hear every footfall and conversation of other guests passing by your door. The hotel has a helpful tour desk.

INEXPENSIVE

Hotel Bienvenido. Calle 10 between Avenidas 1 and 3 (Apdo. 389-2200), San José. ☎ **506/233-2161.** Fax 506/221-1872. 48 units (44 with bathroom). $13 double; $20 triple. AE, MC, V. Parking nearby.

This very basic hotel is one of the most popular in the city for travelers on a tight budget. The rooms are clean, though a bit dark, and there is always ample hot water. There are a few very inexpensive rooms with collective bathrooms, for groups of four or more. The hotel was created from an old movie theater, and there are still a few architectural details remaining from this incarnation. The place fills up by early afternoon in the high season, so call ahead for a reservation and ask for a quiet room in the back.

Hotel Diplomat. Calle 6 between Avenida Central and Avenida 2 (Apdo. 6606-1000), San José. ☎ **506/221-8133** or 506/221-8744. Fax 506/233-7474. 29 units. TEL. $28 double. AE, MC, V. Parking nearby.

It's easy to miss the entrance to this hotel. Watch for it on the east side of the street. The place is what you might expect from a worn yet perennially popular downtown

Family-Friendly Hotels

Meliá Cariari Hotel *(see p. 103)* Not only is there a big pool and recreation area that the kids will love, but there's a baby-sitting service that allows Mom and Dad some time to themselves.

Hotel Herradura *(see p. 102)* The large grounds and three swimming pools give the kids plenty of places to burn off excess energy, and baby-sitting services are also available.

budget hotel. The lobby is narrow, and the front door is fairly nondescript. The carpeted rooms are rather small, and the appointments have seen better days, but they're comfortable nonetheless, and some rooms on the upper floors even have nice views of the mountains. The tiled baths are clean, and the water is hot. If you get too claustrophobic in your room, there's a sitting area on each floor. The hotel's restaurant is a dark, attractive room with pink tablecloths, flowers on every table, and pastel walls. For those seeking an intimate dinner, try one of the tiny booths for two. Prices range from $2.50 for a sandwich to $15 for a lobster dinner.

Hotel Ritz and Pension Continental. Calle Central between Avenidas 8 and 10 (Apdo. 6783-1000), San José. ☎ **506/222-4103.** Fax 506/222-8849. 25 units (5 with bathroom). $12–$20 double without bath, $24 double with bath; $15–$24 triple without bath, $27 triple with bath; $27 quad without bath, $31 quad with bath. AE, MC, V. Parking nearby.

These two side-by-side budget hotels are under the same management and together have rooms to fit most budget travelers' needs. There is even a travel agency and tour company on the first floor, so you can arrange all of your travels around Costa Rica without leaving the hotel. Rooms vary greatly in size and comfort levels and can be dark and a bit musty. Bathrooms are old, and those showers that do have hot water use showerhead heaters that just barely work. If the first room you see isn't to your liking, just ask to see another, or make a small jump up in price category. The current owners are Swiss, so you'll probably meet quite a few Swiss travelers if you stay here. The hotel is in a bit of a bad neighborhood, so be careful walking around, especially if you're carrying a pack on your back.

Joluva Guesthouse. 936 Calle 3B between Avenidas 9 and 11 (Apdo. 1998-1002), San José. ☎ **800/298-2418** in the U.S., or 506/223-7961. Fax 506/257-7668. www.hotels.co.cr/joluva.html. E-mail: joluva@sol.racsa.co.cr. 8 units (6 with bathroom). TV. $25 double without bath, $40 double with bath. Rates include continental breakfast. AE, MC, V. Parking nearby.

Though you can find a less expensive hotel, there are few in this price range that offer the old-fashioned architectural detail of the Joluva—old tile and hardwood floors throughout and high ceilings (in one room, beautiful plasterwork on the ceiling). However, the rooms are small and a bit dark, and only two have windows that open onto the small courtyard. The breakfast room has skylights, which help brighten it a bit. This hotel caters to a gay clientele, but guests of all types are welcome.

Pension De La Cuesta. 1332 Cuesta de Nuñez, Avenida 1 between Calles 11 and 15. ☎ and fax **506/255-2896.** www.arweb.com/lacuesta. E-mail: ggmnber@sol.racsa.co.cr. 9 units (none with bathroom). $26 double; $34 triple. Rates include continental breakfast. AE, MC, V. Parking nearby.

If you don't mind a clean collective bathroom down the hall from your room, this little bed-and-breakfast is a real bargain and definitely worth considering. It was once the home of Otto Apuy, a well-known Costa Rican artist, and original artwork abounds. The building itself is a classic example of a tropical wood-frame home and has been painted an eye-catching pink with blue-and-white trim. The rooms can be a bit dark and are very simply furnished, but there's a very sunny and cheery sunken lounge/courtyard area in the center of the house. The owners give you free run of the kitchen and are even offering free use of their Internet connection. If that's not enough free stuff, there's no charge for children under 12. You'll find this hotel on the hill leading up to the Parque Nacional.

HOTELS IN LA SABANA/PASEO COLÓN

VERY EXPENSIVE

Meliá Confort Corobicí. Autopista General Cañas, Sabana Norte (Apdo. 2443-1000), San José. ☎ **888/485-2676** in the U.S., or 506/232-8122 in Costa Rica. Fax 506/231-5834. E-mail: corobici@sol.racsa.co.cr. 203 units. A/C MINIBAR TV TEL. $115 double; $165–$425 suite. AE, MC, V. Free parking.

Located just past the end of Paseo Colón and on the edge of Parque La Sabana, and recently added to the stable of Meliá hotels, the Corobicí offers all the amenities you would expect at a large aiport hotel, with one added bonus—it's much closer to downtown. The lobby is a vast expanse of marble floor faced by blank walls, though the modern art deco furnishings lend a bit of character. Guest rooms are quite modern and comfortable, with good beds and walls of glass through which, on most floors, you get good views of the valley and surrounding mountains. Joggers will enjoy the nearby Parque La Sabana.

Dining/Diversions: Perhaps the hotel's greatest attributes are its restaurants. Fuji serves authentic Japanese meals amid equally authentic surroundings; La Gondola serves good Italian food. These two restaurants are open for lunch and dinner only. At El Tucan Coffee Shop, you can get an inexpensive meal throughout the day. The Guacamaya is a quiet lobby bar, while the Pub Bar is a bit more lively and features karaoke music. There's also a casino.

Amenities: The Corobicí claims to have the largest health spa in Central America; you'll find a well-equipped exercise room, sauna, hot tub, and aerobics classes. The hotel also offers 24-hour room service, valet/laundry service, downtown shuttle, tour desk, car-rental desk, outdoor pool, conference rooms, a beauty parlor, and a gift shop.

San José Palacio. Autopista General Cañas (Apdo. 458-1150), San José. ☎ **506/220-2034.** Fax 506/220-2036. E-mail: palacio@sol.racsa.co.cr. 255 units. A/C MINIBAR TV TEL. $135–$155 double; $195–$430 suite. AE, DC, MC, V. Free parking.

Owned by the Barcelo company, the developer of the controversial Tambor project on the Nicoya Peninsula, the Palacio tries very hard to live up to its name. The Palacio is not in downtown San José, per se, but neither is it as far out of town as the Marriott, Meliá Cariari, or Herradura, and so it's much more convenient for exploring the city. The hilltop location assures good views from nearly every room. Business travelers, visiting celebrities, and conferences seem to be the bulk of the business here.

Rooms are very modern, and all have angled walls of glass to take in the superb views. Furnishings are of the highest quality, and in some rooms there are even leather chairs. If you stay in one of the executive rooms, you'll have access to a fax machine and secretarial services, and receive a complimentary continental breakfast and afternoon coffee.

Dining/Diversions: Ambar is the hotel's premier dining room, and the creative continental cuisine is reasonably priced and among the best in town. Anfora is a larger and more casual dining room that does an impressive, though expensive, lunch buffet. El Bosque is the hotel's main lounge and is adjacent to the small casino.

Amenities: Room service, massage, car-rental desk, travel agency, baby-sitting, free-form pool with adjacent grill and piano bar, exercise room, sauna, Jacuzzi, two tennis courts, three racquetball/squash courts, business center, conference center, shopping arcade, barber shop, beauty parlor.

MODERATE

✪ **Hotel Grano de Oro.** Calle 30 no. 251 between Avenidas 2 and 4, 150 meters south of Paseo Colón (Apdo. 1157-1007, Centro Colón), San José (mailing address in the U.S.: SJO 36, P.O. Box 025216, Miami, FL 33102-5216). ☎ **506/255-3322.** Fax 506/221-2782. E-mail: granoro@sol.racsa.co.cr. 35 units. TV TEL. $72–$103 double; $125–$160 suite. AE, MC, V. Free parking.

San José boasts dozens of old homes that have been converted into hotels, but few offer the luxurious accommodations or professional service that can be found at the Grano de Oro. Located on a quiet side street off of Paseo Colón, this small hotel offers a variety of room types to fit most budgets and tastes. Personally, I prefer the patio rooms, which have French doors opening onto private patios. However, if you want a room with plenty of space, ask for one of the deluxe rooms, which have large, modern, tiled baths with big tubs. Throughout all the guest rooms, you'll find attractive hardwood furniture, including old-fashioned wardrobes in some rooms. For additional luxuries, you can stay in one of the suites, which have whirlpool tubs. If you don't grab a suite, you still have access to the hotel's two rooftop Jacuzzis. The hotel's patio garden restaurant serves excellent international cuisine and some of the best desserts in the city.

Hotel Rosa del Paseo. 2862 Paseo Colón (Apdo. 287-1007), San José. ☎ **506/257-3213** or 506/257-3258. Fax 506/223-2776. 19 units. A/C TV TEL. $65 double, $75 triple, $100 suite; lower in the off-season. Rates include continental breakfast. AE, MC, V. Parking nearby.

This hotel is housed in one of San José's most beautiful old stucco homes, but unfortunately it's right on busy Paseo Colón. If you are so unfortunate as to get one of the front guest rooms, I doubt you'll be able to sleep at all. However, the rooms in back are well insulated against the noise. Built more than 110 years ago, this old home underwent a complete renovation and modernization a few years ago and is now richly appointed and surprisingly evocative of 19th-century Costa Rica. There are beautiful details throughout the hotel: transoms, ornate stucco door frames, polished hardwood floors. Reproduction antique and wicker furnishings evoke both the tropics and the past century.

There is no restaurant on the premises, but snacks and cold meals are available, and there's a wealth of restaurants nearby. You'll also find 24-hour bar/beverage service, laundry service, airport transportation, a craft shop, and an art gallery.

✪ **Sol Inn Torremolinos.** Calle 40 and Avenida 5 bis (Apdo. 114-1017), San José. ☎ **506/222-9129.** Fax 506/255-3167. E-mail: torremolinos@centralamerica.com. 90 units. TV TEL. $65 double; $75 triple; $75–$85 suite. AE, MC, V. Free parking.

If you want to be close to downtown; have a pool, sauna, Jacuzzi, and exercise room; and not spend a fortune, this is your best choice. Located at the west end of Paseo Colón, the Torremolinos is on a fairly quiet street and is built around a colorful and well-tended garden that makes the hotel's pool a wonderful place to while away an afternoon. The rooms are simply furnished and have plenty of space. There's a moderately priced restaurant serving international dishes, a lobby bar, conference room, tour desk, downtown shuttle bus, and room service.

INEXPENSIVE

Hotel Cacts. 2845 Avenida 3 bis between Calles 28 and 30 (Apdo. 379-1005), San José. ☎ **506/221-2928** or 506/221-6546. Fax 506/221-8616. E-mail: hcacts@sol.racsa.co.cr. 25 units (21 with bathroom). $35–$50 double; $45–$55 triple. Rates include breakfast buffet. MC, V. Free parking.

This is one of the most interesting and unusual budget hotels I've ever seen, housed in an attractive tropical contemporary home on a business and residential street. The original building is a maze of rooms and hallways on several levels (the house is built on a slope). The newer rooms all come with telephones and televisions. My favorite room is the huge bi-level family room with a high beamed ceiling. There's a third-floor open terrace that serves as the breakfast area. The hotel has even recently added a swimming pool and Jacuzzi. Hotel Cacts has its own tour desk and gift shop. The staff here is very helpful, and the hotel will receive mail and faxes, change money, and store baggage for guests.

✪ **Hotel Petite Victoria.** Paseo Colón, Frente a la Sala Garbo (Apdo. 357-1007), San José. ☎ **506/233-1812** or 506/233-1813. Fax 506/233-1812. 16 units. TV. $37–$45 double; $49–$55 triple. Rates include continental breakfast. AE, MC, V. Free parking.

One of the oldest houses in San José, this tropical Victorian home was once the election campaign headquarters for Oscar Arias Sánchez, Costa Rica's Nobel Prize–winning former president. Today, after extensive remodeling and restoration, it's an interesting little hotel that offers a historic setting at inexpensive rates. The big covered patio is perfect for sitting and taking in the warm sun, and it doubles as the hotel's restaurant. Guest rooms have medium to large tiled bathrooms and high ceilings and fans to keep the air cool. Inside, walls are made of wood, so noise can be a bit of a problem, but this is a small price to pay for such old-fashioned elegance. Tour arrangements and laundry service are also offered.

SAN PEDRO/LOS YOSES

✪ **Hotel Le Bergerac.** 50 S. Calle 35 (Apdo. 1107-1002), San José. ☎ **506/234-7850.** Fax 506/225-9103. www.bergerac.co.cr. E-mail: bergerac@sol.racsa.co.cr. 18 units. TV TEL. $68–$88 double; corporate rates available. Rates include full breakfast. AE, MC, V. Free parking.

With all the sophistication and charm of a small French inn, the Hotel Le Bergerac has ingratiated itself with business travelers and members of various diplomatic missions. What these visitors have found (and what you too will find should you stay here) is a tranquil environment in a quiet suburban neighborhood, spacious and comfortable accommodations, personal service, and gourmet meals. The owners have a total of 32 years of hotel experience, which accounts for the professionalism with which Le Bergerac is operated. The hotel is composed of three houses with courtyard gardens in between. Almost all of the rooms are quite large, and each is a little different. My favorite rooms are those with private patio gardens. Some rooms have king-size beds and refrigerators, and in the old master bedroom you'll find a little balcony. In the evenings, candlelight and classical music set a relaxing and romantic mood. The long-standing L'Ile de France restaurant has recently set up shop here, and gourmet French and continental dinners are available for guests and by reservation. The hotel also has a helpful tour desk and provides a wide range of business services to guests.

INEXPENSIVE

D'galah Hotel. Calle Masis, 100 meters past Calle La Cruz (Apdo. 208-2350), San José. ☎ and fax **506/234-1743** or 506/253-7539. 22 units. TV TEL. $35–$45 double. AE, MC, V. Free parking.

If you want to be close to downtown but away from the smog and traffic, this budget hotel is a good choice. Directly across the street from the hotel is the University of Costa Rica, which is an oasis of greenery that attracts many species of birds, especially among the bamboo groves. Rooms are a bit old-fashioned and dark. But, if you aren't too demanding, for the most part they're quite spacious and acceptable. The largest rooms have kitchenettes and sleeping lofts; the newest rooms have carpets and small private patios. Amenities include a small swimming pool, a sauna, and a breakfast room.

Toruma Youth Hostel. Avenida Central between Calles 29 and 31 (Apdo. 1352-1002), San José. ☎ **506/224-4085.** E-mail: recajhi@sol.racsa.co.cr. 100 beds (all with shared bathroom), $8.50 per person per night with an IYHF card; $10 with student ID; $11 general public. MC, V. Free parking.

This attractive old building, with its long veranda, is the largest hostel in Costa Rica's system of official youth hostels. Although it's possible to find other accommodations around town in this price range, none would likely be as clean. The atmosphere here is convivial and will be familiar to anyone who has hosteled in Europe. There's a large lounge in the center of the building with a high ceiling and a great deal of light. The dorms have four to six beds per room. The staff here can help you arrange stays at other hostels and trips around the country, and you can store luggage for 25¢ per day.

ESCAZÚ

This affluent suburb about 15 minutes west of San José is popular with North American retirees and expatriates, and quite a few little B&Bs have sprung up to cater to the needs of visiting friends. If you're interested in staying here you might contact the Costa Rica Bed and Breakfast Group (☎ **506/223-4168;** fax 506/223-4157).

VERY EXPENSIVE

✪ **Tara Resort Hotel and Spa.** Apdo. 1459-1250, Escazú. ☎ **800/405-5112** in the U.S. and Canada, or 506/228-6992 in Costa Rica. Fax 506/228-9651. www.crnn.com/tara. E-mail: taraspa@sol.racsa.co.cr. 40 units. TV TEL. $125 double; $190 bungalow; $155–$250 suite; $275 luxury villa. AE, MC, V. Free parking.

Located in San Antonio de Escazú, 600 meters south of the cemetery (once you hit Escazú, just follow the plentiful signs), Tara is perched high on a mountainside overlooking the entire Central Valley and surrounding volcanic peaks. The view is breathtaking and so is the setting. The owner here has a fixation on *Gone With the Wind,* and everything at this spa/resort follows the theme, from the O'Hara Dining Hall down to one of Rhett's Vitality Baths. Rich in antebellum southern grandeur, don't expect a lot of local color here. The suites are all part of the main house, and each has its own balcony (try to get one overlooking the valley). The nicest room here is the penthouse suite, with its high ceilings, private Jacuzzi, and 360° views. Villas and bungalows vary in size, but in the larger rooms you might find a seating area, a big bathroom with two sinks, a tub, a heat lamp, and perhaps even two balconies. Furnishings are traditional American styles that fit right in with the architecture. The luxury villas even come with a a full stereo system, fax, and complete computer setup, including Internet access and a printer.

Dining/Diversions: The Atlanta Dining Gallery is an elegant setting for fine meals; unfortunately, the windows do not do justice to the view. In the evenings there is live jazz and piano music. Meals are often served on the large back patio, which has an unobstructed view of the valley.

Amenities: Full assortment of spa treatments, including massage, facials, and aromatherapy; outdoor swimming pool, hot tub, sauna, small gym, various lawn and indoor games, conference facilities, and a tour desk.

MODERATE

Costa Verde Inn. Apdo. 89, Escazú (mailing address in the U.S.: SJO 1313, Box 025216, Miami, FL 33102). ☎ **506/228-4080.** Fax 506/289-8591. 14 units. $55 double; $65 triple; $70 suite; lower during the off-season. Rates include continental breakfast. AE, MC, V. Free parking.

This sprawling, modern home is one of the many very nice smaller hotels here in Escazú. It incorporates flagstone and stone walls throughout and has a vaguely colonial feel. A large and lush garden, complete with lighted tennis court, surrounds the inn. My favorite rooms are the two by the tennis courts, one of which has a sunken, stone-floored shower. Other rooms have hardwood floors, and in all the rooms you'll find king-size beds. The suites are larger and have complete kitchens. Common areas include a large living room with fireplace and a wide tiled patio that overlooks the garden. Throughout the inn, you'll see old black-and-white photos that have been hand colored; ask the innkeeper about the photographer. You can also find out here about various excursions around the country, and airport pickups are available. The inn is located 100 meters west and 300 meters south of the cemetery in Escazú (follow the signs). After you go the 100 meters west of the first cemetery, there's actually another smaller one. Don't let it throw you.

Villa Escazú. Apdo. 1401-1250, Escazú. ☎ and fax **506/228-9566.** E-mail: villaescazu@yellowweb.co.cr. 6 units (all with shared bathroom). $40–$60 double; lower rates during the off-season. Rates include full breakfast. No credit cards.

If you're looking for a quiet little inn with a homey feel, this converted private home fits the bill. Service is friendly and personable. The rooms are large and immaculate, with plenty of varnished wood. The upstairs rooms have balconies, and the shared bathroom features a tub. The complimentary breakfasts are extensive and creative. The hotel has well-tended grounds and gardens, with quiet sitting areas. There is a new studio for rent by the week or month. To find the place, triangulate from the Banco Nacional in Escazú: Go 600 meters west, 300 meters south (this is actually just one road, with a severe dogleg), and watch for the sign marking the driveway.

INEXPENSIVE

Hotel Mirador Pico Blanco. Apdo. 900 (1km south of the church in San Antonio de Escazú), Escazú. ☎ **506/289-6197.** Fax 506/289-5189. 23 units. $45 double; $55 triple. AE, MC, V. Free parking.

If you'd like a room with a view but can't afford the prices charged at most mountainside inns around the area, check out this cozy and casual hotel. There's nothing fancy about the rooms here, but most offer absolutely fabulous views. Some rooms have high ceilings, creating an appearance of spaciousness, and almost all of them have balconies (albeit small ones). There's also a small pool with an inviting terrace. A few resident macaws fly around the hillsides here during the day but come home each evening. The restaurant is a popular and inexpensive spot, probably the cheapest view restaurant in the valley. A taxi up here from the airport will cost you about $15.

HEREDIA/ALAJUELA/AIRPORT AREA

Alajuela and Heredia are two colonial era cities that lie much closer to the airport than San José. Alajuela is the closest city to the airport, with Heredia lying about midway between Alajuela and the capital. These are two great places to find small, distinct, and charming hotels. If you'd like to learn more about either of these cities look under "Side Trips from San José," later in this chapter. If your plans are to get yourself to a remote beach or rain-forest lodge as quickly as possible and use San José and the Central Valley purely as a transportation hub, or you just detest urban clutter, noise, and pollution, you might do well to choose one of the hotels listed below.

VERY EXPENSIVE

✪ **Finca Rosa Blanca Country Inn.** Santa Bárbara de Heredia (mailing address in the U.S.: SJO 1201, P.O. Box 025216, Miami, FL 33102-5216). ☎ **506/269-9392.** Fax 506/269-9555. www.finca-rblanca.co.cr. E-mail: rblanca@sol.racsa.co.cr. 6 units, 2 villas. $145–$230 double; $25 each additional person. Rates include breakfast. AE, MC, V. Free parking.

This is another Central Valley inn that is difficult to find but well worth searching out. If the cookie-cutter rooms of international resorts leave you cold, then perhaps the fascinatingly unique rooms of this unusual inn will be more your style. Finca Rosa Blanca is an eclectic architectural confection set amid the lush green hillsides of a coffee plantation. Square corners seem to have been prohibited in the design of this beautiful home. There are turrets and curving walls of glass, arched windows, and a semicircular built-in couch. Everywhere the glow of polished hardwood blends with blindingly white stucco walls and brightly painted murals. The best way I can describe the architecture of this inn is 21st-century pueblo.

Inside, there's original artwork everywhere, and each room is decidedly different and unique. There's the black-and-white room with a patio and bed made from coffee-tree wood. Another room has a bed built into a corner and a handmade tub with windows on two sides. The view is fabulous. If breathtaking bathrooms are your idea of the ultimate luxury, then consider splurging on the master suite, which has a stone waterfall that cascades into a tub in front of a huge picture window. This suite also has a spiral staircase that leads to the top of the turret. Two new villas have been added with the same sense of eclectic luxury, plus a free-form swimming pool.

Dining/Diversions: A four-course gourmet dinner served in the small dining room will run you $25 per person. Be sure to reserve early because there's limited seating. In a tiny space off of the living room, there's an honor bar tucked into a reproduction of a typical Costa Rican oxcart.

Amenities: Car rentals and guide services can be arranged through the hotel, as well as transportation to and from the airport.

Hotel Herradura, Autopista General Cañas. Ciudad Cariari (Apdo. 7-1880), San José. ☎ **800/245-8420** in the U.S. and Canada, or 506/239-0033 in Costa Rica. Fax 506/239-0210, or 305/858-7478 in the U.S. www.costasol.co.cr. E-mail: hherradu@sol.racsa.co.cr. 234 units. A/C TV TEL. $130–$190 double; $210–$795 suite. AE, DC, MC, V. Free parking.

Big and sprawling, the Herradura still possesses San José's largest and most flexible conference facilities, and so it's often bustling with businesspeople and assorted convention traffic. However, despite the crowds, service here never seems to falter. The superior rooms (there are no standard rooms) have all been recently remodeled, and so the accommodations and furnishings are all up to snuff. Still, bathrooms in these rooms are small, and most have no view. The deluxe rooms, on the other hand, are very attractive and luxurious. The walls of glass let in plenty of light and usually a good view (pool-view rooms cost $30 extra). There are balconies and marble-topped cafe tables, and in the bathrooms there are green-marble counters, phones, and hair dryers.

Dining/Diversions: For quiet dining, there is Sakura, a Japanese restaurant with an indoor garden setting, sushi bar, and table-side teppanyaki preparations. The Sancho Panza Restaurant specializes in formal Spanish meals. Casual meals, including buffets, are available at the 24-hour Tiffany's Restaurant coffee shop. Bambolleo is a lounge that offers nightly piano music and light snacks. Gamblers can spend their time at the elegant Casino Krystal.

Amenities: The Herradura's main swimming pool (there are three) is one of the largest and most attractive in San José, with a beachlike patio, a swim-up bar, tiled cafe tables in the water, and attractive landscaping around the edges of the pool. Guests have access to the neighboring Meliá Cariari's 18-hole golf course, 11 tennis courts, pro shop, and health club. The hotel also offers 24-hour room service, city and airport shuttle, car-rental desk, tour desk, baby-sitting. Other facilities include extensive conference and banquet facilities, and a gift shop.

✪ **Marriott Hotel and Resort.** San Antonio de Belén (Apdo. 502-4005). ☎ **800/228-9290** in the U.S. and Canada, or 506/298-0000 in Costa Rica. Fax 506/298-0011. 252 units. A/C MINIBAR TV TEL. $120–$160 double. AE, DC, MC, V.

For my money, the Marriott is the only luxury resort hotel in the San José area to be hitting on all cylinders. Amenities are plentiful, and service here reaches a level and attention to detail uncommon in Costa Rica. The hotel is designed in a mixed Colonial style, with hand-painted Mexican tiles, antique red clay roof tiles, weathered columns, and heavy wooden doors, lintels, and trim. The centerpiece is a large open-air interior patio, which somewhat replicates Old Havana's Plaza de Armas. The rooms are all comfortable and well appointed, with either a king-size or two double beds, two telephones, a working desk, an elegant wooden armoire holding the large television, plenty of closet space, a comfortable sitting chair and ottoman, and a small "Juliet" balcony. The bathrooms are up to par but might seem slightly small at this price.

Dining/Diversions: There are several dining options here. The most elegant restaurant is La Isabela, housed in a re-created wine cellar, which has an extensive menu of creative international fare. For more intimacy, you can reserve La Cava, a private room off of Isabela's main dining room. For more casual dining, the Villa Hermosa restaurant serves "nouvelle Costa Rican" dishes, and there also are the outdoor Casa del Sol grill and the Casa del Café coffee house. The lobby bar features daily piano music and weekend nights of jazz, as well as a tapas bar, a cigar bar, and both indoor and patio seating.

Amenities: The two pools are adjacent but on separate levels of the large outdoor patio area. There is a small but well-appointed health club, outdoor Jacuzzi, saunas, three tennis courts, hiking and jogging trails, golf driving range, golf pro shop, conference rooms, car-rental and tour desks, beauty salon, private chapel, casino, two gift shops, a concierge, room service, laundry service, newspaper delivery, nightly turndown, and express checkout. In-room massage, baby-sitting and secretarial services are all available, and there's a regular shuttle to the airport.

Meliá Cariari Conference Center and Golf Resort. Autopista General Cañas, Ciudad Cariari (Apdo. 737-1007 Centro Colón), San José. ☎ **800/336-3542** in North America, or 506/239-0022 in Costa Rica. Fax 506/239-2803. www.solmelia.es. E-mail: cariari@sol.racsa.co.cr. 244 units. A/C MINIBAR TV TEL. $135–$145 double; $215–$435 suite. AE, DC, MC, V. Free parking.

Located about halfway into San José from the airport, the Cariari is the only resort hotel in the Central Valley with its own golf course, and as such is a must for golfers vacationing in San José. The Cariari, with its use of stone walls, an open-air lobby, and lush garden plantings, also has more of a tropical feel than the city's other luxury hotels. However, the landscaping is not as impeccably manicured as that at the Herradura, nor is the hotel as elegant as the Marriott. Still, the Cariari has recently come under the management of the large Meliá chain, many of the guest rooms were remodeled, and all have plenty of space. The basic rooms have either one king-size or two double beds and small bathrooms. The suites are more spacious and better appointed. All in all, the rooms lack the sort of quality furnishings and styling that you would expect in this price range. Try to get an upper-floor room; those on the lower floor tend to be a bit dark.

Dining/Diversions: Los Vitrales is the hotel's most formal restaurant and serves well-prepared French and continental fare. For more casual meals, you can try Las Tejas Coffee Shop, which offers a breakfast buffet. For seafood and cocktails, there's the tropical, open-air atmosphere of Los Mariscos, which also has live Latin and jazz music in the evenings. More entertainment is provided by the hotel's casino, which is open nightly until 2am.

Amenities: The large pool is surrounded by plenty of patio space and lots of lounge chairs, and has a swim-up bar. In addition to the 18-hole golf course, there are eight tennis courts, a pro shop, and a health club with saunas, whirlpool tubs, an exercise room, a game room, and an Olympic-size swimming pool. Other facilities include a gift shop, beauty parlor, and barber shop. Services include 24-hour room service, concierge, complimentary city shuttle, tour desk, car-rental desk, golf lessons and club rentals, baby-sitting, massage.

✪ **Vista del Valle Plantation Inn.** Apdo. 185-4003, Alajuela. ☎ **506/451-1165**, 506/450-0800, or ☎ and fax 506/450-0900. www.vistadelvalle.com. E-mail: mibrejo@sol.racsa.co.cr. 9 units. $95–$120 double; lower in the off-season. Rates include full breakfast. V.

If you have little need for, or interest in, San José and would like a comfortable base for exploring the rest of Costa Rica, you should consider this fine little country inn. Originally a converted private home, the owners have been adding elegant little cottages around their grounds, which command an impressive view over the Río Grande and its steep-walled canyon. The architecture here has a strong Japanese influence. Most of the accommodations are in independent cottages or bungalows. The cottages are open and airy, with lots of windows letting in lots of light. You'll also find plenty of varnished woodwork, small kitchenettes, and comfortable wraparound decks. The grounds are wonderfully landscaped, with several inviting seating areas set among a wealth of flowering tropical plants. The last time I visited, there were plans to add a few more cottages and a tennis court. The hotel is located 20 minutes north of the Juan Santamaría Airport, and staying here can cut as much as an hour off your travel time to the Pacific coast beaches, Arenal volcano, and Monteverde Cloud Forest.

Dining/Diversions: The resident chef here has studied with Costa Rica's famed Isabel Campabadal, and meals are adventurous and filling.

Amenities: The tile pool has an interesting little fountain/waterfall, and there's an inviting Jacuzzi here, too. There is also a new horse stable and an athletic trail down to a 300-foot waterfall.

MODERATE

Hampton Airport Inn. Autopista General Cañas, by the airport (Apdo. 195-4003), San José. ☎ **800/426-7866** in the U.S., or 506/443-0043. Fax 506/442-9532. www.hamptonhotel.co.cr. E-mail: hampton@sol.racsa.co.cr. 100 units. A/C TV TEL. $69 double to quad. Rates include continental breakfast. AE, DC, MC, V. Free parking.

If familiarity, basic comfort, and proximity to the airport are important to you, then the Hampton Airport Inn is your best bet. The rooms are what you'd expect from a budget chain, and since the hotel is new, they don't show much wear and tear. There's an outdoor swimming pool, free parking, airport shuttle, and free local phone calls. This is a good choice if your plane arrives very late or leaves very early and you don't plan on spending any time in San José.

✪ **Hotel Bougainvillea.** Apdo. 69-2120 (in Santo Tomás de Santo Domingo de Heredia, 150 meters west of the Escuela de Santo Tomás), San José. ☎ **506/244-1414.** Fax 506/244-1313. E-mail: bougain@sol.racsa.co.cr. 86 units. TV TEL. $65 double. AE, MC, V. Free parking.

The Hotel Bougainvillea is an excellent choice and great value if you're looking for a hotel in a quiet residential neighborhood not far from downtown. The hotel offers most of the amenities of the more expensive resort hotels around the Central Valley but charges considerably less. The views across the valley from this hillside location are wonderful, and the gardens are beautifully designed and well tended. Guest rooms, though they lack any Costa Rican style, are as well-done as those in most international hotels. Rooms are carpeted and have small triangular balconies oriented to the views. Though there is no air-conditioning, there are fans, and temperatures rarely get too hot here. The hotel's dining room features continental dishes, several preparations of the local sea bass, or corvina, anchoring the menu. Prices here are quite reasonable. There is also a quiet bar just off the lobby, and room service. A complimentary hourly downtown shuttle bus will take you in and out of town. The hotel's swimming pool is in its own private, walled garden and is quite attractive. There are also tennis courts, a sauna, a jogging trail, conference facilities, and a business center.

✪ **Orquideas Inn.** Apdo. 394, Alajuela. ☎ 506/433-9346. ☎ and fax **506/433-9740.** www.hotels.co.cr/orquideas.html. E-mail: orchid@sol.racsa.co.cr. 20 units. $65 double; $120–$130 suite. Rates include breakfast buffet. V.

This small country inn is just 10 minutes from the airport on the road heading up to the Poás Volcano. The rooms are all spacious and comfortable, with tile floors, private bathrooms, and colorful Guatemalan bedspreads. There are a few larger minisuites located around the small pool, as well as a separate geodesic dome, with a big king-size bed in a loft reached by a spiral staircase, a large sunken tub in the bathroom, and a full kitchen and living room area. The entire grounds are lush and tropical. The Marilyn Monroe bar serves up good drinks, *bocas*, and some seriously spicy buffalo wings. A wide range of tours are available.

4 Dining

For decades, Costa Rican cuisine has been dismissed and disparaged. Rice and beans are served at nearly every meal, the selection of other dishes is minimal, and Ticos generally don't go for spicy food—or so the criticism goes. In recent years, though, some contemporary and creative chefs have been trying to educate and enlighten the Costa Rican palate, particularly in San José, and the early results are promising. Still, most visitors to the capital city quickly tire of Tico fare, even in its more chichi incarnation, and start seeking out the many local restaurants serving international cuisines. They are richly rewarded.

San José has a rather amazing variety of restaurants serving cuisines from all over the world, and you'll never pay much even at the best restaurants. In fact, you really have to work at it to spend more than $40 per person for an extravagant six- or seven-course meal (not including liquor). Most restaurants fall into the moderately priced range. However, service can be indifferent at many restaurants, since the gratuity is already tacked on to the check, and tipping is not common among locals.

If you'd really like to sample the local flavor, head to a *soda,* the equivalent of a diner in the United States, where you can get good, cheap, and filling Tico food. Rice and beans are the staples here and show up at breakfast, lunch, and dinner. (When mixed together, they're called *gallo pinto.*) For breakfast, they're garnished with everything from fried eggs to steak. At lunch and dinner, rice and beans are the main components of a *casado* (which means "married"), the Costa Rican equivalent of a "blue plate special." A casado generally is served with a salad of cabbage and tomatoes, fried bananas, and steak, chicken, or fish. A plate of gallo pinto might cost $2, and a casado might cost $2.75–$3.50, usually with a *fresco* (a fresh fruit drink) thrown into the bargain.

While in Costa Rica, be sure to taste a few of these frescos. They're a bit like a fresh fruit milkshake without the ice cream, and when made with mangoes, papayas, bananas, or any of the other delicious tropical fruits of Costa Rica, they're pure ambrosia. These frescos can also be made with water (*con agua*), and preferences vary. Certain fruits like carambola (star fruit), maracuya (a type of passion fruit), and cas (you'll just have to try it) are made only with water. But remember, while the water in Costa Rica is generally very safe to drink, those with tender stomachs and/or intestinal tracts should stick to frescos made with milk (*con leche*).

For the following listings, I considered a restaurant expensive if a meal without wine or beer costs more than $15 for one person. Moderate restaurants serve complete dinners for between $8 and $15, and inexpensive places are those where you can get a complete meal for less than $8. You should note that in the price ranges for the following restaurants, the highest prices are almost always for shrimp or lobster dishes. Other fish and meat dishes are considerably less expensive. If you want to save money on a meal, skip wine, which is almost always imported and expensive. Beer and soft drinks are more affordable as long as you don't order enormous quantities.

DOWNTOWN SAN JOSÉ

MODERATE

✪ **Café Mundo.** Calle 15 and Avenida 9, 200 meters east and 100 meters north of the INS building. ☎ **506/222-6190.** Main courses $5–$10. AE, MC, V. Mon–Thur 11am–11pm, Fri 11am–midnight, Sat 5pm–midnight. INTERNATIONAL.

This is one of the only places in San José to successfully create an ambience of casual elegance. Wood tables and art deco wrought-iron chairs are spread spaciously around several rooms in this former colonial mansion. There's additional seating on the open-air veranda and in the small garden. The tables and chairs here are just plastic lawn furniture, but the lush tropical foliage and small tile fountain make the trade-off worthwhile, especially during the day. Chef Ray Johnson has a passion for fresh local ingredients prepared with a balanced mix of adventurous creativity and classical finesse. The appetizers include vegetable tempura and fried clam cakes alongside more traditional Tico standards like tamales and fried yuca. There's a long list of pastas and pizzas, as well as more substantial main courses. The nightly special on my last visit was a macadamia nut–crusted corvina fillet with a mint-papaya chutney. Desserts here are high art, and the chocolate cake may just be the best I've ever tasted. One room here is a lively bar with colorful wall murals by Costa Rican artist Miguel Cassafonte that has become the popular hangout for a mix of San José's gay, bohemian, and university crowds.

Café Parisien. Gran Hotel Costa Rica, Avenida 2 between Calles 1 and 3. ☎ **506/221-4011.** Sandwiches $2–$4; main courses $3.50–$20. AE, DC, MC, V. Daily 24 hours. INTERNATIONAL.

The Gran Hotel Costa Rica is hardly the best hotel in San José, but it does have a picturesque patio cafe right on the Plaza de la Cultura. A wrought-iron railing, white columns, and arches create an old-world atmosphere, and on the plaza in front of the cafe a marimba band performs and vendors sell handcrafts. It's open 24 hours a day and is one of the best spots in town to people-watch. Stop by for the breakfast buffet ($7) and watch the plaza vendors set up their booths, peruse the *Tico Times* over coffee while you have your shoes polished, or simply bask in the tropical sunshine while you sip a beer. Lunch and dinner buffets are also offered for $8.50. This is one of the best spots in town on a sunny afternoon, or just before or after a show at the National Theater.

La Cocina de Leña. Centro Comercial El Pueblo. ☎ **506/255-1360** or 506/223-3704. Main courses $7–$25. AE, DC, MC, V. Daily 11am–11pm. COSTA RICAN.

Located in the unusual El Pueblo shopping, dining, and entertainment center, La Cocina de Leña (The Wood Stove) has a rustic feel to it. There are stacks of firewood on shelves above the booths, long stalks of bananas hanging from pillars, tables suspended from the ceiling by heavy ropes, and, most unusual of all, menus printed on paper bags. If you're adventurous, you could try some of the more unusual dishes—perhaps oxtail stew served with yuca and plátano might appeal to you; if not, there are plenty of steaks and seafood dishes on the menu. *Chilasuilas* are delicious tortillas filled with fried meat. Black-bean soup with egg is a Costa Rican standard and is mighty fine here, and the corn soup with pork is equally satisfying. For dessert, there's tres leches cake as well as the more unusual sweetened *chiverre,* which is a type of squash that looks remarkably like a watermelon.

✪ **Tin Jo.** Calle 11 between Avenidas 6 and 8. ☎ **506/221-7605.** Fax 506/222-3942. Main courses $4.50–$12. AE, MC, V. Mon–Sat 11:30am–3pm and 5:30–10:30pm, Sun 11:30am–10pm. CHINESE/THAI/ASIAN.

San José has hundreds of Chinese restaurants, but most simply serve up tired takes on chop suey, chow mein, and fried rice. In contrast, Tin Jo has a wide and varied menu, with an assortment of Cantonese and Szechuan staples as well as a few Thai and Malaysian dishes and even some Indian food. This is as close to an elegant pan-Asian restaurant as you'll find in these latitudes. The mu shu is so good here you'll forgive the fact that the pancakes are actually thin flour tortillas. Some of the dishes are served in edible rice noodle bowls, and the pineapple shrimp in coconut milk curry is served in the hollowed-out half of a fresh pineapple. You can start things off with a Mai Tai or Siamese Kiss, or any of a number of fresh tropical fruit juices. The bow-tied and vested waiters here are helpful, and you'll have real tablecloths and cloth napkins. There's one table set in a small courtyard garden that adds a touch of romance to the meal.

INEXPENSIVE

✪ **La Esmeralda.** Avenida 2 between Calles 5 and 7. ☎ **506/221-0530.** Main courses $3.50–$7. AE, DC, MC, V. Daily 11:30am–5am. COSTA RICAN.

No one should visit San José without stopping in at La Esmeralda at least once—and the later at night, the better. This is much more than just a restaurant serving

Tico food: It's the Grand Central Station of Costa Rican mariachi bands. In fact, mariachis and other bands from throughout Central America and Mexico hang out here every night waiting for work. While they wait they often serenade diners in the cavernous open-air dining hall of the restaurant. Friday and Saturday nights are always the busiest, but you'll probably hear lots of excellent music any night of the week. A personal concert will cost you anywhere from $3 to $7 per song, depending on the size of the group, but if you're on a tight budget you will still be able to hear just fine eavesdropping on your neighbors. The classic Tico food is quite good. Try the coconut flan for dessert.

La Perla. Avenida 2 and Calle Central. ☎ **506/222-7492.** Reservations not accepted. Main courses $2–$7. AE, DC, MC, V. Daily 24 hours. INTERNATIONAL.

It's easy to walk right past this place (I did) the first time you try to find it. The entrance is right on the corner looking across at the National Cathedral, and the restaurant itself is a little bit below street level. This place isn't long on atmosphere, but the food is good and the portions are large. The special here is paella, a Spanish rice-and-seafood dish, for only $5. Other good choices are *sopa de mariscos,* which is a seafood soup with mussels and clams in a delicious broth, or *huevos à la ranchera,* which is prepared a bit differently from the Mexican version and makes a filling meal any time of the night or day. This is a good place to come after a show at the Melico Salazar Theater.

Manolo's Restaurante. Avenida Central between Calle Central and Calle2. ☎ **506/221-2041.** All items $3–$9. AE, MC, V. Daily 11:30am–10pm upstairs; 24 hours downstairs. COSTA RICAN.

Spread out over three floors, on a busy corner on Avenida Central, you'll find this roomy restaurant popular with Ticos and travelers alike. You can view the action in the street below or catch the live folk-dance performance that's staged nightly. The open kitchen serves up steaks and fish, but there is also a popular buffet that includes several typical Costa Rican dishes, such as plátanos and black-bean soup, for about $5. Downstairs, you'll find Manolo's Churreria, a good place for a quick sandwich or one of the fried dough *"churros"* and a cup of coffee—they even have espresso.

✪ **Ruiseñor Café.** Teatro Nacional, Avenida 2 between Calles 3 and 5. ☎ **506/256-6094.** Sandwiches and soups $3.50–$4.50; main courses $4.50–$9. AE, MC, V. Mon–Sat 10:30am–6pm. CONTINENTAL.

This is one of my favorite places to eat in all of San José. Even if there's no show at the Teatro Nacional during your visit, you can enjoy a meal or a cup of coffee here and soak up the neoclassical atmosphere. The theater was built in the 1890s from the designs of European architects, and the art nouveau chandeliers, ceiling murals, and marble floors and tables are pure Parisienne. There are changing art exhibits by local artists to complete the chic cafe atmosphere. The menu includes such continental dishes as quiche, Hungarian goulash soup, and Wiener schnitzel, but the main attractions here are the specialty cakes and tortes that are displayed under glass. Ice cream dishes (including "passionate love" and "spaghetti" ice cream) are raised to a high art here. The ambience is classic French cafe, but the marimba music drifting in from outside the open window will remind you that you're still in Costa Rica. On sunny days, there's even outdoor seating at wrought-iron tables on the side of the theater. The same folks run restaurants with similar menus at the Contemporary Art Museum in the Sabana Park and on Avenida Central in Los Yoses.

Only in the Central Valley: Dining Under the Stars on a Mountain's Edge

While there are myriad unique experiences to be had in Costa Rica, one of my favorites is dining on the side of a volcanic mountain, with the lights of San José shimmering below. These hanging restaurants, called *miradores,* are a resourceful response to the city's topography. Because San José is set in a broad valley surrounded on all sides by volcanic mountains, people who live in these mountainous areas have no place to go but up—so they do, building roadside cafes vertically up the sides of the volcanoes. Many of the roads through these mountains are studded with these hillside hanging restaurants.

While the food at most of these establishments is not usually spectacular, the views often are, particularly at night, when the whole wide valley sparkles in a wash of lights. The town of **Aserri**, 6 miles (9.6km) south of downtown San José, is the king of miradores and **Mirador Ram Luna** (☎ **506/230-3060**) is the king of Aserri. Grab a window seat and, if you've got the fortitude, order a plate of *chicharrones* (fried pork rinds). There's often live music at Ram Luna, just in case the whole thing makes you feel like dancing. You can hire a cab for around $8 or take the Aserri bus at Avenida 6 between Calle Central and Calle 2. Just ask the driver where to get off.

There are also miradores in the hills above Escazú and in San Ramon de Trés Ríos and Heredia.

Soda B y B. Calle 5 and Avenida Central. ☎ **506/222-7316.** Sandwiches $1.50–$3.50; breakfasts $1.20–$2.50; main courses $2–$3.50. AE, DC, MC, V. Mon–Thu 8:30am–10pm, Fri–Sat 9am–10pm. COSTA RICAN.

Located on the corner across from the Tourist Information Center on the Plaza de la Cultura, this spot is popular with downtown shoppers and office workers. Service is prompt, prices (and noise level) are low, and the food is surprisingly good for a sandwich shop. Slide into a high-backed wooden booth and order the *chalupa de pollo B y B*—it's a sort of toasted sandwich piled high with chicken salad and drenched with sour cream and guacamole.

Soda Vishnu. Avenida 1 between Calles 1 and 3. ☎ **506/222-2549.** Reservations not accepted. Main courses $1.25–$3. No credit cards. Daily 7:30am–9:30pm. VEGETARIAN.

Vegetarians will most certainly find their way here. There are booths for two or four people and photo murals on the walls. At the cashier's counter, you can buy natural cosmetics, honey, and bags of granola. However, most people just come for the filling *plato de dia* that includes soup, salad, veggies, an entree, and dessert for around $2. There are also bean burgers and cheese sandwiches on whole wheat bread. There is another Vishnu around the corner on Calle 3 between Avenida Central and Avenida 1.

IN LA SABANA/PASEO COLÓN

EXPENSIVE

✪ **La Masía de Triquel.** Sabana Norte, 175 meters west and 175 meters north of the Datsun Agency. ☎ **506/296-3528** or 506/232-3584. Reservations recommended. Main courses $10–$15. AE, DC, MC, V. Mon–Sat 11:30am–2pm and 6:30–10:30pm. SPANISH.

Despite relocation, a healthy field of competitors, and the death of founding chef Francisco Triquel, La Masía de Triquel is still San José's finest Spanish restaurant. Francisco Triquel Jr. has seen to that. Service is extremely formal, and the regular clientele includes most of the city's upper crust. Although Costa Rica is known for its beef, here you'll also find wonderfully prepared lamb, quail, and rabbit. Seafood dishes include the usual shrimp and lobster, but also squid and octopus. However, there is really no decision to be made when perusing the menu: Start with a big bowl of gazpacho and then spend the rest of the evening enjoying all the succulent surprises you'll find in a big dish of paella.

✪ **La Piazzetta.** Paseo Colón near Calle 40 (opposite Banco de Costa Rica). ☎ **506/222-7896** or 506/221-8451. Reservations recommended. Main courses $8–$24. AE, DC, MC, V. Mon–Sat noon–2:30pm and 6:30–11pm. ITALIAN.

With an amazingly long menu and service by waiters in suits and bow ties, this restaurant harks back to the Italian restaurants of old in the United States, when southern Italian cooking was still an exotic ethnic cuisine.

The menu includes quite a few risotto (rice) dishes, which is a surprise, since most Italian restaurants in Costa Rica stick to spaghetti. Some other unexpected dishes also make appearances here, including several lobster dishes, and veal scallopine in a truffle sauce. Salads are colorful and artistically arranged. If you're in no danger of a coronary, try the *baugna cauda*—anchovies and peppers in an olive oil–based broth. For dessert, sample a classic chocolate mousse, or tiramisù.

MODERATE

Machu Pichu Bar and Restaurant. Calle 32 between Avenidas 1 and 3, 150 meters north of the Kentucky Fried Chicken on Paseo Colón. ☎ **506/222-7384** or 506/225-2243. Main courses $3.50–$12. AE, DC, MC, V. Mon–Sat 11am–3pm and 6–10pm, Sun 11am–3pm. PERUVIAN/CONTINENTAL.

Located just off Paseo Colón near the Kentucky Fried Chicken, Machu Pichu is an unpretentious little restaurant that has become one of the most popular places in San José. The menu is primarily seafood (especially sea bass), and consequently most dishes tend toward the upper end of the menu's price range. Also, many of these fish dishes come in thick cream sauces. You're better off sticking with the two-person seafood sampler, combined with different appetizers. One of my favorite entrees is the *causa limeña,* lemon-flavored mashed potatoes stuffed with shrimp. The ceviche here is excellent, as is the *aji de gallina,* a dish of chopped chicken in a fragrant cream sauce, and octopus with garlic butter. Be sure to ask for a pisco sour, a Peruvian specialty drink.

INEXPENSIVE

Pasteleria Francesa Boudsocq. Calle 30 at Paseo Colón. ☎ **506/222-6732.** Pastries $1.05–$2.75; breakfast $3.50–$4.50; lunch $4–$5.50. AE, MC, V. Mon–Sat 7am–7pm. PASTRIES/FRENCH.

Ticos love their pastries and bakeries, and pastry shops abound all over San José. However, this little place on Paseo Colón is one of the best I've found. They have savory meat-filled pastries that make good lunches, as well as plenty of unusual sweets that are great afternoon snacks. There are only a couple of tables here, so most folks get their goodies to go. Boudsocq recently celebrated its 20th anniversary, so they must be doing something right.

Soda Coppelia. Paseo Colón between Calles 26 and 28. ☎ **506/223-8013.** Reservations not necessary. Most items $1.75–$5. No credit cards. Mon–Fri 8am–6pm, Sat 8am–4pm. COSTA RICAN.

If you're looking for a filling, cheap, and quick breakfast in the Paseo Colón area, I recommend this soda. You'll find it near the Universal movie theater. The wooden booths and a few tables on the (rather noisy) covered walkway are frequently full of local businesspeople because the meals are so reasonably priced. A thin steak will run you just over $2, and for lighter fare, try the burgers, sandwiches, or some of the good-looking pastries such as flaky empanadas or carrot bread.

SAN PEDRO/LOS YOSES

In addition to the restaurants listed below, my vegetarian friends swear that the best vegetarian restaurant in San José is the little **Restaurante Vegetariano San Pedro** (☎ **506/224-1103**), located 125 meters north of the San Pedro Church.

EXPENSIVE

Le Chandelier. 100 meters west and 100 meters south of the ICE office in San Pedro. ☎ **506/225-3980.** Reservations recommended. Main courses $11–$26; fixed-price lunch $14, fixed-price dinner $50. AE, MC, V. Mon–Fri 11:30am–2pm and 6:30–11pm, Sat 6:30–11pm. FRENCH.

Located in a large old house in a quiet residential neighborhood east of downtown San José, Le Chandelier is one of the most elegant restaurants in town. The neighborhood, landscaping, and architectural styling give it the feel of an older Hollywood or Beverly Hills restaurant. The menu includes delicious renditions of French classics such as onion soup, escargots bourguignonne, and chicken à l'orange. There are also some unexpected and less familiar dishes, such as tenderloin with cranberry sauce, carpaccio with smoked salmon and palmito, and roast duck in green pepper sauce. The set dinner is a true feast and might start with an appetizer of carpaccio, followed by gratin of Camembert with shrimp, sorbet, tournedos in Cabernet Sauvignon and green pepper, cheese and fruit, and a dessert of tiramisù.

MODERATE

Ambrosia. Centro Comercial Calle Real. ☎ **506/253-8012.** Reservations not necessary. Sandwiches and salads $3.50–$4.50, main courses $4.50–$8.70. AE, DC, MC, V. Mon–Sat 11:30am–3pm and 6–10:30pm, Sun 11:30am–3pm. CONTINENTAL.

This elegant little restaurant is a good choice for lunch or dinner. Greek and Latin mythology is the dominant menu theme here, with Ulysses, Circe, and Poseidon all having seafood dishes named after them; Zeus, Apollo, and Orion providing namesakes for the different steaks; and the pasta selections anchored by Ravioli Romulus, of course. Behind the mythology, what you will find are well-prepared meals made with fresh ingredients and interesting spices. The Crepe Aphrodite is a delicate crepe filled with chunks of fish and shrimp in a Gouda cheese sauce. The Corvina Cassiopeia is a grilled sea bass fillet topped with a light almond sauce. The ambience here is relaxed, and the service can be a bit inattentive. There's a small bar at the center of the restaurant, and live piano music is sometimes offered in the evenings.

✪ **Il Ponte Vecchio.** San Pedro, 75 meters east and 10 meters north of the Salón de Patines Music. ☎ **506/283-1810.** Main courses $4.50–$12. Mon–Sat noon–2:30pm, 5:30–10:30pm. AE, MC, V. ITALIAN.

Everyone should have a favorite neighborhood Italian restaurant, and this is mine. Not too formal, but no simple pasteria, Il Ponte Vecchio is consistent, comfortable, and personal. Chef Tony D'Alaimo has years of experience, having cut his teeth in New York's Little Italy before settling in San José. There's a small bar just as you enter, then three separate rooms with tables draped in linen tablecloths and set with glass-lanterned candles. The service is attentive and professional but never overbearing. My favorite dish here is the Chicken Valdostana, a delicate breast fillet rolled around some fresh mozzarella, Italian prosciutto, and porcini mushrooms, covered in tangy pomodoro sauce and baked in the oven. You should also check out the homemade ravioli in a cream sauce, with hints of nutmeg.

ESCAZÚ

EXPENSIVE

Atlanta Dining Gallery. Tara Resort Hotel, 600 meters south of the San Antonio de Escazú cemetery. ☎ **506/228-6992.** Reservations recommended. Main courses $7–$22. AE, MC, V. Daily 7am–11pm. CONTINENTAL.

For elegance, excellent service, delicious food, and fabulous views in the Escazú area, you just can't beat the Atlanta Dining Gallery. Located in a reproduction antebellum mansion, this place is straight out of the Deep South, except for the view of the Central Valley. Elegant dark-wood furnishings and a hardwood floor set the tone, but it's the view that keeps grabbing your attention. Scarlett O'Hara never had it so good. Most nights of the week the view is accompanied by such dishes as filet mignon with mushrooms, shrimp scampi, chicken with a mango and avocado sauce, and corvina with a red-pepper and wine sauce. A tempting assortment of desserts accompanies a choice of after-dinner aperitifs and cognacs.

✪ **La Luz.** On the old road to Santa Ana, inside Hotel Alta. ☎ **506/282-4160.** Fax 506/282-4162. Main courses: $6–14. Daily 7am–3pm and 6–10pm. AE, DC, MC, V. CALIFORNIA/PACIFIC RIM/FUSION.

La Luz serves up some of the most adventurous food in Costa Rica. Mixing fresh local ingredients with the best of a whole host of international ethnic cuisines, chef Sherman Johnson is quickly making his mark on the local restaurant scene. The fiery garlic prawns are sauteed in ancho chili oil and sage and served over a roast garlic potato. Then the whole thing is served with a garnish of fried leeks and a tequila lime butter and cilantro oil sauce. There's also pan-seared veal chop stuffed with a cilantro chashew pesto. On top of all this there are nightly specials, fresh baked rolls and breads, and a wide selection of inventive appetizers and desserts. The glass walled dining room is one of the most elegant in town, with a view of the city lights, and tables set with a full setting of fine flatware, thin-walled wineglasses, and linen tablecloths. The wait staff is attentive and knowledgeable, and the chef makes the rounds most nights. La Luz is also open for breakfast and lunch.

MODERATE

✪ **Ritmos Culinarios.** 280 meters south of "El Cruce" on the road to Escazú center. ☎ **506/228-7978.** Fax 506/228-7970. Main courses: $3.50–$8. Mon–Fri 9am–7pm, Sat 9am–5pm. No credit cards. GOURMET DELI/INTERNATIONAL.

The outgrowth of a successful catering business, this place is perfect for everything from a coffee break to a sit-down lunch to a take-home feast. A few art deco tables and chairs are set below a giant painting by artist Francisca Vitto. Several more tables are set on the outdoor patio. The menu features gourmet soups, salads, hot and cold entrees, and desserts. Both the gazpacho and tortilla soups are standouts, as are the stuffed chiles in Nogado sauce. In a deli cooler you'll see the daily offering of cold salads, entrees, and desserts. Off of the main restaurant you'll find a gourmet food shop featuring a wide range of hard-to-find items, local ingredients, and homemade jarred goodies. Ritmos Culinarios also holds regular cooking classes led by an alternating list of leading local chefs.

STREET FOOD & LATE-NIGHT BITES

On almost every street corner in downtown San José you'll find a fruit vendor. If you're lucky enough to be in town between April and June, you can sample more varieties of mangoes than you ever knew existed. I like buying them already cut up in a little bag; they cost a little more this way but you don't get nearly as messy. Be sure to try a green mango with salt and chili peppers. That's the way they seem to like mangoes best in the steamy tropics—guaranteed to wake up your taste buds. Another common street food that you might be wondering about is called *pejibaye,* a bright orange palm nut about the size of a plum. They're boiled in big pots on carts, you eat them in much the same way you eat an avocado, and they taste a bit like squash.

If it's 1am and you've just got to grab a bite, you're in luck. San José has quite a few all-night restaurants, including La Perla, La Esmeralda, and Café Parisien, all of which are described above. Another popular place, which is almost exclusively for men, is the Soda Palace on Avenida 2 and Calle 2 (see "San José After Dark," below, for more information).

5 Seeing the Sights

Most visitors to Costa Rica try to get out of the city as fast as possible so they can spend more time on the beach or off in the rain forests. However, San José is the country's main metropolis, and there are quite a few attractions here to keep you busy for a while. Some of the best and most modern museums in Central America are here, and together these museums have a wealth of fascinating pre-Columbian artifacts. New additions include a modern and expansive children's museum, as well as a centrally located National Arts Center, featuring yet another museum and several performing arts spaces. There are also several great things to see and do just outside San José in the Central Valley. If you start doing day trips out of the city, you can spend quite a few days in this region.

There are literally dozens of tour companies operating in San José, and the barrage of advertising brochures can be quite intimidating. There really isn't much reason to take a tour of San José—it's so compact, you can easily visit all the major sites on your own (see below). However, if you want to take a city tour, which will run you between $15 and $20, here are some companies: **Otec Tours**, Edeficio Ferencz, Calle 3 between Avenidas 1 and 3 (Apdo. 323-1002), San José (☎ **506/256-0633**); **TAM/Adventureland**, Calle Central between Avenida Central and Avenida 1 (☎ **506/256-0203**); **Horizontes Travel,** Calle 32 between Avenidas 3 and 5, (☎ **506/222-2022**); **Ecole Travel**, Calle 7 between Avenida Central and 1; (☎ **506/223-2240**) and **Swiss Travel Service** (☎ **506/282-4898**). These same companies also offer a whole range of day trips out of San José (See "Side Trips from San José," later in the chapter). Almost all of the major hotels have a tour desk, and most of the smaller hotels will also help arrange tours and day trips.

SUGGESTED ITINERARIES

If You Have 1 Day

Start your day on the Plaza de la Cultura. Visit the Gold Museum and see if you can get tickets for a performance that night at the Teatro Nacional. From the Plaza de la Cultura, stroll up Avenida Central to the Museo Nacional. After lunch, head over to the Jade Museum or the neighboring National Arts Center (if you have the energy for another museum). After all this culture, a stroll through the chaos of the Mercado Central is in order. Try dinner at either Bijahua or La Cocina De Leña before going to the Teatro Nacional. After the performance you absolutely must swing by La Esmeralda for some live mariachi music before calling it a day.

If You Have 2 Days

Follow the itinerary above for Day 1. On Day 2, visit the Serpentarium, the Children's Museum (a must if you've brought the kids along), or the Spyrogyra Butterfly Garden, do a bit of shopping, and then head out Paseo Colón to the Museo de Arte Costarricense and La Sabana Park.

If You Have 3 Days

Follow the itinerary for the 2 days outlined above. On Day 3, head out to Irazú Volcano, Orosi Valley, Lankester Gardens, and Cartago. Start your day at the volcano and work your way back toward San José.

If You Have 4 Days or More

Follow the itinerary for 3 days outlined above. Then spend Days 4 and 5 on other excursions from San José. You can go white-water rafting, hiking in a cloud forest, or horseback riding for a day if you're an active type. If you prefer less strenuous activities, try a cruise around the Gulf of Nicoya and a trip to the Rain Forest Aerial Tram.

THE TOP ATTRACTIONS

✪ **Centro Nacional de Arte y Cultura (National Arts Center).** Calle 13 between Avenidas 3 and 5. ☎ **506/257-7202** or 506/257-9370. Free admission. Musuem hours: Tues–Sun 10am–5pm. Any downtown bus.

Occupying a full city block, this was once the National Liquor Factory (FANAL). Now it houses the offices of the Cultural Ministry, several performing arts centers, and the Museum of Contemporary Art and Design. The latter has featured several impressive traveling international exhibits since its inception, including large retrospectives by Mexican painter José Cuevas and Ecuadorian painter Oswaldo Guayasamin. If you're looking for modern dance, experimental theater or a lecture on Costa Rican video, this is the place to be.

Museo de Arte Costarricense. Calle 42 and Paseo Colón, Parque la Sabana este. ☎ **506/222-7155.** Admission $1.50 adults, children and students free. Tues–Sun 10am–4pm. Bus: Sabana-Cementerio.

This small museum at the end of Paseo Colón in Parque la Sabana was formerly an airport terminal. Today, however, it houses a collection of works in all media by Costa Rica's most celebrated artists. On display are some exceptionally beautiful pieces in a wide range of artistic styles, demonstrating how Costa Rican artists have interpreted and imitated the major European artistic movements over the years. In addition to the permanent collection of sculptures, paintings, and prints, there are regular temporary exhibits. If the second floor is open during your visit, be sure to go up and have a look at the conference room's unusual bas-relief walls, which chronicle the history of Costa Rica from pre-Columbian times to the present with evocative images of its people. The Ruiseñor Café here makes a wonderful pit stop.

✪ **Museo de Jade Marco Fidel Tristan (Jade Museum).** Avenida 7 between Calles 9 and 9B, 11th Floor, INS Building. ☎ **506/287-6034**. Admission $2 adults, children under 12 free. Mon–Fri 8:30am–4:30pm. Any downtown bus.

Jade was the most valuable commodity among the pre-Columbian cultures of Mexico and Central America, worth more than gold. This modern museum displays a huge collection of jade artifacts dating from 330 B.C. to A.D. 700. Most are large pendants that were parts of necklaces and are primarily human and animal figures. A fascinating display illustrates how the primitive peoples of this region carved this extremely hard stone.

There is also an extensive collection of pre-Columbian polychromed terra-cotta vases, bowls, and figurines. Some of these pieces are amazingly modern in design and exhibit a surprisingly advanced technique. Particularly fascinating is a vase that incorporates real human teeth, and a display that shows how jade was imbedded in human teeth merely for decorative reasons. Most of the identifying labels and explanations are in Spanish, but there are a few in English.

Before you leave, be sure to check out the splendid view of San José from the lounge area.

✪ **Museo de Los Niños (Children's Museum).** Calle 4 and Avenida 9. ☎ **506/233-2734.** Admission $2 adults, $1 students and children under 12. Tues–Fri 8am–3pm, Sat–Sun 10am–5. Any downtown bus.

This museum is located a few blocks north of downtown, on Calle 4. It's within easy walking distance, but you might want to take a cab, as you'll have to walk right through the worst part of the red-light district.

Recently converted from use as a prison, the museum houses an extensive collection of exhibits designed for the edification and entertainment of children of all ages. Experience a simulated earthquake, or make music by dancing across the floor. Many of the exhibits encourage hands-on play. If you have children with you, you will definitely want to come here, and you may want to visit even if you don't. Be careful, though: The museum is large and spread out, and it's easy to lose track of a family member or friend.

✪ **Museo de Oro Banco Central (Gold Museum).** Calle 5 between Avenida Central and Avenida 2, underneath the Plaza de la Cultura. ☎ **506/223-0528.** Admission $4.50 adults, $1.25 students, 75¢ children under 12. Tues–Sun 10am–4:30pm. Any downtown bus.

Located directly beneath the Plaza de la Cultura, this unusual underground museum houses one of the largest collections of pre-Columbian gold in the Americas. On display are more than 20,000 troy ounces of gold in more than 2,000 objects. The sheer number of small pieces can be overwhelming and seem redundant; however, the unusual display cases and complex lighting systems show off every piece to its utmost. This museum complex also includes a gallery for temporary art exhibits, separate numismatic and philatelic museums, and a modest gift shop.

✪ **Museo Nacional de Costa Rica.** Calle 17 between Avenida Central and Avenida 2, on the Plaza de la Democracia. ☎ **506/257-1433.** Admission $1 adults, students and children under 10 free. Tues–Sun 8:30am–4:30pm. Closed Dec 25 and 31. Any downtown bus.

Costa Rica's most important historical museum is housed in a former army barracks that was the scene of fighting during the civil war of 1948. You can still see hundreds of bullet holes on the turrets at the corners of the building. Inside this traditional Spanish-style courtyard building, you will find displays on Costa Rican history and culture from pre-Columbian times to the present. In the pre-Columbian rooms, you'll see a 2,500-year-old jade carving that is shaped like a seashell and etched with an image of a hand holding a small animal. Among the most fascinating objects unearthed at Costa Rica's numerous archaeological sites are many metates, or grinding stones. This type of grinding stone is still in use today throughout Central America; however, the ones on display here are more ornately decorated than those that you will see anywhere else. Some of the metates are the size of a small bed and are believed to have been part of funeral rites. A separate vault houses the museum's collection of pre-Columbian gold jewelry and figurines. In the courtyard, you'll be treated to a wonderful view of the city and see some of Costa Rica's mysterious stone spheres.

Museo Nacional de Ciencias Naturales "La Salle." Across from the southeast corner of Parque la Sabana. ☎ **506/232-1306.** Admission $1 adults, 75¢ children. Mon–Fri 8am–4pm, Sat 8am–noon, Sun 9am–4pm. Escazú or Pavas bus from Avenida 1 and Calle 18.

Before heading out to the wilds of the Costa Rican jungles, you might want to stop by this natural-history museum and find out more about the animals you will encounter. There are stuffed and mounted anteaters, monkeys, tapirs, and many others, from Costa Rica and from around the world as well. There are also 1,200 birds, 12,500 insects, and 13,500 seashells displayed.

Museo de Entomología. In the basement of the University of Costa Rica's School of Music, San Pedro. ☎ **506/207-5647.** Admission $1.50. Mon–Fri 1–4:45pm. San Pedro bus from Avenida 2 between Calles 5 and 7.

The tropics are home to the world's greatest concentrations and diversity of insects, and at this small museum you can see more than one million mounted insects from around the world. The butterfly collection is the star attraction here.

MORE ATTRACTIONS

Parque Zoológico Simon Bolívar. Avenida 11 and Calle 7, in Barrio Amón. ☎ **506/233-6701.** Admission $1.25 adults, children under 3 free. Mon–Fri 8am–3:30pm, Sat–Sun 9am–4:30pm. Any downtown bus, then walk.

This zoo recently received a major facelift and has shed its former air of neglect and despair. Heck, it's almost lively here now. The collection includes Asian, African, and Costa Rican animals. The zoo is really geared toward locals and school groups. There's a new children's discovery area, snake and reptile house, and gift shop. There's even a McDonald's here. I still recommend heading out into the forests and jungles, where you're less likely to see great concentrations of wildlife, but you'll feel better about it when you do.

Serpentarium. Avenida 1 between Calles 9 and 11. ☎ **506/255-4210.** Admission $4 adults, 1¢ children under 13. Mon–Fri 9am–6pm, Sat–Sun 10am–5pm. Any downtown bus.

Reptiles and amphibians abound in the tropics, and the Serpentarium is an excellent introduction to all that slithers and hops through the jungles of Costa Rica. The live snakes, lizards, and frogs are kept in beautiful large terrariums that simulate their natural environments. Poisonous snakes make up a large part of the collection, with the dreaded fer-de-lance pit viper eliciting the most gasps from enthralled visitors. Also fascinating to see are the tiny, brilliantly colored poison arrow frogs. Iguanas and Jesus Christ lizards are two of the more commonly spotted of Costa Rica's reptiles, and both are represented here. Also on display is an Asian import: a giant Burmese python, which is one of the largest I have ever seen. This little zoological museum is well worth a visit, especially if you plan to go bashing about in the jungles: It will help you identify the numerous poisonous snakes you'll want to avoid. If you show up around 3pm, you may catch them feeding the piranhas and perhaps some of the snakes.

Spyrogyra Butterfly Garden. 100 meters east and 100 meters south of El Pueblo Shopping Center. ☎ and fax **506/222-2937.** www.infocostarica.com/butterfly. E-mail: parcar@sol.racsa.co.cr. Admission $7. Daily 8am–4pm. Calle Blancos bus from Calle 3 and Avenida 5.

Butterflies have been likened to self-propelled flowers, so it comes as no surprise that butterfly gardens are becoming all the rage throughout the tropics these days.

If you'd like to find out why, drop in here at Spyrogyra. Though this butterfly garden is smaller and less spectacular than the other one listed below, it's a good introduction to the life cycle of butterflies and it's the closest to downtown San José. You'll find Spyrogyra near El Pueblo, a 20-minute walk from the center of San José.

OUTSIDE SAN JOSÉ

The Butterfly Farm. In front of Los Reyes Country Club, La Guácima de Alajuela. ☎ **506/438-0400.** www.butterflyfarm.co.cr. E-mail: info@butterflyfarm.co.cr. Admission $14 adults, $10.50 students; $7 children ages 7 to 11. Daily 9am–5pm. San Antonio/Ojo de Agua bus on Avenida 1 between Calles 20 and 22.

At any given time, you may see around 30 of the 80 different species of butterflies raised at this butterfly farm south of Alajuela. The butterflies live in a large enclosed garden similar to an aviary and flutter about the heads of visitors during tours of the gardens. You should be certain to spot glittering blue morphos and a large butterfly that mimics the eyes of an owl. The admission includes a 2-hour guided tour. In the demonstration room you'll see butterfly eggs, caterpillars, and pupae. Among the latter, there are cocoons trimmed in a shimmering gold color and cocoons that mimic a snake's head in order to frighten away predators. The last guided tour of the day begins at 3pm. If you make reservations in advance, the Butterfly Farm has three daily bus tours that stop at several major San José hotels for $20, including round-trip transportation and the tour of the garden. Buses pick up passengers at more than 20 different hotels in the San José area.

Café Britt Farm. North of Heredia on the road to Barva. ☎ **506/260-2748**. Admission $20 per person, including transportation from downtown San José. Three tours daily: 9am, 11am, and 3pm. Tours Nov–Feb during the harvest season; store open daily 8am–5pm all year.

Though bananas are the main export of Costa Rica, people are far more interested in the country's second most important export crop: coffee. Café Britt is one of the leading brands of coffee here, and the company has put together an interesting tour and stage production at its farm, which is 20 minutes outside of San José. Here, you'll see how coffee is grown. You'll also visit the roasting plant to learn how a coffee "cherry" is turned into a delicious roasted bean. Tasting sessions are offered for visitors to experience the different qualities of coffee. There is also a store where you can buy very reasonably priced coffee, and coffee-related gift items.

✪ **Lankester Gardens.** Paraíso de Cartago. ☎ **506/552-3247** or 506/552-3151. Admission $4 adults, 50¢ children. Daily 8:30am–3:30pm. Closed on all national holidays. Cartago bus from San José, then the Paraíso bus from the south side of the Parque Central in Cartago (ride takes 30–40 minutes).

There are more than 1,200 varieties of orchids in Costa Rica, and no fewer than 800 species are on display at this botanical garden in Cartago province. Created in the 1940s by English naturalist Charles Lankester, the gardens are now administered by the University of Costa Rica. The primary goal of the gardens is to preserve the local flora, with an emphasis on orchids and bromeliads. Paved trails wander from open, sunny gardens into shady forests. In each environment, different species of orchids are in bloom. There's an information center, and the trails are well tended and well marked.

✪ **Joyas del Tropico Humedo (Jewels of the Rain Forest).** Grecia. ☎ **506/494-5620.** Admission $5 adults, $2.50 children under 12. Daily 9am–noon and 1–5pm. Buses leave hourly for Grecia from the Coca-Cola station, Calle 16 between Avenidas 1 and 3. The museum is located right downtown, next to the Municipal Building.

Far more than just another bug collection, this exhibit takes the position that insects are works of art, tiny tropical jewels. The displays are artistically arranged and include more than 50,000 arthropods and insects (including thousands of different butterflies) collected from around the world by biologist Richard Whitten (formerly of Oregon) and his wife, Maggie. Make note, this collection used to be housed in Santo Domingo de Heredia.

✪ **Zoo Ave. La Garita, Alajuela.** ☎ **506/433-8989.** Admission $9 adults, $1 children under 12. Daily 9am–5pm. Bus: Catch an Alajuela bus on Avenida 2 between Calles 12 and 14. In Alajuela, transfer to a bus for Atenas and get off at Zoo Ave. before you get to La Garita.

Dozens of scarlet macaws, reclusive owls, majestic raptors, several different species of toucans, and a host of brilliantly colored birds from Costa Rica and around the world make this one exciting place to visit. Bird-watching enthusiasts will be able to get a closer look at birds they may have seen in the wild. There are also large iguana, deer, and monkey exhibits—and look out for the 12-foot-long crocodile. Zoo Ave. houses only injured, donated, or confiscated animals.

WALKING TOUR
Downtown San José

Start: Plaza de la Cultura.
Finish: Plaza de la Cultura.
Time: Allow a full day for this tour, though most of your time will be spent touring the four museums mentioned.
Best Time: Any day of the week except Monday, when the Gold Museum is closed.
Worst Time: Monday, see above.
Because San José is so compact, it's possible to visit nearly all of the city's major sites in a single day's walking tour. Begin your tour on the Plaza de la Cultura, perhaps after having breakfast at the Gran Hotel Costa Rica.

Begin by walking to the:

1. **Teatro Nacional,** which faces the entrance to the Gran Hotel Costa Rica. Be sure to take a walk around inside this baroque masterpiece. The cafe here is another great place to have a meal or a pastry and coffee. Around the back of the theater is the:
2. **Gold Museum,** which is built beneath the Plaza de la Cultura, to the left of the Teatro Nacional. This museum houses the largest collection of pre-Columbian gold in Central America. From the Gold Museum, walk 2 blocks west on Avenida 2 to reach the:
3. **National Cathedral,** a neoclassical structure with a tropical twist. The roof is tin, and the ceiling is wood. A statue of the Virgin Mary is surrounded by neon stars and a crescent moon. Diagonally across the street is the:
4. **Melico Salazar Theater.** This theater has an impressive pillared facade. Though the interior is not nearly as ornate, there are often interesting art and photo exhibits in the lobby. Continue west on Avenida 2 and turn right on Calle 6. In 2 blocks, you will be in the:
5. **Mercado Central,** a fragrant (not necessarily pleasantly so) district of streets crowded with produce vendors. A covered market, with its dark warren of stalls, takes up an entire block and is the center of activity. Beware of pickpockets in this area. Head back toward the Teatro Nacional on Avenida Central, and in 7 blocks you will come to an excellent place for lunch.

Walking Tour—San José

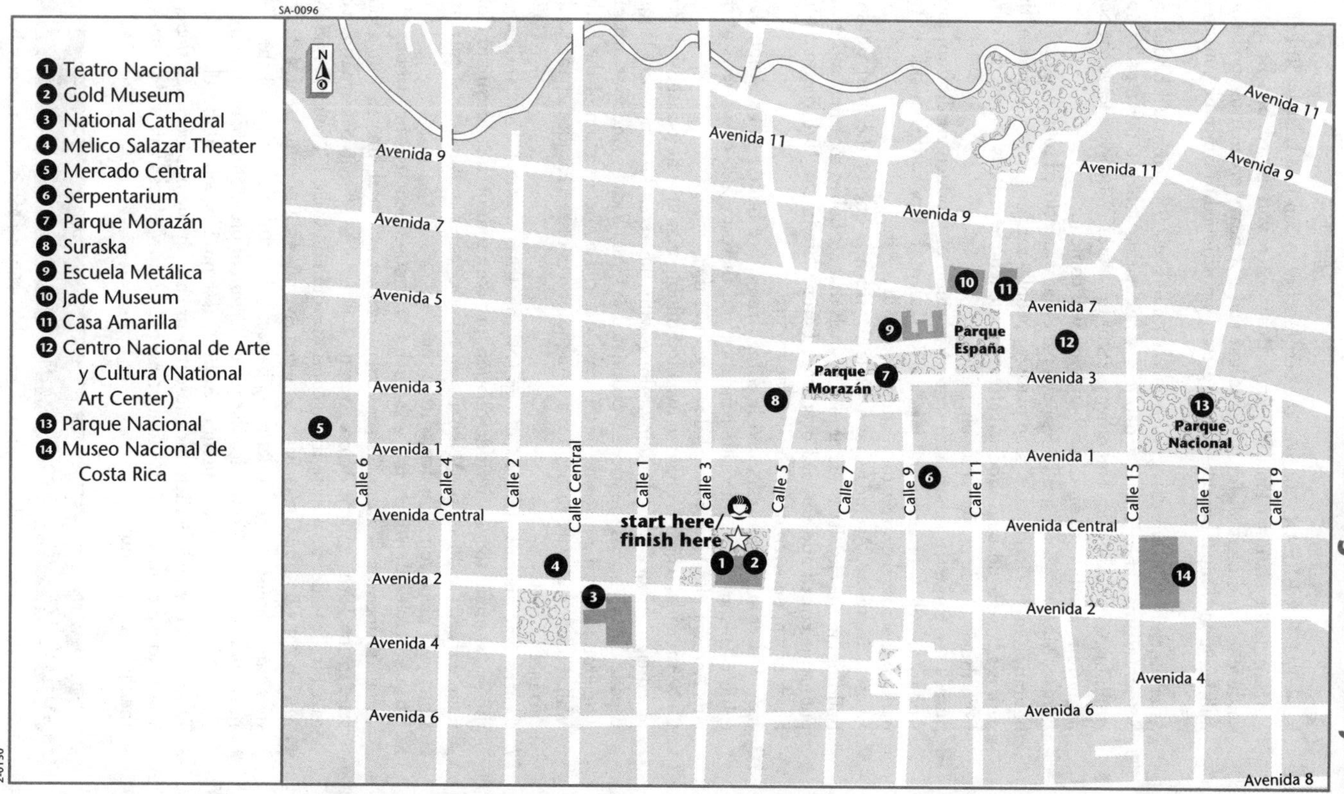

TAKE A BREAK One of the best lunches in San José is at the Ruiseñor Café inside the National Theater. I know this is where you started, but the soups, sandwiches, and main dishes are excellent and not heavy enough to spoil your walking mood. You'll be well fed and perfectly positioned to continue your tour.

After lunch head to the corner of Avenida 1 and Calle 9 where you'll find the:

6. **Serpentarium.** This indoor zoo offers a fascinating look at the reptiles and amphibians of Costa Rica and other parts of the world. When you leave the Serpentarium, head north on Calle 9 and you will come to:
7. **Parque Morazán,** a classically designed park that was restored to its original configuration in 1991. This is a good place for people-watching. At the center of the park is a large bandstand modeled after a music temple in Paris. Across the street from the west side of the park you'll find:
8. **Suraska,** a handcrafts shop with a good selection of products made from local woods, as well as ceramics and jewelry. Retrace your steps to the far side of the park, and across the street to the north you will see the:
9. **Escuela Metálica,** Avenida 5 and Calle 9, which is one of the most unusual buildings in the city. It's made of metal panels that are bolted together, and it was premanufactured and shipped over from Europe late in the 19th century. One block north, on Avenida 7, you'll come to the:
10. **Jade Museum,** which is located in a high-rise office building. The cool, dark exhibit halls are filled with jade pendants, and there are also great views of the city. Across Calle 11 from the Jade Museum is the:
11. **Casa Amarilla,** which is an attractive old building that now houses the Ministry of Foreign Affairs. This building, along with the recently remodeled Parque España directly across the street, was donated to Costa Rica by Andrew Carnegie. The grounds on the east side of the Casa Amarila house a section of the Berlin Wall. From here, walk through the bamboo groves of the Parque España to the entrance of the:
12. **Centro Nacional de Arte y Cultura (National Art Center).** You can just use this as a shortcut to your next destination, or take a tour of the Museum of Contemporary Art and Design. Make sure to exit the center at its southeast entrance, which will place you right across from the:
13. **Parque Nacional,** which has a large bronze monument to the nations that defeated American William Walker's attempt to turn Central America into a slave state in the 19th century. Across Avenida 1 is a statue of Juan Santamaría, who gave his life to defeat Walker. If you continue south on Calle 17, you will find the:
14. **Museo Nacional de Costa Rica,** between Avenida Central and Avenida 2. This museum is housed in a former army barracks that still shows signs of the 1948 revolution. Inside is Costa Rica's largest collection of pre-Columbian art and artifacts. After touring the museum, you can rest on a bench at the Plaza de la Democracia (which borders the museum) or shop at the outdoor mall there. If you head west on Avenida Central or Avenida 2, in 7 blocks you will be back at the Plaza de la Cultura.

6 Outdoor Activities

Due to the smog and pollution, you'll probably want to get out of the city before undertaking any strenuous or aerobic activity. However, there are some options available in and around San José, if you want to brave the elements.

La Sabana Park (at the western end of Paseo Colón), formerly San José's international airport, is the city's center for active sports and recreation. Here you'll find everything from jogging trails, soccer fields, and a few public tennis courts to the National Stadium. All the facilities are free and open to the public. If you really want to experience the local culture, try getting into a pick-up soccer game here. However, be careful in this park, especially at dusk or after dark, because it is so expansive, it has become a favorite haunt for youth gangs and muggers.

For information on horseback riding, hiking, and white-water rafting trips from San José, see "Side Trips from San José," at the end of this chapter.

BIKING & JOGGING Bicycle riding in and around San José is only for the suicidal, and I don't recommend it. If you want ride your bike or jog, you could try **La Sabana Park** mentioned above, or head to **Parque del Este**, which is east of town, in the foothills above San Pedro. Take the San Ramón/Parque del Este bus from Avenida 2 between Calles 9 and 11. It's never a good idea to jog at night, on busy streets, or alone. Women should be particularly careful about jogging alone. And remember, Tico drivers are not accustomed to sport joggers on residential streets, so don't expect drivers to give you much berth.

GOLF & TENNIS If you want to play tennis or golf, take your racket and some balls down to Parque La Sabana or check with the hotels **Herradura** and **Cariari** (see listings above).

SWIMMING If you aren't going to get to the beach anytime soon and want to cool off, check out **Ojo de Agua** (☎ **506/441-2808**), which is on the road to San Antonio de Belén. The spring-fed waters are cool and refreshing, and even if it seems a bit chilly in San José, it's always several degrees warmer out here. This place is very popular with Ticos and can get quite crowded on weekends. Unfortunately, you do have to keep an eye on your valuables here. Admission is $4.50. Buses leave almost hourly for Ojo de Agua, departing from Avenida 1 between Calles 18 and 20.

7 Spectator Sports

Ticos take their *fútbol* seriously. Although not up to European or World Cup standards, Costa Rican professional soccer is some of the best in Central America. The soccer season runs from September through June, with the finals spread out over several weeks in late June and early July. You don't need to buy tickets in advance. Tickets generally run between $2.50 and $12.50. It's worth paying a little extra for *sombra numerado* (reserved seats in the shade). Other options include *sombra* (general admission in the shade), *palco* and *palco numerado* (general admission and reserved mezzanine), and *sol general* (general admission in full sun). The main San José team is Saprissa (affectionately called *El Monstro,* or The Monster). **Saprissa's stadium** is in Tibás (take any Tibás bus from Calle 2 between Avenidas 3 and 7). Games are usually held on Sunday at 11am, but occasionally they are scheduled for Saturday afternoon or Wednesday evening. Check the local newspapers for game times and locations.

The **Vuelta de Costa Rica** is a Central American version of the Tour de France. Bicycle racers from around the region spend several weeks each December battling each other up and over the mountains on the roads of Costa Rica. If you're traveling around the country during December, check the local papers for routes and racing times, and you may be able to watch the pack pass by.

During the first week of January, Costa Rica hosts the **Copa del Café** (Coffee Cup), which is an important international event on the junior tennis tour. Matches are held at the Costa Rica Country Club (☎ **506/228-9333**) in Escazú. Admission is $5, and you can buy tickets at the box office at the Country Club; there's no need to buy tickets in advance. The club is located 800 meters east and 200 meters south of the Mas X Menos Supermarket in Escazú.

Although I hesitate to call it a sport, **Las Corridas a la Tica** (Costa Rican bullfighting) is a popular and frequently comic stadium event. Instead of the blood-and-gore/life-and-death confrontation of traditional bullfighting, Ticos just like to tease the bull. In a typical corrida, anywhere from 50 to 150 *toreadores improvisados* (literally, improvised bullfighters) stand in the ring waiting for the bull. What follows is a slapstick scramble to safety whenever the bull heads toward a crowd of bullfighters. The braver bullfighters try to slap the bull's backside as the beast chases down one of his buddies. You can see a bullfight during the Festejos Populares in Zapote, a suburb east of San José. The corridas run all day and well into the night during Christmas week and the first week in January. Admission is $2 to $5. Take the Zapote bus from Calle 1 between Avenidas 4 and 6. If you don't make it out to the stadium, but are in Costa Rica during the holiday time, don't despair—the local TV stations all show nothing but live broadcasts from Zapote.

8 Shopping

Serious shoppers will be disappointed in Costa Rica. Aside from coffee and oxcarts, there isn't much that's distinctly Costa Rican for you to buy. In fact, there's so little that you probably won't be overwhelmed by souvenir mania the way you might be in countries that have a variety of indigenous handcrafts. To compensate for its own relative lack, Costa Rica does a brisk business in selling crafts and clothes imported from Guatemala, Panama, and Ecuador. Still, there are some interesting and unique items to buy, as discussed under "Best Buys," below (see also "The Best Places to Shop," in chapter 1).

THE SHOPPING SCENE

Shopping in San José centers around an area marked by the parallel streets of Avenida 1 and Avenida 2, from about Calle 14 in the west to Calle 13 in the east. For several blocks west of the Plaza de la Cultura, Avenida Central is a pedestrians-only street where you'll find store after store of inexpensive clothes for men, women, and children. Depending on the mood of the police that day, you may find a lot of street vendors as well.

Most shops in the downtown district are open Monday through Saturday from about 8am to 6pm. Some shops close for lunch, while others remain open (it's just the luck of the draw for shoppers). When you do purchase something, you'll be happy to find that the sales and import taxes have already been figured into the display price.

International laws prohibit trade in endangered wildlife, so visitors to Costa Rica should not buy any wildlife or plants, even if they're readily for sale. The Audubon Society does not tolerate sales of any kind of sea turtle product (including jewelry); wild birds; lizards, snakes, or cat skins; corals; or orchids (except those grown commercially).

It's especially hard to capture the subtle shades and colors of the rain and cloud forests, and many a traveler has gone home thinking his or her undeveloped film contained the full beauty of the jungle, only to discover upon development

36 bright green blurs. To avoid this heartache, you might want to buy one of the picture books on Costa Rica mentioned in the "Recommended Books" section of chapter 2.

BEST BUYS

Two words of advice: **Buy coffee**. Lots of it. Buy as much as you can carry. Coffee is the best shopping deal in all of Costa Rica. Although the best Costa Rican coffee is supposedly shipped off to North American and European markets, it's hard to beat the coffee that's roasted right in front of you here. **Café Britt** is the big name in Costa Rican coffee, but though it's the most expensive brand, it's not necessarily the best. My favorites are the coffees roasted and packaged in Monteverde and by the **Cafe Milagro** folks in Manuel Antonio. If you're going to either of these places, definitely pick up their blends. For good flavor and value, I recommend that you visit **Café Trebol**, on Calle 8 between Avenida Central and Avenida 1. Be sure to ask for whole beans; Costa Rican grinds are often too fine for standard coffee filters. They'll pack the beans for you in whatever size bag you want. Best of all is the price: One pound of coffee sells for about $1.85. It makes a great gift and keeps for a long time in your refrigerator or freezer. If you should happen to buy prepackaged coffee in a supermarket in Costa Rica, the whole beans will be marked either *grano* (grain) or *grano entero* (whole bean). If you opt for ground varieties (*molido*), be sure the package is marked *puro;* otherwise, it will likely be mixed with a good amount of sugar, the way Ticos like it.

One good coffee-related gift to bring home is a coffee sock and stand. This is the most common mechanism for brewing coffee beans in Costa Rica. It consists of a simple circular stand, made out of wood or wire, which holds a sock. Put the ground beans in the sock, place a pot or cup below, and pour boiling water through. You can find the socks and stands at most supermarkets and in the Mercado Central. In fancier craft shops, you'll find them made out of ceramics. Depending on its construction, a stand will cost you between $1.50 and $15; socks run around 30¢, so buy a few spares.

If your interest is in handcrafts, there are many places for you to visit. As I've said, the quality of Costa Rican handcrafts is generally very low, and the offerings are limited. The most typical item you'll find are hand-painted wooden oxcarts. These come in a variety of sizes, and the big ones can be shipped to your home for a very reasonable price.

One notable exception is the fine wooden creations of **Barry Biesanz** (☎ **506/228-1811**; www.biesanz.com). His work is sold in many of the finer gift shops around, but beware, Biesanz's work is often imitated, so make sure what you buy is the real deal (he generally burns his signature into the bottom of the piece).

You may also run across carved masks made by the indigenous Boruca people of southern Costa Rica. These full-sized balsa wood masks come in a variety of styles, both painted and unpainted, and run anywhere from $10 to $70, depending on the quality of workmanship.

SUBURBAN MALLS

In recent years, large suburban malls have been springing up all around San José and its neighboring suburbs. There's **Multiplaza** in Escazú, **Plaza del Sol** in Curridabat, and the still unfinished but already bustling **Mall San Pedro**. The Mall San Pedro is on the main road into San Pedro from downtown at the Fuente de Hispanidad. Inside, you'll find all the familiar name-brand favorites from Victoria's Secret lingerie to Benetton jeans and shirts. Due to high import taxes, prices are substantially higher here than in North America or Europe. Since fakes are always around, it's best to examine merchandise carefully to be sure you're getting the quality you're paying for.

MARKETS

There are several markets near downtown, but by far the largest is the **Mercado Central**, which is located between Avenida Central and Avenida 1 and Calles 6 and 8. Although this dark maze of stalls is primarily a food market, inside you'll find all manner of vendors, including a few selling Costa Rican souvenirs, crude leather goods, and musical instruments. Be especially careful about your wallet or purse and any prominent jewelry, because this area is frequented by very skilled pick-pockets. All the streets surrounding the Mercado Central are jammed with produce vendors selling from small carts or loading and unloading trucks. It's always a hive of activity, with crowds of people jostling for space on the streets. In the hot days of the dry season, the aromas can get quite heady.

There is also a daily street market on the west side of the **Plaza de la Democracia**. Here you'll find two long rows of temporary stalls selling T-shirts, Guatemalan and Ecuadorian handcrafts and clothing, small ceramic ocarinas (a small musical wind instrument), and handmade jewelry. You may be able to bargain the price down a little bit, but bargaining is not a traditional part of the vendor culture here, so you'll have to work hard to save a few dollars.

SHOPPING A TO Z

ART GALLERIES

Arte Latino. Calle 5 and Avenida 1. ☎ **506/258-3306.** Mon–Sat 9am–7pm, Sun 10am–5pm. AE, DC, MC, V.

This gallery carries original artworks in a variety of mediums featuring predominantly Central American themes. Some of it is pretty gaudy, but this is a good place to find Nicaraguan and Costa Rican "primitive" paintings. The gallery also has storefronts in the Multiplaza Mall in Escazú and at the Mall Cariari, which is located on the Interamerican Highway, about halfway between the airport and downtown, across the street from the Hotel Herradura.

Galleria Andromeda. Calle 9 at Avenida 9. ☎ **506/223-3529.** Mon–Fri 9am–noon and 1–7pm. AE, MC, V.

This small, personal gallery features contemporary national artists of good quality. There are usually prints and paintings by several artists on display, and prices are very reasonable.

✪ **Galleria 11-12.** Avenida 15 and Calle 35. Casa 3506, in Barrio Escalante (from the Farolito, 200 meters east, 100 meters north). ☎ **506/280-8441.** Mon–Sat 9am–7pm, Sun by appointment. AE, V.

This gallery deals mainly in high-end Costa Rican art, from neoclassical painters like Teodorico Quirós to modern stars like Rafa Fernandez and Fabio Herrera.

HANDCRAFTS

The most appealing artisans' market close to San José is **La Garzas Handicraft Market** in Moravia (see below). You'll find another collection of shops at the **Artisans Plaza** across from the Mall San Pedro. If you want to stick to downtown San José, try the outdoor market on the **Plaza de la Democracia**, though prices here tend to be high and bargaining can be difficult. If you prefer to do your craft shopping in a flea-market atmosphere, head over to **La Casona** on Calle Central between Avenida Central and Avenida 1. Also be sure to visit the excellent **Annemarie Souvenir Shop** in the lobby of the Hotel Don Carlos.

Scores of shops around San José sell a wide variety of crafts, from the truly tacky to the divinely inspired. Here are some of the better places to look for such items.

Angie Theologos's Gallery. San Pedro (call for appointment and directions). ☎ **506/225-6565.**

Angie makes sumptuous handcrafted jackets from handwoven and embroidered Guatemalan textiles. Her work also includes bolero jackets, plus T-shirts made with Panamanian molas (appliquéd panels).

✪ **Annemarie Souvenir Shop.** Calle 9 between Avenidas 7 and 9. ☎ **506/221-6063.** Daily 9am–7pm. AE, MC, V.

Now occupying two floors at the Hotel Don Carlos, this shop has an amazing array of wood products, leather goods, papier-mâché figurines, paintings, books, cards, posters, and jewelry, to mention just a few of the things you'll find here. You'll see most of this stuff at the other shops but not in such a relaxed and pressure-free environment. Don't miss this shopping experience.

✪ **Atmosfera.** Calle 5 between Avenidas 1 and 3. ☎ **506/222-4322.** Mon–Sat 9am–6pm, sometimes open Sundays. AE, DC, MC, V.

This place has high-quality Costa Rican arts and crafts, from primitivist paintings and sculpture to skillfully made turned-wood bowls. It consists of several small rooms spread over three floors, so be sure you explore every nook and cranny—you'll see stuff here that's not available anywhere else in town.

✪ **Biesanz Woodworks.** Bello Horizonte, Escazú. ☎ **506/228-1811.** Mon–Fri 9am–5pm (call for directions and off-hour appointments). AE, MC, V.

Biesanz makes a wide range of high-quality items, including bowls, jewelry boxes, humidors, and some wonderful sets of wooden chopsticks. The showroom is adjoined to the artist's house. One of the nicest things about Biesanz Woodworks is that they are actively involved in reforestation, and you can even pick up a hardwood seedling here.

La Casona. Calle Central between Avenida Central and Avenida 1. No phone. Daily 9am–6pm. MC, V.

This is actually a large collection of individual shops selling a wide selection of crafts and clothing in a tight maze covering two floors of this covered bazaar. The different shops are piled one on top of the other, and it's often difficult to tell where one ends and another begins. Many of the offerings come from other Latin American countries, but there are a fair number of local items for sale here too.

Las Garzas Handicraft Market. In Moravia, 100 meters south and 50 meters east of the Red Cross Station. ☎ **506/236-0037.** Mon–Sat 9:30am–6pm, Sat 9:30am–4pm. AE, MC, V.

This artisans' market is a short ride out of San José and includes more than 25 shops selling wood, metal, and ceramic crafts, among a large variety of other items. There's a huge selection, and you can get some really good buys here.

Madera Magia. Calle 5 between Avenidas 1 and 3. ☎ **506/233-2630.** Mon–Fri 9am–6pm, Sat 9am–2pm. MC, V.

What you'll notice here is that almost everything is made of wood. The shop is filled with elegant, thin bowls of native hardwood, a big selection of wooden boxes, mirrors framed in wood, and very handsome handmade furniture. All items are of high quality, created by skilled artisans under the guidance of designer J. Morrison. These folks also have a large showroom in the suburb of Santa Ana.

Maya-Quiche. Avenida Central between Calles 5 and 7, Locale #147. ☎ **506/223-5030.** Mon–Sat 10am–6pm. AE, MC, V.

Located in the Galería Central Ramírez Valido shopping mall, this shop sells handcrafts from Central American countries, including gaily painted animals, boxes, and wooden letters from El Salvador, and molas from Panama.

Mercado Nacional De Artesanias. Calle 11 and Avenida 4 bis. ☎ **506/221-5012.** Daily 9am–6pm. AE, DC, MC, V.

Located behind the lovely yellow Iglesia de la Soledad, this store carries a wide variety of typical Costa Rican handcrafts, including large, comfortable woven-rope hammocks; reproductions of pre-Columbian gold jewelry and pottery bowls; coffee-wood carvings; and many other carvings from rare Costa Rican hardwoods. In general, however, the crafts you'll find here are of low quality.

Suraska. Calle 5 and Avenida 3. ☎ **506/222-0129.** Mon–Sat 9am–5pm. AE, V.

Among the selections here are ceramics, mobiles, and jewelry. This store tends to carry higher quality items than most gift shops downtown. Be warned, however, that the prices here are accordingly more expensive.

Jewelry

Esmeraldas Y Diseños. Avenida Las Americas, Sabana Norte; from the Restaurante Chicote, go 100 meters north, 50 meters west, and 150 meters north. ☎ **506/231-4808** or 506/231-5428. Mon–Sat 8am–6pm, Sun 8am–4pm. AE, MC, V.

Notice the location given above for this jewelry store—it's truly a classic San José address. You'll find here copies of pre-Columbian jewelry designs in gold, plus jewelry featuring semiprecious stones from Brazil and emeralds from Colombia.

Leather Goods

Malety. Avenida 1 between Calles 1 and 3. ☎ **506/221-1670.** Mon–Fri 9am–6pm, Sat 9am–5pm. AE, MC, V.

The quality of leather products found in Costa Rica is not as good as in North America, and prices are high, but take a look and see for yourself. This is one of the outlets in San José where you can shop for locally produced leather bags, briefcases, purses, wallets, and other such items. A second store is located on Calle 1 between Avenida Central and Avenida 2.

Liquor

Café Rica, similar to Kahlúa, and **Salicsa,** a cream liqueur, are two delicious coffee liqueurs made in Costa Rica. You can buy them in most supermarkets, liquor stores, and tourist shops, but the best prices I've seen are at the supermarket chain Mas X Menos. There is a Mas X Menos outlet on Paseo Colón and another on Avenida Central at the east end of town, just below the Museo Nacional de Costa Rica.

9 San José After Dark

In order to keep up with the tourism boom and steady urban expansion, San José has made strides to meet the nocturnal needs of visitors and residents alike. You'll find plenty of interesting clubs and bars, a wide range of theaters, and some very lively discos and dance salons.

To find out what's going on in San José while you're in town, pick up a copy of the *Tico Times* (English) or *La Nación* (Spanish). The former is a good place to find out where local expatriates are hanging out; the latter's "Viva" section has extensive listings of discos, movie theaters, and live music.

THE PERFORMING ARTS

Theater is very popular in Costa Rica, and downtown San José is studded with small theaters. However, tastes tend toward the burlesque, and the crowd pleasers are almost always simplistic sexual comedies. **The National Theater Company** (☎ **506/257-8305**) is one major exception, tackling works from Lope de Vega to Lorca to Mamet. Almost all of the theater offerings are in Spanish, though there are two amateur theater groups that periodically stage works in English. Check the *Tico Times* to see if anything is running during your stay.

Costa Rica has a strong modern dance scene. Both the University of Costa Rica and the National University have modern dance companies that perform regularly in San José. Two independent companies—**Los Denmedium** and **Diquis Tiquis**—are excellent. Sadly, however, you're almost more likely to catch these troupes performing in New York or Caracas than in San José.

The National Symphony Orchestra is a respectable orchestra by regional standards, though their repertoire tends to be rather conservative. The symphony season runs from March through November, with concerts roughly every other week at the **Teatro Nacional**, Avenida 2 between Calles 3 and 5 (☎ **506/221-1329**). Tickets cost between $2.50 and $15 and can be purchased at the box office.

Visiting artists also stop in Costa Rica from time to time. Recent concerts have featured Spanish pop diva Ana Belen, Argentine legend Mercedes Sosa, and Cuban-American jazz great Paquito D'Rivera. Revival tours of pop rockers are also popular, with recent visits by Emerson, Lake and Palmer and Deep Purple topping the bill. Many of these concerts and guest performances take place in San José's two historic theaters, the Teatro Nacional and the Teatro Melico Salazar, Avenida 2 between Calle Central and Calle 2 (☎ **506/222-2653**).

Costa Rica's cultural panorama changes drastically every March, when the country hosts large arts festivals. On odd-numbered years **El Festival Nacional de las Artes** reigns supreme, featuring purely local talent. On even-numbered years, the month-long fete is **El Festival Internacional de las Artes**, which offers a nightly smorgasbord of dance, theater, music, and monologue from around the world. Most nights of the festival you will have between four and ten shows to choose from. Many are free, and the most expensive ticket is $5. For exact dates and details of the program, you can contact the Ministry of Youth, Culture and Sports (☎ **506/255-3188**), though you might have trouble getting any info if you don't speak Spanish.

THE CLUB & MUSIC SCENE

If you like to dance, you'll find plenty of places to get down in San José. Salsa and merengue are the main beats that move people here, and many of the dance clubs, discos, and salons feature live music on the weekends. You'll find a pretty limited selection, though, if you're looking to catch some small-club jazz, rock, or blues.

The "Viva" section of *La Nación* newspaper has weekly performance schedules. A couple of dance bands to watch for are Marfil and Los Brillanticos. El Parque and Bruno Porter are two popular local rock groups, Expresso is a good cover band, both Blues Machine and The Blind Pig Blues Band are electric blues outfits, and if you're looking for jazz, check out Jazz Garbo, Editus, or pianist Manuel Obregon. Two very good local bands that don't seem to play that frequently are Cantoamerica and Adrian Goizueta's Grupo Experimental.

A good place to sample a range of San José's nightlife is in **El Pueblo**, a shopping, dining, and entertainment complex done up like an old Spanish village. It's just across the river to the north of town. The best way to get there is by taxi; all the drivers know El Pueblo well. Within the alleyways that wind through El Pueblo are a dozen or more bars, clubs, and discos; there's even a roller-skating rink. **Cocoloco** (☎ **506/222-8782**) features nightly "fiestas," and **Discoteque Infinito** (☎ **506/221-9134**) has three different environments under one roof. Across the street you'll find **La Plaza** (☎ **506/222-5143**), one of my favorite dance spots.

Live Music

Akelarre. Calle 21 between Avenidas 4 and 6. ☎ **506/223-0345.** Mon–Sat 6pm–3am. AE, MC, V.

This popular club is located in a renovated old house near the Museo Nacional. There are several rooms in which to check out the action and a garden out back. There are frequent live performances by hot Costa Rican groups.

La Esmeralda. Avenida 2 between Calles 5 and 7. ☎ **506/233-7386.** 24 hours daily. AE, DC, MC, V.

A sort of mariachi Grand Central Station, La Esmeralda is a cavernous open-air restaurant and bar that stays open 24 hours a day. In the evenings, mariachi bands park their vans out front and wait to be hired for a moonlight serenade or perhaps a surprise party. While they wait, they often fill the restaurant with loud trumpet blasts and the sound of the big bass *guitarón.* If you've never been serenaded at your table before, this place is a must. A song will cost you anywhere from $3 to $10, depending on the size of the group you hire.

DISCOS & SALONS

✪ **El Tobogan.** 200 meters north and 100 meters east of the La Republica main office, off the Guapiles highway. ☎ **506/257-3396.** Fri–Sat 8pm–2am. AE, MC, V.

The dance floor in this place is about the size of a football field, and yet it still fills up. This is a place where Ticos come with their loved ones and dance partners. There's always a live band here, and sometimes it's very good.

La Plaza. Across from the El Pueblo shopping center. ☎ **506/222-5143.** Daily 6:30–4am. AE, DC, MC, V.

This large, open, upscale disco seems to be the favored dance venue for the young and beautiful of San José. The interior is designed to resemble a colonial plaza. This place gets a younger crowd than many of the other spots around town.

Las Tunas. Sabana North, 500 meters west of the ICE office. ☎ **506/231-1802.** Daily 7pm–2am. AE, DC, MC, V.

This happening place serves Mexican food and barbecue, but it's the bar and discotheque that're really cookin'. Live Costa Rican pop music is featured weekly.

Salsa 54. Calle 3 between Avenidas 1 and 3. ☎ **506/233-3814.** Daily 8pm–2am. AE, MC, V.

This is the place to go to watch expert salsa dancers and to try some yourself. In addition to the informal instruction, you might learn something just by watching; you might even be able to take a Latin dance class here.

THE BAR SCENE

There seems to be something for every taste here. Lounge lizards will be happy in most hotel bars in the downtown area, while students and the young at heart will have no problem mixing in at the livelier spots around town. Sports fans can even find a place to catch the most important games of the day.

The best part of the varied bar scene in San José is something called a *boca,* the equivalent of a *tapa* in Spain: a little dish of snacks that arrives at your table when you order a drink. In most bars, the bocas are free; but in some, where the dishes are more sophisticated, you'll have to pay for the treats. You'll find drinks reasonably priced, with beer costing around $1 or $1.50 and mixed drinks $2 or $3.50.

Beatle Bar. Calle 9 between Avenida Central and Avenida 1. ☎ **506/256-9085.** Daily 1pm–2am. No credit cards.

Photos of the Fab Four line the walls here, and the music is a mix of Beatles and other 60s and 70s rock classics. Sit at the bar, or take a turn on the dance floor. There are even a couple of outdoor tables at the front of the bar. The location is one of the liveliest in the downtown area.

✪ **El Cuartel De La Boca Del Monte.** Avenida 1 between Calles 21 and 23. ☎ **506/221-0327.** Daily noon–1am. AE, DC, MC, V.

This popular bar began life as an artist and bohemian hangout, and over the years it's evolved into the leading meat market for the young and well-heeled. However, artists still come, as do foreign exchange students, visitors, and, for some reason, many of the river-rafting guides, so there's always a diverse mix. There's usually live music here on Monday, Wednesday, and Friday nights, and when there is, the place is packed shoulder to shoulder.

Key Largo. Calle 7 between Avenidas 1 and 3. ☎ **506/221-0277.** Daily 6pm–4am. V.

Housed in a beautiful old building just off Parque Morazan in downtown San José, Key Largo is the best-known nightclub in Costa Rica. It's worth a visit just to see the interior of the building, but be warned: This is San José's number-one prostitute pick-up spot.

Rio. Avenida Central, Los Yoses. ☎ **506/225-8371.** Daily noon–3am. AE, DC, MC, V.

This bar and restaurant is close to the University of Costa Rica, and consequently attracts a younger clientele. At night, Rio is always packed to overflowing with the wealthy and the wanna-bes of San José.

Risa's Bar. Calle 1 between Avenida Central and Avenida 1. ☎ **506/223-2803.** Mon–Sat 11:30–3am, Sun 7pm–3am. V.

This restaurant and bar now occupies all four floors of this beautiful old building in the heart of downtown San José. The first floor has a U.S. tavern motif, with wood-panel walls, while the second floor is a casual cafe–cum–fern bar. The third and fourth floors are where the disco rages. The music up here is loud! At the end of the night, you can either walk back down the stairs or take the curving slide out.

✪ **Shakespeare Bar.** Avenida 2 and Calle 28. ☎ **506/257-1288.** Daily 5pm–1am. V.

Located next to the Sala Garbo movie theater, this quiet and classy little spot is a good place to meet after a movie or a show at the Sala Garbo or Laurence Olivier Theater next door.

Soda Palace. Calle 2 and Avenida 2. ☎ **506/221-3441.** 24 hours daily. MC, V.

This dingy but brightly lit bar hardly lives up to its name, but it's a Costa Rican institution. It opens directly onto busy Avenida 2 and is open 24 hours a day. There's a bit of a rough edge to the Soda Palace. Men of all ages sit at the tables conversing loudly and watching the world pass by. Mariachis stroll in, linger for a while, then continue on their way. Legend has it that the revolution of 1948 was planned right here.

HANGING OUT IN SAN PEDRO

The 2-block stretch of San Pedro just south of the University of Costa Rica is the closest thing to Paris's Left Bank or New York's East Village you'll find in Costa Rica. Bars and cafes are mixed in with bookstores and copy shops. It's one of the few places in town where you can sit calmly at an outdoor table or walk the streets without constantly looking over your shoulder and checking that your wallet's still with you. You can just stroll the strip until someplace strikes your fancy—or trust me and try one of the following.

✪ **La Maga.** 100 meters west and 100 meters south of La Fuente de Hispanidad. ☎ **506/283-5047.** Daily 11am–1am. AE, MC, V.

This artsy cafe is named after a character in Julio Cortázar's novel *Hopscotch.* It has recently moved from its original location and is now about 6 blocks away, in a small shopping center across from the Mall San Pedro. Inside, you'll find a long bar, comfortable wooden tables, and racks of magazines and newspapers for perusing. The walls are lined with pictures of literary and musical luminaries. There is some nice outdoor seating and the occasional live music act.

✪ **La Villa.** 200 meters east and 100 meters north of the Church in San Pedro. ☎ **506/225-9612.** Mon–Sat 11am–1am. AE, MC, V.

This converted Victorian house holds the ghosts of Che Guevara and Camilo Cienfuegos—or at least you'll see posters of them and other Latin American revolutionaries on the walls. Around the tables you'll find poets and painters mixing with a new generation of student activists, all in a lively atmosphere. There's even a foosball table in the far back, and, consistent with the revolutionary ethos, everything is priced reasonably.

THE GAY & LESBIAN SCENE

Because Costa Rica is such a conservative Catholic country, the gay and lesbian communities here are rather discreet. Homosexuality is not generally under attack, but many gay and lesbian organizations guard their privacy, and the club scene is not entirely stable. For a general overview of the current situation, news of any special events or meetings, and up-to-date information, gay and lesbian travelers should check in with either **The International Gay and Lesbian Association** (☎ **506/234-2411**) or **La Asociación Triangulo Rosa** (☎ **506/258-0214**). The first number will generally get you an English-speaking person, whereas the latter will generally get you someone in Spanish.

The most established and happening gay and lesbian bars and dance clubs in San José are **Deja Vu,** Calle 2 between Avenidas 14 and 16 (no phone), and **La Avispa,** Calle 1 between Avenidas 8 and 10 (☎ **506/223-5343**). The former is predominantly a guysÕ bar, while the latter is popular with both men and women, although they sometimes set certain nights of the week or month aside for specific communities. There's also **Buenas Vibraciones** and **Bochinche** out on Paseo de los

Estudiantes, **Boy Bar International** in Tibás, and **La Tertulia**, **Faces,** and **Bambú** in San Pedro. None of these advertise their phone numbers, but you can call the organizations listed above for directions and more specific information.

MOVIES & MORE

Most of the movies shown in San José are first-run U.S. productions (in English with Spanish subtitles) that get here about 3 months after their openings in the States. Ticos tend toward action flicks, so there's almost always a Schwarzenegger or Van Damme film to choose from. Even if you aren't interested in what's playing, it's worth the $2.50 or $3 admission just to see a movie in an old-style theater with a full-size screen. Try out the **Cine Magaly,** Calle 23 between Avenida Central and Avenida 1 (☎ **506/223-0085**); **Cine Rex,** Calle Central between Avenidas 2 and 4, just off the Parque Central (☎ **506/221-0041**); or **Cine Variedades,** Calle 3 between Avenida Central and Avenida 1 (☎ **506/223-0085**). These theaters even have balconies (remember those?). Check the "Viva" section of *La Nación* or the *Tico Times* for movie listings and times.

Sala Garbo, 100 meters south of the Pizza Hut on Paseo Colón (☎ **506/222-1034**), shows foreign and art films, usually with Spanish subtitles but sometimes with English subtitles.

Gambling is legal in Costa Rica, and there are casinos at virtually every major hotel. However, as in Tico bullfighting, there are some idiosyncrasies involved in *gambling a la tica.* If blackjack is your game, you'll want to play "rummy." The rules are almost identical, except the house doesn't pay double on blackjack—instead it pays double on any three of a kind or three-card straight flush. If you're looking for roulette, what you'll find here is a bingolike spinning cage of numbered balls. The betting is the same, but some of the glamour is lost. You'll also find a version of five-card draw poker, but the rule differences are so complex that I advise you sit down and watch for a while and then ask some questions before joining in. That's about all you'll find. There are no craps tables or baccarat. There's some controversy over slot machines—one-armed bandits are currently outlawed—but you will be able to play electronic slots and poker games. Most of the casinos here are quite casual and small by international standards. You may have to dress up slightly at some of the fancier hotels, but most are accustomed to tropical vacation attire.

10 Side Trips from San José

San José makes an excellent base for exploring the beautiful Central Valley and the surrounding mountains, and, in fact, it's possible to explore much of the country on day tours from here. Probably the best way to make the most of these excursions is on guided tours, but if you rent a car you'll have greater independence. There are also some day trips that can be done by public bus. Below is information on many of the day tours offered by tour companies in San José. I've arranged these by type of activity. In addition to these, there are many other tours, some of which combine two or three different activities or destinations. Companies offering a wide variety of primarily nature-related day tours out of San José include: **Costa Rica Expeditions** (☎ **506/257-0766**); **Costa Rica Sun Tours** (☎ **506/255-3418**); **Ecole Travel** (☎ **506/223-2240**); **Fantasy Tours** (☎ **800/272-6654** in the U.S., 800/463-6654 in Canada, or 506/290-2098); **Otec Tours** (☎ **506/256-0633**); **Swiss Travel Service** (☎ **506/282-4898**); and **TAM/Adventureland** (☎ **506/256-0203**).

Before signing on for a tour of any sort, find out how much time will be spent in transit and eating lunch, and how much time will actually be spent doing the primary activity. I've had complaints about tours that were rushed, or that spent too much time on secondary activities.

ADVENTUROUS ACTIVITIES

BICYCLING Narrow mountain roads with spectacular views make for some great, though strenuous, bicycling in Costa Rica. However, the best bicycle riding is well outside of San José and far from the dangers of larger vehicular traffic. This means it's best to go off track, on dirt roads, where you're not likely to be run off the road by a semi truck or run head-on into someone coming around a blind curve in the wrong lane. **Costa Rica Sun Tours** (☎ **506/255-3418**) and **Aguas Bravas** (☎ **506/292-2072**) both run a variety of mountain-biking tours, including descents of Irazú Volcano. A 1-day trip should cost between $70 and $90 per person.

Another company offering bicycling trips is **Velero del Rey Tours** (☎ **506/235-4982**). You might also contact **Coast To Coast Adventures** (☎ **506/225-6055**), which, in addition to its 2-week namesake adventure, will also design customized mountain-biking trips of shorter duration.

BUNGEE JUMPING There's nothing unique about bungee jumping in Costa Rica, but it's a little bit less expensive than a similar experience farther north. If you've always had the bug, **Tropical Bungee** (☎ **506/233-6455**; fax 506/255-4354; e-mail: galagui@sol.racsa.co.cr) will let you jump off a 265-foot bridge for $45; two jumps cost $70. Transportation is $7 each way.

CRUISES Several companies offer cruises to the lovely Tortuga Island in the Gulf of Nicoya. The original and most dependable company running these trips is **Calypso Tours** (☎ **506/256-2727**). The cruise costs $95 per person and includes transportation from San José to Puntarenas and back, a basic continental breakfast during the bus ride to the boat, all drinks on the cruise, and an excellent lunch on the beach at the island. Calypso Tours also conducts cruises to a private nature reserve at Punta Coral.

HIKING If you don't plan to visit Monteverde or one of Costa Rica's other cloud-forest reserves, consider doing a day tour to a cloud forest. One popular hiking tour goes to the **Los Angeles Cloud Forest Reserve.** This full-day excursion and guided walk through the cloud forest is operated by **Hotel Villablanca** (☎ **506/228-4603**). The cost is $77, which includes transportation, breakfast, and lunch.

Velero del Rey Tours (☎ **506/235-4982**), mentioned above under bicycling, also organizes guided 1-day hiking tours out of San José.

HORSEBACK RIDING If you enjoy horseback riding, you have your choice of many fascinating locations near San José for day-long trips. **The Valle de Yos-Oy Riding Center** (☎ **506/282-6934** or 506/282-7850) is located in Santa Ana and offers riding classes as well as guided trail rides. **Sacramento Horseback Ride** (☎ **506/237-2116**) offers rides through mountain forests and pastures. A 3-hour tour with them will cost just $35, including lunch.

HOT-AIR BALLOONING One of the most fascinating ways to see Costa Rica is from a balloon floating above the forest. **Serendipity Adventures** (☎ **800/635-2325** in the U.S., or 506/556-2592) offers a half-day tour above the countryside around Naranjo (25 miles from San José). Serendipity will pick you up at your

The Central Valley: Side Trips from San José

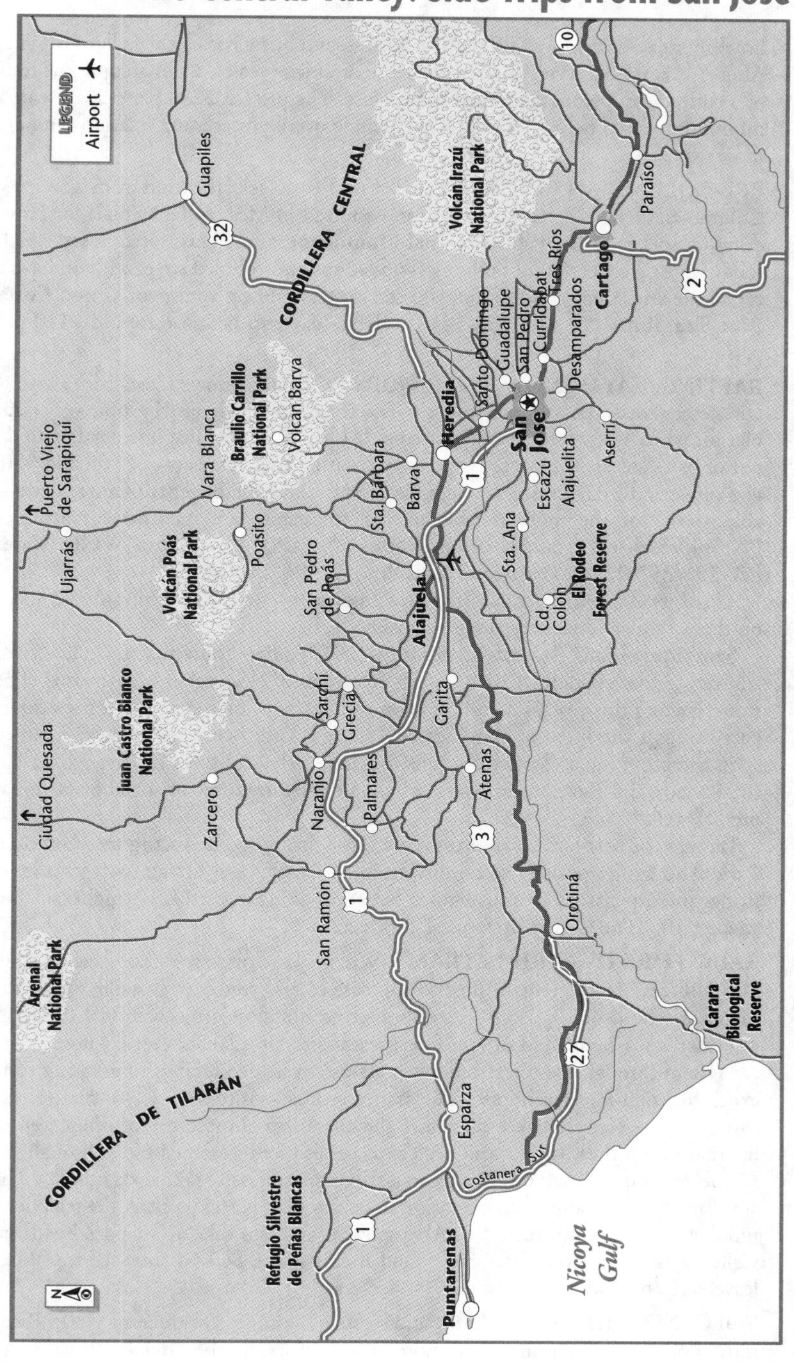

hotel room at 4:30am—that's right, 4:30am—and bring you to the ballooning site. After a several-hour soar, you'll be treated to a tipico breakfast and an optional tour of a coffee farm before the return to San José. The price is $235 per person with a minimum of two persons. Other trips include overnight accommodations and are more expensive.

PRE-COLUMBIAN RUINS Though Costa Rica lacks the kind of massive pre-Columbian archaeological sites that can be found in Mexico, Guatemala, or Honduras, it does have **Guayabo National Monument**, a small excavated town, which today is just a collection of building foundations and cobbled streets. If you have a car, or are an intrepid bus hound, you can do this tour on your own. If not, **Costa Rica Sun Tours** (☎ **506/255-3418**) offers a day trip here for around $110 per person.

RAFTING, KAYAKING & RIVER TRIPS Cascading down Costa Rica's mountain ranges are dozens of tumultuous rivers, several of which have become very popular for white-water rafting and kayaking. If I had to choose just one day trip to do out of San José, it would be a white-water rafting trip. For between $65 and $90, you can spend a day rafting through lush tropical forests; longer trips are also available. Some of the more reliable rafting companies are **Aventuras Naturales** (☎ **800/514-0411** in the U.S., or 506/225-3939), **Costa Rica White Water** (☎ **506/257-0766**), and **Rios Tropicales** (☎ **506/233-6455**).

There are also some raft and boat trips on calmer waters. These trips usually focus on the wildlife and scenery along the river.

Sarapiquí Aguas Bravas (☎ **506/292-2072**) offers tours that include a boat trip down the Sarapiquí River, a quiet river fed by clear mountain streams. The scenery along this river is a combination of rain forest and farms, and these tours pass through the lush Braulio Carrillo National Park before reaching the put-in spot. Sarapiquí Aguas Bravas also runs rougher sections of the same river, as well as the Pacuare and Reventazón rivers, which are plied by most of the above companies, as well.

Perhaps the best-known river tours are those that go up to **Tortuguero National Park**. Though it's possible to do this tour as a day trip out of San José, it's a long, tiring, and expensive day. You're much better off doing it as a 1- or 2-night trip. See chapter 10, "The Caribbean Coast," for details.

RAIN FOREST AERIAL TRAM When you first see the Aerial Tram (☎ **506/257-5961**; e-mail: dosela@sol.racsa.co.cr), you may wonder where the slopes are. Built on a private reserve bordering Braulio Carillo National Park, the tramway is the brainchild of rain-forest researcher Dr. Donald Perry, whose cable-car system through the forest canopy at Rara Avis helped establish him as an early expert on rain-forest canopies. The tramway takes visitors on a 90-minute ride through the treetops, where they have the chance to glimpse the complex web of life that makes these forests unique. There are also well-groomed trails through the rain forest and a restaurant on site, so a trip here can easily take up a full day. The cost for tours, including transportation from San José, is $65 (contact the telephone number above for information). Alternatively, you can take a Guapiles bus from Calle 12 between Avenidas 7 and 9 and then pay the $47.50 entrance fee. Buses leave every half hour and cost $2.

VOLCANO TRIPS Poás, Irazú, and Arenal volcanoes are three of Costa Rica's most popular destinations. For more information on the Arenal Volcano, see chapter 7, and for more information on Poás and Irazú, see below. Numerous tour companies in San José offer trips to all three volcanoes, and though the trips to Poás and Irazú take only half a day, the trips to Arenal take all day. I don't recommend these latter trips because there's at least 3½ hours of travel time in each direction, so you usually arrive when the volcano is hidden by clouds and leave before the night's darkness shows off its glowing eruptions. Tour companies offering trips to Poás and Irazú include **Costa Rica Expeditions** (☎ **506/257-0766**); **Costa Rica Sun Tours** (☎ **506/255-3418**); **Otec Tours**, Edeficio Ferencz, Calle 3 between Avenidas 1 and 3 (Apdo. 323-1002), San José (☎ **506/256-0633**); **TAM/Adventureland**, Calle Central between Avenida Central and Avenida 1 (☎ **506/256-0203**); **San Jose Travel,** Calle 11 and Avenida 2 (☎ **506/257-4511**); and **Swiss Travel Service**, which has several offices around San José (☎ **506/282-4898**). Prices range from $25 to $35 for a half-day trip to $50 to $75 for a full-day trip.

CARTAGO, THE OROSI VALLEY & IRAZÚ VOLCANO

Located about 15 miles (24.2km) southeast of San José, Cartago is the former capital of Costa Rica. Founded in 1563, it was Costa Rica's first city, and was in fact its *only* city for almost 150 years. Irazú Volcano rises up from the edge of town, and although it's quiet these days, it has not always been so peaceful. Earthquakes have damaged Cartago repeatedly over the years, so that today there are few of the old colonial buildings left standing. In the center of the city, a public park winds through the ruins of a large church that was destroyed in 1910, before it could be finished. Construction was abandoned after the quake, and today the ruins are a neatly manicured park, with quiet paths and plenty of benches.

Cartago's most famous building, however, is the **Basilica de Nuestra Señora de Los Angeles** (the Basilica of Our Lady of the Angels), which is dedicated to the patron saint of Costa Rica and stands on the east side of town. Within the walls of this Byzantine-style church is a shrine containing the tiny figure of **La Negrita**, the Black Virgin, which is nearly lost amid its ornate altar. Legend has it that La Negrita first revealed herself on this site to a peasant girl in 1635. Miraculous healing powers have been attributed to La Negrita, and over the years thousands of pilgrims have come to the shrine seeking cures for their illnesses and difficulties. The walls of the shrine are covered with a fascinating array of tiny silver images left as thanks for cures affected by La Negrita. Amid the plethora of diminutive silver arms and legs, there are also hands, feet, hearts, lungs, kidneys, eyes, torsós, breasts, and—peculiarly—guns, trucks, beds, and planes. There are even dozens of sports trophies that I assume were left in thanks for helping teams win big games. Outside the church, vendors sell a wide selection of these trinkets, as well as little candle replicas of La Negrita. August 2 is the day dedicated to La Negrita, and on this day tens of thousands of people walk to Cartago from San José and elsewhere in the country, in devotion to this powerful statue.

If you'd like to soak in a warm-water swimming pool, head 2½ miles (4km) south of Cartago to **Aguas Calientes**. A little over a mile east of Cartago, you'll find Lankester Gardens (☎ **506/552-3247** or 506/552-3151) a botanical garden known for its orchid collection. (See "Attractions," above, for details.)

Buses for Cartago leave San José every 10 minutes from Calle 5 between Avenidas 18 and 20. You can also pick it up en route at any of the covered little bus stops along Avenida Central in Los Yoses and San Pedro. The length of the trip is 45 minutes; the fare is about 35¢.

IRAZÚ VOLCANO Located 20 miles (32.2km) north of Cartago, the 11,260-foot-tall Irazú Volcano is one of Costa Rica's more active volcanoes, although at this time it's relatively quiet. It last erupted on March 19, 1963, on the day that

President John F. Kennedy arrived in Costa Rica. The eruption showered ash on the Meseta Central for months after, destroying crops and collapsing roofs but enriching the soil. There's a good paved road right to the rim of the crater, where a desolate expanse of gray sand nurtures few plants and the air smells of sulfur. The landscape here is often compared to that of the moon. There are magnificent views of the fertile Meseta Central and Orosi Valley as you drive up from Cartago, and if you're very lucky you may be able to see both the Pacific Ocean and Caribbean Sea. Clouds usually descend by noon, so schedule your trip up here as early in the day as possible. From the parking area, a short trail leads to the rim of the volcano's two craters, their walls a maze of eroded gullies feeding onto the flat floor far below. This is a national park, and admission is $6 at the gate (see "Costa Rica's National Parks & Bioreserves" in chapter 4 for more information). Wear warm clothes: This may be the tropics, but it can be cold up at the top. On you way back down, stop for breakfast at **Restaurant Linda Vista** (☎ **506/225-5808**). It's on the right as you come down the mountain. Located at an elevation of 10,075 feet, it claims to be the highest restaurant in Central America; there are walls of windows looking out over the valley far below. A hearty Tico breakfast of gallo pinto with ham will cost about $2.50.

Buses leave for Irazú Volcano Saturday, Sunday, and holidays from Avenida 2 between Calles 1 and 3 (in front of the Gran Hotel Costa Rica). The fare is $4, and the trip takes about 1½ hours. To make sure the buses are running, phone ☎ **506/272-0651**. If you're driving, head northeast out of Cartago toward San Rafael, then continue driving uphill toward the volcano, passing the turnoffs for Cot and Tierra Blanca en route.

OROSI VALLEY The Orosi Valley, southeast of Cartago and visible from the top of Irazú on a clear day, is generally considered one of the most beautiful valleys in Costa Rica. The Reventazón River meanders through this steep-sided valley until it collects in the lake formed by the Cachí Dam. There are scenic overlooks near the town of Orosi, which is at the head of the valley, and in Ujarrás, which is on the banks of the lake. Near Ujarrás are the ruins of Costa Rica's oldest church (built in 1693), whose tranquil gardens are a great place to sit and gaze at the surrounding mountains. Across the lake is a popular recreation center, called **Charrarra**, where you'll find a picnic area, swimming pool, and hiking trails. In the town of Orosi there is yet another colonial church, built in 1743. A small museum here displays religious artifacts.

It would be difficult to explore this whole area by public bus, since this is not a densely populated region. However, there are buses from Cartago to the town of Orosi. During the week, these buses run every hour and leave from a spot 1 block east and 3 blocks south of the church ruins in Cartago. Saturday and Sunday, the bus runs roughly every 45 minutes from the same block and will drop you at the Orosi lookout point. The trip takes 30 minutes, and the fare is 30¢. If you're driving, take the road to Paraíso from Cartago, head toward Ujarrás, continue around the lake, then pass through Cachí and on to Orosi. From Orosi, the road leads back to Paraíso. There are also guided day tours of this area from San José (call any of the companies listed under "Organized Tours," above).

POÁS VOLCANO

This is another active volcano accessible from San José in a day trip. It's 23 miles (37km) from San José on narrow roads that wind through a landscape of fertile farms and dark forests. As at Irazú, there's a paved road right to the top. The volcano stands 8,800 feet tall and is located within a national park, which preserves not only the volcano but also dense stands of virgin forest. Poás's crater is over a mile across and is said to be the second-largest crater in the world. Geysers in the crater sometimes spew steam and muddy water 600 feet into the air, which distinguishes it as the largest geyser in the world. There's an information center where you can see a slide show about the volcano, and there are marked hiking trails through the cloud forest that rings the crater. About 20 minutes from the parking area, along a forest trail, is an overlook onto beautiful Botos Lake, which has formed in one of the volcano's extinct craters.

Be prepared when you come to Poás: This volcano is often enveloped in dense clouds. If you want to see the crater, it's best to come early, and during the dry season. Moreover, it can get cold up here, especially when the sun isn't shining, so dress appropriately. This is a national park and admission is $6 at the gate. For more information see "Costa Rica's National Parks & Bioreserves," in chapter 4.

There is a daily bus from Calle 12 and Avenidas 2 and 4 at 8:30am and returning at 2:30pm. The fare is $3 for the round-trip. The bus is always crowded, so arrive early. Alternatively, you can take a bus to Alajuela, then a bus to San Pedro de Poás. From there you will have to hitchhike or take a taxi ($15 round-trip), which makes this alternative almost as costly as a tour. All the tour companies in San José offer excursions to Poás, although they often don't arrive until after the clouds have closed in. If you're traveling by car, head for Alajuela and continue on the main road through town toward Varablanca. Just before reaching Varablanca, turn left toward Poasito and continue to the rim of the volcano.

HEREDIA, ALAJUELA, GRECIA, SARCHÍ & ZARCERO

All of these cities and towns are northwest of San José and can be combined into a long day trip (if you have a car), perhaps in conjunction with a visit to Poás Volcano. The scenery here is rich and verdant, and the small towns and scattered farming communities are truly representative of Costa Rica's agricultural heartland and campesino tradition. If you're relying on buses, you'll be able to visit any of the towns listed below, but probably just one or two per day.

The road to Heredia turns north off the highway from San José to the airport. To reach Alajuela from Heredia, take the scenic road that heads west through the town of San Joaquín. To continue on to Sarchí, it's best to return to the highway south of Alajuela and drive west toward Puntarenas. Turn north to Grecia and then west to Sarchí. There'll be plenty of signs.

HEREDIA This city was founded in 1706, and a colonial church dedicated in 1763 stands in the central park. The stone facade leaves no questions as to the age of the church, but the altar inside is decorated with neon stars and a crescent moon surrounding a statue of the Virgin Mary. In the middle of the palm-shaded park is a music temple, and across the street, beside several tile-roofed municipal buildings, is the tower of an old Spanish fort. Of all the cities in the Meseta Central, this is the only one with some colonial feeling to it—you'll still see adobe buildings with Spanish tile roofs along narrow streets. Heredia is also the site of the **National Autonomous University**, so you'll find some nice coffee shops and bookstores near the school. Buses leave for Heredia almost every 10 minutes from Calle 12 and Avenida 2, and from Calle 1 between Avenidas 7 and 9. Bus fare is 40¢.

ALAJUELA One of Costa Rica's oldest cities, Alajuela is located only 12 miles (19.3km) from San José. Although it's an attractive little city filled with parks, there isn't much to see or do here. The Juan Santamaría Historical Museum, Avenida 3 between Calle Central and Calle 2 (☎ **506/442-1838**), commemorates Costa Rica's national hero, who gave his life defending the country against a small army led by William Walker, a U.S. citizen who invaded Costa Rica in 1856, attempting to set up a slave state. The museum is open Tuesday through Sunday from 10am to 6pm; admission is free. Buses leave for Alajuela every 10 minutes from two separate and prominent stations on Avenida 2 between Calles 10 and 12 and between Calles 12 and 14; the fare is 55¢.

GRECIA From Alajuela, a narrow, winding road leads to the town of Grecia, which is noteworthy for its unusual metal church, which is painted a deep red and has white gingerbread trim. Grecia is now also home to the interesting Jewels of the Rain Forest Museum (see under "More Attractions," above). Buses leave hourly for Grecia from the Coca-Cola bus station at Calle 16 between Avenidas 1 and 3. The road to Sarchí is to the left as you face the church in Grecia, but due to all the one-way streets you'll have to drive around it.

SARCHÍ Sarchí is Costa Rica's main artisan town. It's here that the colorfully painted miniature oxcarts you see all over the country are made. Oxcarts such as these were once used to haul coffee beans to market. Today, though you may occasionally see oxcarts in use, most are purely decorative. However, they remain a well-known symbol of Costa Rica. In addition to miniature oxcarts, many carved wooden souvenirs are made here with rare hardwoods from the nation's forests. There are dozens of shops in town, and all have similar prices. Aside from handcrafts, the other reason to visit Sarchí is to see its unforgettable church. Built between 1950 and 1958, the church is painted pink with aquamarine trim and looks strangely like a child's birthday cake. Buses leave for Sarchí every 25 minutes from Calle 8 between Avenida Central and Avenida 1 in Alajuela. Bus fare is 65¢. There are also express buses from San José at noon and 5:30pm from Calle 16 and Avenidas 1 and 3. Fare is $1.

ZARCERO Beyond Sarchí, on picturesque roads lined with cedar trees, you'll find the town of Zarcero. In a small park in the middle of town is a menagerie of sculpted shrubs that includes a monkey on a motorcycle, people and animals dancing, an ox pulling a cart, a man wearing a top hat, and a large elephant. Behind all the topiary is a wonderful rural church. It's worth the drive to see this park—or, better yet, you can stop here on the way to La Fortuna and Arenal Volcano. Buses for Zarcero leave from San José hourly from the Coca-Cola bus station at Calle 16 between Avenidas 1 and 3. This is actually the Ciudad Quesada/San Carlos bus. Just tell the driver you want to get off in Zarcero and keep an eye out for the topiary.

TURRIALBA

This attractive little town 33 miles (53km) east of San José is best known as the starting point and home base for many popular white-water rafting trips. However, it's also worth a visit if you have an interest in pre-Columbian history or tropical botany. Buses leave hourly for Turrialba throughout the day from Calle 13 between Avenidas 6 and 8. The fare is $2.

Guayabo National Monument is one of Costa Rica's only pre-Columbian sites that have been excavated and are open to the public. It's located 12 miles (19.3km) northeast of Turrialba and preserves a town site that dates from between 1000 B.C. and A.D. 1400. Archaeologists believe that Guayabo may have supported a population of as many as 10,000 people, but there is no clue yet as to why the city was eventually abandoned only shortly before the Spanish arrived in the New World. Excavated ruins at Guayabo consist of paved roads, aqueducts, stone bridges, and house and temple foundations. There are also grave sites and petroglyphs.

The monument is open daily from 8am to 4pm. This is a national park, and admission is $6 at the gate. For more information, see "Costa Rica's National Parks & Bioreserves," in chapter 4.

Botanists and gardeners will want to pay a visit to the **Center for Agronomy Research and Development** (CATIE), which is located 3 miles (4.8km) southeast of Turrialba on the road to Siquerres. This center is one of the world's foremost facilities for research into tropical agriculture. Among the plants on CATIE's 2,000 acres are hundreds of varieties of cacao and thousands of varieties of coffee. The plants here have been collected from all over the world. In addition to trees used for food and other purposes, there are plants grown strictly for ornamental purposes. CATIE is open Monday through Friday from 7am to 4pm. For information on guided tours, call ☎ **506/556-6431**.

While you're in the area, don't miss an opportunity to spend a little time at **Turrialtico** (☎ **506/556-1111**), a lively open-air restaurant and small hotel high on a hill overlooking the Turrialba Valley. The view from here is one of the finest in the country, with lush greenery far below and volcanoes in the distance. Meals are quite inexpensive, and a room will cost you only $20. This place is popular with rafting companies who bring groups here for meals and for overnights before, after, and during multiday rafting trips. You'll find Turrialtico about 6 miles (9.7km) out of Turrialba on the road to Siquierres.

If you're looking for some luxury in this area, check out **Casa Turire** (☎ **506/531-1111**; fax 506/531-1075; e-mail: casaturire@ticonet.co.cr), where well-appointed rooms and suites in an elegant country mansion run between $110 and $200.

6 Guanacaste & the Nicoya Peninsula

Guanacaste province is Costa Rica's hottest and driest region. The rainy season starts later and ends earlier here, and overall it's more dependably sunny here than in other parts of the country. Combine this climate with a coastline that stretches from the Nicaraguan border to the southern tip of the Nicoya Peninsula, and you have an equation that yields beach bliss. Beautiful beaches abound along this coastline. Some are pristine and deserted, some are dotted with luxury resort hotels, and still others are backed by little villages where you can still get a clean double room for less than $30 a night. These beaches vary from long, straight stretches of sand to tiny coves bordered by rocky headlands. Whatever your passion in beaches, you're likely to find something that comes close to perfection.

This is Costa Rica's most coveted vacation region and the site of its greatest tourism development. The change is dramatic and ongoing. Large resorts have sprung up, and more are in the works. In the past year two regulation golf courses have opened up here, and several more are under construction. The long-awaited international airport in Liberia is finally getting on its feet, and it will soon be possible to fly directly in and out of Liberia—and on to any one of the numerous beaches below—without having to go through San José.

There is, however, one caveat: During the dry season (from mid-November through April), when sunshine is most reliable, the hillsides in Guanacaste turn browner than the chaparral of Southern California. Dust from dirt roads blankets the trees in many areas, and the vistas are far from tropical. Driving these dirt roads without air-conditioning and hermetically sealed windows can be extremely unpleasant. However, if you can't tolerate the least bit of rain on your holiday in the sun, the beaches up here are where you'll want to be.

On the other hand, if you happen to visit this area in the rainy season (May to mid-November), the hillsides are a beautiful rich green, and the sun usually shines all morning, giving way to an afternoon shower—just in time for a nice siesta.

Guanacaste is also Costa Rica's "Wild West," a dry landscape of cattle ranches and cowboys who are known here as *sabaneros*, a name that derives from the Spanish word for savannah or grassland.

Guanacaste & The Nicoya Peninsula

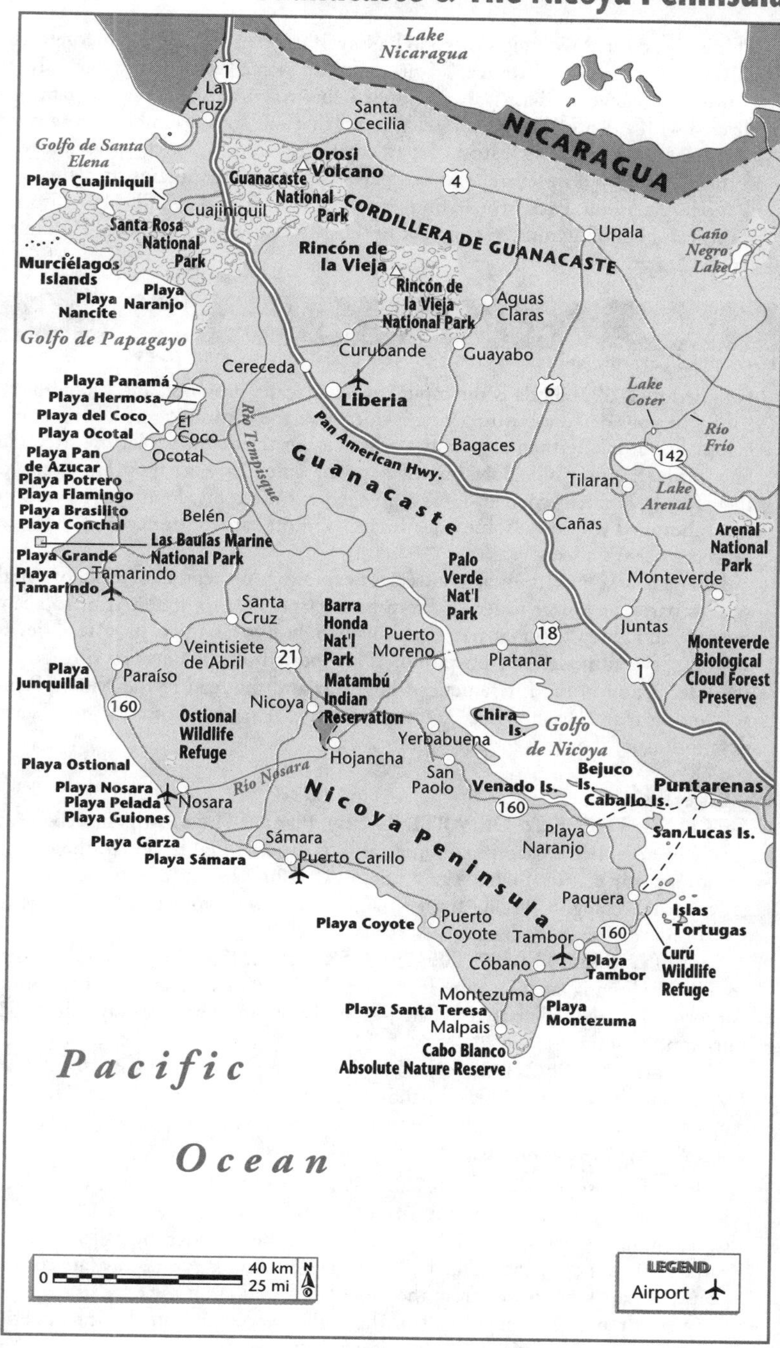

Lake Nicaragua
NICARAGUA
La Cruz
Santa Cecilia
Golfo de Santa Elena
Orosi Volcano
Guanacaste National Park
Playa Cuajiniquil
Cuajiniquil
CORDILLERA DE GUANACASTE
Upala
Caño Negro Lake
Santa Rosa National Park
Murciélagos Islands
Rincón de la Vieja
Rincón de la Vieja National Park
Playa Naranjo
Playa Nancite
Aguas Claras
Golfo de Papagayo
Curubande
Guayabo
Cereceda
Liberia
Playa Panamá
Playa Hermosa
Playa del Coco
Playa Ocotal
El Coco
Ocotal
Lake Coter
Río Frío
Pan American Hwy.
Bagaces
Río Tempisque
Guanacaste
Playa Pan de Azucar
Playa Potrero
Playa Flamingo
Playa Brasilito
Playa Conchal
Tilaran
Lake Arenal
Belén
Cañas
Arenal National Park
Las Baulas Marine National Park
Playa Grande
Playa Tamarindo
Tamarindo
Palo Verde Nat'l Park
Monteverde
Santa Cruz
Barra Honda Nat'l Park
Juntas
Puerto Moreno
Platanar
Veintisiete de Abril
Monteverde Biological Cloud Forest Preserve
Playa Junquillal
Paraíso
Matambú Indian Reservation
Nicoya
Ostional Wildlife Refuge
Chira Is.
Golfo de Nicoya
Yerbabuena
Hojancha
Playa Ostional
Río Nosara
Nicoya Peninsula
San Paolo
Bejuco Is.
Venado Is.
Caballo Is.
Puntarenas
Playa Nosara
Playa Pelada
Playa Guiones
Nosara
Playa Naranjo
San Lucas Is.
Sámara
Playa Garza
Playa Sámara
Puerto Carillo
Paquera
Islas Tortugas
Playa Coyote
Puerto Coyote
Tambor
Cóbano
Playa Tambor
Curú Wildlife Refuge
Montezuma
Playa Montezuma
Playa Santa Teresa
Malpais
Cabo Blanco Absolute Nature Reserve
Pacific Ocean
0
40 km
25 mi
N
LEGEND
Airport

This is big country, with big views and big sky. If it weren't for those rain forest–clad volcanoes in the distance, you might swear you were in Texas. However, Guanacaste hasn't always looked this way. At one time this land was covered with a dense, though fairly dry, forest that was cut for lumber and to create pasturelands for grazing cattle. Today, that dry tropical forest exists only in remnants preserved in several national parks. Up in the mountains, in **Rincón de la Vieja National Park**, you'll find not only forests and wildlife but also hot springs and bubbling mud pots similar to those in Yellowstone National Park in the United States.

1 Liberia

134½ miles (217km) NW of San José; 82 miles (132km) NW of Puntarenas

Founded in 1769, Liberia is the capital of Guanacaste province, and though it can hardly be considered a bustling city, it does have the distinction of having a more colonial atmosphere than almost any other city in the country. Narrow streets are lined with charming old adobe homes, many of which have ornate stone accents on their facades, carved wooden doors, and aged red-tile roofs. Many have beautiful, large shuttered windows (some don't even have iron bars for protection) that open onto the narrow streets.

Liberia is best looked upon as a base for exploring this region, or as an overnight stop as part of a longer itinerary. From here it's possible to do day trips to nearby beaches and three national parks, although only two of them have facilities for visitors. Several moderately priced hotels are located on the outskirts of Liberia at the intersection of the Interamerican Highway and the road to the Nicoya Peninsula and its many beaches. See "Accommodations," later in this section, for detailed descriptions of the area's lodging options.

ESSENTIALS

GETTING THERE & DEPARTING **By Plane** The airstrip in Liberia has finally been cleared to accept commercial international flights. So far, the traffic is predominantly charter flights. Only **Lacsa** (☎ **800/225-2272**) flies in here regularly, with two flights weekly from Miami. Check with your travel agent, as this situation is expected to change.

Sansa (☎ **506/233-0397**, 506/233-3258, or 506/233-5330) has a daily flight to Liberia leaving at 11:45am from San José's Juan Santamaría International Airport. This flight departs for San José at 12:50pm. The one-way fare is $55; duration, 55 minutes.

Travelair (☎ **506/220-3054** or 506/232-7883) has daily flights to Liberia at 8:20am and 3pm from Tobías Bolaños International Airport in Pavas. This flight stops first in Tamarindo. Return flights leave Liberia at 9:20am and 4pm. Fares are $88 one way; $146 round-trip.

By Bus Express buses (☎ **506/222-1650**) leave **San José** daily at 6, 7, 9, and 11:30am and 1, 3, 4, 6, and 8pm from Calle 14 between Avenidas 1 and 3. The ride is 4 hours. A one-way fare costs $3.20. From **Puntarenas**, buses leave at 5:30, 7, and 9:30am, noon, and 5pm. The ride takes 2½ hours. A one-way fare costs $2.

Buses depart for San José from the Liberia bus station on the edge of town, 200 meters north and 100 meters east of the main intersection on the Interamerican Highway. Express buses for San José leave daily at 4:30, 6, 7:30, and 10am and 12:30, 2, 4, 6, and 8pm. To reach **Monteverde**, take any Puntarenas or San José bus leaving before 1pm. Get off at the Río Lagarto Bridge, walk to the dirt road up to Santa Elena, and catch the Puntarenas/Santa Elena bus, which passes here at approximately 3:15pm. For information on getting to various beaches, see the sections below. The ride takes around 2½ to 3 hours.

By Car Take the Interamerican Highway west from San José and follow the signs for Nicaragua and the Guanacaste beaches. It takes approximately 4 hours to get to Liberia.

ORIENTATION The highway passes slightly to the west of town. There are several hotels and gas stations at the intersection with the main road into town. If you turn east into town, you'll come to the central park in less than a kilometer.

NEARBY GUIDED TOURS

If you're staying in Liberia and want to tour the surrounding national parks with a guide or even visit one of the nearby beaches, contact **TAM Tours** (☎ and fax **506/667-0098**) or **Guanacaste Tours** (☎ and fax **506/222-9047**). Both of these companies offer a wide range of tours in the region. One of the more popular is a boat tour down the Bebedero River to Palo Verde National Park, which is south of Cañas and is best known for its migratory bird populations. There's also a horseback trip up through the cloud forest on Miravalles Volcano, which is north of Cañas.

NEARBY RAFTING TRIPS

Leisurely raft trips (with little white water) are offered by **Safaris Corobici** (☎ and fax **506/669-1091**; e-mail: safaris@sol.racsa.co.cr), about 25 miles (40km) south of Liberia. They have 2-hour ($35), 3-hour ($43), and half-day ($60) trips that are great for families and bird-watchers. Along the way you may see many of the area's more exotic animal residents: howler monkeys, iguanas, caimans, coatimundis, otters, toucans, parrots, motmots, trogons, and many other species of birds. Aside from your binoculars and camera, a bathing suit and sunscreen are the only things you'll need. Safaris Corobici is based on the main highway, just before the Hotel Hacienda La Pacifica. They also run trips on the Bebedero River.

EXPLORING RINCÓN DE LA VIEJA NATIONAL PARK

This national park begins on the flanks of the Rincón de la Vieja volcano and includes this volcano's active crater, as well as several others. Down lower, you'll find an area of geothermal activity similar to Yellowstone National Park in the United States. Fumaroles, geysers, and hot pools cover this small area, creating a bizarre, otherworldly landscape. Its main entrance is situated 15½ miles (25km) northeast of Liberia, down a badly rutted dirt road. There are several lodges located around the perimeter of the park, and all offer guided hikes and horseback rides into the park. In addition to hot springs and mud pots, you can explore waterfalls, a lake, and volcanic craters. The bird watching here is excellent, and the views out across the pasturelands to the Pacific Ocean are stunning.

There are several excellent trails inside the Rincón de la Vieja National Park. More energetic hikers can tackle the 5 miles (8km) up to the summit and explore the several craters and beautiful lakes up here. On a clear day, you'll be rewarded with a fabulous view of the plains of Guanacaste and the Pacific Ocean below. The easiest hiking is the gentle **Las Pailas loop**. This 2-mile (3km) trail is just off Las Espuelas park entrance and passes by several bubbling mudpots and steaming fumaroles. Crossing one river you'll either have to take off your shoes or get them wet. The whole loop takes around 2 hours.

My favorite hike here is to the **Blue Lake and La Cangrega Waterfall**. This 3-mile (5km) trail passes through several different life zones, including dry forest, transitional moist forest, and open savannah. A variety of birds and mammals are commonly sighted. At the end of your 2-hour hike, you can take a lunch break at the aptly named Blue Lake, where a 100-foot waterfall empties into the small pond, whose crystal blue hues are amazing.

The entrance fee for this park is $6 per person per day. Camping will cost you an extra $1.50 per person per day. There are actually two entrances and camping areas here, the **Santa Maria** and **Las Espuelas** ranger stations. The latter is by far the more popular and accessible, and it's closer to the action. Here you'll find two small camping areas near each other. I recommend the one closer to the river, although the bathroom and shower facilities are 100 yards away, at the other site.

ACCOMMODATIONS

IN TOWN

Moderate

Hotel El Sitio. Apdo. 134-5000, Liberia, Guanacaste. ☎ **506/666-1211.** Fax 506/666-2059. 52 units. A/C TV TEL. $65 double; $75 triple; $85 quad. AE, MC, V.

Located about 80 yards west of the main intersection on the road to Santa Cruz and the beaches, this hotel follows the same basic Spanish-influenced hacienda style as Las Espuelas and offers similar amenities. Throughout the hotel, there are red-tile floors and original paintings of local Guanacaste scenes on the walls. All the rooms have been remodeled, and they now have cool tile floors instead of carpeting and newer air-conditioning units. The pool area is shady (a welcome relief from the strong Guanacaste sun), and there's even one of the famous pre-Columbian stone spheres in the garden. Beside the large pool, there's a rancho-style bar/restaurant. Other amenities and services include horseback riding, bike rentals, a children's play area, a whirlpool tub, tour arrangements, and a car-rental desk.

Hotel Las Espuelas. Apdo. 88-5000, Liberia, Guanacaste. ☎ **800/245-8420** in the U.S. and Canada, or 506/239-2000. Fax 506/239-2405. www.costasol.co.cr. E-mail: hherradu@sol.racsa.co.cr. 44 units. A/C TV TEL. $68 double; $78 triple. AE, DC, MC, V.

This hotel is located on the Interamerican Highway, 1¼ miles (2km) south of Liberia. The name means "spurs" and is a reference to this being cowboy country, but despite the rugged epithet, this is the most luxurious hotel in Liberia. The open-air lobby and adjacent dining room and bar all have the feel of a modern hacienda. Surrounding the hotel are spacious gardens shaded by huge old guanacaste trees. The trees and garden together give this hotel an oasislike feel. The guest rooms are attractive, though a bit small, and have polished tile floors. In the bathroom, you'll find a basket of toiletries, which is a rarity in Costa Rican hotels.

The restaurant here serves moderately priced international and Costa Rican meals. There's a small bar adjacent to the restaurant and a modest casino open nightly from 7pm until the last bettor calls it quits. Las Espuelas has a helpful tour desk, conference facilities, and a small swimming pool.

Inexpensive

Hotel Guanacaste. Apdo. 251-5000 (25 meters west and 100 meters south of the bus station), Liberia, Guanacaste. ☎ **506/666-0085.** Fax 506/666-2287. 29 units. $15 double; $19 triple; $23 quad. MC, V.

This economical little hotel is primarily a hostel-type establishment catering to young travelers on a tight budget. In addition to the simply furnished rooms, there's a basic soda serving cheap Tico meals. The management here can help arrange trips to nearby national parks and tell you about other interesting budget accommodations, including campgrounds, in the area. The two newest rooms here are doubles with air-conditioning and cost slightly more. You'll find this basic hotel around the corner from Hotel Bramadero.

✪ **Nuevo Hotel Boyeros.** Apdo. 85, Liberia, Guanacaste. ☎ **506/666-0722** or 506/666-0995. Fax 506/666-2529. 70 units. A/C TEL. $32 double; $39 triple. AE, MC, V.

You'll find this economical hotel just before the main Liberia intersection on the Interamerican Highway, and though it isn't as attractively landscaped as other hotels in town, it's good in a pinch (especially at these prices). Arches with turned wooden railings and a red-tile roof give this two-story, motel-style building a Spanish feel. In the courtyard of the hotel are two pools—one for adults and one for children—and a rancho bar/snack bar. All the rooms have a private balcony or patio overlooking the pool. The best and coolest rooms are on the second floor of the east wing. The small restaurant is open 24 hours and serves meals ranging in price from $3 to $8.

✪ **Posada del Tope.** Calle Real, Liberia, Guanacaste. ☎ **506/666-3876.** Fax 506/666-2136. 8 units (2 with bathroom). $10–$13 double; $13–$15 triple. Rates include breakfast. AE, MC, V.

This humble little pension is nothing fancy, but the rooms and shared baths are clean, the owners are friendly and helpful, and it's a real bargain. Only one room has a real double bed; the rest have either one, two, or three single beds. There's safe parking, and guests have kitchen privileges. The nicest thing about this hotel is the fact that it's housed in a wonderfully restored traditional colonial home, with high ceilings, big shuttered windows facing the street, and hefty wooden trim all around. The hotel is located 1½ blocks south of the central park.

Near Cañas

Moderate

✪ **Hotel Hacienda La Pacífica.** Apdo. 8-5700, Cañas, Guanacaste. ☎ **506/669-0266** or 506/669-0050. Fax 506/669-0555. 33 units. $70 double; $80 triple; $90 quad. AE, MC, V.

If you want a central location for exploring the national parks of this region, there are few better choices than the Hacienda La Pacífica. Originally started as a research facility and wild-animal rehabilitation center, the hotel is now a spacious mini–resort hotel with attractive grounds, organized tours and activities, marked trails, and an inviting pool. The hotel is located near the banks of the gentle Corobici River, which is a good place for bird watching. Though the hotel is 25 miles (40km) south of Liberia, it's still convenient for visiting Palo Verde National Park and the Lomas Barbudal Biological Reserve, as well as Santa Rosa and Rincón de la Vieja national parks. Rooms vary in size, though all have tile floors and a patio of some sort. The larger rooms have private sun patios as well as small, courtyardlike walled-in patios accessed through sliding glass doors that make the rooms quite bright. High ceilings keep them cool. The open-air restaurant is shady and cool and serves moderately priced meals. The lodge offers a number of services, including horseback riding ($10 per hour), bike rentals ($3 per hour), guided walks ($15), rafting trips ($35 for 2 hours), and tours to the different national parks. On the grounds, you'll also find a restored 19th-century adobe house and trails that pass through some dry forest along the banks of the Corobici River.

Near Rincón de la Vieja National Park

Moderate

Rincón de la Vieja Mountain Lodge. Apdo. 114-5000, Liberia, Guanacaste. ☎ **506/256-8206** or 506/695-5553. Fax 506/256-5410. E-mail: rincon@sol.racsa.co.cr. 27 units. $51 double; $69 triple; $84 quad. AE, MC, V.

This is the closest lodge to the Las Pailas mud pots and the Azufrale hot springs. The rustic lodge is surrounded by grasslands that conjure up images of the African savannah. It's at the end of a very rough road and feels very remote. The polished-wood main lodge looks like a cross between a ranch hacienda and a mountain cabin. There's a long veranda set with chairs, and inside are a small lounge and dining room with long tables for communal meals. Some of the rooms are quite small, while others have lots of space. Most have hammocks on their verandas, and several back up to a small stream. Camping is permitted here, but it's best to reserve the space in advance. Meals, which are simple but hearty Tico fare, will cost you $26 to $30 a day (depending on whether you take a box lunch with you into the park, or eat a full sit-down lunch back at the hotel). The lodge offers numerous day-long tours either on foot or on horseback and also runs an extensive canopy tour, which takes you on a high-wire trip to nine different treetop platforms, beginning with a manual ascent up a towering ceiba tree. If you're driving, follow the directions to the Hacienda Lodge Guachepelin and continue driving on this dirt road for another 4¼ miles (7km), bearing right at the turnoff for the park entrance. Transportation from Liberia can be arranged at an additional cost.

Santa Clara Lodge. Apdo. 17-5000, Quebrada Grande de Liberia, Guanacaste. ☎ **506/666-4054** or 506/391-8766. Fax 506/666-4047. E-mail: stclodge@asstcar.co.cr. 9 units (none with bathroom), 1 cabin (with bathroom). $30–$40 double; $45 cabin. Meals are an additional $17 per person per day. AE, MC, V.

Santa Clara Lodge is located in the foothills of Guanacaste's volcanic mountains on a working dairy farm, where guests are even invited to participate in the morning milking. With shady grounds on the banks of a small river, the setting is quite tranquil. You can sip a drink beneath the thatch-roofed palapa and listen to the chickens clucking in the yard, or go for a swim in the mineral-water pool. The lodge is well suited for exploring the region if you have your own car or want to arrange tours. Santa Rosa, Guanacaste, and Rincón de la Vieja national parks are all within an hour's drive. You can also hike through field and forest to four different waterfalls. Guided hikes ($10) and horseback rides ($20 to $50) can be arranged, and I particularly recommend the trip to the hot springs. Rooms are simply furnished, as you might expect on a working ranch, and only the cabin has a private bathroom. For those wishing to rough it (up to a point), it's also possible to camp here. Meals are filling Tico fare, with steaks, chicken and fries, salads, and fruits, along with the requisite rice and beans. To reach the lodge, head north from Liberia for about 14¼ miles (23km) and turn right on the road to Quebrada Grande. In Quebrada Grande, turn right at the soccer field and continue for another 2½ miles (4km). You can also arrange transportation from Liberia to the lodge if you phone in advance.

Inexpensive

Hacienda Lodge Guachipelin. Apdo. 636-4050, Alajuela. ☎ **506/442-2818** or 506/284-2049. Fax 506/442-1910. www.guachipelin.com. E-mail: hacienda@intnet.co.cr. 13 units (5 with bathroom). $24–$37 double. Rates include breakfast. AE, MC, V.

Located 14¼ miles (23km) northeast of Liberia on the edge of Rincón de la Vieja National Park, this rustic lodge is housed in a 112-year-old ranch house. The rooms are pretty basic, and some are actually in an old bunkhouse. The ranch is still in operation today, and in addition to exploring the park, you can ride horses and commune with the pigs, dairy cows, and beef cattle. It isn't easy to get to the lodge, and once you arrive you'll need a few days to explore the park, so plan on taking all your meals here and going on a few guided tours. A horseback tour with a bilingual guide will cost around $34 per person for a half-day ride. This is one of the closest lodges to the thermal springs (6.2 miles) and bubbling mud pots (3 miles) of Rincón de la Vieja National Park. Horseback rides can be arranged to the geothermal areas, as well as to various lakes, the top of a nearby dormant volcano, and some beautiful waterfalls. If you're driving a car, you'd better have four-wheel drive or high clearance (though in the dry season, mid-November through April, it's sometimes passable in a regular car). To reach the lodge, drive about 3 miles (5km) north of Liberia and turn right on the dirt road to Curubande, which you'll pass through in about 7½ miles (12km). Continue on this road for another 3½ miles (6km), passing through the ranch's gate, before arriving at the lodge. When you contact the lodge to make a reservation, you can arrange to be picked up in Liberia for around $8 per person.

DINING

There are plenty of standard Tico dining choices in Liberia, yet most visitors choose to eat in their hotel's dining room. In town, the most popular alternatives are **Pizzeria Pronto**, which is located 100 meters north of the visitor information center and serves a wide range of pizzas baked in a clay oven, or one of the sodas around the central park. Other choices include:

Restaurant Rincón Corobici. Interamerican Highway, 3 miles (5km) north of Cañas. ☎ **506/669-1234.** Reservations accepted. Main courses $2.50–$25. AE, MC, V. Daily 8am–10pm. COSTA RICAN/INTERNATIONAL.

The food here is decidedly mediocre, but the setting, particularly during the day, more than makes up for it. While there's plenty of covered seating in the main open-air dining room, you'll want to choose a table on the wooden deck, which overlooks a beautiful section of the Corobici River. The sound of rushing water tumbling over the rocks in the riverbed is soothing accompaniment to the simple but filling meals. The whole fried fish is your best choice here, though you can also have steaks, lobster, shrimp, and sandwiches. This restaurant makes an ideal lunch stop if you're heading to or coming from Liberia, or have just done a rafting trip on the Corobici River. Be sure to try the fried yuca chips—you may never go back to french fries.

Restaurante Pókopí. 100 meters west of the main intersection in Liberia on the road to Santa Cruz. ☎ **506/666-1036.** Fax 506/666-1528. Main courses $4.50–$16. AE, MC, V. Daily 11am–10pm. CONTINENTAL.

It doesn't look like much from the outside, but this tiny restaurant has a surprising amount of class. An even more pleasant surprise is the unusual (for rural Costa Rica) variety of continental dishes on the menu. Order one of their delicious daiquiris while you peruse the menu, which is on a wooden cutting board. You have your choice of mahimahi prepared five different ways, pizza, chicken cordon bleu, chicken in wine sauce, and other equally delectable dishes. However, for a real surprise, order the chateaubriand. It comes to your table with great flair, surrounded by succulent fresh vegetables and a tomato stuffed with peas. Be sure to dine early if you want a quiet meal; attached to the restaurant is a disco that swings into action most nights at 9pm. If you want to milk the local nightlife, you can combine dinner and disco. And you thought you were out in the sticks.

2 La Cruz

172 miles (277km) NW of San José; 37 miles (59km) NW of Liberia; 12 miles (20km) S of Peñas Blancas

La Cruz is a tiny hilltop town near the Nicaraguan border. The town itself has little to offer beyond a fabulous view of Bahia Salinas, but it does serve as a gateway to the nearly deserted beaches down below, a few mountain lodges bordering the nearby Santa Rosa and Guanacaste national parks, and the Nicaraguan border crossing at Peñas Blancas.

ESSENTIALS

GETTING THERE & DEPARTING **By Plane** The nearest airport with regularly scheduled service is in Liberia.

By Bus Buses (☎ 506/222-3006) leave San José daily for **Peñas Blancas** at 5, 7:30, and 10am and 1:30 and 4pm from Calle 14 between Avenidas 3 and 5. These buses stop in La Cruz and will also let you off at the entrance to Santa Rosa National Park. The ride to La Cruz takes 6 hours. A one-way fare costs $5.40. Alternatively, you can take a bus from San José to Liberia. Buses leave Liberia for Peñas Blancas at 5:30, 8:30, and 11am and 2 and 4:30pm. The ride takes about 1 hour to La Cruz and costs $1.75.

Buses depart for San José from Peñas Blancas daily at 5, 7:15, and 10:30am, noon, and 1:30 and 3:30pm, passing through La Cruz about 20 minutes later. Buses leave Liberia for San José daily at 4:30, 6, 7:30, and 10am and 12:30, 2, 4, 6, and 8pm.

By Car Take the Interamerican Highway west from San José and follow the signs for Nicaragua and the Guanacaste beaches. When you reach Liberia, head straight through the major intersection, following signs to Peñas Blancas and the Nicaraguan border. It takes approximately 5 hours to get to La Cruz.

ORIENTATION The highway passes slightly to the east of town. You'll pass the turnoffs to Santa Rosa National Park, Playa Cuajiniquil and Los Inocentes Lodge before reaching the town. To reach the beaches of Bahia Salinas, head into La Cruz to El Mirador Ehecatl and then follow the roads and signs down to the water.

EXPLORING SANTA ROSA NATIONAL PARK

Best known for its remote, pristine beaches, reached by several kilometers of hiking trails or a four-wheel-drive vehicle, Santa Rosa National Park is a fine place to ramble, watch sea turtles nest, and surf. Located 18½ miles (30km) north of Liberia and 18½ miles (13km) south of La Cruz on the Interamerican Highway, it covers the Santa Elena Peninsula and has the distinction of being Costa Rica's first national park. Unlike other national parks, it was founded not to preserve the land but to preserve a building, known as **La Casona**, which played an important role in Costa Rican independence. It was here, in 1856, that Costa Rican forces fought the decisive Battle of Santa Rosa, forcing the U.S.-backed soldier of fortune William Walker and his men to flee into Nicaragua. Inside the restored ranch house you'll find relics from and representations of that historic battle. This small museum and monument is open daily from 8am until 4:30pm.

It costs $6 per person to enter the park. Camping is allowed at several sites within the park, but generally you must reserve in advance. A campsite costs $1.50 per person per day. There's camping near the entrance and principal ranger station, as well as at La Casona, and down by Playas Naranjo and Nancite.

THE BEACHES Five miles (8km) west of La Casona down a rugged road that is impassable during the rainy season is **Playa Naranjo**. Even during the dry season, this road is rough on four-wheel-drive vehicles. Two and a half miles (4km) north of Playa Naranjo along a hiking trail that follows the beach you'll find **Playa Nancite**. **Playa Blanca** is 13 miles (21km) down a dirt road from Caujiniquil, which itself is 12½ miles (20km) north of the park entrance.

Playa Nancite is known for its *arribadas* (grouped egg-layings) of olive Ridley sea turtles, which come ashore to nest by the tens of thousands each year in October. Playa Naranjo is best known for its perfect surfing waves, which break at Witch's Rock just offshore. On the northern side of the peninsula is Playa Blanca, a beautiful, remote white-sand beach with calm waters. This beach is reached by way of the village of Caujiniquil and is accessible only during the dry season. However, if you reach the small village of Caujiniquil and then head north for a few kilometers, you will come to a small annex to the national park system at Playa Junquillal (not to be confused with the more-developed beach of the same name farther south in Guanacaste). This is a lovely little beach that is also often good for swimming. The park entrance is $6 per person per day, and it costs $1.50 per person to camp. There are basic bathroom and shower facilities here.

WHAT TO DO IN LA CRUZ

There's not really much to do in La Cruz except catch a sunset and some ceviche at the **El Mirador Ehecatl** (no phone). This humble little restaurant holds a commanding view of Bahia Salinas and serves up hearty Tico standards at only slghtly inflated prices. Similarly, there's not really much reason to stay in La Cruz, but if you must, check out **Amalia's Inn** (☎ and fax **506/679-9181**), which is a simple little hotel with a small pool and good views of the bay.

ACCOMMODATIONS NEAR LA CRUZ

Three Corners Bolaños Bay. P.O. Box 773019, Heredia. ☎ and fax **506/260-0527,** or ☎ 506/283-8901. E-mail: suschrcr@sol.racsa.co.cr. 72 units. $89 double; $114 suite. AE, MC, V.

This new hotel occupies a beautiful spot in front of Isla Bolaños on Bahia Salinas. However, this hotel is quickly becoming a specialized destination appealing primarily to windsurfers, due to the fact that strong, steady winds buffet the bay throughout the Guanacaste dry season and periodically during the rainy season. When these winds are really howling, it makes most other activities here impossible or uncomfortable, and simply sitting by the pool reading a book can be quite a challenge. The rooms are rather disappointing for this price range. They have all the standard ammenities, including bidets, but lack any sense of style or individuality. Only 18 of the rooms have an ocean view. All have small patios. The suites have two bedrooms sharing one bathroom. The restaurant is located under one of the hotel's two immense peaked thatch roofs, and the reception area is under the other. Food and service here are inconsistent at best. In addition to a full-service wind-surfing center, the hotel can arrange a wide range of tours and activities. To reach Three Corners Bolaños Bay, go into La Cruz and head toward the water, or ask directions to El Mirador Ehecatl. Take the dirt road that passes to the right of this popular restaurant (as you face the water) and then follow the roads and signs to the hotel. If you arrive in La Cruz by bus, you'll either have to arrange pick up with the hotel or hire a cab, which should cost around $10.

✪ **Los Inocentes Lodge.** Apdo. 228-3000, Heredia. ☎ and fax **506/265-5484** or 506/679-9190. Fax 506/265-4385. www.arweb.com/orosi. E-mail: orosina@sol.racsa.co.cr. 11 units, 8 cabins. $59 per person (includes 3 meals). AE, V.

Set on a ranch 8½ miles (14km) from La Cruz, near the Nicaraguan border and bordering Guanacaste National Park, Los Inocentes is popular with naturalists interested in exploring the nearby dry and transitional forests. Horseback rides through the ranch ($5 per hour, with guide) are the most popular activities, and in fact, the ranch does a brisk business in tours coming up here from various Guanacaste beaches to do some riding. The rooms are all located in the main lodge building, which dates back to 1890. They are comfortable, though basic, and have tile or wood floors. Some have high ceilings, and most open onto large verandas with hammocks and wicker rocking chairs. Each room has access to a private bathroom, but most are not attached to the room and some folks on the second floor even have to go downstairs to their bathroom on the first floor. There are eight separate cabins located about 100 yards away from the main lodge. These are two-bedroom affairs better suited for families and small groups. Meals are simple but filling. In addition to horseback riding, there are nature trails and a swimming pool. There's a great view of Orosi Volcano from the lodge, and the bird watching here is excellent.

3 Playa Hermosa & Playa Panamá

160 miles (258km) NW of San José; 25 miles (40km) SW of Liberia

Playa Hermosa means "beautiful beach," which is an appropriate name for this crescent of sand. Surrounded by dry, rocky hills, this curving gray-sand beach is long and wide and rarely crowded, despite the presence of the Costa del Cacique condo development and the Meliá Sol Playa Hermosa Hotel on the hill at the north end of the beach. Fringing the beach is a swath of trees that stays surprisingly green right through the dry season. The shade provided by these trees is a big part of the beach's appeal. Rocky headlands jut out into the surf at both ends of the beach, and at the base of these rocks you'll find tide pools that are fun to explore.

Beyond Playa Hermosa, you'll find Playa Panamá and the calm waters of Bahia Culebra, which has recently been transformed from one of the most remote and underdeveloped spots in Guanacaste to host not one, but two large resort hotels. However, since these resorts are located slightly north of Playa Panamá proper, it's still possible to enjoy the quiet beauty of this big, calm beach.

ESSENTIALS

GETTING THERE & DEPARTING **By Plane** The nearest airport with regularly scheduled service is in Liberia. From here you can arrange a taxi to bring you the rest of the way. The ride takes about 45 minutes and should cost around $20.

By Bus Express buses leave San José daily at 3:20pm from Calle 12 between Avenidas 5 and 7, stopping first at Playa Hermosa and next at Playa Panamá, 2 miles (3km) farther north. One-way fare for the 5-hour trip is $3.50.

Alternatively, you can take a bus from San José to Liberia (see "Liberia," above, for details) and then take a bus from Liberia to Playa Hermosa and Playa Panamá. Buses (☎ **506/666-1249**) leave Liberia for these two beaches daily at 7:30 and 11:30am and 3:30, 5:30, and 7pm. The trip lasts 45 minutes. A one-way fare costs $1. During the high season, extra buses from Liberia are sometimes added. Alternatively, you can take a bus to Playa del Coco, from which the playas are a quick taxi ride away.

One bus departs for San José daily at 5am from Playa Panamá, with a stop in Playa Hermosa along the way. Buses to Liberia leave Playa Panamá at 6 and 8:30am

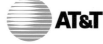

and 12:30, 4:30, and 7pm, stopping in Playa Hermosa a few minutes later. Ask at your hotel where to catch the bus.

By Car Follow the directions for getting to Liberia, then head west toward Santa Cruz. Just past the village of Comunidad, turn right. In about 7 miles (11km) you'll come to a fork in the road. Take the right fork. These roads are relatively well marked, and a host of prominent hotel billboards should make it easy enough to find the beach. It takes about 5 hours from San José.

ORIENTATION There are no real towns here, just a few houses and hotels on and near the beach. You'll come to Playa Hermosa first, followed by Playa Panamá a few kilometers farther along the same road. The road ends at the Blue Bay Village Beach Resort.

Playa Hermosa is about a 500-yard-long stretch of beach, with all the hotels laid out along this stretch. From the main road, which continues on to Playa Panamá, there are about three access roads heading off perpendicular, directly toward the beach, and connected by other access roads. All the hotels are well marked, with signs pointing guests down the right access road.

VISITOR INFORMATION & EQUIPMENT RENTAL In the middle of Playa Hermosa, you'll find **Aqua Sport** (☎ **506/672-0050**; fax 506/672-0060), which is both the visitor information center and water-sports equipment rental center for Playa Hermosa. Kayaks, sailboards, canoes, bicycles, beach umbrellas, snorkel gear, and parasails are all available for rental at fairly reasonable rates. This is also where you'll find the local post office, public phones, a small supermarket, and a restaurant (see "Dining," below).

OUTDOOR PURSUITS

Both beaches are usually good for swimming, although Playa Panamá is slightly more protected. If you want to do some diving while you're here, check in with **Bill Beard's Diving Safaris** (☎ **506/672-0012;** fax 506/672-0231; 800-779-0055 in the U.S.; e-mail for reservations: billbeards@netrunner.net; e-mail for weather conditions: diving@sol.racsa.co.cr; web page: www.diving-safaris.com) at the Sol Playa Hermosa Hotel at the north end of the beach. Bill Beard is a long-established and respected dive operator. He's got a large shop and offers a wide range of trips to numerous dive spots and also offers night dives, multiday packages, certification classes, and Nitrox dives. Alternatively, you can check out the Costa Smeralda Hotel or Blue Bay Village Beach Resort. A two-tank dive should run between $60 and $90 per person.

For Guided National Park Tours, both **Tam** (☎ **506/670-0336**) and **Swiss Travel Services** (☎ and fax **506/667-0100**) run a wide range of trips and tours and will pick you up at any hotel in either Playa Hermosa or Playa Panamá.

ACCOMMODATIONS

VERY EXPENSIVE

Blue Bay Village Resort. Playa Arenilla, Guanacaste. ☎ **800/BLUE BAY** in the U.S., or ☎ and fax 506/672-0130. www.bluebayresorts.com. E-mail: costarica@bluebayresorts.com. 160 units. A/C TV TEL. $250 double; $345 triple; children under 12 are $50 per day. Rates are all-inclusive (including drinks). Rates slightly higher peak weeks, lower in off-season. AE, MC, V.

Just a few kilometers north of the Costa Smeralda, this was the first all-inclusive resort in the Guanacaste region. It recently changed its name and management. Most of the independent villas can be separated into two rooms or shared by a family or pair of friends. Inside, one room is equipped with a king-size bed, the other with two queen-size beds. All rooms have marble floors, pine ceilings, large bathrooms, and small private patios or balconies. The resort is quite spread out, so if you don't want to do a lot of walking or wait for the golf cart shuttles, ask for a room near the pool and restaurants. If you want a good view, ask for one on the hill overlooking the bay. For those seeking more isolation, there are rooms located in the dry forest behind the resort. The hotel has a host of organized sports and activities, including daily programs for children. All nonmotorized sports equipment, activities, and classes are included. The hotel has its own small crescent-shaped swath of beach, which is very calm and protected for swimming.

Dining/Diversions: The hotel's most formal restaurant is Da Vinci, serving northern Italian cuisine in an elegant indoor setting. Reservations and proper attire are required. Breakfasts and more casual meals can be taken at the open-air El Papagayo restaurant, overlooking the pool. There's also a pool-side bar and a snack bar down at the spa. You can spend your evenings at the new theater or disco complex.

Amenities: A three-tiered main pool, a small lap pool, and a resistance lap pool; a well-equipped fitness center, with Nautilus machines, free weights, Jacuzzis, a steam room, sauna, health bar, and daily classes. There's also a tennis court, volleyball courts, water-sports equipment, nature trails, children's programs, game room, conference center, tour desk, beauty salon, boutique, room service, laundry service, and valet parking.

EXPENSIVE

Sol Playa Hermosa Hotel and Villas. Playa Hermosa, Guanacaste. ☎ **800/572-9934** or 506/290-0565. Fax 506/290-0566. E-mail: hermosol@sol.racsa.co.cr www.loria.com/sol. 54 units, 47 villas. A/C TV TEL. Dec–Apr and July, $110 double, $195–$225; villa May–June and Aug–Nov, $81 double, $146–$169 villa. AE, DC, MC, V.

This is the oldest and most established resort in the area. In 1997, it was taken over by the Meliá hotel chain, and it remains the lone major hotel on Playa Hermosa. Set on a steep hillside at the north end of the beach, the Sol Playa Hermosa was built with Mediterranean styling. The hotel is at the top of the hill, about 300 yards from the beach—you'll need to be in good shape to stay here. Luckily, the two pools are both at the top of the hill, so if you're staying up here, you don't have to walk down to the beach to take a swim. The villas are new units located just off the entrance. All have kitchens, satellite TVs, and modern furnishings. Quite a few even have their own small swimming pool or Jacuzzi, although only a few of the newest villas, built high on the hill, have really worthwile views. The hotel rooms are all well maintained and quite standard for this price range; most have excellent views.

Just so you don't get too confused, this whole complex was formerly the Condovac Hotel and Villas. However, the Meliá chain has divorced itself from the older villas, which are spread along the hillside below the main hotel, and now only operates the new villas near the entrance.

Dining/Diversions: The hotel has numerous dining options. El Roble is the hotel's most formal dining room and specializes in steaks. El Pelicano is a casual buffet that is open throughout the day. Heliconias is a snack bar by the pool at the villas. Bars include Frutas y Flores, the lobby bar, and Chico and Pepe, the hotel's poolside disco/bar.

Amenities: There are two freshwater swimming pools, a tennis court, a dive shop, a tour desk, a minimarket, and a gift shop. Services include diving-equipment rentals, scuba classes, dive trips, and jet-ski rentals.

Moderate

✪ **El Velero Hotel.** Playa Hermosa, Guanacaste. ☎ **506/672-0036.** Fax 506/672-0016. 13 units. $58–$86 double; rates slightly higher during Christmas and Easter, and slightly lower during off-season. AE, MC, V.

This small Canadian-owned hotel is the nicest moderately priced place on Playa Hermosa. It's located right on the beach and has its own small swimming pool beside an open-air bar. White walls and polished tile floors give El Velero a Mediterranean flavor. The guest rooms are large, and those on the second floor have high ceilings. The upper third of these room's walls are screens, so there's plenty of cross ventilation. Fans also help keep the rooms cool. The more expensive rooms have air-conditioning. Bathrooms are small and have showers only. Various tours, horseback riding, and fishing trips can be arranged through the hotel; however, the most popular excursions are the full-day and sunset cruises on the hotel's 38-foot sailboat. The hotel has its own popular little restaurant, which offers a good selection of meat, fish, and shrimp dishes in the $6 to $14 range.

Sula Sula. Playa Panamá, Guanacaste. ☎ **506/672-0116.** Fax 506/672-0117. 20 units, 4 cabins. A/C TV TEL. $78 double; $108 cabin; lower rates in the off-season. MC, V.

This new complex is the only real hotel right on Playa Panamá. Spread out under the shade of numerous guanacaste trees, Sula Sula has the feel of a miniresort. The rooms are all large, cool, and clean, with high ceilings, red Mexican tile floors, and large desk and bureau. Each ahas a small patio facing the pool. The cabins have two bedrooms, a sitting room, and a kitchenette but no air-conditioning. There's a snack bar out by the pool and a more formal restaurant near the reception.

✪ **Villa del Sueño.** Playa Hermosa, Guanacaste. ☎ and fax **506/672-0027.** Fax 506/672-0028. E-mail: delsueno@sol.racsa.co.cr. 15 units. $44.50–$54.50 double; lower rates in the off-season. AE, MC, V.

Although this hotel is not right on the beach (it's located on the first road to your left as you reach Playa Hermosa), its well-groomed lawns and gardens feel like an oasis in the dust and heat of a Guanacaste dry season. Villa del Sueño offers clean and comfortable rooms at a good price, and the restaurant here is one of the best in Playa Hermosa. All the rooms have cool tiled floors, high hardwood ceilings, ceiling fans, and well-placed windows for cross ventilation. The second-floor superior rooms have more space and larger windows. For an extra $10 you can have one of the four air-conditioned rooms. There's a small pool in the center courtyard. Meals are served in an open-air restaurant in the main building. The folks here manage a neighboring condominium development, which has additional apartment and efficiency units available for nightly and weekly rental. They can also help with a variety of tour arrangements and have a small gift shop.

Inexpensive

Cabinas Playa Hermosa. Apdo. 117, Liberia, Guanacaste. ☎ and fax **506/672-0046.** 22 units. $34 double; $42 triple; $50 quad; lower rates available in the off-season. V.

This little hotel, tucked away under shady trees, is a sprawling beachfront spread at the south end of Playa Hermosa. Each large room has a pair of Adirondack chairs on its front porch, and the beach is only a few steps away. Rooms 1 through 4 directly face the ocean, but they're also very close to the restaurant and bar and so can be noisy. The rest are located in several low buildings that run perpendicular to the beach. Even though most of the rooms are rather dark and can feel run-down, they're large, with two double beds each and a lot of closet space. Horseback riding and boat trips can be arranged. The open-air restaurant has a rustic tropical feel to it, with unfinished tree trunks holding up the roof. Seafood and homemade pasta are the specialties. Menu prices range from $3.50 to $10; service can be quite slow and inattentive. To find the hotel, turn left at the first road into Playa Hermosa. The hotel's white archway gate is down this dirt road about 1 kilometer.

DINING

In addition to the place listed below, you'll find one of the best restaurants in Playa Hermosa at the hotel **Villa del Sueño** (☎ **506/672-0026**). There is no fixed menu here, but the nightly selection of blackboard specials will please almost any palate.

Aqua Sport. On the beach in Playa Hermosa. ☎ **506/670-0450.** Reservations not necessary. Main courses $4.50–$16. AE, MC, V. Daily 9am–10pm (noon–9pm in the rainy season). CONTINENTAL.

Part of the Aqua Sport market and equipment-rental shop is a small open-air restaurant with tables of polished hardwood. The beach is only steps away, the atmosphere is very casual, and the food is much better than you'd expect from such a place. The focus is on seafood—grilled lobster for $16, shrimp à la diabla for $7.50, and huge paella or assorted seafood platters that feed four and cost $45 and $50, respectively.

4 Playa del Coco & Playa Ocotal

157 miles (253km) NW of San José; 21½ miles (35km) W of Liberia

Playa del Coco is one of the most easily accessible beaches in Guanacaste, with a paved road right down to the water, and has been a longtime popular destination with middle-class Ticos from San José. Unfortunately, many of the hotels right in town are quite run-down, and the water is neither very clean nor appealing (this is a busy fishing port). The crowds that come here like their music loud and constant, so if you're in search of a quiet retreat, stay away. On the other hand, if you're looking for a beach with inexpensive hotels, a lively nightlife, and plenty of cheap food and beer close at hand, you may enjoy Playa del Coco.

The beach, which has grayish-brown sand, is quite wide at low tide and almost nonexistent at high tide. In between high and low, it's just right. Trash can be a bit of a problem right in town; however, if you walk down the long, curving beach to the north of town, you're bound to find a nice clean spot to unfold your blanket. Better still, if you have a car, head over to **Playa Ocotal**, which is a couple of kilometers down a dirt road. This is a tiny pocket of a cove bordered by high bluffs and is quite beautiful. Playas Hermosa and Panamá are also quite close to the north.

ESSENTIALS

GETTING THERE & DEPARTING **By Plane** The nearest airport with regularly scheduled flights is in Liberia. From there you can take a bus or arrange for a taxi to take you to Playa del Coco or Playa Ocotal, which is about a 45-minute drive.

By Bus An express bus (☎ **506/222-1650**) leaves San José for Playa del Coco at 8am and 2pm daily from Calle 14 between Avenidas 1 and 3. Allow 5 hours for the trip. A one-way ticket is $3.80. From Liberia, buses to Playa del Coco leave at 5:30 and 8:15am, and 12:30, 2, and 4:30pm. A one-way ticket for the 45-minute trip costs $1.10.

The direct bus for San José leaves Playa del Coco daily at 8am and 2pm. Buses for Liberia leave at 7 and 9:15am and 2 and 6pm.

Depending on demand, the Playa del Coco buses sometimes go as far as Playa Ocotal; it's worth checking beforehand if possible. Otherwise, a taxi should cost around $5.

By Car Follow the directions for getting to Liberia and Playa Hermosa, but at the turnoff for Playa Hermosa, take the left fork instead. It takes about 5 hours from San José.

ORIENTATION Playa del Coco is a small but busy beach town. Most of its hotels and restaurants are either on the water, on the road leading into town, or on the road that heads north from San Francisco Treats. Playa Ocotal is south of Playa del Coco on a dirt road that leaves the main road just before the beach. Playa Ocotal is a collection of vacation homes, condos, and hotels, and has one bar on the beach.

FUN ON & OFF THE BEACH

There are plenty of boats anchored here at Playa del Coco, and that means plenty of opportunities to go fishing, diving, or sailing. However, the most popular activities, especially among the hordes of Ticos who come here, are hanging out on the beach, hanging out in the sodas and bars, and cruising the discos at night. If you're interested, you might be able to join a soccer match (the soccer field is in the middle of town). It's also possible to arrange horseback rides; ask at your hotel.

SCUBA DIVING Scuba diving is the most popular water sport in the area, and dive shops abound. **Mario Vargas Expeditions** (☎ **506/670-0351;** e-mail: mvexped@sol.racsa.co.cr) and **Rich Coast Diving** (☎ **506/670-0176**) are the most established and offer equipment rentals and dive trips. A two-tank dive, with equipment, should cost between $65 and $90 per person. Both also offer PADI certification courses. Rich Coast now offers multiday trips aboard a 35-foot trimaran. A 3-day/2-night excursion, with food, equipment, and diving, costs $350 to $500 per person, depending on the size of your group and the dive destinations. This trimaran is also available for the surf or fishing excursions described below.

SPORTFISHING & SAILBOAT CHARTERS Full- and half-day sportfishing excursions can be arranged through **Papagayo Sportfishing** (☎ **506/670-0354**) or **Agua Rica Yacht Charters** (☎ **506/670-0332**). A half day of fishing, with boat, captain, food, and tackle, should cost between $200 and $375; a full day should run between $400 and $700. Papagayo also arranges trips to ferry surfers up to Witches Rock for around $175 each way. Agua Rica, for its part, also charters out a couple of sailboats. The most economical option is a 4-hour cruise on its catamaran, which costs just $35 per person.

ACCOMMODATIONS

EXPENSIVE

El Ocotal Beach Resort. Apdo. 1, Playa del Coco, Guanacaste. ☎ **506/670-0321.** Fax 506/670-0083. E-mail: elocotal@sol.racsa.co.cr. 46 units, 12 bungalows,. A/C TV TEL. $80 double, $105 bungalow, $145 suite; rates higher during peak weeks and lower in the off-season. AE, DC, MC, V.

This is the most luxurious hotel in the Playa del Coco area, although, unfortunately, I've received some complaints about the quality of service. The guest rooms vary in age, though all are fairly spacious and attractively furnished. The older rooms are closer to the beach, while the rooms with the best views and greatest comfort are atop a hill overlooking a dramatic stretch of rocky coastline. Scuba diving and sportfishing are the main draws here, and package tours are available. Diminutive Playa Ocotal is one of the prettiest little beaches along this stretch of coast and offers good swimming.

Dining/Diversions: El Ocotal's primary restaurant is one of its greatest assets. The large room is surrounded on three sides by glass walls and has a stunning view of Playa Ocotal and miles of coastline. There's also patio dining. Seafood is the specialty, and the prices are moderate. El Ocotal also runs the Father Rooster restaurant on the beach, with more casual meals and service.

Amenities: Scuba classes, rentals, and trips are some of the hotel's most popular services. There are also boat excursions, fishing charters, surfing excursions, a car-rental desk, and a tour desk. The hotel's main swimming pool is quite attractive and has a little artificial waterfall. Thatched ranchos beside the pool provide shady shelter when the sun gets too strong. There are also two other pools, tennis courts, a hot tub, and a dive shop.

MODERATE

Hotel La Flor De Itabo. Apdo. 32, Playa del Coco, Guanacaste. ☎ **506/670-0292** or 506/670-0003. 16 units, 8 apts. $35–$50 double; $70 apt. for 1 to 4 people. AE, DC, MC, V.

This is perhaps the nicest hotel right in Playa del Coco, although that's not saying an awful lot, and it's not on the beach. Still, the pool is large and the grounds are lushly planted. Toucans and parrots squawk and talk amid the flowers, adding their own bright colors to an already colorful garden, and stone reproductions of pre-Columbian statues provide a touch of the mysterious. With fewer than two dozen rooms, the service here is reliably good. The most inexpensive rooms are in four bungalows, with screened windows and fans. The standard rooms are more spacious, have air-conditioning, and are attractively decorated with wood carvings and Guatemalan textiles. The apartments are located a little bit away from the main building. While they're larger than the standard and bungalow rooms, have air-conditioning, and include kitchenettes, they tend to feel a bit spartan. Italian dishes are the specialty of the restaurant, with main courses ranging from $6 to $12. The bar is decorated with flags from all over the world and is a popular hangout with sport fishers. There's even a small casino here. In addition to a pool, the hotel has a volleyball court, a children's play area, and a small park.

✪ **Hotel Villa Casa Blanca.** Apdo. 176-5019, Playa del Coco, Guanacaste. ☎ and fax **506/670-0448.** E-mail: vcblanca@sol.racsa.co.cr. 14 units. $59 double; $69 triple; $85–$95 suite. Rates include breakfast buffet. AE, MC, V.

With friendly, helpful owners, beautiful gardens, and attractive rooms, this bed-and-breakfast inn is my favorite spot in the area. Located in a new development about 500 meters from the beach, it was built in the style of a Spanish villa. All the guest rooms have their own distinct characters, and though some are a tad small, others feel quite roomy. One room has a canopy bed and a beautiful bathroom with a step-up bath. The suites are higher up and have ocean views. My favorite has a secluded patio with lush flowering plants all around. A little rancho serves as an open-air bar and breakfast area, and beside this is a pretty little lap pool with a bridge over it. Villa Casa Blanca also manages several rental houses and condos in the area, so if you plan to stay for a week or more, or need lots of room, ask about these.

INEXPENSIVE

La Luna Tica. Playa del Coco, Guanacaste. ☎ **506/670-0127.** Fax 506/670-0279. 34 units. $17 double; $22 triple; $28 quad. Lower rates in the off-season. V.

This is your best budget choice if you want to be real close to the beach. It's located just south of the soccer field, and the 15 oldest rooms are located right on the beach. These are very basic, have polished concrete floors, and are kept very clean. The newer rooms are in the annex just across the street. Five of these have air-conditioning. The nicest rooms are on the second floor; each has hardwood floors and is flanked by a cool veranda. La Luna Tica also has a restaurant right on the beach, serving Tico standards, Tex-Mex, Creole cuisine, and fish dishes at very reasonable prices.

Villa del Sol B&B. Playa del Coco, Guanacaste. ☎ and fax **506/670-0085.** E-mail: villasol@sol.racsa.co.cr. 7 units (5 with bathroom). $35–$40 double; lower rates in the off-season. MC, V.

This new bed-and-breakfast, located a kilometer north of Playa del Coco village, is a good, quiet option, with four rooms upstairs and three downstairs. All are spacious and clean and receive plenty of light. The most interesting room has a round queen-size bed, high ceilings, and views of the gardens. There's an inviting small pool with a covered barbecue area. A continental breakfast is included in the rates, and tasty dinners are prepared nightly for guests from a small menu of European-influenced dishes. There's plenty of protected parking, and the hotel can arrange a wide range of tours, diving, and fishing options. To find the hotel, just turn onto the dirt road at San Francisco Treats restaurant.

DINING

There are dozens of cheap open-air sodas at the traffic circle in the center of El Coco village. These restaurants serve Tico standards, with an emphasis on fried fish. Prices are quite low, and so is the quality for the most part. For views, you can't beat the restaurant at **El Ocotal Beach Resort**, and for desserts, lunch, or snacks there's **San Francisco Treats**, which is located on the main road into Playa del Coco, about 300 yards before you hit the beach. In addition to the places listed below, you can get excellent Italian food at the new hotel/restaurant **La Puerta del Sol** (☎ **506/670-0195**) located 200 meters north and 100 meters east of San Francisco Treats.

Helen's. 100 meters south of the ice factory. ☎ **506/670-0121.** Reservations not accepted. Main courses $4.50–$12. No credit cards. Daily 11am–10pm. COSTA RICAN/SEAFOOD.

This is a local favorite, and because Helen's husband is a fisherman, the seafood is always absolutely fresh. The ceviche comes in a big bowl and is enough for a meal. Be sure to try the lobster soup if it's on the menu.

✪ **Pato Loco Inn.** 800 meters before the beach on the main road. ☎ **506/670-0145.** Reservations not necessary. Main courses $3–$4. AE, MC, V. Fri–Wed 6–10pm. ITALIAN/PASTA.

This small Italian-run inn serves up the best pasta in these parts. Choose a spaghetti, penne, linguine, or fettucine in one of their innumerable fresh sauces, or opt for the nightly special. If you're lucky, they might have some fresh homemade ravioli in a creamy ricotta sauce. If not, the penne melanzana on the regular menu is a standout. Service is friendly and informal at the six tables spread out underneath the exposed red-tile roof. You'll even find a good selection of Italian wines at fair prices here.

PLAYA DEL COCO AFTER DARK

Playa del Coco is one of Costa Rica's liveliest beach towns after dark. **Coconuts** (no phone) is the main disco in town and is located just off the the little park right on the beach. If these directions don't get you there, don't worry, you'll hear it. Alternatively you can head across the park to **Sambuka** (☎ **506/670-0272**), a lively night spot with a crowded dance floor. On the road into town, you'll find the new bar and restaurant **Kachetto** (no phone), a comfortable second-floor affair with good bocas and some outdoor tables on the veranda overlooking Coco's main street. Finally, if you want to test your luck, check out the casino at **Flor de Itabo** (see "Accommodations," above).

5 Playas Flamingo, Potrero, Brasilito & Conchal

173 miles (280km) NW of San José; 41 miles (66km) SW of Liberia

These beaches were among the first in Costa Rica to attract international attention, and for many years Playa Flamingo was the beach resort in this neck of the woods. However, with attention and development shifting toward the Papagayo Gulf a little farther north, Playa Flamingo has been somewhat forgotten. Hotels and condo developments here have fallen on hard times, and there's a sense of neglect at some of the local establishments. However, I wouldn't count Playa Flamingo out. The beach here is a beautiful stretch of white sand, and the hard times might just force this once exclusive resort town to bring its prices down to earth. Moreover, the combination of Playa Flamingo with a plethora of other nearby beaches still makes this a destination to consider. The views from Playa Potrero are beautiful; on Playa Brasilito, budget travelers have a chance at some fun in the sun without spending a fortune; and Playa Conchal is a shell collector's dream come true.

The centerpiece of the section of coast is still Playa Flamingo, with its luxury hotels, full-service marina, private airstrip, retirement and vacation homes, and, best of all, one of the only white-sand beaches in the area. In fact, the old name for this beach was Playa Blanca, which made plenty of sense. When the developers moved in, they needed a more romantic name than "White Beach," so it became Playa Flamingo, even though there are no flamingos.

You'll probably want to spend some time on this beautiful beach. Playa Flamingo is on a long spit of land that forms part of Potrero Bay. On the ocean side of the peninsula, there's the long white-sand beach, behind which is a dusty road and then a mangrove swamp. At the end of the sand spit is a fortresslike rock outcropping upon which most of Playa Flamingo's hotels and vacation homes are built. There are great views from this rocky hill. If you're not staying on Playa Flamingo, you should know that there are (unprotected) parking spots all along the beach road where you can park your car for the day. There is, however, little shade on the beach, so be sure to use plenty of sunscreen and bring an umbrella if you can. The marina is located on the bay side of the peninsula.

About 2½ miles away on **Playa Brasilito,** you'll find one of the only two real villages in the area. The soccer field is the center of the village, and around its edges you'll find a couple of little *pulperías* (general stores). There's a long stretch of beach, and though it's of gray sand, it still has a quiet, undiscovered feel to it (at least on weekdays). However, Playa Brasilito is rapidly becoming popular both with Ticos and budget travelers from abroad. There's now a disco here, and on weekends it can get pretty crowded and noisy.

Just south of Brasilito is the small, crushed-shell beach of **Conchal**. In 1997, the 310-room Meliá Playa Conchal opened here, and this is no longer the semiprivate haunt of a few beach cognoscenti. The Meliá company owns almost all the land behind the beach, so the only access is along the soft sand road that follows the beach south of Brasilito. Just before the road hits Conchal, you'll have to ford a small river and then climb a steep rocky hill, so four wheel drive is recommended. Luckily, all beaches in Costa Rica are public property. Unfortunately, as Conchal's popularity has spread, unscrupulous builders have been bringing in dump trucks to haul away the namesake seashells for landscaping and construction, and the impact is noticeable.

If you continue along the road from Brasilito without taking the turn for Playa Flamingo, you'll soon come to **Playa Potrero**. The sand here is a brownish gray, but the beach is long, clean, deserted, and quite calm for swimming. You can see the hotels of Playa Flamingo across the bay. Drive a little farther and you'll find the still-underdeveloped **Playa La Penca** and, finally, **Sugar Beach**.

ESSENTIALS

GETTING THERE & DEPARTING **By Plane** The nearest airports with regularly scheduled flights are in Liberia and Tamarindo. From either of these places you can arrange for a taxi to drive you to any one of these beaches. Playa Brasilito and Conhal are about 45 minutes from Liberia and 25 from Tamarindo (add about 5 more minutes for Flamingo and 10 for Portero). A taxi from Liberia should cost around $30; $25 from Tamarindo.

By Bus Express buses (☎ **506/221-7202**) leave San José daily at 8 and 10am from the corner of Calle 20 and Avenida 3, stopping at Playas Brasilito, Flamingo, and Potrero, in that order. The ride takes 6 hours. A one-way ticket costs $5.50.

Express buses depart **Playa Potrero** for San José at 9am and 2pm, stopping a few minutes later in Playa Flamingo and Brasilito. Ask at your hotel where the best place is for catching the bus. Buses to **Santa Cruz** leave Potrero at 9am and 5pm and take about 45 mimutes. If you're heading north toward Liberia, get off the bus at Belén and wait for a bus going north. Buses leave Santa Cruz regularly for San José.

By Car There are two major routes to these beaches. The most direct route is by way of the **Tempisque River ferry**. Take the Interamerican Highway west from San José. Twenty-nine miles (47km) past the turnoff for Puntarenas, turn left for the ferry. The ferry operates continually from 5am to 7pm daily. After crossing the Tempisque River, follow the signs for Nicoya, continuing north to Santa Cruz. About 10 miles (16km) north of Santa Cruz, just before the village of Belén, take the turnoff for Playas Flamingo, Brasilito, and Potrero. After another 12½ miles (20km), take the right fork to reach these beaches. The drive takes about 6 hours.

It's often slightly quicker, particularly on Fridays and Saturdays when beach traffic is heavy, to drive north all the way to Liberia and then come back south, thus avoiding the lines of cars waiting to take the ferry. This also applies if you're heading back to San José on a Sunday. After you reach Liberia, follow the directions for Playa Hermosa but continue on the main road past the town of Filadelfia, until the village of Belén. Turn right here until you reach Huacas, where there will be signs pointing you toward Playa Flamingo. The ride from Liberia should take about an hour.

ORIENTATION These beaches are strung out over several miles of deeply rutted dirt roads. Playa Flamingo is by far the most developed. It's located down a side road, while the villages of Brasilito and Potrero are right on the main road.

FUN ON & OFF THE BEACH

Though **Playa Flamingo** is the prettiest beach in this area, **Playa Potrero** has the gentlest surf and therefore is the best swimming beach. **Playa Conchal**, which is nearly legendary for its crushed seashells, is a short walk south of **Brasilito**. Though it's beautiful, the drop-off is quite steep, and it's known for its dangerous riptides. The water at Playa Brasilito is often fairly calm, which makes it another good swimming choice. However, my favorites for a full day of swimming and sunbathing are **Playas La Penca** and **Sugar Beach**.

SCUBA DIVING Scuba diving is quite popular here. **Eco Treks** (☎ **506/654-4578;** e-mail: ecotreks@ecotreks.com) and **Costa Rica Diving** (☎ **506/654-4148**) both have shops on the roads into Flamingo. These companies offer trips out to the Catalina and Bat Islands for between $65 and $90. Both also offer PADI certification courses, as well as multiday packages. Alternatively, you check in with Flamingo Divers at the **Flamingo Marina Hotel and Club** (see below).

SPORTFISHING If you want to go sportfishing, you'll have plenty of options here. Head out to **The Marina Flamingo Yacht Club** (☎ **506/654-4203**), where you can hook with a variety of boats based along its docks. A full-day fishing excursion can cost between $450 and $1,200, depending on the size of the boat. Half-day trips cost between $250 and $550.

Alternatively, you can contact the **Bahia Potrero Resort Hotel and Club** (☎ **506/654-4183**), the **Flamingo Marina Hotel and Club** (☎ **506/290-1858**), **Dream Catcher International** (☎ **506/654-4227**), **Club Villas Pacífica** (☎ **506/654-4137**), or **Blue Marlin Sport Fishing** (☎ **506/654-4043**). The choices are many and competition is fierce here, so shop around to find the boat, skipper, and price that best fit your needs.

HORSEBACK RIDING If you'd rather stay on dry land, you can arrange a horseback ride with **Costa Rica Riding Adventures** (☎ 506/654-4106), **Bo-Mar Tours** (☎ 506/654-4469), or **Finca Montejicar** (☎ 506/654-4237). This latter place works in conjunction with the Hotel Brasilito. Depending on the size of your group, it should cost between $10 and $20 per person per hour.

MOUNTAIN BIKING & OTHER ADVENTURE TOURS You can rent a mountain bike from **Eco Treks** (☎ **506/654-4578;** e-mail: ecotreks@ecotreks.com). The folks at Eco Treks will point you to a ride suited to your ability and conditioning level. They can also arrange multiday biking tours to other parts of Costa Rica, as well as kayaking, hiking, and rafting trips. Alternatively, check in with the Fantasy Tours desk at the **Flamingo Marina Hotel and Club**.

ACCOMMODATIONS

If you plan to be here for a while or are coming down with friends or a large family, you might want to consider renting a condo or house. They rent for anywhere between $100 and $300 per day in the high season (slightly less during the low season). For information and reservations, contact **Sea View Rentals**, Apdo. 77, Santa Cruz, Guanacaste (☎ **506/654-4007**; fax 506/654-4009), or **The Trading Post** (☎ and fax **506/654-4430**).

VERY EXPENSIVE

✪ **Meliá Playa Conchal.** Apdo. 232-5150, Santa Cruz, Guanacaste. ☎ **800/336-3542** in the U.S., or 506/654-4123. Fax 506/654-4181. E-mail: mconchal@sol.racsa.co.cr. 310 suites. A/C TV TEL. $165 suite; $400 master suite; rates lower in the off-season and higher during Christmas and Easter weeks. AE, MC, V.

This sprawling hotel is the largest and most luxurious resort yet to open in Costa Rica. And while this is far from the norm for tourism here, if you're looking for a big-resort vacation in Costa Rica, this is the best option. From the massive open-air reception building down to the free-form swimming pool (the largest in Central America), everything here has been done on a grand scale. There's a small village feel to the layout, with all of the rooms located in one of the 40 separate bungalows, which are reached by way of the constantly circulating golf-cart-towed commuter cars. All of the rooms come with either one king or two double beds in a raised bedroom nook. Down below, there's a comfortable sitting area, with a couch, coffee table, and chairs with ottomans. The bathrooms are large and modern, with marble tiles, full tubs, bidets, and even a telephone. Depending on whether you're on the first or second floor, you'll either have a garden patio or a small balcony. Only three of the bungalows actually have ocean views, and two of these contain the master suites, which have double the living area of the standard suites and slightly more luxurious appointments.

Because of the golf course and its ponds and wetlands, there's good bird watching here, with healthy populations of parrots, roseate spoonbills, and wood storks. If you venture off the hotel grounds, you'll find yourself on Playa Conchal, which for years had been one of the best-kept secrets in Guanacaste.

Dining/Diversions: Guests generally take all their meals here, and there are a variety of options. There's a large generic international buffet restaurant, which seats 400 and has the most extensive hours. Off of this you'll find an open-air bar and large lounge where nightly entertainment revues are staged. There's also an outdoor grill, a poolside snack bar, and La Faisanela, a semifancy Italian restaurant. Up on a high bluff you'll find the Astrea restaurant, serving elegant continental dishes, as well as the hotel's casino and discotheque.

Amenities: Aside from the massive pool and its scattered Jacuzzis, there's a regulation 18-hole golf course designed by Robert Trent Jones, a pro shop, four lighted tennis courts, water-sports equipment, a dive shop, and a small gym with exercise equipment and three more Jacuzzis. There's also a conference facility, a small shopping arcade with an assortment of gift shops and galleries, car- rental desk, tour desk, concierge, 24-hour room service, laundry service, and valet parking.

EXPENSIVE

Flamingo Marina Hotel and Club. Playa Flamingo (Apdo. 321-1002, Paseo de los Estudiantes, San José), Guanacaste. ☎ **506/290-1858.** Fax 506/231-1858. www.Flamingo.com. E-mail: hotflam@sol.racsa.co.cr. 30 units, 21 condos, 4 apts. A/C TV TEL. $58–$78 double; $90–$120 suite; $100–$180 apt; $145–$200 condo; rates slightly higher during peak periods. AE, DC, MC, V.

Located up the hill from the beach, the Flamingo Marina Hotel offers one of the most attractive settings at Flamingo Beach. The open-air lobby overlooks both the swimming pool and the bay. There are a variety of room types to choose from, all of which have air-conditioning and refrigerators. The standard rooms have tile floors and lots of wood accents, while the suites have wet bars in the seating area and tiled whirlpool tubs. All the rooms have patios or balconies, and most have bay views. The suites even have their own Jacuzzis.

Dining: The Sunrise Cafe serves reasonably priced continental dishes with an emphasis on seafood.

Amenities: There's a tennis court here, as well as two adjacent swimming pools, one with a popular swim-up bar. You'll also find a tour desk, offering up a wide range of tours around the region, as well as sportfishing charters; sea kayaking, and boogie board rentals. You'll also find Flamingo Divers headquartered here, offering snorkeling and diving trips and classes.

Hotel Aurola Playa Flamingo Holiday Inn. Playa Flamingo (Apdo. 7802-1000, San José), Guanacaste. ☎ **506/233-7233.** Fax 506/255-1171. 88 units. A/C TV TEL. $100–$120 double; $150–$250 suite. AE, DC, MC, V.

This hotel, right across the road from the beach at Playa Flamingo, has long been a favorite of vacationing gringos. In late 1995, it received a total facelift that has spruced it up quite a bit. The hotel is constructed in a horseshoe shape around a large pool and opens out on the ocean. Half the rooms have a clear view of the ocean, across a narrow dirt road. All the rooms are clean and cool, with tile floors, modern bathrooms, and many amenities, including VCRs. The pool- and beach-view rooms are slightly nicer, and you'll pay more for them. The suites all have a sitting room, wet bar, two TVs, and two balconies.

Dining: The most popular meeting and eating place here is the poolside bar and restaurant.

Amenities: There's a modest gym, a large game room, and a children's playroom.

Hotel Fantasias Flamingo. Playa Flamingo (Apdo. 12270-1000, San José), Guanacaste. ☎ **506/654-4350** or 506/222-9847. Fax 506/257-5002. www.multicr.com/fantasias. E-mail: flamingo@sol.racsa.co.cr. 42 units. A/C TEL. $110–$120 double; lower rates in the off-season. AE, MC, V.

This new hotel is located up on the bluff, a little bit beyond the Flamingo Marina Hotel and Club. The rooms are all identical, with wall-to-wall carpeting, two double beds, large dressers and plenty of closet space, and private bathrooms with tubs. The nicest rooms enjoy a view of Potrero Bay and have large sliding glass doors that open onto either a private patio or a balcony. Several of these patios adjoin the swimming pool and have stairs leading down into the water.

Dining/Diversions: There's only one restaurant here, located up on the second floor with stunning views of Bahia Potrero. Breakfast, lunch, and dinner are served, pretty standard continental fare, at reasonable prices. Your best bet is usually the catch of the day. Just off the restaurant, you'll find the hotel's small bar.

Amenities: The free-form pool has a swim-up bar and a footbridge over it, and even adjoins several of the rooms. Golf is available at Rancho Las Colinas, 30 minutes away. Tour desk, laundry service.

✪ **Hotel Sugar Beach.** Playa Pan de Azucar (Apdo. 90, Santa Cruz), Guanacaste. ☎ **800/458-4735** in the U.S., or 506/654-4242. Fax 506/654-4239. www.sugar-beach.com. E-mail: sugarb@sol.racsa.co.cr. 31 units. A/C. $100–$138 double; $165–$225 suite. AE, MC, V.

Just as the name implies, the Hotel Sugar Beach is located on a white-sand beach—one of the few in the area and therefore one of the most attractive, in my opinion. So far, this hotel is the only thing out here, giving it a strong measure of seclusion and privacy. The beach is on a small cove surrounded by rocky hills. Unfortunately, the hills become very brown and desolate in the dry season, so don't expect the verdant tropics if you come down here in March or April. The hotel itself is perched above the water. Nature lovers will be thrilled to find wild howler monkeys and iguanas almost on their doorsteps. Snorkelers should be happy here, too; this cove has some good snorkeling in the dry season. The newest rooms are set back amid the trees and are quite large. Tile floors, wicker furniture, beautiful carved doors, and big bathrooms all add up to first-class comfort. The oldest rooms are the most basic, though they're in an interesting circular building. Hammocks under the trees provide a great way to while away a hot afternoon.

Dining: The open-air dining room is in a circular building with a panoramic vista of ocean, islands, and hills. The menu is long and there are daily specials with entree prices from $6 to $15.

Amenities: Scuba-diving and snorkeling trips, horseback riding, and fishing-boat charters can be arranged. The hotel rents masks and fins, sea kayaks, and boogie boards.

MODERATE

Hotel Bahia Potrero Beach Resort. Playa Potrero (Apdo. 45-5051, Santa Cruz), Guanacaste. ☎ **506/654-4183.** Fax 506/654-4093. 10 units. $50–$89 double. Rates include continental breakfast. AE, MC, V.

This comfortable little beach hotel is on Playa Potrero and, from the beach in front, has a view of Playa Flamingo across the bay. Set in a green garden with a white wooden fence surrounding the property, the Bahia Flamingo feels like a private home in the country. A laid-back atmosphere prevails, with hammocks for dozing, a pool, and miles of nearly deserted beach for strolling and swimming. The rooms are large and cool, though a little dark. They all have refrigerators and a small patio. Fishing and snorkeling trips can be arranged, and horses are available at $15 per hour. To find this hotel, watch for the sign pointing down a road to the left a mile or so after you pass the turnoff for Playa Flamingo. The hotel's restaurant is a breezy, high-ceilinged room and has a nice view of green lawns, white fence, and blue ocean. Fresh seafood and hearty steaks average $5 to $10. When I last visited, there was a lot of construction going on. The hotel is going to get a new dining room and some extra rooms. A group of condominiums were also being built next door.

INEXPENSIVE

Cabinas Conchal. Playa Brasilito, Santa Cruz, Guanacaste. ☎ **506/654-4257.** 9 units. $20 double; $30 triple; $40 quad. No credit cards.

Located on the south edge of Brasilito, Cabinas Conchal consists of several yellow buildings inside a walled compound. The stucco-and-stone construction gives the buildings a bit of character as well as added security. Some rooms have just a double bed, while others have a double and a pair of bunk beds. All are quite clean. Table fans help keep the rooms cool. The beach is about 200 meters away.

Cabinas Cristina. Playa Potrero (Apdo. 121, Santa Cruz), Guanacaste. ☎ **506/654-4006.** Fax 506/654-4128. 5 units. $30 double; $35 triple; $40 quad. MC, V.

This little place is located on Playa Potrero across the bay from Playa Flamingo and a few kilometers north of Brasilito. Although Cabinas Cristina isn't right on the beach, it's still a great value in this area of high-priced hotels. The rooms are spacious and very clean (they fill up fast), with hot plates, refrigerators, dressers, bars with stools, tiled bathrooms, and double and bunk beds. On the veranda there are large rocking chairs. There's a small pool in the middle of a grassy green yard, and a thatched-roof palapa. Playa Potrero is just a 5-minute walk down a dirt road.

Hotel Brasilito. Playa Brasilito, Santa Cruz, Guanacaste. ☎ **506/654-4237.** Fax 506/654-4247. 15 units. $20–$30 double. V.

This hotel, right in Brasilito and just across a sand road from the beach, offers basic, small rooms that are generally quite clean. There's also a bar and big open-air restaurant serving economical meals. This is still one of the best values in town, though the building across the street is a disco, which makes it difficult to go to bed early on the weekends. The higher prices are for rooms with air-conditioning; rates also rise during Christmas and Easter. Rooms A and B have nice balconies and ocean views. The hotel also rents snorkeling equipment, bodyboards, and horses, and can arrange a variety of tours.

CAMPING ON THE BEACH

It's possible to camp on Playas Potrero and Brasilito. At the former, contact **Maiyra's** (☎ **506/654-4213**), and at the latter try **Camping Brasilito** (☎ **506/654-4452**). Each charges around $3 per person to make camp and use the basic bathroom facilities. Each also has some basic cabins for around $10 per person.

DINING

Amberes. Playa Flamingo near the Flamingo Marina Hotel. ☎ **506/654-4001.** Reservations recommended in high season. Main courses $5.50–$17. MC, V. Daily 6:30–10pm. CONTINENTAL.

This is the happening spot in Flamingo. Not only is it the most upscale restaurant outside of a hotel, but it also boasts a bar, a disco, and even a tiny casino. You can come for dinner and make it an evening. Though the menu changes daily, you'll always find a wide selection of dishes, with the emphasis on seafood. Fresh fish served either meunière or Provence style are two of the best dishes here. People with sensitive ears should take note: The music can become way too loud at dinner. Luckily the open-air disco doesn't usually get cranking until 10pm. The bar opens at 5:30pm.

✪ **Marie's.** Playa Flamingo near the Flamingo Marina Hotel. ☎ **506/654-4136.** Reservations not accepted. Sandwiches $2.50–$6, main courses $6–$17. V. Daily 6:30am–9pm.

Right in the middle of all the luxury hotels at Playa Flamingo is a great little place for a snack or a full meal. The menu is primarily sandwiches and other lunch foods, but on the blackboard behind the bar you'll find daily specials such as mahimahi (called "dorado" down here) and, from August to December, lobster and conch. You'll also find such Tico favorites as casados and ceviche. Tables in the open-air restaurant are made from slabs of tree trunks. Be sure to try the three-milks cake (a Nicaraguan specialty), which just might be the moistest cake on earth.

PLAYA FLAMINGO AFTER DARK

If you don't head to the disco and casino at Amberes, you might want to check out the poolside bar at the **Mariner Inn** (☎ **506/654-4081**), which seems to be the liveliest spot in town.

6 Playa Tamarindo & Playa Grande

183 miles (295km) NW of San José; 45 miles (73km) SW of Liberia

Tamarindo is a bit of a boomtown and one of the few beach towns where the construction and real estate businesses are still robust. So far, the development remains a mixture of mostly small hotels in a variety of price ranges and an eclectic array of restaurants. Most of the continuing development seems to be creeping up the hills inland from the beach and south beyond Punta Langosta. The beach itself is a long, wide swath of white sand that curves gently from one rocky headland to another. Behind the beach are low, dry hills that can be a very dreary brown in the dry season but instantly turn green with the first brief showers of the rainy season. The dust that turns the hills brown can also make the main street through Tamarindo extremely unpleasant to walk along, so stick to the beach.

Though there's only one major resort hotel in town, the proximity to great surfing and an abundance of stylish smaller hotels have made Tamarindo one of the most popular beaches on this coast. Fishing boats bob at their moorings at the south end of the beach, and brown pelicans fish just outside the breakers. A sandy islet offshore makes a great destination if you're a strong swimmer; if you're not, it makes a great foreground for sunsets. As I said above, Tamarindo is popular with surfers, who ply the break right here or use the town as a jumping-off place for Playas Grande, Langosta, Avellana, and Negra.

Just to the north of Tamarindo lies Playa Grande, one of the principal nesting sites for the giant leatherback turtle, the largest turtle in the world. This beach is usually too rough for swimming, but the well-formed and consistent beach break is very popular with surfers. I almost hate to mention places to stay in Playa Negra, because the steady influx of tourists and development could doom this beach as a turtle nesting site.

ESSENTIALS

GETTING THERE & DEPARTING **By Plane** **Sansa** (☎ **506/233-0397**, 506/233-5330, or 506/233-3258 in San José) flies to Tamarindo from San José's Juan Santamaría International Airport daily at 5:15am, 11:35am, and 3pm. On Tuesday, Thursday, Saturday, and Sunday, there is an additional flight at 9:45am. The flight takes 50 minutes. The fare is $55 each way.

Travelair (☎ **506/220-3054** or 506/232-7883) flies to Tamarindo daily at 8:20am, 11:45am, and 3pm from Tobías Bolaños International Airport in Pavas. The duration is 50 minutes, and the fare is $88 one way, $146 round-trip.

Sansa flights leave Tamarindo for San José at 6:20am, 12:50pm and 4:05pm daily, with the additional flight leaving at 10:50am. Travelair flights leave for San José at 9:35am, 12:45pm, and 4pm daily. The return flights are sometimes quite lengthy, with one or more intermediary stops often added at the airline's discretion.

By Bus An express bus (☎ **506/222-2666**) leaves San José daily for Tamarindo at 3:30pm, departing from Calle 14 between Avenidas 3 and 5, and takes 5½ hours. The one-way fare is $5.

Alternatively, you can catch a bus to Santa Cruz from the same station. Buses (☎ **506/221-7202**) leave San José for Santa Cruz daily at 7, 9, 10, and 11am and 3:30 and 6pm. The trip's duration is 5 hours; one-way fare is $4. Buses leave Santa Cruz for Tamarindo daily at 4:30, 6:30, 8:30, and 11:30am and 1 and 8:30pm. The trip lasts 1½ hours; one-way fare is $1.50.

If you're coming from Liberia, you can take a Santa Cruz or Nicoya bus (which run almost hourly), get off in the village of Belén, south of Filadelfia, and wait for the next Tamarindo-bound bus. However, since buses to Tamarindo are infrequent, you may have a long wait. It's generally best to go to Santa Cruz and pick up a Tamarindo-bound bus there.

A direct bus leaves Tamarindo for San José daily at 5:45am. Buses to Santa Cruz leave at 6, 6:30, 7, and 9am, noon, and 3pm. In Santa Cruz you must transfer to one of the frequent San José buses.

By Car The most direct route is by way of the Tempisque River ferry. Take the Interamerican Highway west from San José, and 29 miles (47km) past the turnoff for Puntarenas, turn left toward the ferry. The ferry operates daily from am to 7pm. The ferry costs about $2 per car and driver, with a nominal 20¢ fee per passenger. The ferries that ply this crossing are quite small, and on busy days you may have to wait for several crossings before making it on board. After crossing the Tempisque River, follow the signs for Nicoya, continuing north to Santa Cruz. About 10 miles (16km) north of Santa Cruz, just before the village of Belén, take the turnoff for

Tamarindo. In another 12½ miles (20km), take the left fork for Playa Tamarindo. The drive takes about 6 hours.

On Fridays and Saturdays, when beach traffic is heavy, it's often quicker to drive all the way north to Liberia and then come back south, thus avoiding the lines of cars waiting to take the ferry. This also applies if you're heading back to San José on a Sunday. See the section "Playas Flamingo, Potrero, Brasilito & Conchal," above, for more specific directions.

ORIENTATION The unpaved road leading into town runs parallel to the beach and dead-ends just past Cabinas Zully Mar. There are a couple of side roads off this main road that lead farther on to Playas Langosta, Avellana and Negra. You'll find several of the newer hotels mentioned below off of these side roads.

GETTING AROUND If you need to rent a car there's an **Elegante Rent A Car** office at the Pueblo Dorado Hotel (☎ **506/653-0015**).

FUN ON & OFF THE BEACH

Tamarindo is a long beach, and though it can sometimes be great for swimming, it's often too rough. You also have to be careful when and where you swim on Tamarindo Beach. There are rocks just offshore in several places, some of which are exposed only at low tide. An encounter with one of these rocks could be nasty, especially if you're bodysurfing. Also, you should avoid swimming near the estuary mouth, where the currents can carry you out away from the beach. That said, the best swimming is always down at the southern end of the beach, toward Punta Langosta.

If you just want to laze on the beach, you can pick up beach chairs, umbrellas, and mats at **Tamarindo Tour/Rentals** (☎ **506/653-0078**), located on the right as you come into town. It's open daily. There's a little storefront and gift shop here, which doubles as a local information center and clearinghouse for condo and apartment rentals around the area.

BIKING, HORSEBACK RIDING & OTHER ACTIVITIES **Bikes** are available for rent at **Tamarindo Tour/Rentals** (☎ **506/653-0078**) and **Iguana Surf** (☎ and fax **506/653-0148**). You'll probably see plenty of horses and riders running up and down the beach. You can flag one of these down and ask about rates, or set up a riding date with **Tamarindo Tour/Rentals** or **Papagayo Excursions**. Rates for horse rental, with a guide, are around $10 to $15 per hour. Both companies, as well as **Iguana Tours**, also offer boat or kayak tours of the nearby estuary for around $20 per person. Papagayo Excursions offers the widest selection of full-day and multiday trips, including raft floats on the Corobici River ($80) and tours to Palo Verde and Rincón de la Vieja National Parks ($80).

If you want to brush up on your Spanish or learn how to dance salsa, check in with the folks at **Wayra Instituto de Español** (☎ and fax **506/653-0264**). This place is located up a side street from Iguana Surf.

GOLF Golf has come to this region in a big way, with not one but two courses. The better course and facilities are at the **Melia Playa Conchal Resort** (☎ **506/654-4123**). This Robert Trent Jones–designed course is still open to the walk-in public, but as the resort itself gets more and more popular, they may restrict public access. Currently, it will cost you $90 in greens fees for 18 holes, including a cart and a bucket of balls for the driving range. Closer to Tamarindo, in Playa Grande, you'll find **Rancho Las Colinas** (☎ and fax **506/654-4089**), a Ron Garl–designed 18-hole course, which charges $42 in greens fees plus $20 for the cart.

SAILBOAT CHARTERS The folks who run the **Finca Monte Fresco** (☎ **506/653-0241;** e-mail: samoniqe@sol.racsa.co.cr) just outside of Tamarindo also own the 52-foot ketch *Samonique III.* They charter this boat for anything from sunset cruises to week-long trips out to Cocos Island. A half-day cruise costs $60 per person, and a full day is just $80 per person. This includes an open bar and snacks on the half-day cruise, lunch on the full-day trip. Beyond this, the charter rates are around $175 per person per day, including all board, and vary depending on the size of your group.

SNORKELING, SURFING & SEA KAYAKING If you want to try any of these water sports while in Tamarindo, **Iguana Surf** (☎ and fax **506/653-0148**) is your one-stop source for equipment. To get there, head up the main road, turning left just before the Zully Mar cabins (in the direction of the Hotel Pasatiempo) and then follow this road as it turns right. The shop will be prominently on your left. These folks are open daily and rent snorkeling equipment ($15 per day), boogie boards ($10 per day), sea kayaks ($35 per day), and surfboards ($20 per day). They also have half-day and hourly rates for many of these items. Iguana Surf, by the way, has been earning rave reviews for its hearty breakfasts.

You can also rent similar equipment of slightly lesser quality, and at slightly lower rates, from **Tamarindo Tour/Rentals.**

Finally, if you want to do any scuba diving while you're here, check in with **Agua Rica** (☎ **506/653-0094**), which you'll find on the main road, near Cabinas Marielos. They have a full-service dive shop and offer day trips, multiday dive cruises, and the standard resort and full certification courses.

SPORTFISHING **Papagayo Excursions** (☎ **506/653-0254** or 506/653-0227; e-mail: papagayo@sol.racsa.co.cr), which has its office and a small gift shop in the commercial center across from the Hotel Tamarindo Diria, offers folks a chance to go after the "big ones" that abound in the waters offshore. From here it takes only 20 minutes to reach the edge of the continental shelf and the waters preferred by marlin and sailfish. Although fishing is good all year, the peak season for billfish is between mid-April and August. Rates for the boat are $250 to $450 for a half day and $350 to $750 for a full day. Alternatively, you can contact **Tamarindo Sportfishing** (☎ **506/653-0090**), **Warren Sellers Sportfishing** (☎ **506/653-0186**), or **Capullo Sportfishing** (☎ **506/653-0048**), which is located on the road between Capitain Suizo and Sueño del Mar. All offer half-day trips for between $250 and $500 and full-day trips for between $350 and $800.

WATCHING NESTING SEA TURTLES On nearby **Playa Grande**, leatherback sea turtles nest between late September and mid-March. The only time to see this activity is at night. During the nesting season you'll be inundated with opportunities to sign up for the nightly tours—they usually cost $12 per person. If your hotel can't set it up for you, you'll see signs all over town offering tours. Make sure you go with someone licensed and reputable. No flash photography is allowed because any sort of light can confuse the turtles and prevent them from laying their eggs; guides must use red-tinted flashlights. Basically, there are two organizations running the tours, a local cooperative of guides called **Coopetamarindo** (no phone; office located on the road into town) and **Papagayo Excursions** (☎ **506/653-0254** or 506/653-0227). The latter seems to have better-informed guides and slightly more personal service. Playa Grande is just north of Tamarindo across a small river mouth. The trips simply ferry visitors across in small *pangas* (outboard-driven boats), and then it's a 10- to 25-minute walk up Playa Grande until you find a nesting mother.

Alternatively, you can drive over to Playa Grande, where the tours cost just $5 per person. You'll find a small shack administered by the Matapalo Conservation Association next to the Hotel Las Tortugas. Part of the money goes to support local schools and a medical clinic. Try to arrive early (around 6pm) to sign up for a tour, because only a limited number of people are allowed on the beach at one time. The list fills up fast, and if you arrive late, you may have to wait until real late.

If the turtles are not nesting, or you've got some time to kill before your turtle tour, check out **El Mundo de la Tortuga** (☎ **506/653-0471**), a small turtle museum/exhibit at Playa Grande. Visitors take the half-hour self-guided tour by picking up a cassette player and choosing a tour cassette in English, Spanish, German, or Italian. The museum opens each afternoon at 4pm and stays open until the turtle tours are done for the night. Admission $6.

ACCOMMODATIONS

IN TOWN

Very Expensive

✪ **Hotel and Villas Cala Luna.** Playa Tamarindo, Guanacaste. ☎ **506/653-0214.** Fax 506/653-0213. http://calaluna.racsa.co.cr:895. E-mail: calaluna@sol.racsa.co.cr. 40 units, 21 villas. A/C TV TEL MINIBAR. $130 double room; $280–$360 villas; rates slightly lower in the off-season. AE, MC, V.

If you're looking for serious luxury in Tamarindo, stay in one of the two or three bedroom villas here. These independent villas are the size of a small home and just as well equipped. The living rooms are huge, with a high peaked ceiling, couches, table and chair, satellite television, and complete sound system. The full kitchen comes with a microwave oven and cappuccino machine, and there's even a washing machine. If this isn't enough, each villa has its own private swimming pool. The bedrooms are spacious and elegant with either a king or two double beds. Everything is done in soft pastels with hand-painted accents, and the red tile roofs and Mexican tile floors add to the elegance while helping to keep things cool. Rooms in the hotel are similarly spacious and well-done, but you'll have to share the hotel's main swimming pool with the rest of the guests. The biggest drawback here is that the gardens still need some time to fill in and truly isolate each villa, which are rather close to each other; you also have to cross the street and walk a short path to reach the beach.

Dining: The restaurant here serves a wide selection of continental and Italian dishes.

Amenities: Aside from the villas with their private pools, there's a large free-form pool with a swim-up bar. The hotel has its own boat for fishing and diving trips and can arrange a whole host of other tours around the region. Bicycle rentals, room service, and baby-sitting are also available.

✪ **Hotel El Jardín Del Eden.** Playa Tamarindo, Guanacaste. ☎ and fax **506/653-0111** or ☎ 506/653-0137. www.jardin-eden.com. E-mail: hotel@jardin-eden.com. 18 units, 2 apts. A/C FAN TV TEL. $120–$140 double; $160 apt. Rates include breakfast buffet. AE, MC, V.

Though it isn't right on the beach, this is one of the most luxurious and comfortable hotels in Tamarindo. It also offers the best service and some of the best meals in town. There are excellent views from the guest rooms, which are in Mediterranean-style buildings on a hill 150 yards from the beach. The owners of the hotel are French and have brought a touch of sophistication that's often lacking at beach hotels in Costa Rica. Almost all the guest rooms have a balcony or private terrace with views of the Pacific. The large stone-tiled terraces, in particular, give you the sense of staying at your own private villa. The honeymoon room has a large bathroom with a tub, while other rooms have showers only. Service here is very personal, and the staff can help you arrange various tours and excursions.

Dining: The thatched-roof, open-air dining room features excellent French and Italian meals with nightly specials and the occasional live band.

Amenities: There are two swimming pools, one of which has a swim-up bar. There's also a whirlpool tub. The terraces surrounding the pools and tub have thatched palapas for shade, and there's even a little artificial waterfall flowing into the pool. Just off the reception you'll find a small open-air gym. The beach is 150 yards away, down the hill along a private path.

Expensive

✪ **Hotel Capitan Suizo.** Playa Tamarindo, Guanacaste. ☎ **506/653-0353** or 506/653-0075. Fax 506/653-0292. E-mail: capitansuizo@ticonet.co.cr. 22 units, 8 bungalows. TEL. $95–$125 double; $130–$150 bungalow; lower rates in off-season. AE, MC, V.

This quiet, luxurious hotel is located on the southern end of Tamarindo. The rooms are located in a series of two-story buildings. The lower rooms have air-conditioning and private patios; the upper units have plenty of cross ventilation and small balconies. All have large bathrooms and sitting rooms with fold-down futon couches. In effect, all the rooms are really suites, with their separate sitting/living room area. The spacious bungalows are spread around the shady grounds, near the large free-form pool. These all come with a tub in the bathroom and an inviting outdoor shower among the trees.

Dining: All the meals are served in the open-air rancho.

Amenities: There is a small gift shop on the premises, as well as a small gym. The hotel can arrange a wide variety of tours and activities and has its own horses.

✪ **Sueño del Mar.** Playa Tamarindo, Guanacaste. ☎ and fax **506/653-0284.** www.tamarindo.com/sdmar. E-mail: suenodem@sol.racsa.co.cr. 4 units, 1 casita. $75–$95 double; $95–$150 suite or casita. Rates include breakfast. AE, MC, V.

This place is such a gem I was hesitant to let the secret out. Now it's nearly impossible to get a room, and I often jokingly threaten to drop them from the book, so I can stay here. Located at the south end of Tamarindo beach on Punta Langosta, it's the little touches and innovative design that set Sueño del Mar apart. The rooms are actually small, but they feature four-poster beds made from driftwood, African dolls on the windowsills, Kokopeli candleholders, and open-air showers with sculpted angelfish, hand-painted tiles, and lush tropical plants. Fabrics are from Bali and Guatemala. Somehow, all this works well together, and the requisite hammocks nestled under shade trees right on the beach add the crowning touch. The separate small casita has its own kitchen, veranda, and sleeping loft, while the suite is a spacious second-floor room, with wraparound screened-in windows, a delightful open-air bath and shower, and an ocean view. The beach right out front is rocky and a bit rough but does reveal some nice, quiet tidal pools at low tide.

Dining: Breakfasts are huge and creative and have earned local renown. In fact, co-owner Susan Money has even published her own breakfast cookbook.

Tamarindo Diriá. Playa Tamarindo (Apdo. 476-1007, San José), Guanacaste. ☎ **506/653-0031** or 506/290-4340. Fax 506/653-0032 or 506/290-4367. E-mail: tnodiria@sol.racsa.co.cr. 80 units. A/C TV TEL. $85–$112 double; $105–$139 triple. AE, MC, V.

This is Tamarindo's old (and only) reliable beachfront resort. A 1997 remodeling and steady upkeep have kept the hotel in pretty good shape. Wedged into a narrow piece of land between a dusty road and the beach, the Diriá manages to create its own little world of tropical gardens and palm trees. The remodeled rooms are done in contemporary pastel colors with red-tile floors. Some rooms have separate seating areas, and most have hair dryers, clock radios, and a basket of toiletries in the small bathroom. It's the beachfront location and attractive gardens that make this hotel a worthwhile place to stay.

Dining: The big open-air bar/restaurant beside the pool features a different menu nightly, with prices for main dishes ranging from $5 to $12. The new Matapalo restaurant serves a continental menu out by the beach under an immense matapalo tree. There's also a lunch buffet in the garden most days.

Amenities: There's a swimming pool, gift shop, tour desk, and game room, and both beach-equipment rentals and car rentals can be arranged on premises. Across the street, there's a small commercial center with a minimart.

Villa Alegre. Playa Tamarindo, Guanacaste. ☎ **506/653-0270.** Fax 506/653-0287. www.crica.com/hotels. E-mail: vialegre@sol.racsa. 4 units (2 with bathroom), 2 casitas. $95–$100 double; $175 casita. MC, V.

This new bed-and-breakfast out on Playa Langosta is yet another well-run and homey option here in Tamarindo. Each of the rooms has a different motif, culled from the owners' years of globe-trotting. The Guatemalan and United States rooms share a large bathroom; however, these can easily be joined to form one larger suite. The Mexican room is wheelchair accessible, and each room actually has its own private patio. The casitas were still under construction when I last visited, but each will be quite spacious and luxurious, with one slated for a Japanese design, while the other will have a Russian flavor.

Dining: Breakfasts here are a full-on four-course affair.

Amenities: There's a small pool, horseshoe and shuffleboard courts, and the beach is about 100 yards away through the trees.

Moderate

Hotel El Milagro. Playa Tamarindo (Apdo. 145-5150, Santa Cruz), Guanacaste. ☎ **506/653-0042.** Fax 506/653-0050. E-mail: flokiro@sol.racsa.co.cr. 32 units. $45–$60 double with fan; $55–$70 double with A/C. Additional persons $10. Rates include breakfast buffet. AE, MC, V.

This place started out as a restaurant but has expanded into an attractive little hotel on the edge of town. It's located across the road from the beach, and the rooms are lined up in two long rows facing each other behind the restaurant. The front wall of each room is made of louvered doors that open onto small semicircular patios. Rooms are comfortable and have high ceilings. Pretty gardens and some big old shade trees make El Milagro even more attractive. The restaurant serves well-prepared continental dishes, and there's a swimming pool with a swim-up bar. There's also a children's pool. Various tours and excursions can be arranged through the hotel.

✪ **Hotel Pasatiempo.** Playa Tamarindo, Santa Cruz, Guanacaste. ☎ **506/653-0096.** Fax 506/653-0275. www.tamarindo.com. E-mail: passtime@sol.racsa.co.cr. 11 units. Nov–Mar, $49 double; Apr–Oct, $39 double. AE, MC, V.

A good value, this hotel is set back from the beach a couple of hundred yards in a grove of shady trees. The guest rooms are housed in duplex buildings with thatch roofs, and each room has its own patio with a hammock or chairs. There's plenty of space in every room, and some even sleep five people. Each room bears the name of a different beach, and the bedroom walls all have hand-painted murals. In the center of the five duplexes is a small yet very inviting pool. There's also a popular rancho-style open-air bar that has a pool table, nightly happy hour, good snacks, and occasional live music. The adjacent restaurant, one of the best in town, serves excellent pastas, fresh fish, and Tex-Mex specialties.

Inexpensive

In addition to the cabinas and hotel listed below, there's **Tito's Camping**, located out toward the Hotel Capitan Suizo in Tamarindo. It charges $2.50 per person.

✪ **Cabinas Marielos.** Playa Tamarindo, Guanacaste. ☎ and fax **506/653-0141.** 16 units. $22–$30 double; $29–$34 triple; $38 quad. V.

This place is located down a palm-shaded driveway across the road from the beach. Rooms are clean and fairly new, though small and simply furnished. There are tile floors and wooden chairs on the patios. Some of the bathrooms do not have doors, but they're clean. There's a kitchen that guests can use, and the garden provides a bit of shade. The hotel provides a laundry service and can arrange turtle tours and horseback riding.

Cabinas Zully Mar. Tamarindo, Guanacaste. ☎ **506/653-0140** or 506/226-4732. Fax 506/653-0028. 44 units. $25–$50 double; $35–$57 triple. AE, MC, V.

The Zully Mar has long been a favorite of budget travelers staying in Tamarindo. The newer rooms, which are in a two-story, white-stucco building with a wide, curving staircase on the outside, have air-conditioning and are more comfortable. The doors to these guest rooms are hand-carved with pre-Columbian motifs. These rooms also have high ceilings with fans, tile floors, a long veranda, and large bathrooms. The older rooms are much smaller and more spartan. Although there are mango trees out front for shade, there's little other landscaping, and the sandy grounds look a bit unkempt. Don't let this bother you: Miles of beach are just across the street, as are the hotel's popular restaurant and bar.

In Playa Grande

Moderate

Hotel El Bucanero. Playa Grande, Guanacaste. ☎ and fax **506/653-0480.** 8 units. $45 double; $50 triple; $55 quad. MC, V.

This new hotel is a good choice in Playa Grande. The rooms are all clean and cool, with tile floors and private bathrooms. The rooms come in several sizes and a mix of bed arrangements: several singles, a double and a single, two doubles—take your pick or mix and match. Three of the rooms have air-conditioning. The hotel's restaurant and bar are located on the second floor of the octagonal main building. They serve reasonably priced seafood dishes and Tico standards, but the best part about it is the fact that it's an open-air affair and gets a nice breeze. The hotel is located about 150 yards from the beach.

✪ **Las Tortugas Hotel.** Apdo. 164, Playa Grande, Guanacaste. ☎ and fax **506/653-0458.** www.cool.co.cr/usr/turtles. E-mail: nela@cool.co.cr. 11 units. A/C. Nov–Mar, $50 double, $80 suite; rates slightly higher during peak weeks, lower in the off- season. No credit cards.

Playa Grande is best known for the leatherback turtles that nest here, and much of the beach is now part of Las Baulas National Park, which was created to protect the turtles. However, this beach is also very popular with surfers, who make up a large percentage of the clientele at this beachfront hotel. Several of the rooms here are quite large, and most have interesting stone floors and shower stalls. The upper suite has a curving staircase that leads up to its second room. The owners led the fight to have the area declared a national park and continue to do everything possible to protect the turtles. The hotel's restaurant serves well-prepared local and continental dishes. The restaurant is on the second floor, but as part of the hotel's turtle-friendly design, its view of the ocean is obscured by a natural wall of shrubs and trees. There's also a small bar, a turtle-shaped swimming pool, and a Jacuzzi. The hotel keeps a few canoes on the nearby estuary for gentle paddling among the mangroves. Las Tortugas also manages some nearby houses for longer stays.

DINING

In addition to the restaurants listed below, **Stella's** (☎ **506/653-0127**), located 200 yards beyond Pasatiempo, is a local favorite for Italian food and fresh-baked pizzas.

EXPENSIVE

✪ **La Meridiana.** About 100 meters off the main road, turn left just before Zully Mar. ☎ and fax **506/653-0230.** Reservations recommended in the high season. Main courses $6–$20. AE, MC, V. Daily noon–10pm. ITALIAN.

This is no run-of-the-mill pasta and pizza joint at the beach. Loosen your belt a notch and prepare for some very good Italian food at this family-run place. The restaurant takes up most of the terraced outdoor patio of a large house. There are lush gardens all around and a pool down below. Ceiling fans keep things cool, but there are also a few tables in an indoor air-conditioned room. The setting is elegant, yet the service is casual and friendly. The extensive menu covers all the bases with a wide range of antipasti, pasta, meat, and seafood to choose from. The fish is fresh (usually dorado, tuna, and snapper are on hand) and can be done *al limone, alla siciliana,* or *al vino bianco.* The filetto tartufato is a tender piece of tenderloin in a truffle-butter sauce. However, don't rush past the pastas. The house tagliatelle is a delicious seafood pasta in a light cream sauce, the gnocchi comes in delicate medallions, and the homemade ravioli with lobster is to die for. The wine list features Italian vintages exclusively at a fair price. Whether or not you choose one of the delicious desserts, you should definitely wash everything down with a glass of grappa, which is a contraband brew made by an uncle somewhere in northern Italy.

MODERATE

Coconut Café. On the left as you come into town. ☎ and fax **506/653-0086.** Reservations not necessary. Main courses $8–$18. V. Daily 5–10pm. INTERNATIONAL.

This is one of Tamarindo's more atmospheric restaurants. A thatch roof, wicker furniture, and fresh flower arrangements all set on a raised deck add up to a gringo fantasy of the tropics, but isn't that what you came down here for anyway? The Coconut Café serves some of the most creative food in town, including such dishes as red chicken curry, mahimahi teriyaki, shrimp brochettes, and fondue. However, because the menu changes periodically, you can expect other equally enticing dishes when you visit. The only drawback here is that the very dusty road is only a few feet away.

El Milagro. On the left as you enter town. ☎ **506/653-0042.** Reservations not accepted. Main courses $5–$16. AE, MC, V. Daily 7am–11pm. CONTINENTAL/COSTA RICAN.

Lush gardens and wide terraces make this a pleasant choice, and you can even go for a swim in the adjacent pool. Reproductions of pre-Columbian stone statues stand in the gardens, and the bar has carved-wood columns. On those rare occasions when it's raining, you can retreat to one of the indoor dining rooms. Though the emphasis here is on seafood, you'll also find such unexpected offerings as chicken cordon bleu, fried Camembert, bananas flambé, crepes with ice cream, and hot fruits in amaretto sauce.

INEXPENSIVE

In addition to the places listed below, **Nogui's Sunset Café** (☎ **506/653-0029**) is one of the most popular places in town—and rightly so. This simple open-air cafe is just off the beach on the small traffic circle and serves hearty breakfasts and well-prepared salads, sandwiches, and quiche for lunch. **Soda Natural**, next to Coconut Café, is also a good, inexpensive spot for breakfasts and lunch. Finally, there's **Pedro's Fish Shack**, just a basic wooden shanty next to Nogui's Sunset Café, where I've had some of the freshest fish dinners of my life.

Cantina Las Olas. On the side road toward Punta Langosta before Iguana Surf. No phone. Reservations not necessary. Main courses $2.50–$7. No credit cards. Daily 6–12pm (kitchen closes at 9:30pm). MEXICAN.

A real bargain, this casual open-air restaurant is painted in light blue pastel, with bright geometric designs for trim. There's a large and popular bar in the back and a pool table off to the side. Dining is at one of the three wooden picnic tables or several smaller bare wood tables. The tacos, burritos, and fajitas here are all well-prepared Tex-Mex standards and come with a very spicy hot sauce on the side. There are even several vegetarian entrees. I recommend the fish burritos, but ask about the nightly specials, which might feature blackened fish tacos or shrimp enchiladas. Wash the whole thing down with some mango margaritas. This is a surfer hangout, and they often have surf videos on the TV screen and loud rock and roll or reggae going.

Fiesta del Mar. At the end of the main road. No phone. Reservations not accepted. Main courses $3.50–$14. No credit cards. Daily 8am–11pm. STEAK/SEAFOOD.

Another bargain spot, the Fiesta del Mar is located across the circle from the beach and specializes in steaks and seafood cooked over a wood fire. Try the grilled steak in garlic sauce for $7 or the whole fried fish for $4.50. The open-air dining area is edged with greenery and has a thatched roof, so it feels very tropical. There's live music several nights a week.

✪ **Panadería Johann.** On the road into town. No phone. Reservations not accepted. Prices: $2–$9. No credit cards. Daily 6am–7pm. BAKERY/PIZZA.

There are always fresh-baked goodies at this popular bakery on the outskirts of Tamarindo, although what you will find on any given day is never certain. Possibilities include buttery croissants, vegetarian pizzas, chocolate éclairs, and different types of French pastries and breads. A whole pizza goes for around $9. If you're heading out to the beach for the day, be sure to stop by and pick up some bread or pastries. There are a few tables out back where you can eat your pizza. This place recently changed hands, and the new French owners have transformed the neighboring El Cocodrilo restaurant into a French restaurant. Club 21, a bar and disco, is also attached.

EN ROUTE SOUTH: PLAYA AVELLANAS AND PLAYA NEGRA

As you head south from Tamarindo you will come to several as yet underdeveloped beaches, most of which are quite popular with surfers. Beyond Tamarindo and Playa Langosta are **Playa Avellanas** and then **Playa Negra**, both of which have a few basic cabinas catering to surfers.

INEXPENSIVE

Hotel Playa Negra. Apdo. 31, Santa Cruz, Guanacaste. ☎ **506/382-1301,** or ☎ and fax 506/293-0332. 10 bungalows. $60 up to 4 persons. MC, V.

This collection of thatch-roofed bungalows is right in front of the famous Playa Negra point break. However, even if you're not a surfer, the beach and coast along this area are quite beautiful, with coral and rock outcroppings and calm tide pools. The round bungalows each have one queen and two single beds, two desks, a ceiling fan, and private bathroom. They have concrete floors, but everything is painted in contrasting pastels and feels quite comfortabe. Out by the oval pool is the large open-air rancho that houses the hotel's restauant and serves as a social hub for guests and surfers staying at more basic cabinas inland from the beach.

✪ **Mono Congo Lodge.** Apdo. 177-5150, Santa Cruz, Guanacaste. ☎ **506/382-6926.** Fax 506/680-0280. 5 units (1 with bathroom). $35–$40 double; $60 apt. No credit cards.

This overgrown jungle house has morphed into a popular surf and nature lodge. The main house is a huge three-story affair that is almost entirely open—no exterior walls—and has the feel of a giant tree house. There are ample open areas for lounging on both the second and third floors, where you will find the rooms. The rooms are rather basic but clean and comfortable, and the beds have mosquito netting. Off the main building you'll find the separate two-bedroom apartment, which is more swank, with its arched door and rounded windows, full kitchen, and tile floors. The restaurant is in the main building and serves three meals daily, with nightly dinner specials. The owners are friendly and have horses available for riding. The hotel is about a 10-minute walk from Playa Negra through Pacific dry forest. The last time I visited there were plans to add a few more individual cabins and a swimming pool.

7 Playa Junquillal

18½ miles (30km) W of Santa Cruz; 12½ miles (20km) S of Tamarindo

Playa Junquillal (pronounced hoon-key-AL) is a long, windswept beach that, for most of its length, is backed by grasslands. This gives it a very different feel from other beaches on this coast. There's really no village to speak of here, so if you're heading out this way, plan on getting away from it all. Not a cliché but simply the truth: Junquillal really is off the beaten path. Once here, your options for what to do are limited to whatever's being offered at your chosen hotel. However, the long beach is great for strolling, and the sunsets are superb. When the waves are up and the sea is rough, this beach can be dangerous for swimming. When it's calm, jump right on in.

ESSENTIALS

GETTING THERE & DEPARTING **By Plane** The nearest airport with regularly scheduled flights is in Tamarindo. You can arrange a taxi from the airport to Playa Junquillal. The taxi ride should take 45 minutes and costs about $25.

By Bus An express bus (☎ **506/221-7202**) leaves San José daily at 2pm from the corner of Calle 20 and Avenida 3. The trip takes 5 hours; one-way fare is $5.

Alternatively, you can take a bus to Santa Cruz (see "Playas Flamingo, Potrero, Brasilito & Conchal," earlier in this chapter, for details) and from there, take the 6:30pm bus to Playa Junquillal. The ride takes 1½ hours, and the one-way fare is $1.20.

The one express bus to San José departs Playa Junquillal daily at 5am. There's also a daily bus to Santa Cruz that departs at the same time.

By Car Take the Interamerican Highway from San José. Twenty-nine miles (47km) past the turnoff for Puntarenas, turn left toward the Tempisque ferry. After crossing the Tempisque River, continue north through Nicoya to Santa Cruz. In Santa Cruz, head west 8½ miles (14km) to the town of 27 de Abril, which is where the pavement ends. From here it's another rough 11 miles (18km) to Playa Junquillal.

Other than walking on the beach, swimming when the surf isn't too strong, and exploring tide pools, there isn't much to do here, which is just fine with me. This beach is ideal for anyone who just wants to relax without any distractions. Bring a few good books. The larger hotels here—**Antumalal**, **Iguanazul**, and **Villa Serena**—all offer plenty of activities and facilities, including volleyball, swimming pools, and tennis courts. Sportfishing trips can also be arranged at most hotels. At the Iguanazul, guests can rent bikes, which is a good way to get up and down to the beach.

If you're a surfer, the beach break right in Junquillal is sometimes pretty good. I've also heard that if you look hard enough, there are a few hidden reef and point breaks around.

Finally, if you want to do some **diving**, check in with Micke and Maarten **at El Lugarcito** (☎ **506/653-0436**; e-mail: lugarcito@sol.racsa.co.cr). These folks offer day trips to the Catalina Islands as well as resort and full certification courses.

ACCOMMODATIONS & DINING

Most of the hotels listed below have their own restaurant, and guests usually take their meals right where they're staying. In addition, you can get good Italian meals, pizza, and pasta at the **Coco Flotante** (no phone, up near the Iguanazul) and the **Restaurante Tatanka** (☎ **506/653-0426;** on your left about 200 meters from the beach). The latter place also has some new, moderately priced rooms.

EXPENSIVE

✪ **Hotel Antumalal.** Playa Junquillal (Apdo. 49-5150, Santa Cruz), Guanacaste. ☎ and fax **506/653-0425.** E-mail: antumal@sol.racsa.co.cr. 30 units. Dec 15–Apr 30, $85 double, $95 triple, $100 suite; May 1–Dec 14, $65 double, $70 triple, $80 suite. AE, DC, MC, V.

Located at the end of the road into Playa Junquillal, the Antumalal is the most extensive and oldest hotel on the beach. However, everything is well maintained. The big, old shade trees and lush gardens create a world of tropical tranquility that's perfect for romance and relaxation. Guest rooms are all in duplex buildings with stucco walls on the outside and beautiful murals on the inside. Out front, you'll find a big patio with a hammock, while inside there are brick floors, colorful Guatemalan bedspreads, and big bathrooms. The suites are located in a large two-story building closer to the beach; each suite has a sitting room, kitchenette, and lots of space. Oddly, the views are best from those on the ground floor, at least until the many coconut palms grow a bit more. Right now, the second-floor balconies put you right at the level of the palm fronds, which largely block the view of the sea.

Dining/Diversions: The dining room is housed under a huge, high-peaked rancho that has a fascinating driftwood chandelier hanging from the ceiling. However, when I last visited they were planing on moving the primary restaurant down to a new building beside the pool. The menu includes plenty of good Italian dishes, as well as fresh seafood and Tico standards. There's a bar up in the original dining room and another beside the pool.

Amenities: The swimming pool, with its swim-up bar, is only a few steps from the beach and is beautiful at night when the underwater lights are on. There is also a tennis court, horseback riding, and boat charters for fishing and scuba diving.

MODERATE

Hotel Villa Serena. Playa Junquillal (Apdo. 17, Santa Cruz), Guanacaste. ☎ and fax **506/653-0430.** 10 units. $50 double; $60 triple; $70 quad. Rates are lower during off-season. No credit cards.

Villa Serena is directly across the street from the beach and has long been a popular choice in Playa Junquillal. It is also the closest hotel to the beach (with the exception of one very rustic collection of cabinas). Each of the individual bungalows is surrounded by neatly manicured lawns and gardens. The hotel's main building houses the second-floor dining room, which serves filling and tasty European-style meals and has an enticing view of the sea. Art nouveau decorations and European art abound throughout the building, giving the hotel a very sophisticated feel for such a remote location. The rooms are quite spacious and have ceiling fans, dressing rooms, and large bathrooms. Each has its own covered patio, and only steps away is the small pool. The last time I visited, everything seemed quite run-down, but a little elbow grease and some fresh paint could quickly change that around. The German owner is very friendly and helpful and can arrange horseback riding or fishing tours.

✪ **Iguanazul Hotel.** Playa Junquillal (Apdo. 130-1550, Santa Cruz), Guanacaste. ☎ **800/948-3770** in the U.S. and Canada, or ☎ and fax 506/653-0123. www.ticonet.co.cr/iguanazul. E-mail: iguanazul@ticonet.co.cr. 24 units. Dec 1–Apr 15, $65–$72 double, $80–$87 triple; Apr 16–Nov 30, $49–$62 double, $59–$72 triple. Rates include continental breakfast. AE, MC, V.

Set on a windswept, grassy bluff above a rocky beach, Iguanazul is far from the madding crowd. Originally catering to surfers, this is definitely a spot for sun worshipers who like to have a good time, and the clientele tends to be young and active. The pool is large, as is the surrounding patio area, and there's a volleyball court. However, that's not to say you can't relax here. Head down to one of the quiet coves or grab a hammock set in a covered palapa on the hillside. Don't, however, expect a tropical setting; grasslands surround the hotel, which gives the area the feel of Cape Cod or the Outer Banks. Guest rooms are nicely decorated with basket lampshades, wicker furniture, red-tile floors, high ceilings, and blue-and-white tile bathrooms. The higher prices are for air-conditioned rooms, and two of these even have televisions.

There are plenty of things to do around here. You can rent horses, bikes, and body boards. Captain Gene runs sportfishing charters out of the hotel, and there are board games, dartboards, and table tennis for those who find the sun and sea monotonous. The hotel maintains a little gift shop. Even if you're not staying here, this is a good place to dine; the food is excellent and the sunsets are phenomenal.

INEXPENSIVE

In addition to the lodgings listed below, **Camping Los Malinches** has wonderful campsites on fluffy grass, amid manicured gardens, set on a bluff above the beach. Camping will run you $7 per tent, but the fee entitles you to bathroom and shower privileges. You'll see a sign on the right as you drive toward Playa Junquillal, a little bit beyond the Iguanazul Hotel. The campground is located about 1 kilometer down this dirt road.

Hibiscus Hotel. Playa Junquillal (Apdo. 163-5150, Santa Cruz), Guanacaste. ☎ **506/653-0437**. 5 units. $34 double; $40 triple. No credit cards.

Though the accommodations here are very simple, the friendly German owner makes sure that everything is always clean and in top shape. The grounds are pleasantly shady, and the beach is just across the road. The rooms have cool Mexican-tile floors and firm beds. The hotel now has a restaurant. For years now, I've been getting glowing reports about both the service and general ambience here.

Hotel El Castillo Divertido. Playa Junquillal, Santa Cruz, Guanacaste. ☎ and fax **506/653-0428**. 7 units. Dec–Apr, $26–$32 double; May–Nov, $23–$26 double. MC, V.

Quite a few people have moved to Costa Rica from around the world in hopes of living out fantasy lives impossible in their home countries. This fanciful hotel is just such a creation. Built by a young German, the hotel is a tropical rendition of a classic medieval castle (well, sort of). Ramparts and a turret with a rooftop bar certainly grab the attention of passersby. Guest rooms here are fairly small, though rates are also some of the lowest in the area. Ask for an upstairs room with a balcony. If you don't get one of these, you'll still have a good view from the hotel's rooftop bar. The hotel is about 500 meters from the beach.

8 Playa Sámara

21½ miles (35km) S of Nicoya; 152 miles (245km) W of San José

Playa Sámara is a pretty beach on a long, horseshoe-shaped bay. Unlike most of the rest of the Pacific coast, the water here is excellent for swimming, since an offshore island and rocky headlands break up most of the surf. Because Playa Sámara is easily accessible by bus or car along a well-paved road, and because there are quite a few cheap cabinas, sodas, and a raging disco here, this beach is popular both with families seeking a quick and inexpensive getaway and with young Ticos out for a weekend of beach partying. In the wake of this heavy traffic, the beach can get trashed; however, the calm waters and steep cliffs on the far side of the bay make this a very attractive spot, and the beach is long and wide. Directly behind the main beach is a wide, flat valley that stretches inland and to the north.

ESSENTIALS

GETTING THERE & DEPARTING By Plane Sansa (in San José: ☎ **506/233-0397**, 506/233-3258, or 506/233-5330) flies to Carillo (15 minutes south of Sámara) daily at 7:30am, from San José's Juan Santamaría International Airport. The flight's duration is 1 hour and 10 minutes, with one stop en route; fare is $55 each way.

Travelair (in San José: ☎ **506/220-3054** or 506/232-7883) flies to Carillo daily at 1:20pm from Tobías Bolaños International Airport in Pavas. The flight stops at Punta Islita en route. The flight's duration is 55 minutes; fare is $80 one way, $131 round-trip.

Most hotels will arrange to pick you up in Carillo. If not, you'll have to hire a cab for around $7.

The Sansa flight leaves Carillo for San José at 8:40am. Travelair flies out of Carillo daily at 2:25pm.

By Bus An express bus (☎ **506/222-2666**) leaves San José daily at noon from Calle 14 between Avenidas 3 and 5. The trip lasts 6 hours; one-way fare is $5.

Alternatively, you can take a bus from this same San José station to Nicoya and then catch a second bus from Nicoya to Sámara. Buses leave San José for Nicoya daily at 6, 8, and 10am and 1, 2, 3, and 5pm. The trip takes 6 hours; fare is $4. Buses leave Nicoya for Sámara and Carillo daily at 8am, 3pm, and 4pm. The trip's duration is 1½ hours. The fare to Sámara is $1.25; fare to Carillo is $1.50.

The express bus to San José leaves daily at 4am. Buses for Nicoya leave daily at 5:30 and 6:30am. Buses leave Nicoya for San José daily at 4, 7:30, and 9am, noon, and 2:30 and 5pm.

By Car Take the Interamerican Highway from San José. Twenty-nine miles (47km) past the turnoff for Puntarenas, turn left toward the Tempisque ferry. After crossing the Tempisque River, continue north to Nicoya. In Nicoya, head more or less straight through town until you see signs for Playa Samara. From here it's a paved road almost all the way to the beach. (By way of explaining the pavement, rumor has it an important government official has a beach house here.) Alternatively, you can reach Nicoya via Liberia. This route is longer but comes in handy when the ferry is down or extremely busy.

ORIENTATION Sámara is a busy little town at the bottom of a steep hill. The main road heads straight into town, passing the soccer field before coming to an end at the beach. Just before the beach is a road to the left that leads to most of the hotels listed below. This road also leads to Playa Carillo and the Guanamar Resort.

FUN ON & OFF THE BEACH

Aside from sitting on the sand and soaking up the sun, the main activities in Playa Sámara seem to be hanging out in the sodas and dancing into the early morning hours. If you stay close to the center of town (by the soccer field), expect to stay up until the disco closes down.

You'll find that the beach is nicer and cleaner down at the south end, near **Las Brisas del Pacifico** hotel. The masses don't usually head south to Playa Carillo, a long, flat beach about 20 minutes from Sámara.

Caving Cavers will want to head 38½ miles (62km) northeast of Playa Sámara on the road to the Tempisque ferry. If you don't have a car, your best bet is to get to Nicoya, which is about half an a hour away by car, and then take a taxi to the park, which should cost about $10. Here, at **Barra Honda National Park**, there's an extensive system of caves, some of which reach more than 200 meters in depth. Human remains and indigenous relics have been found in other caves, but these are not open to the public. Since this is a national park, you'll have to pay the $6 entrance fee. If you plan to descend the one publicly accessible cave, you'll also need to rent (or bring your own) equipment and hire a local guide at the park/entrance station. Expect to pay around $50 to $60 per person for a visit to the Terciopelo cave. Furthermore, the cave is open only during the dry season (mid-November through April). Inside you'll see plenty of impressive stalactites and stalagmites and enough bats to last you till the next *Batman* sequel. Even if you don't descend, the trails around Barra Honda and its prominent limestone plateau are good for hiking and bird watching.

ACCOMMODATIONS

EXPENSIVE

✪ Villas Playa Sámara. Playa Sámara (Apdo 111-1007, Centro Colón, San José), Guanacaste. ☎ **506/256-8228.** Fax 506/221-7222. www.crica.com/hotels/vilsam.html. E-mail: htlvilla@sol.racsa.co.cr. 56 units. $95–$125 double; $185 quad. Off-season rates available. AE, MC, V.

Located 5 minutes south of town, right on the beach, this is the most luxurious hotel in Sámara. Built to resemble a small village, the resort consists of numerous bungalows varying in size from one to three bedrooms. Attractive though not overly luxurious, the villas are outfitted with bamboo furniture, and there are tiled bathrooms. All the villas have kitchens and patios, and some of the nice touches include colorful bedspreads and artwork, basket lampshades, and vertical blinds on the windows. White-stucco exterior walls and red-tile roofs give the villas a Mediterranean look.

Dining/Diversions: The open-air restaurant overlooks the pool and serves good seafood with an Italian tinge. There's a casino (open only in the high season) above the restaurant.

Amenities: Horse and bicycle rentals. A wide range of tours around the region can be arranged, as well as sportfishing and scuba diving. The swimming pool here is beautiful at night and has a swim-up bar and adjacent cold-water whirlpool tub. Other facilities include volleyball and badminton courts.

MODERATE

✪ Hotel Las Brisas del Pacífico. Playa Sámara (Apdo. 11917-1000, San José), Guanacaste. ☎ **506/656-0250.** Fax 506/656-0076. 36 units. Nov–Apr, $60–$75 double, $70–$85 triple; May–Oct, $40–$70 double or triple. AE, MC, V.

Located on the same road as the Marbella, this hotel is set amid very shady grounds right on a quiet section of the beach and backs up a steep hill. Most of the rooms are up a long and steep flight of stairs at the top of the hill and have large balconies and walls of glass that provide an excellent view of the bay. The third-floor rooms are the largest here, but due to the design, the second-floor rooms actually have the best views. At the base of the hill, there are rooms in stucco duplexes with steeply pitched tile roofs and red-tile patios. These rooms have cold-water showers only, but it's never cool enough here to warrant hot showers. Only a few steps from the beach, there's a small pool with a cold-water whirlpool. The main dining room is a breezy open-air restaurant surrounded by lush garden plantings. The menu changes daily, but the emphasis is always on German and European cuisine. Entree prices range from $6 to $14. There's also a second pool and bar at the top of the hill.

INEXPENSIVE

In addition to the accommodations listed below, you'll find a slew of very inexpensive places to stay along the road into town and around the soccer field. Many of the rooms at these places are less accommodating than your average jail cell. As an alternative, you can pitch a tent right by the beach for a few dollars at **Camping Cocos**, where you can also use their basic showers and bathrooms. You'll find Camping Cocos about 400 meters north of the center of town. It can be reached from the beach or from the main road heading north, parallel to the beach.

Cabinas Belvedere. Playa Sámara, Guanacaste. Fax **506/685-5004.** 9 units. $27 double. Includes continental breakfast. V.

This tropical Swiss chalet is located on the hillside across the street from the Hotel Marbella on the inland edge of town. The rooms are rather small, but they're immaculate and have fans and mosquito nets. There's a Jacuzzi here, but the clincher for me is the framed velvet paintings on the walls.

Hotel Giada. Playa Sámara, Nicoya, Guanacaste. ☎ **506/656-0132.** Fax 506/656-0131. 13 units. $37 double; $42 triple; $50 quad. Rates include breakfast. AE, MC, V.

This new Italian-owned hotel is located on the left-hand side of the main road into town, about 150 meters before the beach. The rooms are all very clean and comfortable and even have a small balcony. Breakfasts are served in a cool, shady central gazebo. The management is very helpful and can arrange dive or fishing expeditions and horseback riding trips.

Hotel Marbella. Playa Sámara, Guanacaste. ☎ **506/656-0122.** Fax 506/656-0121. 12 units. $25 double; $30 triple. Weekly and off-season discounts available. AE, MC, V.

Though it's a bit of a walk to the beach, and the immediate surroundings are none too appealing, this small German-run hotel is properly tropical in decor. You'll find the Marbella just around the corner from the road that leads down to the soccer fields and the beach. Guest rooms are fairly large and have red-tile floors and woven mats for ceilings. There are open closets and modern bathrooms with hot water. There's a small swimming pool in a gravel courtyard and a second-floor dining room with rattan chairs and a bamboo-fronted bar. All the rooms have a small balcony or porch, though not necessarily any sort of a view. The dining room serves only breakfast these days but is expected to prepare a dinner menu soon. You'll also find a bar and snack bar here.

DINING

There are numerous inexpensive sodas in Sámara, and most of the hotels have their own dining rooms. In town, try the following:

Colochos Bar. On the main street through town. No phone. Reservations not accepted. Main courses $4–$12. No credit cards. Daily 11am–10pm. COSTA RICAN/SEAFOOD.

This open-air rancho restaurant on the main road into town offers a wide selection of seafood. There are four different types of ceviche, lobster dishes, paella, and plenty of shrimp plates. Prices are very reasonable and portions are large. Though there's a thatch roof over your head, you'll find lace doilies on the tables.

NEARBY PLACES TO STAY & DINE

✪ **Hotel Punta Islita.** Apdo. 6054-1000, San José. ☎ **506/231-6122.** Fax 506/296-5773. www.nacion.co.cr/netinc/puntaislita.E-mail: ptaisl@sol.racsa.co.cr. 24 units, 1 casita. A/C TV. $132 double; $175 suite; $350 casita. AE, MC, V.

Set on a high bluff between two mountain ridges that meet the sea, Punta Islita is isolated. Although it's possible to drive here, most guests opt to fly into the nearby airstrip (see "Getting There," above). Punta Islita is just one beach down from Guanamar, but if you do drive, it's best to come over on the Naranjo ferry from Puntarenas and then up through Jicarral and Coyote. The rooms here are done in a Santa Fe style, with red Mexican floor tiles, neo-Navajo print bedspreads, and calm, adobe-colored walls offset with sky-blue doors and trim. Each room has a king-size bed, stocked minibar, and a private patio with a hammock. The suites come with a separate sitting room and a private two-person Jacuzzi. The hotel also rents one larger villa, with a fully equipped kitchenette, for longer stays or larger groups or families. The beach below the hotel is a small crescent of gray-white sand with a calm, protected section at the northern end. The hotel will shuttle you up and back. Otherwise, it's about a 10-minute walk away.

Dining: Meals are all served in the large, thatched rancho, which also houses the hotel's bar and sitting area. When you're this isolated, the meals better measure up, and so far Punta Islita has met the challenge. The emphasis is on fresh seafood in light nouvelle French sauces, but the steak in two-pepper sauce is also excellent.

Amenities: The small tile pool and adjoining Jacuzzi are set on the edge of the bluff and create the illusion of blending into the ocean far below. The hotel also has two tennis courts, a small gym, a golf driving range, water-sports equipment, bicycle and four-by-four rentals, a conference center, a shuttle to the beach, a tour desk, a small gift shop, laundry service, and nightly turndown. The hotel will send someone to pick you up at the airport.

PLAYA SAMARA AFTER DARK

Right at the entrance to Playa Samara, where the main road into town dead-ends into the sea, you'll find the town's small soccer field. Most of the nightlife in town is centered around this soccer field, where you'll find several very basic bars and a popular disco. Alternatively, you can check out what's happening down on the southern edge of town at the **Villas Playa Samara**, which is the largest resort in the area and therefore has one of the liveliest hotel bars. However, my favorite evening activity is still walking the long wide expanse of beach and watching the stars.

9 Playa Nosara

34 miles (55km) SW of Nicoya; 165 miles (266km) W of San José

Playa Nosara is actually several beaches, almost all of which are nearly deserted most of the time. Because the village of Nosara is several kilometers from the beach, and because the land near the beach has been turned into a large, spread-out resort community, Nosara has been spared the sort of ugly, uncontrolled growth characteristic of many other Guanacaste beaches. All of the hotels are spread out and most are tucked away down side roads. There is not the hotels-on-top-of-hotels feeling that you get at Playas Flamingo, Tamarindo, or Coco. In fact, on first arriving here, it's hard to believe there are any hotels around at all. Nosara has long been popular with North American retirees, and they too have made sure that their homes are not crammed cheek-by-jowl in one spot, hiding them instead among the profusion of trees that make Nosara one of the greenest spots on the Nicoya Peninsula. So, if you're looking for reliably sunny weather and a bit of tropical greenery, this is a good bet.

The best way to get to Nosara is to fly; however, with everything so spread out, that makes getting around once you've arrived difficult. The roads to and in Nosara are in horrendous shape, and though there has long been talk of some sections being widened and paved, it will probably still be quite a few years before the blacktop reaches here.

ESSENTIALS

GETTING THERE & DEPARTING By Plane Sansa (in San José: ☎ **506/233-0397**, 506/233-3258, or 506/233-5330) has one flight daily to Nosara, departing from San José's Juan Santamaría International Airport at 7:30am. Flight duration is 1 hour 20 minutes; fare is $50 each way. The flight stops first in Punta Islita and Puerto Carillo.

The Sansa flight departs Nosara daily at 8:57am.

By Bus An express bus (☎ **506/222-2666**) leaves San José daily at 6:15am from Calle 14 between Avenidas 3 and 5. The trip's duration is 6½ hours; one-way fare is $4.50.

You can also take a bus from San José to Nicoya (see "Playa Sámara," above, for details) and then catch a second bus from Nicoya to Nosara. A bus leaves Nicoya for Nosara daily at 1pm. Trip duration is 3 hours; one-way fare is $1.25.

The bus to San José leaves daily at 4pm. The bus to Nicoya leaves daily at 6am. Buses leave Nicoya for San José daily at 4, 7:30, and 9am, noon, and 2:30 and 5pm.

By Car Follow the directions above for getting to Playa Sámara but watch for a well-marked fork in the road a few kilometers before you reach that beach. The right-hand fork leads, after another 13½ miles (22km) of terrible road, to Nosara.

ORIENTATION The village of Nosara is about 3 miles (5km) inland from the beach; however, most of the hotels listed here are on the beach itself.

FUN ON & OFF THE BEACH

There are several beaches at Nosara, including the long, curving **Playa Guiones**, **Playa Nosara**, and, my personal favorite, diminutive **Playa Pelada**. This latter is a short white-sand beach lined with sea grasses and mangroves. However, there isn't too much sand at high tide, so you'll want to hit the beach when the tide's out. At either end of the beach there are rocky outcroppings that reveal tide pools at low tide. Surfing and bodysurfing are both good here; Playa Guiones in particular is garnering quite a reputation as a consistent and rideable beach break. Because the village of Nosara is several miles inland, these beaches are very clean, secluded, and quiet.

When evening rolls around, don't expect a major party scene. Nightlife in Nosara seems to be centered around the two bars located across from each other by the town's soccer field.

Fishing Charters Most of the hotels in the area can arrange fishing charters for $250 to $300 for a half day or $400 to $600 for a full day. These rates are for one to four people. You can also contact **Pesca Bahia Garza** (☎ **506/680-0856**) and arrange a half-day or full-day fishing trip.

Bird & Sea Turtle Watching Bird-watchers should explore the mangrove swamps around the estuary mouth of the Río Nosara. Just walk north from Playa Peleada and follow the riverbank; explore the paths into the mangroves.

If you time your trip right, you can do a night tour to nearby **Playa Ostional** to watch nesting olive Ridley sea turtles. These turtles come ashore by the thousands in a mass egg-laying phenomenon known as an arribada. These arribadas take place 4 to 10 times between July and November, with each lasting between 3 and 10 days. Consider yourself very lucky if you happen to be around during one of these fascinating natural phenomena. Even if it's not turtle-nesting season, you might still want to look into visiting Playa Ostional, just to have a long, wide expanse of beach to yourself. However, be careful swimming here, as the surf and riptides can be formidable. During the dry season (mid-November through April), you can usually get there in a regular car, but during the rainy season, you'll need four-wheel drive. This beach is part of Ostional National Wildlife Refuge. At the northwest end of the refuge is India Point, which is known for its tide pools and rocky outcrops.

A LANGUAGE SCHOOL & YOGA RETREAT

You can brush up or start up your Spanish in Nosara at the **Rey de Nosara Language School** (☎ and fax **506/382-8735**). A 2-week course, with 3 hours a day of lessons, costs $150.

If your pursuits are more physical and/or spiritual, you can check out the **Nosara Retreat** (☎ **888/803-0580** in the U.S., or fax 506/255-3351), which is a yoga retreat run by former instructors at the Kripalu Center. Rates here run around $200 per person per day, including room and board and yoga classes.

ACCOMMODATIONS

MODERATE

Estancia Nosara. Playa Nosara (Apdo. 37, Bocas de Nosara), Guanacaste. ☎ and fax **506/680-0378.** www.nosara.com. E-mail: estancia@nosara.com. 10 units. $40–$62 double; $50–$68 triple; $58–$82 quad. MC, V.

Although Estancia Nosara is a mile or so from the beach (located inland on the main road heading toward town and the airport), it's set amid shady jungle trees and has a swimming pool and tennis court, which together make this hotel a good value. There's an artificial waterfall tumbling from a small hill of stones near the pool and reproductions of pre-Columbian stone statues in the lush garden. The guest rooms are in two buildings and have red-tile floors, kitchenettes, high ceilings, overhead fans, showers with hot water, and plenty of closet space. There's a large open-air restaurant that serves moderately priced meals, and the hotel rents out horses, boogie boards, snorkeling equipment, and bikes. A full day of fishing arranged through the hotel will cost $400 for the boat, which can take up to four people.

Hotel Playas de Nosara. Playa Nosara (Apdo. 4, Bocas de Nosara), Guanacaste. ☎ and fax **506/680-0495.** www.nosara.com. E-mail: playasdenosara@nosara.com. 17 units. $75 double; $85 triple. Rates higher during peak weeks and lower in the off-season. AE, DC, MC, V.

Perched high on a hill above both Playa Pelada and Playa Guiones, this older hotel has the best views in the area, if not necessarily the best accommodations. In the 5 years I've been visiting, the place has always had the feeling of someone's unfinished backyard project. After years of delays, the large kidney-shaped pool is finally open, but the unfinished construction all around it will probably continue for some time. So far, all the rooms overlook Playa Guiones and have balconies so you can take in the great view. The gardens, though fairly lush, seem untended. The circular restaurant holds a high perch over Playa Pelada and is an excellent spot to take in the sunset.

Hotel Villa Taype. Playa Nosara (Apdo. 8-5233, Bocas de Nosara), Guanacaste. ☎ and fax **506/382-7715.** E-mail: taype@nosara.com. 12 units, 5 bungalows. $50–$60 double; $60–$70 triple. Rates include breakfast buffet. V.

Although a relatively new hotel, this place has already changed its name and management once. It's located down a side road that leads from the main road to Playa Guiones. The room decor is very simple but quite attractive. There are white-tile floors, high ceilings, overhead fans, and well-designed bathrooms. The higher prices are for rooms with air- conditioning. All have patios, but the bungalows have their own little *ranchito,* with a sitting area and hammock. The dining room, with its wood ceiling and arched windows overlooking the pool, serves moderately priced meals; the swimming pool has a swim-up bar. There's also a tennis court here, and you can rent bodyboards, surfboards, tennis rackets, and snorkeling gear. Best of all, the beach is only 100 yards away.

INEXPENSIVE

✪ **Almost Paradise.** Playa Nosara (Apdo. 15-5233, Bocas de Nosara), Guanacaste. No phone. Fax **506/685-5004.** E-mail: almost@nosara.com. 6 units. $34 double. No credit cards.

Located on the hill above Playa Pelada, this delightful little hotel is aptly named. This older wood building is a welcome relief from all the concrete and cinder block so common in Costa Rican construction. The rooms are simple and clean and feature colorful local artwork. All have access to an inviting covered veranda with strung hammocks and an ocean view. The attached restaurant has gone through several incarnations over the years yet has remained a local favorite.

A Cabina

Cabinas Chorotega. Nosara, Guanacaste. ☎ **506/680-0836** (public phone, Spanish only). 8 units (2 with bathroom). $10–$15 double. No credit cards.

Located on the outskirts of Nosara village, Cabinas Chorotega is about 3 miles (5km) from the beach, so you'll need to have some sort of transportation if you stay here and want to go the beach. The rooms are very basic but clean, and the rooms with private bathrooms are a particularly good value. Some rooms have more windows and are quite a bit brighter than others, so look at a couple of rooms if you can.

DINING

In addition to the place mentioned below, I've been getting rave reviews about the Italian food found at **La Dolce Vita** (no phone) found on the main road into town, about 1¼ miles (2km) before the sign that says "Bienvenidos a Playas de Nosara."

Doña Olga's. On the beach at Playa Pelada. No phone. Reservations not accepted. Main courses $1.50–$15. No credit cards. Daily 6:30am–10pm. COSTA RICAN.

Little more than a roof over a concrete slab, with some tables in between, Olga's is still one of the most popular restaurants in Nosara. Gringos and Ticos alike hang out here, savoring fried-fish casados, sandwiches, and breakfasts that include huge helpings of bacon. On the weekends the cavernous structure beside the restaurant becomes a lively disco.

10 Playa Tambor

93–104 miles (150–168km) W of San José (not including ferry ride); 12½ miles (20km) S of Paquera; 23½ miles (38km) S of Naranjo

Once a sleepy fishing village, Tambor became, in 1993, the site of Costa Rica's first all-inclusive beach resort. Though the original plans called for a sprawling mega resort with several hotels, controversy and shifting fortunes have stalled work on future development. Playa Tambor Resort currently has 402 units, which still makes it, for the moment, the largest beach resort in Costa Rica. It appears that 1999 may see the inauguration of a condominum and private bungalow development, as well as a 9-hole golf course.

Playa Tambor itself is a long scimitar of beach protected on either end by rocky headlands. These headlands give the waters a certain amount of protection from Pacific swells, making this a good beach for swimming. However, the sand is a rather hard-packed, dull gray-brown color, which often receives a large amount of flotsam and jetsam brought in by the sea. I also find this beach much less attractive than those located farther south along the Nicoya Peninsula.

Aside from the hotels listed here, there are a few inexpensive cabinas available near the town of Tambor, at the southern end of the beach. Your two best bets are **Cabinas El Bosque** (☎ **506/683-0039**) on the main road, and **Hotel Dos Largatos** (☎ **506/683-0236**), on the beach next to Tambor Tropical.

ESSENTIALS

GETTING THERE & DEPARTING **By Plane** **Sansa** (☎ **506/233-0397**, 506/233-3258, or 506/233-5330) flies twice daily to Tambor from San José's Juan Santamaría International Airport at 10:05am and 2:40pm. Flight duration is 30 minutes; fare is $45 each way.

Travelair (☎ **506/220-3054** or 506/232-7883) flies to Tambor daily at 11:30am from Tobías Bolaños International Airport in Pavas. Flight duration is 30 minutes; fare is $66 one way, $105 round-trip.

By Bus & Ferry If you're traveling from San José by public transportation, it takes two buses and a ferry ride to get to Tambor. If you miss your connections you might have to spend the night in Puntarenas, so plan ahead and give yourself plenty of time.

Express buses (☎ **506/221-5749**) leave for Puntarenas from San José daily every 30 minutes between 6:30am and 9pm from Calle 16 between Avenidas 10 and 12. Trip duration is 2 hours; fare is $2.50.

From Puntarenas take the passenger launch **Paquereña** (☎ **506/661-2830**), which leaves from the pier behind the market at 6am, 11am, and 3pm. This passenger launch (*la lancha*) should not be confused with the several car ferries that also leave from Puntarenas, and you should always check the schedule before making plans. Ferry-trip duration is 1½ hours; fare is $1.50. The bus south to Montezuma (this will drop you off in Tambor) will be waiting to meet the lancha when it arrives in Paquera. The bus ride takes about 45 minutes; fare is $2.

When you're ready to head back, the Paquera bus, which originates in Montezuma, passes through Tambor at approximately 6:15am, 10:45am, and 2:45pm to meet the Paquereña ferry, which leaves for Puntarenas at 8am, 12:30pm, and 5pm. Total trip duration is 3½ hours. Buses to San José leave Puntarenas daily every 30 minutes between 6:30am and 7pm.

By Car Take the Interamerican Highway from San José to Puntarenas and catch either the Naranjo ferry or the Paquera ferry.

In 1998, a new company was given permission to operate a car ferry between Puntarenas and Paquera, easing some of the load on this popular route. Lines and waits are much shorter now, but I still recommend arriving a little bit early during the peak season and on weekends. **Ferries to Paquera** leave daily at 5 and 8:45am and 12:30, 2, 5, and 8:15pm. The trip takes 1½ hours. Fare is around $10 for a car and driver; $1.50 for additional adults, $4 for adults in first class; $1 for children, and $2 for children in first class.

The **Naranjo ferry** (☎ **506/661-1069**) leaves daily at 3, 7, and 10:50am and 2:50 and 7pm. The trip takes 1½ hours. Fare is $9.50 for cars, $1.50 for adults, and 75¢ for children.

The car ferry from Paquera to Puntarenas leaves daily at 6, 8, and 8:45am and 2:30, 6, and 8:30pm. The car ferry from Naranjo leaves at 5:10 and 8:50am and 12:50, 5, and 9pm.

Tambor is about 45 minutes south of Paquera and 2 hours south of Naranjo. The road from Paquera to Tambor was upgraded when the resort was built, and taking the Paquera ferry will save you time and some very rough, dusty driving. The Naranjo road, until Paquera, is all dirt and gravel and in very bad shape.

ORIENTATION Though there's a small village of Tambor, through which the main road passes, the hotels themselves are scattered along several kilometers. You'll see signs for these hotels as the road circles around Playa Tambor.

FUN ON & OFF THE BEACH

Playa Tambor Beach Resort is an all-inclusive, full-service resort, so if you're staying here, you'll have access to all manner of beach toys. If you're staying at Hotel Tango Mar, you won't have access to so many toys, but you will have the Nicoya Peninsula's only golf course on the premises. All the hotels listed below offer horseback riding and tours around this part of the peninsula and can arrange dive trips.

Curú Wildlife Refuge (☎ **506/661-2392**), 10 miles (16km) north of Tambor, is a private reserve that has several pretty, secluded beaches, as well as forests and mangrove swamps. This area is extremely rich in wildlife. Howler and white-faced monkeys are often spotted here, as are quite a few species of birds. Admission for the day is $5 per person. Camping is also permitted for a nominal fee, and there are some basic cabins available with advance notice. If you don't have a car, you should arrange pickup with the folks who manage this refuge. Alternatively, you could hire a taxi in Paquera to take you there for around $6.

ACCOMMODATIONS

VERY EXPENSIVE

Barcelo Playa Tambor Beach Resort. Bahia Ballena, Puntarenas (mailing address: Barceló Hotels, P.O. Box 771-1150, La Uruca, San José). ☎ **506/683-0303.** Fax 506/683-0304. www.barcelo.com. E-mail: tambor@sol.racsa.co.cr. 402 units. A/C MINIBAR TV TEL. $182–$312 double; lower rates available in the off-season. Rates are all-inclusive. AE, DC, MC, V.

All-inclusive beach resorts can be found all over the Caribbean, but this was Costa Rica's first. Still, the beach here is mediocre at best, and the new resorts opening up farther north in Guanacaste would be my first choice if an all-inclusive, large resort vacation is what you're looking for. Moreover, the Playa Tambor development has been surrounded by controversy since its inception, and charges of violating Costa Rica's environmental laws and mistreating workers were leveled against the Spanish developers.

A huge complex of open-air buildings forms the lobby, theater, restaurants, and bars. The guest rooms are in attractively designed two-story buildings that are reminiscent of banana plantation houses. The rooms themselves are built to international standards, and though they have not even a hint of Costa Rican character, they're quite comfortable. Around the resort, hundreds of vacationers soak up the sun, splash in the pool and the waves, and indulge all day in the endless supply of free refreshments.

Dining/Diversions: The cost of all your meals and bar drinks is included in the room rates here, and when it comes time to eat, you can choose from a buffet at El Tucán, à la carte meals at El Rancho, or fast food from the poolside El Palenque. There are also a couple of different bars, a disco, an open-air theater that stages nightly entertainment revues, and a large casino.

Amenities: The free-form pool, one of the largest in the country, is surrounded by hundreds of lounge chairs and has a swim-up bar. Other facilities include lighted tennis courts, a basketball court, an outdoor exercise facility, and a whirlpool tub. Tours, cruises, jet skis, parasailing, sportfishing and sunset sailboat excursions, and scuba trips can be arranged for an additional cost. Sports equipment available for use by guests free of charge includes sailboards, sea kayaks, snorkeling gear, small sailboats (Hobie Cats and Sunfish), and boogie boards. Table tennis, croquet, and badminton are also available.

✪ **Hotel Tango Mar.** Tambor, Puntarenas (mailing address: Apdo. 3877-1000, San José). ☎ **506/683-0002**, or 800/648-1136 in the U.S. Fax 506/683-0003. www.tangomar.com. 35 units, 3 villas. A/C TV. $125 double; $140–$175 suites; $195–$275 villa. Rates include breakfast. DC, V.

Before the Playa Tambor Beach Resort was built, Tango Mar was the luxury resort in this neck of the woods. Today, it's still a great place to get away from it all. With only 18 rooms and scattered suites and villas, there are never any crowds. The water is wonderfully clear, and the beach is fronted by coconut palms and luxuriant lawns. If you choose to go exploring, you'll find seaside cliffs and even a waterfall that pours into a tide pool. The hotel rooms all have big balconies and glass walls to soak up the ocean views; some rooms even have their own Jacuzzi. The suites are set back among shade trees and flowering vegetation. Each has a carved four-poster canopy bed and indoor Jacuzzi. The villas are all different, but all are spacious and relatively secluded. Some of the suites and villas are a bit far from the beach and main hotel, so you'll either need your own car, or you'll have to rent a golf cart. My favorite suites are the five octagonal Tiki suites located close to the main lodge and beach.

Dining/Diversions: The small open-air restaurant overlooks the beach and has plenty of patio space. The varied menu includes plenty of fresh fish with prices ranging from $9 to $18 for entrees. There's also an adjacent bar.

Amenities: The swimming pool, though small, is set in a lush, secluded garden that is reached by way of a sidewalk across a frog pond. Tango Mar's 10-hole golf course is the only golf course on the Nicoya Peninsula (it has a $25 greens fee, which is for a full day of unlimited play). There are also tennis courts, guided horseback rides ($20 to $40), boat and snorkeling tours ($35 to $70), fishing charters ($250 to $500 for a half day, $800 for a full day for up to six people), limited room service, golf club and bike rentals, and massages.

Tambor Tropical. Tambor, Puntarenas (mailing address in the U.S.: Public Affairs Counsel, 867 Liberty St. NE, Salem, OR 97301). ☎ **506/683-0011**. Fax 506/683-0013. members.aol.com/tambort/tambor.htm. E-mail: tamborcr@sol.racsa.co.cr. 10 units. $125–$150 double. Rates include a continental breakfast. AE, MC, V.

If you're looking for upscale accommodations right in Tambor, this should be your first choice. The rooms here are located in five two-story octagonal cabins, and the whole place is an orgy of varnished hardwoods, with purpleheart and cocobolo offsetting each other at every turn. The rooms are enormous and come with large, complete kitchens and a spacious sitting area. The bed is located on a slightly raised platform beneath a ceiling fan. The walls are in effect nothing but shuttered picture windows, which give you the choice of gazing out at the ocean or shutting in for a bit of privacy. The upstairs rooms have large wraparound verandas, while the lower rooms have garden-level decks. The beach is only steps away. Plenty of coconut palms and flowering plants provide a very tropical feel.

Dining: The restaurant serves well-prepared meals and great desserts at very reasonable prices.

Amenities: There's an inviting free-form tile pool and Jacuzzi. A wide range of tours and activities can be arranged here, from horseback riding to scuba diving, with plenty of nature hikes mixed in between.

11 Playa Montezuma

103–114 miles (166–184km) W of San José (not including the ferry ride); 22½ miles (36km) SE of Paquera; 33½ miles (54km) S of Naranjo

For years, Montezuma has enjoyed near legendary status among backpackers, hippie expatriates, and European budget travelers. This fame and tourist traffic have had their price. The haphazard collection of budget lodgings that sprang up were generally pretty ratty, long-term campers were trashing the beach, and Montezuma earned a nasty reputation for having a sewage problem. In recent years, local businesspeople and hotel owners have joined together and addressed most of these problems. Now the town has a well-tended feel, and there are lodgings of value and quality in all price ranges. The local community even passed an ordinance shutting down all loud discos in the town center, so it's possible to get a good night's sleep as well.

Still, it's the natural beauty, miles of almost abandoned beaches, rich wildlife, and jungle waterfalls that first made Montezuma famous, and they are what keep this one of my favorite beach towns in Costa Rica. The water here is a gorgeous royal blue, and beautiful beaches stretch out along the coast on either side of town. Be careful, though: The waves can occasionally be too rough for casual swimming, and you need to be aware of stray rocks at your feet. Be sure you know where the rocks and tide are before doing any bodysurfing. The best places to swim are a couple hundred yards north of town in front of the El Rincón de los Monos campground, or several kilometers farther north at Playa Grande.

ESSENTIALS

GETTING THERE & DEPARTING **By Plane** The nearest airport to Montezuma is in Tambor, 10½ miles (17km) away. See above for flight details. Some of the hotels listed below may be willing to pick you up in Tambor for a reasonable fee. If not, you will have to see about hiring a taxi, which could cost anywhere between $10 and $20. Taxis are generally waiting to meet most regularly scheduled planes. Budget travelers can just walk the 50 meters out to the main road and hitchhike or flag down the next bus. Finally, you can call **Gilberto Rodríguez** (☎ **506/642-0241,** or beeper ☎ **506/296-2626**) for a cab.

By Bus & Ferry If you're traveling from San José by public transportation, it takes two buses and a ferry ride to get to Montezuma. If you miss your connections you might have to spend the night in Puntarenas, so plan ahead and give yourself plenty of time.

Express buses (☎ **506/221-5749**) leave San José for Puntarenas daily every 30 minutes between 6:30am and 9pm from Calle 16 between Avenidas 10 and 12. Trip duration is 2 hours; fare is $2.50.

From Puntarenas take the passenger launch Paquereña (☎ **506/661-2830**), which leaves from the pier behind the market at 6am, 11am, and 3pm. This passenger launch should not be confused with the several car ferries that also leave from Puntarenas, and you should always check the schedule before making plans. Ferry-trip duration is 1½ hours; fare is $1.50. The bus south to Montezuma will be waiting to meet the launch when it arrives in Paquera. The bus ride takes 1¾ hours; fare is $3.

When you're ready to return, the bus for Paquera leaves Montezuma daily at 5:30am, 10am, and 2pm and meets the Paquereña ferry, which leaves for Puntarenas at 8am, 12:30pm, and 5pm. Buses to San José leave Puntarenas daily every 30 minutes between 6:30am and 7pm.

By Car Take the Interamerican Highway from San José to Puntarenas and catch either the Naranjo ferry or the Paquera ferry.

In 1998 a new company was given permission to operate a car ferry between Puntarenas and Paquera, easing some of the load on this popular route. Lines and waits are much shorter now, but I still recommend arriving a little bit early during the peak season and on weekends. Ferries to Paquera leave daily at 5 and 8:45am and 12:30, 2, 5, and 8:15pm. The trip takes 1½ hours. Fare is around $10 for a car and driver; $1.50 for additional adults, $4 for adults in first class; $1 for children, and $2 for children in first class.

The Naranjo ferry (☎ **506/661-1069**) leaves daily at 3, 7, and 10:50am and 2:50 and 7pm. The trip takes 1½ hours. Fare is $9.50 for cars, $1.50 for adults, and 75¢ for children.

The car ferry from Paquera to Puntarenas leaves daily at 6, 8, and 8:45am and 2:30, 6, and 8:30pm. The car ferry from Naranjo leaves at 5:10 and 8:50am and 12:50, 5, and 9pm.

Montezuma is about 1½ hours south of Paquera and 3 hours south of Naranjo. The road from Paquera to Tambor has been upgraded with the arrival of the resort hotel, and taking the Paquera ferry will save you both time and some very rough, dusty driving. Beyond Tambor, it's approximately another 50 minutes to Montezuma.

ORIENTATION & INFORMATION As the winding mountain road that descends into Monteverde bottoms out, you turn left onto a small dirt road that defines the village proper. On this 1-block road, you will find the Sano Banano restuarant and across from it a small park with its own brand-new basketball court. The bus stops at the end of this road. From here, hotels are scattered up and down the beach and around the village's few sand streets.

Buses these days are met by hordes of locals trying to corral you to one of the many budget hotels. Remember, they are getting a small commission for every body they bring in, so their information is biased.

Your best one-stop resource is **Aventuras Montezuma** (☎ and fax **506/642-0050**), which functions as a tour and information clearinghouse. Located next to the Sano Banano restaurant, Aventuras Montezuma can arrange boat tours and rafting trips and offers car and motorcycle rentals, airport transfers, international phone and fax service, and currency exchange. However, since this is pretty much the only game in town, I've received complaints that the service can be gruff and indifferent. Most hotels can also arrange most of these tours and services.

FUN ON & OFF THE BEACH

In Montezuma, mostly you just hang out on the beach, hang out in a restaurant, hang out in a bar, or hang out in a hammock at your hotel. However, if you're interested in more than just hanging out, head for the waterfall just south of town. This waterfall is one of those tropical fantasies where water comes pouring down into a deep pool. It's a popular spot, but it's a bit of a hike up the stream. There are actually a couple of waterfalls up this stream, but the upper falls are by far the more spectacular. You'll find the trail to the falls just over the bridge south of the village (on your right just past Las Cascadas restaurant). At the first major outcropping of rocks, the trail disappears and you have to scramble up the rocks and river for a bit. A trail occasionally reappears for short stretches. Just stick close to the stream and you'll eventually hit the falls.

HORSEBACK RIDING & VISITING A GREAT TIDE POOL Several people around the village will rent you horses for around $5 to $8 an hour, though most people choose to do a guided 4-hour horseback tour for $25 to $35. These latter rides usually go to a second waterfall 5 miles (8km) north of Montezuma. This waterfall cascades straight down into a deep tide pool at the edge of the ocean. The pool here is a delightful mix of fresh and sea water, and you can bathe while gazing out over the sea and rocky coastline. When the water is clear and calm, this is one of my favorite swimming holes in all of Costa Rica. However, the pool here is dependent upon the tides—it disappears entirely at very high tide, when all you can do is visually admire the falls and physically enjoy the horse ride. You can also ride a horse to Cabo Blanco (see below). **Luis**, whose rental place is down the road that leads from town out to the beach, is a reliable source for horses, as is Roger, or **"Roger the horse guy"**—any local can direct you to him. However, you'll find the best-cared-for and -kept horses at **Finca Los Caballos** (☎ **506/642-0124**), which is located up the hill on the road leading into Montezuma.

OTHER ACTIVITIES There are a couple of rental shops in the center of the village where you can rent a bicycle by the day or hour, as well as boogie boards and snorkeling equipment (although the water must be very calm for snorkeling here). If you'd like to get out on the water and visit yet another beautiful beach, ask at your hotel or **Aventuras Montezuma** (see above) about boat trips to **Tortuga Island**. These tours last 5 hours and cost around $25, which is a considerable savings over similar trips offered by companies in San José—although the trips out of San José include a gourmet lunch that isn't a part of the trips from Montezuma.

AN EXCURSION TO CABO BLANCO NATURE RESERVE: PELICANS, HOWLER MONKEYS & BEAUTIFUL BEACHES

As beautiful as the beaches around Montezuma are, the beaches at **Cabo Blanco Absolute Nature Reserve**, 6¾ miles (11km) south of the village, are even more beautiful. Located at the southernmost tip of the Nicoya Peninsula, Cabo Blanco is a national park that preserves a nesting site for brown pelicans, magnificent frigate birds, and brown boobies. The beaches are backed by lush tropical forest that is home to howler monkeys. You can hike through the preserve's lush forest right down to the deserted, pristine beach. This is Costa Rica's oldest official bioreserve and was set up thanks to the pioneering efforts of conservationists Karen Mogensen and Nicholas Wessberg. Admission is $6.

On your way out to Cabo Blanco you'll pass through the tiny village of **Cabuya**. Some very basic cabinas and hotels have sprung up out here. There are nice deserted stretches of beach and very few travelers.

There are usually shared taxis heading out this way from Montezuma in the morning. The fare is around $5 per person. Taxis here are generally red 4 × 4s, clearly marked. They tend to hang around Montezuma center. Some enterprising locals also function as pirate taxis. The general rule is, "Don't call us, we'll find you." However, the most dependable *taxista* is **Gilberto Rodríguez** (☎ **506/642-0241**).

ACCOMMODATIONS

MODERATE

✪ **Amor de Mar.** Montezuma, Cóbano de Puntarenas. ☎ and fax **506/642-0262.** E-mail: shoebox@sol.racsa.co.cr. 11 units (9 with bathroom). $30–35 double with shared bathroom; $40–$60 double or triple with private bathroom. Rates slightly lower in the off-season. AE, MC, V.

It would be difficult to imagine a more idyllic spot in this price range. In fact, it's hard to imagine a much more idyllic spot at all. With its wide expanse of neatly trimmed grass sloping down to the sea, tide pools (one of which is as big as a small swimming pool), and hammocks slung from the mango trees, this is the perfect place for anyone who wants to do some serious relaxing. The owners, who have young children, love to have other families as guests, and there's always a cheerful family atmosphere. Couples and individuals will also enjoy a stay at Amor de Mar simply for the stunning location and beautifully appointed main building, which abounds in varnished hardwoods. Most of the rooms have plenty of space, and all are very clean and receive lots of sunlight. The big porch on the second floor is a great place for reading or just gazing out to sea. Only breakfast is served here, but it's one of the best in town, with the specialties including big banana pancakes and fresh homemade whole-wheat French bread.

✪ **El Sano Banano.** Montezuma, Cóbano de Puntarenas. ☎ and fax **506/642-0068.** www.efn.org/~timbl/cr/elbanano.htm. E-mail: elbanano@sol.racsa.co.cr. 3 units, 8 cabins, 1 apt. Dec–Mar, $45 double, $60–$70 cabin, $90–$140 apt; rates lower in off-season. AE, MC, V.

El Sano Banano is the sort of tropical retreat many travelers dream about. If you walk down the beach (toward your left as you face the water), after about 10 minutes you'll find it on the left. From the front porch of your cabin you can sit and listen to the waves crashing on the beach a few feet away. Please don't try to drive up the beach, even if you have a four-wheel-drive vehicle—seclusion and quiet are the main offerings of this place, and cars would ruin the atmosphere. If you don't want to carry all your bags, the hotel will be pleased to bring it to your room. There are two types of cabins here—most are white ferroconcrete geodesic domes that look like igloos, and there is one octagonal, hardwood Polynesian-style bungalow. There are also three standard rooms and one large apartment in a separate building. All have refrigerators, coffeemakers, and hot plates, and many guests opt for extended stays. All the rooms and cabins are set amid a lush garden planted with lots of banana and elephant-ear plants, and there are big rocks scattered beneath the shady old trees. One other thing you should know is that the showers, though private, are outside of the cabins, in the trees. This is the tropics. Why not?

✪ **Finca Los Caballos.** Apdo. 22, Cóbano de Puntarenas. ☎ and fax **506/642-0124.** E-mail: naturelc@sol.racsa.co.cr. 8 units, 1 apt. $50 double. V.

This new lodge is located on a high ridge about 1¾ miles (3km) above and before Montezuma. The rooms are in two separate concrete block buildings. Each room has one double and one single bed, private bathroom, and cement floors. Spanish-style tile roofs, hardwood trim, and some nice painting accents make this place feel a lot nicer than most budget lodges. I prefer the end rooms of each building as they have open gables (screened, of course) that allow for more cross ventillation. Every room has a small patio, and there are plenty of hammocks hung around. There's a small pool here, with a wonderful view of rolling hills down to the Pacific Ocean. The restaurant serves creative, well-prepared meals using fresh and natural ingredients.

The name of the lodge translates to "horse ranch," and riding is taken seriously here. The owners have 40 acres of land and access to many neighboring ranches and trail systems. The horses are well tended and trained. The standard trips to Montezuma's waterfalls and Cabo Blanco are available, as are overnight rides to Malpais and other adventure tour options.

Los Mangos. Montezuma, Cóbano de Puntarenas. ☎ **506/642-0259** or 506/642-0076. Fax 506/642-0050. 14 unitss (6 with bathroom), 10 bungalows. Dec–Mar, $30 double without bathroom, $45 double with bathroom, $60 bungalow. Apr–Nov, $20 double without bathroom, $30 double with bathroom, $40 bungalow. V.

This is still the only hotel in Montezuma with its own swimming pool. Situated across the road from the water and near Amor de Mar, it takes its name from the many mango trees under which the bungalows are built. (If mango is your passion, come in May, when they're in season.) The rooms are fairly basic, and those in the older building close to the road are a good value. However, it's the octagonal bungalows built of Costa Rican hardwoods that are the most attractively appointed. Each has a small porch with rocking chairs, a thatched roof, a good amount of space, and ceiling fans. The swimming pool is built to look like a natural pond, and there's even an artificial waterfall flowing into it. Beside the pool is a large rancho-style restaurant and bar serving reasonably priced Italian meals.

INEXPENSIVE

Now that camping on the beach is discouraged (although many folks still get away with it), most campers make do at **El Rincón de los Monos** (no phone), which is about 100 yards north of town along the beach, charges about $3 per tent, and provides showers and bathrooms. Others head south toward Cabuya and Cabo Blanco.

Hotel La Aurora. Montezuma, Apdo. 2, Cóbano de Puntarenas. ☎ and fax **506/642-0051.** 9 units. $15–$25 double; $5 each additional person. AE, MC, V (add 10% surcharge).

Just to the left as you enter the village of Montezuma, you'll see this large, white house. The rooms are spread around the spacious three-story building, which also features a small library of books, some hammocks and comfortable chairs, and flowering vines growing up the walls. In fact, there are vines all over La Aurora, which give it a tropical yet gothic feel. Most rooms are of average size and have wood walls that don't go all the way to the ceiling, which improves air circulation but reduces privacy. There are two new rooms up on the third floor with balconies and an ocean view over the treetops. Fresh coffee, tea, and hearty breakfasts are served each morning, and there's a kitchen available for guest use.

✪ **Hotel Lucy.** Montezuma, Cóbano de Puntarenas. ☎ and fax **506/642-0273.** 10 units (all with shared bathroom). $10 double; $15 triple. Lower rates available in the off-season. No credit cards.

This converted two-story home has the best location of any budget lodging in Montezuma, right on a pretty section of beach a bit south of town, in front of Los Mangos. If you can snag a second-floor room with an ocean view, you'll be in budget heaven. The beach here is a bit rough and rocky for swimming, but the sunbathing and sunsets are beautiful. There's a small restaurant here serving Tico standards at very reasonable prices all day long.

Hotel Moctezuma. Montezuma, Cóbano de Puntarenas. ☎ and fax **506/642-0058.** 21 units (12 with bathroom). $7 double without bathroom; $14 double with bathroom; $18 triple with bathroom; $22 quad with bathroom. Rates lower in the off-season. V (add 6% surcharge).

Located right in the center of the village and overlooking the small bay, the Hotel Moctezuma offers basic but clean rooms with fans, in two facing buildings. Some of the rooms are upstairs from the hotel's bar and restaurant; it may be noisy here, but you get a veranda with an ocean view. If you like to go to sleep early, try to get a room at the back of the building across the street instead. The walls don't go all the way to the ceiling, which is great for air circulation but lousy for privacy.

DINING

In addition to the places listed below, you'll find several basic sodas and casual restaurants right in the village. There is also the new **Bakery Idalie** (☎ **506/642-0458**), which is a great place to pick up a snack, something sweet, or the makings of a bag lunch.

El Sano Banano. On the main road into the village. ☎ **506/642-0272.** Reservations not accepted. Main courses $4–$8. AE, MC, V. Daily 7am–9:30pm. VEGETARIAN/INTERNATIONAL.

Delicious vegetarian meals including nightly specials, sandwiches, and salads are the specialty of this ever-popular Montezuma restaurant, although fish and chicken dishes are also served. Lunches feature some hefty sandwiches and fresh pizzas. You can even order a sandwich with cheese from the cheese factory in Monteverde, and there are always fish and vegetarian casados available for around $5. The nightly dinner menu specials are posted on a blackboard out front early in the afternoon so you can be savoring the thought of dinner all day. Any time at all, the yogurt-fruit shakes are fabulous, but I like to get a little more decadent and have one of the mocha shakes. El Sano Banano also doubles as the local movie house. They show nightly laser disc releases projected on a large screen and have a library of more than 300 movies. The movies begin at 7:30pm and require a $2.50 minimum purchase.

Las Cascadas. On the road out of town toward Cabo Blanco. ☎ **506/642-0589.** Reservations not accepted. Main courses $3–$10. AE, MC, V. Daily 7:30am–9pm. COSTA RICAN/SEAFOOD.

This little open-air restaurant is built on the banks of the stream just outside of the village and takes its name from the nearby waterfalls. The menu sometimes includes fresh fish fillets, whole red snapper, or shrimp in salsa ranchera. Las Cascadas even added a few vegetarian items recently (as well as some budget rooms). As one of the more enjoyable places in Costa Rica to have a meal, you can sit for hours beneath the thatched roof listening to the stream rushing past.

✪ **Playa de Los Artistas.** Across from Hotel Los Mangos. ☎ **506/661-2550.** Reservations not accepted. Main courses $6–$16. No credit cards. Mon–Sat 5–10:30pm. ITALIAN/MEDITERRANEAN.

If you're craving Italian food for dinner, this is the place to find it in Montezuma. The open-air restaurant is beside an old house fronting the beach, and there are only a few tables. This place is popular, so arrive early if you want to be sure of getting a seat. If you don't get a seat and you feel hearty, try the low wooden table surrounded by tatami mats on the sand. Meals are served in large, broad wooden bowls set on ceramic-ringed coasters and come with plenty of fresh bread for soaking up the sauces. The menu changes nightly but always features several fish dishes. The fresh grouper in a black pepper sauce is phenomenal. They recently added an outdoor grill for some great grilled fish and seafood.

MONTEZUMA AFTER DARK

Ever since the local bars were required to turn down their music at 10pm, most of Montezuma's raging nightlife has moved slightly out of town. On the road into Montezuma you'll find the **Kaliolin Disco**, which is open Wednesday, Friday, and Saturday nights. Last I heard, this place was for sale and rumored to be closing. Heading in the other direction, located about 1 kilometer toward Cabo Blanco, the new Las Manchas Disco is open nightly during the high season and more sporadically during the off-season. Both discos have been offering free round-trip taxi service in order to lure the crowds.

Before the discos get going, on slow nights and for those without enough impetus to get out of town, the local action seems to base itself either at **Chico's Bar** or at the **bar at the Hotel Moctezuma.** Both are located on the main strip in town facing the water. I also enjoy **El Chiringuito,** which has natural wood tables set in the sand under thatch-roofed palapas and serves some hearty bocas with their drinks. You can even borrow a chess or backgammon board here. It is located in downtown Montezuma, on the same road as Chico's and Hotel Moctezuma.

If your evening tastes are even mellower, El Sano Banano Restaurant also doubles as the local movie house. See their listing under "Dining," above, for more information.

12 Malpais & Santa Teresa

93 miles (150km) W of San José; 7½ miles (12km) S of Cóbano

Malpais translates as "badlands" and I can't decide if this is an accurate description or a deliberate local ploy to keep this place private. The beach here is a long, wide expanse of light sand dotted with rocky outcroppings. Sure, it can get rough here, but the surfers seem to like it. The road out here from Cóbano is perhaps even rougher than the surf, but this promises to keep out the madding crowds for some time to come. What you will find in Malpais and Santa Teresa are a scattering of beach hotels and simple restaurants, miles of nearly deserted beach, and easy access to some nice jungle and the nearby Cabo Blanco Reserve.

ESSENTIALS

GETTING THERE & DEPARTING **By Bus and Ferry** Follow the directions above for getting to Montezuma, but get off the Montezuma bus in Cóbano. From Cóbano there are two buses daily for Malpais and Santa Teresa, one in the morning and one in the afternoon (fare: $1.75), which in theory wait for the above buses. If you miss this bus connection, you can hire a cab for around $15.

By Car Follow the directions above to Montezuma. At Cóbano, follow the signs to Malpais and Playa Santa Teresa. It's another 7½ miles (12km) or so down a very rough dirt road, that pretty much requires four-wheel drive year-round and is sometimes impassable during the rainy season.

ORIENTATION Malpais and Santa Teresa are two tiny beach villages. As you reach the ocean the road will fork; Malpais is to your left, Santa Teresa is to your right.

FUN ON & OFF THE BEACH

If you do decide to do anything here besides lie on or walk the beach and body-, boogie-, or board-surf, your primary options include nature hikes and horseback riding. Most hotels here can help you arrange either, as well as trips to the nearby Cabo Blanco Reserve.

WHERE TO STAY & DINE

In addition to the hotels listed below, budget travelers should probably head over to **Cabinas Bosque Mar** (☎ **506/226-0475**), which is on the Malpais road and has a few basic rooms. You may also be able to pitch a tent. Look for camping signs; you should get bathroom and shower access for a few bucks.

If you venture away from your hotel for meals, you'll probably end up at **Frank's Place** (☎ **506/642-0296**), which is located at the crossroads where you enter town. Frank's is a notch above most sodas and seems to be the most happening spot in town.

✪ **Star Mountain Eco Resort.** Malpais, Cóbano, Puntarenas (Apdo. 1486-1250, Escazú). ☎ **506/296-5656.** Fax 506/642-0047. www.starmountaineco.com. E-mail: info@starmountaineco.com. 5 units (4 with bathroom). $25 per person shared bathroom; $65 double with bathroom. Rates include breakfast. No credit cards.

If you don't mind being a few rough kilometers away from the beach, this mountain lodge is an excellent place to escape it all and get very close to nature. The hotel has 86 hectares of its own land and basically borders the Cabo Blanco Reserve. The rooms are all wonderfully done in lively pastel colors, with cool tile floors and nice artwork on the walls. The bunkhouse is clean and comfortable and good for groups or students. There's a free-form tile pool and Jacuzzi, and guests can hike or ride horseback through the surrounding jungle. The restaurant features French/Belgian cuisine, and a full dinner should run you between $10 and $15. To get here, head toward Malpais and turn left at the sign for the lodge. It's another 2 miles (3km) or so up a dirt road, and you'll have to ford a river, so come by four-wheel-drive vehicle or horse.

✪ **Tropico Latino Lodge.** Playa Santa Teresa, Cóbano, Puntarenas. ☎ and fax **506/640-0062.** www.centralamerica.com/cr/hotel/tropico.htm. E-mail: tropico@centralamerica.com. 6 units. $56 double; lower rates in the off-season. No credit cards.

This simple hotel is still the nicest place in Malpais/Santa Teresa. The rooms, housed in three duplex bungalows, are massive. The king-size bamboo bed barely makes a dent in the floor space. There's also a separate sofa bed, as well as a small desk and wall unit of shelves and closet space. The bathrooms are modern and comfortable. Although none of the rooms has an unobstructed ocean view, they do all have private patios with a hammock. You'll find more hammocks and some chaise longues out on the beach. The shady grounds are rich in the native pochote tree, which is conspicuous for its spiky trunk. There's a swimming pool and Jacuzzi, if the ocean is too rough. The small restaurant here has excellent fresh fish and plenty of pasta dishes, probably just to please the palate of the Italian owners. A wide range of tours and activities can be arranged, as well as transport to Cóbano or the Tambor airport.

7 The Northern Zone

If you like your ecotourism rough and gritty but don't think you can take the heat and humidity of the Osa Peninsula (covered in chapter 9, "The Southern Zone"), this is the area for you. The northern zone, roughly defined here as the area north of San José and between Guanacaste province on the west and the lowlands of the Caribbean coast on the east, is a naturalist's dream come true. There are rain forests and cloud forests, jungle rivers, and an unbelievable diversity of birds and other wildlife. In addition to its reputation for muddy hiking trails and crocodile-filled rivers, the northern zone claims one of the best windsurfing spots in the world (on Lake Arenal, which is free of crocodiles, by the way) and Costa Rica's most active volcano. **Arenal Volcano**, when free of clouds, puts on spectacular nighttime light shows and by day is reflected in the waters of nearby **Lake Arenal**. Adding a touch of comfort to a visit to the northern zone are several hot springs and a variety of hotel options that vary in their levels of luxury.

1 Puerto Viejo de Sarapiquí

51 miles (82km) N of San José; 63¼ miles (102km) E of La Fortuna

The Sarapiquí region, named for the river that drains this area, lies at the foot of the Cordillera Central mountain range. To the west is the rain forest of Braulio Carrillo National Park, and to the east are Tortuguero National Park and Barra del Colorado National Wildlife Refuge. In between these protected areas lie thousands of acres of banana, pineapple, and palm plantations. It's here that you can see the great contradiction of Costa Rica: On the one hand, the country is known for its national parks, which preserve some of the largest tracts of rain forest left in Central America; on the other hand, nearly every acre of land outside of these parks has been clear-cut and converted into plantations—and the cutting continues.

Within the remaining rain forests, there are several lodges that attract naturalists (both amateur and professional). Two of these lodges, La Selva and Rara Avis, have become well known for the research that's conducted on their surrounding reserves.

The Northern Zone

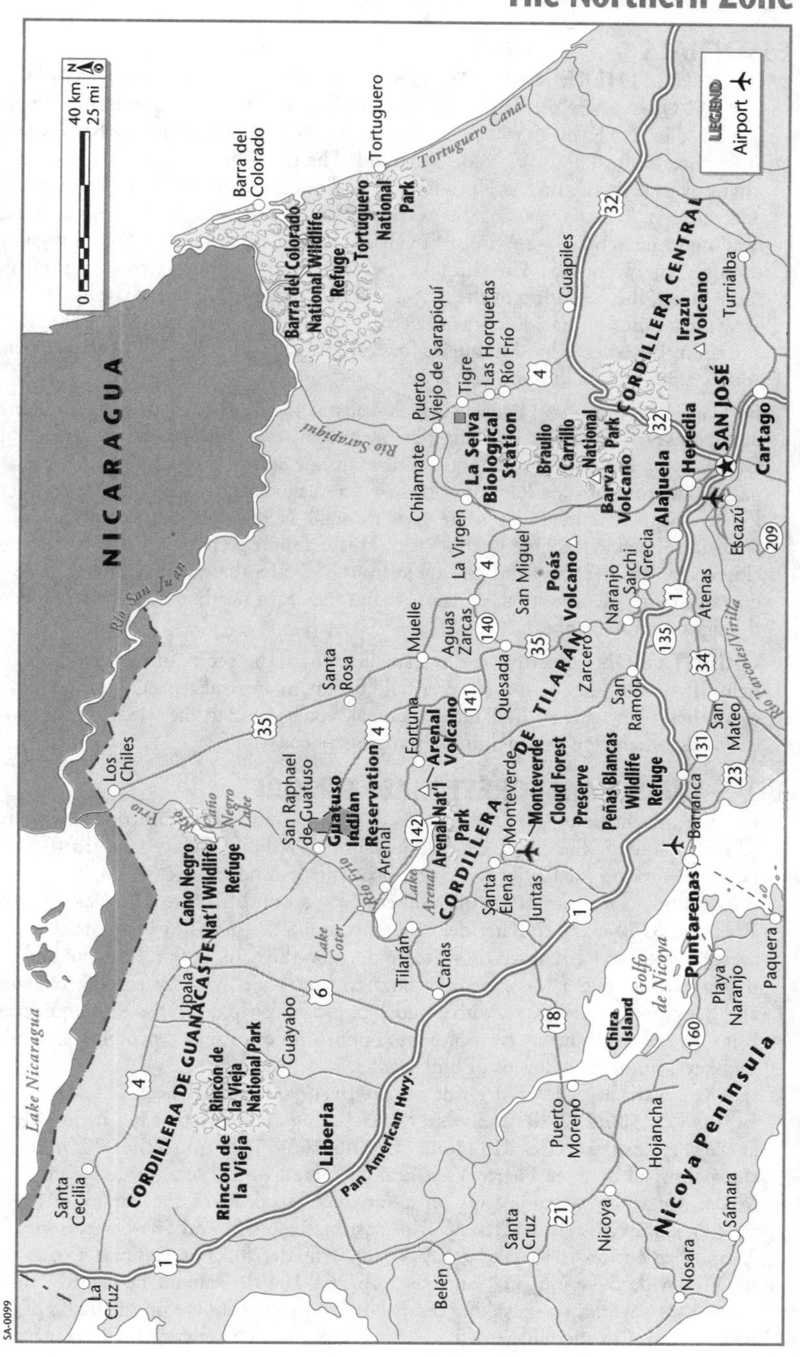

ESSENTIALS

GETTING THERE & DEPARTING **By Bus** Express buses (☎ **506/259-8571**) leave San José daily at 8, 10, and 11am and 1, 3, and 4pm from Avenida 9 and Calle 12. The buses will be marked "Rio Frio," "Puerto Viejo," or both. There are two routes to Puerto Viejo de Sarapiquí. The faster heads out on the Guápiles Highway and then past Las Horquetas. The slower, but more scenic, route heads out through Heredia, passing between the Barva and Poás volcanoes. If you're heading to La Selva, Rara Avis, or El Gavilán lodges, be sure you're on a bus going through Las Horquetas. The trip takes between 2 and 4 hours, depending on the route taken, the condition of the roads, and the frequency of stops; fare is $3.50.

Express buses for San José leave Puerto Viejo daily at 7, 8, and 11am and 1, 3, and 4pm. Buses leave Las Horquetas for San José daily at 7:30, 8:30, and 11:30am and 2, 3:30, 4:30, and 6pm; fare is $2.50.

By Car The Guápiles Highway, which leads to the Caribbean coast, heads north out of downtown San José on Calle 3 before heading east. Turn north before reaching Guápiles on the road to Río Frío and continue north through Las Horquetas, passing the turn-offs for Rara Avis, La Selva, and El Gavilán lodges, before reaching Puerto Viejo. An alternative route goes through Heredia, Barva, Varablanca, and San Miguel before reaching Puerto Viejo. This is a more scenic route and passes very close to the Poás Volcano and directly in front of the La Paz waterfall. If you want to take this route, head west out of San José and then turn north to Heredia and follow the signs for Varablanca.

ORIENTATION Puerto Viejo is a small town, at the center of which is a soccer field. If you continue past the soccer field on the main road and stay on the paved road, then turn right at the Banco Nacional, you'll come to the Río Sarapiquí and the dock, where you can look into arranging a boat trip.

BOAT TRIPS, RAIN-FOREST HIKES & MORE

For the adventurous, Puerto Viejo is a jumping-off point for trips down the Río Sarapiquí to Barra del Colorado National Wildlife Refuge and Tortuguero National Park on the Caribbean coast. Boat trips can be arranged at most hotels in town. A boat for up to 10 people will cost you around $100 to Oro Verde Lodge and back, $250–$275 to Barra del Colorado, and $275–$300 to Tortuguero. Alternatively, you can head down to the town dock on the bank of the Sarapiquí and see if you can arrange a less-expensive boat trip on your own, by tagging on with another group, or better yet, with a bunch of locals. A trip down the Sarapiquí, even if it's for only an hour or two, provides opportunities to spot crocodiles, caimans, monkeys, sloths, and dozens of bird species.

If you want a faster, wilder ride on the river, you should check in with **Aguas Bravas** (☎ **506/292-2072**) a white-water-rafting company that has its local base at the very basic **Islas del Rio Hotel** (☎ **506/766-6574**). You'll find this hotel on the main road between Puerto Viejo and Chilamate on the left a little before Selva Verde. Aguas Bravas runs trips on a variety of sections of the Sarapiquí River, ranging from Class III to Class V. Trips cost between $55 and $75 per person.

Another option is to take a kayak trip with the folks at **Rancho Leona**, in La Virgen de Sarapiquí (☎ and fax **506/761-1019**). Rancho Leona is a small stained-glass workshop, kayaking center, and rustic guest house on the banks of the Río Sarapiquí in the village of La Virgen. The trips are offered as a package that includes 2 nights' lodging in simple, dormitory-style accommodations and an all-day kayak trip with some basic instruction and lunch on the river. The cost for the

2-day trip is $75 per person. No experience is necessary, and the river is very calm. More extensive trips, and trips for experienced kayakers, can be arranged, and these folks have a very isolated geodesic dome cabin deep in the rain forest.

If you're driving to Puerto Viejo de Sarapiquí via the Guápiles Highway, you might want to stop at the **Aerial Tram**. Entrance into the facility, which includes a guided tour and hike on their rain-forest trails, video presentation, and 90-minute ride on the tram. The entrance fee is $47.50 per person, but it allows you to spend the whole day exploring their network of trails, in addition to the above. You'll see the entrance to the Aerial Tram on your right, a little bit after passing through the Zurquí tunnel. For more information, see chapter 5, "Side Trips from San José."

Finally, if you want to visit the Sarapiquí region on a day trip from San José, call **Costa Rica Fun Adventures** (☎ **506/228-4354**), which runs a jam-packed day trip up here that combines a bus ride and stop at the La Paz waterfall, a visit to a banana plantation, a rain-forest hike and a boat ride on the river for $75 per person.

ACCOMMODATIONS & DINING

All of the lodges listed below arrange excursions throughout the region, including boat trips on the Sarapiquí, guided hikes in the rain forest, and horseback or mountain-bike rides.

IN PUERTO VIEJO

Hotel El Bambú. Apdo. 1518-2100, Puerto Viejo, Sarapiquí. ☎ **506/766-6005.** Fax 506/766-6132. 14 units. TV TEL. $58 single or double, $64 triple, $75 quad. Rates include continental breakfast. AE, MC, V.

This is the most luxurious hotel in Puerto Viejo, although that's not saying a whole heck of a lot. The best rooms here are up on the second floor facing away from the main road. The rooms have high ceilings, tile floors, and attractive bamboo furniture. Three of the rooms have air-conditioning. Downstairs, just off the lobby, you'll find the big open-air restaurant that overlooks the dense grove of bamboo for which the hotel is named. The restaurant serves basic Tico and Chinese standards. You'll find the hotel directly across the street from the soccer field in the middle of town. Tours around the region, as well as boat trips down the Río Sarapiquí as far as Barra del Colorado and Tortuguero, can be arranged.

Mi Lindo Sarapiquí. Puerto Viejo, Sarapiquí. ☎ **506/766-6281.** 7 units. $12 double, $18 triple. AE, MC, V.

This little family-run lodging is located in the center of town overlooking the soccer field. The rooms are on the second floor above the large restaurant and bar. Nothing fancy, but this is the most popular budget lodging around. Although, be warned, the bar/restaurant is popular with locals and can be noisy.

SOUTH OF PUERTO VIEJO

✪ **El Gavilán Lodge.** Apdo. 445-2010, Zapote, San José. ☎ **506/234-9507.** Fax 506/253-6556. http//:costarica.tourism.co.cr/hotels/gavilan. E-mail: gavilan@sol.racsa.co.cr. 15 units (13 with bathroom). $50 double, $75 triple. Lower rates during off-season. MC, V.

Located on the banks of the Río Sarapiquí just south of Puerto Viejo on the road to Río Frío, El Gavilán is surrounded by 250 acres of forest reserve (secondary forest) and 25 acres of gardens planted with lots of flowering ginger, heliconia, and bromeliads. If you're interested in orchids, plan a visit in December, when many of these beautiful flowers are in bloom. Guest rooms are simply furnished but do have fans and hot water, and there are always fresh-cut flowers. What El Gavilán lacks in luxurious comfort, it makes up for in friendliness and attentive service. The rooms in the main building are quite basic but have huge bathrooms with two sinks. Other rooms are in rustic duplexes with cement floors. Most have one single and one double bed, but there are variations. There's a Jacuzzi in the garden and several open-air ranchos, some of which have hammocks strung up for afternoon siestas. Tico and continental meals are served buffet style, and there's always plenty of fresh fruits and juices. Breakfast will run you $5, and lunch and dinner each cost $12. Travelers interested in the outdoors and nature will most enjoy a stay here. There's a kilometer-long nature trail at the lodge, and various excursions can be arranged. Guided hikes through the forest, horseback rides, and river trips are all offered for around $20 per person. Multiday packages, as well as day trips to the Arenal Volcano, are also available.

La Selva Biological Station. South of Puerto Viejo (U.S. mailing address: Interlink 341, P.O. Box 02-5635, Miami, FL 33152). ☎ **506/240-6696.** Fax 506/240-6783. www.ots.ac.cr. E-mail: reservas@ns.ots.ac.cr. 10 units. $60 per person double occupancy. Lower rates for researchers. Rates include 3 meals daily. MC, V.

Located a few kilometers south of Puerto Viejo, La Selva Biological Station caters primarily to students and researchers but also accepts visitors seeking a rustic rain-forest adventure. The atmosphere is definitely that of a scientific research center. La Selva, which is operated by the Organization for Tropical Studies, covers 3,700 acres and is contiguous with Braulio Carrillo National Park. Researchers estimate that more than 2,000 species of flora exist in this private reserve, and 400-plus species of birds have been identified here. Rooms are basic, but they are large, and the high ceilings help keep them cool. Most have bunk beds and shared bathrooms. The dining hall is a big, bright place where students and scientists swap data over fried chicken or fish and rice and beans. Because scientific research is the primary objective of La Selva, researchers receive priority over casual, short-term visitors. However, very informative guided tours are available most days, even if you are staying at another hotel in the area. Call the local number (☎ **506/766-6565**) at least 1 day in advance to arrange one of these. If you wish to stay overnight at La Selva, you must have a reservation with the San José office. Since there are very few rooms here, it pays to book well in advance. Direct transportation to and from La Selva costs $10 each way, and is available only on Monday, Wednesday, and Friday.

Rara Avis. Apdo. 8105-1000, San José (mailing address in the U.S.: Dept. 1389, Box 025216, Miami, FL 33102). ☎ and fax **506/253-0844** or 506/764-3131. www.cool.co.cr/raravis. E-mail: raraavis@sol.racsa.co.cr. 17 units (10 with bathroom). $75 double with shared bathroom, $135 double with private bathroom. Rates include transportation from Las Horquetas, guided hikes, and 3 meals daily. MC, V.

Once the exclusive stomping grounds of scientists and students, Rara Avis was made famous by the pioneering canopy research of Dr. Donald Perry, who first erected his famous canopy cable-car system in the rain forest here. Since that time, Rara Avis has become a very popular destination for people with a more casual interest in the rain forest. Though Perry's canopy cable car is no longer here, this rain-forest research facility is still a fascinating place to visit. To get here, you must first travel to the village of Las Horquetas, which is between Guápiles and Puerto Viejo de Sarapiquí. In Las Horquetas, you're met by a tractor that takes 3 hours to cover the 9¼ miles (15km) to Rara Avis's more popular lodge (there are two lodges and one cabina here). The road is periodically graded, but the last 2 miles (3km) are still over a road made of fallen logs and deep, deep mud. You should always confirm your travel arrangements with the lodge. If you don't have a car, you'll have to rely on the bus—take the 7am "Rio Frio" bus out of San José (Calle 12 between Avenidas 7 and 9); this bus does not continue on to Puerto Viejo. In Río Frío, you will then have to grab a taxi to take you the rest of the way to Las Horquetas (cost around $2.50). On special occasions, the lodge may hold up its tractor to allow for folks who take the 8am Puerto Viejo bus, but you must confirm this in advance with the lodge.

The Waterfall Lodge is by far the more comfortable and has rustic rooms and a wraparound porch. The more economical El Plastico Lodge was at one time a penal colony, and though it's been renovated and converted, it's still very spartan. There's a new cabina set deep in the forest beside a river, with two comfortable rooms for those wanting closer communion with nature. (It's a 10-minute walk from the main lodge.) Finally, there's a treetop cabin that requires an athletic 100-foot ascent with harness and climbing gear, and then a rappel back down. There are beds up here, and you can spend the night, but there is no bathroom or other facilities, and it gets expensive, as you can't book this aerie by itself—you also have to keep a room in either El Plastico or the Waterfall Lodge. Meals are basic Tico-style dishes with lots of beans and rice. Rara Avis is adjacent to Braulio Carrillo National Park, and together the two have many miles of trails for you to explore. Bird-watchers take note: More than 320 species of birds have been sighted here. When making reservations, be sure to get directions for how to get to Las Horquetas.

West of Puerto Viejo

La Quinta de Sarapiquí Country Inn. Chilamate, Sarapiquí. ☎ and fax **506/761-1052.** 15 units. $45 double. MC, V.

This small family-run lodge makes a good base for exploring the Sarapiquí region. Located on the banks of the Sardinal River about 15 minutes west of Puerto Viejo, La Quinta caters primarily to nature lovers and bird-watchers. The rooms are located in four buildings dispersed around the grounds among richly flowering gardens. The rooms are simple but clean and have either two or three single beds. There are no double or queen-size beds here, so couples beware. Each room has a small patio with a sitting chair or two for gazing out into the garden. Meals are served family style in the main lodge and will run you an extra $20 per day. There's a small pool, and it's even safe to swim in the river. There's also a small gift shop, a small butterfly garden, and a reforestation project on hand. Horses are available for guests to ride free of charge, and a host of tours around the region are offered as well. If you don't have a car, call the hotel to see if you can arrange a pickup in Puerto Viejo.

Selva Verde Lodge. Apdo. 55, Chilamate, Sarapiquí. ☎ **800/451-7111** in the U.S. and Canada, or 506/766-6800. Fax 506/766-6803. www.hlbrooktravel.com. E-mail: travel@holbrooktravel.com. 40 units, 5 bungalows. $100 double, $125 triple; rates slightly lower during the off-season. Rates include 3 meals daily. MC, V.

For years, this was one of the showcase ecotourist lodges in Costa Rica. A recent remodeling included the building of a new reception area and a covered bus port for the numerous tour buses that come here. Frankly, I think the success has gone to their heads. Service, food, and personal attention have all suffered. Located right off the main highway a few kilometers west of Puerto Viejo, Selva Verde is bounded by the Río Sarapiquí, across which is a large rain-forest preserve. The rooms here are all connected by covered walkways that keep you dry even though this area receives more than 150 inches of rain each year. The lodge buildings are all built of varnished hardwoods, inside and out, and are built on pilings so that all the rooms are on the second floor. These are without doubt the nicest rooms in the area. The bungalows are located across the road and 500 meters into the forest and are not nearly as comfortable as the rooms in the main compound, but they do offer somewhat more privacy. Meals are served buffet style in a beautiful large dining room that overlooks the river; they're well prepared and filling but not too creative. There are several trails on the grounds, a wonderful suspension bridge across the Sarapiquí River to more trails, and modest butterfly and botanical gardens. Excursions that can be arranged through the lodge include river trips ($25 per person), rafting trips ($45 per person), horseback riding ($20 per person), and guided walks ($15 per person).

2 Arenal Volcano & La Fortuna

87 miles (140km) NW of San José; 37¾ miles (61km) E of Tilarán

If you've never experienced it firsthand, the sight and sound of an active volcano erupting are awesome. Until 1937 when the mountain just west of La Fortuna was first scaled, no one ever dreamed that it might be a volcano. Gazing up at the cinder-strewn slopes of Arenal Volcano today, it's hard to believe that people could not have recognized this perfectly cone-shaped volcano for what it is. However, in July 1968, the volcano, which had lain dormant for hundreds of years, surprised everybody by erupting with sudden and unexpected violence. The nearby village of Tabacón was destroyed, and nearly 80 of its inhabitants were killed. Since that eruption 30 years ago, 5,358-foot Arenal has been Costa Rica's most active volcano. Frequent powerful explosions send cascades of red-hot lava rocks tumbling down the western slope, and during the day the lava flows steam and rumble. However, it's at night that the volcano puts on its most mesmerizing show. If you are lucky enough to be here on a clear night, you'll see the night sky turned red by lava spewing from Arenal's crater. In the past few years, the forests to the south of the volcano have been declared Arenal National Park. Eventually, this park should stretch all the way to Monteverde Biological Cloud Forest Preserve.

Lying at the eastern foot of this natural spectacle is the tiny farming community of La Fortuna. In recent years, this town has become a center for volcano-watchers from around the world. There are a host of moderately priced hotels in and near La Fortuna, and it's here that you can arrange night tours to the best volcano-viewing spots, which are 10½ miles (17km) away on the western slope, past the Tabacón Hot Springs.

ESSENTIALS

GETTING THERE & DEPARTING By Bus Buses (☎ **506/255-4318**) leave San José for La Fortuna daily at 6:15, 8:40, and 11:30am from the Atlantico del Norte bus station at Avenida 9 and Calle 12. The trip's duration is 4½ hours; fare is $2.75.

Alternatively, you can take a bus to Ciudad Quesada from the same location in San José and then take a local bus from Ciudad Quesada to La Fortuna. Ciudad Quesada buses leave San José daily every hour on the hour, but the schedule is flexible. Buses are sometimes added or canceled depending on demand and hours may vary. You'll never have to wait more than an hour for the next bus, but if you want to be sure, it's best to call (☎ **506/255-4318**). The fare for the 3-hour trip is $2. The bus you take may be labeled "Tilarán." Don't worry, this bus stops in La Fortuna. The schedule for these buses changes frequently depending on demand, so it is best to check, but generally it is not hard to get from Ciudad Quesada to La Fortuna by bus. The trip lasts 1 hour; fare is $1.25.

Buses depart La Fortuna for San José daily at 5am, 11am, and 2:45pm. Buses to Ciudad Quesada leave at 6, 7, 8:30, 10, and 11:30am and 1, 2, and 4pm daily. From there, you can catch one of the hourly buses to San José.

By Car There are several routes to La Fortuna from San José. The most popular is to head west on the Interamerican Highway and then turn north at Naranjo, continuing north through Zarcero to Ciudad Quesada. From Ciudad Quesada, one route goes through Jabillos, while the other goes through Muelle. The former route is more popular and was repaved in 1997. However, the severe weather and heavy traffic up here quickly take their toll, and I don't expect the smooth roads to last very long. You can also go first to Alajuela or Heredia and then head north to Varablanca before continuing on to San Miguel, where you turn west toward Río Cuarto and Aguas Zarcas. From Aguas Zarcas, continue west through Muelle to the turnoff for La Fortuna. This is the longest route and recommended only if you really want to combine your visit here with a stop at the Poás Volcano and La Paz waterfall, and if you're staying at one of the lodges closer to Aguas Zarcas. Travel time on most of the other routes is between 3 and 4 hours. A new route from San Ramón (west of Naranjo) north through La Tigra is very scenic and passes the Villablanca and Valle Escondido lodges and is currently the fastest route to La Fortuna.

ORIENTATION As you enter La Fortuna, you will see the massive volcano directly in front of you. La Fortuna is only a few streets wide, with almost all the hotels, restaurants, and shops clustered along the main road that leads out of town toward Tabacón and the volcano. There are several small information and tour-booking offices across the street from the soccer field.

EXPERIENCING THE VOLCANO

The first thing you should know is that you can't climb Arenal Volcano; it's not safe due to the constant activity. Several foolish people who have ignored this warning have lost their lives, and others have been severely injured. The second thing you should know is that Arenal Volcano borders a region of cloud and rain forests, and the volcano's cone is often socked in. Many people come to Arenal and never get to see the exposed cone. Moreover, the volcano does go through periods when it is relatively quiet. Still, waiting for and watching Arenal's nearly constant eruptions is the main activity in La Fortuna and is best done at night when the orange lava glows against the starry sky. Though it's possible simply to look up from the middle of town and see Arenal erupting, the view is better from the west side of the volcano. If you have a car, you can drive to the west side, but if you've arrived by bus, you will need to take a taxi or tour. Arenal National Park constitutes an area of 2,920 hectares, which include the viewing and parking areas closest to the volcano. The park is open from 8am to 10pm daily and charges $6 admission per person. However, unless you need actually to feel the heat of a lava flow, you will probably find the view of the natural fireworks perfectly acceptable from the dirt road just outside the park entrance. One other option for good viewing is to dine at the Arenal Observatory Lodge and then hang out on their deck for the nightly light show.

If you don't have a car and are staying in La Fortuna, night tours are offered through every hotel in town and at several tour offices on the main street, at a cost of $7 to $15 per person. Almost all of the tours include a stop at one of the hot

Taking a Soothing Soak in Tabacón Hot Springs

One of the primary fringe benefits that Arenal Volcano has bestowed on the area around it are several naturally heated thermal springs. Located at the site of the former village, Tabacón Hot Springs Resort is the most extensive and luxurious spot to soak your tired bones. A series of variously sized pools, fed by natural springs, are spread out among lush gardens. At the center is a large pool with a slide, a swim-up bar, and a perfect view of the volcano. One of the stronger streams flows over a sculpted waterfall, with a rock ledge underneath that provides a perfect place to sit and receive a free hydraulic shoulder massage. The resort also offers professional massages, mud masks, and an excellent restaurant serving local and Italian dishes. Entrance fees are $14 for adults; $7 for children.

Across the street from the resort and down a gravel driveway is another bathing spot fed by the same springs. You'll find several large pools here but far more basic facilities and no view. Admission is $5.

Finally, there's a free public spot located in a densely forested section of the road between Tabacón and the park entrance. This area has some very rudimentary dams set in a section of a warm side-stream. To find it, keep going past the Tabacón Hot Springs Resort away from La Fortuna. You'll soon enter the forested section. After a few tight turns, the path leading down to the springs is on your left. There's a small sign and this is a well-known and popular spot, so you'll usually see several cars parked on the side of the road here.

springs, but they don't actually enter the park proper. You can watch the volcano only from the road that runs between the park entrance and the Arenal Observatory Lodge.

OTHER ADVENTUROUS PURSUITS IN THE AREA

Aside from the impressive volcanic activity, the area around Arenal Volcano is packed with other natural wonders.

Leading the list of side attractions is the **Río Fortuna waterfall**, which is located about 3½ miles (5.5km) outside of town in a lush jungle setting. There's a sign in town to indicate the road that leads out to the falls. Depending on recent rainfall, you can hike or drive to just within viewing distance. Once you get to a makeshift entrance to the lookout, you'll have to pay the $3 entrance fee actually to check out the falls. It's another 15- to 20-minute hike down a steep and often muddy path to the pool formed by the waterfall. You can swim here, but stay away from the turbulent water at the base of the falls—several people have drowned here. Instead, check out and enjoy the calm pool just around the bend.

If this seems like too much exercise, you can rent a horse and guide for transportation. Another good ride is up to Cerro Chato, an extinct side cone on the flank of Arenal. There's a pretty little lake up here. Either of these tours should cost around $15 to $20 per person. You can arrange either tour through your hotel, through **Aventuras Arenal** (☎ **506/479-9133;** fax 506/479-9295), or through **Sunset Tours** (☎ and fax **506/479-9099**). In addition to the above tours, each of these companies offers most of the tours listed below, as well as fishing trips and sightseeing excursions on the lake.

From La Fortuna, you can also arrange a tour to the **Venado Caverns**, a 45-minute drive away. You'll see plenty of stalactites, stalagmites, and other limestone formations, of course, but you'll also see bats and cave fish. Tours here cost between $25 and $30 and can be arranged through most hotels and any of the local tour operators.

La Fortuna is also a great place from which to make a day trip to the **Caño Negro National Wildlife Refuge**. This vast network of marshes and rivers is 62 miles (100km) north of La Fortuna near the town of Los Chiles. This refuge is best known for its amazing abundance of bird life, including roseate spoonbills, jabiru storks, herons, and egrets, but you can also see caimans and crocodiles. Bird-watchers should not miss this refuge, though keep in mind that the main lake dries up in the dry season (mid-April through November), which reduces the number of wading birds. Full-day tours to Caño Negro average between $35 and $45 per person. Desafio Raft, Aquas Bravas, and Aventuras Arenal all offer trips. Ask at your hotel for more information.

For adventure tours in the area check out **Desafio Raft** (☎ **506/479-9464**; fax 506/479-9178; e-mail: desafio@sol.racsa.co.cr) or **Aguas Brava** (☎ **506/479-9025**). Both of these companies offer daily raft rides of Class 1–2, 3, and 4–5 on different sections of the Peñas Blancas and Sarapiquí rivers. A half-day trip leaving from Fortuna costs just $37 per person; a full day of rafting costs $60 to $80 per person. Both of these companies also offer mountain biking and most of the standard local guided trips, and they each have a horseback trip from La Fortuna/Arenal to Monteverde for around $65 per person. They will even drive your car around for you while you take the scenic (and sore) route.

Finally, kids and the young at heart may enjoy the pool, fountain, and water slide at **Jungla y Senderos Los Lagos** (☎ **506/479-9126**). I personally come here more for the network of trails and small lakes that are also on this property. You'll find Los Lagos on the road to Tabacón a few kilometers out of La Fortuna.

ACCOMMODATIONS IN LA FORTUNA

MODERATE

✪ **Hotel-Rancho El Corcovado.** El Tanque de La Fortuna, San Carlos. ☎ **506/479-9300.** Fax 506/479-9090. 23 units. $42 double, $52 triple; low-season rates available. AE, MC, V.

This hotel is located 4½ miles (7km) east of La Fortuna. While only the west-facing rooms offer a volcano view (and only from their porches), all rooms are clean and spacious and have good beds. There are nice views from the central swimming pool's patio. The hotel has colorful gardens, its own small lake and forest trails, and an inexpensive restaurant serving Tico standards from 6am to 7pm. This hotel isn't quite as attractive as Las Cabañitas up the road, but neither is it as expensive.

Las Cabañitas Resort. Apdo. 5-4417, La Fortuna, San Carlos. ☎ **506/479-9400** or 506/293-0780. Fax 506/479-9408. E-mail: gasguis@sol.racsa.co.cr. 30 cabins. Dec–Apr, $72.50 double, May–Nov, $65 double. AE, MC, V.

Located 1 kilometer east of town, these rustic mountain cabins are spacious and immaculate. About half of the cabins face the volcano and have little porches where you can sit and enjoy the show by day or night. Each cabin is built of varnished hardwoods and has a beautiful floor, a high ceiling, louvered walls to let in the breezes, a modern tile bathroom down a few steps from the sleeping area, and rocking chairs on the porch. There's a small kidney-shaped swimming pool with a snack bar beside it and also a larger, full-service restaurant specializing in Costa Rican cuisine. A full meal plan will run you $22 per day. Some of the rooms are wheelchair accessible. A wide variety of tours can be arranged through the hotel.

INEXPENSIVE

La Fortuna is a tourist boomtown, and basic cabins have popped up here at a phenomenal rate. Right in La Fortuna you'll find a score of budget options. If you have time, it's worth walking around and checking out a couple. If you have a car, drive a little bit out of town toward Tabacón and you'll find several more basic cabins, some even with views of the volcano.

In addition to the inexpensive lodgings listed below, there is **Jungla y Senderos Los Lagos** (☎ **506/479-9126**) campground a few minutes west of La Fortuna. This small complex recently installed some basic cabins, as well as a swimming pool, water slide, and recreation area up near the main road. However, its nicest attractions are the small lakes and jungle trails located a couple of kilometers down a dirt road. This is where you'll find the campground. Los Lagos charges around $4 per person for camping and has cooking and bathroom facilities.

Hotel La Fortuna. La Fortuna, San Carlos. ☎ and fax **506/479-9197.** 10 units. $15 double, $21 triple. AE, MC, V.

Located 1 block south of the gas station, this perennial budget travelers' favorite has risen from the ashes. A 1997 fire destroyed most of the original hotel, but reconstruction was quick and the Hotel La Fortuna is back in business. Most of the rooms are back on the original site, but there are three rooms in a new annex across the street. Accommodations are very basic, but what do you expect at these prices? At least the rooms are clean and have private bathrooms. There is an open-air restaurant at the front of the hotel, and a wide range of tours can be arranged with the helpful owners.

Hotel Las Colinas. Apdo. 06 (150 meters south of the National Bank), La Fortuna, San Carlos. ☎ and fax **506/479-9107.** 17 units. $25 double, $35 triple. MC, V.

This three-story building in the center of town offers clean but basic rooms. You'll need to be in good shape if you stay in one of the third-floor rooms, which have the best views, as the stairs are very steep. There are a few rooms on the ground floor, but they don't even have windows to the outside and are very dark. My favorite room is no. 33, with a private balcony and an unobstructed view of Arenal Volcano.

✪ **Hotel San Bosco.** La Fortuna, San Carlos (200 meters north of the gas station). ☎ **506/479-9050.** Fax 506/479-9109. 32 units. $30–$39 double, $34–$42 triple; rates lower in the off-season. MC, V.

Located a block off La Fortuna's main street, the San Bosco has two styles of rooms. The older, cheaper rooms are small and dark and have cement floors, while the newer rooms are much more attractive and have stone walls, tile floors, air-conditioning, reading lights, and benches on the veranda in front. There's an observation deck for volcano viewing up on the top floor of the hotel, and they recently added a swimming pool and Jacuzzi. The San Bosco can help you arrange a wide variety of tours and even has a small gift shop.

DINING IN LA FORTUNA

Dining in La Fortuna is nowhere near as spectacular as volcano viewing. Most folks either eat at their hotel or go to any one of a number of basic sodas serving Tico standards. The favorite meeting place in town is the **El Jardin Restaurant** (☎ **506/479-9360**), on the main road, right in the center of La Fortuna. Other choices include **La Choza de Laurel** (no phone) and **La Pradera** (☎ **506/479-9167**). Heading out of town, you'll find your best alternative at **El Vagabundo** (☎ **506/479-9565**), an Italian pizza and spaghetti joint.

ACCOMMODATIONS & DINING NEAR THE VOLCANO

EXPENSIVE

Tabacón Lodge. P.O. Box 181-1007, Centro Colón, San José. ☎ **506/256-1500.** Fax 506/221-3076. www.tabacon.com. E-mail: tabacon@sol.racsa.co.cr. 42 units. A/C TV TEL. $100 double, $120 suite. AE, MC, V.

This new hotel is a sister project to the very popular neighboring Tabacón Hot Springs and part of the Tabacón Hot Springs Resort. Together they pack a pretty good one-two punch. Every room here has a direct view of the volcano, although those toward the west end of the property have the best views. The rooms are in a series of long, low buildings stacked up on a small hill. The rooms are all spacious and new, with nice wooden furniture. They also each have a private terrace with a couple of chairs for volcano viewing. Nine of the rooms here are truly designed to be accessible to travelers with disabilites. The one suite is quite a bit larger and has its own Jacuzzi. However, if you opt for a standard room, don't worry—there's a hot and cold pool here, and free run of the hot springs across the street is included in the price of the room. There's no restaurant yet, but one is planned, as is a gift shop, tour desk, and ample reception area. The hotel is located on the main road between La Fortuna and Lake Arenal. As you drive along this road, you will hit the lodge on your right, and then about 100 yards later, around a sharp bend, the hot springs will be on your left.

MODERATE

Arenal Lodge. Apdo. 1139-1250, Escazú. ☎ **506/228-3189.** Fax 506/289-6798. 29 units. $55 double, $87 junior suite, $107 chalet, $128 master. Rates slightly higher on peak weeks, lower in off-season. AE, MC, V.

For stunning location and spectacular views, it's hard to beat the Arenal Lodge. Located high on a hillside a mile from Lake Arenal, this lodge has a direct, unobstructed view of Arenal Volcano's most active slope, which is 6 miles (9.7km) away on the far side of a deep valley. If you reserve one of the huge junior suites, you can actually lie in bed and gaze out at the volcano through a wall of glass. The light show on clear nights is enough to keep you awake for hours. These rooms have two queen-size beds, balconies, large picture windows, two sinks in the bathroom, and lots of space. The standard rooms, though attractively decorated, have no views at all. However, if you choose to stay in one of these more economical rooms, it's only a few steps to a large viewing deck. Five separate chalets on a hill behind the main building house 10 new rooms. These rooms all have plenty of space, good views from their balcony or patio, and small kitchenettes. Meals, which will run you around $30 per person per day, are served in a dining room with a wall of glass, so you can ooh and aah at the volcano between bites of corvina or steak. After dinner, you can retire to the library, where there's a huge stone fireplace and a pool table. A separate lounge has a TV and VCR. The lodge can also arrange night tours ($15 per person), trips to the base of Arenal and Tabacón hot springs ($25 to $30 per person), and fishing for rainbow bass in Lake Arenal ($250 for two people with lunch and a guide). Situated on a macadamia plantation between two strips of virgin forest, the lodge has several trails that are great for bird watching.

✪ **Arenal Observatory Lodge.** Apdo. 321-1007, Centro Colón, San José. ☎ **506/257-9489.** Fax 506/257-4220. E-mail: arenalob@sol.racsa.co.cr. 28 units (23 with bathroom). $42–94 double, $72–$92 triple; rates slightly lower in the off-season. AE, MC, V.

This once-rustic lodge was originally built for the use of volcanologists from the Smithsonian Institution but has turned into my favorite lodge in the Arenal area.

The hotel is only 2½ miles (4km) from the volcano and is built on a high ridge, which gives it the best view of any of the local lodges. Lying in bed at night listening to the eruptions, it's easy to think you're in imminent danger. The superior rooms feature massive picture windows, with a spectacular view of the volcano. The nicest of these are the four new rooms in the Observatory Block. Room no. 29 even has a view of both the lake and the volcano. The most basic rooms here are in the original *casona* (big house) and are located about 500 meters from the main lodge; bathrooms are shared. Surrounding the lodge is the Arenal National Park, which includes thousands of acres of forest and many kilometers of excellent trails. The lodge offers a number of guided and unguided hiking options, including a free morning trip to one of the cooled-off lava flows. To get here, head to the national park entrance, keep on the dirt road past the entrance, and follow the signs to the Observatory Lodge. A four-wheel-drive vehicle was recommended for the 5½-mile (9km) dirt road up to the lodge, but two bridges now eliminate the need to ford any major rivers and a two-wheel-drive vehicle will usually make it in the dry season.

Arenal Vista Lodge. Apdo. 818-1200, Pavas, San José. ☎ **506/220-1712** or 506/381-1428. Fax 506/232-3321. E-mail: explore@sol.racsa.co.cr. 24 units. $70 double, $80 triple, $90 quad. AE, MC, V.

This comfortable lodge is a decent choice if you want to be real close to the volcano when the Arenal Observatory Lodge is full. All the rooms have great views of Arenal Volcano, so you can sit back and watch the volcano's fireworks displays in comfort. Meals will cost you an additional $24 per person per day. The lodge is located above the shore of Lake Arenal. To reach it, drive toward the Arenal Observatory Lodge; after crossing your first major bridge and then fording a little stream, turn right. The lodge is several kilometers and several streams farther along this dirt road. Be warned: Even with a four-wheel-drive vehicle, some of these rivers can be too high to cross during, or just after, heavy rains.

✪ **Montaña De Fuego Inn.** La Palma de la Fortuna, San Carlos. ☎ **506/382-0759.** Fax 506/479-9579. 25 units. $50 double, $55 triple. MC, V.

This hotel offers bed-rattling volcano proximity at prices well below the fancier northern-slope lodges. Located 5 miles (8km) outside La Fortuna on the road to Tabacón, these individual cabins have wonderful volcano views from their spacious glass-enclosed porches. Inside, the cabins are all varnished wood, with sparse but new appointments. When I last visited, construction was underway on a new restaurant and reception area, and plans were in the works for a swimming pool. If this place is full, check next door at the Cabañas Arenal Paraiso (☎ **506/479-9006**), which has very similar accommodations at similar prices and is run by the same family (the owners of the two lodges are brothers).

ACCOMMODATIONS & DINING EAST OF LA FORTUNA

MODERATE

✪ **El Tucano Resort and Spa.** (Apdo. 114-1017, San José) Aguas Calientes de San Carlos. ☎ **506/460-6000** or 506/460-3152. Fax 506/460-1692. 90 units. TV TEL. $85 double, $105 junior suite, $130–$195 suite. AE, MC, V.

Located 5 miles (8.5km) north of Ciudad Quesada (San Carlos) on the road to Aguas Zarcas, El Tucano was Costa Rica's first true spa resort, and though you won't find the sort of services you'd get in Palm Springs, you will find the most elegant spa facility in Costa Rica, as well as natural hot springs, Jacuzzis, indoor and natural steam rooms, a small gym, and in-house massage therapists. The resort is located in a steep-walled valley and faces a lush rain forest. The rooms are set into the steep hillside and are connected by narrow, winding alleys and stairways. Most rooms are carpeted and very comfortable, with attractive decorations. If you want extra space, ask for one of the suites, junior suites, or luxury suites. The suite designations just differentiate rooms with slightly more space and amenities. There are even two presidential suites, which come with private terrace, in-room Jacuzzi, and large-screen television. This is a great place just to kick back and relax for a day or two. There is a wide range of spa treatments and services available at extra cost. Room service is also available, as is shuttle service to San José ($35 per person one-way), horseback riding, and tours around the region. There's a swimming pool, two tennis courts, whirlpool tubs with natural hot-spring waters, natural steam rooms, miniature golf course, gift shop, and hiking trails. Just hanging around, you should see plenty of colorful toucans, the hotel's namesake, as well as many other birds. The dining room here is large and formal, with excellent service and a continental menu that includes such dishes as chicken à l'orange and pasta with shrimp. The best tables here, when the weather is nice, are on an outdoor balcony overlooking the river.

Hotel La Garza. (Apdo. 100-2250, Tres Rios) Plantanar, San Carlos. ☎ **506/475-5222** or 506/222-7355. Fax 506/475-5015. E-mail: lagarza@sol.racsa.co.cr. 12 units. TEL. Nov–Apr, $74 double, $84 triple; May–Oct, lower rates available. AE, MC, V.

This comfortable lodge is set on a large working ranch just south of Muelle. La Garza means "the egret" in Spanish, and you will see plenty of these birds here, as they roost nearby. Also, the ranch includes 750 acres of primary rain forest where many other species of birds can be spotted. Built on the banks of the San Carlos River, the hotel consists of six duplex bungalows, each of which has a deck overlooking the river. Large trees provide shade, and the sound of the river lulls you to sleep at night. High ceilings and overhead fans help keep the rooms cool, and all the rooms are attractively decorated and have views of Arenal Volcano in the distance. The hotel's restaurant and bar are reached via a small suspension bridge over the lazy little river that runs through the property. You can arrange tours of the region, or wander around the ranch observing the day-to-day activity. The hotel has a pool and a Jacuzzi, but the ranch's rain forest, with all its birds and other wildlife, is the primary attraction here.

✪ **Tilajari Hotel Resort.** Muelle (Apdo. 81-4100), San Carlos. ☎ **506/469-9091.** Fax 506/469-9095. E-mail: tilajari@ns.goldnet.co.cr. 64 units. A/C TV TEL. Nov–Apr, $82 double, $110 suite double, May–Oct, $63 double, $80 suite double. AE, MC, V.

This sprawling resort just outside the farming community of Muelle (17.4 miles from La Fortuna) is a sort of country club for wealthy Costa Ricans, but it also makes a good base for exploring this area. Covering 30 acres and built on the banks of the San Carlos River, the Tilajari Hotel offers some of the most luxurious accommodations in the region. The modern buildings are painted a blinding white and have red-tile roofs. Most of the rooms have views of the river, while the others open on to rich flowering gardens. The oldest rooms are farthest from the main lodge, are slightly smaller, and have smaller patios. These nicest rooms have river-view balconies. The suites come with a separate living room and kitchenette. Large iguanas are frequently sighted on the grounds, as are crocodiles, which live in the San Carlos River. There's a large open-air dining room that has both formal and informal sections and a bar. The menu consists primarily of moderately priced Tico and international dishes. There's also a swimming pool, tennis courts, racquetball court, mountain bikes, soccer field, sauna, game room with pool tables and table tennis, gift shop, orchid garden, tropical fruit and vegetable garden, and a well-maintained butterfly garden to keep guests busy. The tennis is taken quite seriously here, with two indoor and several lighted courts.

The lodge arranges tours around the region, including trips to Caño Negro ($48 per person), Arenal Volcano and Tabacón Hot Springs ($43 per person), Venado Caverns ($45 per person), and Fortuna Falls ($45 per person). Trips into the nearby rain forest, either on foot, on horseback, or by tractor, can also be arranged, as can gentle floats on the Peñas Blancas River and multiday packages.

INEXPENSIVE

Termales del Bosque. Ciudad Quesada, San Carlos. ☎ **506/460-4740.** Fax 506/460-1356. E-mail: canopy@sol.racsa.co.cr. 15 units (10 with bathroom). $30–$40 double, $36–$42 triple. MC, V.

This new place packs a lot of ecotourism punch for the buck. The ten new rooms are in five duplex buildings set on a small hill. Each comes with a private bathroom, two double beds, and front and back patios. The restaurant is in one of the property's original buildings, where you'll also find several more basic rooms with shared bathrooms. Meals will run you around $20 per day. Nowhere near as fancy as the neighboring El Tucano Resort, Termales del Bosque does have some wonderful natural hot springs set in rich rain forest. The series of sculpted pools are set on the banks of a small river. Down by the pools, there's a natural steam room (scented each day with fresh eucalyptus), a massage room, and a snack and juice bar. The trail down here winds through the thick forest and, if you want to keep on walking, you can take guided or self-guided tours on a network of well-marked trails. You can rent horses right at the lodge, and there's even a new canopy tour here. If you aren't staying here, you can use the pools and hike the trails for $8, or do the canopy tour for $45. You'll find Termales del Bosque on the road from San Carlos to Aguas Zarcas just before El Tucano.

ACCOMMODATIONS & DINING SOUTH OF LA FORTUNA

MODERATE

Valle Escondido Lodge. Apdo. 452-1150, La Uruca. ☎ **506/231-0906.** Fax 506/232-9591. www.cmnet.co.cr. E-mail: valle@ns.goldnet.co.cr. 25 units. $65 double, $77 triple. AE, MC, V.

South of La Fortuna, just off the road between San Ramón and La Fortuna, is a modest hotel that provides access to some of the region's rain forests. Valle Escondido (Hidden Valley) is situated on a 990-acre farm that includes primary and secondary forest as well as fields of ornamental plants that are grown for export. The rooms are spacious and comfortable, and all are carpeted. In front of the rooms run long verandas where you can sit and enjoy the tranquillity of the surroundings. The lodge restaurant serves Tico and Italian meals, and there's also a small bar where you can wet your whistle and a small pool and Jacuzzi where you can wet the rest of you. Hiking, horseback riding ($7 per hour), mountain biking ($4 per hour), and bird watching are the primary activities here; a wide range of tours are available for an additional charge.

Villablanca Hotel. (Apdo. 247-1250, San Rafael de Escazú), San Ramón, Alajuela. ☎ **506/228-4603** or 506/289-6569. Fax 506/228-4004. E-mail: vilablan@sol.racsa.co.cr. 5 units, 54 casitas. $73 double room, $89 double, $104 triple, $152 quad casita. AE, DC, MC, V.

Villablanca is certainly out of the way, but if you're interested in bird watching or exploring the cloud forest and want to avoid the crowds of Monteverde, this is a good choice. Owned and operated by a former president of Costa Rica, this lodge consists of 54 Tico-style casitas surrounded by 2,000 acres of farm and forest. There are five new rooms in the main building, and while all the rooms are up to par, the rustic casitas are a better bet. Each is built of adobe and has traditional tile floors and whitewashed walls with deep blue trim. (This is the classic color scheme of 19th-century adobe homes throughout the country.) Inside, you'll find a rounded fireplace in one corner, window seats, comfortable hardwood chairs, colorful curtains, and twin beds covered with attractive bedspreads. Rooms also have electric teapots and small refrigerators. The tiled bathrooms have tubs that look out through a wall of windows. In the hacienda-style main lodge, you'll find the dining room, where simple-but-filling buffet meals are served. An unusual atrium garden, library, lounge, gift shop, and small bar round out the amenities. Adjacent to the lodge are 6¾ miles (11km) of trails through the Los Angeles Cloud Forest Reserve. Admission to the reserve is $22 per person and includes a guided hike. You can also rent horses (for $10 per hour). Transportation to and from the lodge to San José is $35 each way. Alternatively, you can take a public bus from San José to San Ramón and then take a taxi for around $10. If you're driving, head west out of San José to San Ramón and then head north, following the signs to Villablanca.

3 Tilarán & Lake Arenal

124 miles (200km) NW of San José; 12½ miles (20km) NW of Monteverde; 43½ miles (70km) SE of Liberia

This remains one of the least-developed tourism regions in Costa Rica but not for lack of resources or charms. It does, after all, have Lake Arenal, an artificial lake with an area of 33 square miles (making it the largest lake in Costa Rica), surrounded by rolling hills that are partly pastured and partly forested. At the opposite (east) end of the lake from Tilarán lies the perfect cone of Arenal Volcano. The volcano's barren slopes are a stunning sight from here, especially when reflected in the waters of the lake. The north side of Lake Arenal is a dry region of rolling hills and pastures, distinctly different from the lusher landscape near La Fortuna.

People around here used to curse the winds, which often come blasting across this end of the lake at 60 knots or greater. However, since the first sailboarders caught wind of Lake Arenal's combination of warm fresh water, steady blows, and spectacular scenery, things have been changing quickly. Although the town of Tilarán is still little more than a quiet farm community, hotels are proliferating out along the shores of the lake. Even if you aren't a fanatical sailboarder, you still might enjoy hanging out by the lake, hiking in the nearby forests, and catching glimpses of Arenal Volcano.

The lake's other claim to fame is its rainbow bass fishing. These fighting fish are known in their native South America as *guapote* and are large members of the cichlid family. Their sharp teeth and fighting nature make them a real challenge.

ESSENTIALS

GETTING THERE & DEPARTING **By Bus** Express buses leave San José for Tilarán daily at 7:30 and 9:30am and 12:45, 3:45, and 6:30pm from Calle 14 between Avenidas 9 and 11. The trip lasts from 4 to 5½ hours, depending on road conditions; fare is $3.

There are also morning and afternoon buses from Puntarenas to Tilarán. The ride takes 3 hours; fare is $2.10. To get to Puntarenas, see the information on getting to Puntarenas in chapter 6.

From Monteverde (Santa Elena), there is a bus daily at 7am. The fare for the 3-hour trip is $1.25.

From Tilarán, direct buses to San José leave daily at 4:45, 7, and 7:45am and 2 and 4:45pm. Buses to Puntarenas leave at 6am and 1pm daily. The bus to Santa Elena (Monteverde) leaves daily at 1pm. Buses also leave regularly for Cañas, where you can catch buses north or south along the Interamerican Highway. Buses for La Fortuna, at the south end of Lake Arenal, leave daily at 7am and 3pm.

By Car From San José, take the Interamerican Highway west toward Puntarenas and then continue north on this road to Cañas. In Cañas, turn east toward Tilarán. The drive takes 4 hours. If you're thinking of heading up this way from La Fortuna, be aware that for several kilometers the road is unpaved and in very bad shape and should not be tried in a regular car, except during the dry season.

ORIENTATION Tilarán is about 3 miles (5km) from Lake Arenal. All roads into town lead to the central park, which is Tilarán's main point of reference for addresses. If you need to exchange money, check at one of the hotels listed here, or go to the Banco Nacional. If you need a taxi to get to a lodge on Lake Arenal, call **Taxis Unidos Tilaran** (☎ **506/695-5324**).

WINDSURFING, FISHING & OTHER ACTIVE SPORTS

WINDSURFING If you want to try windsurfing, you can rent equipment from **Tilawa Windsurfing Center** (☎ **506/695-5050**), which has its facilities on one of the lake's few accessible beaches, about 5 miles (8km) from Tilarán on the road along the west end of the lake. Boards rent for $40 to $46 per day, and lessons are also available. You can also ask at **Rock River Lodge (☎ 506/695-5644)** (see "Accommodations" below), which rents equipment for around $50 per day or $275 per week. Rock River Lodge also has some high-end mountain bikes, which will run you around $35 per day.

FISHING If you want to try your hand at fishing for rainbow bass, contact **J.J.'s Fishing and Outdoor Tours** (☎ **506/695-5825**). A half-day fishing trip will cost around $125, and a full day goes for $175. J.J.'s can also arrange non-fishing boat trips out on the lake and other outdoor tours.

HORSEBACK RIDING & HIKING If you're looking for another way to get around on dry land, the folks at **Tilawa** or **Rock River Lodge** can arrange for you to rent a horse for $15 per hour. If you feel like strapping on your hiking boots, there are some trails for hiking on the far side of Lake Arenal, near the smaller Coter Lake.

SWIMMING Up above Lake Arenal on the far side of the lake from Tilarán, you'll find the beautiful little heart-shaped **Coter Lake**. This lake is surrounded by forest and has good swimming. UFO watchers also claim this is a popular pit stop for extraterrestrials.

EXPLORING THE BOTANICAL GARDENS

A taxi to Coter Lake will cost around $12. Continuing south on the road around the lake will bring you to the town of Nuevo Arenal, where the pavement ends. If you continue another 2½ miles (4km) on this road, you'll come to the **Arenal Botanical Gardens** (☎ **506/694-4273**), which is open daily from 9am to 5pm and charges $4 admission. This private garden was started only in 1991, but it's already quite beautiful and extensive. Not only are there many tropical plants and flowers to be seen, but there are always butterflies and hummingbirds here.

ACCOMMODATIONS

MODERATE

Chalet Nicholas. Apdo. 72-5710, Tilarán, Guanacaste. ☎ and fax **506/694-4041.** 3 units. $49 double. Rates include full breakfast. No credit cards.

This friendly American-owned bed-and-breakfast is located 1½ miles west of Nuevo Arenal and sits on a hill above the road. There are great views from the garden, and all of three rooms have a view of Arenal Volcano. This modern home is set on 3 acres and has pretty flower gardens, an organic vegetable garden, an orchid garden, and an aviary full of toucans and other colorful birds. Behind the property are acres of forest through which you can hike in search of birds, orchids, butterflies, and other tropical beauties. If you don't mind the lack of privacy, the upstairs loft room is the largest. It even has its own private deck. No smoking is allowed in the house or on the grounds. A 3-hour horseback-riding tour costs $20 per person. Owners John and Catherine Nichols go out of their way to make their guests feel at home. All around, it's a really good deal.

Hotel Tilawa. Apdo. 92-5710, Tilarán, Guanacaste. ☎ **800/851-8929** in the U.S., or 506/695-5050. Fax 506/695-5766. www.hotel-tilawa.com. E-mail: tilawa@sol.racsa.co.cr. 28 units. TEL. $65 double, $85 triple. AE, MC, V.

Built to resemble the Palace of Knossos on the island of Crete, the Hotel Tilawa sits high on the slopes above the lake, has a sweeping vista down to the water, and is primarily a windsurfer's hangout. Unusual colors and antique paint effects give the hotel a weathered look (even though it's actually only a few years old); inside there are wall murals and other artistic paint treatments throughout. Rooms have dyed cement floors, Guatemalan bedspreads, and big windows. Some have kitchenettes. Amenities include a swimming pool and tennis court. There's a bar/disco beside the pool, as well as a moderately priced restaurant in the main building. For a fee, the Tilawa can arrange windsurfing, mountain biking, horseback riding, and fishing trips. They've even begun their own Spanish-language school, with week-long intensive programs available.

Lake Coter Eco-Lodge. Apdo. 8-5570, 1000 San José. ☎ **506/257-5075.** Fax 506/257-7065. 37 units. $49–$66 double, $57–$75 triple. AE, DC, MC, V.

Tucked into the forested hills above Lake Arenal is the much smaller—but natural, not artificial—Lake Coter. Near this pretty lake (up a very rough gravel road), you'll find this rustic lodge. While the older rooms in the main lodge are dark and depressing, there are 12 much nicer rooms on a hill, a short walk from the main lodge. These all have porches and great views; be sure to request one of these rooms. Surrounding the lodge are more than 1,300 acres of cloud forest and 10 miles (16km) of hiking trails.

Meals are served family style in the rustic dining room in the main lodge. Tico standards and some international dishes are the fare here, and meals will run you $25 per person per day. Transportation to and from the lodge can be arranged at additional cost. Activities available include hiking, horseback riding, mountain biking, windsurfing, canoeing, and swimming on Lake Coter. Excursions to Arenal Volcano and Venado Caverns can also be arranged. This hotel specializes in large groups and package tours; if you decide to stay here and are interested in various tours around the region, be sure to ask about their package rates and you could save a lot over the à la carte prices.

✪ **Rock River Lodge.** Apdo. 95, Tilarán, Guanacaste. ☎ and fax **506/695-5644.** http://rockriver.mastermind.net. E-mail: rokriver@sol.racsa.co.cr. 6 units, 8 bungalows. $45–$65 double, $55–$75 triple. V.

Set high on a grassy hill above the lake, this small lodge looks as if it might have been transported from Hawaii. The rooms are in a long, low lodge set on stilts. Walls and floors are made of hardwood, and there are bamboo railings along the veranda. Wind chimes let you know when the winds are up, and there are sling chairs on the porch. Rooms are of medium size and have one double bed and a bunk bed, as well as modern tiled bathrooms. Though fairly simple in style, this is one of the most attractive lodges in the area. The newer bungalows are farther up the hill, offer more privacy, and some even have sculpted bathtubs. It's a long walk down to the lake (not to mention the walk back up), so a car is recommended. Meals will cost you around $25 per person per day and are served in the spacious open-air restaurant, where there's a large stone fireplace. This hotel caters to sailboarders and other active travelers. When the wind isn't up, owner Norman List offers mountain-biking trips and horseback and hiking adventures to a nearby waterfall.

✪ **Villa Decary.** Nuevo Arenal, 5717 Tilarán, Guanacaste. No phone. Fax **506/694-4330.** 4 units, 1 casita. $59 double, $69 casita. No credit cards.

Named after a French explorer (and a rare palm species he discovered and named), this new bed-and-breakfast is nestled on a hill above Lake Arenal, midway between the town of Nuevo Arenal and the Arenal Botanical Gardens (see above). Each room comes with two double beds, large picture windows, and a spacious private balcony with a lake view. The rooms get plenty of light, which, combined with the bright Guatemalan bedspreads and white-tile floors, give the place a very lively feel. The separate casita has a full kitchen and the best view on the premises. Breakfasts are extravagant and memorable, with a steady stream of fresh fruits; fresh juice; strong coffee; homemade pancakes, waffles, or muffins; and usually an excellent omelet or soufflé. You might not want to stop eating, but eventually you'll just have to call it quits and get on with your day. There's great bird watching on the hotel grounds, and howler monkeys are common guests here as well.

INEXPENSIVE

Cabinas El Sueño. Tilarán, Guanacaste. ☎ **506/695-5347.** Fax 506/695-6072. 12 units. $14 double, $20 triple. MC, V.

Situated in the middle of this small town, Cabinas El Sueño is a simple two-story accommodation, but it is clean and the management is friendly. There's parking in back and a small courtyard complete with a fountain on the second floor of the building. Some of the rooms can be a bit cramped. For an extra $2, they'll put a TV in your room. Downstairs, there's a restaurant and bar.

Cabinas Mary. Apdo. 89 (on the south side of the park), Tilarán, Guanacaste. ☎ **506/695-5479** or 506/695-5758. 18 units. $15 double. No credit cards.

Located right on Tilarán's large and sunny central park, Cabinas Mary is a very basic, but fairly clean, lodging. It's upstairs from the restaurant of the same name and has safe parking in back. Rooms are large, and most have plenty of windows. You even get hot water here, which is a surprise at this price. The restaurant downstairs is a popular hangout. It's open daily from 6am to 10pm; meals cost between $3 and $7.

Hotel Naralit. Tilarán, Guanacaste. ☎ **506/695-5393.** Fax 506/695-6767. 23 units. TV. $20–23 double, $25–$30 triple. V.

This newer budget hotel is a good bet in Tilarán. The rooms are clean and comfortable and even have cable TV. There are three second-floor rooms that have a nice shared balcony with views of the town's church.

DINING

If you're staying in Tilarán, there are numerous inexpensive places to eat, including the restaurants at Cabinas Mary and Cabinas El Sueño, both of which are mentioned above. Also, around the corner from Cabinas Mary is **El Lugar**, a popular restaurant and bar that's worth checking out. If you're staying outside of town, it's likely you'll eat in your hotel's dining room, since there are few restaurants around the shores of the lake. Also worth mentioning is **Equus BBQ**, a small open-air restaurant in front of Xiloe Lodge that has a view of the lake. It specializes in roast chicken and steaks. If you're staying down near Nuevo Arenal, try the following places.

Congo Cafe. On the main street through town. No phone. Reservations not accepted. Main courses $3–$4. No credit cards. Wed–Mon 11am–9pm. MEXICAN/INTERNATIONAL.

This new restaurant is a relaxed and eclectic place to pass some time with a cup of iced espresso and a macadamia nut tart, or pick up a tasty light meal. The menu shifts daily, with typical entrees including quesadillas, eggplant parmesan subs, veggie burgers, fresh crepes, and hefty omelets. There are a couple of folding card tables outside and a bar and more tables inside.

Restaurant Lajas. On the main street through town. ☎ **506/694-4169.** Reservations not accepted. Main courses $2.50–$5. No credit cards. Daily 10am–10pm. COSTA RICAN.

This surprisingly fancy little restaurant is one of the best values in Costa Rica. There are red tablecloths on every table, waiters in bow ties, and a wall of mirrors to make the tiny dining room look larger than it really is—but these are only the incidentals. The real reason to eat here is good Tico cooking at rock-bottom prices. The deal of the day is always the casado. You won't walk away hungry or poor.

4 Monteverde

103 miles (167km) NW of San José; 51 miles (82km) NW of Puntarenas

To be frank, I have a love-hate relationship with Monteverde. Next to Manuel Antonio, this is Costa Rica's most internationally recognized tourist destination. The fame and accompanying traffic have led me to dub it the Monteverde Crowd Forest. Nevertheless, the preserve itself and the extensive network of private reserves around it are incredibly rich in biodiversity, and a well-organized infrastructure helps guarantee a rewarding experience for first-time ecoadventurers.

Monteverde translates as "Green Mountain," and that's exactly what you'll find at the end of the steep and windy rutted dirt road that leads here. Along the way, you'll pass through mile after mile of often dry, brown pasturelands. All of these pastures were once covered with dense forest, but now only small pieces of that original forest remain.

The village of Monteverde was founded in 1951 by Quakers from the United States who wished to leave behind a constant fear of war as well as an obligation to support continued militarism through paying U.S. taxes. They chose Costa Rica primarily because it had no standing army. Although Monteverde's founders came here to farm the land, they wisely recognized the need to preserve the rare cloud forest that covered the mountain slopes above their fields, and to that end they dedicated the largest adjacent tract of cloud forest as the Monteverde Biological Cloud Forest Preserve.

Perched on a high mountain ridge, this tiny, scattered village and surrounding cloud forest are well known both among scientific researchers and ecotravelers. Cloud forests are a mountaintop phenomenon. Moist, warm air sweeping in off the nearby ocean is forced upward by mountain slopes, and as this moist air rises it cools, forming clouds. The mountaintops of Costa Rica are blanketed almost daily in dense clouds, and as these clouds cling to the slopes, moisture condenses on forest trees. This constant level of moisture has given rise to an incredible diversity of innovative life-forms and a forest in which nearly every square inch of space has some sort of plant growing. Within the cloud forest, the branches of huge trees are draped with epiphytic plants: orchids, ferns, and bromeliads. This intense botanic competition has created an almost equally diverse population of insects, birds, and other wildlife. Monteverde Biological Cloud Forest Preserve covers 26,000 acres of forest, including several different life zones that are characterized by different types of plants and animals. Within this small area are more than 2,000 species of plants, 400 species of birds, and 100 different species of mammals. It's no wonder that the preserve has been the site of constant scientific investigations since its founding in 1972.

The preserve was originally known only to the handful of researchers who came here to study different aspects of life in the cloud forest. However, as the beauty and biological diversity of the area became known outside of academic circles, casual visitors began arriving. For many, the primary goal was a chance to glimpse the rare and elusive **quetzal**, a bird once revered by the pre-Columbian peoples of the Americas. As the number of visitors began to grow, lodges began opening, word spread, more lodges opened, and so on. Today Monteverde is a prime example of too many people chasing after the same little piece of nature. Monteverde is akin to the Yosemite Valley, only on a much smaller scale—a place of great and fragile beauty whose popularity threatens to destroy the very beauty that draws people to it. That said, and despite the hordes of ecotourists traipsing its trails, Monteverde is still a beautiful place and offers a glimpse into the life of one of the world's most threatened ecosystems. However, if your primary goal is to sight a quetzal, you should seriously consider visiting other cloud-forest areas around Costa Rica. Other options include Villablanca and the Los Angeles Cloud Forest Reserve, or the Tapantí National Wildlife Refuge, near Cerro de la Muerte, which has several nearby lodges (see chapter 8). At the latter, you'll find far fewer crowds and usually better chances of seeing the famed quetzal.

ESSENTIALS

GETTING THERE & DEPARTING **By Bus** Express buses (☎ **506/222-3854**) leave San José daily at 6:30am and 2:30pm from Calle 14 between Avenidas 9 and 11. The trip takes 3½ hours; fare is $5.25.

There's also a daily bus that departs Puntarenas for Santa Elena, only a few kilometers from Monteverde, at 2:15pm. The bus stop in Puntarenas is across the street from the main bus station. The fare for the 2½-hour trip is $2.50.

There is a daily bus from Tilarán (Lake Arenal) at 1pm. Trip duration, believe it or not, is 2 hours (for a 25-mile trip); fare is $1.20.

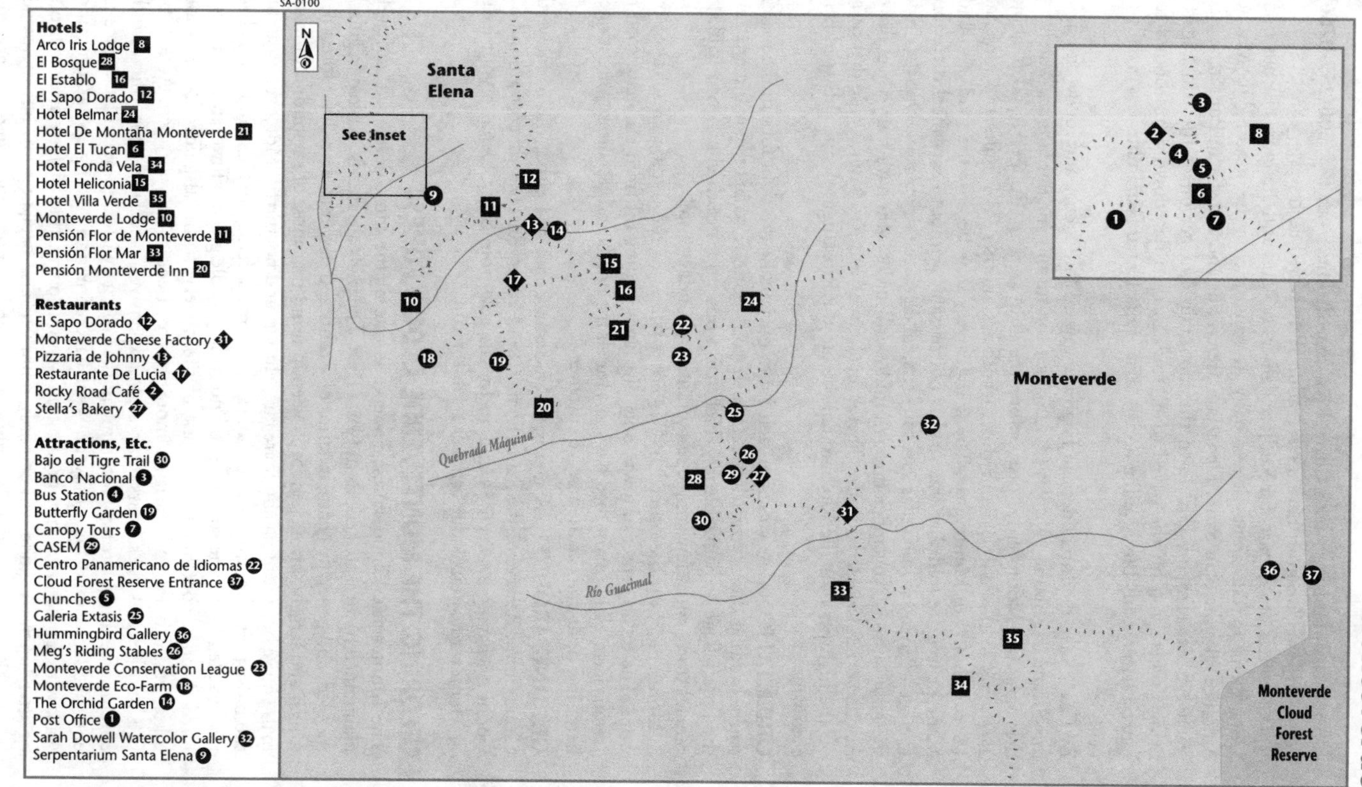
SA-0100
Hotels
Arco Iris Lodge 8
El Bosque 28
El Establo 16
El Sapo Dorado 12
Hotel Belmar 24
Hotel De Montaña Monteverde 21
Hotel El Tucan 6
Hotel Fonda Vela 34
Hotel Heliconia 15
Hotel Villa Verde 35
Monteverde Lodge 10
Pensión Flor de Monteverde 11
Pensión Flor Mar 33
Pensión Monteverde Inn 20
Restaurants
El Sapo Dorado 12
Monteverde Cheese Factory 31
Pizzaria de Johnny 13
Restaurante De Lucia 17
Rocky Road Café 2
Stella's Bakery 27
Attractions, Etc.
Bajo del Tigre Trail 30
Banco Nacional 3
Bus Station 4
Butterfly Garden 19
Canopy Tours 7
CASEM 29
Centro Panamericano de Idiomas 22
Cloud Forest Reserve Entrance 37
Chunches 5
Galeria Extasis 25
Hummingbird Gallery 36
Meg's Riding Stables 26
Monteverde Conservation League 23
Monteverde Eco-Farm 18
The Orchid Garden 14
Post Office 1
Sarah Dowell Watercolor Gallery 32
Serpentarium Santa Elena 9
N
Santa Elena
See Inset
Monteverde
Quebrada Máquina
Río Guacimal
Monteverde Cloud Forest Reserve

Another option is to take **Costa Rica Expeditions**'s van (☎ **506/257-0766**) from San José. You must have a reservation. Fare is $40 each way.

The express bus departs for San José daily at 6:30am and 2:30pm. The bus from Santa Elena to Puntarenas leaves daily at 6am. If you are heading to Manuel Antonio, take the 6am Santa Elena/Puntarenas bus and transfer in Puntarenas. To reach Liberia, take any bus down the mountain and get off at the Río Lagarto Bridge, where you hit the paved road. You can then flag down a bus bound for Liberia (almost any bus heading north). The Santa Elena/Tilarán bus leaves daily at 7am.

By Car Take the Interamerican Highway toward Puntarenas and follow the signs for Nicaragua. About 19 miles (31km) past the turnoff for Puntarenas, watch for the signs for Monteverde, just before the Río Lagarto Bridge. It takes about 2¼ hours to this point. From this turnoff, it's another 23½ miles (38 km) and 1½ to 2 hours to Monteverde. The going is very slow because the road is so bad. Many people are told that this road is not passable without four-wheel drive, but I've been driving it in regular cars for years, albeit in the dry season. Don't try it in the rainy season (November through mid-April) unless you have four-wheel drive. Also, be careful where you turn: There's an alternate route to Monteverde that turns off the highway near the Río Sardinal (before the Río Largato), and this road is in even worse shape.

ORIENTATION As you approach Santa Elena, take the right fork in the road if you're heading directly to Monteverde. If you continue straight, you'll come into the little village of Santa Elena, which has a bus stop, health clinic, two banks, a general store, and a few simple restaurants and budget hotels.

Monteverde, on the other hand, is not a village in the traditional sense of the word. There's no center of town, only dirt lanes leading off from the main road to various farms. This main road has signs for all the hotels and restaurants mentioned here, and dead-ends at the reserve entrance.

GETTING AROUND A taxi between Santa Elena and either the Monteverde Cloud Forest Reserve or the Santa Elena Cloud Forest Reserve will cost around $7. Count on paying between $4 and $6 for the ride from Santa Elena to your lodge in Monteverde. Your lodge can call a cab for you.

EXPLORING THE MONTEVERDE CLOUD FOREST

The Monteverde Cloud Forest Preserve is one of the most developed and well-maintained natural attractions in Costa Rica. The trails are clearly marked, regularly traveled, and generally gentle in terms of ascents and descents. The cloud forest here is lush and largely untouched. Still, keep in mind that most of the birds and mammals you've been reading about are rare, elusive, and nocturnal. Moreover, to all but the most trained of eyes, those thousands of exotic ferns, orchids, and bromeliads tend to blend into one large mass of indistinguishable green. However, with a guide hired through your hotel or on one of the preserve's official guided 2- to 3-hour hikes, you can see and learn far more than you could on your own. At $15 per person, the preserve's tours may seem expensive, especially after you pay the entrance fee, but I strongly recommend that you go with a guide. In fact, since the entrance fee is valid for a full day, what I recommend is taking an early-morning walk with a guide and then heading off on your own either directly after that hike or after lunch. A guide will certainly point out and explain a lot, but there's also much to be said for walking quietly through the forest on your own or in very small groups.

Perhaps the most famous resident of the cloud forests of Costa Rica is the quetzal, a robin-size bird with iridescent-green wings and a ruby-red breast, which has become extremely rare due to habitat destruction. The male quetzal also has two long tail feathers that make it one of the most spectacular birds on earth. The best time to see quetzals is early to midmorning, and the best months are February through April (mating season).

Other animals that have been seen in Monteverde include jaguars, ocelots, and tapirs. After the quetzal, Monteverde's most beautiful resident was the golden toad (*sapo dorado*), a rare, native species. However, the golden toad seems to have disappeared from the forest and is feared extinct. Various avenues of speculation are that the toad was adversely affected by a natural drought cycle, the disappearing ozone layer, pesticides, or acid rain. Photos of the golden toad abound in Monteverde, and I'm sure you'll be as saddened as I was by the disappearance of such a beautiful creature.

The preserve is open daily from 7am to 4pm, and the entrance fee is $8 per person, $4 for students. Because only 100 people are allowed into the preserve at any one time, you may be forced to wait for a while. Most hotels can reserve you a guided walk and entrance to the preserve for the following day, or you can get tickets in advance directly at the preserve entrance. The trails can be very muddy, depending on the season, so ask about current conditions. If the mud is heavy, you can rent rubber boots at the preserve entrance for $1 per day. They may make your hike much more pleasant.

Before venturing into the forest, have a look around the information center. There are several guidebooks available, as well as posters and postcards of some of the preserve's more famous animal inhabitants.

To learn even more about Monteverde, stop in at the **Monteverde Conservation League** (☎ **506/645-5003**; e-mail: acmmcl@sol.racsa.co.cr), which is located across the street from the gas station. Their office is open Monday through Friday from 8am to noon and from 1 to 5pm, and from 8am to noon on Saturdays. They sell informative books, T-shirts, and cards, and all proceeds go to purchase more land for the Bosque Eterno de Los Niños (Children's Eternal Forest).

BIRD WATCHING & HIKING OUTSIDE THE PRESERVE

Ample bird-watching and hiking opportunities can also be found outside the preserve boundaries. You can avoid the crowds at Monteverde by heading 3 miles (5km) north from the village of Santa Elena to the **Santa Elena Cloud Forest Reserve** (☎ **506/645-5014**). This 900-acre reserve has a maximum elevation of 5,600 feet, which makes it the highest cloud forest in the Monteverde area. There are 5 miles (8km) of hiking trails as well as an information center. As it borders the Monteverde Preserve, a similar richness of flora and fauna is to be found here, although quetzals are not nearly as common. The $6 entry fee at this reserve goes directly to support local schools. The reserve is open daily from 7am to 5pm. Guided tours are available for $20 per person, including the entrance fee.

The Bajo del Tigre Trail is a 2-mile-long trail that's home to several different bird species not usually found within the reserve. The trail starts a little past the CASEM artisans' shop (see "Shopping" below) and is open daily from 8am to 5pm. The trail has been undergoing some upkeep and improvements, and there is now a small visitors center, which has good views out to the Nicoya Gulf. Admission is $5.

You can also go on guided 3-hour hikes at the **Reserva Sendero Tranquilo** (☎ **506/645-5010**), which has 200 acres of land, two-thirds of which is in virgin forest. This reserve is located up the hill from the cheese factory, charges $15 for its tours, and is open daily from 5am to 2pm seasonally.

The Monteverde Eco-Farm (☎ **506/645-5222**) is open daily from 7am to 5pm. More than 100 species of birds have been seen here. There are also good views and two waterfalls. Admission is $5.

CANOPY TOURS, NIGHT TOURS & HORSEBACK RIDING

For an elevated look at the cloud forest, check out the local branch of **Canopy Tours** (☎ **506/645-5243**), which has an office across from Hotel El Tucan. This is one of my favorite canopy tours in Costa Rica, since the ascent is made by climbing up the hollowed-out interior of a giant strangler fig. The 2½-hour tours run three times daily and cost $45 for adults, $35 for students, and $25 for children under 12.

For those less adventurous, it's still possible to get up into the canopy on the new **Skywalk** (☎ **506/645-5238**). A network of forest paths and suspension bridges give visitors a view otherwise reserved for birds, monkeys, and more serious climbers. The bridges reach 130 feet above the ground at their highest point. The Skywalk is located about 2 miles (3.5km) outside of the town of Santa Elena, on the road to the Santa Elena Cloud Forest Reserve. It is open daily from 7am to 4pm. Admission $8.

Almost all of the area hotels can arrange a variety of other tour and activity options, including night trips to the Arenal Volcano (a grueling 4-hour ride away), guided night tours of the cloud forest, and, of course, horseback riding. The going rate for horseback rides with a guide is between $7 and $10 per person per hour. **Meg's Riding Stables** (☎ **506/645-5052**) and **La Estrella Stables** (☎ **506/645-5075**) are two of the more-established operators and offer guided rides for around $8 per hour.

OTHER ADVENTURES IN MONTEVERDE

Because the vegetation in the cloud forest is so dense, most of the forest's animal residents are rather difficult to spot. If you were unsatisfied with your sightings, even with a naturalist guide leading you, you might want to consider attending a slide show of photographs taken in the preserve. Many of the hotels offer nightly slide shows; if yours doesn't, check with the Monteverde Lodge and Hotel Belmar.

There's also a daily slide show at 4:30pm at the **Hummingbird Gallery** (☎ **506/645-5030**). Admission is $3. You'll find the gallery just outside the preserve entrance. Hanging from trees around it are several hummingbird feeders that attract more than seven species of these tiny birds. At any given moment, there might be several dozen hummingbirds buzzing and chattering around the building and your head. Inside, you will, of course, find a lot of beautiful mounted and unmounted color prints of hummingbirds. There are also many other beautiful photos from Monteverde available in prints or postcards. This is one of the better stocked gift shops in the area and is open Monday through Saturday from 9am to 5pm, Sunday from 9am to 2pm.

Birds are not the only colorful fauna in the Monteverde cloud forest. Butterflies abound here, and the **Butterfly Garden**, located near the Pensión Monteverde Inn, displays many of Costa Rica's most beautiful species. Besides the hundreds of preserved and mounted butterflies, there are gardens and a greenhouse where you can watch live butterflies. The garden is open daily from 9:30am to 4pm, and the admission is $6 for adults and $3 for children, which includes a guided tour. The best time to visit is between 11am and 1pm, when the butterflies are most active.

If your taste runs toward the slithery, don't miss the quaint **Serpentarium Santa Elena** (☎ **506/645-5238**) on the road to the preserve. It's open daily from 8am to 5pm and charges $3 for admission.

Finally, after you've seen the birds and snakes and butterflies, you might want to stop in at **The Orchid Garden** (☎ **506/645-5510**), on the main road toward the preserve. This new attraction boasts more than 400 species of orchids. Admission $5.

You can glimpse another part of the area's history at **El Trapiche** (☎ **506/645-6054**), where the process of making *tapa dulce* (local brown sugar sold in solid blocks) is demonstrated on Tuesday, Thursday, and Saturday on an old-fashioned sugar mill. El Trapiche is open Tuesday through Sunday from 11am to 10pm, serves tipico food, and sells homemade sugar products. You'll find El Trapiche 1 mile north of Santa Elena on the road to Tilarán.

SHOPPING

If you're in the mood to do some shopping, stop in at **CASEM** (☎ **506/645-5190**), which is on the right just past Restaurant El Bosque. This crafts co-operative sells embroidered clothing, T-shirts, posters, and postcards with photos of the local flora and fauna, Boruca weavings, locally grown and roasted coffee, and many other items to remind you of your visit to Monteverde. CASEM is open Monday through Saturday from 8am to 5pm and Sunday from 10am to 4pm (closed Sunday from May through October). There is also a well-stocked gift shop at the entrance to the preserve. You'll find plenty of T-shirts, postcards, and assorted crafts here, as well as a well stocked selection of science and natural history books. Finally, don't forget that perhaps the best gift shop in Monteverde is at the **Hummingbird Gallery** (☎ **506/645-5030,** see above).

Between November and April, you can also visit the **Sarah Dowell Watercolor Gallery** (☎ **506/645-5047**), which is up the hill from the cheese factory and sells paintings by this local artist. You might also check out **Galeria Extasis** (☎ **506/645-5548**), off the main road to the reserve, which sells the intriguing wooden sculptures of artist Marco Tulio Brenes. If you are interested in taking a class or workshop with one of the many local artists, check in with the newly formed **Monteverde Studio of the Arts** (☎ **800/370-3331** in the U.S. and Canada; e-mail: mstudios@sol.racsa.co.cr).

TAKE A BREAK Finally, if all the above has worn you out, stop in at **Chunches** (☎ **506/645-5147**), a new coffee/espresso bar and bookstore in Santa Elena, which also doubles as a Laundromat. Chunches is open Monday through Saturday from 9am to 6pm.

A LANGUAGE SCHOOL IN THE MOUNTAINS

The Centro Panamericano de Idiomas (☎ **800/903-8950** in the U.S. and Canada, or 506/645-5026; www.cpi-edu.com; e-mail: anajarro@sol.racsa.co.cr), offers immersion language classes in a wonderful setting. A 2-week program, with 4 hours of class per day and a homestay with a Costa Rican family, costs $570.

ACCOMMODATIONS

When choosing a place to stay in Monteverde, be sure to check whether the rates include a meal plan. In the past, all the lodges operated on the American plan (three meals a day), but this practice is on the wane. Check before you assume anything.

MODERATE

✪ **El Sapo Dorado.** Apdo. 9-5655, Monteverde, Puntarenas. ☎ **506/645-5010** or 506/645-5184. Fax 506/645-5180 or 506/645-5181. E-mail: elsapo@sol.racsa.co.cr. 20 cabin suites. $70–$80 double, $83–$96 triple; Rates lower in the off-season. V.

Located on a steep hill between Santa Elena and the preserve, El Sapo Dorado (named for Monteverde's famous "golden toad") offers attractive cabins with good views. The cabins are built of hardwoods both inside and out and are surrounded by a grassy lawn. Big windows let in lots of light, and high ceilings keep the rooms cool during the day. The older cabins also have fireplaces, which are a welcome feature on chilly nights and during the peak parts of the rainy season. The newer rooms all have spacious terraces with sunset views. The hotel has modern mountain bikes for rent and a massage room with a local therapist on call. There's also an excellent restaurant here, which is open to the public and serves three meals daily. From the large patio terrace, you can watch the sunset while listening to classical music. The bar stays open until 11pm and is usually fairly quiet. Not only does El Sapo Dorado own and manage the Reserva Sendero Tranquilo, but they also have a network of well-maintained trails into primary forest right on sight. To find the hotel and restaurant, watch for the sign on the left-hand side of the main road to the preserve, just as you're leaving Santa Elena.

✪ **Hotel Belmar.** Apdo. 17-5655, Monteverde, Puntarenas. ☎ **506/645-5201.** Fax 506/645-5135. E-mail: belmar@sol.racsa.co.cr. 32 units. $60 double, $70 triple; discounts are available in the off-season. V.

You'll think you're in the Alps when you stay at this beautiful Swiss chalet–style hotel. Set on the top of a grassy hill, the Belmar has stunning views of the Nicoya Gulf and the Pacific. Afternoons in the dining room or lounge are idyllic, with bright sunlight streaming in through a west-facing glass wall. Sunsets are spectacular. Most of the guest rooms are fitted with wood paneling, French doors, and little balconies that open onto splendid views. Meals usually live up to the surroundings and run around $21 per person per day. The Belmar is up a road to the left of the gas station as you come into the village of Monteverde.

Hotel De Montaña Monteverde. Apdo. 2070-1002, Paseo Los Estudiantes, San José. ☎ **506/224-3050** or 506/645-5046. Fax 506/222-6184. E-mail: monteverde@ticonet.co.cr. 27 units, 5 cabins. $65 double, $78 triple, $78–$110 suite. AE, MC, V.

This long, low motel-style building is one of the oldest hotels in Monteverde and is frequently filled with tour groups. The hotel is surrounded by 15 acres of farm and woods, and there are horses available for rent. Older rooms are rustic and have wood paneling. Newer rooms have queen-size beds, more light, and spectacular views of the Nicoya Gulf. There are also several spacious suites, including a honeymoon suite with its own whirlpool tub and a view. For family privacy, there are five cabins across the lawn from the main lodge. The rustic glass-walled dining room offers excellent views. Attached to the restaurant is a small bar that's busy in the evening, when people sit around swapping stories of their day's adventures and wildlife sightings. Meals will run you around $27 per person per day. On cold nights, you can warm up in the sauna or hot tub.

Hotel Fonda Vela. Apdo. 70060-1000, San José. ☎ **506/257-1413** or 506/645-5125. Fax 506/257-1416. E-mail: fondavel@sol.racsa.co.cr. 25 units. $68 double, $77 triple, $75–$83 suite double, $84–$92 suite triple. AE, MC, V.

Located on the right after the sign for the Pensíon Flor Mar, the Fonda Vela is one of the more luxurious lodges in Monteverde. Guest rooms are in five buildings scattered among the forests and pastures of this former farm, and most have views of the Nicoya Gulf. Lots of hardwood has been used throughout, and there are flagstone floors in some rooms. About half of the rooms have bathtubs, which is a rarity in Costa Rica. Several large suites, two of which have sleeping lofts, are the most spacious accommodations available, but unfortunately they do not have views. The dining room has great sunset views. Meals will run you $30 per person per day. You'll also find a bar and a gift shop here, as well as laundry service and horse rentals. Throughout the hotel you'll see paintings by owner Paul Smith, who also handcrafts guitars and violins and is a musician himself.

Hotel Heliconia. Apartado 10921-1000, San José. ☎ **506/645-5109.** Fax 506/645-5007. E-mail: heliconi@sol.racsa.co.cr. 22 units. $66 double, $77 triple. No credit cards.

The Heliconia, named after one of the tropics' most fascinating flowers, is one of the more comfortable and luxurious hotels in Monteverde. The main lodge building has varnished wood walls and a hardwood-floored balcony that runs the length of the second floor. Guest rooms in the main building are also done in floor-to-ceiling hardwoods that give them a rustic, mountain-resort feel. Behind the main lodge, there are paths that lead through attractive gardens to rooms with more space. These rooms have carpeting and full-size bathrooms with bathtubs. There's a hot tub in a bamboo grove, just outside the main building. The hotel's restaurant serves a changing nightly menu with both Tico and international dishes. There's also a small bar and trails that lead from the hotel up to an area of virgin forest with a scenic view of the Golfo de Nicoya.

Hotel Villa Verde. Apdo. 16-5655, Monteverde, Puntarenas. ☎ **506/645-5025.** Fax 506/645-5115. E-mail: estefany@sol.racsa.co.cr. 21 units. $49 double, $78 suite. Rates include breakfast. AE, MC, V.

This is the closest hotel to the preserve and is built on a grand scale. The main lodge features a huge dining room with floor-to-ceiling windows that reach all the way to the two-story-high roof. Each suite has a living room and a fireplace and is identified not by a number but by the likeness of a specific bird carved into the door. Standard rooms are spacious and comfortable, although the textured sand bathroom walls and pale blue tiles are an aesthetic disaster. The food here is favored by many of the local residents and guides.

✪ **Monteverde Lodge.** Calle Central and Avenida 1 (Apdo. 6941), San José. ☎ **506/257-0766.** Fax 506/257-1665. www.expeditions.co.cr. E-mail: costaric@expeditions.co.cr. 27 units. Dec 15–Apr 30, $76 double, $88 triple; May 1–Dec 14, $67 double, $76 triple. AE, MC, V.

Operated by Costa Rica Expeditions, the Monteverde Lodge is one of the most upscale hotels in Monteverde. It's located 3 miles (5km) from the preserve entrance in a secluded setting near Santa Elena. Guest rooms are large and comfortable and have angled walls of glass with chairs and a table placed so that avid bird-watchers can do a bit of birding in the morning before even leaving their rooms. The gardens and secondary forest surrounding the lodge now have some gentle groomed trails and are also home to quite a few species of birds. This lodge's most popular feature is a large hot tub in a big atrium garden just off the lobby. After hiking all day, you can soak your bones under the stars.

The hotel's dining room offers great views, good Tico and international food, and excellent formal service provided by bow-tied waiters. Meals will cost an additional $35 (plus tax and tip) per person per day. The bar adjacent to the dining room is a very popular gathering spot, especially with the many groups that use this lodge.

There are regular evening slide shows focusing on the cloud forest.

Bus service to and from San José is available ($40 each way), as is a shuttle to the preserve ($4 each way), horseback riding, and a variety of optional tours.

INEXPENSIVE

✪ **Arco Iris Lodge.** Apdo. 003-5655, Monteverde, Puntarenas. ☎ **506/645-5067.** Fax 506/645-5022. E-mail: arcoiris@sol.racsa.co.cr. 9 units. $25–$38 double. V.

This is by far the nicest hotel right in Santa Elena. The nine rooms are spread out in five separate buildings. All have wood or tile floors and plenty of wood accents. My favorite room is the "honeymoon cabin," which has its own private balcony with a forest view and good bird watching. There's a small garden on the premises, which supplies the restaurant with fresh vegetables and herbs in season. The menu is heavy on Tico standards but does feature some more adventurous dishes, like shrimp in coconut sauce and pork in peanut sauce. The management here is extremely helpful, speaks five languages, and can arrange a wide variety of tours.

Cabinas El Gran Mirador. Monteverde, Puntarenas. ☎ and fax **506/645-5354** or ☎ 506/381-7277. 22 units. $38 double, $15 per person students with valid ID. Rates include breakfast. No credit cards.

If you're looking for a bit more adventure and rusticity than are offered at any of the lodges in Monteverde, give these friendly folks a call. Once a very isolated and very rustic little lodge, this place has become quite popular and now has 22 rooms in 10 cabins. The wooden cabins are all very simply furnished and have great views of Arenal Volcano (when it's clear). The rooms have a dormitory feel, and if you're alone, you probably will be grouped with other travelers. El Gran Mirador is a long way from the Monteverde Cloud Forest Preserve, but it's close to the Santa Elena Cloud Forest Reserve. You can now reach El Gran Mirador year-round, so it's no longer necessary to be taken in by horseback—although you can still rent horses for $8 per hour. To get here, head out toward Santa Elena following signs to the Santa Elena Reserve and Skywalk. As you get close to the Skywalk, you will see the sign and turn-off for El Gran Mirador. This hotel also offers popular tours by horseback and boat to the Arenal Volcano.

El Bosque. Apdo. 27-5655, Monteverde. ☎ **506/645-5129** or 506/645-5158. Fax 506/645-5129. 23 units. $30 double, $38 triple, $46 quad. AE, MC, V.

Hidden down the hill behind El Bosque restaurant (on the main road to the preserve) is one of Monteverde's best values. Though the rooms are very basic, they're clean and fairly large and have high ceilings, picture windows, and double beds. The cement floors and simple furnishings are what help keep the rates down. The rooms are arranged in a semicircle around a minimally landscaped garden. The setting may not be spectacular, but if you're going to spend all day in the preserve, this shouldn't bother you too much. The hotel also has a camping area ($2.50 per person per night).

The hotel's restaurant is 100 yards up a dirt road and down a path that crosses a jungly ravine by footbridge, which turns going for breakfast into a morning bird-watching trip. Tico standards and international dishes are served here, with prices ranging from $3.50 to $15.

El Establo. Apdo. 549-2050, San Pedro. ☎ **506/645-5110** or 506/645-5033. Fax 506/645-5041. 20 units. $40 double, $50 triple, $60 quad. MC, V.

Horses are an integral part of Costa Rican culture and a common sight in Monteverde. El Establo, as its name implies, is a working stable and incorporates this theme in its architectural design. Though the hotel is next to the road, there are 120 acres of farm behind it, and half of this area is in primary forest. Most of the rooms are situated off a large enclosed porch that contains plenty of comfortable chairs and a fireplace. Guest-room doors look as if they were salvaged from a stable, but inside, the rooms are carpeted and have orthopedic mattresses and modern bathrooms, though with showers only. The end rooms have a bit more light than others. Of course, the hotel also has plenty of horses for rent at $7 per hour, with a guide. Meals will run you around $25 per person per day.

Hotel El Tucan. Santa Elena, Puntarenas. ☎ **506/645-5017.** Fax 506/645-5462. 14 units (7 with bathroom). $14 double without bathroom; $20 double with bathroom. No credit cards.

This very basic lodging is located on the edge of Santa Elena (on the back road from the village's main street that leads to Monteverde) and consequently does not have the rural feel of many of the area's other accommodations. Though the rooms without bathrooms are only slightly larger than closets, they are fairly clean. Rooms with a private bathroom are slightly larger, with some housed in a separate building across the street. Very inexpensive Costa Rican–style meals are served in a very basic dining room on the ground floor. Keep in mind that this hotel is 3 miles (5km) from the preserve. If you don't have a car, transportation to and from the preserve by taxi is going to add a bit to the cost of the room.

Pensión Flor de Monteverde. Apdo. 99-5655, Santa Elena, Monteverde. ☎ and fax **506/645-5236.** 8 units (4 with bathroom). $14 double, $21 triple (shared bathroom); $20 double, $30 triple (private bathroom). No credit cards.

This new pension is my favorite budget option in Monteverde. Located 75 meters up a dirt road, just outside Santa Elena on the way to the preserve, this hotel has an authentic rural feel. The rooms are very simple, but immaculately clean. The owners will make you feel part of the family. They also know and love the area, and are eager to share it with guests. A full meal plan will cost you $15 per person per day, including taxes.

Pensión Flor Mar. Apdo. 2498-1000, San José. ☎ **506/645-5009.** Fax 506/645-5580. 13 units (3 with bathroom). $26 per person without bathroom; $30 per person with bathroom. Rates include 3 meals daily. No credit cards.

The Flor Mar was one of the first lodges to open in Monteverde and initially catered almost exclusively to professors and students doing scientific research in the preserve. Study groups still make up the bulk of the Flor Mar's business, but casual visitors are also welcome. The rooms are very simply furnished, which means bunk beds in some rooms. There are no views to speak of here; however, this lodge is close to the park entrance, a definite plus if you don't have a car. The dining room is large and rather dark, but there's a much more appealing lounge in the lower of the lodge's two main buildings. The rates include all three meals a day.

Pensión Monteverde Inn. Monteverde. ☎ **506/645-5156.** Fax 506/645-4052. 10 units (8 with bathroom). $8 per person with shared bathroom; $11 per person with private bathroom. No credit cards.

Of the numerous inexpensive lodgings in the area, this one has the most pleasant surroundings. Located about 150 meters past the Monteverde Butterfly Garden, the Monteverde Inn itself is a couple of hundred yards off the main road on a small farm. Owner David Savage and his family have operated this simple, rustic lodge for years. The rooms are small and come with two twin beds or a double bed. Hardwood floors keep the rooms from seeming too spartan. It's a bit of a walk up to the park entrance, but once you reach the main road, you can try hitching a ride. Horse rentals are available for $6 per hour. Also, economical meals are available, making this is a good choice for those who have to watch their colónes.

DINING

Most lodges in Monteverde have their own dining rooms, and these are the most convenient places to eat. Because most visitors to Monteverde want to get an early start, they usually grab a quick breakfast at their hotel. It's also common for people to have their lodge pack them a bag lunch to take with them to the preserve. If you're in the mood to eat out, though, there are now several inexpensive restaurants scattered along the road between Santa Elena and Monteverde. One worth mentioning is the **Pizzeria de Johnny** (☎ **506/645-5066**), which now has new digs on the road to the reserve near El Sapo Dorado. Upstairs from the pizzeria is the **Neotropica Cafe** another new place specializing in gourmet and vegetarian deli sandwiches, as well as burritos and other Tex-Mex standards.

Alternatively, stop in at **Stella's Bakery** (no phone) across the road from the CASEM gift shop, for some fresh bread and maybe a piece of cake or some cookies. Stella's is open daily from 6am to 6pm and also has a small cafe where you can get pizzas, eggplant parmigiana, salads, and deliciously decadent baked goods. Next, stop by the **Monteverde Cheese Factory** (☎ **506/645-5136**) and pick up some of the best cheese in Costa Rica (you can even see it being made). The cheese factory is open Monday through Saturday from 7:30am to 4pm and Sunday from 7:30am to 12:30pm. Between the two places, you should be able to put together a great picnic lunch. You can also get fresh, homemade ice cream at the Cheese Factory these days.

In Santa Elena, you might want to check out **Rocky Road Café** (☎ **506/645-5035**) for hefty sandwiches, excellent burgers, and a wide range of desserts. They'll also prepare you a box/bag lunch.

✪ **El Sapo Dorado.** Road to the left as you leave Santa Elena. ☎ **506/645-5010.** Reservations recommended during high season. Main courses $6–$14. AE, MC, V. Daily 6:30am–9:30am, noon–3pm, and 6–9pm. INTERNATIONAL.

Located high on a hill above the main road, El Sapo Dorado provides great sunsets and good food. The menu is a little bit more imaginative than at most restaurants in Monteverde, which makes it well worth a visit even if you miss the sunset. A recent menu included grilled corvina in a Sambuca sauce, fettuccine in peanut-squid sauce, and filet mignon in pepper-cream sauce. There are always vegetarian options, as well. In addition to a large, formal dining room, there's a patio that's a great spot for lunch or an early dinner. Taped classical music and jazz are played in the evenings.

Restaurante De Lucía. On the road down to the Butterfly Farm, on your right. ☎ **506/645-5337.** Reservations recommended during the high season. Main courses $8–$12; lunch $2.50–$6. AE, MC, V. Daily 11am–10pm. COSTA RICAN/INTERNATIONAL.

In just a few years here, De Lucía's has earned some local renown. There's really no menu, but your waiter will bring out a platter with the nightly selection of meats and fresh fish, which are then grilled to order. One of the more interesting dishes here is the chicken in orange sauce. All meals come with fresh homemade tortillas and a full accompaniment of side orders and vegetables. The sweet plátanos prepared on the open grill are delicious. Service is informal and friendly. The heavy wood tables and chairs are spread comfortably around the large dining room.

The Central Pacific Coast

8

The central Pacific coast is home to some of the most accessible beaches in Costa Rica. They range from the somewhat seedy Puntarenas and the cut-rate, fun-in-the-sun Jacó to the jungle-clad hillsides of Manuel Antonio and Dominical. For the most part, this coast is not as spectacular as that of the more rugged Nicoya Peninsula, but neither does it get as brown and desolate-looking as the peninsula gets in the dry season. The climate here is considerably more humid than farther north but not nearly as steamy as along the south Pacific or Caribbean coasts. Jacó and Manuel Antonio are Costa Rica's two most developed beaches, while Puntarenas, a former seaport, offers the most urban beach setting in the country (it's just a short day trip away from San José). If you're looking to get away from it all, without traveling too far or spending too much, Dominical should be your top choice on this coast.

This is also where you'll find some of Costa Rica's most popular and spectacular national parks and biological reserves: **Manuel Antonio National Park**, home of three-toed sloths and white-faced monkeys; **Chirripó National Park**, a misty cloud forest that becomes a barren páramo at the peak of its namesake, **Mt. Chirripó**; and **Carara Biological Reserve**, one of the last places in Costa Rica where you can see the disappearing dry forest join the damp, humid forests that extend south down the coast and glimpse an occasional scarlet macaw.

1 Puntarenas

71 miles (115km) W of San José; 118 miles (191km) S of Liberia; 46 miles (75km) N of Playa de Jacó

Some see Puntarenas as a fallen jewel, others see nothing more than a run-down, rough-and-tumble port town. After decades of decay and neglect, Puntarenas has been targeted for some long-overdue attention and renovation, though the much-trumpeted work has been progressing at a snail's pace. A 10-mile-long spit of land jutting into the Gulf of Nicoya, Puntarenas was once Costa Rica's busiest port, but that changed several years ago when the government inaugurated nearby Puerto Caldera, a modern container port facility. After losing its port, the city survived primarily on commercial fishing. Watching the tourist boom bring big bucks to other cities, Puntarenas decided to try to grab its piece of the pie. To that end, the city built a sewage treatment plant to clean up its water and now has the only beach-cleaning machine in Costa Rica. The town's beachfront **Paseo de los Turistas** (Tourist Walk), a 10-block promenade of ice cream stands, small restaurants, and arcades, will be the next spruced up area. Work is underway on a modern cruise ship dock that will accommodate two ships at a time. When all the work is finished, Puntarenas should also have a convention and recreation center, a seaside aquarium, a museum, and an artisans' row where visitors will be able to stock up on regional arts and crafts.

With a good highway leading all the way from San José, Puntarenas can be reached (on a good day, with no traffic) in 1½ hours by car, which makes it the closest beach to San José—at least in elapsed time if not in actual mileage. Because Puntarenas is a city, a former port town, and commercial fishing center, this beach has a very different character from any other in Costa Rica. A long, straight stretch of sand with gentle surf, the beach is backed for most of its length by the Paseo de los Turistas. Across a wide boulevard from the paseo are hotels, restaurants, bars, discos, and shops. The sunsets and the views across the Gulf of Nicoya are quite beautiful, and there's almost always a cooling breeze blowing in off the water. All around town you'll find unusual old buildings, reminders of the important role Puntarenas once played in Costa Rican history. It was from here that much of the Central Valley's coffee crop was once shipped, and while the coffee barons in the highlands were getting rich, so too were the merchants of Puntarenas.

If you're in Costa Rica for only a short time and want to get in some time on the beach, Puntarenas is certainly an option, though I recommend driving (or being driven) the extra hour or so that it takes to reach some of the nicer beaches farther south. Swimming here still seems more the exception than the rule, and Puntarenas is still primarily a place to spend the night during transit. It is here you must pick up the ferries to Nicoya, and many folks like to arrive the night before and get an early start. It's also a good place to break up the longer trip up to, or back from, Guanacaste. Puntarenas is most popular as a weekend holiday spot for Ticos from San José and is at its liveliest on weekends.

One final note, in 1997 and 1998, Puntarenas was the site of Costa Rica's worst outbreak of dengue fever (see chapter 3 for more information). This has subsided, but you should always wear insect repellent in Puntarenas, especially during the day, since dengue is spread by a mosquito that is active only during the daytime.

ESSENTIALS

FESTIVAL If you're in Puntarenas on the Saturday closest to July 16, you can witness the **Fiesta of the Virgin of the Sea.** During this festival, a regatta of colorfully decorated boats carry a statue of Puntarenas's patron saint.

GETTING THERE & DEPARTING By Bus Express buses (☎ **506/221-5749**) leave San José daily every 30 minutes between 6:30am and 9pm from Calle 16 between Avenidas 10 and 12. Trip duration is 2 hours; fare is $2.50.

The main Puntarenas bus station is a block east of the Hotel Imperial, which is in front of the old main dock on the Paseo de los Turistas. Buses to San José leave daily every 30 minutes between 6:30am and 7pm. The bus to Santa Elena leaves daily at 2:15pm from a stop across the railroad tracks from the main bus station. Buses to Quepos (Manuel Antonio) leave daily at 5am, 11am, and 2:30pm.

By Car Head west out of San José on the Interamerican Highway, passing the airport and Alajuela, and follow the signs to Puntarenas. The drive takes about 1½ hours.

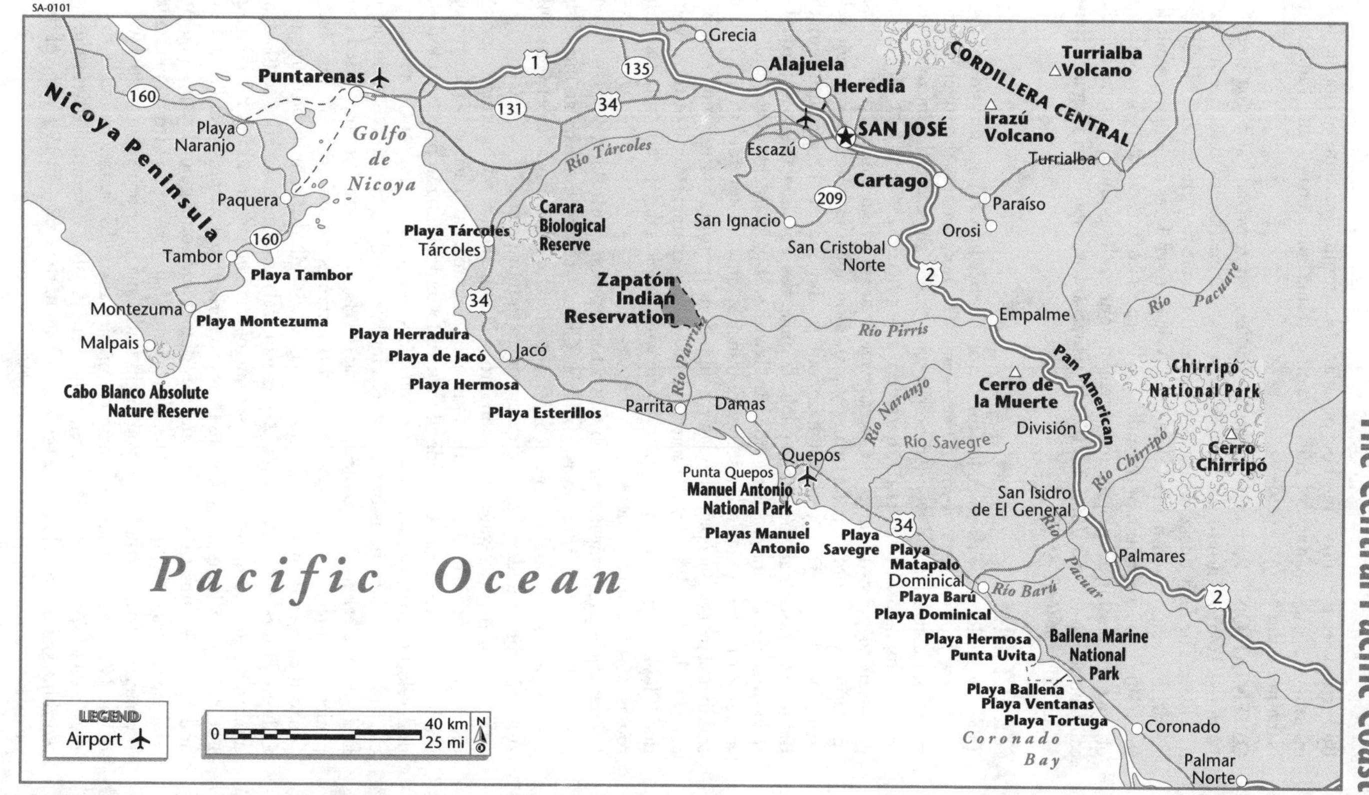
SA-0101
Grecia
Alajuela
Heredia
SAN JOSÉ
CORDILLERA CENTRAL
Turrialba Volcano
Irazú Volcano
Turrialba
Escazú
Cartago
Paraíso
Orosi
San Ignacio
San Cristobal Norte
Puntarenas
Nicoya Peninsula
Playa Naranjo
Golfo de Nicoya
Paquera
Tambor
Playa Tambor
Montezuma
Playa Montezuma
Malpais
Cabo Blanco Absolute Nature Reserve
Río Tárcoles
Playa Tárcoles
Tárcoles
Carara Biological Reserve
Zapatón Indian Reservation
Playa Herradura
Playa de Jacó
Jacó
Playa Hermosa
Playa Esterillos
Parrita
Río Parrita
Damas
Río Pirrís
Empalme
Río Pacuare
Pan American
Cerro de la Muerte
Chirripó National Park
Cerro Chirripó
División
Río Naranjo
Río Savegre
Río Chirripó
Quepos
Punta Quepos
Manuel Antonio National Park
Playas Manuel Antonio
Playa Savegre
Playa Matapalo
San Isidro de El General
Palmares
Río Pacuar
Dominical
Río Barú
Playa Barú
Playa Dominical
Playa Hermosa
Punta Uvita
Ballena Marine National Park
Playa Ballena
Playa Ventanas
Playa Tortuga
Coronado
Coronado Bay
Palmar Norte
Pacific Ocean
1
135
160
131
34
209
2
LEGEND
Airport
0
40 km
25 mi
N

By Ferry See the "Playa Tambor" or "Playa Montezuma" sections of chapter 6 for information on crossing to and returning from Puntarenas from Paquera or Naranjo on the Nicoya Peninsula.

ORIENTATION Puntarenas is built on a long, narrow sand spit that stretches 10 miles (16km) out into the Gulf of Nicoya and is marked by only five streets at its widest. The ferry docks for the Nicoya Peninsula are near the far end of town, as are the bus station and market. The north side of town faces an estuary, while the south side faces the mouth of the gulf. The Paseo de los Turistas is on the south side of town, beginning at the pier and extending out to the point. If you need a taxi, call **Coopetico** (☎ **506/663-2020**). Car rentals are available from **Elegante Rent-a-Car** (☎ **506/661-1958**).

ATTRACTIONS

Take a walk along the Paseo de los Turistas and notice how similar this side of town is to a few Florida beach towns 50 years ago. The hotels across the street range in style from converted old wooden homes with bright gingerbread trim to modern concrete monstrosities to tasteful art deco relics needing a new coat of paint. If you want to go swimming, the ocean waters are now said to be perfectly safe (pollution was a problem for many years), although the beach is still not very attractive. Alternatively, you can head out to the end of the peninsula to the **Balneario Municipal**, the public pool. It's huge, has a great view (albeit through a chain-link fence), and is surrounded by lawns and gardens. However, this place is pretty run-down and a bit seedy. Entrance is only $1 for adults and 50¢ for children. The pool is open Tuesday through Sunday from 9am to 4pm. Your best bet is to head back down the spit, and just a few kilometers out of town you'll find **Playa Dona Aña**, a popular beach with picnic tables, bath and changing rooms, and a couple of sodas.

Puntarenas isn't known as one of Costa Rica's prime sportfishing ports, but there are usually a few charter boats available. Check at your hotel or at the **Hotel Yadran**. Rates are usually between $250 and $400 for a half day and between $400 and $600 for a full day. These rates are for up to four people.

The most popular water excursions from Puntarenas are yacht cruises through the tiny, uninhabited islands of the Guayabo, Negritos, and Pajaros Islands Biological Reserve. These cruises include a lunch buffet and relaxing stop on beautiful and undeveloped **Tortuga Island**, where you can swim, snorkel, and sun. The water is clear blue and the sand is bright white. However, as this trip has surged in popularity, a cattle-car element to these tours has developed. Several San José–based companies offer these excursions, with round-trip transportation from San José, but if you're already in Puntarenas, you might receive a slight discount by boarding here. **Calypso Tours** (☎ **506/256-2727;** e-mail: calypso@centraamerica.com) is the most reputable company that cruises out of Puntarenas. In addition to Tortuga Island, Calypso Tours takes folks to their own private nature reserve at Punta Coral and even on a sunset cruise that includes dinner and some guided stargazing. Any of these cruises will run you $99 per person from San José, or $94 from Puntarenas. If you check down at the docks, you might find some other boats that ply the waters of the Nicoya Gulf. Some of these companies also offer sunset cruises with live music, snacks, and a bar. However, make sure you feel comfortable with the seaworthiness of the vessel and the professionalism of the crew—in 1997, one of these boats capsized, and two passengers drowned.

ACCOMMODATIONS

VERY EXPENSIVE

Caribbean Village Fiesta Hotel. Apdo. 171-5400, Puntarenas. ☎ **800/662-2990** in the U.S., or 506/663-0808. Fax 506/663-1516. E-mail: fiesta@sol.racsa.co.cr. 220 units. A/C TV TEL. Dec 16–Apr 15, $187 double, $233 suite; Apr 16–Dec 15, $139 double, $175 suite. AE, MC, V.

This large-scale resort hotel changed hands and decided to go the "all-inclusive" route. They also changed their name without apparently consulting a map; this hotel is on the Pacific Ocean. It's greatest asset is its proximity to San José, so if you're looking for a place in the sun and you don't want to waste time getting there, this may be your best bet. On the downside, the beach the resort sits on isn't that appealing for swimming, so you'll probably find most of your water activities confined to the giant swimming pool. As the name implies, the Fiesta is meant for partying, or at least keeping active. There are nightly musical theater revues, live music in the Mastil Bar, a popular casino, a disco that cranks up at 10pm each evening, and the frequent "beach parties" the hotel puts on to attract a young Tico clientele, so don't expect peace and quiet. Do expect crowds.

All the rooms come with either two doubles or one king-size bed. Though there are large TVs in all the rooms, the bathrooms in the standard rooms are small and have showers only. If you opt for a deluxe room or suite, you'll get more comfortable and spacious accommodations and a better view. The hotel is located a couple of miles south of town on the road from Puntarenas to Caldera.

Dining/Diversions: This is an all-inclusive resort, so all of your food and local beers and spirits are included. A giant rancho at the back of the hotel serves as the principal restaurant and bar. Muelle 49 is an outdoor seafood restaurant with a view of the ocean and pier. There's also an Italian restaurant that offers the most formal atmosphere, but even here, "dress shorts" are permitted. My favorite bar is located on an island in the middle of the main pool. The casino is housed in a large atrium.

Amenities: The free-form main swimming pool is huge, has an island in the middle, and is surrounded by hundreds of lounge chairs. Artificial boulders give it a more natural look. In addition, you'll find a second pool, whirlpool tub, volleyball court, two tennis courts, exercise room, game room, gift shop, and jewelry shop. Free use of all the land-sports equipment (tennis rackets, basketballs, volleyballs, bicycles) and water-sports equipment (kayaks, boogie boards). You can make arrangements for tours and excursions here, including scuba trips, sportfishing charters, national-park visits, and day cruises. There are also jet skis and windsurfers available for rent.

EXPENSIVE

Yadran Hotel. At the end of the Paseo de los Turistas (Apdo. 14-5400), Puntarenas. ☎ **506/661-2662.** Fax 506/661-1944. 42 units. A/C TV TEL. $77–$97 double, $98–$118 triple; slightly lower rates in the off-season. AE, DC, MC, V.

Located at the far end of Puntarenas, at the tip of the spit, this is the most luxurious in-town choice. I find it a bit overpriced, for what you get, but because it's in town, you'll have access to other restaurants and can stroll the Paseo de los Turistas. Also, the car-ferry dock is only a few blocks away. The range in room prices reflects whether or not you get an ocean view. I like the upper-floor rooms, with a balcony and a view, but even the priciest rooms can seem a bit dreary.

Dining/Diversions: The hotel has two small restaurants. One is a poolside patio restaurant and the other is a slightly more formal indoor dining room with a view out over the water. The seafood here is good, if a bit pricey. Entree prices range from $6.50 to $20. A small casino is open every evening from 6pm on. The disco is open on Friday and Saturday beginning at 7pm. It's located underground, so the beat won't keep you awake if you decide not to dance the night away.

Amenities: The hotel has a helpful tour desk, bicycle rentals, and a gift shop.

MODERATE

✪ **Hotel Las Brisas.** Paseo de los Turistas (Apdo. 83-5400), Puntarenas. ☎ **506/661-4040.** Fax 506/661-2120. 20 units. A/C TV. $42 double, $49 triple; lower rates in the off-season. Rates include breakfast. AE, MC, V.

Out near the end of the Paseo de los Turistas, you'll find this very clean hotel with large air-conditioned rooms, a small pool out front, and the beach right across the street. All the rooms have tile floors, double or twin beds, and small televisions and tables. Large picture windows keep the rooms sunny and bright during the day. The hotel's small open-air dining room serves some of the best food in town, with the emphasis on continental dishes. The bouillabaisse is excellent, and if you're lucky you might happen on a Greek-style fish special or homemade moussaka. It's worth staying here just to enjoy the food. There's complimentary coffee and a secure parking lot, and this is where I often stay if I've got a ferry to catch in the morning.

Hotel Tioga. Paseo de los Turistas (Apdo. 96-5400), Puntarenas. ☎ **506/661-0271,** or 506/255-3115 in San José. Fax 506/661-0127. www.cmnet.co.cr. E-mail: tiogacr@sol.racsa.co.cr. 46 units. A/C. $38–$63 double. Rates include breakfast. AE, MC, V.

This 1950s modern-style hotel is the old standard on the Paseo de los Turistas. The beach is across the street, and there are plenty of nearby restaurants. When you walk through the front door, you enter a courtyard with a pool that's been painted a brilliant shade of blue. In the middle of the pool, there's a tiny island with a tree growing on it. Rooms vary in size, and most have air-conditioning, telephone, and television, but if you must have these perks, be sure to request them. The larger rooms are attractive, with huge closets, modern bathrooms, and private balconies with a view of the ocean. The smaller, less-expensive rooms have louvered, frosted-glass windows to let in lots of light and air while maintaining some privacy. The restaurant and bar are on the second floor, and there's a breakfast room and lounge on the fourth floor, so you can look out across the water as you enjoy your complimentary breakfast. There's a new casino.

INEXPENSIVE

✪ **Hotel Ayi Con.** 50 meters south of the market (Apdo. 358), Puntarenas. ☎ **506/661-0164.** 44 units (22 with bathroom). $11 double without bathroom, $16 double with bathroom, $20 double with bathroom and A/C. No credit cards.

Centrally located near the market and the ferry-boat docks, the Ayi Con is your basic low-budget Tico accommodation. It's above a row of shops in a very busy shopping district of Puntarenas and is frequented primarily by Costa Ricans. Backpackers will find that this is probably the best and the cleanest of the cheap hotels in Puntarenas. If you're just passing through and have to spend a night in town, this place is convenient and acceptable.

DINING

Since you're in a seaport, you should be sure to try corvina, the national fish dish of Costa Rica, at least once. The most economical option is to pull up a table at one of the many open-air snack bars along the Paseo de los Turistas. They have names like **Soda Rio de Janeiro** and **Soda Acapulco**, and serve everything from sandwiches, drinks, and ice cream to ceviche and whole fish meals. Sandwiches are priced at around $1.00, and a fish fillet with rice and beans should cost around $3.50.

If you want meat, you might try **La Yunta Steakhouse**. Another popular spot is the **Restaurant Aloha.** Both of these restaurants are on the Paseo de los Turistas.

✪ **Bierstube.** Paseo de los Turistas between Calles 21 and 23, Paseo de los Turistas. ☎ **506/661-0330.** Main courses $3–$9. DC, MC, V. Wed–Mon noon–1am, Tue 6pm–10:30pm. GERMAN/SEAFOOD.

This German-Tico beer garden also happens to serve excellent seafood. The restaurant is a huge open room with a high ceiling; louvered windows swing open and provide fresh breezes and a view of the bay. There's beer on tap and good hearty meals. The "filete bierstube" is a fresh piece of corvina in a light tomato sauce, with mushrooms and peppers.

La Caravelle. Paseo de los Turistas between Calles 21 and 23, Paseo de los Turistas. ☎ **506/661-2262.** Reservations recommended in high season and on weekends. Main courses $5.50–$15. MC, V. Wed–Sat noon–2:30pm and 6–10:30pm, Sun 11:30am–10pm. FRENCH.

For more than 16 years, La Caravelle has been serving fine French dinners in an eclectically decorated cafe atmosphere. The restaurant's walls are decorated with a curious assortment of paintings, as well as a carousel horse, which gives La Caravelle a very playful feel. The menu, however, is strictly traditional French, with such flavorful and well-prepared dishes as tenderloin with bourguignonne sauce or a tarragon béarnaise. There are quite a few good seafood dishes, as well as a salade Niçoise. There's a modest assortment of both French and Chilean wines to accompany your meal, though wine prices are a bit high (as they are all over Costa Rica).

2 Playa de Jacó

72 miles (117km) W of San José; 46 miles (75km) S of Puntarenas

Playa de Jacó is the closest thing Costa Rica has to Fort Lauderdale during spring break. This long stretch of beach is strung with a dense hodgepodge of hotels in all price categories, cheap souvenir shops, seafood restaurants, pizza joints, and even a miniature golf course. If you're looking for a cheap place not far from San José where you can spend a week in the sun, Jacó continues to be the top choice.

However, the beach here is not particularly appealing. It's made of dark gray sand with lots of little rocks and it's often very rough. Charter flights arrive weekly from Montreal and Toronto, and consequently many of the hotels here are owned and populated by Canadians. Jacó is also now gaining popularity with Germans and young Ticos. However, the number-one attraction here is the surf, and this is definitely a surfer-dominated beach town. This is the most touristy beach in Costa Rica and is a prime example of what happens when rapid growth hits a beach town. However, on the outskirts of town and close to the beach there's still plenty of greenery to offset the excess of cement along the town's main street. In fact, this is the first beach on the Pacific coast that actually has a tropical feel to it, after the dryness of Guanacaste. The humidity is palpable, and the lushness of the tropical forest is visible on the hillsides surrounding town. In hotel gardens, flowers bloom profusely throughout the year.

ESSENTIALS

GETTING THERE & DEPARTING **By Bus** Express buses (☎ **506/223-1109** or 506/643-3135) leave San José daily at 7:30am, 10:30am, and 3:30pm from the Coca-Cola bus terminal at Calle 16 between Avenidas 1 and 3. The trip takes 3 hours; fare is $2.50. On weekends and holidays, extra buses are often added, so it's worth calling to check.

Buses from San José to Quepos and Manuel Antonio also pass by Jacó (they let passengers off on the highway about 1 kilometer from town). These buses leave San José daily at 6, 7, and 10am, noon, and 2, 4, 5, and 6pm. Trip duration is 3 hours; fare is $2.50 for the indirect bus to Quepos, $5 for the direct bus to Manuel Antonio. However, during the busy months, some of these buses will refuse passengers getting off in Jacó, or accept them only if they pay the full fare to Quepos or Manuel Antonio.

From Puntarenas, there are two buses daily to Jacó at 5am and 3pm, or you can catch Quepos-bound buses daily at 5am, 11am, and 2pm and get off in Jacó. Either way, the trip's duration is 1 hour; fare is $1.50.

The Jacó bus station is at the north end of town, at a small mall across from the Jacó Fiesta Hotel. Buses for San José leave daily at 5am, 11am, and 3pm. Buses bound for Quepos stop in Jacó around 6am, noon, and 4pm. Since schedules can change, it's best to ask at your hotel about current departure times.

By Car There are two main routes to Jacó. The easier, though longer, route is to take the Interamerican Highway west out of San José and get off at the Puntarenas exit. From here, head south on the Costanera, the coast road. Alternatively, you can take the narrow and winding, though more scenic, old highway, which turns off the Interamerican Highway just west of Alajuela near the town of Atenas. This highway meets the Costanera a few kilometers west of Orotina.

ORIENTATION Playa de Jacó is a short distance off the southern highway. One main road runs parallel to the beach, with a host of arteries heading toward the water; it's off these roads that you'll find most of the hotels and restaurants.

GETTING AROUND While almost everything is within walking distance in Jacó, you can rent a bicycle or scooter from several shops on the main street or call **Jaco Taxi** (☎ **506/643-3030**). For longer excursions, you can rent a car from **Ada** (☎ **506/643-3207**), **Economy** (☎ **506/643-3280**), or **Elegante** (☎ **506/643-3224**). Expect to pay approximately $50 for a 1-day rental. You might also consider talking to any of the local taxi drivers, who would probably take you wherever you wanted to go for the same $50 per day, thus saving you some hassle and headache.

FAST FACTS Both the **Banco Nacional** (☎ **506/643-3072**) and the **Banco de Costa Rica** (☎ **506/643-3334**) have branches in town on the main road and are open Monday through Friday from 9am to 3pm. **Botiquín Garabito** (☎ **506/643-3205**), the town's pharmacy, is down the street from the Banco Nacional. There's a gas station out on the main highway, at the south end of town. The health center and post office are at the Municipal Center at the south end of town, across from El Naranjal restaurant. A public phone office, from which you can make international calls, is located in the ICE building on the main road. This office is open Monday through Saturday from 8am to 12pm and from 1 to 5pm. The **Banana Bath Laundry** (☎ **506/643-3786**) is located on the main strip next to the Red Cross and is open Monday through Saturday from 8am to 5pm.

Same-day service is available. Finally, there's a Western Union office in a small strip mall across from La Hacienda Restaurant.

FUN ON & OFF THE BEACH

Unfortunately, the water here has a nasty reputation for riptides, as does most of the water off Costa Rica's Pacific coast. Even strong swimmers have been known to drown in the power rips. At times, storms far offshore cause huge waves to pound on the beach, making it impossible to go in the water much beyond your waist. If this is the case, you'll have to be content with the hotel pool (if the hotel you stay in has one).

After you've spent some time on Playa de Jacó, you might want to visit some of the other nearby beaches. **Playa Esterillos**, 13½ miles (22km) southeast of Jacó, is long and wide and almost always nearly deserted. **Playa Hermosa**, 6.2 miles (10km) southeast of Jacó, where sea turtles lay eggs from July to December, is also well-known for its great surfing waves. **Playa Herradura**, about 4 miles (6.5km) northwest of Jacó, is ringed by lush hillsides. Although this beach currently has just a few basic cabins and campgrounds, the Marriott corporation is well underway in construction of a megaresort and golf course at Playa Herradura, which is slated to open in late 1999. All of these beaches are beautiful and easily reached by car, moped, or bicycle—if you've got a lot of energy. All are signposted, so you'll have no trouble finding them.

Conversely, the same waves that often make Playa de Jacó unsafe for swimming make it one of the most popular beaches in the country with surfers. Nearby **Playa Hermosa** and **Playa Escondida** are also excellent surfing beaches. Those who want to challenge the waves can rent surfboards for around $2.50 an hour or $10 per day, and boogie boards for $1.50 an hour, from any one of the numerous surf shops along the main road.

One great day trip from Jacó is to the nearby **Iguana Park** (☎ **506/240-6712**). Don't let the iguana burgers and tacos on sale at the restaurant here or the iguana "leather" wallets and belts on sale at the gift shop fool you—this place is actually an iguana preservation project. When you're not eating and buying iguana products, you can take a walk through a forest trail in an area massively repopulated with green iguanas and visit the park's education center (where you can touch and hold iguanas). The park is also the site of one of the original canopy tour operations. The canopy tour here takes a full 3½ hours and costs $50, including the separate $10 entrance fee for the Iguana Park. You'll find Iguana Park about 10km from Orotina—to get here from Jacó, head back toward San José via Orotina. In Oritina, follow the signs to Iguana Park, which is about 20 minutes south.

Finally, if all the activity here has worn you out, contact **The Serenity Spa** (☎ **506/643-1254**), which offers massage, as well as mud packs and face and body treatments. The spa is located on the second floor, among a tiny little cul-de-sac of shops next to Ada Rent-A-Car and Wishbone Eatery.

BIKING If you would rather stay out of the surf but still want to get some exercise, you can rent a bike for around $8 per day or $1.50 per hour. Bikes are available from a slew of shops along the main road.

SPORTFISHING If you're interested in doing some sportfishing, check down around Playa Herradura, call **J.D. Watersports** (☎ **506/257-3857**), which works out of Punta Leona, or ask at **Hotel Club del Mar** (☎ **506/643-3194**). A half-day fishing trip for four people will cost around $250 to $325, and a full day will cost between $450 and $800.

CARARA BIOLOGICAL RESERVE: A FAMOUS NESTING GROUND FOR SCARLET MACAWS & A PLACE TO SEE CROCODILES

A little over 9 miles (15km) north of Jacó is Carara Biological Reserve, a world-renowned nesting ground for scarlet macaws. It has several miles of trails open to visitors. There's a loop trail that takes about an hour and another trail that's open only to tour groups. The macaws migrate daily, spending their days in the park and their nights among the coastal mangroves. It's best to view them in the early morning when they arrive, or around sunset when they head back to the coast for the evening, but a good guide can usually find them for you during the day. Whether or not you see them, you should hear their loud squawks. Among the other wildlife you might see here are caimans, coatimundis, armadillos, pacas, peccaries, river otters, kinkajous, and, of course, hundreds of species of birds. Be sure to bring along insect repellent, or, better yet, wear light cotton long sleeves and pants. I was once foolish enough to attempt a quick hike while returning from Manuel Antonio—still in beach clothes and flip-flops—not a good idea. The reserve is open daily from 8am to 4pm. This is a national park, so admission is a flat $6 per person at the gate. There are several companies offering tours to Carara Biological Reserve for around $30 to $35. Check at your hotel or contact **Fantasy Tours** (☎ **506/643-3231** or 506/643-3383) for schedules and more information.

The muddy banks of the Tárcoles River are home to a healthy population of American crocodiles, and just north of the entrance to the Carara Biological Reserve is a bridge that's a prime spot for viewing both the crocs and the macaw migrations. It's worth a stop, but be careful: Thieves and pickpockets work this spot regularly. Don't leave your car or valuables unguarded, and be wary if yours is the only car parked here.

ORGANIZED TOURS OF NEARBY SITES

If you will be spending your entire Costa Rican visit in Jacó but would like to see some other parts of the country, you can arrange tours through the local offices of **Explorica** (☎ **506/643-3586**) or **Fantasy Tours** (☎ **506/643-3231** or 506/643-3383). Both companies offer day tours to Arenal, Poás, and Irazú volcanoes, white-water-rafting trips, cruises to Tortuga Island, and trips to Braulio Carillo and Manuel Antonio national parks and other places. They also offer overnight trips. Rates range from $50 to $85 for day trips. Horseback-riding tours are also very popular. These trips give you a chance to get away from all the development in Jacó and see a bit of nature. Contact **Fantasy Tours** (see above), **Sanchez Madrigal Bros.** (☎ **506/643-3203**), or **Hermanos Salazar** (☎ **506/643-3203**) to make a reservation. Tours lasting 3 to 4 hours cost around $25 to $35.

ACCOMMODATIONS IN PLAYA DE JACÓ

Since Playa Leona, Playa Herradura, and Playa Hermosa de Jacó (not to be confused with Playa Hermosa in Guanacaste) are close by, many people choose accommodations in these beach towns as well. Selected listings for these towns follow this section.

EXPENSIVE

Best Western Jacó Beach Hotel. Playa de Jacó (Apdo. 962-1000, San José), Puntarenas. ☎ **800/272-6654** in the U.S., 800/463-6654 in Canada, or 506/220-1725. Fax 506/232-3159. E-mail: jacohote@sol.racsa.co.cr. 130 units. A/C TV TEL. Nov–Apr, $88 double or triple; May–Oct, $69 double or triple. AE, MC, V.

This is Jacó's main Canadian charter-flight hotel and is packed throughout the high season with crowds fleeing the cold in Ontario and Quebec. Situated right on the beach, this five-story hotel is just what you would expect of a tropical beach resort. The open-air lobby is surrounded by lush gardens, and there are covered walkways connecting the hotel's buildings. The hotel underwent remodeling in 1993 and now has a more modern look about it. In 1997, it was taken over by the Best Western chain. Rooms are adequate and have tile floors and walls of glass facing onto balconies; however, not all of the rooms have good views (some face another building). Ask for a view room on a higher floor, if possible. Bathrooms tend to be a bit battered, but they do have bathtubs. If you'd like more space and a kitchen, ask about the Villas Jacó Princess across the road.

Dining/Diversions: El Muelle, the hotel's open-air restaurant, overlooks the pool and serves local and international dishes in the $5 to $20 price range. Out by the beach, there's the Bar Guipipías, which overlooks the water and doubles as a disco.

Amenities: Facilities include a round swimming pool (which seems small by today's resort standards and is often crowded), a tennis court ($7 per hour), a volleyball court, and a gift shop. Room service; a tour desk; car, motorcycle, and surfboard rentals; laundry service; and shuttle service from San José are all available. In addition, bicycles are provided free of charge to guests.

✪ **Hotel Amampola.** Apdo. 133, Playa de Jacó, Puntarenas. ☎ **506/643-3337.** Fax 506/643-3668. 53 units. A/C TV TEL. $86 double, $135 suite, $150 villa. AE, MC, V.

Although it's 4 blocks from the beach, this is still the best luxury option in Jacó, if only because it's one of the newest. The rooms are cool and comfortable, with white-tile floors, two double beds, plenty of closet and shelf space, a desk and chair, and either a small patio or balcony, depending on whether you're on the ground or second floor. The bathrooms have sleek European fixtures and a bidet. The suites have an extra living/sitting room with a fold-out sofa bed and just a king-size bed in the master bedroom. The villas come with two bedrooms, a living room, full kitchen, and small patio, but frankly I find the rooms much nicer and more comfortable.

Dining: Near the reception area you'll find the open-air restaurant, which specializes in Italian food, as well as the hotel's small casino and bar/disco.

Amenities: There's a gift shop, a midsize pool with a swim-up bar and two Jacuzzis, and bicycles for rent.

Hotel Cocal. Apdo. 54, Playa de Jacó, Puntarenas. ☎ **800/732-9266** in the U.S., or 506/643-3067. Fax 506/643-3082. E-mail: cocalcr@sol.racsa.co.cr. 45 units. A/C. $85 double, lower in the off-season. Rates include breakfast buffet and $10 match play at the casino. AE, MC, V.

No children are allowed at this hotel, so the atmosphere is usually very peaceful. Located right on the beach, the building is done in colonial style, with arched porticos surrounding a courtyard that contains two medium-size pools, a few palapas for shade, and a thatched-roof bar. Each guest room is well proportioned, with a tile floor, a double and a single bed, a desk, and a porch or balcony. The Cocal is on one of the nameless streets leading down to the beach from the main road through Jacó; watch for their sign in the middle of town.

Dining/Diversions: There are two dining rooms here (one on each floor) serving three meals a day. It's the upstairs dining room that has the best view of the beach. Service is generally quite good, and so is the food. Prices range from $5 to $18 for entrees. The hotel also has a small casino if you have the gaming instinct.

Amenities: The hotel is located right on the beach and has a small outdoor swimming pool. Bicycle and water-sports equipment rentals, laundry service, baby-sitting, limited room service (7am-10pm), and free coffee in the lobby.

MODERATE

Hotel Balcón del Mar. Playa de Jacó. ☎ **506/643-3251.** Fax 506/229-2222. www.asstcard.co.cr/guia. E-mail: balcomar@asstcard.co.cr. 21 units. A/C TV. $50 double, rates lower in the off-season. MC, V.

If you want a hotel right on the beach and a good view of the ocean, one of the higher rooms in this four-story hotel might fit the bill. The rooms are nothing special, but they are clean and comfortable, with most of the modern amenities, and even have a small balcony looking out to sea. When I last visited, construction was underway on a new wing that is supposed to include several deluxe suites. In addition, they were planning on replacing the current swimming pool with a much larger one. However, despite all the work going on, the rooms I did see were in need of some upkeep. There is also a restaurant here serving standard Tico fare at moderate prices. The hotel is located right on the beach, next to the Jacó police station.

✪ **Hotel Club del Mar.** Apdo. 107-4023, Playa de Jacó, Puntarenas. ☎ and fax **506/643-3194.** 18 units. $48–$95 double, rates 25% lower in the off-season. AE, MC, V.

Because of its location, friendly owners, and attractively designed rooms, this has long been my favorite Playa de Jacó hotel. The Club del Mar is at the far southern end of the beach where the rocky hills meet the sand. The best rooms are in two newer two-story shell-pink buildings, each of which has eight rooms. The rooms have green-tile floors, pastel bedspreads, fascinating custom-made lampshades, tile bathroom counters, and French doors that open onto private patios or balconies. The older rooms are also attractive and have Guatemalan throw rugs, bamboo furniture, full kitchens, and glass front walls. Twelve of the rooms here have air-conditioning and all have small, unstocked refrigerators. A small swimming pool is right by the beach, and there's a first-class restaurant on the premises (closed Tuesdays). Owner Philip Edwardes oversees the kitchen and at times personally prepares such dishes as lemon chicken and chateaubriand. However, it's the conviviality and helpfulness of Edwardes, his wife Marilyn and son Simon, that make a stay here so enjoyable. All are avid gardeners, and the hotel grounds contain many rare palms, heliconias, and flowering gingers. The Edwardeses also arrange sportfishing outings, horseback rides, raft trips, and various other tours.

Hotel Copacabana. Apdo. 150, Playa de Jacó, Puntarenas. ☎ and fax **506/643-3131.** 29 units. $39 double, $59 double with A/C, $79–$99 suite. AE, MC, V.

This Canadian-owned hotel is right on the beach and is popular with sportfishers and sports lovers in general. The standard rooms are all on the second floor and have one double and one single bed, a ceiling fan, and little bay windows with bamboo shades. On the shared veranda, strung hammocks alternate with small tables and chairs. Although they have the benefit of air-conditioning and kitchenettes, most of the suites are located on the first floor and are a bit claustrophobic. If you can get one on the second floor with an ocean view, it's worth the splurge. Most of the activity here is centered around the pool and its neighboring bar. A 24-foot satellite dish ensures a steady stream of televised sports events, and the food here is surprisingly good. In addition to hearty breakfasts, the restaurant serves up a creative pasta bar, fresh seafood, and perhaps the best french fries in Costa Rica.

✪ **Pochote Grande.** Apdo. 42, Playa de Jacó, Puntarenas. ☎ **506/643-3236.** Fax 506/220-4979. 24 units. $45 double, $55 triple; lower rates available in the off-season. AE, MC, V.

Named for a huge, old pochote tree on the grounds, this very attractive hotel is located right on the beach at the far north end of Jacó. The grounds are shady and lush, and there's a small pool. Guest rooms are large enough to sleep four comfortably and have kitchenettes. All the rooms have white-tile floors and a balcony or patio, and the second-floor rooms are blessed with high ceilings. The restaurant and snack bar serve a mixture of Tico, German, and American meals (the owners are German by way of Africa). Prices for meals range from $3 to $15. There's also a gift shop. This place stays full with charter groups in the high season.

Villas Estrellamar. Apdo. 3, Playa de Jacó, Puntarenas. ☎ **506/643-3102.** Fax 506/643-3453. E-mail: brunot@sol.racsa.co.cr. 20 units. TEL. Dec–Apr, $44–$53 double, May–Nov, $22–$27 double. AE, MC, V.

This hotel is located on the landward side of Jacó's main road and is a 200-yard walk to the beach. However, what you give up in proximity to the beach, you make up in attractive gardens and a quiet setting. Catering primarily to a French- and German-speaking clientele, Estrellamar's accommodations are all bungalows and apartments, all with kitchenettes, tile floors, and patios. Try to get a room facing the hotel's attractive pool. The more expensive rooms have air conditioners; the less-expensive ones come with fans. For $3 per day, you can rent a television with cable. In addition to seating around the pool, there are two shady ranchos; one with a Ping-Pong table.

Villas Miramar. Playa de Jacó, Puntarenas. ☎ **506/643-3003.** Fax 506/643-3617. 12 units. Dec–Apr, $49 double, $59 triple; May–Nov, $33 double or triple. AE, MC, V.

Located down a narrow lane off the main road through town, the Miramar is about 100 feet from the beach. It has its own small pool surrounded by a terrace and flowering hibiscus. Guest rooms sport a Spanish architectural style with arched doorways, wrought-iron wall lamps, and red-tile floors throughout. There are large patios, and all of the rooms have kitchenettes with unstocked refrigerators. There are also barbecues in the gardens in case you'd like to grill some fish or steaks. The apartments vary in size; the largest can sleep up to six people. Everything is clean and well maintained. This is a good deal.

INEXPENSIVE

Cabinas Alice. 100 meters south of the Red Cross, Playa de Jacó, Puntarenas. ☎ and fax **506/643-3061.** 22 units. $31 double, $36–$48 triple or quad. AE, MC, V.

Cabinas Alice, though a small and modest Tico-run place, is one of the best values in Jacó. The rooms are in the shade of large old mango trees, and the beach is right outside the gate. Since the rooms vary in age, ask to take a look at a couple before accepting one. The largest rooms have kitchens and also happen to be closest to the small pool and the beach. The rooms in back each come with a carved-wood headboard and matching nightstand, a tile floor, a large shower, and potted plants. The other rooms are pretty basic, with nothing but a double and a single bed in the room. The road down to Cabinas Alice is across from the Red Cross center. Meals are served in the small attached soda, where you can get a fish fillet fried in garlic and butter for under $5. This place is popular with young Ticos and fills up fast during the high season.

Flamboyant Hotel. Apdo. 18, Playa de Jacó, Puntarenas. ☎ **506/643-3146.** Fax 506/643-1068. 8 units. $46 double, triple or quad. AE, MC, V.

The Flamboyant doesn't quite live up to its name, but it's still a good value. The rooms are arranged around a small swimming pool and are only a few steps from the beach. All the rooms are spacious and have kitchenettes, but the furnishings are quite simple. You'll find the hotel down a narrow lane toward the ocean from the Flamboyant Restaurant, which is on the main road in the middle of Jacó.

✪ **Hotel Mar de Luz.** Playa de Jacó, Puntarenas. ☎ and fax **506/643-3259.** 20 units. A/C. $38 double, lower during off-season. No credit cards.

This is one of Playa de Jacó's best deals and a comfortable alternative to the typical string of cut-rate cabinas you'll find crowding this popular beach town. The rooms here are divided into two basic types. All come with air-conditioning, small kitchenettes, full-size refrigerators, private bathrooms with heated water, and room safes. The most interesting rooms here feature stone walls, small sitting areas, and either one or two double beds placed on a raised sleeping nook. My only complaint is that the windows are too small and mostly sealed, so you're forced to use the air-conditioning. There's a refreshing pool, with plenty of chaise longues around, as well as a kids' pool. In the gardens just off the pools, there's a grill available for guest use. There is also a comfortable common sitting area, with a selection of magazines and books in several languages and cable television. Dutch owners Victor and Carmen Keulen seem driven to offer as much comfort, quality, and service as they can for the price. You'll find the hotel 50 meters east of the Hotel Tangeri right in the center of Jacó.

Hotel Zabamar. Playa de Jacó, Puntarenas. ☎ and fax **506/643-3174.** 20 units. $24.50 double, $32.60 triple, $36.70 double with A/C, $44.80 triple with A/C. MC, V.

The Zabamar is set back from the beach in a shady compound. The older rooms have red-tile floors, small refrigerators, ceiling fans, hammocks on their front porches, and showers in enclosed, private patios. There are also 10 newer rooms with air-conditioning. There are even *pilas* (laundry sinks) in little gravel-and-palm gardens behind the older rooms. Some rooms have rustic wooden benches and chairs. The shallow swimming pool stays quite warm. Travelers on tight budgets will appreciate the size of the older, less-expensive rooms. Special rates can be negotiated for longer stays, and prices for all rooms are lower from April 15 to December 15. The small open-air bar/restaurant serves inexpensive seafood and burgers, as well as the standard Tico *gallo pinto* for breakfast.

CAMPING

There are several campgrounds in or near Playa de Jacó. **Madrigal** (☎ **506/643-3521**), at the south end of town at the foot of some jungly cliffs, is my favorite. The campground is just off the beach and has a bar/restaurant that's open from 7am to 10pm. You can also try **Camping Garibito** (no phone), which is centrally located, or El Hicaco (☎ **506/643-3004**), which is close to the beach but right next door to Disco Los Tucanes, so don't expect to get much sleep if you stay here. Campsites run between $2 and $5 per night.

ACCOMMODATIONS AROUND PLAYA DE JACÓ

VERY EXPENSIVE

✪ **Villa Caletas.** Apdo. 12358-1000, San José. ☎ **506/257-3653.** Fax 506/222-2059. E-mail: caletas@ticonet.co.cr. 9 units, 19 villas. $130 double, $160–$190 villa, $230 master suite; rates slightly lower during the off-season. AE, MC, V.

It's hard to find a luxury hotel in Costa Rica with a more spectacular setting. Perched 350 meters above the sea, Villa Caletas enjoys commanding views of the Pacific. While the rooms are all elegantly appointed and spacious, you'll want to stay in a villa here. Each individual villa is situated on a patch of hillside facing the sea or surrounding forests. Inside, you'll find a main bedroom with a queen-size bed and a comfortable sitting room with couches that convert into two single beds. The villas feature white-tile floors, modern bathrooms, and a private terrace for sitting around and soaking up the views. The junior suites are larger, and some have either a Jacuzzi or small private pool. The master suite has both. All of the suites have air-conditioning, but I prefer to open all the windows and the sliding door and soak in the breezes. It's a long way to the beach down below (or a short drive to Jacó or Herradura), but most guests are happy to lounge around and swim in the free-form "infinity" pool that seems to blend into the sea below and beyond.

Dining/Diversions: The hotel has two restaurants featuring French and continental cuisine. The food has been Villas Caletas's Achilles' heel for some time, but the last time I visited, it was quite good. The hotel also has a Greek-style amphitheater where you can sometimes catch sunset concerts of jazz and classical music.

Facilities: Swimming pool, conference room.

EXPENSIVE

Punta Leona Hotel and Club. (Apdo. 8592-1000, San José) Punta Leona. ☎ **506/231-3131.** Fax 506/232-0791. E-mail: puntaleo@sol.racsa.co.cr. 108 units, 72 apts. A/C TV. $77–$87 double, $97–$165 for 4 to 8 people. AE, DC, MC, V.

Located 6.2 miles (10km) north of Jacó, this gated resort and residential community boasts the most impressive grounds of any easily accessible hotel in Costa Rica. Rain forest, white-sand beaches (two of them), and a rocky promontory jutting out into the Pacific all add up to a drama rarely encountered in Costa Rican resorts. After passing through the resort's guarded gate, you drive more than a mile down a gravel road that passes through dense primary rain forest before arriving at the grassy lawns that sprawl beneath huge trees. The main guest rooms are not as luxurious as one would hope, and in fact some of them are downright run-down. The standard hotel rooms are housed in Spanish-style buildings with red-tile roofs and white stucco walls. Inside, you'll find that the beds and bedspreads are a bit dated and worn, but otherwise the rooms are comfortable. In addition to these rooms, there are a variety of different apartment types, including some unusual small chalets, and some coveted railroad cars (which feel a lot like mobile homes).

Dining/Diversions: Restaurant Léon Marino serves a variety of Costa Rican and international dishes. Prices are moderate. There's also a more informal outdoor restaurant that serves grilled meats and typical meals, as well as two bars. The one on Playa Mantas doubles as a disco.

Amenities: Facilities include two swimming pools, 4 miles (6.5km) of beach, tennis court, boutique, supermarket, conference room. There's regular daily bus service between the guest accommodations and Playa Blanca. Sportfishing, sunset cruises, and rental of sailboards, jet skis, and horses are all available. Scuba lessons and equipment rental are also offered (there's decent diving at Playa Blanca).

DINING

Playa de Jacó has a wide range of restaurants. Most cater to surfers and budget travelers. Budget travelers who really want to save money on meals can always stay at a hotel that provides kitchenettes for its guests, shop at the local *supermercado*, and fix their own meals. Most hotels here have restaurants, even most inexpensive lodgings, so you won't have to venture far.

If you end up walking the strip and want to eat in town, I've listed some places I recommend below. In addition, **The Garden Cafe**, **Ceviche del Rey**, and **The Wishbone Eatery** are all local favorites, and **Pizzeria Terraza** has excellent clay-oven pizzas and homemade pastas. If you're looking for simply prepared, fresh seafood, **El Recreo** and **Restaurante Santimar** are both good bets, serving standard Tico beach fare—fresh seafood, sandwiches, chicken, and steak. For a filling American-style breakfast, try **Chatty Cathy's**. Actually, one of the best restaurants in town is the dining room at the Hotel Club del Mar, which is open to the public with reservations.

Killer Munchies. 300 meters south of the Best Western Jacó Beach Hotel. ☎ **506/643-3354.** Reservations not accepted. Main courses $2.50–$11. No credit cards. Mon–Fri 5:30–9pm, Sat–Sun 10am–9pm.

The name says it all. This restaurant serves hearty burritos, simple pasta dishes, and a wide array of freshly baked pizzas. With vines covering latticed walls and an abundance of potted palms, the ambience is somewhere between an early '80s fern bar and a college beer hall. Try to get a table on the covered deck, so you can watch the people passing by and the pizzas being made in the outdoor wood-burning oven. My favorite item is the Greek pizza, with olives, feta cheese, and anchovies, but the barbecue chicken pizza is also delicious.

✪ **Villa Creole.** 400 meters east and then 200 meters north and 100 meters west of Apartotel Las Gaviotas. ☎ **506/643-3298.** Fax 506/643-3882. Reservations recommended. Main courses $8–$16. MC, V. Daily 6:30–10pm.

Playa de Jacó is one of the more unlikely places on this planet to find fine French cuisine. But Belgian-born chef Jean-Claude Vankrinkelveldt decided several years ago to seek sunnier climes and set up shop here. With a handful of plastic tables spread around an open-air rancho, and a simple small kitchen located just behind the small bar, Villa Creole doesn't look like the haunt of a former Michelin master—but looks can be deceiving. The choice of appetizers includes a *turin de lapin au poivre ver* (rabbit pâté with green peppercorns), as well as a *soupe de poissons* that is definitely not your ordinary fish stew. Main dishes feature fresh fish and lobster, as well as beef, chicken, and rabbit prepared in classic French sauces. I opted for the *lapin a la mutard y a la biere* (rabbit in a mustard and beer sauce), while my companion devoured the *suprême de volalle dijonaise* (chicken dijonaise). Vankrinkelveldt has a secret source for gourmet vegetables that include delicate brussels sprouts, baby carrots, green beans, and fresh endive. Each meal comes accompanied by a homemade baguette that puts most breads baked in this country to shame. Several dessert choices are available nightly, shifting according to the chef's whim, but often include a classic crème brûlée, chocolate mousse, and fresh tarts and pies. To find the hotel, head inland from the Apartotel Las Gaviotas and follow the signs.

PLAYA DE JACÓ AFTER DARK

Playa de Jacó is the central Pacific's party town, and there are several discos that are packed every night of the high season and every weekend during the low season. The most popular is **Disco La Central** (☎ **506/643-3076**), right on the beach near the south end of town. Located in a huge open-air hall, it features the requisite '70s flashing lights and suspended mirrored ball. A garden bar in a thatched-roof building provides a slightly quieter place to have a drink. **Los Tucanes Disco Club** (no phone) is another happening place located one street over from Disco La Central. Both charge a nominal cover charge of around $3. On the north end of town, **Los Faroles Restaurant** (☎ **506/643-3167**) is the most popular night spot. If you're looking for a surfer hangout, check out **La Hacienda** (☎ **506/643-3191**), a second-floor bar with a laid-back feel, a beat-up pool table, a dartboard, and surf videos on the TVs. Lately, they've been having live rock and roll bands here on weekends. La Hacienda is located on the main drag toward the north end of town. Sports freaks can catch the latest games at **Hotel Copacabana** (☎ **506/643-3131**) or **El Zarpe** (☎ **506/643-3473**). The latter serves up good, reasonably priced burritos, burgers, and other assorted bar food. The very late-night crowd always seems to end up at the **Pancho Villa Restaurant**.

EN ROUTE TO MANUEL ANTONIO: PLAYA HERMOSA

Playa Hermosa is the first beach you'll hit as you head south from Playa de Jacó. This is primarily a surfers' beach, but it is still a lovely spot to spend some beach time. The hotels listed here are both in Playa Hermosa. If you're looking for something even more remote and undeveloped, head out to Playa Esterrillos Este for the **Auberge du Pelican** (fax **506/779-9108** or 779-9236).

MODERATE

Terraza del Pacifico. Playa Hermosa de Jacó (Apdo. 168), Jacó, Puntarenas. ☎ **506/643-3222.** Fax 506/643-3424. 43 units. A/C TV TEL. $70 double or triple. AE, MC, V.

Located just over the hill at the start of Playa Hermosa, this hotel has a wonderful setting on a mostly undeveloped section of beach. However, last time I visited it was up for sale and very run-down. Rooms are built so that they all have ocean views, and in the middle of the hotel complex is a circular pool with a swim-up bar and plenty of chaise longues for sunbathing and siestas. Red-tile roofs and white walls give the buildings a very Mediterranean look, while hardwood balcony railings add a touch of the tropics. The guest rooms all have either a patio or balcony, and the room curtains are hand-painted with colorful bird and flower images. The hotel's restaurant is located within a few feet of the high-tide mark and serves Italian food.

INEXPENSIVE

Cabinas Las Olas. Playa Hermosa de Jacó, Puntarenas. ☎ and fax **506/643-3687.** E-mail: lasolas@sol.racsa.co.cr. 4 units, 3 ranchos. $35 double, $45 triple, $55 rancho cabina (sleeps up to 5 people). No credit cards.

Playa Hermosa is a renowned surfing beach, and this is its most popular surfer hotel. The main building is on a hill by the road. Two of the rooms are located upstairs and have two double beds, a veranda with a hammock, and ocean views; downstairs are a couple of smaller budget rooms that are fine for a single traveler. The rooms are basic but comfortable. Closer to the beach are three A-frame cabins or ranchos, which have a roomy bedroom on the second floor (in the peak of the A), and a single bed, bunk bed, kitchenette, and bathroom on the ground floor. Between the main building and the cabins is a pool with a small stone waterfall. Out by the ocean there's the Hard Charger's Cafe, which serves three meals daily. The breakfast burritos provide just the carbo load needed for a full day of surfing. If you don't surf, there's a thatch palapa strung with hammocks for watching the waves, the sunsets, and the folks riding horses on the beach.

3 Manuel Antonio National Park

87 miles (140km) SW of San José; 43 miles (69km) S of Playa de Jacó

No other destination in Costa Rica has received more international attention than Manuel Antonio. Many first-time visitors to Costa Rica plan their vacation around seeing it. It's no surprise why: The views from the hills overlooking Manuel Antonio are spectacular, the beaches inside the park are idyllic, and its jungles are crawling with white-faced and squirrel monkeys, among other forms of exotic wildlife. The flip side is that you'll have to pay more dearly to see it, and you'll have to share it with far more fellow travelers than you might prefer. Still, this is one of the most beautiful locations in the entire country. Gazing down on the blue Pacific from high on the mountainsides of Manuel Antonio, it's almost impossible to hold back a gasp of delight. Offshore rocky islands dot the vast expanse of blue, and in the foreground the rich deep green of the rain forest sweeps down to the water. Even cheap Instamatics regularly produce postcard-perfect snapshots. It's this superb view that hotels at Manuel Antonio sell and that keeps people transfixed on decks, patios, and balconies along the 4¼ miles (7km) of road between Quepos and the national park entrance.

One of the most popular national parks in the country, Manuel Antonio is also one of the smallest, covering fewer than 1,700 acres. Its several nearly perfect small beaches are connected by trails that meander through the rain forest. One of its most striking features is how quickly the mountains surrounding its beaches rise as you head inland from the water; however, the park was created to preserve not its beautiful beaches but its forests, home to endangered squirrel monkeys, three-toed sloths, purple-and-orange crabs, and hundreds of other species of birds, mammals, and plants. Whereas once this entire stretch of coast was a rain forest teeming with wildlife, now just this small rocky outcrop of forest remains.

Unfortunately, the popularity of Manual Antonio has brought rampant development and ever-growing crowds of beachgoers. In just the last few years, these factors have turned what was once a peaceful and pristine spot into an area full of hastily built, overpriced hotels, packed parking areas, and noisy crowds. Frankly, Manuel Antonio has become completely overburdened with adoring throngs, some of whom have taken to feeding the wild animals, which is a dangerous distortion of what ecotourism should be. On weekends, the beaches are packed with people, and the disco down near the park entrance blares its music until early morning, drowning out the sounds of crickets and frogs that once lulled visitors to sleep here. A shantytown of snack shacks lines the road just outside the park, which makes this area look more like a slum than a national park.

Those views that are so bewitching also have their own set of drawbacks. If you want a great view, you aren't going to be staying on the beach and, in fact, you probably won't be able to walk to the beach. This means that you'll be driving back and forth, taking a lot of taxis, or riding the public bus a lot. Also keep in mind that it's hot and humid here, and it rains a lot. However, the rain is what keeps Manuel Antonio lush and green, and this wouldn't be the tropics if things were otherwise.

If you're traveling on a budget, you'll likely end up staying in the nearby town of Quepos, which was once a quiet banana port—the land to the north was used by Chiquita to grow its bananas. Disease wiped out most of the banana plantations, and now the land is planted with African oil-palm trees. To reach Quepos by road, you must pass through miles and miles of these oil-palm plantations. Today, Quepos is finally shaking its image as a dirty, run-down port town. More and more,

Quepos is filling up with a wide variety of restaurants, sourvenir and craft shops, and lively bars.

Despite the above caveats, Manuel Antonio is still worth visiting. If you plan carefully, you can escape many of the problems that detract from its appeal. If you avoid the peak months of December to March, you'll avoid most of the crowds. If you must come during the peak months, try to avoid weekends, when the beach is packed with families from San José. If you stay at a hotel partway up the hill from the park entrance, you'll have relatively easy access to the beach, you may get a view, and best of all, you'll be out of earshot of the disco. If you visit the park early in the morning, you can leave when the crowds begin to show up at midday. In the afternoon, you can lounge by your pool or on your patio.

ESSENTIALS

GETTING THERE & DEPARTING **By Plane** **Sansa** (☎ **506/233-0397**, 506/233-3258, or 506/233-5330 in San José) flies to Quepos daily at 8:10 and 8:25am and 1:25 and 4pm. On Monday, Wednesday, and Friday there is an additional flight at 9:45am. All flights leave from San José's Juan Santamaría International Airport. The flight's duration is 25 minutes; fare is $35 each way.

Travelair (☎ **506/220-3054**, or 506/232-7883 in San José) also flies to Quepos daily at 7:20 and 8:45am and 1:15 and 4pm from Tobías Bolaños International Airport in Pavas. Flight duration is 20 minutes; fare is $48 one way, $77 round-trip.

There's an airport transfer service that charges $4 per person to any hotel in Manuel Antonio and Quepos. Speak to a gate agent at either Sansa or Travelair to arrange a ride. Taxis occasionally meet incoming flights as well. Expect to be charged between $7.50 and $10 per car for up to four people, depending on the distance to your hotel and your bargaining abilities.

When you're ready to depart, **Sansa** (☎ **506/771-0161** in Quepos) has daily flights to San José leaving at 8:50 and 9:05am and 2:25 and 4:55pm, with an extra departure at 12:55pm on Monday, Wednesday, and Friday.

Travelair flights leave for San José daily at 7:50 and 11:15am and 1:45 and 4:30pm.

By Bus **Express buses** (☎ **506/223-5567**) to Manuel Antonio leave San José daily at 6am, noon, and 5pm from the Coca-Cola bus terminal at Calle 16 between Avenidas 1 and 3. Trip duration is 3½ hours; fare is $5.50. These buses go all the way to the park entrance and will drop you off at any of the hotels along the way.

Regular buses (☎ **506/223-5567**) to Quepos leave San José daily at 7 and 10am and 2, 4, and 6pm. Trip duration is 4 hours; fare is $4. These buses stop in Quepos. From here, if you're staying at one of the hotels on the road to Manuel Antonio, you must take a local bus or taxi to your hotel.

Buses leave Puntarenas for Quepos daily at 5am, 11am, and 2:30pm. The ride takes 3½ hours; fare is $3.

Many of the buses for Quepos stop to unload and pick up passengers in Playa de Jacó. If you're in Jacó heading toward Manuel Antonio, you can try your luck at one of the covered bus stops out on the Interamerican Highway (see the section on Playa de Jacó, above).

From Quepos, buses leave for Manuel Antonio daily, roughly every hour, from 6am to 10pm. Fare is 35¢. The ride takes about 15 minutes.

When you're ready to depart, the Quepos bus station is next to the market, which is 3 blocks east of the water and 2 blocks north of the road to Manuel Antonio. Express buses to San José leave daily at 6am, noon, and 5pm. Local buses to San José (duration is 4 hours) leave at 5 and 8am and 2 and 4pm.

Manuel Antonio

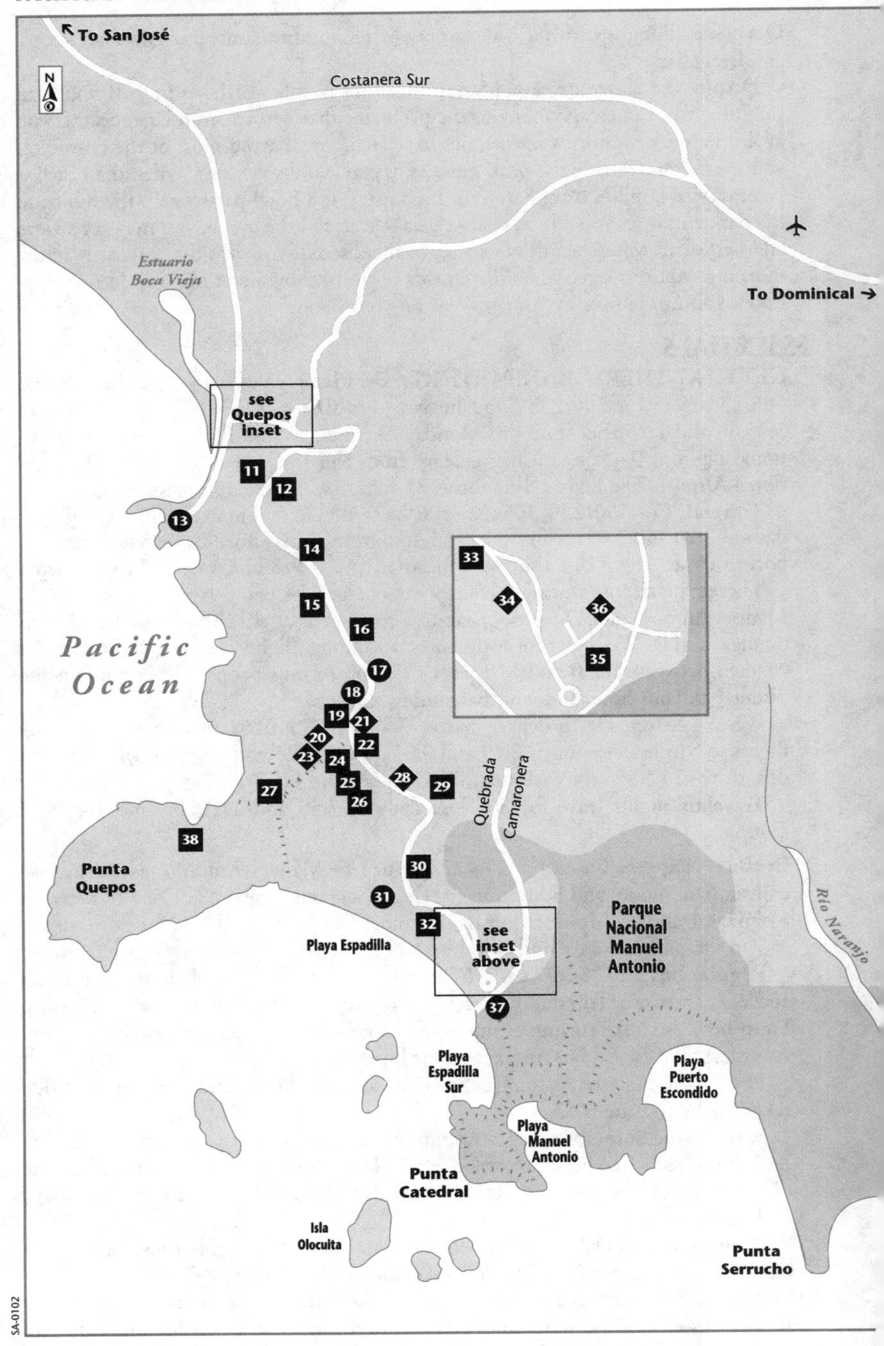
To San José
Costanera Sur
Estuario
Boca Vieja
To Dominical
see
Quepos
inset
Pacific
Ocean
Quebrada
Camaronera
Punta
Quepos
Playa Espadilla
see
inset
above
Parque
Nacional
Manuel
Antonio
Río Naranjo
Playa
Espadilla
Sur
Playa
Puerto
Escondido
Playa
Manuel
Antonio
Punta
Catedral
Isla
Olocuita
Punta
Serrucho
SA-0102

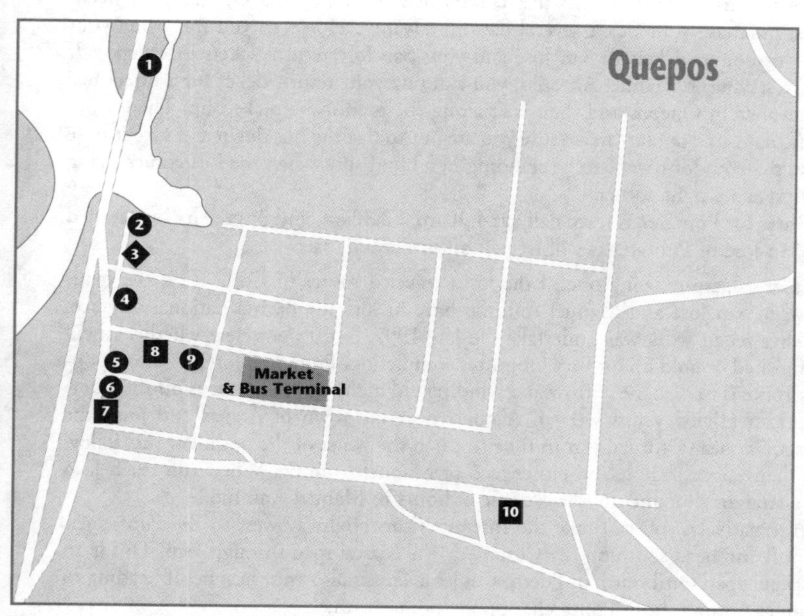

Hotels
Cabinas Pedro Miguel 11
Cabinas Ramirez 33
Cabinas Vela-Bar 36
El Dorado Mojado 22
El Lirio 16
El Parador 38
Hotel and Cabanas Playa Espadilla 35
Hotel Casitas Eclipse 28
Hotel Costa Verde 29
Hotel Malinche 9
Hotel Plinio 12
Hotel Quepos 10
Hotel Si Como No 26
Karahé 30
La Colina 15
La Mariposa 24
Makanda-By-The-Sea 27
Tulemar Bungalows 19
Verde Del Mar 32
Villas Nicolas 25

Restaurants
Barba Roja 20
Cafe Milagro 3
Casa de Cafe 21
El Gran Escape 4
Jardín Gourmet 28
Karola's 23
Plinio Restaurant 12
Restaurant Vela-Bar 36

Attractions, Etc.
Botíca Quepos 7
Disco Arco Iris 1
El Banco Bar 8
Elegante Rent A Car 2
Hotel Kamuk Casino 5
Jardin Gaia 14
L'Aventura Boutique 6
La Buena Nota 31
La Escuela de Idiomas D'Amore 18
Maracas Disco 13
Mar y Sombra Restaurante & Disco 34
National Park Entrance 37
Stable Equus 17

In the busy winter months tickets sell out well in advance, especially on weekends; purchase your ticket several days in advance. However, you must buy your Quepos-bound tickets in San José and your San José return tickets in Quepos. If you're staying in Manuel Antonio, you can buy your return ticket for a direct bus in advance in Quepos and then wait along the road to be picked up. There is no particular bus stop; just make sure you are out to flag the bus down and give it time to stop—you don't want to be standing in a blind spot when the bus comes flying around some tight corner.

Buses for Puntarenas leave daily at 4:30am, 10:30am, and 3pm. Any bus headed for San José or Puntarenas will let you off in Playa de Jacó.

By Car Despite being one of the most traveled routes in Costa Rica, the roads between San José and Manuel Antonio have historically been a national disgrace. Massive repair work was undertaken in late 1997, but it's not clear whether it will be finished or hold up for very long after completion. From San José, the most popular route is to take the narrow and winding old highway, which turns off the Interamerican Highway just west of Alajuela near the town of Atenas and joins the Costanera near Orotina, just in time to catch the worst of the potholes. Just follow the many signs to hotels in either Jacó or Manuel Antonio. When you reach Jacó it's a straight shot and another couple of hours to Manuel Antonio.

Alternatively, you can take the Interamerican Highway west to the Puntarenas turnoff and head south on the Costanera, the coastal road through Jacó. This is an excellent road until south of Puerto Caldera. This is also your best bet if heading to Manuel Antonio from Puntarenas or any point north.

ORIENTATION Quepos is a little port town at the mouth of the Boca Vieja Estuary. After crossing the bridge into town, take the lower road (to the left of the high road). In 4 blocks, turn left, and you'll be on the road to Manuel Antonio. This road winds through town a bit before starting over the hill to all the hotels and the national park.

GETTING AROUND A taxi between Quepos, any hotel along the road toward the park, and Manuel Antonio costs around $4. The return trip from the park to your hotel should only cost 75¢ per person. I know this system doesn't make much sense, but this is a fixed price, so watch out for drivers who try to charge more. If the taxi must leave the main road (for hotels like La Mariposa, El Parador, and Makanda) the charge is higher.

The bus from Quepos to Manuel Antonio, and vice versa, takes 15 minutes and runs roughly every half hour, from 6am to 10pm daily, from the main bus terminal in Quepos, near the market. Fare is 30¢.

You can also rent a car from **Elegante Rent-a-Car** (☎ **506/777-0115**) for around $50 a day. They're located in downtown Quepos, on the left just as you cross the bridge into town. With advance notice, they'll meet you at the airport with your car for no extra charge.

If you rent a car, never leave anything of value in it unless you intend to stay within sight of the car at all times. Car break-ins are commonplace here. Children will offer to watch your car for a small price when you leave it anywhere near the beach. Take them up on the offer if you want to avoid damage by thieves trying to find out what's in your trunk. Alternatively, there is now a parking lot just outside the park entrance, which costs around $3 for the whole day—well worth it.

FAST FACTS The **Lucimax Laundromat** is located out on the edge of town on the road toward Manuel Antonio. **Botíca Quepos** is the main pharmacy in town.

It's on the corner of the main street where you make the turn for Manuel Antonio (☎ **506/777-0038**) and is open daily from 7am to 7pm. If you need to call a taxi, dial ☎ **506/777-1693** or **506/777-0425**. The telephone number of the **Quepos Hospital** is ☎ **506/777-1397**; and for the **Rural Guard** (local police), call ☎ **506/777-0308.**

EXPLORING THE NATIONAL PARK

Manuel Antonio is a small park with only three major trails. Most visitors come primarily to lie on one of the beaches and check out the white-faced monkeys, which sometimes seem as common as tourists. A guide is not essential here, but as I've said before, unless you're experienced in rain-forest hiking, you'll see and learn a lot more with one. A 2- or 3-hour guided hike should cost between $20 and $30 per person. Almost any of the hotels in town can help you set up a tour of the park. Alternatively, you can call **Costa Rica Adventure Travel** (☎ **506/777-1262;** e-mail: iguana@sol.racsa.co.cr), which charges $35 per person, including the $6 entrance fee. If you decide to explore the park on your own, a basic map is available at the park entrance.

ENTRY POINT, FEES & REGULATIONS The park is closed on Monday, but open Tuesday through Sunday from 8am to 4pm year-round. You'll find the park entrance at **Playa Espadilla**, the beach at the end of the road from Quepos. To reach the park station, you must cross a small, sometimes polluted stream that's little more than ankle-deep at low tide but can be knee- or even waist-deep at high tide. Just after crossing the stream, you'll come to a small ranger station. You will have to pay a fee of $6 per person to enter. This is where you can pick up the small map of the park I mentioned above. The Parks Service allows only 600 visitors to enter each day, which may mean that you won't get in if you arrive in midafternoon during the high season. Camping is not allowed.

THE BEACHES **Playa Espadilla**, the gray-sand beach from which you enter the park, is often perfect for board-surfing and bodysurfing but can be a bit rough for casual swimming. This beach is not technically in the park and so there's no entrance fee; consequently, it's the most popular beach with locals and visiting Ticos. There are a couple of little shops by the water that rent boogie boards, beach chairs, and beach umbrellas. A full-day rental of a beach umbrella and two chaise longues will cost around $10. (These are not available inside the park).

Playa Espadilla Sur is the first beach you come to within the park boundaries and is usually the least-crowded beach in the park and one of the best places to find a quiet shade tree to plant yourself under. If you want to explore further, you can walk along this soft sand beach or follow a trail through the forest parallel to the beach. At the far end there's a short connecting trail to **Playa Manuel Antonio**, which is sometimes clear enough to offer good snorkeling along the rocks at either end. A branch trail from this beach leads up and around **Punta Catedral** (Cathedral Point), a high promontory bluff where there are some spectacular views. The full hike up, down, and around takes only about 25 minutes, but it's a little rough: If you take this trail, wear good shoes. Cathedral Point is one of the best places to spot monkeys, though you're more likely to see a white-faced monkey than a rare squirrel monkey. At low tide, Playa Manuel Antonio shows a very interesting relic: a circular stone turtle trap left by its pre-Columbian residents. From Playa Manuel Antonio, there's another slightly longer trail to the **Puerto Escondido**, where there's a blowhole that sends up plumes of spray at high tide. Beyond here, at **Punta Surrucho**, there are some sea caves. Be careful when hiking beyond Puerto Escondido:

What seems like easy beach hiking at low tide becomes treacherous to impassable at high tide. Two other trails wind their way inland from the trail between Playa Manuel Antonio and Puerto Escondido. It's great to spend hours exploring the steamy jungle and then take a refreshing dip in the ocean.

OUTDOOR PURSUITS IN MANUEL ANTONIO

As a popular destination with scores of hotels, a national park, good deep-sea fishing, and nearby jungles and estuaries, Manuel Antonio offers plenty of activities besides sunbathing.

Rainmaker Rainforest Tours (☎ and fax **506/777-1262**) arranges rafting, mangrove tours, and guided tours. These folks have an office in the small mall just outside of Villas Si Como No.

There are several rafting companies in Quepos that ply the same rivers. Among them are **Amigos del Río** (☎ **506/777-0082**) and **Iguana Tours** (☎ **506/777-1262**). All offer full-day rafting trips for around $65 to $85. Large multi-person rafts are used during the rainy season, and single person "duckies" are broken out when the water levels drop.

If your tropical fantasy is to ride a horse down a beach between jungle and ocean, contact **Stable Equus** (☎ **506/777-0001**), which charges $30 for a 2-hour ride in Manuel Antonio. This stable allegedly treats its animals more humanely than other stables in the area and is also concerned with keeping horse droppings off the beaches. Full-day horseback-riding excursions to a typical Costa Rican farm are provided by **Rancho Savegre Tours** (☎ **506/777-0528**). Tours cost $60 per person and include hotel transfers, lunch, and several swimming stops.

Finally, if you want to do some mountain biking while you're here, check in with **Cycling Estrella** (☎ and fax **506/777-1286**), which is in downtown Quepos. Well-maintained bikes rent for $15 per day. You can also do guided tours for $40 per day, as well as multiday expeditions.

THINGS TO SEE & DO IN QUEPOS

For a closer look at some exotic birds and other assorted wildlife, check out **Jardin Gaia**, a wildlife rescue center that rehabilitates and breeds injured and confiscated animals, many of them endangered. The center is located on the road between Quepos and Manuel Antonio. Jardin Gaia is open daily from 8am to 4pm and charges $5 per person, which includes a guided tour and plenty of print information. The tours generally begin at 9:30am and 1:30pm.

One new attraction in the area is a private rain-forest reserve called **Rainmaker**, which is owned and run by the folks at Si Como No. Located in the lush hills outside of Quepos, about 25 minutes by car, you can currently walk the well-groomed trails here, ride around on horseback, and swim in the waterfall-fed pools ($39 per person for half-day tours, including transportation and lunch). An aluminum canopy skywalk, which has been long in the development stage, should be open by the time this book hits the stands. This place is best visited by an arranged tour (which includes transportation).

Quepos is one of Costa Rica's billfish centers, and sailfish, marlin, and tuna are all common in these waters. If you're into sportfishing, try hooking up with **Blue Fin Sportfishing** (☎ 506/777-1676), **Costa Rican Dreams** (☎ 506/777-0593), **Marlin Azul** (☎ 506/777-0191), **Sportfishing Costa Rica** (☎ 506/257-3553), **Sportfishing Quepos** (☎ 506/777-0493), or **Poseidon Adventures** (☎ 506/777-0935). A full day of fishing should cost between $450 and $850, depending on the size of the boat. There's a lot of competition here so it pays to shop around and investigate. Try asking at the **Gran Escape** restaurant and also down at the **Manuel Antonio Marina**.

If you're staying at a budget hotel in Quepos and don't want to go all the way over the hill to the national park, you can swim and lounge at **Nahomi Lagoon** (☎ **506/777-0707**), Quepos's public swimming pool. You'll find this pool on a tiny peninsula at the end of the road that runs parallel to the water. Admission is around $1, and the pool is open Tuesday through Sunday from 10am to 8pm. The rocky promontory on which the pool is built feels like an island and is surrounded by the turquoise waters of a small cove. There's a snack bar and restaurant here, and on weekends the **Maracas** disco rages.

LEARN SPANISH IN PARADISE

I've never understood why all the language schools in Costa Rica are clustered in San José. **La Escuela de Idiomas D'Amore** (☎ and fax **506/777-1143;** e-mail: damore@sol.racsa.co.cr) runs immersion programs out of a former hotel with a fabulous view on the road to Manuel Antonio. A 2-week conversational Spanish course, including a homestay and two meals daily, costs $850.

SHOPPING

If you're looking for souvenirs, you'll find plenty of beach towels, beachwear, and handmade jewelry in a variety of small shops in Quepos and at impromptu stalls down near the national park. For a good selection in one spot try **La Buena Nota** (☎ **506/777-1002**), which is in its new home on the road to Manuel Antonio, right near the Hotel Karahé. This shop is jam-packed with all sorts of beachwear, souvenirs, and U.S. magazines and newspapers and also acts as an informal information center for the area. They recently put in a few basic rooms upstairs, and if you'd like to find out about renting a house, this is a good place to ask.

If you're looking for higher-end gifts, check out **L'Aventura Boutique** (☎ **506/777-1019**) on Avenida Central in Quepos. This small shop has a nice collection of woodwork by Barry Biesanz, banana-fabric works by Lil Mena, and pottery by Cecilia "Pefi" Figueres.

One of my favorite hangouts in Quepos has always been the **Cafe Milagro** (☎ and fax **506/777-1707**), which is one of the few homey coffeehouses I've found in Costa Rica. The folks here roast their own beans and also have a mail-order service to keep you in Costa Rican coffee year-round. You'll find local art for sale on the walls and a good selection of Cuban cigars, too. They've also opened another shop, **Casa de Cafe**, located on the main road to Manuel Antonio right near La Mariposa.

ACCOMMODATIONS

There are very few beachfront hotels in Manuel Antonio, so you won't have much luck finding a hotel where you can walk directly out of your room onto the beach. In fact, most of the nicer hotels here are a kilometer or so away from the beach, high on the hill overlooking the ocean. If you're traveling on a rock-bottom budget, you'll get more for your money by staying in Quepos and taking the bus to the beaches at Manuel Antonio every day. The rooms in Quepos may be small, but they're much cleaner and more appealing than those available in the same price category on the other side of the hill.

Remember, there is still a considerable glut of hotel rooms in Manuel Antonio. It's a good idea to have a reservation during the high season, or at least for your first night or two, but if you happen to come into town by car and can afford to make a few stops, you should be able to shop around and bargain for a room here at all but the busiest times of year.

Very Expensive

El Parador. Apdo. 284, Quepos. ☎ **506/777-1414.** Fax 506/777-1437. E-mail: parador@sol.racsa.co.cr. 60 units. A/C TV TEL. $145 standard, $185 deluxe, $265 junior suite, $710 presidential suite. Rates are based on double occupancy; children or third person must pay for breakfast. Rates slightly higher during peak weeks, lower during off-season. AE, MC, V.

What is luxurious opulence to one person can seem blindingly ostentatious to another. The jury is still out on El Parador. The hotel itself is spread out over more than 12 acres of land on a low peninsula, down a dirt road from La Mariposa. Its design aims to imitate Spanish Mediterranean grandeur, and the main building is loaded with antiques, including 17th-century Dutch and Flemish oil paintings, a 300-year-old carved wooden horse, and 16th-century church and castle doors. The standard rooms, although small, are new and well appointed. All have private patios, but few have any view to speak of. Most look out on the miniature golf course. Deluxe rooms offer slightly more space, and the second-floor units have private balconies. The junior suites are located on the top of a hill, giving a good view of the sea and Cathedral Point in the distance. All are equipped with a VCR, Jacuzzi, wet bar, and refrigerator. The three-bedroom presidential suite is in the main building and has the amenities of the other suites, plus a fully equipped kitchenette and decorative antiques. The hotel can arrange a wide variety of tours and activities in the area and runs a shuttle van to the national park. There's also a small secluded beach about 500 meters from the hotel. El Parador shoots for a level of luxury and service not commonly found in Costa Rica, and if this is what you're looking for in Manuel Antonio, then this is the place for you.

Dining: Most of the meals are served in the main La Galeria dining room and its adjoining terrace. Breakfast is served buffet style, and dinners are four-course, fixed-price affairs, chosen from a menu that changes nightly and generally includes eight main-course selections. There are three private dining rooms of varying sizes that can be reserved for special occasions. Sunsets are best enjoyed from the Mirador Lounge, above and behind the main building.

Amenities: The small kidney-shaped pool has a swim-up bar and central fountain. There's also a modest fitness center, Jacuzzi, steam room, tennis court, private helipad, tour desk, and small gift shop.

✪ **Hotel Si Como No.** Apdo. 5-6350, Quepos. ☎ **800/237-8201** in the U.S., or 506/777-0777. Fax 506/777-1093. www.sicomono.com. E-mail: information@sicomono.com. 39 units. A/C. Dec 1–Apr 15, $150–$190 double, Apr 16–Nov 30, $135–$150 double. Rates include breakfast. AE, MC, V.

This new complex seeks to combine modern amenities with an ecologically conscious attitude. All the wood used is farm grown, and although all the rooms have air-conditioning, guests are asked to use it only when necessary. The rooms are all classified as suites, and most are housed in a series of duplex villas, with treetop views out over the forest and onto the Pacific. These rooms all have a bedroom, living room, private balcony, and either a kitchenette or wet bar. You'll find the best views in villas 4, 6, 8, and 14. A few rooms are housed in the hotel's main building or on the ground floor of a villa, and while these are quite acceptable, it's worth the small splurge for a deluxe suite. The hotel has bought a large chunk of property for its own private reserve, and nature trails are planned.

Dining/Diversions: There are two dining options here. The Claro Que Sí restaurant in the main building is the more formal option, with a moderately priced menu of "nouvelle Costa Rican" cuisine. Try the fish of the day in an avacodo butter sauce, or the pork tenderloin in a mint sauce. Down by the pool, you'll find the Rico Tico Bar and Grill, which serves excellent ceviche, fresh fish, and grilled meats, plus Mexican snacks such as nachos and quesadillas.

Amenities: A free-form tile pool with waterfall, Jacuzzi, and slide; conference center and 50-seat laser-projection theater. Every night, a movie on laser disc is shown at 8pm. Nonguests who dine here can watch the movie for free. The hotel also has a full-time concierge.

La Mariposa. Playa Manuel Antonio, Quepos. ☎ **800/416-2747** in the U.S., or 506/777-0456. Fax 506/777-0050. 15 units, 6 villas. $120–$140 double room, $180 suite or villa. TV TEL. Rates include continental breakfast. MC, V (6% surcharge added). No children under 12 allowed.

While this is still one of Manuel Antonio's premier accommodations, I think it's been coasting on its reputation for some time. Perched on a ridge at the top of the hill between Quepos and Manuel Antonio, La Mariposa (the Butterfly) commands a mountains-to-the-sea vista of more than 270°. Needless to say, the sunsets here are knockouts, and the daytime views are pretty captivating themselves. La Mariposa offers spacious, attractively designed and decorated rooms, but the service and meals here fall far below the mark. Keep in mind that if you decide to abandon the view and the attractive little pool, it'll take either a steep hike or a short drive to get to the beach.

The nicest accommodations here are the bi-level villas. Each has a large bedroom and bathroom on the upper floor and a spacious living room and deck on the lower floor. There are huge tropical murals behind the two queen-size beds in the bedrooms, plus high ceilings, skylights, blue-and-white-tile counters, and shelves of plants. The bathrooms are spacious and even have small atrium gardens. Several of these villas have recently been split into separate junior suites and deluxe rooms. The junior suites each have a Jacuzzi out on the small balcony or just inside its sliding glass door. There are also several spacious rooms, most of which are quite comfortable but do not have views. Take note: No children under 12 are allowed.

Dining/Diversions: The open-air restaurant is set on a red-tiled terrace that takes in all the views. The emphasis is on seafood. On my three most recent visits, the food has fallen far short of what one would expect at these surroundings and at these prices. A continental breakfast is always included in the rates, and some people opt for the modified American plan, but I strongly advise against it. There's also a small bar.

Amenities: The small swimming pool is set on its own terrace. Services include room service, concierge, tour desk. The hotel provides a complimentary shuttle to and from the Quepos airport.

✪ **Makanda-By-The-Sea.** P.O. Box 29, Quepos. ☎ **506/777-0442.** Fax 506/777-1032. www.makanda.com. E-mail: makanda@makanda.com. 7 units. Dec 1–Apr 30, $135 studio, $185 villa; May 1–Nov 30, $90 studio, $125 villa. Rates include continental breakfast. AE, MC, V.

Located halfway down the road to El Parador and Punta Quepos, Makanda is a wonderfully luxurious collection of studio apartments and private villas. Each is individually decorated, with flair and a sense of style. If you combine Villa 1 with the three studios, you get one very large four-bedroom villa, great for a family or small group. Every choice comes with a full kitchenette and either a terrace or balcony. The grounds are well tended, intermixed with tropical flowers and Japanese gardens. A continental breakfast is delivered to your room each morning. The hotel's pool and Jacuzzi combine colorful tile work and interesting geometry with an infinity effect and a view of the jungle-covered hillsides and Pacific Ocean.

Dining: Makanda's Sunset Bar & Grill, is one of the better restaurants in Manuel Antonio, with just a few tables set under open-sided cloth tents, serving creative continental dishes and rich desserts. Be sure to make reservations in the high season.

Amenities: Pool, Jacuzzi, laundry service, and concierge.

Tulemar Bungalows. Quepos (mailing address in the U.S.: SJO 042, P.O. Box 025369, Miami, FL 33102). ☎ **506/777-0580** or 506/777-1325. Fax 506/777-1579. www.tulemar.com. E-mail: tulemar@sol.racsa.co.cr. 14 units. A/C TV TEL. Dec 16–Apr 31, $180; May 1–Dec 15, $129. Rates include full breakfast. AE, MC, V.

These individual octagonal bungalows are some of the more interesting and exclusive accomodations in Manuel Antonio. Each bungalow has a spacious living room, full kitchenette, two queen-size beds, and 180° views over jungle and ocean. The couches in the living room fold out into beds, and extra cots for children can be placed in the rooms. The furnishings are fine but a bit sparse and lacking in style. My biggest complaint here is that the hotel continues to feed the local monkey population in order to thrill and please guests—a pet peeve of mine, since these animals are not pets.

Dining: The hotel's restaurant serves only breakfast, lunch, and snacks. Although sometimes during the high season, they also do dinner.

Amenities: The hotel's private road winds steeply down to a small cove and semi-private beach where you'll find chaise longues, kayaks, boogie boards, and a snack bar. The pool here is small yet elegant, with its infinity effect blending in with the Pacific Ocean and breathtaking view.

EXPENSIVE

✪ **Hotel Casitas Eclipse.** Apdo. 11-6350, Quepos. ☎ **506/777-0408.** Fax 506/777-1738. www.crica.com/hotels. E-mail: eclipse@sol.racsa.co.cr. 25 units. A/C TEL. Dec 16–Apr 15, $91–$119 double, $200 two-bedroom casita; Apr 16–Dec 15, $60–$75 double, $133 two-bedroom casita. AE, MC, V.

Located close to the top of the hill between Quepos and Manuel Antonio, these beautiful casitas are some of the most boldly styled structures in Manuel Antonio. While the villas have a distinctly Mediterranean flavor, the owner swears they're inspired by Mesoamerican and Pueblo Indian villages. Their styling makes them seem much larger than they actually are, although they're certainly plenty roomy. All are painted a blinding white and are topped with red-tile roofs. Though simply furnished, the rooms are very comfortable and attractive inside. You can rent either the entire casita or split it up. The larger downstairs suites have tile floors, built-in banquettes, high ceilings, large patios, and full kitchens. If you don't need all that space, you can opt for the upstairs room, which has a separate entrance, private bathroom, and balcony of its own. There are three attractive tiled pools spread out among the lush grounds. Only the restaurant and a couple of villas have ocean views here, and even these are rather blocked by trees. Nevertheless, I prefer the units farther from the road, where you're more likely to hear and see squirrel monkeys passing by than trucks and buses. Considering what's available in this price range, this is a good choice.

Dining/Diversions: The Jardin Gourmet restaurant (see "Dining," below) serves breakfast, lunch, and dinner. There's a small bar just off the restaurant, as well as the more lively Cockatoo Bar on the terrace above.

Amenities: Three swimming pools, concierge, and tour desk.

MODERATE

El Dorado Mojado. Apdo. 238-6350, Quepos. ☎ **506/777-0368.** Fax 506/777-1248. 4 units, 4 villas. A/C. Dec–Apr, $50 double, $74 villa; May–Nov, $49 double, $60 villa. High-season rates include breakfast. MC, V.

The architectural uniqueness of the buildings at this small hotel makes it one of the most interesting places to stay in Manuel Antonio. Both the villas (with full kitchens) and the smaller standard rooms are very comfortable. The buildings are set back in the forest and are connected by a raised walkway below which grow lush tropical plants. The buildings resemble modernized banana plantation houses, with glass walls that extend vertically for two stories before angling in to form an atrium effect. Standard rooms are located either upstairs (with hardwood floors and more light) or downstairs (with painted red-tile floors). Other interesting and attractive touches include cane-sided cupboards, open-air showers with walls of glass block, and Guatemalan bedspreads. The villas also have TVs, carved antique headboards, and Murphy beds. Some people might find the forest shade a bit dark, but it's still a beautiful setting. I would request Villa A, which has earned the title "monkey villa" for the frequent visits local primates pay to it, or Villa D, which sits beside a flowing stream and offers the most privacy.

Hotel and Cabinas Playa Espadilla. Manuel Antonio, Quepos. ☎ and fax **506/777-0416,** or 506/777-0903. www.maqbeach.com. E-mail: spadilla@sol.racsa.co.cr. 15 units, 16 cabinas. $40–$50 double with fan, $50–$70 double with air-conditioning. AE, MC, V.

There isn't much charm or personality here, but it is clean and close to the beach. The newer rooms all have air-conditioning and full kitchenettes. These are also closest to the pool. The older cabinas are more basic, and most just have fans. Although there isn't much in the way of decor or closet space in any of them, there are enough beds to sleep up to four people comfortably (a double bed and a bunk bed). You'll find this hotel down the side road that runs perpendicular to Playa Espadilla, the first beach outside the national park.

✪ **Hotel Costa Verde.** Apdo. 106-6350, Quepos (mailing address in the U.S.: SJO 1313, P.O. Box 025216, Miami, FL 33102). ☎ **506/777-0584,** or in the U.S. and Canada 888/412-3800. Fax 506/777-0506. www.Costaverde.co.cr. E-mail: costaver@sol.racsa.co.cr. 43 units. Dec 15–Apr 15, $65–$90 double, $120 penthouse; Apr 16–Dec 14, $40–$70 double, $100 penthouse. AE, DC, MC, V.

The guest rooms at Costa Verde have long been some of my favorites in the area. With their screen walls they seem to sum up the sensual climate of the tropics—no need for walls when they only keep out the breezes. Over the years, Costa Verde has continued to add new rooms, and today the original rooms are some of the least expensive but are still quite pleasant. Most of the rooms have ocean views, kitchenettes, and balconies, and the more expensive rooms have loads of space. The newest addition this year is the huge penthouse suite, which has a commanding view of the spectacular surroundings. There are two small pools set into the hillside, with views out to the ocean. The lodge's open-air restaurant looks into the forest trees, where you can sometimes get a look at a sloth. To one side of the dining room is a long bar, and there's also a small gift shop. Costa Verde is more than halfway down the hill to Manuel Antonio, about a 10-minute walk from the beach.

Hotel Plinio. Apdo. 71-6350, Quepos. ☎ **506/777-0055.** Fax 506/777-0558. www.hotelplinio.com. E-mail: plinio@sol.racsa.co.cr. 13 units. Dec–Apr, $60–$70 double, $75 standard suite or house, $90 deluxe suite; May–Nov, lower rates are available. Rates include a breakfast buffet. AE, MC, V (7% surcharge).

The Plinio was for many years a favorite of budget travelers visiting Manuel Antonio, and although its room rates have crept up over the years, it's still a good value. The hotel is built into a steep hillside, so it's a bit of a climb from the parking lot up to the guest rooms and restaurant (roughly the equivalent of three flights of stairs). Once you are up top, though, you'll think you're in a tree house. Floors and walls are polished hardwood, and there are even rooms with tree-trunk pillars. The hotel's suites are the best value. These are built on either two or three levels. Both types have sleeping lofts, while the three-story rooms also have rooftop decks. My favorite room is known as the "jungle house" and is set back in the forest. The restaurant, which is one of the more popular places to eat in Manuel Antonio, serves a variety of good Italian and international dishes, with entree prices ranging from $4.50 to $10. Behind the hotel there's a forest with 3 miles (5km) of trails and, at the top of the hill, a 50-foot-tall observation tower with an incredible view. There's also a snack bar near the pool, for lunches. A lap pool, kids' pool, and recreation room with library round out the amenities.

Karahé. Apdo. 100-6350, Quepos. ☎ **506/777-0170.** Fax 506/777-0175. 24 units, 9 villas. $50–$80 double. Rates include continental breakfast. AE, DC, MC, V.

The Karahé has long been one of the better beachfront hotels in Manuel Antonio, but competition is increasing, and in order to keep up, the hotel has had to lower its rates, which is good news for travelers. The bad news is that the management can be gruff and innattentive. Note that if you opt for one of the villas (the cheapest and oldest rooms in the hotel), you'll be a steep uphill climb from the beach and won't have air-conditioning. On the other hand, you'll have a much better view.

If you choose to stay in one of the more expensive beachfront units, you'll have a new room with cool tile floors, two double beds, air-conditioning, and a small patio. With the exception of the cheapest rooms, all rooms have balconies and full bathtubs. The gardens that surround the upper half of the hotel are quite lush and are planted with flowering ginger that often attracts hummingbirds. The gardens are not nearly as attractive down in the lower part of the hotel grounds, but this is where you'll find the small pool. The hotel is located on both sides of the road about 500 yards before you reach the end of the road at Manuel Antonio.

The hotel's restaurant is built at treetop level midway between the hotel's two levels of accommodations. Entree prices range from $5 to $15, and the specialty of the house is shish kebab cooked over an indoor barbecue. There's also a snack bar near the pool, which serves lunch and doubles as the hotel's bar. The hotel can arrange a wide range of tours and charters, including sportfishing ($750 for a full day).

✪ **La Colina.** Apdo. 191, Quepos. ☎ **506/777-0231.** Fax 506/777-1553. 11 units. Dec–Apr, $40 double, $55 suite; May–Nov, $25 double, $35 suite. Rates include breakfast. V.

This casual little bed-and-breakfast is operated by a couple of Colorado natives who moved down to Manuel Antonio a few years ago and converted their home into a B&B. Although the original rooms here are fairly small, they're decorated with style. They have black-and-white-tile floors, louvered French doors, and, despite the small size of the rooms, a good writing desk. Outside each room, there's a small patio area with a few chairs. The new suites are built on the highest spot on this property and have front and back balconies with views of both the ocean and the mountains. The suites are all large and comfortable and come with air-conditioning. Breakfast is served in your room, out on the patio, or in the open-air rancho restaurant. The Sunset Grill (closed for dinner on Tuesday) serves a mix of international dishes with a hefty emphasis on fresh seafood. La Colina also rents out two fully equipped apartments and can accommodate longer-term stays. The hotel is on your right as you head toward Manuel Antonio, right at a sharp switchback on a steep hill, hence the name, La Colina.

Verde Del Mar. Manuel Antonio (Apdo. 348-6350), Quepos. ☎ **506/777-1805.** Fax 506/777-1311. E-mail: verdemar@sol.racsa.co.cr. 20 units. $55–$70 double. AE, MC, V.

This new hotel is one of the better choices down toward the national park. From your room, it's just a 50-meter walk from the beach (Playa Espadilla) via a raised wooden walkway. All but two of the rooms come with a basic kitchenette; six of them have air-conditioning. All have plenty of room, nice wrought-iron queen-size beds, red tile-floors, a desk and chair, a fan, and a small porch. Some of the larger rooms even have two queen-size beds. The hotel has no restaurant, but there are plenty within walking distance. There's a small pool here if the surf is too rough. You'll find Verde del Mar (which had to change its name from La Casa del Sol) on the beach side of the road just before the Mar y Sombra.

✪ **Villas Nicolas.** Apdo. 236, Quepos. ☎ **506/777-0481.** Fax 506/777-0451. www.hotels.co.cr/nicolas. E-mail: nicolas@sol.racsa.co.cr. 20 units. $59–$90 double, $75–$105 triple, $90–$150 quad. Weekly, monthly, and low-season rates available. V.

These large villas pack a big punch for the buck. Built as terraced units up a steep hill in deep forest, they really give you the feeling you're in the jungle. Spacious and well appointed, with wood floors, throw rugs, separate living rooms, and large bathrooms, some rooms even have full kitchenettes, which make longer stays comfortable and feasible. My favorite features, though, are the huge balconies, with both sitting chairs and a hammock. There's also a small pool. The rooms highest up the hill have views I'd be willing to pay a lot more for.

INEXPENSIVE

Cabinas Pedro Miguel. Apdo. 17, Manuel Antonio, Quepos. ☎ and fax **506/777-0035.** 14 units. $22–$28 double, $37 quad. AE, DC, MC, V.

Located a kilometer outside Quepos on the road to Manuel Antonio (across from Hotel Plinio), these cabinas are very basic, with cement floors and cinder-block walls, but at least they're away from the fray and surrounded by forest. The second-floor rooms are newer and cleaner and have carpeting as well as a glimpse of the water from the common veranda. One of them is huge, with a kitchen and a back wall made entirely of screen. From it, guests can look out over a lush stand of trees. During the high season, you can dine at the restaurant, which serves Costa Rican standards, and the owners encourage guests to participate in meal preparation. There's a tiny swimming pool, and the management here is very friendly.

Cabinas Ramirez. Playas Manuel Antonio, Quepos. ☎ **506/777-0003.** 16 units. $15–$27 double. No credit cards.

These basic beachside cabinas are the most popular budget choices near the park, especially among young Ticos. The hotel is next door to the restaurant/bar and disco Mar y Sombra, so evenings can be loud. The rooms are basic cinder-block affairs with concrete floors. Some are quite dark and prisonlike, but all are clean. The owner also allows camping for backpackers with tents, for $5 per tent.

Cabinas Vela-Bar. Apdo. 13, Manuel Antonio, Quepos. ☎ **506/777-0413.** Fax 506/777-1071. www.maqbeach.com. E-mail: velabar@maqbeach.com. 11 units. $22–$35 double, $35–$59 triple, $52–$75 quad. AE, DC, MC, V.

You'll find this unusual little hotel up the dirt road that leads off to the left just before the end of the road to Manuel Antonio National Park. It has a wide variety of room choices: If you're on an exceedingly tight budget, you can stay in a tiny room or, if you have a little more money to spend, you can opt for a spacious one-bedroom house that has tile floors and arched windows. There are double beds and tiled bathrooms in all rooms. The open-air restaurant/bar is deservedly very popular; check the chalkboard for the day's special. Entrees range in price from $5.10 to $11.50. This is one of the best budget options in Manuel Antonio, and it's only 100 meters from the beach.

El Lirio. Apdo. 123, Quepos. ☎ **506/777-0403.** Fax 506/777-1182. 9 units. Dec–Apr, $25–$46 double, May–Nov, $17–$30 double. Rates include continental breakfast. AE, MC, V.

Although the nicest rooms overlook the road and consequently can be a bit noisy, there are some quieter rooms at the back of the grounds, near the swimming pool. A Mediterranean style prevails here, with arches, stucco walls, and red-tile floors and roofs. The rooms have high ceilings, mosquito nets over the beds, and tiled bathrooms. The grounds are quiet and lush, planted with orchids and other tropical flowers and overhung by large, shady trees. You'll find El Lirio on the left, near the top of the hill as you drive from Quepos to Manuel Antonio. All in all, this is a very attractive place and a pretty good deal.

Hotel Malinche. Quepos. ☎ and fax **505/777-0093.** 24 units. $10–$35 double. MC, V.

Another good choice for backpackers, the Hotel Malinche is located on the first street to your left as you come into Quepos. You can't miss the hotel's arched brick entrance. Inside, you'll find bright rooms with louvered windows. The rooms are small but have hardwood floors and clean bathrooms. The more expensive rooms are new and have air-conditioning and carpets.

Hotel Quepos. Quepos. ☎ **506/777-0274.** 20 units (11 with bathroom). $10 double without bathroom, $15 double with bathroom. No credit cards.

This little budget hotel is both comfortable and clean. There are hardwood floors, ceiling fans, a large, sunny TV lounge, and even a parking lot and laundry service. The management is very friendly, and there's an interesting souvenir shop and a charter-fishing office on the first floor. This hotel is across from the soccer field on the way out of town toward Manuel Antonio.

DINING

There are scores of dining options around Manuel Antonio and Quepos, and almost every hotel has some sort of restaurant. My favorite of these is the small restaurant at **Makanda** (see "Accommodations," above). I've also recently got good reports on the Italian food at **Il Pirata** in downtown Quepos.

For the cheapest meals around, try a simple soda in Quepos, or head to one of the dozen or so open-air shacks near the side of the road just before the circle at the entrance to the national park. The standard Tico menu prevails, with prices in the $2.50 to $8 range. Though these little places lack atmosphere, they do have views of the ocean. The best of the batch is **Las Olas**, which is on the beach side of the main road, just before you get into the main cluster of activity in Manuel Antonio. In Quepos, **La Marquesa** on the main road is a good bet. The fish is fresh daily, the portions are large, and the prices are bargains.

If you have a room with a kitchenette, you can shop at one of several supermarkets in Quepos, or brave the cluttered stalls of its central market, right next to the bus station.

For a picnic lunch, complete with cooler, check out **Pickles Deli** in the small shopping center next to Hotel Si Como No. Another option for light meals and well-prepared sandwiches is **L'Angelo Italian Deli** in Quepos, located 1 block west of the Bus Terminal.

MODERATE

Barba Roja. Quepos–Manuel Antonio Road. ☎ **506/777-0331.** Reservations not accepted. Main courses $5–$11.30; sandwiches $2.50–$6. V. Tues–Sun 7am–10pm, Monday 4–10pm. SEAFOOD/CONTINENTAL.

Perched high on a hill, with stunning views over jungle and ocean, the Barba Roja has long been one of the more popular restaurants in Manuel Antonio. The rustic interior is done with local hardwoods and bamboo, which gives the open-air dining room a warm glow, and there's an outdoor patio where you can sit for hours taking in the view or the stars. There's even a gallery attached to the restaurant, so if you tire of the view you can take a gander at some original art by local artists. On the blackboard, there are daily specials such as grilled fish steak served with a salad and baked potato. Portions here are massive. The restaurant is open for breakfast and serves delicious whole-wheat French toast. For lunch, there are a number of different sandwiches, all served on whole-wheat bread. If you're in the mood to hang out and meet some of locals and other fellow travelers, spend some time at the bar sipping piña coladas or margaritas.

✪ **El Gran Escape.** On the main road into Quepos, on your left just after the bridge. ☎ **506/777-0395.** Reservations not accepted. Main courses $6–$16. Wed–Mon 6am–11pm. MC, V.

This Quepos landmark is a favorite with locals and fisherman—for good reason. The fish is fresh and well prepared, and the prices are reasonable. If that's not enough of a recommendation, the atmosphere is lively and the service is darn good for a beach town in Costa Rica. Wooden tables and chairs fill up this big room, and sportfishing photos and an exotic collection of masks fill up the walls. If you venture away from the fish, there are hearty steaks, giant burgers, and a wide assortment of delicious appetizers. The Gran Escape's small bar is often crowded, and if there's a game going on, it will be on the television here. At press time, I learned that the owners here have opened a new restaurant, Sushi Mar, directly above the original restaurant. Odds are it's as well-done as the Gran Escape.

Jardín Gourmet. Quepos–Manuel Antonio Road at Hotel Casitas Eclipse. ☎ and fax **506/777-1728.** Reservations recommended during high season. Main courses $5–$20. AE, MC, V. Daily 6:30–9:30am, 11am–5pm, and 6–10pm. ITALIAN.

Perched at the highest part of the Hotel Casitas Eclipse, this has added a bit of class to the dining options in Manuel Antonio. The menu leans heavily toward excellently prepared seafood dishes. Fresh fillets of red snapper and dorado ($8 to $12) come either grilled or in light sauces with fresh basil or thyme. The *tagliatelle ai frutti di mare* ($11) is fresh pasta piled with clams, shrimp, chunks of fish, and a half lobster, served in a light tomato sauce. There are plenty of meat and chicken choices, as well as a healthy and reasonably priced selection of wines for the area. The restaurant is an open-air affair with rattan tables and chairs, cloth tablecloths, and oil lanterns. You can also get breakfast and light lunches here. Upstairs on the open terrace is the new Cockatoo Bar, which has great panoramic views of Manuel Antonio.

Karola's. Quepos–Manuel Antonio Road. ☎ **506/777-1557.** Reservations not accepted. Main courses $5–$25. V. Daily 7am–10pm (closed May and June). SEAFOOD/CONTINENTAL.

The steep driveway leading down to this open-air restaurant is within a few feet of the Barba Roja parking lot but is easily overlooked. Watch closely when you're up at the top of the hill. The restaurant is across a footbridge from its parking lot and is set against a jungle-covered hillside. Far below you can see the ocean if you're here during the day. Grilled seafoods are the specialty, but they also do peel-and-eat shrimp with a great house sauce. Desserts (such as macadamia pie) are good, and you can order margaritas by the pitcher. Not to be topped by the Barba Roja, there's a separate art gallery here as well.

✪ **Plinio Restaurant.** 1 kilometer out of Quepos toward Manuel Antonio. ☎ **506/777-0055.** Main courses $4.50–$10. AE, MC, V. Daily 6–10am and 5–10pm. ITALIAN/INTERNATIONAL.

This is a long-standing, popular restaurant in Manuel Antonio, located at an equally popular hotel. The open-air restaurant is a sort of covered deck about three stories above the parking lot, so be prepared to climb some steps before you get to eat. It's worth it, though. The basket of bread that arrives at your table shortly after you sit down is filled with delicious treats, and the menu is also full of tempting dishes. Italian is the primary cuisine here, but you may also encounter a German or Indonesian dish as one of the nightly specials. Two of my favorite dishes here are the spaghetti with pesto and the broccoli-and-cauliflower parmigiana. There's also a great antipasto platter that includes prosciutto, salami, and cheese. At lunchtime, a separate chef takes over the restaurant at the poolside snack bar, preparing some wonderful lunches, with frequent Asian and Creole specials.

Restaurant Vela-Bar. 100 meters down side road near the park entrance. ☎ **506/777-0413.** Reservations not accepted. Main courses $5–$12. AE, MC, V. Daily 7–10am, 11:30am–2:30pm, and 5:30–11pm (closed at lunch June–Nov). INTERNATIONAL.

The Vela-Bar is a small and casual place that serves some of the more creative cuisine in Manuel Antonio. This is also the best of the restaurants closest to the park entrance. Seafood and vegetarian meals are the specialties here, and the most interesting dishes are almost always the specials posted on the blackboard. A typical day's choice might include fresh fish in sherry or wine sauce with curried vegetables.

MANUEL ANTONIO AFTER DARK

Discos are becoming almost as common in Manuel Antonio as capuchin monkeys. Night owls and dancing fools have their choice. The local favorite appears to be **Maracas** (☎ **506/777-0707**), which is located at the Nahomi Pool on the pier south of Quepos. The disco here is open Thursday through Saturday from 10pm to 2am and frequently features live music. Admission fees depend on whether or not there is a live band and range between $1 and $5. Another popular Quepos disco is the **Arco Iris** (☎ **506/777-0449**), which is located just over the bridge heading out of town. Admission here is usually around $2.50. Down near the beach, folks get going at the restaurant **Mar y Sombra** (☎ **506/777-0591**), which has the nicest setting of any disco around and almost never charge a cover.

The bars at the **Barba Roja** restaurant and **Villas Si Como No** are also good places to hang out and meet people in the evenings. You can also hang out at the **Vela-Bar**, which seems to be popular with gay men.

Back in Quepos, **El Banco Bar** is the most popular gringo hangout.

If you enjoy the gaming tables, the **Hotel Kamuk** (☎ **506/777-0379**) in Quepos has a small casino and will even foot your cab bill if you try your luck and lay your money down. You'll also find a small casino at the **Hotel Divisamar** (☎ **506/777-0371**) on the Manuel Antonio Road, across from the Barba Roja.

Finally, if you want to see a flick, check what's playing at **Hotel Si Como No**'s little theater, although you have to eat at the restaurant or spend a minimum at the bar to earn admission.

EN ROUTE TO DOMINICAL: PLAYA MATAPALO

Playa Matapalo is a long strand of flat beach that's about midway between Quepos and Dominical. It's nowhere near as developed as either of those two beaches, but this is part of its charm. The beach here seems to stretch on forever, and it's almost always nearly deserted. Unfortunately, the surf is often too rough for swimming, although boogie boarding can be good. Foremost among this beach's charms are peace and quiet. With only a few places to stay, there are no crowds, and Matapalo is basically a little village. The beach itself is about a kilometer from the village. In addition to the hotel listed here, there's an Italian restaurant that serves economical meals, a Tico cabina with a disco, and other projects in the works.

El Coquito del Pacífico. Playa Matapalo (Apdo. 6783-1000, San José). ☎ **506/233-1731.** Fax 506/222-8849. 6 units. $38 double, $47 triple, $54 quad. No credit cards.

This little collection of cabinas is operated by the same people who run the Hotel Ritz/Pension Continental, a budget travelers' standard in San José. The cabinas are all quite large and have white-tile floors, high ceilings, colorful sheets on the beds, and overhead fans. There's a small restaurant/bar, and guests can use the mountain bikes and boogie boards for free. Horseback rides can also be arranged. When you hit the beach, turn right, and the hotel will be a hundred yards or so north.

4 Dominical

18 miles (29km) SW of San Isidro; 26 miles (42km) S of Quepos; 99 miles (160km) S of San José

This area is no longer the best-kept secret in Costa Rica, but Dominical and the coastline south of Dominical remain excellent places to find isolated beaches, spectacular views, remote jungle waterfalls, and abundant budget lodgings. The beach at Dominical itself has both right and left beach breaks, which means there are usually plenty of surfers in town. In fact, the beach in Dominical really has appeal only to surfers; it's too rough and rocky for regular folk.

Leaving Manuel Antonio, the road south to Dominical runs by mile after mile of oil-palm plantations. However, just before Dominical, the mountains once again meet the sea. From Dominical south, the coastline is dotted with tide pools, tiny coves, and cliffside vistas, all of which bring Big Sur, California, to mind. Dominical is the largest village in the area and has several small lodges both in town and along the beach to the south. The village enjoys an enviable location on the banks of Río Barú, right where it widens considerably before emptying into the ocean. There's good bird watching along the banks of the river and throughout the surrounding forests.

ESSENTIALS

GETTING THERE & DEPARTING **By Plane** The nearest airport with regular service is in Quepos (see "Essentials" in the "Manuel Antonio National Park" section, above). From there you can hire a taxi, rent a car, or take the bus.

By Bus To reach Dominical, you must first go to San Isidro de El General or Quepos. Buses leave San José for San Isidro at 5:30, 7:30, 10:30, and 11:30am and 1:30, 2:30, 4:30 and 5pm from Calle 16 between Avenidas 1 and 3. Leave no later than 9:30am if you want to catch the 1:30pm bus to Dominical. The trip takes 3 hours; fare is $3.

From San Isidro de El General, buses leave for Dominical at 7 and 8am and 1:30 and 4pm. The bus station for Dominical is 1 block south of the main bus station and 2 blocks west of the church. Trip duration is 1½ hours; fare is $1.50.

From Quepos, buses leave daily at 5am and 1:30pm. Trip duration is 3½ hours; fare is $3.50.

When you're ready to leave, note that buses depart Dominical for San Isidro de El General only twice daily: at 6am and 2pm. If you want to get to San José the same day, you'll have to catch the morning bus. Buses to Quepos leave at approximately 7am and 1:30pm. Buses leave San Isidro for San José daily at 5, 5:30, 7:30, 8:30, 10:30 and 11:30am and 1:30 and 4:30pm.

By Car From San José, head south (toward Cartago) on the Interamerican Highway. Continue on this road all the way to San Isidro de El General, where you turn right and head down toward the coast. The entire drive takes about 5 hours.

Alternatively, you can drive here from Manuel Antonio/Quepos. Just take the road out of Quepos toward the hospital and airport. Follow the signs for Dominical. It's a straight, albeit bumpy, shot. The 25 miles (40km) should take you only 3 hours at most to cover.

ORIENTATION Dominical is a small village on the banks of Río Barú. The village is to the right after you cross the bridge and stretches out along the main road parallel to the beach. As you first come into town, there's a soccer field and general store, where there's a public telephone.

FAST FACTS You can purchase stamps and send mail from the **San Clemente Bar & Grill**. If you need a taxi, ask around for **Beto** (no phone). The gas station is located about 1¼ miles (2km) north of town on the road to Quepos.

EXPLORING THE BEACHES & BALLENA MARINE NATIONAL PARK

Because the beach in the village of Dominical is unprotected and at the mouth of a river, it's often much too rough for swimming; however, you can go for a swim in the calm waters at the mouth of the Río Barú, or head down the beach a few kilometers to the little sheltered cove at **Roca Verde**. If you have a car, you should continue driving south, exploring beaches as you go. You will first come to **Dominicalito**, a small beach and cove that shelters the local fishing fleet and can be a decent place to swim, but I recommend continuing on a bit. You will soon hit **Playa Hermosa**, a long stretch of desolate beach with fine sand. As in Dominical, this is unprotected and can be rough, but it's a nicer place to sunbathe and swim than Dominical. At the village of Uvita, 10 miles (16km) south of Dominical, you'll reach the northern end of the Ballena Marine National Park, which protects a coral reef that stretches from Uvita south to Playa Piñuela and includes the little Isla Ballena, just offshore. To get to Playa Uvita, turn in at the village of Bahia and continue until you hit the ocean. The beach here is actually well protected and good for swimming. At low tide, an exposed sandbar allows you to walk about and explore another tiny island. This park is named for the whales that are sometimes sighted close to shore in the winter months. If you ever fly over this area, you'll also notice that this little island and the spit of land that's formed at low tide form the perfect outline of a whale's tail.

HORSEBACK TOURS, RAIN-FOREST HIKES & WATERFALLS

Although the beaches stretching south from Dominical should be beautiful enough to keep most people content, there are lots of other things to do. Several local farms offer horseback tours through forests and orchards, and at some of these farms you can even spend the night. **Hacienda Baru** (☎ **506/787-0003**; fax 506/787-0004) offers several different hikes and tours, including a walk through mangroves and along the river bank (for some good bird watching), a rain-forest hike through 200 acres of virgin jungle, an all-day trek from beach to mangrove to jungle that includes a visit to some Indian petroglyphs, an overnight camping trip, and a combination horseback-and-hiking tour. They even have tree-climbing tours and a small canopy platform 100 feet above the ground. Tour prices range from $15 (for the mangrove hike) to $60 (for the jungle overnight). If you're traveling with a group, you'll be charged a lower per-person rate, depending on the number of people in your group. Hacienda Baru also has six comfortable cabins with two bedrooms each, full kitchens, and even a living room ($50 double, $60 triple).

The jungles just outside of Dominical are home to two spectacular waterfalls. The most popular and impressive is the **Santo Cristo** or **Nauyaca Waterfalls**, a two-tiered beauty with an excellent swimming hole. Most of the hotels in town can arrange for the horseback ride up here, or you can call **Don Lulo** at ☎ **506/771-3187**. A half-day tour here, with both breakfast and lunch, should cost around $35 to $40 per person. This site has become so popular that Don Lulo has set up a little welcome center at the entrance (just off the road into Dominical from San Isidro) and even allows camping here. It is also possible to reach these falls by horseback from an entrance near the small village of Tinamaste (you will see signs on the road); however, I still recommend the tours with Don Lulo.

Similar tours (at similar prices) are offered to the **Terciopelo Waterfalls**, which are a three-tiered set of falls with a 120-foot drop but not quite as spacious and inviting a pool as the one at Santa Cristo. Hacienda Baru is located about a mile north of Dominical on the road to Manuel Antonio.

A FARM STAY

Finca Brian y Milena, Apdo. 2-8000, San Isidro de El General, (☎ **506/771-4582;** fax 506/771-1903), offers day and overnight trips to their farm in the hills above Dominical.

Here you can bird watch, explore the tropical rain forest, and visit a working farm where tropical fruits, nuts, and spices are grown. If you stay for several nights, you can visit the Santo Cristo or Diamante waterfalls by horseback or on foot. At night here, you can soak in the hot tub. Rates begin at $30 per person per day. Horse rentals and overnight excursions are additional.

ACCOMMODATIONS

VERY EXPENSIVE

Villas Escaleras. (mailing address in the U.S.:Suite 2277 SJO, P.O. Box 025216, Miami, FL 33102), Dominical, Pérez Zeledón. ☎ and fax **506/771-5247.** 3 villas. $125–$350 nightly per villa, most with a 3-night minimum. MC, V.

If you're looking for an isolated, luxurious getaway with breathtaking views, this place is for you. Located 1,200 feet above Dominical, the three separate villas here are all meticulously crafted and finished, with combination hardwood and

Mexican tile floors, Guatemalan fabrics, and interesting decorative crafts from around the world. The main three-bedroom villa sleeps up to 10 people. Its massive library/sitting room opens on to an equally spacious wraparound balcony, with tables and chairs and several hammocks for soaking in the views. When not soaking in the views, you can soak in the villa's kidney-shaped pool. The other villas are smaller but equally luxurious and oriented toward the view. There's another private pool at the newest two-bedroom villa and one planned for the "small villa." You'll need a sturdy four-wheel-drive vehicle to get up here, and you'll have to do most of your own cooking (in the well-equipped full kitchens) or drive back down into Dominical, although catering is sometimes available on request.

Moderate

Hotel Roca Verde. Dominical, Pérez Zeledón. ☎ **506/787-0036.** Fax 506/787-0013. E-mail: doshnos@sol.racsa.co.cr. 12 units. $60 double. MC, V.

This former budget hotel has a wonderful location a couple of kilometers south of Dominical. The setting is superb—on a little cove with rocks and tide pools. In 1998, all the original buildings were torn down, and a new, fancier hotel was built. I visited only in the building stage, but expect to find new, spacious rooms with cool, clean tile floors, orthopedic matresses, private terraces, and ocean views. The restaurant is slated to have both Tico and international fare, and the bar will once again feature satellite TV and the occasional live band on weekends. There should also be a swimming pool. If you're driving, head south out of town on the main road and you'll see their sign a couple of kilometers down on the right.

✪ **Pacific Edge.** Apdo. 531-8000, Dominical, Pérez Zeledón. ☎ and fax **506/787-0031.** 4 units. $40 double, $45 triple. MC, V (20% surcharge added).

Located 2½ miles (4km) south of Dominical and then another ¾ mile (1.2km) up a steep and rocky road, four-wheel-drive vehicles are highly recommended—I'd say required. This place is a bit of a way from the beach, but the views from each individual bungalow are so breathtaking that you may not mind. Spread along a lushly planted ridge on the hillside over Dominical, these comfortable cabins have wood floors, solar-heated water, solar reading lights, and small kitchenettes. Their best feature is surely the spacious private porch with a comfortable hammock in which to laze about and enjoy the view. Their worst feature is that they come with only single beds (up to three), so couples will have to push two together or cuddle tightly. The restaurant serves breakfast and dinner daily, which will run you around an extra $20 per person per day. A wide range of tours and activities can be arranged here.

Punta Dominical. Apdo. 196-8000, Dominical. ☎ **506/787-0016.** 4 cabins. $42 double, $52 triple, $62 quad. No credit cards.

Located about 2½ miles (4km) south of Dominical on a rocky point, this place has a stony cove on one side and a sandy beach on the other. The cabins and restaurant are set among shady old trees high above the surf and have excellent views of both coves. All the cabinas have good views, but the best are to be had from the ones higher up the hill. The cabins, built on stilts and constructed of dark polished hardwood, all have big porches with chairs and hammocks. Screened and louvered walls are designed to catch the breezes. The bathrooms are large and have separate changing areas. The hotel's open-air restaurant specializes in seafood and is very reasonable, with entree prices ranging from $3 to $15.

Villas Río Mar. (Apdo. 1350-2050, San José) Dominical, Pérez Zeledón. ☎ **506/787-0052** or 506/787-0053. Fax 506/787-0054. E-mail: riomar@sol.racsa.co.cr. 40 units. Dec 15–Apr 15, $80 double, Apr 16–Dec 14, $57 double. AE, MC, V.

This is the closest thing to a resort in this neck of the woods. The bamboo-accented rooms are in 20 separate thatch-roofed duplex bungalows. While the rooms themselves seem a bit overwhelmed by queen-size beds, each has a spacious and comfortable porch with several sitting chairs, a small couch, coffee table, wet bar, and minifridge. At night, you can drop the tulle drapes that enclose each patio for some privacy and mosquito protection. There's a large kidney-shaped pool with a small gym and Jacuzzi, as well as tennis and basketball courts. The grounds are beautifully planted with flowering plants, and the bird watching is excellent. Meals are served in the large open-air rancho, with an emphasis on fresh seafood. A wide range of tours are offered, and mountain bikes are available for rent, as are inner tubes for floating down the Río Barú. The hotel is located up a dirt road a few hundred yards up the Río Barú, just on the right as you enter Dominical.

INEXPENSIVE

In addition to the places listed here, if you continue south another 10 miles (16km) you'll find a campground at Playa Ballena and a couple of basic cabinas in Bahia and Uvita. The best of these is **Cabinas El Cocotico** (no phone, $20 double), owned and operated by Jorge Díaz, a local legend and enjoyable raconteur who also arranges trips to a nearby waterfall. You'll see a sign for Cabinas El Cocotico on your left as you reach Uvita, traveling south from Dominical. Turn here; the hotel is 500 meters up the dirt road.

✪ **Albergue Willdale.** Dominical (c/o Selva Mar, Apdo. 215-8000, San Isidro de El General). ☎ **506/787-0023.** 7 units. $25 double, $30 triple. AE, MC, V.

The Albergue Willdale is located directly across from the soccer field and is by far the friendliest place in Dominical. Directly behind the lodge is the river, where you can go swimming, fishing, or paddling around. The owners Richard and Ani Dale are from Virginia, and they'll gladly fill you in on all there is to do in the area. The rooms are large and have big windows and patios, although the bathrooms are a bit small. I prefer the two rooms in the wooden building, although these are closer to the road. There are reading lights, fans, hot water, and attractive Mexican bedspreads. If you're interested in staying for a while, the Dales also rent two very comfortable houses (with their own swimming pools) up in the hills for $120 a night or $900 per week. There are kayaks and inner tubes available for playing on the river.

Cabinas Nayarit. 200 meters west of Rancho Coco, Dominical. ☎ and fax **506/787-0033.** 18 units. $28–$33 double or triple; rates lower in the off-season. V.

Wedged between the mouth of the Río Barú and the beach, there are several sandy lanes lined with simple houses and some cabinas, which cater primarily to surfers. Of these, Cabinas Nayarit is one of the best. There are several styles of rooms located in a cluster of buildings here, including older rooms with fans, older rooms with air-conditioning, and newer rooms with air-conditioning, skylights, carved wooden headboards, and louvered windows. I recommend the second-floor rooms with ocean views but no air-conditioning. Oddly, despite their size differences and comfort levels, all of them come with one double and one single bed. Definitely take a look at a few of them first if you can, before choosing. There's a small restaurant here serving moderately priced Tico fare.

✪ **Cabinas San Clemente.** Apdo. 703-8000, Dominical, Pérez Zeledón. ☎ **506/787-0026.** Fax 506/787-0055. 20 units (16 with bathroom). $10 double with shared bathroom, $15–$50 double with private bathroom. AE, MC, V.

In addition to running the town's most popular restaurant and serving as the social hub for the surfers, beach bums, and expatriates passing through, this place offers a variety of accommodations to fit most budgets. The cheapest rooms are all located above the restaurant, which is on the main road in the center of town. These are very basic budget affairs, with wood walls and floors, shared bathrooms, and floor or ceiling fans. A couple of kilometers away, at the beach, San Clemente has much nicer rooms in two separate buildings. Some of the newer, second-floor rooms have wood floors and wraparound verandas and are a real steal in this price range. The grounds here are shady, and there are plenty of hammocks. When I last visited they were putting the final touches on the Atardecer Restaurant here at the beach. If you plan an extended stay, ask about one of the houses the San Clemente also rents out. San Clemente also has a surf shop and board rentals, and the owner makes, bottles, and sells a very serious hot sauce.

DINING

The social center of Dominical is definitely the **San Clemente Bar and Grill**, a gringo/surfer hangout and sports bar specializing in massive breakfasts, nightly dinner specials (usually seafood), and a regular menu of hefty sandwiches and tasty Mexican-American food. One interesting (and sobering) thing here is the ceiling full of broken surfboards. If you break a board out on the waves, bring it in, and they'll hang it and even buy you a bucket of beer. Next to the Hotel Río Lindo you'll find the **Restaurant Maui**, which is a good place for fresh seafood. If you head a little bit south of town you can check out the restaurants at either Roca Verde or Punta Dominical. All of the above restaurants are moderately priced, with main courses running between $5 and $15.

Right in town, in front of the soccer field, there's the **Soda Laura** (no phone), which serves basic Tico meals and has a nice view of the river mouth. For light meals with a gringo touch, check out the neighboring **Deli Del Rio**. A little farther on down the main road is the **Soda Nanyoa** (no phone). Dishes at these places range in price from $1.75 to $8.

DOMINICAL AFTER DARK

Don't come to Dominical expecting a raging nightlife. Most folks hang out either at the **San Clemente Bar and Grill** or **Thrusters**, which is located halfway between the soccer field and the beach. Both are surfer bars with pool tables and dartboards. Occasionally there are roving discos that set up shop at one bar or another on weekends. If so, you'll hear about it—and hear it.

EN ROUTE SOUTH

The beaches south of Dominical are some of the nicest and most unexplored in Costa Rica. Basic cabinas and hotels are starting to pop up all along this route. This is a great area to roam in a rental car. The southern highway here (Costanera Sur) is still not paved, but it is relatively well graded and maintained. One good itinerary is to make a loop from San Isidro to Dominical, down the Costanera Sur, hitting several deserted beaches and then returning along the Interamerican Highway.

Among the beaches you'll find down here are **Playa Ballena**, **Playa Piñuelas**, **Playa Ventanas**, and **Playa Tortuga**. There's a bit of development in the area around Playa Tortuga and Ojochal. Most of the owners of the lodges down here are either Canadian or European—so you can expect to find well-maintained accommodations at very reasonable prices.

A REMOTE NATURE LODGE

Hotel Villas Gaia. Playa Tortuga (P.O. Box 11516-1000, San José). ☎ and fax **506/256-9996.** E-mail: hvgaia@sol.racsa.co.cr. 12 units. $60 double. MC, V.

Located just off the Costanera Sur just before the town of Ojochal, this small hotel has the nicest accommodations down in this neck of the woods. All the rooms are actually separate wood bungalows. Each has one single and one double bed, private bathroom, ceiling fan, and a small veranda with a jungle view. The swimming pool here was especially designed for scuba instruction, and Villa Gaia hopes to lure divers with its close proximity to Isla del Caño. The pool (and a poolside bar) is up on a high hill with a good view over mangrove forests out to the sea. There's a large open-air dining room down by the parking lot, which is too close to the highway for my taste. A wide range of tours are available, including Isla del Caño, Corcovado National Park, and Wilson Botanical Gardens.

5 San Isidro de El General: A Base for Exploring Chirripó National Park

75 miles (120km) SE of San José; 76 miles (123km) NW of Palmar Norte; 18 miles (29km) NE of Dominical

San Isidro de El General is the largest town in this region and is located just off the Interamerican Highway in the foothills of the Talamanca Mountains. Although there isn't much to do right in town, this is the jumping-off point for trips to Chirripó National Park. This is also the principal transfer point if you're coming from or going to Dominical, and most buses traveling the Interamerican Highway stop here.

ESSENTIALS

FESTIVAL If you're visiting this area in February, you should head out to nearby Rey Curré village for the **Fiesta of the Diablitos,** where costumed Boruca Indians perform dances representative of the Spanish conquest of Central America. There are fireworks and an Indian handcraft market. The date varies, so it's best to call the Costa Rica Tourist Board (☎**800/327-7033**) for more information.

GETTING THERE & DEPARTING **By Bus** Express buses (**Empresa Musoc ☎ 506/771-0414** or 506/222-2422) leave San José daily at 5:30, 7:30, 10:30, and 11:30am and 1:30, 2:30, 4:30 and 5pm from Calle 16 between Avenidas 1 and 3. Trips take 3 hours; fare is $3.

Buses to or from Golfito and Puerto Jiménez will also drop you off in San Isidro.

There are also buses from Quepos to San Isidro daily at 5:30am and 1:30pm. Trip duration is 3½ hours; fare is $3.50.

Buses depart San Isidro for San José daily every hour between 5:30am and 5pm. Buses to Dominical (onward to Quepos) leave daily at 7am and 1:30pm. Buses to Dominical and Uvita leave daily at 8am and 4pm. Buses to Golfito pass through San Isidro at around 10am, 2pm, and 6pm. Buses to Puerto Jiménez leave daily at 9am and 3pm.

By Car It's a long and winding road from San José to San Isidro; this section of the Interamerican Highway is one of the most difficult sections of road in the country. Not only are there the usual car-eating potholes and periodic landslides, but you must also contend with driving over the 11,000-foot-high Cerro de la Muerte (Mountain of Death). This aptly named mountain pass is legendary for its dense afternoon fogs, blinding torrential downpours, steep drop-offs, constant switchbacks, and unexpectedly breathtaking views. In other words, *drive with extreme care,* and bring a sweater or two—it's cold up at the top. It'll take you about 3 hours to get to San Isidro.

ORIENTATION Downtown San Isidro is just off the Interamerican Highway. There's a large church that fronts the central park. The main bus station is 2 blocks west of the north end of the central park.

OUTDOOR AND INTELLECTUAL PURSUITS

If you're spending any time in San Isidro and you want to undertake any adventures, contact **Brunca Tours** (☎ and fax **506/771-2150**). Brunca Tours's main operation is white-water rafting on the Río General, which has class III and IV sections. Rafting trips run around $50–$65 per person. Brunca Tours can also arrange a wide range of adventure and less-adventurous tours around the region.

If your pursuits are more cerebral, you can study Spanish at the **Spanish Language and Environmental Protection Center** (☎ **506/771-4582**; fax 506/771-8841). The Center has week-long and multiweek courses that combine intensive language classes with lectures and outings.

LAS QUEBRADAS BIOLOGICAL CENTER: A NEARBY COMMUNITY PRESERVATION PROJECT

Located just 4½ miles (7km) from San Isidro, **Las Quebradas Biological Center** (☎ and fax **506/771-4131**) is a community-run private reserve with 1¾ miles (2.7km) of trails through primary rain forest. Camping is permitted. There is an information center here and small souvenir store. From San Isidro, you can take a local bus to Quebradas, but you'll have to walk the last mile to the entrance. Alternatively, you can take a taxi for around $10. If you're driving, take the road to Morazán and Quebradas.

EXPLORING CHIRRIPÓ NATIONAL PARK

At 12,412 feet in elevation, Mount Chirripó is the tallest mountain in Costa Rica. If you're headed up this way, come prepared for chilly weather.

Actually, come prepared for all sorts of weather: Because of the great elevations, temperatures frequently dip below freezing, especially at night. However, during the day, temperatures can soar—remember, you're still only 9° from the equator. The elevation and radical temperatures have produced an environment here that's very different from the Costa Rican norm. Above 10,000 feet, only stunted trees and shrubs can survive in regions known as páramos. If you're driving the Interamerican Highway between San Isidro and San José, you'll pass through a páramo on the Cerro de la Muerte.

Hiking up to the top of Mt. Chirripó is one of Costa Rica's great adventures. On a clear day (usually in the morning), you can see both the Pacific Ocean and the Caribbean Sea from the summit. You can do this trip fairly easily on your own if you've brought gear and are an experienced backpacker. While it's possible to hike from the park entrance to the summit and back down in 2 days, it's best to allow 3 to 4 days for the trip, to give yourself time to enjoy your hike fully and spend some time on top, since that's where the glacier lakes and páramo are. For much of the way you'll be hiking through cloud forests that are home to abundant tropical fauna, including the spectacular quetzal, Costa Rica's most beautiful bird. These cloud forests are cold and damp, so come prepared for rain and fog.

There are several routes to the top of Mount Chirripó. The most popular, by far, leaves from San Gerardo de Rivas. However, it's also possible to start your hike from the nearby towns of Herradura and Canaan. All these places are within a mile or so of each other, reached by the same major road out of San Isidro. San Gerardo is the most popular because it's the easiest route to the top and has the greatest collections of small hotels and lodges. Information on all of these routes are available at the National Parks office in San Gerardo de Rivas.

Once you're at the summit lodge, there are a number of hiking options. The most popular is to the actual summit (the lodge itself is a bit below), which is about a 1½-hour hike passing through the Valle de los Conejos (Rabbit Valley) and the Lago San Juan. There are a number of other hikes and trails leading off from the summit, including trails to neighboring peaks. These hikes should be undertaken only after carefully exploring an accurate map and talking to park rangers and other hikers.

Finally, if you're tired and sore from so much hiking, be sure to check out the small natural hot springs located a short hike off the road between San Gerardo de Rivas and Herradura. The entrance to the springs is about half a mile beyond San Gerardo de Rivas. From here you'll have to hike about 10 minutes and pay a $1 entrance fee before getting in to soak.

ENTRY POINT, FEES & REGULATIONS Although it's not that difficult to get to Chirripó National Park from nearby San Isidro, it's still rather remote. And to see it fully, you have to be prepared to hike. To get to the trailhead, you have three choices: car, taxi, or bus. If you choose to drive, take the road out of San Isidro, heading north toward San Gerardo de Rivas, which is some 12½ miles (20km) down the road. Otherwise, you can catch a bus in San Isidro that will take you directly to the trailhead in San Gerardo de Rivas. Buses leave daily at 5am from the western side of the central park in San Isidro. It costs 85¢ one way and takes 1½ hours. Another bus departs at 1pm from a bus station 200 meters south of the park. Buses return to San Isidro daily at 7am and 4pm. A taxi from town should cost around $15 to $20. Because the hike to the summit of Mt. Chirripó can take between 6 and 12 hours, depending on your physical condition, I recommend taking the earlier bus so you can start hiking when the day is still young, or arriving the day before and spending the night in San Gerardo de Rivas (there are a number of inexpensive cabinas there), before setting out early the following morning.

Park admission is $6 per day. If you plan to stay at the lodge near the summit, you must make reservations in advance, since accommodations there are limited (see "Staying at the Summit Lodge," below). Note that camping is not allowed in the park. Finally, it's possible to have your gear carried up to the summit by horseback during the dry season. A number of guides work outside the park entrance in San Gerardo de Rivas. They charge between $15 and $20 per pack, depending on size and weight. In the rainy season, the same guides work, but they take packs up by themselves, not by horseback.

STAYING AT THE SUMMIT LODGE Reservations for lodging on the summit of Mt. Chirripó must be made with the National Parks office in San Gerardo de

Rivas (☎ and fax **506/771-3155** or 506/771-3297). In 1998, the old buildings were torn down and two new ones were erected. Helicopters and lots of pack horses were used in the construction. This is an increasingly popular destination, and you must reserve well in advance during the dry season. The new lodge still holds only 60 people. There's no food or bedding at the lodge, so be sure to bring your own. There are bunk beds, bathrooms, and a kitchen area, however, and there are even plans for the park service to run a little soda up here, so check before you come. Although I was told the new lodge will have good drinking water, I still recommend you pack your own. It costs $2.50 per person per night to stay here, in addition to the $6 park entrance fee.

WARNING It can be dangerous for more inexperienced or out-of-shape hikers to climb Chirripó, especially by themselves. It's not very technical climbing, but it is a long, arduous hike. Such folks should just take day hikes out of San Isidro and/or San Gerardo de Rivas, and ask at their hotel about guides.

ACCOMMODATIONS & DINING

The following section lists only hotels because there are no notable restaurants in San Isidro. The town has its fair share of local joints, but most visitors are content at their hotel restaurant.

Hotel Chirripó. South side of church, San Isidro de El General. ☎ **506/771-0529.** 41 units (24 with bathroom). $8 double without bathroom, $13 double with bathroom, $20 triple with bathroom. No credit cards.

This budget hotel is fine in a pinch, if you need to spend the night in San Isidro. It's located on the central square within a couple of blocks of all the town's bus stations. Rooms vary considerably, so ask to see some first. Some have windows (and street noise), and some have no windows or street noise. Stay away from the rooms in front, since these are the noisiest. There's a large, popular restaurant at the front of the lobby.

Hotel del Sur. San Isidro de El General. ☎ **506/771-3033.** Fax 506/771-0527. 50 units, 10 bungalows. TV TEL. $30–$50 double. MC, V.

This midsize hotel is located about 3¾ miles (6km) south of San Isidro right on the Interamerican Highway. The hotel has far better facilities and a wider range of services than anything within several hours, but everything here has seen better days. Rooms are generally large. The nicer (and more expensive) rooms have air-conditioning, loads of space, plenty of light, and tile floors; the cheaper rooms have worn carpeting and feel cramped and dingy. The bungalows have basic kitchenettes. There's a large pool here, as well as a basketball court, tennis court, playground equipment, and Ping-Pong table. There's also a tour desk and a host of activities available. The restaurant specializes in steaks and is popular with locals, tour groups, and folks making the longer drive south, or back to San José.

Hotel Iguazu. San Isidro de El General. ☎ **506/771-2571.** 21 units (16 with bathroom). TV. $20 double. No credit cards.

This is a good, clean, safe choice in San Isidro. The rooms are basic and come in different sizes, with a different arrangement of beds, but all have small televisions. The rooms are definitely in better shape than those at the Hotel Chirripó. The hotel is a half block away from the Musoc bus station. Some may find this convenient, others might find it too noisy. The hotel is actually on the second and third floor of the Super Lido department store.

ACCOMMDOATIONS CLOSER TO THE TRAILHEAD

If you're climbing Mount Chirripó, you'll want to spend the night as close to the trailhead as possible. As mentioned above, there are several basic cabinas right in San Gerardo de Rivas that charge between $5 and $10 per person. If you're looking for a little more comfort, check out the following.

Rio Chirripó Pacifico Mountain Lodge. San Gerardo de Rivas, Pérez Zeledón. ☎ **506/771-6096.** Fax 506/771-2003. 8 units. $45 double. Rate includes breakfast. AE, MC, V.

This new lodge is located on a beautiful bend in the Río Chirripó, just 500 meters before the National Park's office. The rooms are in two side-by-side, two-story buildings. All have one single and one double bed, painted cement floors, and a small veranda, with some interesting natural wood latticework on the railings. I prefer the rooms on the second floor, as they have a slightly better view. There's a large open-air rancho that serves as the restaurant here. If you have time before or after your ascent of the big mountain, you can climb on some impressive river-polished rocks or swim in a couple of natural pools.

✪ **Tilari Mountain Lodge.** Rivas, San Isidro (Apdo. 517-8000), Pérez Zeledón. ☎ and fax **506/771-0341.** 8 units. $42 double, $52 triple. Rates include full breakfast. AE, MC, V.

This small mountain getaway, though nothing fancy, is one of the nicer options right around San Isidro and also makes a good base for exploring or climbing Mount Chirripó. The eight rooms are in two separate concrete-block buildings. Most come with one double and one single bed, although one room can handle a family of four in one double and two single beds. All of the rooms come with a small fridge and a small patio. I prefer the four rooms that face the Talamanca mountains, although the morning sun beats down fiercely on these. There are plenty of fruit trees around and good bird watching right on the grounds. Hearty meals are served in the lodge's main dining room. Down by the Río General there's a small pool and separate children's pool. Horseback riding is also available, and the hotel maintains some forest trails. Talari is located 5 miles (8km) outside of San Isidro and will pick you up in town for free if you give them advance notice.

EN ROUTE TO SAN JOSÉ: TWO PLACES TO SEE QUETZALS IN THE WILD

Between San Isidro de El General and San José, the Interamerican Highway climbs to its highest point in Costa Rica and crosses over the Cerro de la Muerte. This area has recently acquired a newfound importance as one of the best places in Costa Rica to see quetzals in the wild. March, April, and May are nesting season for these birds, and this is usually the best time to see them, but in this area it's often possible to see them year-round. On one 2-hour hike here, without a guide, our small group spotted eight of these amazing birds.

All of the lodges listed below, along with some new ones, are located along a 12½-mile (20km) stretch of the Interamerican Highway, between the cities of Cartago and San Isidro. You'll probably start seeing their billboards and quetzal-painted placards long before you see any birds.

In addition to the lodges listed below, if you're looking for a rustic (although not cheap) escape on a private reserve, check in with the folks at **Genesis II Cloud-forest Preserve** (☎ **506/381-0739**; e-mail: genesis@yellowweb.co.cr). This place caters to biologists, students, and folks truly interested in conservation projects. You'll see signs for this place along the Interamerican Highway. There are only five rooms, so reservations (and a very heavy-duty four-wheel-drive vehicle) are highly recommended.

Albergue de Montaña Tapantí. Kilometer 62 Carretera Interamericana Sur, Macho Gaff, Cartago (Apdo. 46d1-1200, Pavas). ☎ and fax **506/232-0436.** 10 units. $55 double, $65 triple, $75 quad. Rates include breakfast. MC, V.

If you want easy access to both the highway and the cloud forest, this cross between a mountain lodge and roadside motel might be your best bet. The buildings at Tapantí are built to resemble Swiss chalets, and you may come to believe you're in Switzerland when you feel how cold it gets here at night: The lodge is at 10,000 feet and frost is not uncommon, but there's a fireplace in the lounge to warm your bones. Most of the guest rooms are actually suites with separate bedrooms and living rooms; although the furnishings here are both sparse and dated. Luckily, the rooms do have heaters. The nicest rooms here have private balconies that provide nice views of the neighboring forests. The lodge's dining room serves such Swiss specialties as beef fondue and raclette, as well as other continental dishes. Guided hikes, horseback rides, trout fishing, and bird-watching walks are all available through the lodge.

Albergue Mirador de Quetzales. Kilometer 70 Carretera Interamericana Sur, Cartago. ☎ **506/534-4415** or 506/381-8456. 11 units (4 with bathroom). $50–$60 double. Rates include breakfast, dinner, and a 2-hour tour. No credit cards.

This family-run lodge is also known as Finca Eddie Serrano. The rooms in the main lodge are quite basic, with wood floors, bunk beds, and shared bathrooms. Four newer A-frames provide a bit more comfort and a private bath. Meals are served family style in the main lodge. But quetzals, not comfort, are the main draw here, and if you come between December and May, you should have no trouble spotting plenty of them. There are good hiking trails through the cloud forest here, and the Serrano family are genial hosts and good guides. The lodge is located about 700 meters down a dirt road from the main highway.

✪ **Savegre Mountain Lodge.** Kilometer 80 Carretera Interamericana Sur, San Gerardo de Dota (Apdo. 1636, Cartago). ☎ and fax **506/771-1732.** www.ecotourism.co.cr. E-mail: ciprotur@sol.racsa.co.cr. 20 cabins. $53 per person. Rates include 3 meals daily. AE, MC, V.

This working apple and pear farm, which also has more than 600 acres of primary forest, has acquired a reputation as one of the best places in the country to see quetzals. The rustic farm has long been popular as a weekend vacation and picnicking spot for Ticos, but now people from all over the world are searching it out. The rooms here are quite basic, but if you're serious about bird watching, this shouldn't matter. In addition to the quetzals, some 150 other species have been spotted. Hearty Tico meals are served here, and if you want to try your hand at trout fishing, you might luck into a fish dinner. You'll find this lodge 5½ miles (9km) down a dirt road off the Interamerican Highway. This road is steep and often muddy, and four-wheel drive is recommended. The signs pointing to the lodge actually read "Savegre Lodge/Cabinas Chacón."

9 The Southern Zone

The southern zone is an area of rugged beauty, vast expanses of virgin lowland rain forest, and few cities or settlements. Lushly forested mountains tumble into the sea, streams still run clear and clean, scarlet macaws squawk raucously in the treetops, and dolphins frolic in the Golfo Dulce.

But this beauty doesn't come easy; you must have plenty of time (or plenty of money, preferably both) and a desire for a bit of adventure. Because it is so far from San José and there are so few roads, most of the really fascinating spots can be reached only by small plane or boat, although hiking and four-wheeling will get you into some memorable surroundings as well.

In many ways this is Costa Rica's final frontier, and the cities of Golfito and Puerto Jimenez are nearly as wild as the jungles that surround them.

Tourism is still underdeveloped in the southern zone. It is, after all, an 8-hour drive from San José to Golfito or Puerto Jimenez. Moreover, the heat and humidity are more than many people can stand. It's best to put some forethought into planning a vacation down here, and it is usually wise to book your rooms and transportation in advance.

1 Drake Bay

90 miles (145km) S of San José; 20 miles (32km) SW of Palmar

Located on the northern end of the Osa Peninsula, Drake Bay is what adventure travel is all about. Little more than a small collection of lodges catering to naturalists, anglers, scuba divers, and assorted vacationers, Drake Bay is a good place to get away from it all. Until 1997, there was no road into Drake Bay, no airstrip in town. Currently, both exist, but how reliable they are is another question—the road is often closed by heavy rains and mudslides, and the airstrip is serviced only by charter flights, and these are restricted by tide conditions. Because of the bay's remoteness, there has been little development here. Accommodations vary from tents on wooden platforms and cement-walled cabinas to very comfortable lodges that border on the luxurious. There are few conventional phones and no power lines in Drake Bay, so most lodges make do with radio and cellular phones and gas-powered electrical generators.

The bay is named after Sir Francis Drake, who is believed to have anchored here in 1579. Emptying into the bay is the tiny **Río Agujitas**, which acts as a protected harbor for small boats and is a great place to do a bit of canoeing or swimming. It's here that many of the local lodges dock their boats. Stretching south from Drake Bay are miles and miles of deserted beaches. Adventurous explorers will find tide pools, spring-fed rivers, waterfalls, forest trails, and some of the best bird watching in all of Costa Rica. If a paradise such as this appeals to you, Drake Bay makes a good base for exploring the peninsula.

South of Drake Bay lie the wilds of the **Osa Peninsula** and **Corcovado National Park**. This is one of Costa Rica's most beautiful regions, yet it's also one of its least accessible. Corcovado National Park covers about half of the peninsula and contains the largest single expanse of virgin lowland rain forest in Central America. For this reason, Corcovado is well-known among naturalists and researchers studying rain-forest ecology, and if you come here you'll learn firsthand why they call them rain forests. It does indeed rain here. Lots. In fact, some parts of the peninsula receive more than 250 inches per year. In addition to producing lush forests, this massive amount of rain produces more than a few disgruntled visitors.

ESSENTIALS

Because Drake Bay is so remote, it's highly recommended that you have a room reservation and transportation arrangements (usually arranged with your hotel) before you arrive. The lodges listed here are scattered along several kilometers of coastline, and it is not easy to go from one to another looking for a room.

Although a flashlight and rain gear are always useful to have on hand in Costa Rica, they're absolutely essential in Drake Bay.

GETTING THERE Depending on your temperament, getting to Drake Bay may be half the fun, or it may be torture. Despite the new road into—and airstrip in—Drake Bay, the traditional route is still the most popular. Most guests still fly first (or take a bus) to **Palmar Sur**. From here, it's a 15-minute bus or taxi ride over dirt roads to the small town of Sierpe. This bumpy ride takes you through several banana plantations and quickly past some important archaeological sites. In Sierpe you will board a small boat for a 25-mile (40km) ride to Drake Bay. The first half of this trip snakes through a maze of mangrove canals and rivers, before heading out to sea for the final leg to the bay. Be warned: Entering and exiting the Sierpe River mouth is often treacherous, and I've had several very white-knuckle moments here.

By Plane The airstrip in Drake Bay itself is currently operating only by charter and is dependent on the tides. Most lodges include transportation in their packages, so check with them about where you will be flying in to. The closest regularly serviced airport to Drake Bay is in **Palmar Sur**, a taxi and boat ride away. **Sansa** (☎ **506/233-0397**, 506/233-3258, or 506/233-5330) flies to Palmar Sur daily at 9:30am from San José's Juan Santamaría International Airport. The flight takes 45 minutes; fare is $55 each way. Note that Sansa frequently alters its schedule and routing; this flight may stop in Quepos on the way down and thus take slightly longer.

Travelair (☎ **506/220-3054** or 506/232-7883) has flights to Palmar Sur that depart daily at 8:45am from Tobías Bolaños International Airport in Pavas. This flight stops at Quepos en route. Flight duration is 55 minutes; fare is $78 one way, $127 round-trip.

It's also possible to charter a seaplane that will fly you directly to the bay. **Alas Anfibias de Costa Rica** (☎ **506/232-9567**) charters a four-passenger seaplane for $750 and an eight-passenger plane for $1,500 (each way).

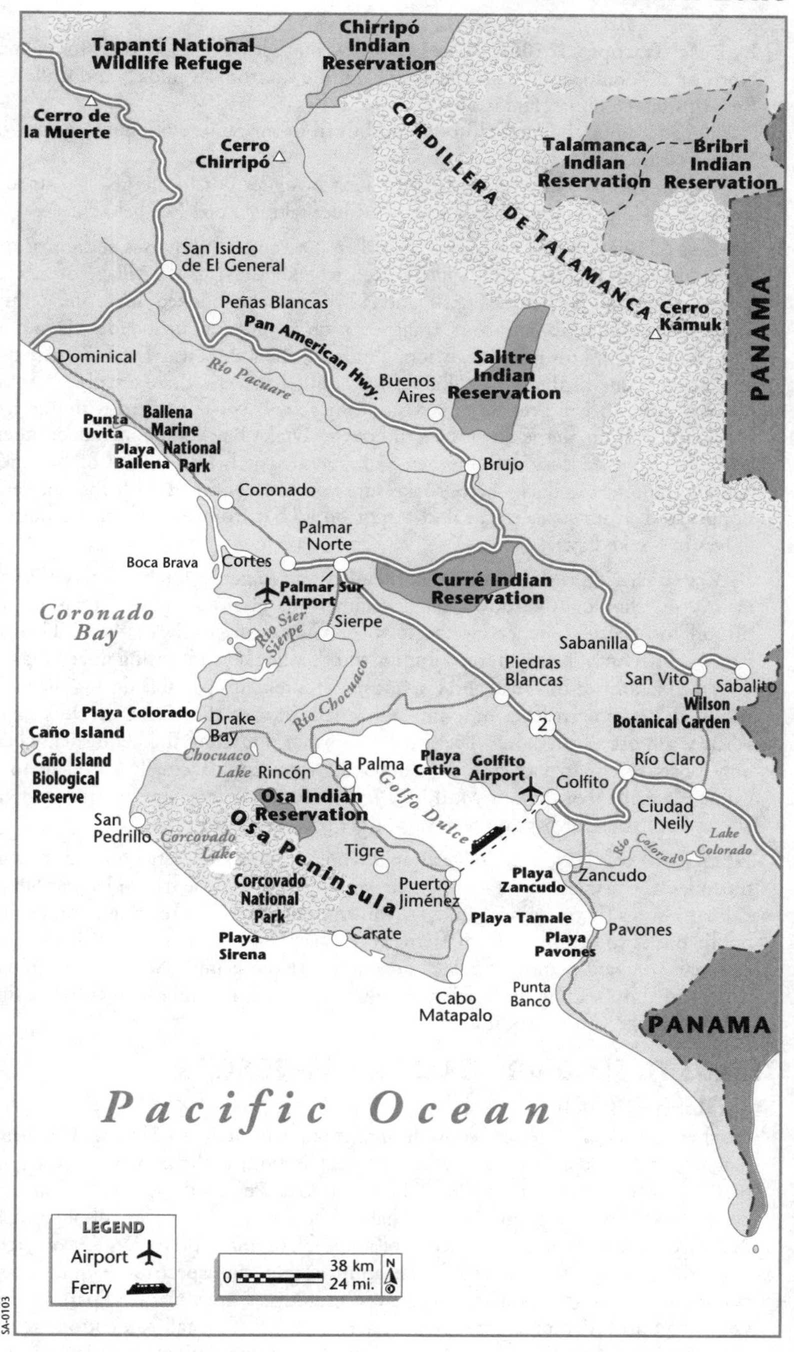
Tapantí National Wildlife Refuge
Chirripó Indian Reservation
Cerro de la Muerte
Cerro Chirripó
CORDILLERA DE TALAMANCA
Talamanca Indian Reservation
Bribri Indian Reservation
San Isidro de El General
Peñas Blancas
Pan American Hwy.
Cerro Kámuk
PANAMA
Dominical
Río Pacuare
Buenos Aires
Salitre Indian Reservation
Punta Uvita
Ballena Marine National Park
Playa Ballena
Brujo
Coronado
Palmar Norte
Boca Brava
Cortes
Palmar Sur Airport
Curré Indian Reservation
Coronado Bay
Sierpe
Río Sierpe
Sabanilla
Piedras Blancas
San Vito
Sabalito
Río Chocuaco
2
Wilson Botanical Garden
Playa Colorado
Caño Island
Drake Bay
Caño Island Biological Reserve
Chocuaco Lake
Rincón
La Palma
Playa Cativa
Golfito Airport
Río Claro
Golfito
Osa Indian Reservation
Golfo Dulce
Ciudad Neily
San Pedrillo
Corcovado Lake
Osa Peninsula
Lake Colorado
Río Colorado
Tigre
Playa Zancudo
Zancudo
Corcovado National Park
Puerto Jiménez
Playa Tamale
Carate
Pavones
Playa Sirena
Playa Pavones
Punta Banco
Cabo Matapalo
PANAMA
Pacific Ocean
LEGEND
Airport
Ferry
0
38 km
24 mi.
N
SA-0103

By Bus **Tracopa** (☎**506/221-4214**) express buses leave San José daily for Palmar Norte at 5, 7, 8:30, and 10am and 1, 2:30, and 6pm from Avenida 5 and Calle 14. Bus trips take 6 hours; fare is $4.

You can also catch any Golfito-bound bus from this same station and get off in Palmar Norte.

Once in Palmar Norte, ask when the next bus goes out to Sierpe. If it doesn't leave for a while (they aren't frequent), consider taking a taxi (see below).

By Taxi & Boat Once you arrive at either the Palmar Norte bus station or the Palmar Sur airstrip, you'll most likely need to take a taxi to the village of Sierpe. The fare should be between $10 and $15. If you're booked into one of the main lodges, chances are your transportation is already included—via a guy named Rainer and his minibus, whom almost all the lodges use. Even if you're not booked into one of the lodges, Rainer (or another driver—there are always some hanging around) will probably have room for you. If you're booked with a lodge, the boat fare from Sierpe downriver and out to Drake Bay will be included; otherwise, the trip will cost you another $15. Again, you'll find plenty of boatmen hanging around the docks here. Make sure you feel confident with the boat and skipper and, if possible, try to find a spot on a boat from one of the established lodges in Drake Bay.

By Car Driving is still not a recommended way to get to Drake Bay. But if you insist, you should drive down the Interamerican Highway, past Palmar to the turnoff for Puerto Jimenez (at the town of Chacarita; clearly marked). Then at Rincón, turn onto the rough road leading into Drake Bay. I'm getting mixed reports as to the viability of this road and I'm not sure if it remains passable during the rainy season. It certainly reaches only into the small heart of the village of Drake Bay, whereas almost all the hotels I've listed are farther out along the peninsula, where only boats reach. In fact, the only hotel that you could actually drive up to is Cabinas Cecilia. For the rest you'd have to find some place secure to leave your car and either haul your bags quite a way, or get picked up in a boat.

DEPARTING Have your lodge arrange a boat trip back to Sierpe for you. Be sure the lodge also arranges for a taxi to meet you in Sierpe for the trip to Palmar Sur or Palmar Norte. (If you're on a budget, you can ask around to see if a late-morning public bus is still running from Sierpe to Palmar Norte.) In the two Palmars, you can make onward plane and bus connections. At the Palmar Norte bus terminal, almost any bus heading north will take you to San José, and almost any bus heading south will take you to Golfito.

THINGS TO SEE & DO: BEACHES, RAIN FORESTS, WILDLIFE & HIKING

Beaches, forests, wildlife, and solitude are the main attractions of Drake Bay. While Corcovado National Park (covered in the next section) is the area's star attraction, there's plenty to soak up in Drake Bay. The **Osa Peninsula** is home to an unbelievable variety of plants and animals: more than 140 species of mammals, 267 species of birds, and 117 species of amphibians and reptiles. While you aren't likely to see a high percentage of these animals, you can expect to see quite a few, including several species of monkeys, coatimundis, scarlet macaws, parrots, and hummingbirds. The tallest tree in Costa Rica, a 230-foot-tall silk-cotton tree, is located within Corcovado, as is Costa Rica's largest population of scarlet macaws. Other park inhabitants include jaguars, tapirs, sloths, and crocodiles. If you're lucky, you might even see one of the region's osas, the giant anteaters.

Those Mysterious Stone Spheres

While Costa Rica lacks the great cities, giant temples, and bas-relief carvings of the Maya, Aztec, and Olmec civilizations of northern Mesoamerica, its pre-Columbian residents did leave a unique legacy that continues to cause archaeologists and anthropologists to scratch their heads and wonder. Over a period of several centuries, hundreds of painstakingly carved and carefully positioned granite spheres were left by the peoples who lived throughout the Diquis Delta, which flanks the Terraba River in southern Costa Rica. The spheres, which range from grapefruit-size to more than 7 feet in diameter, can weigh up to 15 tons, and many reach near spherical perfection.

Archaeologists believe that the spheres were created during two defined cultural periods. The first, called the Aguas Buenas period, dates from around A.D. 100 to 500. Few spheres survive from this time. The second phase, during which spheres were created in apparently greater numbers, is called the Chiriquí period and lasted from approximately A.D. 800 to 1500. The "balls" believed to have been carved during this time frame are widely dispersed along the entire length of the lower section of the Terraba River. To date, only one known quarry for the spheres has been discovered, in the mountains above the Diquis Delta, which points to a difficult and lengthy transportation process. Archaeologists believe the spheres were hand carved in a very time-consuming process, using stone tools, perhaps aided by some sort of firing process. However, an alternative theory holds that granite blocks were placed at the bases of powerful waterfalls, and the hydraulic beating of the water eventually turned and carved the rock into these near-perfect spheres. Finally, there are quite a few proponents of theories claiming that extraterrestrial intervention is the obvious explanation for the stone balls.

Most of the stone balls have been found at the archaeological remains of defined settlements and are associated with either central plazas or known burial sites. Their size and placement have been interpreted to have both social and celestial importance, although their exact significance remains a mystery. Unfortunately, many of the stone balls have been plundered and are currently used as lawn ornaments in the fancier neighborhoods of San José. Some have even been shipped out of the country. The Museo Nacional de Costa Rica (see chapter 5) has a nice collection, including one massive sphere in its center courtyard. With the city laid out behind you, this ball provides a never-fail photo op. You can also see the stone balls near the small airport in Palmar Sur and on Caño Island (which is located 12 miles (19km) off the Pacific coast near Drake Bay).

Around Drake Bay and within the national park there are many miles of trails through rain forests and swamps, down beaches, and around rock headlands. All of the lodges listed below offer guided excursions into the park. It's also possible to begin a hike around the peninsula from Drake Bay.

AN EXCURSION TO CAÑO ISLAND BIOLOGICAL RESERVE

One of the most popular excursions from Drake Bay is a trip out to **Caño Island** and the **Caño Island Biological Reserve** for a bit of exploring and snorkeling or scuba diving. The island is located about 12 miles (19km) offshore from Drake Bay and was once home to a pre-Columbian culture about which little is known. A trip to the island will include a visit to one of this culture's cemeteries, and you'll also be able to see some of the stone spheres that are commonly believed to have been carved by the people who once lived in this area. Few animals or birds live on the island, but the coral reefs just offshore teem with life and are the main reason most people come here. This is one of Costa Rica's prime scuba diving spots. Visibilty is often quite good here, and there's even easily accessible snorkeling from the beach.

Most of the lodges listed below offer trips to Caño Island. You can also do some sportfishing while you're in the area—almost any of the lodges can arrange a charter boat for you.

ACCOMMODATIONS & DINING

All but the least expensive lodges listed below are all-inclusive, but to simplify matters (so that rates can be judged on the same scale as others in this book) I've chosen to list nightly room rates; the price categories have been shifted to take this factor into account (a "very expensive" room is classified here as "expensive," and so on). Also, please note that these lodges do most of their business in package trips that include several nights' lodging, all meals, transportation, and tours. If you intend to do several tours while you're here, be sure to ask about these packages. They could constitute a significant savings for you.

VERY EXPENSIVE

✪ **Aguila De Osa Inn.** Apdo. 10486-1000, San José (mailing address in the U.S.: Isla Fantasma, Interlink no. 898, P.O. Box 025635, Miami, FL 33102). ☎ and fax **506/296-2190** or 506/232-7722. www.centralamerica.com/cr/hotel/aguila. E-mail: Aguilacr@sol.racsa.co.cr. 14 units. $220–$270 double, $330–$400 triple, $500 master suite. Rates include 3 meals daily. MC, V.

The most expensive lodge in Drake Bay, this is also the most comfortable. Situated high on a hill overlooking Drake Bay and the Pacific Ocean, the Aguila de Osa Inn offers large, attractively decorated rooms located a vigorous hike up a steep hillside. This could pose a problem for guests who have trouble walking. There's a bar built atop some rocks on the bank of the Río Agujitas and a dining room with a good view of the bay. Meals are simply prepared but tasty and filling, and the kitchen leaves a fresh thermos of coffee outside each room every morning. All the guest rooms have hardwood or tile floors, ceiling fans, large bathrooms, and excellent views. Excursions available through the lodge include hikes in Corcovado National Park ($65 per person), trips to Caño Island ($65 per person for snorkelers, $110 per person for scuba divers), horseback rides ($55 per person), and sportfishing ($450 to $850 for a full day's rental, depending on the size of the boat and the number of people in your party). Packages generally do not include air transportation. Round-trip boat transportation from Sierpe is $45 per person. Round-trip van transportation between Palmar Sur and Sierpe is $40 for a 4-passenger van and $60 for a 7-passenger van.

Dining: Meals are served in the open-air dining room. Since most folks are either fishing or on one of the organized tours, lunches are often picnic affairs on the boat, in Corcovado National Park, or on Caño Island. Dinners feature fresh fish, meat, and chicken, often prepared with a tropical or Caribbean flair.

Amenities: A fresh pot of coffee is left outside your door each morning; laundry service.

EXPENSIVE

Casa Corcovado Jungle Lodge. Apdo. 1482-1250, Escazú (mailing address the in U.S.: Interlink #253, P.O. Box 526770, Miami, FL 33152). ☎ **506/256-3181.** Fax 506/256-7409.

www.crica.com/hotels. E-mail: corcovado@sol.racsa.co.cr. 7 units. Packages available. $527 3 days/2 nights with one tour, and $605 4 days/3 nights with two tours, including round-trip transportation from San José, all meals, park fees, and taxes. MC, V.

This very isolated jungle lodge is the closest accommodation to Corcovado National Park on this end of the Osa Peninsula. The rooms are all private bungalows built on the jungle's edge. These are all spacious, with one or two double beds (each with mosquito netting) and a large tiled bathroom. Electricity and hot water are supplied by a combination solar and hydroelectric energy system. Excellent family style meals are served in the main lodge, although lunch is often taken down by the beach. All the standard tours, including fishing and diving, are available, and the lodge seems to cater to the more serious naturalist tourist. Access is strictly by small boat here, and sometimes the beach landing can be a bit rough, so it's recommended that guests be in decent physical shape. The beach here is great for swimming when the sea's not too rough. The lodge has a few hammocks set up in the shade where you can await delivery of one of the wonderful picnic lunches.

Amenities: There's a swimming pool, nature trails, and laundry service. They were planning a little gift shop and small conference center the last time I visited.

Drake Bay Wilderness Resort. Apdo. 98-8150, Palmar Norte, Osa. ☎ and fax **506/771-2436** or 506/284-4107; in San José ☎ **506/256-7394.** www.drakebay.com. E-mail: emichaud@drakebay.com. 4 tents (all with shared bathroom), 20 units. Tents $96 double, rooms, $136 double, $204 triple. Rates include 3 meals daily. Packages available. $534 per package, 4 days/3 nights (two tours), including round-trip transportation from San José, all meals, and lodging in a cabin. Tax not included. MC, V.

This is one of the most convenient and best-located lodges at Drake Bay. It backs onto the Río Agujitas and fronts onto the Pacific. The lodge offers a variety of accommodations of different ages and styles. Travelers who want to rough it a bit or economize can opt for a large tent with a double bed, small table and lamp, and nearby communal bathroom and shower. Those seeking more comfort should opt for one of the rooms. All of the rooms have ceiling fans, small verandas, good mattresses on the beds, and private bathrooms. The family style meals are filling, with an emphasis on fresh seafood and fresh fruits. Because it's on a rocky spit, there isn't a good swimming beach right here, but, depending on the tide, you can swim in a small tide pool formed by the rocks.

Amenities: The lodge provides free use of its canoes, free same-day laundry service, and fax service for guests. Tours offered by Drake Bay Wilderness Resort include hikes within the national park ($60 per person), trips to Caño Island ($60 per person for snorkelers, $95 per person for scuba divers), horseback-riding tours ($40 per person), and sportfishing charters ($250 per day for one to three persons). Mountain bikes are also available, as are sea kayaks. One of the new tours offered here is a trip inland (by mountain bike or horse) to a private farm the owners have. There are small butterfly- and iguana-breeding projects here, and you can even spend the night if you want.

✪ **La Paloma Lodge.** Apdo. 97-4005, San Antonio de Belen, Heredia. ☎ **506/239-2801,** or ☎ and fax 506/239-0954. www.lapalomalodge.com. E-mail: lapaloma@lapalomalodge.com. 10 units. Rooms, $170 double, cabins, $230 double, $345 triple. Rates include 3 meals daily. Packages available, including round-trip transportation from San José, all meals, indicated tours, and taxes. High season (Nov 16–May 15): $625 standard, $725 deluxe 4 days/3 nights (two tours); $715 standard; $850 deluxe 5 days/4 nights (two tours). Low season (May 1–Nov 15): $560 standard, $665 deluxe 4 days/3 nights (two tours); $635 standard, $770 deluxe, 5 days/4 nights (two tours). MC, V.

Situated on a steep hill overlooking the Pacific, with Caño Island in the distance, the individual bungalows at La Paloma offer expansive ocean views worth every huff and puff it takes to get up here. The main lodge building is a huge, thatched, open-air structure with a long veranda. In one corner is a sitting area that's a pleasant place to meet other lodge guests. All of the cabins are built on stilts, feature large verandas, and are set among lush foliage facing the Pacific Ocean. The three older cabins are my favorites simply for their spaciousness and seclusion. Four screen walls keep you in touch with nature and let the ocean breezes blow through. The newer cabins provide wonderful ocean views from their main sleeping lofts. The rooms, though much smaller than the cabins, are still attractive and have good views from their verandas (which, like the cabins, have hammocks).

Dining: Meals are generally fixed menu—everyone gets the same main dish, although accommodations are made for vegetarians or special needs with advance warning. Meals are generally a fish or chicken fillet, or pasta with a shrimp/tomato sauce, along with sides of steamed vegetables, rice, mashed potatoes, etc. There's always delicious fresh-baked bread here.

Amenities: The beach is down at the bottom of the hill (about a 10-minute hike away), and there's a new tiled pool with superb sunset views. The electricity is shut off each evening at 9:30pm, which might irritate some late-night bookworms, but if you're like me, you'll want to get up at dawn to watch the early-morning birds. Excursions available include hikes in the park ($65 per person), trips to Caño Island ($65 per person), horseback rides ($50 per person), scuba trips ($100 per person), and sportfishing charters ($450 for a full day's boat rental). There are also canoes, kayaks, and snorkeling equipment for rent.

MODERATE

Cabinas Jinetes de Osa. Drake Bay, Osa Peninsula (mailing address in the U.S.: P.O. Box 833, Conifer, CO 80433). ☎ **506/385-9541,** or 800/317-0333 in the U.S. and Canada. www.costaricadiving.com. E-mail: crventur@costaricadiving.com. 9 units (6 with shared bathroom). $80–$100 double. Rates include 3 meals daily. Dive packages available. MC, V (6% surcharge added).

This perennial budget option in the village of Drake Bay has been renovated recently. A new set of U.S. owners have put some effort into sprucing it up and turning Jinetes de Osa into a serious dive operation. Its wooden construction and location directly above the beach give it an edge over the other lodges in the village of Drake Bay. It is also the closest of the less-expensive places to the docks on the Río Agujitas, which is nice for those traveling independently or with heavy bags. Basic Tico-style meals are served in a small open-air dining room. More rooms are apparently in the works. A wide range of tours and activities are available, as are dive packages, weekly packages, and PADI certification courses.

NEARBY PLACES TO STAY & DINE

EXPENSIVE

Río Sierpe Lodge. Apdo. 85, Palmar Norte. ☎ **506/257-7010** or 506/284-5595. Fax 506/257-7012. 11 units. $130 double, $195 triple. Rates include 3 meals daily and transportation to and from Palmar. AE, MC, V (add 7% surcharge).

This lodge is located on the south bank of the Río Sierpe near the river mouth and is best known as a fishing lodge, with various fishing packages available. You won't be right on the beach if you stay here, but the lodge will ferry you to one of two beaches, and all the excursions that are offered in Drake Bay are available here at comparable prices. The lodge is surrounded by forests, and there are hiking trails on the property. Meals in the dining room feature international cuisine with an emphasis on fresh fruits, fish, and chicken. Naturalists, anglers, and scuba divers are all catered to here. Adventurous types can do a 2-day horseback trek that includes camping in the rain forest, and they also specialize in overnight trips into Panama.

2 Puerto Jiménez: Gateway to Corcovado National Park

21½ miles (35km) W of Golfito by water (56 miles by road); 53 miles (85km) S of Palmar Norte

Despite its small size and languid pace, Puerto Jiménez is a double boomtown, where rough jungle gold panners mix with wealthy ecotourists, budget backpackers, and a surprising number of celebrities seeking a small dose of anonymity and escape. Located on the southeastern tip of the Osa Peninsula, the town itself is just a couple of gravel streets, with the ubiquitous soccer field, a block of general stores, some inexpensive sodas, a butcher shop, and several bars. Scarlet macaws fly overhead, and mealy parrots provide wake-up calls.

On first glance, it's hard to imagine anything ever happening here, but looks are often deceiving. Signs in English on walls around town advertise a variety of tours, with most of the excursions going to nearby Corcovado National Park. The national park has its headquarters here, and this town makes an excellent base or embarkation point for exploring this vast wilderness. If the in-town accommodations are too budget-oriented, you will find several far more luxurious places farther south on the Osa Peninsula. However, not only the highbrow are making their way to this remote spot. You will also find a burgeoning surfer community out here. It's no secret any longer—**Cabo Matapalo** (the southern tip of the Osa Peninsula) is home to several very dependable right point breaks.

Finally, if you're worried the nightlife is going to be too sleepy for you, don't forget about all those gold miners lurking about. As the home base and resupply station for miners (most of them panning illegally) seeking to strike it rich in the jungles in and around the park, Puerto Jiménez's streets can actually get pretty rowdy at night, especially when panners cash in a find.

ESSENTIALS

GETTING THERE & DEPARTING **By Plane** **Sansa** (☎ **506/233-0397**, 506/233-3258, or 506/233-5330) has flights departing for Puerto Jiménez daily at 9:45am and 12:20pm on Tuesday, Thursday, Saturday, and Sunday, from San José's Juan Santamaría International Airport. The flight takes 55 minutes; cost is $55 each way.

Travelair (☎ **506/220-3054** or 506/232-7883) has flights to Puerto Jiménez departing at 8:50am daily. The flight takes 55 minutes; fare is $87 dollars one way, $146 round-trip.

Sansa flights depart Puerto Jimenéz daily at 10:45am and 1:25pm on Tuesday, Thursday, Saturday, and Sunday. The Travelair flight leaves for San José daily at 9:55am.

Note that due to the remoteness of this area and the unpredictable flux of traffic here, both Sansa and Travelair frequently improvise on scheduling. Sometimes this means an unscheduled stop in Quepos or Golfito either on the way down from or back to San José, which can add some time to your flight. Less frequently it may mean a change in departure time, so it is always best to confirm.

By Bus Express buses (☎ **506/257-4121**) leave San José daily at 6am and noon from Calle 12 between Avenidas 7 and 9. The trip takes 9 hours; fare is $7.50.

Buses depart Puerto Jiménez for San José daily at 5 and 11am.

By Boat There is daily passenger launch service from Golfito to Puerto Jiménez at 11am. The boat leaves from the municipal dock. Trip duration is 1½ hours; fare is $4. It's also possible to charter a water taxi in Golfito for the trip across to Puerto Jiménez. You'll have to pay between $30 and $55 for an entire launch, some of which can carry up to 12 people. One scheduled launch a day departs Puerto Jiménez for Golfito from the public dock at 6am; fare is $4.

By Car Take the Interamerican Highway east out of San José (through San Pedro and Cartago) and continue south on this road. In about 3 hours, you'll pass through San Isidro de El General. In another 3 hours or so, take the turnoff for La Palma and Puerto Jiménez. This road is paved at first, but at Rincón it turns to gravel. The last 22 miles (35km) are slow and rough, and, if it's the rainy season (mid-April through November), it'll be too muddy for anything but a four-wheel-drive vehicle.

ORIENTATION Puerto Jiménez is a dirt-laned town on the southern coast of the Osa Peninsula. The public dock is over a bridge past the north end of the soccer field; the bus stop is 2 blocks east of the center of town. Puerto Jiménez is the most popular base for exploring Corcovado National Park.

EXPLORING CORCOVADO NATIONAL PARK

Although a few gringos have, over the years, come to Puerto Jiménez to try their luck at gold panning, the primary reason for coming here these days is to visit Corcovado National Park. Within a couple of hours of the town (by four-wheel-drive vehicle) there are several entrances to the park; however, there are no roads in the park, so once you reach any of the entrances, you'll have to start hiking. Exploring Corcovado National Park is not something to be undertaken lightly, but neither is it the expedition that some people make it out to be. The biggest problems of overnight backpacking trips through the park are the heat and humidity. Frequent rainstorms cause the trails to be quite muddy, and should you choose the alternative—hiking on the beach—you'll have to plan your hiking around the tides. Often there is no beach at all at high tide.

Because of its size and remoteness, Corcovado National Park is best explored over several days; however, it is possible to enter and hike a bit of it for day trips. The best way to do this is to book a tour with your lodge on the Osa Peninsula, from a tour company in Puerto Jiménez, or through a lodge in Drake Bay (see "Accommodations & Dining," in the Drake Bay section, above).

GETTING THERE & ENTRY POINTS There are four primary entrances to the park, which are really just ranger stations reached by rough dirt roads. Once you've reached them, you'll have to strap on a backpack and hike. Perhaps the easiest one to reach from Puerto Jiménez is La Leona ranger station, accessible by car, bus, or taxi. If you choose to drive, take the dirt road from Puerto Jiménez to Carate (Carate is at the end of the road). From Carate, it's a 2-mile (3km) hike to La Leona. To travel there by bus, pick up one of the collective buses (actually a four-wheel-drive pickup truck with slat seats in the back) that leave Puerto Jiménez for Carate daily at 6am and 2:30pm (and return at 8am and 4:30pm). Remember, these "buses" are very informal and change there schedules regularly to meet demand or avoid bad weather, so always ask in town. One-way fare is around $3. These buses leave from the main road in town that heads out to Carate, more or less in front of the soda Carolina, and will stop to pick up anyone who flags it down along the way. Your other option is to hire a taxi, which will charge approximately $35 each way to Carate. En route to Carate, you will pass several campgrounds

Trail Distances in Corcovado National Park

It's 10 miles (16km) from La Leona to Sirena; Sirena is 15½ miles (25km) along the beach to San Pedrillo; from San Pedrillo, it's another 5½ miles (9km) to Marenco Biological Reserve.

and small lodges as you approach the park. If you are unable to get a spot at one of the campsites in the park, you can stay at one of these and hike the park during the day.

Alternatively, you can travel to **El Tigre**, about 8¾ miles (14km) by dirt road from Puerto Jiménez, where there's another ranger station. But note that trails from El Tigre go only a short distance into the park. The third entrance is in **Los Patos**, which is reached from the town of La Palma, northwest of Puerto Jiménez. From here, there's an 11¾-mile (19km) trail through the center of the park to Sirena, a ranger station and research facility (see "Beach Treks & Rain Forest Hikes," below). Sirena has a landing strip that is used by charter flights. The northern entrance to the park is **San Pedrillo**, which you can reach by hiking from Sirena or by taking a boat from Drake Bay or Sierpe (see "Beach Treks & Rain Forest Hikes," below). It's 8¾ miles (14km) from Drake Bay.

If you're not into hiking in the heat, you can charter a plane in Puerto Jiménez to take you to Carate, Sirena, Drake Bay, or even Tiskita Jungle Lodge (See "Where to Stay in Playa Pavones," later in this chapter), which is across the gulf, south of Playa Pavones. Contact **Alfa Romeo Aero Taxi** (☎ **506/775-1515** or 506/296-5596) for details.

FEES & REGULATIONS Park admission is $6 per person per day. Most of the ranger stations have simple dormitory-style lodgings, cantinas, and campsites, but all must be reserved in advance through the Parks Service at their offices in Puerto Jiménez (☎ **506/735-5036** or 506/735-5282), 1 block east of the main street at the end of town near the soccer field. Only a limited number of persons are allowed to camp at each ranger station, so make your reservations well in advance. There is an extra $1.50 per day fee for camping, and meals can be prepared for you at around $15 more per day, but you must also reserve your meals in advance.

VISITOR INFORMATION If you plan to hike the beach trails from La Leona or San Pedrillo, be sure to pick up a tide table at the park headquarters' office in Puerto Jiménez. The tide changes rapidly; when it's high, the trails and river crossings can be impassable.

BEACH TREKS & RAIN-FOREST HIKES There are quite a few good hiking trails in the park. Two of the better-known ones are the beach routes, starting at either La Leona or San Pedrillo ranger stations. None of the park's hikes are easy, but the forest route from the Los Patos ranger station to Sirena, while long, is less taxing than either of the beach treks, which can be completed only when the tide is low. The Los Patos–Sirena hike is, as mentioned above, 11¾ miles (19km) through rain forest. It's beautiful, and Sirena is a fascinating place to end up. A research facility as well as ranger station, it's frequented primarily by scientists studying the rain forest. One of the longest hikes, from San Pedrillo to Sirena, can be done only during the dry season. Between any two stations, the hiking is arduous and will take all day, so it's best to rest between hikes, if possible.

Remember, this is quite a wild area. Never hike alone and take all the standard precautions for hiking in the rain forest. In addition, be especially careful about swimming in any isolated rivers or river mouths, as most rivers in Corcovado are home to crocodiles.

ACCOMMODATIONS & DINING IN THE PARK: CAMPSITES, CABINS & CANTINAS Reservations are essential at the various ranger stations if you plan on eating or sleeping inside the park (see above under "Fees & Regulations"). **La Leona** ranger station has a campground, some very basic dormitory-style cabins, and a cantina. There is camping and a cantina at **Los Patos** ranger station. **Sirena** has bunks, a campground, and a cantina. Every ranger station has potable water, but it's advisable to pack in your own; whatever you do, don't drink stream water. Campsites in the park are $1.50 per person per night. A dorm bed will run you $2.50, and meals are around $15 per day.

ACTIVE PURSUITS OUTSIDE THE PARK

Closer to Puerto Jiménez, kayaking trips around the estuary and up into the mangroves and out into the gulf are popular. Contact **Escondido Trex** (☎ **506/735-5210;** e-mail: osatrex@sol.racsa.co.cr), which has an office in the Soda Carolina (see "Dining in Puerto Jiménez," below). They have daily paddles through the mangroves, as well as sunset trips, where dolphins are sometimes encountered. These folks also do guided rain forest hikes and can have you rappelling down the face of a jungle waterfall. More adventurous multiday kayak and camping trips are also available, and they'll even take you gold panning (although no guarantees your panning will pay for the trip). Escondido Trex even maintains some kayaks in Matapalo, if you're staying in a hotel out that way.

If you're interested in doing some bill fishing or deep-sea fishing, check around the public dock for notices put up by people with charter boats. Rates usually run between $400–$600 for a full day, or $200–$300 for a half day.

ACCOMMODATIONS IN PUERTO JIMÉNEZ

MODERATE

✪ **Doña Leta's Bungalows.** Apartado 91, Puerto Jiménez. ☎ and fax **506/735-5180.** www.hotles.co.cr/donaleta.html. E-mail: letabell@sol.racsa.co.cr. 7 units. $35 double, $45 triple. Discounts in the off-season. V.

These attractive new cabins are located on a spit of land jutting out into the gulf, just east of town and the airstrip. The smaller cabins are octagonal and have just one double bed, while the larger ones feature a sleeping loft with a double and single bed above and a double bed below. All the cabins come with a refrigerator, two-burner stove, private bathroom, and carved-wood door. There's a small restaurant and bar here and a large central deck built under and around a large fig tree that's frequented by scarlet macaws. The grounds also include a couple of volleyball nets, a small patch of beach, and a semigroomed trail through the mangroves. There are kayaks here available free of charge for guests.

INEXPENSIVE

✪ **Agua Luna.** In front of the public dock, Puerto Jiménez. ☎ and fax **506/735-5034,** or ☎ 506/735-5108. 14 units. TV. $17–$30 double or triple. No credit cards.

These very reasonable rooms offer the most luxury of any of the in-town lodgings in Puerto Jiménez. Agua Luna is located right at the foot of the town's public dock and backs up to a mangrove forest. The six older rooms directly face the gulf across a fenced-in gravel parking area. The most surprising feature in each of these rooms is the huge bathroom, which includes both a shower and a tub facing a picture window that looks into the mangroves. The most disappointing feature is that these windows let you watch the gray water discharge directly into the mangroves. There are two double beds in each room, and on the tiled veranda out front you'll find hammocks for lounging. The newer rooms are located a half block away and are smaller and less attractive than those in the original building. The higher prices are for rooms with air-conditioning.

Cabinas Marcelina. Puerto Jiménez. ☎ **506/735-5007.** Fax 506/735-5045. 6 units. $10 double, $15 triple. No credit cards.

Located at the southern end of Puerto Jiménez's main street, these basic rooms are a good choice for anyone on a shoestring budget. The owner keeps the tile-floored rooms clean, and there's surprisingly little mildew (always a problem in cinder-block buildings). Bathrooms are basic but adequate.

Cabinas Puerto Jiménez. 50 meters north of Bar y Restaurant El Rancho, Puerto Jiménez. ☎ **506/735-5090** or 506/735-5152. 10 units. $12 double, $18 triple. No credit cards.

Located right on the waterfront at the north end of the soccer field, this inexpensive accommodation even offers a few rooms with views of the bay. The exterior of the building, with its varnished wood, is more appealing than the guest rooms. Though large, the basic rooms have cement floors. However, they're kept clean and are the best choice in town for travelers on a tight budget.

ACCOMMODATIONS & DINING AROUND THE OSA PENINSULA

As with most of the lodges in Drake Bay, the accommodations listed in this section include three meals a day in their rates and do a large share of their business in package trips. Per-night rates are listed, but the price categories have been downshifted to take into account the fact that all meals are included. Ask about package rates if you plan to take several tours and stay awhile; they could save you money.

EXPENSIVE

✪ **Lapa Rios.** Apdo. 100, Puerto Jiménez, Osa Peninsula (mailing address in the U.S.: Box 025216, SJO-706, Miami, FL 33102). ☎ **506/735-5130.** Fax 506/735-5179. www.crica.com/hotels/laparios.html. E-mail: laparios@sol.racsa.co.cr. 14 units. Nov–Apr, $276 double, $396 triple, May–Oct, $242 double, $345 triple. Discounts for children up to 10 years old. Rates include 3 meals daily. AE, MC, V.

If you're looking for the ultimate luxury getaway in the jungle, this may be the place for you. However, keep in mind that there are no TVs, no telephones, no air-conditioning, no discos, no shopping, no paved roads, and no crowds. Moreover, the beach is a good 15-minute hike away, and it's not the best for swimming. In fact, other than a beautiful little pool, miles of hiking trails, and a quiet tropical bar, there is nothing around to distract your attentions from the stupendous views of the forest and ocean far below.

The hotel consists of seven duplex buildings perched along three ridges. Each spacious room is totally private and oriented toward the view. Walls have open screening, and the ceiling is a high-peaked thatched roof. Mosquito nets drape languidly over the two queen-size beds. A large deck and small tropical garden, complete with outdoor shower, more than double the living space of each room. The buildings are constructed of local materials such as palm thatch, bamboo, mangrove wood, and other hardwoods. Perhaps the most appealing aspect of each room is the screen-walled shower that lets you drink in the views while you bathe. Be warned, it's a bit of a hike back and forth from the main lodge to the rooms located on the lowest ridge.

Lapa Rios is surrounded by its own 1,000-acre private rain-forest reserve, which is home to scarlet macaws, toucans, parrots, hummingbirds, monkeys, and myriad other wildlife. For a closer look at the rain forest, hire one of the resident naturalists for guided walks or venture out on your own. If bird watching is your thing, you need go no farther than the lodge's outdoor deck, which seems to be a popular spot with numerous avian species.

Dining: The centerpiece of the large open-air dining room is a 50-foot-tall spiral staircase that leads to an observation deck tucked beneath the peak of the building's thatch roof. Each evening there's a choice of two main entrees, with an emphasis on fresh seafood and locally available ingredients.

Amenities: Guided walks, horseback riding, boat trips, sportfishing, sea kayaking, jungle camping trips. Day trips to Corcovado National Park, Caño Island, and Wilson Botanical Gardens. Snorkeling equipment, bodyboard, and surfboard rentals. Tours cost $20 to $40 per person. Round-trip transportation from Puerto Jiménez runs $20 per person. Facilities include a swimming pool and hiking trails.

Moderate

✪ **Bosque del Cabo Wilderness Lodge.** Osa Peninsula (mailing address in the U.S.: Interlink 528, P.O. Box 025635, Miami, FL 33152). ☎ **506/735-5062.** Fax 506/735-5043. E-mail: boscabo@sol.racsa.co.cr. 7 units. $160–$180 double. Rates include 3 meals daily. V (with 5% surcharge).

This simple yet tasteful lodge is located 500 feet above the water at the southern tip of the Osa Peninsula, where the Golfo Dulce meets the Pacific Ocean. It's surrounded by 300 acres of land that the owners purchased in order to preserve a piece of the rain forest. The cabins are all spacious and attractively furnished, have wooden decks or verandas to catch the ocean views, and are set amid beautiful gardens. The deluxe cabins come with king-size beds and slightly larger deck space. Cabin no. 6 is my favorite and offers a spectacular view of the sunrise from your bed. Meals are well prepared and filling and usually feature fruit grown on the premises. These folks also rent out a separate two-bedroom house that's quite popular. There's a trail down to a secluded beach that has some tide pools and ocean-carved caves. Another trail leads to a jungle waterfall. If you're too lazy to hike down to the beach, there's a small pool by the main lodge. Surfing is a popular activity here, as are hiking and horseback riding. Trips to the national park or fishing trips can be arranged. It'll cost you around $25 to take a taxi from Puerto Jiménez to the lodge.

✪ **Corcovado Lodge Tent Camp.** Costa Rica Expeditions, Apdo. 6941-1000, San José. ☎ **506/257-0766** or 506/222-0333. Fax 506/257-1665. www.expeditions.co.cr. E-mail: crexped@sol.racsa.co.cr. 20 tents. $112 double. Rates include 3 meals daily. MC, V.

If you're looking for a good blend of comfort and adventure, check out Costa Rica Expeditions's Corcovado Lodge Tent Camp, which is built on a low bluff right above the beach. Forested mountains rise up behind the tent camp, and just a few minutes' walk away is the entrance to Corcovado National Park.

Just reaching this lodge is an adventure in itself. You can either take a five-seat chartered plane to the gravel landing strip at Carate and then walk for 45 minutes to the lodge, or take the lodge's specially designed pontoon boat from Golfito or Puerto Jiménez. If you have a four-wheel-drive vehicle, you can get as far as the landing strip and then walk the remaining 1½ kilometers. Once you're there, you have a real sense of being away from it all.

Accommodations are in large tents pitched on wooden decks. Each tent has two twin beds, a table, and a couple of folding chairs on the front deck. Toilets and showers are a short walk away, but there are enough so that there's usually no waiting. Meals are served in a large screen-walled dining room furnished with picnic tables. A separate but similar building is furnished with hammocks, a small bar, and a few board games. Services at the lodge include guided walks and boat excursions, both into the national park and out to Caño Island. The newest addition to the lodge is a canopy platform located 120 feet up an ancient ajo tree. If you're truly adventurous, you can spend the night in a tent atop the platform (just don't wake up on the wrong side of the tent). Package rates that include transportation and tours are also available and are the way most people come here.

INEXPENSIVE

Tierra de Milagros. Osa Peninsula, Puerto Jiménez. ☎ and fax **506/735-5045** or 506/735-5210. E-mail: osatrex@sol.racsa.co.cr. 9 units. $80 double. Rate includes 3 meals daily. No credit cards.

Located down by the beach, below the much fancier Lapa Rios, this little place feels more like an international hippie hostel or a small Rainbow Gathering than a hotel. The individual cabins are spread spaciously around the property, which features a large central vegetable garden and many fruit trees. The open-walled cabins have cement floors and foam mattresses with mosquito netting. The larger ones have sleeping lofts. Each has its own shower, but the toilets are communal. Vegetarian meals (mostly from the garden) and sometimes fresh fish are served in the large central thatch-roofed "big house." There are horses on the grounds, and this is a good base to surf the nearby beaches of Pan Dulce and Matapalo. There's usually an acupuncturist, massage therapist, yoga instructor, or tai chi master in residence.

DINING IN PUERTO JIMÉNEZ

Bar Restaurant Agua Luna. 25 meters north of the public pier. ☎ **506/735-5033.** Reservations not accepted. Main courses $2.50–$10. No credit cards. Daily 9am–11pm. COSTA RICAN.

The first restaurant you come to after arriving in Puerto Jiménez by boat is also one of the best. Here's what you'll see: a collection of tiny thatched ranchos (the equivalent of Mexican palapas) set amid shady gardens and one larger building with a nice view of the mangroves. The bar and its dance floor are popular, and the music is usually loud, so don't expect a quiet, romantic dinner for two. Seafood is plentiful and fresh, and prices for fish dinners are low even for Costa Rica.

Soda Carolina. On the main street. ☎ **506/735-5185.** Reservations not accepted. All items $2–$8. No credit cards. Daily 6am–11pm. COSTA RICAN.

Set in the center of the town's main street, and otherwise known as the "Bar, Restaurante y Cabinas Carolina," this is Puerto Jiménez's budget travelers' hangout and also serves as an unofficial information center. The walls are painted with colorful jungle and wildlife scenes to whet the appetites of new arrivals and satisfy the needs of armchair travelers. As for the fare, seafood is the way to go. They've got good fried fish as well as a variety of ceviches. The black-bean soup is usually good, and the casados are filling and cost less than $3. If you need a place to stay, there are five basic rooms with cement floors and private bathrooms behind the kitchen. The rooms cost around $5 per person and front a very unattractive yard.

3 Golfito: A Place for Sportfishing & Touring Botanical Gardens

54 miles (87km) S of Palmar Norte; 209 miles (337km) S of San José

Golfito is an odd and unlikely destination for foreign travelers. In its prime this was a major banana port, but United Fruit pulled out in 1985 following a few years of rising taxes, falling prices, and labor disputes. Ticos come here in droves on weekends and throughout December to take advantage of cheaper prices on name-brand goods and clothing sold at the Duty Free Zone. Be warned: Sometimes all these shoppers make finding a room difficult. Golfito is also a major sportfishing center and a more and more popular gateway to a slew of nature lodges spread along the quiet waters, isolated bays, and lush rain forests of the Golfo Dulce.

Golfito itself is an old banana port set on the north side of the Golfo Dulce, at the foot of lush green mountains. The setting alone is enough to make this one of the most attractive cities in the country, but Golfito also has a certain charm all its own. Sure, the areas around the municipal park and public dock are kind of seedy, but if you go a little bit farther along the bay, you come to the old United Fruit Company housing. Here you'll find well-maintained wooden houses painted bright colors and surrounded by neatly manicured gardens. Toucans are commonly sighted here. It's all very lush and green and clean—an altogether different picture from that painted by most port towns in this country. These old homes are experiencing a sort of renaissance as they become small hotels catering to shoppers visiting the adjacent duty-free shopping center.

Sportfishing cognoscenti know that Golfito's real draw is the marlin and sailfish just beyond its bay. Arguably one of the best fishing spots in Costa Rica, it provides pleasant, uncrowded surroundings in which die-hard sportfishers can indulge their greatest fantasies of catching the great one to end all great ones. Landlubbers, take heed: Golfito has great opportunities for bird watching and is also close to some lovely botanical gardens that you can easily spend a day or more touring.

ESSENTIALS

GETTING THERE & DEPARTING **By Plane** **Sansa** (☎ **506/233-0397**, 506/233-3258, or 506/233-5330) has two daily flights to Golfito departing at 6am and 2:20pm from San José's Juan Santamaría International Airport. Trip duration is 55 minutes; fare is $55 each way. Sansa flights return to San José daily at 7:05am and 3:45pm. **Travelair** (☎ **506/220-3054** or 506/232-7883) has one flight to Golfito daily at 8:50am from Tobías Bolaños International Airport in Pavas. The flight stops in Puerto Jiménez en route, and returns to San José at 10:15am. The flight takes 1 hour; fare is $81 one way, $138 round-trip.

By Bus Express buses leave San José daily at 7am and 3pm from the Tracopa station (☎ **506/221-4214**) at Avenida 5 and Calle 14. The trip takes 8 hours; fare is $6.

Buses depart Golfito for San José daily at 5am and 1pm from the bus station near the municipal dock.

By Boat A passenger launch leaves Puerto Jiménez, on the Osa Peninsula, daily at 6am. The trip takes 1½ hours; fare is $4. You can also hire a boat to take you across the Golfo Dulce to Golfito. However, as there are not very many available in Puerto Jiménez, you're likely to have to pay quite a bit ($30 to $55 each way) for such a service. The passenger launch departs Golfito for Puerto Jiménez daily at 11:30am.

By Car It's a straight shot down the Interamerican Highway south from San José to Golfito, but it's a long and arduous straight shot. In the 8 hours it takes to drive the 209 miles (337km) from San José, you'll pass over the Cerro de la Muerte, which is famous for its dense fog and torrential downpours. Also, you'll have to contend with potholes of gargantuan proportions for almost the entire length of this road. Just remember, if the road is suddenly smooth and in great shape, you can bet that around the next bend there will be a bottomless pothole that you can't swerve around. Take it easy. When you get to Río Claro you'll notice a couple of gas stations and quite a bit of activity. Turn right here and follow the signs to Golfito. If you end up at the Panama border, you've missed the turnoff by about 20 miles.

GETTING AROUND If you can't get to your next destination by boat, bus, or car, **Alfa Romeo Aero Taxi** (☎ **506/775-1515** or 506/296-5596) runs charters to most of the nearby destinations, including Carate, Drake Bay, Sirena, and Puerto Jiménez. A taxi ride anywhere in town should cost around 75¢ each way.

FAST FACTS If you need to exchange money, you can do so at the gas station, or "La Bomba," in the middle of town. There is a Laundromat on the upper street of the small downtown that charges $3 for a 5-pound load. If you drop off your clothes in the morning, they'll be ready in the afternoon.

ACTIVE PURSUITS IN AND AROUND GOLFITO

If you want to explore the waters of the Golfo Dulce, check out **Yak Yak Kayaks** (☎ **506/775-1179**). These folks offer a variety of tours for everyone from beginners to advanced kayakers. Trips include nearby mangrove explorations, trips to an island with a waterfall and freshwater swimming hole, and overnight tours to Playa Zancudo and other points around the gulf. Rates are $7 per hour for single kayaks, $10 per hour for two-person kayaks. A half-day tour, including lunch, runs around $50 per person. Yak Yak Kayaks has its "office" on the beach in front of Las Gaviotas Hotel. They also have a couple basic cabins and can arrange hikes into the rain forests surrounding Golfito.

BEACHES AND SWIMMING There's no really good swimming or beaches right in Golfito. The closest spot is **Playa Cacao**, a short boat ride away, although this is not one of my favorite beaches in Costa Rica. You can probably get a ride here for a few dollars from one of the boat taxis down at the public docks, or ask at **Yak Yak Kayaks** about getting there.

SPORTFISHING The waters off Golfito also offer some of the best sportfishing in Costa Rica, and if you'd like to try hooking into a possible world-record marlin or sailfish, contact **Golfito Sportfishing** (☎ **506/776-0007**) or Roy's **Zancudo Lodge** (☎ **506/776-0008**), both of these operations are based in nearby Playa Zancudo, but they can arrange pickup in Golfito. A full-day fishing trip will cost between $500 and $800. Another company to check with is **Leomar Sportfishing and Diving** (☎ **506/775-0230**), which offers similar trips at similar prices.

TOURING THE BOTANICAL GARDENS

About 30 minutes by boat out of Golfito, you'll find **Casa Orchideas**, a private botanical garden lovingly built and maintained by Ron and Trudy MacAllister. Two-hour tours of the gardens (Sunday through Thursday) cost $5 per person, with a minimum of four people. During the tour, you'll sample a load of fresh fruits picked right off the tree. Most hotels in the region can organize a tour to the gardens; if not, you'll have to hire a boat to get there, which should cost you around $75 round-trip, including the boat pilot's waiting time.

If you have a serious interest in botanical gardens or bird watching, consider an excursion to **Wilson Botanical Gardens** (☎ **506/773-3278** or 506/240-6696; fax 506/240-6783; e-mail: reservas@ns.ots.ac.cr), located just outside the town of San Vito, about 40 miles (65km) to the northeast. The gardens are owned by the Organization for Tropical Studies and include more than 7,000 species of tropical plants from around the world. Among the plants grown here are many endangered species, which makes the gardens of interest to botanical researchers. Despite the scientific aspects of the gardens, there are so many beautiful and unusual flowers amid the manicured grounds that even a neophyte cannot help but be astounded. All this luscious flora has attracted at least 330 species of birds. A full day in the gardens, including lunch, will cost you $16 ($8 without lunch); a half-day walk around costs $4. Naturalist guides can be hired for around $20. If you'd like to stay the night here, there are 12 well-appointed rooms and 4 cabins. Rates, which include three meals, run between $65 and $80 per person; you need to make reservations beforehand if you wish to spend the night.

You'll find the gardens about 3¾ miles (6km) before San Vito. To get here from Golfito, drive back out to the Interamerican Highway and continue south toward Panama. In Cuidad Neily, turn north. A taxi would cost about $35 each way.

EXPLORING THE TOWN

Other than sportfishing off its waters, exploring nearby botanical gardens, and making connections to other places, there isn't a whole lot to do in Golfito. You can admire the United Fruit Company buildings, and have a drink overlooking the gulf. The recently organized **Golfito Ecotourist Guide Association** (☎ **506/775-0518** or 506/775-1179) can hook you up with a guide to help you explore the town, as well as a few trails through the nearby rain forest.

WHERE TO STAY IN GOLFITO

MODERATE

Las Gaviotas Hotel. Apdo. 12-8201, Golfito. ☎ **506/775-0062.** Fax 506/775-0544. 18 units, 3 cabanas. $40–$55 double, $45–$60 triple, $84 cabaña. AE, MC, V.

If you want to be right on the water, this is a good option in Golfito. Situated a short taxi ride out of town on the road that leads to the Interamerican Highway, Las Gaviotas has long been the hotel of choice on the Golfo Dulce. There is a long pier that attracts the sailboat and sportfishing crowd. For landlubbers, there's a small pool built out near the gulf water. Guest rooms, which are set amid attractive gardens, all face the ocean, and though they're quite large, they're a bit spartan and are starting to show their age. There are small tiled patios in front of all the rooms, and the cabanas have little kitchens. The more expensive rooms have air-conditioning. A large open-air restaurant looks over the pool to the gulf; it's a great view, but the food leaves much to be desired. Just around the corner is a large open-air bar. In addition, there's a small gift shop. The waterfront location is this hotel's greatest asset.

INEXPENSIVE

Cabinas Jardin Cervecero Alamedas. 100 meters south of the Depósito Libre, Golfito. ☎ **506/775-0126.** 6 units. $20 double or triple. AE, MC, V.

These six new rooms have been built across the gravel driveway from one of the more popular restaurants in the area around the free port. The rooms are clean, and each has one double, one single, and one bunk bed. I prefer the upstairs rooms, which have wood (instead of concrete) floors and more air circulation.

Casa Blanca Lodge. 300 meters south of the Depósito Libre, Golfito. ☎ **506/775-0124.** 12 units. $10–$15 double, $15–$20 triple or quad. No credit cards.

In the old United Fruit Company neighborhood near the airport, there are many pretty old houses surrounded by attractive, neatly manicured gardens. Several of these old homes have been turned into inexpensive hotels catering to shoppers visiting the free port. This is one of the nicer of the small family run hotels. The rooms in the new annex are more attractive and more comfortable than those in the main building, which tend to be dark and musty.

Complejo Turistico Samoa del Sur. 100 meters north of the public dock, Golfito. ☎ **506/775-0233.** Fax 506/775-0573. 14 units. TV TEL. $30 double, $40 triple to quad. AE, MC, V.

It's hard to miss the two giant thatched spires that house this new hotel's already-established restaurant and bar. The rooms are spacious and clean. Varnished wood headboards complement two firm and comfortable double beds. With red-tile floors, modern bathrooms, and carved-wood doors, the rooms all share a long, covered veranda that's set perpendicular to the gulf, so the views aren't great. If you want to watch the water, you're better off grabbing a table at the restaurant.

Golfo Azul. Barrio Alameda, 300 meters south of the Depósito Libre, Golfito. ☎ **506/775-0871.** Fax 506/775-1849. 24 units. $15–$20 double or triple with fan; $23–$27 double, triple, or quad with air-conditioning. No credit cards.

Azul offers a quiet location in the most attractive part of Golfito. Many of the people who stay here are Ticos in town to shop at the nearby Depósito Libre (free port), but anyone will appreciate the clean rooms. The smallest rooms are cramped, but there are larger rooms, some with high ceilings that make them feel even more spacious. Bathrooms are tiled and have hot water, and rooms have either fans or air-conditioning. The hotel's restaurant is in an older building and is brilliantly white inside and out. Meals are quite reasonably priced.

PLACES TO STAY ON THE GOLFO DULCE

The three lodges listed here are all located on the shores of the Golfo Dulce. There are no roads into this area, so you must get to the lodges by boat. It is recommended that you visit this area with firm reservations, so your transportation should be arranged. If worse comes to worse you can hire a boat taxi at the *muellecito* (little dock), which is located on the water just beyond the gas station, or "La Bomba," in Golfito, for between $25 and $35.

EXPENSIVE

Gulfo Dulce Lodge. Apartado 137, Golfito. ☎ **506/222-2900** or 506/735-5062. Fax 506/222-5173 or 506/735-5043. www.crica.com/hotels. E-mail: aratur@sol.racsa.co.cr. 6 units. $160 double, $200 triple. Rates include 3 meals daily and transportation to and from Golfito or Puerto Jiménez. Two-night minimum stay. No credit cards.

This small Swiss-run lodge is just down the beach from Casa Orquideas and Dolphin Quest, about a 30-minute boat ride from Golfito. The five separate cabins and main lodge buildings are all set back away from the beach 500 meters into the forest. The cabins are spacious, airy, and feature either a twin and a single bed or three single beds. In addition, there are large modern bathrooms, solar hot-water showers, a small sitting area, and a porch with a hammock. Meals are served in an open thatch-roofed building beside the small swimming pool. One room, attached to the building that houses the kitchen and laundry, is almost an afterthought but would do in a pinch if none of the cabins are available. The lodge also offers jungle hikes, river trips, and other guided tours.

Rainbow Adventures. Apdo. 63, Golfito (mailing address in the U.S.: Michael Medill, 5875 NW Kaiser Rd., Portland, OR 97229). ☎ **800/565-0722** or 503/690-7750 in the U.S., or ☎ and fax 506/775-0220 in Costa Rica. Fax 503/690-7735 in the U.S. www.travelsource.com/ecotours/rainbow. 4 units, 2 cabins. $255–$285 double, $60 each additional person. Rates include 3 meals daily and round-trip transportation between the lodge and Golfito or Puerto Jiménez. AE, DC, MC, V.

If you're looking for a place to kick back, explore the tropical rain forest, and still have some of the trappings of luxury, Rainbow Adventures might be just what you're looking for. This isolated lodge is surrounded by 1,000 acres of rain forest that abuts the Piedras Blancas National Park. The grounds immediately surrounding the lodge are neatly manicured gardens planted with exotic fruit trees, flowering shrubs, and palms from around the world. Days are spent lounging in hammocks, swimming, sunning, exploring the jungle, reading, bird watching, wild animal–watching, and maybe a bit of fishing. But mostly you get to do nothing and not feel guilty about it. Be warned, however, that if you need TV, telephone, crowds, shopping, or discos, you should stay away from Rainbow Adventures.

Rooms in the main lodge, which is constructed entirely of tropical hardwoods, are decorated with antiques, stained glass, and oriental carpets. The second-floor rooms are the smallest and least expensive. For just a little more, you can have the penthouse, a large third-floor room with four open walls and treetop views of the gulf. Only slightly more expensive are the spacious cabins, which are located a hundred or so yards away from the main building and built on stilts. Cabins have open living rooms and a large bedroom that can be divided into two small rooms. The owner has just opened up eight more rooms in the sister lodge, Buena Vista, which is located several hundred yards up Playa Cativa.

Dining: Meals are generally served buffet or family style, with a set menu each evening. However, the creativity of the chef and the quantities of food guarantee that everyone leaves the table satisfied. Though beer and wine are available, you should bring your own liquor.

Amenities: Fishing trips (barracuda, roosterfish, snook, and red snapper are plentiful), boat charters ($35 per hour for a boat that can carry four passengers), and guided hikes can all be arranged, as well as trips to the nearby Casa Orquideas (see "Touring the Botanical Gardens," above). The lodge has several well-maintained trails through primary rain forest, with jungle waterfalls and wonderful swimming holes. A private beach provides protected swimming and, when it's calm, there's some good snorkeling nearby (equipment is available at no charge). If neither the natural swimming holes nor Gulfo Dulce appeals to you, there's also a new spring-fed pool just off the main lodge.

INEXPENSIVE

Dolphin Quest. Apdo. 141, Golfito. ☎ **506/735-5062.** Fax 506/775-0373. 6 units. $40–$100 double. Rates include 3 meals daily. No credit cards.

This expansive and rustic spread is located right by the beach, in between Casa Orquideas and Golfo Dulce Lodge. There are a variety of accommodations. Each of three separate, octagonal ranchos has a roomy sleeping loft, open half-walls, cement floors, and a small kitchenette. My favorite rooms are in the separate, older wooden house, which is built up on stilts and has spacious front and back porches, two bedrooms, full kitchen, and a comfortable living area. Camping is permitted, and there are also dormitory beds available, for those looking for a real budget stay in the Golfo Dulce. Scuba diving, snorkeling, horseback riding, and transport between the lodge and Golfito are all available. Dolphin Quest is a family-run operation—they welcome families and give discounts for children.

DINING

In addition to the restaurants listed below, **Coconut Cafe** (☎ **506/775-0518,** across from the gas station) is a popular hangout. Open for breakfast and lunch, this place specializes in espresso and exotic coffee concoctions as well as desserts. It's a good place to gather information on trips and tours around the gulf.

Bar & Restaurant La Cubana. 150 meters east of the gas station, on the upper road through downtown Golfito. No phone. Main courses $2.50–$7.50. No credit cards. Tue–Sun 6am–10pm. COSTA RICAN.

This small, open-air restaurant commands a good view of the gulf and serves hearty meals at rock-bottom prices. The menu is pretty basic, but a fresh, whole fish in garlic sauce will cost you just $4. The restaurant is located on the bluff of a small hill and even has a view of the gulf. They recently added the bar, which may either liven up or totally destroy the ambience.

Jardin Cervecero Alamedas. 100 meters south of the Depósito Libre. ☎ **506/775-0126.** Main courses $2.50–$12. AE, MC, V. Daily 7am–11pm (closed Sun and Mon during the off-season). COSTA RICAN/SEAFOOD.

If you are staying at any of the other hotels near the Depósito Libre, this should be your first choice when deciding where to eat. The restaurant is located underneath an old house that's built on stilts. White chairs and dark green tablecloths provide a sort of fern-bar feel inside, while outside real tropical gardens surround the house. There are great deals on seafood here, including a long list of ceviches. The only drawback is that they tend to play the stereo too loud.

Samoa del Sur. 100 meters north of the public dock. ☎ **506/775-0233.** Main courses $2.50–$17. AE, MC, V. Daily 7am–midnight. CONTINENTAL.

It's hard to miss the Samoa del Sur: It's that huge circular rancho just north of the public dock. This oversized jungle structure seems out of place in a town where cinder blocks are the preferred construction material, but its tropical atmosphere is certainly appreciated (at least by this writer). The restaurant's biggest surprise is its extensive menu of familiar continental and French dishes, such as onion soup, salad Niçoise, fillet of fish meunière, and paella. There are also pizzas and spaghetti. The view of the gulf makes this a great spot for a sunset drink or dinner. In addition to the food, the giant rancho houses a pool table, several high-quality dartboards, and a big-screen television. The bar sometimes stays open all night.

4 Playa Zancudo

12 miles (19km) S of Golfito (by boat); 22 miles (35km) S of Golfito (by road)

Although the word leaked out in recent years, Playa Zancudo remains one of Costa Rica's most isolated beach getaways. It's a popular backpacker hangout, which means there are plenty of cheap rooms, some cheap places to eat, and lots of young gringos and Europeans around. These factors alone are enough to keep Zancudo jumping through the winter months. The beach itself is long and flat, and because it's protected from the full force of Pacific waves, it's one of the calmest beaches on this coast and relatively good for swimming, especially toward the northern end.

There's a splendid view across the Golfo Dulce, and the sunsets are hard to beat. Because there's a mangrove swamp directly behind the beach, mosquitoes and biting sandflies can be a problem—so be sure to bring insect repellent.

ESSENTIALS

GETTING THERE **By Plane** The nearest airport is in Golfito. See the Golfito section, above, for details. To get from the airport to Playa Zancundo, you can take a boat (see "By Boat," below) or a taxi (see "By Car," below).

By Boat Water taxis can be hired in Golfito to make the trip out to Playa Zancudo; however, trips depend on the tides and weather conditions. When the tide is high, the boats take a route through the mangroves. This is by far the calmest and most scenic way to get to Zancudo. When the tide is low, they must stay out in the gulf, which can get choppy at times. Currently it costs around $7–$10 per person for a water taxi, with a minimum charge of $20. If you can round up any sort of group, be sure to negotiate. The ride takes about 40 minutes.

Alternatively, there's a passenger launch from the muellecito (little dock) in Golfito, which normally leaves twice daily at around 4:30am and noon. Because the schedule sometimes changes, be sure to ask in town about current departure times. The trip lasts 45 minutes; fare is $2.50.

Finally, if you'd like to plan ahead, you can call **Zancudo Boat Tours** (☎ **506/776-0012**) and arrange for pickup in Golfito. They charge $10 per person each way, with a $20 minimum.

By Bus It's possible to get to Zancudo by bus, but I recommend the above water-borne routes. If you insist, though, you can catch the 2pm Pavones bus in front of the gas station "La Bomba" in downtown Golfito and get off in the village of Conte (at around 3:30). A Zancudo-bound bus should be there waiting. The whole trip takes about 3 hours; fare is $3.

By Car If you've got a four-wheel-drive vehicle, you should be able to make it out to Zancudo even in the rainy season, but be sure to ask in Golfito before leaving the paved road. The turnoff for Playas Zancudo and Pavones is at El Rodeo, about 2½ miles (4km) outside of Golfito, on the road in from the Interamerican Highway. Pretty quickly after the turnoff, you'll have to wait and take a small diesel-operated crank ferry (fare is $2 per vehicle). A four-wheel-drive taxi will cost around $30 from Golfito. It takes about 2 hours when the road is in good condition. To get here from San José, see "Getting Here by Car," above, in the Golfito section.

DEPARTING The public launch to Golfito leaves twice daily at 7am and 1pm from the dock near the school, in the center of Zancudo. If you're heading to Pavones or the Osa Peninsula next, contact **Zancudo Boat Tours** (☎ **506/776-0012**; leave a message), which is willing to make the trips to these two places. They charge $10–$15 per person, with a minimum charge of $20 for either trip. You can also arrange a water taxi back to Golfito, but work with your hotel owner and make a reservation at least one day in advance. The bus to Golfito leaves Zancudo each morning at 5am.

ORIENTATION Zancudo is a long, narrow peninsula (sometimes only 100 yards or so wide) at the mouth of the Río Colorado. On one side is the beach, on the other is a mangrove swamp. There is only one road that runs the length of the beach, and it's along this road, spread out over several kilometers of long, flat beach, that you'll find the hotels I've mentioned here. It's about a 20-minute walk from the public dock near the school to the popular Cabinas Sol y Mar.

RELAXING AND OUTDOOR PURSUITS

The main activity at Zancudo is relaxing, and people take it seriously. There are hammocks at almost every lodge, and if you bring a few good books, you can spend quite a number of hours swinging slowly in the tropical breezes. The beach along Zancundo is great for swimming. It's generally a little calmer on the northern end and gets rougher (good for body surfing) as you head south. There's a bar that doubles as a disco, but visitors are more likely to spend their time just hanging out in restaurants, meeting like-minded folks or playing board games.

Susan and Andrew Robertson, who run Cabinas Los Cocos, also operate **Zancudo Boat Tours** (☎ **506/776-0012**; leave a message), which offers snorkeling trips, trips to the Casa Orquideas Botanical Garden, a trip up the Río Coto to watch birds and wildlife, and others. Tour prices are $30 per person per tour, with discounts available for larger groups.

For fishing, contact **Big Al's Sportfishing** (☎ **506/776-0016**). A full day's fishing, with food, tackle, licenses, and beer, costs $300 for two people. Each additional person costs $50. You can also hook up with **Golfito Sportfishing** (☎ **506/776-0007**), which, despite the name, is located in Zancudo. Golfito Sportfishing charges between $350 and $550 per boat for a full day of fishing.

ACCOMMODATIONS

VERY EXPENSIVE

Roy's Zancudo Lodge. Apdo. 41, Playa Zancudo, Golfito. ☎ **506/776-0007.** Fax 506/776-0011. www.kaosfree.com/zancudo. 14 units. A/C. $75 per person nonfishing; $360 per person including full-day fishing. Rates include all meals and beer. Packages available. V.

Primarily a fishing lodge, this pricey hotel is located at the north end of Zancudo. All of the rooms look out onto a bright green lawn of soft grass and the small swimming pool and Jacuzzi, with the beach just a few steps beyond. The rooms are in several long row buildings up on stilts. All have hardwood floors, small, clean bathrooms, ceiling fans, air conditioners, and small verandas. There are four suites that have a separate sitting room and stocked minifridge.

Dining: There's an open-air restaurant that, naturally, specializes in fresh fish.

Amenities: The lodge offers many different types of fishing excursions and packages and boasts more than 20 world-record catches.

INEXPENSIVE

✪ **Cabinas Sol y Mar.** Apdo. 87, Playa Zancudo, Golfito. ☎ **506/776-0014.** Fax 506/776-0015. www.zancudo.com. E-mail: solymar@zancudo.com. 4 units. Dec 1–Apr 30, $30 double, May 1–Nov 30, $20 double. V (add 6% surcharge).

Although there are only four rooms here, this is the most popular lodging in Zancudo. Two of the rooms are modified geodesic domes with tile floors, verandas, and tin roofs. The bathrooms have unusual showers that feature a tiled platform set amid smooth river rocks and translucent roofs that flood them with light. The other two rooms are larger and newer but aren't as interesting. You'll have to decide between space and character. There's an adjacent open-air restaurant that's one of the most popular places to eat in Zancudo. Seafood dishes are the specialty here (the whole fried fish is good), and prices are very reasonable.

✪ **Los Cocos.** Apdo. 88, Golfito. ☎ and fax **506/776-0012.** www.zancudo.com. E-mail: loscocos@sol.racsa.co.cr. 4 units. $30–$35 per night; $180–$210 per week; prices lower in the off-season. No credit cards.

If you've ever pondered throwing it all away and setting up shop in a simple house by the beach, these kitchen-equipped cabins might be a good place for a trial run. Set under the trees and only a few yards from the beach, the four cabins here are quiet and semi-isolated from one another. Two of them served as banana-plantation housing in a former life, until they were salvaged and moved here. These wood houses have big verandas and bedrooms and large eat-in kitchens. Bathrooms are down a few steps in back and have hot water. The two newer cabins also offer plenty of space, small kitchenettes, and a private veranda, as well as comfortable sleeping lofts. If you plan to stay in Zancudo for a while, this is a perennially good choice. There are complimentary boogie boards for guest use. The owners, Susan and Andrew Robertson, also run Zancudo Boat tours, so if you want to do some exploring or need a ride into Golfito or Puerto Jiménez, they're the folks to see.

DINING

The most popular restaurant in Zancudo has traditionally been at **Cabinas Sol y Mar**. This small open-air spot is a de rigueur hangout for resident gringos as well as travelers. You might also try the tasty Italian meals at **Restaurante Maconda**. And if you want basic Tico fare and some local company, head to **Soda Suzy**.

5 Playa Pavones: A Surfer's Mecca

25 miles (40km) S of Golfito

Touted as the world's longest rideable left break, Pavones is a legendary surf spot. It takes around 6 feet of swell to get this wave cranking, but when the surf's up, you're in for a long, long ride—so long, in fact, that it's easier to walk back up the beach to where the wave is breaking than to paddle back. The swells are most consistent during the rainy season, but you're likely to find surfers here year-round. Locals tend to be pretty possessive around here (both the wave and local properties have engendered bitter disputes), so don't be surprised if you receive a cool welcome in Pavones. Other than surfing, nothing much goes on here; however, the beach is quite nice, with some rocky areas that give Pavones a bit more visual appeal than Zancudo. If you're feeling energetic here, you can also go for a horseback ride or hike into the rain forests that back up this beach town.

Various lodges are starting to sprout up, but so far most accommodations here are very basic. Pavones is a tiny village with few amenities. The one exception is **Tiskita Lodge**, a jungle getaway several kilometers south of Pavones.

For the past 20 or so years, Pavones has been the site of some fierce and ongoing land battles among locals, foreign investors, and squatters. In 1997 the conflict turned bloody, and one foreign landholder and one squatter were killed in a gun battle. The U.S. State Department quickly issued a traveler's advisory. However, if you stick to tourism and stay away from real estate speculation, you really should have no problems down here.

ESSENTIALS

GETTING THERE & DEPARTING **By Plane** The nearest airport is in Golfito. See the Golfito section, above, for details. See below on how to get to Pavones from the Golfito airport.

By Bus There is a bus to Pavones from Golfito daily at 2pm. Trip duration is 3½ hours; fare is $1.80. The bus to Golfito departs Pavones daily at 5am.

By Car If you have a four-wheel-drive vehicle, you should be able to get to Pavones even in the rainy season, but be sure to ask in Golfito before leaving the paved road. The turnoff for Playas Zancudo and Pavones is at El Rodeo, about 2½ miles (4km) outside of Golfito, on the road in from the Interamerican Highway. Pretty quickly after the turnoff, you'll have to wait and take a small diesel-operated crank ferry (fare is $2 per vehicle). A four-wheel-drive taxi from Golfito to Pavones will cost between $30 and $40. It takes around 2 hours.

ACCOMMODATIONS & DINING

Right in Pavones, there are several very basic lodges catering to itinerant surfers and renting rooms for between $10 and $20 per night for a double room. There are also a couple of sodas where you can get Tico meals. The most popular of these is **Esquina del Mar**, which is located right on the beach's edge, in front of the fattest part of the surf break.

Casa Impact. Apdo. 133, Golfito. ☎ **407/683-1429** in the U.S., or 506/775-0637. 3 units (none with bathroom). $28 single, $56 double. Rates include breakfast and dinner. No credit cards.

Casa Impact is composed of two octagonal houses with simple rooms on the second floor and a communal bathroom on the ground floor. Actually, one of the houses has just one bedroom, so in effect you have a private bath. Most of the clientele here is surfers, as is owner Ted Margraff, and of course there are surfboards for rent. You can also rent horses, for $10 per hour, or a sea kayak. Meals are well-prepared and filling and include fresh juices, pizzas, and freshly baked breads and cakes. Electricity here is provided by photovoltaic cells.

✪ **Tiskita Jungle Lodge.** Apdo. 1195-1250, Escazú. ☎ **506/233-6890.** Fax 506/255-3529. 13 units. $455 3 days/2 nights, $535 4 days/3 nights. Package prices are per person, based on double occupancy and including round-trip transportation from San José, all meals, guided walks, and taxes. AE, MC, V.

This small lodge is nearly on the Panamanian border, with the beach on one side and hills covered by rain forest behind. Although originally and primarily an experimental fruit farm growing exotic tropical fruits from around the world, Tiskita has also become a great place to get away from it all. There's a dark-sand swimming beach, tide pools, a farm and forest to explore, and great bird watching (285 species have been sighted). Of the 400 acres here, 250 are in primary rain forest, while the rest are in orchards and pastures. The lodge itself is set on a hill a few hundred yards from the beach and commands a superb view of the ocean.

Accommodations are in deluxe rustic cabins with screen walls and verandas. Constructed of local hardwoods, the cabins have a very tropical feel, and if you're a bird-watcher, you can just sit on the veranda and add to your life list. My favorite cabin is no. 6, which has a great view and ample deck space. Some of the cabins have two or three rooms, making them great for families but less private for couples. Meals are served family style in the open-air main lodge. While they're not fancy, they're certainly tasty and filling, and you'll probably be eating plenty of ingredients straight from the gardens.

The lodge is almost 3 hours from Golfito by car, so most guests take advantage of the package tours, which include air transportation to Tiskita's private landing strip. Although if you've driven down to Pavones, Tiskita is only a few kilometers farther on down the road.

10 The Caribbean Coast

Costa Rica's Caribbean coast feels a world apart from the rest of the country. The pace is slower, the food is spicier, the tropical heat seems more palpable, and the rhythmic lilt of patois and reggae music fill the air.

Although this was the coast Christopher Columbus landed on in 1502 and christened Costa Rica (Rich Coast), it has until recently remained terra incognita. It was not until 1987 that the Guápiles Highway opened between San José and Limón. Before that, the only routes down to this region were the famous jungle train (which is no longer in operation) and the narrow winding road from Turrialba to Siquírres. More than half of this coastline is still inaccessible except by boat or small plane. This inaccessibility has helped preserve large tracts of virgin lowland rain forest, which are now set aside as **Tortuguero National Park** and **Barra del Colorado National Wildlife Refuge**. These two parks, on the northern reaches of this coast, together form one of Costa Rica's most popular destinations with ecotravelers. Of particular interest are the sea turtles that nest along this stretch of coast. Another intriguing national park in this area is in Cahuita, a beach town. The park was set up to preserve 500 acres of coral reef, but its palm tree–lined beaches are stunning.

So remote was the Caribbean coast from Costa Rica's population centers in the Central Valley that it developed a culture all its own. The original inhabitants of the area included people of the Bribrí, Cabécar, and KéköLdi tribes, and each of these groups maintain their cultures on indigenous reserves in the Talamanca mountains. In fact, until the 1870s, there were few non-Indians in this area. However, when Minor Keith built the railroad to San José and began planting bananas, he brought in black laborers from Jamaica and other Caribbean islands to lay the track and work the plantations. These workers and their descendants established fishing and farming communities up and down the coast. Today dreadlocked Rastafarians, reggae music, Creole cooking, and the English-based patois of this Afro-Caribbean culture give this region a distinctly Jamaican flavor. Many visitors find this striking contrast with the Spanish-derived Costa Rican culture fascinating.

The major city on this coast is Limón, a ramshackle and run-down port city that also happens to be the site of the country's liveliest Carnival celebration. Each year, Limonenses throw a street

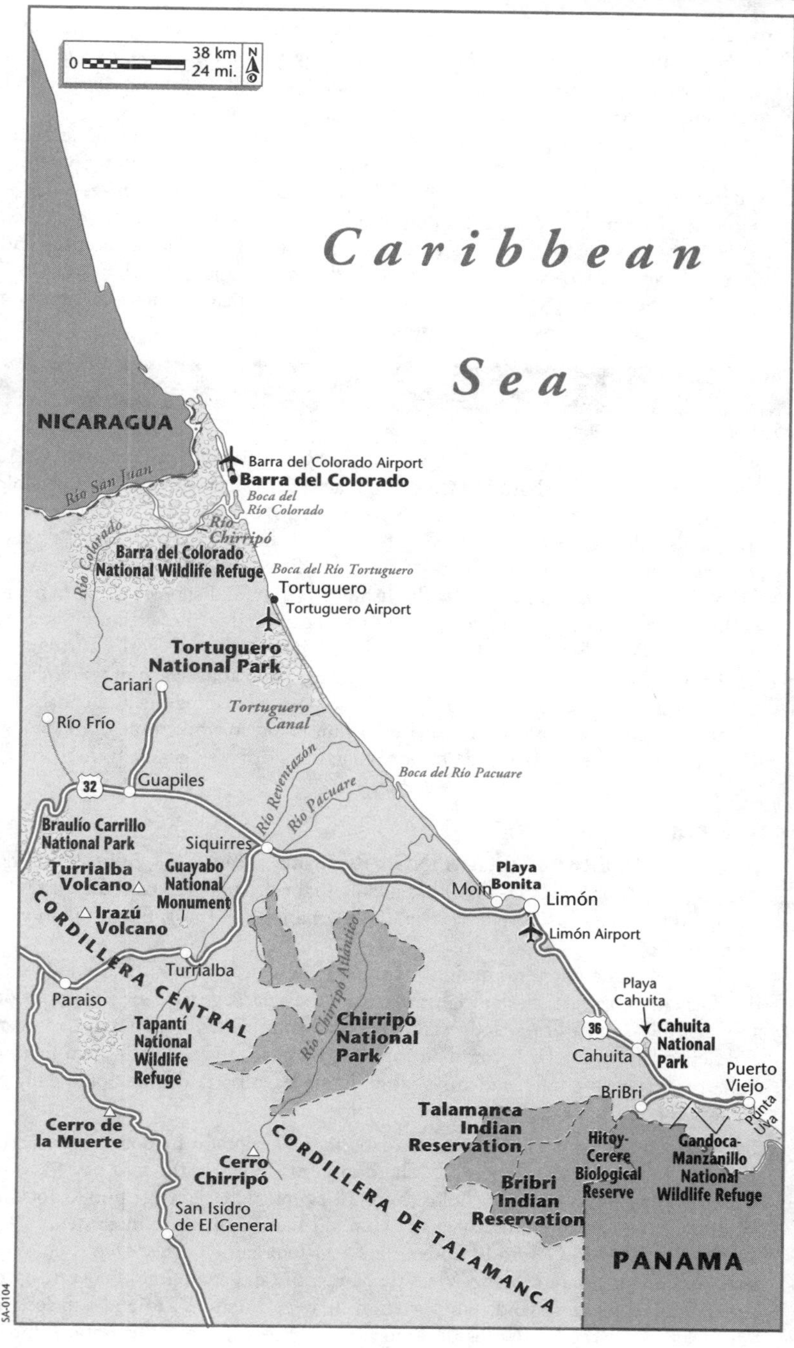
38 km
24 mi.
0
N
Caribbean Sea
NICARAGUA
Barra del Colorado Airport
Barra del Colorado
Boca del Río Colorado
Río San Juan
Río Colorado
Río Chirripó
Barra del Colorado National Wildlife Refuge
Boca del Río Tortuguero
Tortuguero
Tortuguero Airport
Tortuguero National Park
Cariari
Río Frío
Tortuguero Canal
Río Reventazón
Río Pacuare
Boca del Río Pacuare
32
Guapiles
Braulío Carrillo National Park
Siquirres
Turrialba Volcano
Guayabo National Monument
Irazú Volcano
Moin
Playa Bonita
Limón
Limón Airport
CORDILLERA CENTRAL
Turrialba
Paraiso
Río Chirripó Atlántico
Tapantí National Wildlife Refuge
Chirripó National Park
Playa Cahuita
36
Cahuita
Cahuita National Park
Puerto Viejo
BriBri
Punta Uva
Cerro de la Muerte
Talamanca Indian Reservation
Hitoy-Cerere Biological Reserve
Gandoca-Manzanillo National Wildlife Refuge
Cerro Chirripó
CORDILLERA DE TALAMANCA
Bribri Indian Reservation
San Isidro de El General
PANAMA
SA-0104

party of several days' duration, with marching drum bands, colorful floats and costumes, and general revelry. The event officially celebrates the *Día de la Raza* (Day of the People), which falls on October 12, but the party usually stretches out to include the weekend closest to that date.

Over the past few years, the Caribbean Coast has garnered a reputation as being a dangerous, drug infested zone, rife with crime and danger. Part of this reputation is deserved, as there have been several high-profile crimes, and drugs such as marijuana, cocaine, and crack are rather readily available in Limón and at the beach towns here. However, part of this reputation is exaggerated. The same crime and drug problems exist in San José and some of the more popular beach destinations on the Pacific coast. Use common sense and take normal precautions, and you should have no problems on the Caribbean coast.

1 Barra del Colorado

71 miles (115km) NE of San José

Named for its location at the mouth of the Río Colorado up near the Costa Rica–Nicaragua border, Barra del Colorado is an isolated little town solely accessible by boat or small plane. There are no roads in or to Barra del Colorado. The town itself is a small, ramshackle collection of raised stilt houses and supports a diverse population of Afro-Caribbean Blacks, Miskito Indians, and Nicaraguan emigrants.

The reason tourists come here is the fishing. Tarpon and snook fishing here are world-class, and if they don't keep you busy, you can head farther offshore for some deep-sea action. Barra del Colorado shares it's ecosystem with Tortuguero (see below) and, as in Tortuguero, you will find a wide abundance of wildlife and rain-forest fauna accessible only by small boat via a series of rivers and canals. It's hot and humid here most of the year, and it rains a lot, so while some of the lodges have at times risked offering a "tarpon guarantee," they're generally hesitant to promise anything in terms of the weather.

ESSENTIALS

GETTING THERE & DEPARTING **By Plane** **Sansa** (☎ **506/233-0397**, 506/233-3258, or 506/233-5330) has a daily flight departing at 6am for Barra del Colorado from San José's Juan Santamaría International Airport. Flight duration is 35 minutes; fare is $45 each way.

Most folks come here on multiday fishing packages, and most of the lodges in this area either operate charter flights as part of their package trips, or will book you a flight. Also, some of these lodges have been working with Travelair, whose service and dependability are far better than Sansa's, so it pays to check with them first.

If you're traveling independently, Sansa flights leave Barra del Colorado daily at 6:45am for San José.

By Boat It is also possible to travel to Barra del Colorado by boat from Puerto Viejo de Sarapiquí (see chapter 7, "The Northern Zone"). Expect to pay $150 to $200 each way for a boat that holds up to 10 people. Check at the public dock in Puerto Viejo de Sarapiquí or ask at the Hotel El Bambú, if you're interested.

Alternatively, **Rio Colorado Lodge** runs a 34-foot launch, *River Queen*, between Barra del Colorado and Puerto Viejo de Sarapiquí (and sometimes between Barra and Limón), including land transportation between Puerto Viejo and San José. If you're staying at the Rio Colorado Lodge, be sure to ask about this option (for at least one leg of your trip) when booking; the hotel doesn't discriminate—you can arrange transporation even if you aren't staying with them.

ORIENTATION The town of Barra del Colorado is actually split in half—north/south—by the Río Colorado. The airstrip is on the southern half of town, as are most of the lodgings. Those lodges that are farther up the canals will meet you in a small boat at the airstrip.

FISHING, FISHING, AND, WELL, MORE FISHING

Fishing is the primary activity here. Almost all of the lodges specialize in fishing and fishing packages. If you don't fish, you might wonder just what in the world you are doing here. Even though there are excellent opportunities for bird watching and touring the jungle waterways, most lodges here are still merely paying lip service to ecotourists and would rather see you with a rod and reel.

Fishing takes place year-round. You can do it in the rivers and canals, in the very active river mouth, or offshore. Most anglers come in search of the tarpon, or silver king. **Tarpon** can be caught here, both in the river mouth and to a lesser extent in the canals, year-round, but for some reason they seem to take a little time off in July and August—the two rainiest months. And, while you might see plenty of tarpon actually rolling on their sides on the surface, they don't seem to bite very much right around the full moon. **Snook**, an aggressive river fish, peak in April, May, October, and November, while fat snook, or **calba**, run heavy from November through January. Depending how far out to sea you venture, you might hook up with **barracuda**, **jack**, **mackerel (spanish and king)**, **wahoo**, **tuna**, **dorado**, **marlin,** or **sailfish**. In the rivers and canals, fishermen regularly bring in **mojarra**, **machaca,** and **guapote** (rainbow bass). Following recent developments in fishing, anglers have been using traditional rod and reel setups, as well as fly rods, to go for just about all the fish mentioned above. To fish here, you'll need both salt ($32) and fresh ($12) fishing licenses. Most lodges include these in your packages or can readily provide the licenses for you.

Aside from fishing there's not much to do in Barra del Colorado. The town is tiny and tends to be a bit rough-and-tumble due to the large number of transient commercial fishermen and loggers, as well as its border town status. Check if your lodge has a good naturalist guide and/or canoes or kayaks for rent or use. Otherwise, you'll be spending a lot of time sitting around your hotel reading or watching the river flow by.

ACCOMMODATIONS & DINING

As I said, almost all of the hotels here specialize in package tours, including all your meals, fishing and tackle, and usually your liquor too—so rates are high. In addition to the lodges listed below, there is one "budget" lodging in town called **Tarponland Lodge** (☎ **506/383-6097**; fax 506/710-6592). It's located just next to the airstrip and caters to independent travelers

VERY EXPENSIVE

Rio Colorado Lodge. P.O. Box 5094-1000, San José. ☎ **800/243-9777** in the U.S. and Canada, or 506/232-4063 in Costa Rica. Fax 506/231-5987. www.sportsmansweb.com/riocolorado. E-mail: tarpon@sol.racsa.co.cr. 19 units. $1717 per person for 7 days/6 nights/4 full days of fishing, including 2 nights' lodging in San José, all meals at the lodge, boat, guide and fuel, and licenses. Nonfishing guests $90 per person per day. AE, MC, V.

This rustic old lodge was founded and built more than 25 years ago by local legend Archie Fields. It continues to be one of the principal fishing lodges in Costa Rica. The rooms are comfortable but rustic, with some showing the wear and tear of the years. There's some variation in room size and quality. Several rooms have air-conditioning and/or televisions, two are wheelchair accessible, and there's even a "honeymoon suite," which is basically a standard room with a small mirror hung by ropes over the bed. As at Silver King lodge, the whole complex is tied together by covered walkways. The most disappointing aspect for me here is the sad little zoo, which houses a wide range of local birds and mammals in small chicken-wire cages.

Dining/Diversions: The nicest feature here is the large bar and dining area out by the river, where breakfast is served. Dinner is served family style in the second-floor dining room. There's also a large bar (where lunch is served), with satellite TV, pool table, and dartboard, as well as a conference room and well-stocked tackle shop.

Amenities: As at the other lodges in Barra del Colorado, fishing is the main activity here, but this lodge also runs the *River Queen* riverboat (see above) for those interested in cruising either to Puerto Viejo or Limón. Laundry service, free coffee service all day long, and free rum and soft drinks during happy hour.

✪ **Silver King Lodge.** Mailing address in the U.S.: P.O. Box 025216, Dept. 1597, Miami, FL 33102. ☎ **800/847-3474,** 800/309-8125, or 506/381-1403. Fax 506/381-0849. www.silverkinglodge.com. E-mail: slvrkng@sol.racsa.co.cr. 13 units. $1815 per person double occupancy for 4 full days of fishing, air transportation to and from Barra del Colorado from San José, all meals at the lodge, liquor, and up to 2 nights' lodging in San José; $358 per person per day, including all fishing, meals, and liquor. AE, MC, V.

This is by far the most luxurious lodge in Barra del Colorado. Fishing is still taken seriously here, with a large selection of modern boats and equipment, as well as a full tackle shop, but Silver King also emphasizes comfort. The entire complex is built on raised stilts and connected by covered walkways. The rooms are immense, with two double beds, desk and chair, luggage racks, fishing racks, an overhead fan, and a roomy closet. The floors and walls are all varnished hardwood, and the ceilings are finished in bamboo.

Dining/Diversions: The meals here are truly exceptional, by far the best buffet style lodge cooking I've ever had. Each all-you-can eat meal is anchored with at least two main dishes and a wide variety of appetizers, salads, side dishes, and dessert. You should be eating plenty of fish during your stay—coconut-battered snook nuggets with a pineapple-wasabi dip was just one of the highlights of my culinary indulgences here. There's a comfortable bar, with a large satellite television and 24-hour-a-day service, albeit it's self-service during the very off hours. All soft drinks, local beers, and liquors are free, as is wine with dinner, and there's a small charge for all liquor.

Amenities: Silver King provides free daily laundry service. There's also an enclosed Jacuzzi and a small outdoor swimming pool, for those brief breaks between eating, drinking, and fishing.

MODERATE

Samay Lagoon Lodge. Barra del Colorado. ☎ **506/284-7047.** Fax 506/383-6370. www.samay.com. E-mail: samaycr@sol.racsa.co.cr. 22 units. $250 per person 3 days/2 nights, including ground and boat transportation to and from San José, meals, and several tours. MC, V.

This is the only lodge in the Barra del Colorado area that doesn't specifically cater to hard-core fisherman. You can fish here, but Samay Lagoon Lodge is geared more toward ecotourists and is quite popular with European budget travelers and student groups. The hotel is actually about halfway between Barra and Tortuguero on a small spit of land between its namesake lagoon and the Caribbean Sea. The rooms come in a variety of shapes and sizes and are housed in three separate buildings. The beds are all just soft foam matresses, but they have mosquito netting. There is a separate lounge, dining room, and bar where buffet-style meals are served. The lodge has 12 canoes and several boats for tours, and there are plenty of hammocks for just hanging out.

2 Tortuguero National Park

155 miles (250km) NE of San José; 51 miles (79km) from Limón

"Tortuguero" comes from the Spanish name for the giant sea turtles (*tortugas*) that nest on the beaches of this region every year from mid-February to mid-October. The chance to see this nesting attracts many people to this remote region, but just as many come to explore the intricate network of jungle canals that serve as the main transportation arteries. This stretch of coast is connected to Limón, the Caribbean coast's only port city, by a series of rivers and canals that parallel the sea, often running only 100 yards or so from the beach. This aquatic highway is lined for most of its length with a dense rain forest that is home to howler monkeys, three-toed sloths, toucans, and great green macaws. A trip up the canals is like cruising the Amazon but on a much smaller scale.

In 1996, local citizens and certain municipal officials began work on a road into Tortuguero. A large swath was cut to within almost 1 kilometer of the village, with several kilometers of the construction passing through protected parklands. When the project was publicly discovered, it caused a minor local and regional scandal. Work was halted, and several parties are under indictment, but much of the damage is done. Still, this is not a reliable route to Tortuguero and probably won't be for some time.

Overall, remember the climate in this region: more than 200 inches of rain annually, so you can expect rain at any time of the year.

ESSENTIALS

GETTING THERE & DEPARTING **By Plane** **Travelair** (☎ **506/220-3054** and 506/232-7883) has one flight departing daily at 6:30am for Tortuguero from Tobías Bolaños International Airport in Pavas. The flight takes 30 minutes; fare is $45 one way, $90 round-trip.

Sansa (☎ **506/233-0397**, 506/233-3258, or 506/233-5330) has a daily flight departing at 6am for Tortuguero from San José's Juan Santamaría International Airport. Flight duration is 50 minutes (with a stop in Barra del Colorado); fare is $45 each way.

In addition, many lodges in this area operate charter flights as part of their package trips.

If you're traveling independently, Sansa flights leave Tortuguero daily at 7:50am for San José. Travelair departs Tortuguero daily at 7:15am for San José.

It always pays to check with both Sansa and Travelair. Additional flights are often added during the high season, and flights are sometimes dropped during the low season.

By Boat Flying to Tortuguero is convenient if you don't have much time, but a boat trip through the canals and rivers of this region is often the highlight of any visit to Tortuguero. All of the more expensive lodges listed offer their own bus and boat transportation packages, which include a 3-hour boat ride through the canals. However, if you're coming here on the cheap and plan to stay at one of the less-expensive lodges or at a budget cabina in Tortuguero, you will have to arrange your own transportation. In this case, you have a few options.

The most direct method is to get yourself to the public docks in **Moín** (just north of Limón) and try to find a boat on your own. There's a bus that runs from a stop in front of the prominent Radio Casino building, one block north of Limón's central market; it costs 25¢. Otherwise, you can take a taxi for $2.50 (for up to four people). Once at the docks, you should be able to negotiate a fare of between $40 and $60, depending on how many people you can round up to go with you. These boats tend to depart between 8am and 10am every morning. Usually, the fare you pay covers the return trip as well, and you can arrange with the captain to take you back across when you're ready to leave.

You might want to search out **Modesto Watson** (☎ **506/226-0986**), who owns a boat named after his wife, Francesca. The couple offers overnight and multiday packages to Tortuguero. They've been doing this for a long time and are wonderful guides. The trip from Moín to Tortuguero takes between 3 and 4 hours. **Laura's Tropical Tours** (☎ **506/758-2410**) also offers boat tours to Tortuguero from Moín.

It is also possible, albeit expensive, to travel to Tortuguero by boat from Puerto Viejo de Sarapiquí (see chapter 7, "The Northern Zone"). Expect to pay $200 to $250 each way for a boat that holds up to 10 people. Check at the public dock in Puerto Viejo de Sarapiquí or ask at the Hotel El Bambú, if you're interested. The ride usually takes about 3 to 4 hours.

ORIENTATION Tortuguero is one of the most remote locations in Costa Rica. There are no roads into this area and no cars in the village, so all transportation here is by boat or foot. Most of the lodges are spread out over several kilometers to the north of the village of Tortuguero on either side of the main canal and the small airstrip is at the north end of the beach side spit of land. At the far northern end of the main canal you'll see the **Cerro de Tortuguero** (Turtle Hill), which, at some 350 feet, towers over the area. The hike to the top of this hill is a popular half-day tour and offers some good views of the Tortuguero canals and village, as well as the Caribbean Sea.

Tortuguero Village is a tiny collection of houses connected by footpaths. The village is spread out on a thin spit of land, bordered on one side by the Caribbean Sea and on the other by the main canal. At most points, it's less than 300 meters wide. In the center of the village you'll find a small children's playground and a soccer field, as well as a kiosk that has information on the cultural and natural history of this area.

If you stay at a hotel on the ocean side of the canal, you will be able to walk into and explore the town at your leisure, whereas if you're across the canal, you'll be dependent on the lodge's boat transportation. However, some of the lodges across the canal have their own network of jungle trails that may appeal to naturalists.

EXPLORING THE NATIONAL PARK

According to existing records, Tortuguero National Park has hosted sea turtles since at least 1592, largely due to its extreme isolation. Even today, there are no roads into the park. Over the years, turtles have been captured and their eggs harvested by local settlers, but it wasn't until the 1950s that this practice became so widespread that the turtles faced extinction. Regulations controlling this mini-industry were passed in 1963, and in 1970 Tortuguero National Park was established. Today, four different species of sea turtles nest here: the green turtle, the hawksbill, the loggerhead, and the giant leatherback. The prime nesting period is from mid-June to mid-October (with August and September being the peak months). The park's beaches are excellent places to watch sea turtles nest, especially at night. Appealingly long and deserted, however, the beaches are not appropriate for swimming. The surf is usually very rough, and the river mouths have a nasty habit of attracting sharks that feed on the turtle hatchlings and many fish that live here.

Green turtles are perhaps the most common turtle found in Tortuguero, so you're more likely to see one of them than any other species if you visit during the prime nesting season. **Loggerheads** are very rare here, so don't be disappointed if you don't see one. Perhaps the most spectacular sea turtle to watch laying eggs is the **giant leatherback**. The largest of all turtle species, the leatherback can grow to 6½ feet long and weigh well over 1,000 pounds. It nests from mid-February to mid-April, predominately in the southern part of the park.

You can also explore the park's rain forest, either by foot or by boat, and look for some of the incredible varieties of wildlife that live here: jaguars, anteaters, howler monkeys, collared and white-lipped pecaries, some 350 species of birds, and countless butterflies, among others. There are several trails that branch out from the park entrance.

ENTRY POINT, FEES & REGULATIONS The Tortuguero National Park entrance and ranger station are at the south end of Tortuguero Village. Admission to the park is $6. However, there are some caveats: You will need to pay the park fee only if you plan on hiking one of the trails here or touring the canals specifically within the park. Many hotels and private guides take their tours to a series of canals that border the park, and are very similar in terms of flora and fauna. When the turtles are nesting, you will have to arrange a night tour in advance either with your hotel or the **Caribbean Conservation Corporation** (see below). These guided tours generally run $15 and include admission to the park. Flashlights and flash cameras are not permitted on the beach at night, since the lights discourage the turtles from nesting.

ORGANIZED TOURS Most visitors come to Tortuguero on an organized tour. All of the lodges listed below, with the exception of the most budget accommodations in Tortuguero Village, offer complete package tours that include various hikes and night tours, and this is generally the best way to visit the area. For rates, see the individual lodge listings below. In addition, there are several San José–based tour companies that offer budget 2-day/1-night excursions to Tortuguero, which include transportation, all meals, and limited tours around the region. Prices for these trips range between $65 and $90 per person, and guests are generally lodged in one of the basic hotels in Tortuguero Village. These trips are good for travelers who like to be able to say, "Been there, done that." However, if you really want to experience Tortuguero, I recommend staying for at least two nights. In fact, many of these package tours are quite flexible, with the option of adding on an extra day or two, or upgrading your accommodations. Companies offering these excursions include **Ecole Travel** (☎ **506/223-2240**) and **Tortuguero Odyssey Tours** (☎ **506/758-0824**).

BOAT CANAL TOURS Aside from watching the turtles nest, the unique thing to do in Tortuguero is tour the canals by boat. Most of the lodges can arrange a canal tour for you, but you can also arrange a tour through one of the operators in Tortuguero Village. I recommend **Ernesto Castillo**, who can be reached through Cabinas Sabina or by just standing anywhere in the village and shouting his name—Tortuguero's that small. **Daryl Loth** (☎ **506/381-4116**), who lives in the yellow house in front of the Jungle Shop, or **Albert Taylor**, who can be reached through Cabinas Miss Junie (☎ **506/710-0523**), are also good. Daryl is leading the way away from loud and polluting two-stroke engines, and he gives a tour with a combination four-stroke and electric engines, to provide a cleaner, quieter trip around Tortuguero. If none of these guides is available, ask for a recommendation at **Paraiso Tropical Gift Shop** (☎ **506/710-0323**) or at the **Caribbean Conservation Corporation's Museum** (☎ **506/710-0547**). Most guides charge between $12 and $15 per person for a tour of the canals. If you travel through the park, you'll also have to pay the park entrance fee ($6 per person). Expect to pay around $10 per person for a night tour of the canals.

FISHING TRIPS & PACKAGES

All of the lodges along this coast offer fishing trips and fishing packages. If you want to try your hand at reeling in a monster tarpon, it will generally cost you between $35 and $50 per hour, including boat, guide, and tackle.

EXPLORING THE TOWN

The most popular attraction in town is the small **Caribbean Conservation Corporation's Visitors' Center and Museum** (☎ **506/710-0547;** e-mail: ccc@cccturtle.org). While the museum has information and exhibits on a whole range of native flora and fauna, its primary focus is on the life and natural history of the sea turtles. Most visits to the museaum include a short informative video on the turtles. There is a small gift shop here, and all the proceeds go toward conservation and turtle protection. The museum is open daily, 10am until noon and 2 to 5pm. On Sunday the museum is open only from 2 to 5pm. There's no admission charge, but donations are encouraged.

In the village, you can also rent dugout canoes, known here in Costa Rica as *cayucos* or *pangas*. Be careful before renting and taking off in one of these; they tend to be heavy, slow, and hard to maneuver, and you may be getting more than you bargained for.

There are a couple of souvenir shops on the main footpath near the center of the village—the **Jungle Shop** (no phone) donates 10% of its profits to local schools and is open from 9am to 5pm, and **Paraiso Tropical Gift Shop** (☎ **506/710-1323**), which is open from 8:30am to 6pm.

ACCOMMODATIONS & DINING

Although the room rates below appear quite high, keep in mind that they usually include round-trip transportation from San José (which amounts to approximately $100 per person) and all meals. When broken down into nightly room rates, most of the lodges charge between $40 and $60 for a double room.

EXPENSIVE

✪ **Tortuga Lodge.** Avenida 3 and Calle Central (Apdo. 6941-1000), San José. ☎ **506/257-0766** or 506/222-0333. Fax 506/257-1665. www.expeditions.co.cr. E-mail: costaric@expeditions.co.cr. 25 units. $637 double, 2 days/1 night; $771 double, 3 days/2 nights. Rates include round-trip transportation (bus and boat one-way, charter flight the other) from San José and 3 meals daily. MC, V.

The whole Tortuga Lodge operation received a face-lift in 1997, which included the construction of a large new dining room and bar that fronts Tortuguero's main canal. The nicest feature here is the long multilevel deck, where you can sit and dine, sip a cool tropical drink, or just take in the view as the water laps against the docks at your feet. All the rooms have been remodeled and are considered standards, with one double and one single bed, ceiling fans, and a comfortable private bathroom. I'd opt for the second-floor rooms, which feature varnished wood walls and floors and come with a small covered veranda. Despite the high rates (considerably higher than at other area lodgings), the rooms here are not substantially larger or nicer than those at the Mawamba, Laguna, Jungle, or Pachira lodges; what you're paying for is all the years of experience that Costa Rica Expeditions, the lodge's owner, brings to Tortuguero. Service here is generally quite good, as are the meals.

Dining: The meals here are much more creative than those you'll find at other lodges in Tortuguero. Although served family style, the meals go far beyond the typical rice and beans that usually define meals in this region. Meals here include homemade bread and special treats, such as fresh cold seafood salad.

Amenities: There are several acres of forest behind the lodge, and a few kilometers of trails wind their way through the trees. This is a great place to look for colorful poison-arrow frogs. Most packages include a couple of different tours, including boat trips through the canals, visits to Tortuguero Village, and trips to see the turtles laying eggs (in season). There are also several optional tours including fishing trips, hikes to Tortuguero Hill, and night hikes.

MODERATE

Laguna Lodge. Apdo. 7-3180, San José. ☎ **506/225-3740.** Fax 506/283-8031. 14 units. $390 double, 3 days/2 nights. Rates include round-trip transportation from San José, tours, and 3 meals daily. MC, V.

This small lodge is a good choice if you want to be on the ocean side of the main canal. Located 2 kilometers north of Tortuguero Village, the rooms here are all very attractive, with wood walls, waxed hardwood floors, and tiled bathrooms with screened upper walls to let in air and light. Each room also has a little shared veranda. There's a small screen-walled dining room that serves basic family style meals, and a separate screened bar area, with a small deck area out over the water. Another covered deck, also over the water, is strung with four hammocks for lazing away the afternoons. Several covered palapa huts have also been built among the flowering ginger and hibiscus and strung with hammocks. All the standard Tortuguero tours are available.

✪ **Mawamba Lodge.** Apdo. 10050-1000, San José. ☎ **506/223-7490,** 506/223-2421, or 506/222-5463. Fax 506/255-4039. www.crica.com/hotels/mawamba.htm. E-mail: mawamba@sol.racsa.co.cr. 40 units. $338 double, 2 days/1 night; $423 double, 3 days/2 nights. Rates include round-trip transportation from San José, 3 meals daily, and some tours. AE, MC, V.

Located about 500 meters north of Tortuguero Village on the beach side of the canal, Mawamba is a good choice for anyone who would like to be able to wander this isolated stretch of beach or walk into town at will. Rooms have varnished wood floors, twin beds, hot-water showers, ceiling fans, and a veranda with rocking chairs. There are also plenty of hammocks around for anyone who wants to kick back. However, there is also a beach volleyball court for those seeking more active diversion, a Jacuzzi for those who have been too active, and the only swimming pool in Tortuguero. This latter attraction is a big plus, as the ocean here is generally not suitable for bathing. The gardens are lush and overgrown with flowering ginger, heliconia, and hibiscus. Meals are above average for Tortuguero, and might include pasta and lobster or chicken in béchamel sauce. Plus there is usually good, fresh bread. You can dine either in the screened-in dining room or out on the patio. Tours included in the rates include a 4-hour boat ride through the canals and a guided forest hike. There's a small gift shop on the premises and nightly lectures and slide shows that focus on the natural history of this area. Optional tours include a night hike ($17 per person) and fishing trips (prices depend on the season and particular fish being sought).

✪ **Pachira Lodge.** P.O. Box 1818-1002, San José. ☎ **506/256-7080** or 506/256-6340. Fax 506/223-1119. E-mail: paccira@sol.racsa.co.cr. 26 units. $295 double, 2 days/1 night; $402 double, 3 days/2 nights. Rates include round-trip transportation from San José, 3 meals daily, and tours. AE, MC, V.

The rooms in this new lodge are in a series of buildings perched on stilts and connected by covered walkways in a dense section of secondary forest set in a little bit from the main canal. Each room is spacious and clean, with varnished wood floors, painted wood walls, two double beds, ceiling fans, and plenty of cross ventilation. The covered walkways come in handy when it rains. Meals are served family style in a large screened-in dining room, and there's even a small gift shop here. Bilingual guides and all the major tour options are available.

INEXPENSIVE

There are several basic lodges in the village of Tortuguero, offering budget lodgings for between $7 and $15 per person. **Cabinas Miss Junie** (☎ **506/710-0523**) and **Cabinas Sabinas** (no phone) are the traditional favorites, although the best of this batch is the new **Cabinas Tortuguero** (no phone), located at the south end of the village on the way toward the national park entrance. If you choose one of these you'll likely be taking your meals at one of the several small sodas in town and will have to make your own arrangements for touring the canals or renting a canoe.

El Manati Lodge. Tortuguero, Limón. ☎ **506/383-0330.** 6 units. $30 double. No credit cards.

If you'd like to have a Tortuguero jungle lodge experience but don't have the bucks to spend on the above places, this is your best choice. This lodge is located across the canal from Laguna Lodge, about 1¼ miles north of Tortuguero Village. The young owners live here and have slowly built the lodge themselves over the years. Most of the rooms are fairly basic, with cement floors and floor fans, but they have attractive curtains and new fixtures in the bathrooms. There's even hot water. Some of the cabins have several rooms, with a variety of sleeping arrangements, including bunk beds. These are a good deal for families. Breakfast and dinner are available (for $5 and $8, respectively). Canal tours and turtle-watching walks are $10 per person for 2 hours, and there are canoes you can rent for $5 per hour. The honor bar is housed in a separate screened-in building and features a dartboard and Ping-Pong table. Transportation up here and back can be arranged in Moín near Limón for $50 to $60 round-trip. Piece it all together, and you come up with a 3-day, 2-night trip with tours, meals, and transportation from Limón for around $250 for two people!

3 Limón: Gateway to Tortuguero National Park & Southern Coastal Beaches

99 miles (160km) E of San José; 34 miles (55km) from Puerto Viejo

It was just offshore from present-day Limón, in the lee of Isla Uvita, that Christopher Columbus is believed to have anchored in 1502, on his fourth and last voyage to the New World. He felt that this was potentially a very rich land and named it Costa Rica (Rich Coast), but it never quite lived up to his expectations. The spot where he anchored, however, has proved over the centuries to be the best port on the Caribbean coast, so his judgment wasn't all bad. It was from here that the first bananas were shipped to North America in the late 19th century. Today, Limón is primarily a rough-and-tumble port city that ships millions of pounds of bananas northward every year.

Limón is not generally considered a tourist attraction, and I don't recommend it except during Carnival, or as a logistical stop in a more complex itinerary. Most travelers use it primarily as a gateway to Tortuguero to the north and the beaches of Cahuita and Puerto Viejo to the south. If you do spend some time in Limón, you can take a seat in Parque Vargas along the seawall and watch the city's citizens go about their business. There are even some sloths living in the trees here. Maybe you'll spot them. Take a walk around town if you're interested in architecture. When banana shipments built this port, many local merchants erected elaborately decorated buildings, several of which have survived the city's many earthquakes. There's a certain charm in the town's fallen grace, drooping balconies, rotting woodwork, and chipped paint. Just be careful after dark, particularly outside of the city center—Limón has earned a reputation for frequent muggings and robberies.

The biggest event of the year in Limón, and one of the most fascinating festivals in Costa Rica, is the annual **Carnival**, which is held for a week around Columbus Day (October 12). For 1 week of the year, languid Limón shifts into high gear for a nonstop bacchanal orchestrated to the beat of reggae, soca, and calypso music. During the revelries, residents of the city don costumes and take to the streets in a dazzling parade of color. In recent years, the central government has tried to rein in Carnival, citing health and safety concerns, but this hasn't deterred the Limonenses. If you want to experience Carnival, make hotel reservations early, as they fill up fast.

If you're planning on heading up to Tortuguero on your own, see "Tortuguero National Park," above, for details on how to get there from Limón.

ESSENTIALS

GETTING THERE & DEPARTING **By Bus** Buses leave San José roughly every half hour daily, between 5am and 7pm from the new Caribbean Bus terminal (Gran Terminal del Caribe) on Calle Central one block north of Avenida 11. Trip duration is 2½–3 hours. The buses are either direct or local (corriente), and they don't alternate in any particularly predictable fashion. The local buses are generally older and less comfortable and stop en route to pick up passengers from the roadside. I highly recommend taking a direct bus if possible. Fare $2.50 for the local, $3.15 for the direct.

Buses leave Limón for San José roughly every half hour between 5am and 7:30pm and similarly alternate between local and direct. The bus stop is one block east and half a block south of the municipal market. Buses to Cahuita and Puerto Viejo leave daily at 5, 8, and 10am and 1 and 4pm. The Cahuita/Puerto Viejo bus stop is on Avenida 4, near the Radio Casino building, one block north of the municipal market. Buses to Punta Uva and Manzanillo, both of which are south of Puerto Viejo, leave Limón daily at 6am and 2:30pm, from the same block.

By Car The Guápiles Highway heads north out of San José on Calle 3 before turning east and passing close to Barva Volcano and through Braulio Carillo National Park, en route to Limón. The drive takes about 2½ hours. Alternatively, you can take the old highway, which is equally scenic, though slower. This highway heads east out of San José on Avenida Central and passes through San Pedro before reaching Cartago. From Cartago on, the road is narrow and winding and passes through Paraiso and Turrialba before descending out of the mountains to Siquírres, where the old highway meets the new. This route will take you 4 hours or more to get to Limón.

ORIENTATION Nearly all addresses in Limón are measured from the central market, which is aptly found smack-dab in the center of town, or from Parque Vargas, which is at the east end of town fronting the sea. The bus stop for buses out to Moín and Playa Bonita is located in front of the prominent Radio Casino building, just to the north of the Cahuita/Puerto Viejo bus stop.

A NEARBY BEACH: PLAYA BONITA

If you want to get in some beach time while you're in Limón, hop in a taxi or a local bus and head north a few kilometers to **Playa Bonita**, a small public beach. Although the water isn't very clean and is usually too rough for swimming, the setting is much more attractive than downtown. This beach is popular with surfers.

ACCOMMODATIONS & DINING

MODERATE

The first three hotels listed here are a few kilometers out of town toward Playa Bonita, and I seriously recommend them over the options you'll find in Limón proper.

Cabinas Cocori. Playa Bonita (Apdo. 1093), Limón. ☎ and fax **506/758-2930,** or ☎ 506/798-1670. 26 units. A/C TV. $22.50 double, $35 apt. (accommodates up to five people). AE, DC, MC, V.

Located on the water just before you reach Playa Bonita, this hotel and apartment complex commands a fine view of the cove, small beach, and crashing surf. The grounds are in need of landscaping, but the rooms are nice enough. A pair of two-story peach-colored buildings house the rooms. The apartments each have a kitchenette with hot plate and refrigerator, two bedrooms, and a bathroom. A long veranda runs along both floors. The rooms are small and basic but clean. All rooms have air-conditioning, but those on the second floor have better sea breezes and views. The restaurant here serves basic Tico fare but has a fabulous setting overlooking the sea.

Hotel Maribu Caribe. Apdo. 623-7300, San José. ☎ **506/758-4543,** 506/758-4010, or 506/253-1838 in San José. Fax 506/758-3541, or 506/234-0193 in San José. 52 units. A/C TEL. $78 double, $88 triple. AE, DC, MC, V.

Located on top of a hill overlooking the Caribbean and built to resemble an Indian village, the Maribu Caribe is a pleasant, if not overly luxurious, choice if you're looking to spend some time in the sun. The hotel is popular with Tico families from San José because it's easy to get to for weekend trips. The guest rooms are in circular bungalows with white-tile floors and varnished wood ceilings. The furnishings are confortable but a bit old.

The hotel's restaurant has the best view in Limón, or in all of Costa Rica, for that matter. It's built out over the edge of a steep hill, with tide pools and the ocean below. In addition to the formal dining room, there are tables outside on a curving veranda that make the most of the view. Entree prices range from $5 to $20, and the emphasis is on seafood prepared in the continental style. There's a bar here, as well as a bar/snack bar by the pool. The Maribu Caribe can help you with tour arrangements and has a gift shop.

INEXPENSIVE

Hotel Acon. Avenida 3 and Calle 3 (Apdo. 528), Limón. ☎ **506/758-1010.** Fax 506/758-2924. 39 units. A/C TV TEL. $23 double, $27 triple. AE, MC, V.

This older in-town choice is a good bet in Limón. The rooms, all of which are air-conditioned (almost a necessity in this muggy climate), are clean and have two twin beds and a large bathroom. The restaurant on the first floor just off the lobby is a cool, dark haven on steamy afternoons and features a wide selection of typical Tico and Chinese dishes. Prices range from $2.50 to $10. The second-floor disco stays open late on weekends, so don't count on a quiet night.

Park Hotel. Avenida 3 between Calles 1 and 3, Limón. ☎ **506/758-3476** or 506/ 798-0555. Fax 506/758-4364. 32 units. $15–$25 double, $18–$28 triple, $30–$40 suites. AE, MC, V.

You can't miss this pink pastel building across the street from the fire station. It's certainly seen better years, but in Limón there aren't too many choices, and this seems to be where I often end up staying. This place is periodically painted and spruced up, but the climate and sea breezes really take their toll. Still, part of what makes this place memorable is the aging tropical ambience. Try to see the room you'll be getting before putting any money down. Ask for a room on the ocean side of the hotel because these are brighter, quieter, and cooler than those that face the fire station, although they're also slightly more expensive. The suites are generally kept in much better condition and have private ocean-view balconies; moreover, some have either air-conditioning or a television, or both. The large, sunny dining room off the lobby serves standard Tico fare at very reasonable prices.

En Route South

✪ **Selva Bananito Lodge.** P.O. Box 801-1007, San José (mailing address in the U.S.: 850 Juniper Avenue, Kellogg, IA 50135). ☎ and fax **506/253-8118.** Fax 506-224-2640. www.netins.net/showcase/costarica. E-mail: conselva@sol.racsa.co.cr. 7 units. $135 double, lower rates available in the off-season. Rate includes 3 meals daily. No credit cards.

This new nature lodge is a welcome addition to the Caribbean coast, allowing you to combine exploration of a the Talamanca lowland rain forests with some serious beach time in Cahuita or Puerto Viejo. The seven individual raised-stilt cabins here are all spacious and comfortable, with an abundance of varnished woodwork. Inside you'll find two double beds, a desk and chair, and some fresh flowers, as well as a large private bathroom. Outside, there's a wraparound veranda, with a hammock and some sitting chairs. It all adds up to what I call "rustic luxury." Half the cabins have views of the Bananito River and a small valley, the other half have views of the Matama mountains, part of the Talamanca mountain range. There are no electric lights at Selva Bananito, but each evening as you dine by candlelight, your cabin's oil lamps are lit for you. Hot water is provided by gravity-fed solar panels. Tasty family style meals are served in the large, open rancho, which is also a great spot for morning bird watching. There's a wide range of tours and activities including rain-forest hikes and horseback rides in the jungle here, tree climbing, self-guided trail hikes, and even the opportunity to rappel down the face of a jungle waterfall. The owners are very involved in conservation efforts in this area, and approximately two-thirds of the 850 hectares here are primary forest managed as a private reserve. You'll need a four-wheel-drive vehicle to reach the lodge, or arrange pickup in Bananito beforehand.

4 Cahuita

124 miles (200km) E of San José; 26 miles (42km) S of Limón; 8 miles (13km) N of Puerto Viejo.

The influx of tourists and an apparently robust drug trade have changed the face and feel of this quiet Caribbean town. A few notorious crimes against visitors have had a serious impact here, and even though local citizens and business owners have responded to the problem and even organized civilian patrols to monitor the park paths during the day (and unlit streets at night), it's still highly recommended that you take every possible precaution against robbery and avoid walking alone outside of downtown at night.

Any way you cut it, Cahuita is still one of the most laid-back villages you'll find anywhere in Costa Rica. After a short time, you'll likely find yourself slipping into the heat-induced torpor that affects anyone who ends up here. The gravel streets are almost always deserted, and the social heart of the village is the front porches of Salon Vaz and Salon Sarafina, Cahuita's dueling bar/discos. The village traces its roots to Afro-Caribbean fishermen and laborers who settled in this region in the mid-1800s, and today the population is still primarily English-speaking blacks whose culture and language set them apart from other Costa Ricans.

The main reason people come to Cahuita, other than its laid-back atmosphere, is its miles of pristine beaches, which stretch both north and south from town. The beaches to the south, as well as the forest behind them and one of Costa Rica's few coral reefs beneath the waters offshore, are all part of Cahuita National Park. Silt and pesticides washing down from nearby banana plantations have taken a heavy toll on the coral reefs, so don't expect the snorkeling to be world-class. Still, it can be pretty good on a calm day, and the beaches inside the park are idyllic.

ESSENTIALS

GETTING THERE & DEPARTING **By Bus** Express buses leave San José daily at 10am, 1:30pm, and 4pm from the new Caribbean Bus terminal (Gran Terminal del Caribe) on Calle Central one block north of Avenida 11. The trip's duration is 4 hours; fare is $4.50. On Saturday and Sunday there is an extra bus at 8am. However, it is always best to check, as this bus line (Mepe) is one of the most fickle in Costa Rica.

Buses leave from the same station for Sixaola at 6am and 3:30pm and currently stop in Cahuita. Previously, they dropped folks off on the entrance road, about 500 meters from town.

Alternatively, you can catch a bus to Limón (see Limón section, above, for details) and then transfer to a Cahuita- or Puerto Viejo–bound bus in Limón. These latter buses leave daily at 5, 8, and 10am and 1 and 4pm from Radio Casino, which is one block north of the municipal market. Buses from Limón to Manzanillo also stop in Cahuita and leave daily at 6am and 2:30pm. The trip takes 1½ hours; fare is $1.15.

Buses departing Puerto Viejo and Sixaola (on the Panama border) stop in Cahuita at approximately 7, 8, 10, and 11:15am and 2, 4, and 5pm en route to San José. However, these buses are often full, particularly on weekends and throughout the high season. To avoid standing in the aisle all the way to San José, it is sometimes better to take a bus first to Limón and then catch one of the frequent Limón/San José buses. Buses to Limón leave daily at 6:30 and 9am, noon, and 3, 4:30, and 6pm. Another tactic I've used is to take a morning bus to Puerto Viejo, spend the day down there, and board a direct bus to San José at its point of origin, thereby snagging a seat.

By Car Follow the directions above for getting to Limón, and as you enter the outskirts of Limón, watch for a paved road to the right (it's just before the railroad tracks). Take this road south to Cahuita, passing the airstrip and the beach on your left as you leave Limón.

ORIENTATION There are only eight sand streets in Cahuita, so you shouldn't get lost. Three roads lead into town from the highway. Buses usually take the road that leads into the heart of town and drop their passengers in front of the Salon Vaz bar. An alternate route bypasses town and heads toward Playa Negra, which is just north of town. As you're coming from the north, the first road leads to the north end of Playa Negra. If you come in on the bus and are staying at a lodge on Playa Negra, head out of town on the street that runs between Salon Vaz and the small park. This road curves to the left and continues a mile or so out to Playa Negra. The village's main street dead-ends at the entrance to the national park (a footbridge over a small stream). The bus stop is in front of Salon Vaz.

FAST FACTS You can wash your clothes at the self-service Laundromat in front of Cabinas Vaz. One load in the washer or dryer will cost $1.50. The police station is located where the road from Playa Negra turns into town. The post office, next door to the police station, is open Monday through Friday from 8am to 5pm. In addition to tours and bicycle rentals, **Cahuita Tours and Adventure Center** (☎ **506/755-0232**), on the main road to Playa Negra about 2½ blocks from Salon Vaz, offers international fax service and allows travelers to exchange money. If you can't find a cab in town, try calling **René** (☎ **506/755-0243**).

EXPLORING CAHUITA NATIONAL PARK

On arrival, you'll immediately feel the call of the long scimitar of beach that stretches south from the edge of town. This beach is glimpsed through the trees from Cahuita's sun-baked main street and extends a promise of relief from the heat. While the lush coastal forest and picture-perfect palm lines are a tremendous draw, the park was actually created to preserve the 600-acre coral reef that surrounds it. The reef contains 35 species of coral and provides a haven for hundreds of brightly colored tropical fish. You can walk on the beach itself, or follow the trail that runs through the forest just behind the beach to check out the reef.

The best place to swim is just before or beyond the Peresoso (Lazy River), several hundred yards inside Cahuita National Park. The trail behind the beach is great for bird watching, and if you're lucky, you might see some monkeys or a sloth. The loud grunting sounds you hear off in the distance are the calls of howler monkeys, which can be heard from more than a mile away. Nearer at hand, you're likely to hear crabs scuttling amid the dry leaves on the forest floor—there are half a dozen or so species of land crabs living in this region. My favorites are the bright orange-and-purple ones. The trail behind the beach stretches a little more than 4 miles (6.4km) to the southern end of the park at **Puerto Vargas,** where you'll find a beautiful white-sand beach, the park headquarters, and a primitive campground with showers and outhouses. The reef is off the point just north of Puerto Vargas, and you can snorkel here. However, the nicest coral heads are located several hundred yards offshore, and it's best to have a boat take you out. A 3-hour snorkel trip should cost around $20 per person with equipment. These can be arranged with any of the local tour companies listed below. Be warned: These trips are best taken when the seas are calm—for safety's sake, for visibility, and for comfort.

If you don't dawdle, the hike to Puerto Vargas should take no more than 2 hours each way. Bring plenty of mosquito repellent, as this area can be buggy.

ENTRY POINTS, FEES & REGULATIONS The in-town park entrance is just over a footbridge at the end of the village's main street. It has recently been spruced up and now has bathroom facilities, changing rooms, and storage lockers. This is the best place to enter if you're just interested in spending the day on the beach and maybe taking a little hike in the bordering forest. The main park entrance is at the southern end of the park in Puerto Vargas. This is where you should come if you plan to camp at the park, or if you don't feel up to hiking a couple of hours to reach the good snorkeling spots. The road to Puerto Vargas is approximately 3 miles (5km) south of Cahuita on the left. Officially, admission is $6 per person per day, but the last time I visited, the fee was being collected only at the Puerto Vargas entrance, and it was possible to enter the park from the town of Cahuita with just a voluntary contribution. The park is open from dawn to dusk for day visitors. There is an extra $1.50 per person charge for camping. The 50 campsites at Puerto Vargas stretch along for several kilometers and are either right on or just a few steps from the beach. My favorite campsites are those farthest from the entrance. There are basic shower and bathroom facilities at a small ranger station, but these can be a bit far from some of the campsites.

BEACHES & ACTIVE SPORTS OUTSIDE THE PARK

Outside the park, the best place for swimming is **Playa Negra**. The stretch right in front of Atlantida Lodge is my favorite spot.

If you want to take advantage of any organized adventure trips or tours while in Cahuita, there are plenty of options. I recommend **Cahuita Tours and Adventure Center** (☎ **506/755-0232;** fax 506/755-0082), on the village's main street heading out toward Playa Negra. Cahuita Tours has glass-bottom boat and snorkeling trips for $15 to $20 per person. They also arrange jungle tours ($15 to $25), white-water-rafting trips ($65 to $85), and Jeep tours to the Bribri reservation. Cahuita Tours also rents bicycles ($7.50 per day), boogie boards ($12.50 per day), snorkeling equipment ($7.50 per day), and binoculars ($7.50 per day), and also has a decent little gift shop and provides fax and money-changing services.

In addition, **Turistica Cahuita Information Center** (☎ **506/755-0071**), also on the main road heading out toward Playa Negra, and **Roberto Tours** (no phone), a block away from the Salon Vaz toward the park, offer similar tours and rentals at similar prices. Most of the companies also offer multiday trips to Tortuguero, as well as to Bocas del Toro, Panama.

Brigitte (watch for the sign on Playa Negra) rents horses for $5 per hour (you must have experience) and also offers guided horseback tours for $25 to $35.

Bird-watchers who have a car should head north 5½ miles (9km) to the **Aviaros de Caribe Bed-and-Breakfast Lodge** (☎ and fax **506/382-1335**), where guided canoe tours of the Estrella Estuary are available. More than 310 species of birds have been sighted in the immediate area. The 3½-hour tour costs $30 per person and leaves throughout the day, but it's best to leave very early or near dusk and to make reservations in advance. If you would just like to walk their grounds and bird-watch from their covered deck, there's a $3 entrance fee.

SHOPPING

For a wide selection of beach wear, local crafts, cheesy souvenirs, and batik clothing, you can try either **Boutique Coco Miko** or **Boutique Bambata**, which are on the main road near the entrance to the park. The latter is also a good place to have your hair wrapped in colorful threads and strung with beads. Out toward Playa Negra, similar wares are offered at the gift shop at **Cahuita Tours** and the neighboring **Toucan Rasta Boutique**.

Ask around town and you should be able pick up a copy of Paula Palmer's *What Happen: A Folk-History of Costa Rica's Talamanca Coast* (Publications in English, 1993). The book is a history of the region, based on interviews with many of the area's oldest residents. Much of it is in the traditional Creole language, from which the title is taken. It makes fun and interesting reading, and you just might bump into someone mentioned in the book.

Finally, don't forget to check out the handmade jewelry and crafts sold by local and itinerant artisans, who usually set up makeshift stands near the park entrance.

EVENING ENTERTAINMENT

The Salon Vaz, a classic Caribbean bar, has traditionally been the place to spend your nights (or days, for that matter) if you like cold beer and very loud reggae and soca music. **The Salon Sarafina**, located just across the street, is giving Vaz a run for its money. I personally find it ever so slightly nicer and more hospitable. There are usually local women hanging out on the front porches of each establishment, selling fresh pati pies or bowls of run-down stew.

ACCOMMODATIONS

MODERATE

Atlantida Lodge. Cahuita, Limón. ☎ **506/755-0115.** Fax 506/755-0213. www.atlantida.co.cr. E-mail: atlantis@sol.racsa.co.cr. 30 units. $55 double, $65 triple, $75 quad; lower rates available in the off-season. AE, MC, V.

Set amid lush gardens and wide green lawns and run by French Canadians, the Atlantida is a quiet and comfortable retreat, with a great location in front of Playa Negra. The guest rooms are done in a style reminiscent of local Indian architecture, with pale yellow stucco walls and plenty of bamboo trim. A recent remodeling has spruced the place up, and the rooms all now have cool tile floors instead of painted cement. Each room also has a patio with a bamboo screen divider for privacy, which opens onto the hotel's lush gardens. The meals are served in an open rancho dining room. The continental-style dinners are reasonably priced and well prepared, though they're available only to hotel guests. There is complimentary coffee offered all day, and a host of different tours can be arranged here, from snorkeling to horseback riding to white-water rafting. The beach is right across the street, and the hotel also has a conference room, a small gym, and a nice tile pool. You'll find it beside the soccer field on the road to Playa Negra, about a mile out of town.

✪ **Aviarios del Caribe.** Apdo. 569-7300, Limón. ☎ and fax **506/382-1335.** 6 units. $65 double, $80 triple, $95 quad. Rates include full breakfast. AE, MC, V.

If you prefer bird watching to beaching, this B&B, located on the edge of a small river delta, is the place to stay on this section of the Atlantic coast. As the name implies, birds are important here, and the lodge's owners have spotted more than 310 species within the immediate area. You can work on your life list from the lawns, the second-floor open-air dining room and lounge, or a canoe paddling around the nearby canals. This house is built up on stilts and is surrounded by a private wildlife sanctuary that also includes forest trails. The guest rooms are all large and comfortable and have fans, tile floors, potted plants, fresh flowers, and modern bathroom fixtures. Some rooms also have king-size beds. In the lounge area you'll find a fabulous collection of mounted insects, as well as terrariums that house live snakes and poison-arrow frogs. You'll also certainly make friends with Buttercup, the resident three-toed sloth. Only breakfast is served here, so you'll have to take your other meals in Cahuita or at a roadside soda along the way.

Chalet Hibiscus. Apdo. 943, Limón. ☎ **506/755-0021.** Fax 506/755-0015. 7 units. Dec–Apr, $40–$50 cabin, $50–$100 house; lower rates available May–Nov. AE, MC, V.

If you're planning a long stay in Cahuita, I advise checking into this place. Although it's about 1¼ miles from town on the road along Playa Negra, it's well worth the journey. The largest house has two bedrooms and sleeps up to six people.

There's hardwood paneling all around, a full kitchen, hot water, red-tile floors, a *pila* (washbasin) for doing your laundry, and even a garage. A spiral staircase leads to the second floor, where you'll find hammocks on a balcony that looks over a green lawn to the ocean. The attractive little cabins have wicker furniture and walls of stone and wood. If you ever wanted to be marooned on the Mosquito Coast, this is the place to live out your fantasy. You're a kilometer north of Playa Negra here, but there's a tiny swimming pool for cooling off during the day. The other houses are similarly simple yet elegant, and the setting is serene and beautiful. Be sure to ring the bell outside the gate—there are guard dogs on the grounds. If the houses and cabins here are full, the owner can arrange rentals of similar accommodations nearby. The hotel now has a small second-floor bar, with a good billiards table. There is also a TV room for vegging out and a volleyball court for getting active.

✪ **El Encanto Bed and Breakfast.** Apdo. 1234, Limón (just outside of town on the road to Playa Negra). ☎ and fax **506/755-0113.** 3 units. $38 double, $46 triple, lower in the off-season. Rates include complete breakfast. AE, MC, V.

The three individual bungalows at this new bed-and-breakfast are set in from the road, on spacious and well-kept grounds. The bungalows themselves are equally spacious and have interesting touches such as wooden bed frames, arched windows, Mexican tile floors, Guatemalan bedspreads, and framed Panamanian molas hanging on the walls. Hearty breakfasts are served in the open dining room. The owners are friendly and helpful—and don't worry, the two large German shepherds that greet you don't bite.

✪ **Magellan Inn.** Plaza Víquez, Cahuita (Apdo. 1132, Limón). ☎ and fax **506/755-0035.** www.web-span.com/tropinet/magellan1.htm. E-mail: borgato@sol.racsa.co.cr. 6 units. $59 double, $69 triple. Rates include continental breakfast. AE, DC, MC, V.

This small inn is out at the far end of Playa Negra (about 2 kilometers north of Cahuita) and is the most luxurious hotel in the area. The six large rooms are all carpeted and have French doors, vertical blinds, tiled bathrooms with hardwood counters, and two joined single beds with attractive bedspreads. Each room has its own spacious tiled veranda with an overhead fan and bamboo chairs. There is a casually sophisticated combination bar/lounge and sitting room that has oriental-style rugs and wicker furniture. Most memorable of all are the hotel's sunken pool and garden, both of which are built into a crevice in the ancient coral reef that underlies this entire region. There is often good bird watching right here. Quiet breakfasts are served right here, and the sister restaurant Casa Creole is just next door.

INEXPENSIVE

✪ **Alby Lodge.** Apdo. 840, Limón. ☎ and fax **506/755-0031.** 4 units. $30 double, $35 triple, $39 quad. Children under 13 stay for free. No credit cards.

Located about 150 yards down the winding lane to the right just before you reach the park entrance, the Alby Lodge is a fascinating little place hand-built by its German owners. Though the four small cabins are close to the center of the village, they're surrounded by a large lawn and feel secluded. The cabins are quint-essentially tropical, with thatch roofs, mosquito nets, hardwood floors and beams, big shuttered windows, tile bathrooms, and a hammock slung on the front porch. You won't find more appealing rooms in this price range.

Cabinas Atlantic Surf. Cahuita, Limón. ☎ **506/755-0086.** 6 units. $15 double. No credit cards.

These small but attractive rooms are a great choice for budget travelers. In a town where all the newer hotels seem to be built of cement, the rustic, varnished wood walls, floors, and small porches of these rooms are a welcome sight. There are fans and tiled showers within, and Adirondack chairs on the porches. The upstairs rooms have high ceilings but still get pretty warm. The Atlantic Surf is down the lane from the Cabinas Sol y Mar, only 100 yards from the park entrance.

New Cabinas Arrecife. Cahuita (100 meters west of the post office), Limón. ☎ and fax **506/755-0081.** 10 units. $20 double, $30 triple. MC, V.

Located out near the water, next to Restaurant Edith, this new row of basic rooms is another excellent budget choice in Cahuita. Each room comes with a double and a single bed, table fan, and tile floors. There's not a lot of room to move around, but things are pretty clean and new for this price range. There's a shared veranda with some chairs for sitting, where you can catch a glimpse of the sea through a dense stand of coconut palms. If you want to be closer to the sea, grab one of the hammocks strung on those palms, or sit in the small open restaurant, which serves breakfast every day and dinners according to demand.

Seaside Jenny's. Cahuita, Limón. ☎ **506/755-0256.** 8 units. $15–$30 double, slightly lower during off-season. No credit cards.

Located 200 yards straight ahead (toward the water) from the bus stop, Jenny's place has been popular for years, and her newer rooms are some of the best in town in this price range. Best of all, they're right on the water, so you can go to sleep to the sound of the waves. All of the rooms have shuttered windows, and there are sling chairs and hammocks on their porches. The more expensive rooms are on the second floor and have what are arguably the best views in Cahuita. There's one room in an older building, which, even though it has a big porch and plenty of Caribbean atmosphere, is not quite as nice as the others.

Dining

Coconut meat and milk figure in a lot of the regional cuisine. Most nights, local women cook up pots of various local specialties and sell them from the front porches of the two discos; a full meal will cost you about $2.50. For snacks, there's **The Pastry Shop**, a tiny bakery on the left side of the main road as you head toward Playa Negra. The coconut pie, brownies, gingersnaps, banana bread, and corn pudding are all delicious. Prices range from 50¢ to $1.

In addition to the places mentioned below, you might see if anything is happening at **Sobre Las Olas** (no phone), out by the water on the road to Playa Negra. The restaurant here has historically been plagued by sketchy service and inconsistent food quality, and it's constantly changing management. However, the location is one of the best in town, with a great view of the waves crashing on the reef. I've also heard good things about the Italian food at the new **Ristorante Delle Alpi** at the Hotel Cahuita and the pizza at **Emilio's** in front of Cabinas Palmer.

✪ **Casa Creole.** Playa Negra Road, 1½ miles (2.5km) north of Cahuita. ☎ **506/755-0104.** Reservations suggested during the high season. Main courses $6.50–$16. MC, V. Mon–Sat 6–9pm. FRENCH/CREOLE.

While the rest of Cahuita may feel like a misplaced piece of Bob Marley's Jamaica, this new restaurant takes its inspiration from islands a little farther south in the Caribbean—and far more French. The restaurant is an outgrowth of the neighboring Magellan Inn. Tables in the open first floor dining room are set with linen tablecloths, and candles in glass lanterns. The building is painted a lively pastel pink, with plenty of painted gingerbread and varnished wood trim. There's a sense of informal elegance about it all. Start with a dish of the pâté maison or a shrimp, coconut, and pineapple cocktail. The spiced shrimp martiniquaise and the sumbo soconut shrimp are both excellent, as is the fresh fish seasoned and baked inside a banana leaf. The emphasis here is on seafood, but the ample menu includes meat, chicken, and pasta dishes. Top it off with some fresh raspberry coulis, homemade profiteroles, or exquisite homemade fresh fruit sherbet.

✪ **Margaritaville.** Playa Negra Road, 1¼ miles north of Cahuita. ☎ **506/755-0038.** Reservations not necessary. Complete meals $6–$8. No credit cards. Mon–Sat 8–10am and 6–10pm. INTERNATIONAL.

There's usually only one main dish served each night at this little restaurant, but if you drop by ahead of time and make a special request, the friendly owner may try to accommodate you. If you're an adventurous eater, though, I'm sure you'll enjoy whatever is coming from the kitchen, which might be roasted chicken, a local Creole dish made with coconut milk, or eggplant lasagne. All the breads are home-baked and delicious. The tables here are set up on the open second floor of Moray's B&B. It's all very mellow and definitely not to be missed.

Restaurant Edith. By the police station. ☎ **506/755-0248.** Reservations not accepted. Main courses $3.50–$11.50. No credit cards. Mon–Sat 7am–10pm, Sun 6–10pm. CREOLE/SEAFOOD.

This place has become a tradition, and deservedly so. Quite some years ago, Miss Edith decided to start serving up home-cooked meals to all the hungry tourists hanging around. If you want a taste of the local cuisine in a homey sit-down environment, this is the place. While Miss Edith's daughters take the orders, Mom cooks up a storm out back. The menu, when you can get hold of it, is long, with lots of local seafood dishes and Creole combinations such as yuca in coconut milk with meat or vegetables. The sauces here have spice and zest and are a welcome change from the typically bland fare served up throughout the rest of Costa Rica. After you've ordered, it's usually no more than 45 minutes until your meal arrives. It's often crowded here, so don't be bashful about sitting down with total strangers at any of the big tables. Miss Edith's place is at the opposite end of town from the park entrance, just turn right at the police station/post office.

5 Puerto Viejo

124 miles (200km) E of San José; 34 miles (55km) S of Limón

Though Puerto Viejo is even smaller than Cahuita, it has a somewhat livelier atmosphere due to the many surfers who come here from around the country (and around the world) to ride the village's famous Salsa Brava wave. For nonsurfers, there are also some good swimming beaches, and if you head still farther south, you will come to the most beautiful beaches on this coast. When it's calm, the waters down in this region are some of the clearest anywhere in the country, and there is some good snorkeling among the coral reefs. Your best chance to find calm conditions, however, is between August and October.

This is the end of the line along Costa Rica's Caribbean coast. After the tiny town of Manzanillo, just south of Puerto Viejo, a national wildlife reserve stretches a few final kilometers to the Panamanian border.

You may notice, as you make your way into town from the highway, that there are cacao trees planted along the road. Most of these trees continue to suffer from a blight that has greatly reduced the cacao-bean harvest in the area. However, there is still a modest local harvest, and you can get delicious cocoa candies here.

ESSENTIALS

GETTING THERE & DEPARTING **By Bus** Express buses (☎ **506/257-8129**) to Puerto Viejo leave San José daily at 10am, 1:30pm, and 4pm from the new Caribbean Bus terminal (Gran Terminal del Caribe) on Calle Central one block north of Avenida 11. The trip's duration is 5 hours; fare is $5. On Saturday and Sunday there is an extra bus at 8am that goes all the way to Manzanillo. However, it is always best to check, as this bus line is one of the most fickle in Costa Rica. Always ask if the bus is going in to Puerto Viejo, and if it's continuing on to Manzanillo (especially helpful if you're staying in a hotel south of town), then don't be surprised if it doesn't do exactly what you were told.

Buses leave from the same station for Sixaola at 6am and 3:30pm, and will leave you at the turnoff for Puerto Viejo (except when they decide to continue in to Puerto Viejo) about 3 miles (5km) outside of town. However, be warned, there is not much traffic on this road and no taxi will likely be waiting for you. You will have to hike in, hitchhike, or wait for a bus coming from Limón to stop and pick you up.

Alternatively, you can catch a bus to Limón (see Limón section, above, for details) and then transfer to a Puerto Viejo–bound bus in Limón. These latter buses leave daily at 5, 8, and 10am and 1 and 4pm from Radio Casino, which is one block north of the municipal market. Buses from Limón to Manzanillo also stop in Puerto Viejo and leave daily at 6am and 2:30pm. The trip takes 1½ hours; fare is $1.30.

Express buses leave Puerto Viejo for San José daily at 7am, 9am, and 4pm. Buses for Limón leave daily at 6 and 8:40am, and 1, 4, and 5pm. Buses to Punta Uva and Manzanillo leave Puerto Viejo daily around 7am and 4pm. These buses return from Manzanillo at 8:15am and 5:15pm.

By Car To reach Puerto Viejo, continue south from Cahuita for another 10 miles (16km). Watch for a dirt road that forks to the left from the paved highway. The paved road continues on up to Bribri and Sixaola. The dirt road will take you into Puerto Viejo after another 3 miles (5km).

ORIENTATION The dirt road in from the highway runs parallel to Playa Negra, or Black Sand Beach, for a couple hundred meters, before entering the village of Puerto Viejo, which has all of about six dirt streets. The sea will be on your left and forested hills on your right as you come into town. It's another 9¼ miles (15km) or so on a rough dirt and gravel road south to Manzanillo.

FAST FACTS Public phones are located at Hotel Maritza, El Pizote Lodge, the Manuel Leon general store (next to Johnny's Place), and the ATEC office. The latter is your best bet for mailing a postcard and obtaining visitor information. The nearest bank is in **Bribri**, about 6 miles (10km) away. There is a Guardia Rural police post near the park on the beach. The town's main taxi driver is named **Bull** and he drives a beat-up old Isuzu Trooper. You might find him hanging around the parquecito, or ask a local to point you to his house.

EXPLORING PUERTO VIEJO

Most people who show up in this remote village have only one thing on their mind: surfing. Just offshore from the tiny village park is a shallow reef where powerful storm-generated waves sometimes reach 20 feet. These waves are the biggest and most powerful on the Caribbean coast. Even when the waves are small, this spot is recommended only for very experienced surfers because of the danger of the reef. There are also popular beach breaks south of town on Playa Cocles. For swimming, head out to **Playa Negra** (this is not the same one I talked about in Cahuita), along the road into town, or to the beaches south of town around Punta Uva, where the surf is much more manageable.

If you aren't a surfer, the same activities that prevail in Cahuita are the norm here also. Read a book, take a nap, or go for a walk on the beach. If you have more energy, you can rent a bicycle or a horse (watch for signs), or just hike and head south toward Punta Uva. You can either follow the beach or stick to the road. After about 5 miles (8km), you'll be rewarded with some of the nicest beaches on this coast.

You should be sure to stop in at the **Association Talamanqueña de Ecoturismo y Conservacion (ATEC)** office (☎/fax **506/750-0188**; e-mail: atecmail@sol.racsa.co.cr), across the street from the Soda Tamara. This local organization is concerned with preserving both the environment and the cultural heritage of this area and promoting ecologically sound development and tourism in the region. In addition to functioning as the local post office and information center, they have a little shop that sells T-shirts, maps, posters, and books. They also offer quite a few different tours. There are half-day walks that focus on nature and either the local African-Caribbean culture or the indigenous Bribri culture. These walks pass through farms and forests, and along the way you'll learn about local history, customs, medicinal plants, and Indian mythology, and have an opportunity to see sloths, monkeys, iguanas, keel-billed toucans, and other wildlife. There are four different walks through the nearby Bribri Indians' KéköLdi Reserve; there are also more strenuous hikes through the primary rain forest. ATEC offers snorkeling trips to the nearby coral reefs and snorkeling and fishing trips in dugout canoes. Bird walks and night walks will help you spot more of the area wildlife; there are even overnight treks. The local guides who lead these tours have a wealth of information and make a hike through the forest a truly educational experience. Don't miss an opportunity to do a tour with ATEC. Half-day walks (and night walks) are $12.50, and a full-day run between $25 and $40. A half day of snorkeling or fishing will cost around $20 per person. ATEC can also help you arrange overnight camping trips into the Talamanca mountains and through neighboring indigenous reserves, as well as trips to Tortuguero. Some tours require minimum groups of 5 or 10 people and several days' advance notice. The ATEC office is open Monday through Saturday from 8am to 8pm, and Sunday from 8am to noon and 4pm to 8pm. If you're looking to stay here for an extended period of time and would like to contribute to the community, this is the place to ask about volunteering.

One of the nicer ways to spend a day in Puerto Viejo is to visit the local **Botanical Gardens** (☎ **506/750-0046;** e-mail:jardbot@sol.racsa.co.cr), located a couple hundred yards inland from the Black Sand beach on a side road just north of El Pizote Lodge. Hosts Peter and Lindy Kring have devoted an equal share of time and love to create this meandering collection of native and imported tropical flora. There are medicinal, commercial, and just plain wild flowering plants, fruits, herbs, trees, and bushes. Visitors get to gorge on whatever is ripe at the moment. There is also a rigorous rain-forest loop trail leaving from the grounds. The gardens are open Friday through Monday from 10am–4pm. Entrance to the garden or loop trail is $2.50 per person, or $8 including the guided tour.

If you're interested in organized adventure tours to Tortuguero, white-water rafting, or snorkeling, you can check with **Terra Aventura** (☎ **506/750-0004**). They offer a wide range of tour options, including a 4-day/3-night trip to Bocas del Toro, Panama, which costs $200 per person, all transportation, lodging, and meals included. Day trips into the jungle or snorkeling cost between $25 and $50 per person. Last I heard their office was next to the pulpería Manuel Leon, which is next to Johnny's Place, but they were perhaps going to move. Ask around; it shouldn't be hard to track them down.

MANZANILLO & THE MANZANILLO-GANDCA WILDLIFE REFUGE

If you continue south on the coast road from Puerto Viejo, you'll come to a couple of even smaller villages. **Punta Uva** is 5 miles (8km) away, and **Manzanillo** is about 9¼ miles (15km) away. For a good day trip you can catch the 7am bus from Puerto Viejo down to Manzanillo and then catch the 5:15pm bus back. Again, it's always wise to check with ATEC about current local bus schedules. Alternatively, it's about 2 hours each way on bicycle, with only two real hills to contend with. However, since the road and most of the bikes rented in town are rather rugged, expect your wrists and rear end to take quite a beating. It's also possible to walk along the beach from Punta Cocles to Manzanillo, a distance of about 6 miles (10km).

Manzanillo is a tiny village with only a few basic cabinas and funky sodas. The most popular place to eat and hang out is **Restaurant Maxi** (no phone), an open-air joint located on the second floor of an old wooden building facing the sea. There's no menu here, but a fresh fish plate will cost you between $5 and $7; lobster, in season, will cost around $12. Whatever you order will come with rice and beans, patacones, and a small side of cabbage salad.

The Manzanillo-Gandoca Wildlife Refuge encompasses the small village and extends all the way to the Panamanian border. Manatees, crocodiles, and more than 350 species of birds live within the boundaries of the reserve. The reserve also includes the coral reef offshore, and when the seas are calm, this is the best snorkel and diving spot on this coast. Four species of sea turtles nest on one 5½-mile-long (8.9km) stretch of beach within the reserve, between March and July. If you want to explore the refuge, you can easily find the well-maintained trail by walking along the beach just south of town until you have to wade across a small river. On the other side you'll pick up the trailhead. Otherwise you can ask around the village for local guides or check out **Aquamor** (☎ **506/228-9513**; e-mail: aquamor@sol.racsa.co.cr), a kayak and dive operation located on the one main road in town. These folks rent kayaks for $5 per hour, and a guide will accompany your group for another $5 per hour. Depending on tides and sea conditions, this is a great way to explore the mangroves and estuaries and even snorkel or dive the nearby coral reef. A one-tank beach dive, with equipment and guide, costs $30 per person. They have a whole variety of tour and diving options, including PADI dive certification courses. Aquamor also often has a few kayaks for rent down on the beach at Punta Uva near Selvyns.

SHOPPING

Color Caribe (☎ **506/750-0075**), across the street from Cabinas Grant, sells hand-painted T-shirts, batik beachwear, and coconut-shell jewelry. Similar wares, as well as a wider selection of Bob Marley memorabilia, can be found at **Boutique Tabu** (no phone), located near the Mepe bus stop. There are also a couple of *pulperías* in the village.

Puerto Viejo attracts a lot of local and international bohemians, who seem to survive solely on the sale of handmade jewlery and painted ceramic trinkets (mainly pipes and cigarette lighter holders). You'll find them at makeshift stands set up by the town's "little park" or *parquecito*, a few wooden benches in front of the sea between Soda Tamara and Stanford's.

Finally, **the ATEC shop** is a great place to get reading materials relevant to the region. Here, you can usually pick up Paula Palmer's oral history, *What Happen: A Folk-History of Costa Rica's Talamanca Coast* (Publications in English, 1993). If you'd like to learn more about the culture of the local Bribri Indians, look for a copy of *Taking Care of Sibö's Gifts* by Paula Palmer, Juanita Sánchez, and Gloria Mayorga. ATEC itself publishes and sells *Coastal Talamanca, A Cultural and Ecological Guide*, a small booklet packed with information about this area. Another good way to get a feel for the languid pulse of this town is to pick up a copy of *Talamanca's Voice*, the locally produced newsletter of the region.

PUERTO VIEJO AFTER DARK

There are two main disco-bars in town. **Johnny's Place** is near the Rural Guard station, about 100 meters north of the ATEC office. You'll find **Standford's** overlooking the water out near Salsa Brava just as the main road heads south of town. Both have small dance floors with ground-shaking reggae, dub, and rap rhythms blaring. The action usually spills out from the dance floor at both joints on most nights. I like the atmosphere better at Johnny's, where they often have tables and candles set out on the sand, near the water's edge.

Another place I like is **El Bambu**, just beyond Stanford's on the road toward Punta Uva. This place is smaller and more intimate than either of the other bars yet still packs them in and gets them dancing on the Monday or Friday reggae nights.

As in Cahuita and Limón, Puerto Viejo has had its peaceful image tarnished by a couple of rapes and other violent incidents like drug trafficking, and endemic petty theft. Be careful here, especially at night, and never leave valuables unattended, *anywhere.*

ACCOMMODATIONS

MODERATE

El Pizote. Puerto Viejo, Limón. ☎ **506/221-0986.** Fax 506/255-1527, or ☎ and fax (at the Lodge) 506/750-0088. www.hotels.co.cr/pizote.html. E-mail: pizotelg@sol.racsa.co.cr. 8 units (shared bathroom), 6 bungalows. $50 double without bathroom, $75 double with bathroom, $66 triple without bathroom, $87 triple with bathroom, $75 quad without bathroom, $100 quad with bathroom. Lower rates available in the off-season. AE, MC, V.

El Pizote changed ownership recently, and some changes are in the works. The big change will be the addition of a swimming pool, the first and only one in Puerto Viejo proper. There are also plans for four new deluxe bungalows with kitchenettes and air-conditioning. Nevertheless, anyone familiar with El Pizote will have no trouble recognizing the lodge. You still have to walk through a dense grove of trees hung heavy with bromeliads and dracaena plants to reach the rooms, which are in a U-shaped unpainted wooden building on raised stilts. The rooms are cool, with polished wood walls, two double beds, and a shared wraparound veranda. There are burlap-and-bamboo window shades, as well as ceiling fans, a desk, and reading lamps. Two clean communal bathrooms, each with several shower stalls and toilets, are shared by the eight rooms. The bungalows are built in a similar style, but each one has it's own bathroom and private veranda. For activity, there are hiking trails in the adjacent forest and a volleyball court. There is good bird watching here. The restaurant serves breakfast ($8) and dinner ($14.50) only, but drinks are available all day. There is a set menu each evening, which might feature spaghetti with shrimp or a fresh fish plate. The meals are hearty but by no means stellar. The Almendros Bar here has a pool table and is popular with locals. El Pizote is directly in front of Black Sand beach about 300 yards before you enter downtown Puerto Viejo.

INEXPENSIVE

Cabinas Chimuri. Puerto Viejo, Limón. ☎ and fax **506/750-0119.** E-mail: atecmail@sol.racsa.co.cr. 4 units (none with bathroom). $21 double, $32 triple or quad, $8.50 per person in dormitory. Discounts offered in the low season. AE, MC, V.

If you're an inveterate camper and don't mind being a 15-minute walk from the beach, I'm sure you'll enjoy this rustic lodge. It's built in traditional Bribri Indian style with thatched-roof A-frame cabins in a forest setting, a short stroll up a trail from the parking lot to the lodge buildings. (There are other trails on the property as well.) This lodge is definitely for nature lovers who are used to roughing it; accommodations are very basic, but there is a kitchen for guests to use. New this year is a dormitory room that sleeps up to eight people in bunk beds. The lodge also runs several different hiking trips into the rain forest and the adjacent Bribri Indian KéköLdi Reserve ($25 per person). If arriving by bus, be sure to get off at the trail to Cabinas Chimuri before the road reaches the beach.

Cabinas Jacaranda. Puerto Viejo, Limón. ☎ **506/750-0069.** 7 units (3 with bathroom). $12 double without bathroom, $17 double with bathroom, $20 triple with bathroom. No credit cards.

This basic backpackers' special has a few nice touches that set it apart from the others. The floors are cement, but there are mats. Japanese paper lanterns cover the lights, and mosquito nets hang over the beds. The Guatemalan bedspreads add a dash of color and tropical flavor, as do the tables made from sliced tree trunks. If you're traveling in a group, you'll enjoy the space and atmosphere of the big room. If the hotel is full, the owners also rent a few nearby bungalows. The Garden Restaurant, adjacent to the rooms, serves the best food in town.

✪ **Casa Verde.** Puerto Viejo, Limón. ☎ and fax **506/750-0015.** Fax 506/750-0047. E-mail: atecmail@sol.racsa.co.cr. 14 units (6 with bathroom). $15–$20 double without bathroom; $25-$30 double with bathroom. Rates slightly lower in the off-season. AE, MC, V.

This little hotel is located on a side street on the south side of town. The older rooms, with shared bathroom, are in an interesting building with a wide, covered breezeway between the rooms and the showers and toilets out back. The front and back porches of this building are hung with hammocks. A quiet sense of tropical tranquillity pervades this place. The newer rooms are behind the house next door and are a bit larger than the older rooms. These new rooms have high ceilings, tile floors, private bathrooms, and a veranda. There is also a small separate bungalow with a kitchenette. Everything is well maintained, and even the shared bathrooms are kept immaculate.

Escape Caribeño. Puerto Viejo (Apdo. 704-7300, Limón). ☎ and fax **506/750-0103** or 506/382-2572. 12 units. $37 double, $45 triple, $53 quad. AE, MC, V.

Located just outside of Puerto Viejo on the road to Punta Uva, Escape Caribeño consists of 10 individual concrete cabins with brick pillars, spacious bedrooms, and tiled patios in a small compound. Large picture windows, vertical blinds, and hardwood furniture give these cabins the aesthetic edge over many area places in this price range. I actually prefer the two wooden cabins located on the ocean side of the main road, near the hotel's office. There are reading lamps by the beds and small refrigerators in every room. The attractive gardens have been planted with bananas and palms. It's a 5-minute walk into town or out to a beautiful beach that has a small island just offshore.

La Perla Negra Hotel. Puerto Viejo, Limón. ☎ **506/750-0111.** Fax 506/750-0114. 24 units. $34 double, slightly higher Christmas and Easter weeks.

While most new hotels around here have been springing up south of town, this place is currently the last hotel on the northern end of Puerto Viejo's Black Sand Beach. From here it's a long but straight walk up the beach to Cahuita National Park. The rooms in this two-story wood complex are all large and have lots of screened windows to encourage cross ventilation. Every room comes with one double and one single bed, and a few even have additional sleeping lofts for families. There are ceiling fans, clean bathrooms, and plenty of woodwork. Each has its own private balcony or patio. Half the rooms face the ocean and the others face an overgrown farm out back. I'd definitely opt for an ocean-facing room. There's a rectangular tile pool and pool-side bar, and the ocean is only about 20 meters away. The hotel serves breakfast daily and lunch and dinner upon request. There's a large brick barbecue available for guest use.

NEARBY PLACES TO STAY

All the hotels listed below are located along the road south of Puerto Viejo heading toward Manzanillo. This is one of the most beautiful and isolated stretches of beach you'll find in Costa Rica. However, I recommend that you have a vehicle if you plan to stay at one of these hotels, since public transportation is sporadic.

MODERATE

✪ **Almendros and Corales Tent Camp.** Manzanillo, Limón (Apdo. 681-2300, Costa Rica). ☎ **506/272-2024** or 506/272-4175. Fax 506/272-2220. 20 tents. $70 double, rates slightly lower during the off-season. MC, V.

This isn't camping in any traditional sense. So don't expect to be roughing it. What you will find here are large raised platforms, big enough so that within the stretched-tarp roof and screened walls there's another large standing-room tent, providing pretty complete protection against rain and mosquitoes. This second tent takes up about half of the platform's screened-in floor space and still leaves room for a hammock, table, chairs, and a bathroom area with a cold-water shower and toilet. Inside the tent you'll find either two single beds or one double bed, a small table, two oil lamps, and a small closet. If that sounds more luxurious than you'd like, remember that the tents are in some dense secondary forest, with nothing but screen and cloth for walls, so you'll still feel very close to nature. There are wooden walkways connecting the tents to the main lodge and dining area. Meals will run you an extra $25 per person per day. Perhaps the best part of the whole setup is the fact that Manzanillo beach is just 200 yards away through the jungle. Snorkel equipment, sea kayaks, bicycles, and a variety of tours are also available.

Best Western Punta Cocles. Puerto Viejo, Limón (Apdo. 11020-1000, San José). ☎ **800/325-6927** in the U.S., 506/234-8055, or 506/234-8051. Fax 506/234-8033. 60 units. A/C TEL. $70 standard room, can accommodate up to 4 people; $90 with kitchenette, can accommodate up to 6. AE, DC, MC, V.

Though this is one of the largest and most expensive hotels in the area, it is certainly not my first choice. I've seen very little change since the Best Western chain assumed management in 1997. My biggest complaints here are that the whole complex lacks personality or character and you are about 500 meters inland from the beach. Situated in a large jungle clearing, the rooms do not get any sea breezes and consequently must be air-conditioned. Still, the rooms are large and well maintained, and those that come with kitchenettes are a good deal, especially if you're traveling with a large group or family. There's the large open-air La Iguana restaurant, which serves unmemorable meals, and the poolside Rasta Mouse Bar, which sometimes features live music. There's an adult as well as children's pool, and a Jacuzzi. There's also a small playground for children, and you can rent mountain bikes and boogie boards here.

Casa Camarona. Playa Cocles, Puerto Viejo, Limón (Apdo. 2270-1002, Paseo de los Estudiantes, San José). ☎ **506/224-3050.** Fax 506/222-6184. 17 units. $45 double, 60 triple. AE, MC, V.

Casa Camarona is a new hotel and has the enviable distinction of being one of the few hotels in this area right on the beach—no road to cross, no path through the jungle, just a small section of shady gardens separates you from the Caribbean Sea. The rooms here are in two separate two-story buildings. Definitely get a room on the second floor. Up here you'll find spacious rooms painted in pleasant pastels, with plenty of cross ventilation and a wide shared veranda. I don't know who designed the first-floor rooms, but the low ceilings made it feel as if the walls were closing in on me. There's a nice-open air restaurant and bar. The best feature here is the location on a quiet section of Playa Cocles. The hotel keeps some chaise longues on the beach under the shade of palm trees, and there's even a beach bar open during the day, so you barely have to leave that chaise to quench your thirst.

✪ **Playa Chiquita Lodge.** Puerto Viejo, Limón. ☎ **506/750-0062** or 506/233-6613. Fax 506/223-7479. http://infoweb.co.cr/bissinger/. E-mail: wolfbiss@sol.racsa.co.cr. 10 units. $39 double, $49 triple, includes full breakfast. Rates slightly lower in the off-season. V.

This place just oozes jungle atmosphere and is sure to please anyone searching for a steamy retreat on the beach. Set amid the shade of large old trees a few miles south of Puerto Viejo toward Punta Uva (watch for the sign), the lodge consists of unpainted wooden buildings set on stilts and connected by wooden walkways. There are wide verandas with rocking chairs and seashell mobiles hanging everywhere. The rooms have recently been painted, which lightens things up quite a bit. They are still spacious, with wide-board floors and paintings by local Indian artists. The top of the bathroom wall is screened so you can gaze out into the jungle as you shower. There is a short trail that leads down to a private little swimming beach with tide pools and beautiful turquoise water. Lately, this beach has become the site of a daily 4:00pm volleyball game. Meals here cost from $5 to $13, and choices range from spaghetti to lobster; since the management is German you can expect a few German dishes as well. Throughout the day there are free bananas and coffee. When I last visited, construction was underway on a thermal spa, which is expected to feature steam baths and massage services. The owners also rent out fully equipped houses for those interested in longer stays or more privacy and independence.

✪ **Shawandha Lodge.** Puerto Viejo, Limón. ☎ **506/750-0018.** Fax 506/750-0037. 12 units. Dec 15–Apr 15, $80 double, Apr 16–Dec 14, $65 double. Rates include full breakfast. AE, MC, V.

If you're looking for a luxurious, isolated, and romantic getaway, this small collection of individual bungalows is a great choice. Set in a lush patch of forest about 200 yards inland from Playa Chiquita, Shawandha has the feel of a small village. Artistic flourishes abound. The thatch-roofed, raised bungalows feature painted exterior murals, high-pitched ceilings, varnished wood floors, and either one king or a mix of queen and single beds. The bathrooms are practically works of art, each with original, intricate mosaics of hand-cut tile highlighting a large open shower. Every bungalow has its own spacious balcony, with both a hammock and couch, where you can lie and look out on the flowering gardens. There's a large open-air restaurant and lounge, where meals and drinks are served. The menu here is an eclectic mix featuring fresh fish and meats in a variety of French, Caribbean, and Polynesian sauces. The beach is easily accessed by a private path, and a host of activities and tours can be arranged.

Villas del Caribe. Puerto Viejo, Limón (Apdo. 8080-1000, San José). ☎ and fax **506/381-3358**, or ☎ 506/233-2200 in San José). Fax 506/221-2801. 12 units. $69 double, $79 triple, $89 quad. AE, MC, V.

If you want to be right on the beach and have spacious, comfortable accommodations, there isn't a better choice in this area. Villas del Caribe, built in a sort of contemporary Mediterranean style and set on a private 100-acre nature reserve, offers two-story villas with full kitchens and a choice of one or two bedrooms. The living rooms have built-in sofa beds, and just outside there is a large terrace complete with barbecue grill. The kitchens are attractively designed, with blue-tile counters. Bathrooms feature wooden-slat shower doors, potted plants on a platform by the window, louvered and screened walls that let in light and air, and more blue-tile counters. Upstairs, you'll find either a large single bedroom with a king-size bed or two smaller bedrooms (one with bunk beds). Either way, there's a balcony with a hammock and an ocean view. The water, which is usually fairly calm, is only steps away through the coconut palms, and there's some coral just offshore that makes for good snorkeling. The hotel can arrange horseback rides, fishing trips, snorkeling, and diving—even oxcart rides. There's still no restaurant here, so you'll have to cook your own food, use one of the nearby basic sodas, or head back into Puerto Viejo.

INEXPENSIVE

Cabinas Selvyn. Punta Uva, Limón. No phone. 10 units (all with shared bathroom), 2 apts. $7.50–$10 double, $150–$200 per month for an apt. No credit cards.

The atmosphere here is friendly and funky. Rooms are located in two old wooden buildings behind the small open-air restaurant. There are no fans here, so try to get one of the second-floor rooms, which receive a bit of the sea breezes. All the rooms come with mosquito nets, but beyond that, the accommodations are spartan. Nevertheless, the hotel is located 100 meters down a dirt lane from one of the most isolated and beautiful beaches in Costa Rica, and the owner is a great cook.

DINING

To really sample the local cuisine, you need to look up a few local women. Ask around for **Miss Dolly** and see if she has anything cooking. Her specialties are bread (especially banana) and ginger biscuits, but she'll also fix a full Caribbean meal for you if you ask a day in advance and she has time. Miss Daisy also makes pan bon, ginger cakes, patties (meat-filled turnovers), and coconut oil (for tanning). Both **Miss Sam** and **Miss Irma** serve up sit-down meals in their modest little sodas. Just ask around for these women and someone will direct you to them. Be sure to try run-down (or "rondon") soup, which is a spicy coconut-milk stew made with anything the cook can run down.

Puerto Viejo has become a very popular destination for Italian immigrants, and it seems everywhere you turn there's a pretty decent Italian restaurant. In addition to the places listed below, you can get very good Italian cuisine at both **Caramba** and **Marco's Pizzeria and Ristorante**, right in town.

✪ **Amimodo.** On the left hand side of the main road heading south of Puerto Viejo, just after Cabinas Salsa Brava. No phone. Main courses $4–14. Daily 6–11pm. No credit cards. NORTHERN ITALIAN.

I first wandered onto this unlikely wonder one Wednesday, when The Garden was closed. Fortune smiled on me. The meal began with a *bresaula de tiburon*, thin slices of home-smoked shark served on a bed of lettuce, with a light avocado dressing. Next came a plate of homemade ravioli stuffed with lobster in a lobster-based red sauce. My companion opted for the gnocchi, which were some of the most melt-in-your-mouth gnocchi I'd ever tasted. Owner Livio Illusig twisted our arms and we shared a fresh grilled red snapper. Dessert was out of the question. The last time I visited Puerto Viejo they were still putting finishing touches on the new location, which will be closer to the water on the road heading toward Punta Uva. I still expect the atmosphere to be informal, with a few more tables spread around the larger, open-air space in this new building. One day, I'll try to save room for dessert.

Café Pizzeria Coral. On the road to the soccer field. ☎ **506/750-0051.** Reservations not accepted. Pizza $3.50–$5; pasta $4–$5. No credit cards. Tues–Sun 7am–noon and 5:30–9:30pm. ITALIAN/PIZZA.

Although this place bills itself as a pizzeria, your best bets are the breakfasts, desserts, and fresh breads. While the pizza here is mediocre, the chocolate cake is a standout. The morning baskets of bread, fruit, granola plates, and giant pancakes will set you back a few colónes, but they'll also set you up for most of the day. The open-air dining room is up a few steps from the street. The whole place is walled in by flowering hibiscus that attracts plenty of hummingbirds in the morning, which is why this is my favorite breakfast joint in town. You'll find the Café Pizzeria Coral about two blocks from the water in the center of the village.

✪ **The Garden Restaurant.** Cabinas Jacaranda. ☎ **506/750-0069.** Reservations not accepted. Main courses $5–$10. No credit cards. Wed–Mon 5:30–10pm. Closed May–June and September. CARIBBEAN/ASIAN.

Just up the block from Café Coral, this restaurant serves the most creative food in Puerto Viejo and some of the best in all of Costa Rica. The co-owner and chef is from Trinidad by way of Toronto and has created an eclectic menu. You'll find such surprising offerings as chicken satay, fresh garden salad with passion fruit dressing, Jamaican jerk chicken, calypso curry fish, and chicken Bangkok. There are also daily specials and lots of delicious fresh juices. Many of the ambrosial desserts are made with local fruits, and there are also such delights as ginger spice cake and chocolate decadence. Every dish is beautifully presented, usually with edible flowers as garnish. Be forewarned: The closing days here are subject to food availability and the chef's mood, so it's always worthwhile to ask in advance.

The Juice Joint. At the Cabinas Salsa Brava, on the main road heading south toward Punta Uva. No phone. Main courses $2–$5. No credit cards. Daily 7am–12am. COSTA RICAN/CONTINENTAL.

The fresh juices, homemade brownies, iced espresso, and hearty lunches at this small outdoor cafe were what initially won me over. Now they also have an open-air barbeque where fresh fish and lobster, chicken, and meats are grilled nightly. The small collection of wooden tables and chairs are painted in dark African-inspired tones. A few have palm thatch umbrellas for shade, and one has an excellent view of the surf action on Salsa Brava. Breakfasts here feature fresh baked goods, fruit plates, granola, and, of course, *gallo pinto* (rice and beans). And the dinners are a great alternative to the many Italian restaurants and simple sodas. At any point of a hot day, this is a great place for a cool drink, a quick bite, and a quiet break from the rigors of beachcombing.

Soda Tamara. On the main road through the village. ☎ **506/750-0148.** Main courses $3.50–$6. AE, MC, V. Wed–Mon 7am–9pm. COSTA RICAN.

This little Tico-style restaurant has long been popular with budget-conscious travelers and has an attractive setting for such an economical place. There's a patio dining area, which is actually larger and more comfortable than the main dining room, which is a bit dark and cramped. The painted picket fence in front gives the restaurant a homey feel. The menu features standard fish, chicken, and meat entrees, served with a hefty helping of Caribbean-style rice and beans. You can also get *patacones* (fried chips made out of plantains) and a wide selection of fresh fruit juices. However, service can be slow and flies are sometimes a problem. At the counter inside, you'll find homemade cocoa candies and unsweetened cocoa biscuits made by several women in town. They're definitely worth a try.

NEARBY PLACES TO DINE

As the beaches stretching south of Puerto Viejo keep getting more and more popular, there has been a corresponding increase in the number of places to grab a meal. In addition to the restaurant listed below, **Cabinas Selvyn** (Punta Uva) and **Elena Brown's Restaurant** (Playa Chiquita) are two very popular and dependable spots for local cuisine. If you make it as far south as Manzanillo, **Maxi's Restaurant** is your best bet. For fancier fare, check out the restaurant at **Shawandha** (see above). Only Shawandha has a phone.

El Duende Feliz. On the main road, Punta Uva. No phone. Reservations not required. Main courses $3.50–$10. No credit cards. Dec–Apr 8:30am–10pm; May–Nov Fri–Wed 8:30am–10pm. ITALIAN.

Isn't it reassuring to know that even in the middle of nowhere you can get a decent plate of pasta? El Duende Feliz is on the outskirts of Punta Uva Village and serves a wide selection of authentic Italian dishes. Seafood shows up quite a bit, of course. There are also steaks and plenty of pasta dishes, many featuring homemade pasta. The bread here is baked on premises daily. You can even finish off your meal with a scoop of gelato and an espresso. El Duende Feliz is also open for breakfast and lunch. If you're down on the beaches of Punta Uva, stop in around midday for a hearty sandwich served on the aforementioned fresh baked bread.

Appendix

A Basic Spanish Phrases & Vocabulary

English	Spanish	Pronunciation
Hello	**Buenos días**	*bway*-noss *dee*-ahss
How are you?	**Como está usted?**	*koh-moh* ess-*tah* oo-*stead?*
Very well	**Muy bien**	mwee byen
Thank you	**Gracias**	*gra*-see-ahss
Good-bye	**Adiós**	ad-*dyohss*
Please	**Por favór**	pohr fah-*vohr*
Yes	**Sí**	see
No	**No**	noh
Excuse me	**Perdóne me**	pehr-*doh*-neh-may
Give me	**Deme**	*day*-may
Where is . . . ?	**Donde está** . . . ?	*dohn*-day ess-*tah* . . . ?
the station	**la estación**	la ess-*tah*-syohn
the bus stop	**la parada**	la pah-*rah*-da
a hotel	**un hotel**	oon oh-*tel*
a restaurant	**un restaurante**	oon res-tow-*rahn*-tay
the toilet	**el servicio**	el ser-*vee*-see-o
To the right	**A la derecha**	ah lah day-*ray*-chuh
To the left	**A la izquierda**	ah lah is-*kyayr*-duh
Straight ahead	**Adelante**	ah-day-*lahn*-tay
I would like . . .	**Quiero** . . .	*kyehr*-oh . . .
to eat	**comer**	ko-*mayr*
a room	**una habitación**	oo-nah ah-bee-tah-*syohn*
How much is it?	**Cuánto?**	*Kwahn*-toh?
The check	**La cuenta**	la *kwen*-tah
When?	**Cuándo?**	*Kwan*-doh?
Yesterday	**Ayer**	ah-*yayr*
Today	**Hoy**	oy
Tomorrow	**Mañana**	mahn-*yah*-nah
Breakfast	**Desayuno**	deh-sai-*yoo*-noh
Lunch	**Comida**	co-*mee*-dah
Dinner	**Cena**	*say*-nah

Numbers

1	**uno** (*oo*-noh)	18	**dieciocho** (dyays-ee-*oh*-choh)
2	**dos** (dose)	19	**diecinueve** (dyays-ee-*nyway*-bay)
3	**tres** (trayss)	20	**veinte** (*bayn*-tay)
4	**cuatro** (*kwah*-troh)	30	**trienta** (*trayn*-tah)
5	**cinco**(*seen*-koh)	40	**cuarenta** (kwah-*ren*-tah)
6	**seis** (sayss)	50	**cincuenta** (seen-*kween*-tah)
7	**siete** (*syeh*-tay)	60	**sesenta** (say-*sen*-tah)
8	**ocho** (*oh*-choh)	70	**setenta** (say-*ten*-tah)
9	**nueve** (*nway*-bay)	80	**ochenta** (oh-*chen*-tah)
10	**diez** (dee-*ays*)	90	**noventa** (noh-*ben*-tah)
11	**once** (*ohn*-say)	100	**cien** (syen)
12	**doce** (*doh*-say)	1000	**mil** (mil)
13	**trece** (*tray*-say)		
14	**catorce** (kah-*tor*-say)		
15	**quince** (*keen*-say)		
16	**dieciséis** (dyays-ee-*sayss*)		
17	**diecisiete** (dyays-ee-*sye*-tay)		

B Some Typically Tico Words & Phrases

Chunche Knicknack; thing—as in "whatchamacallit."
Con mucho gusto With pleasure.
De hoy en ocho In one week's time.
Diay An untranslatable but common linguistic punctuation, often used to begin a sentence.
Guila A child.
Mae Translates a lot like "man"; used by teenagers as constant verbal punctuation.
Maje A lot like *mae* above, but with a slightly derogatory connotation.
Macha, or machita A blonde woman.
Ponga la maría, por favor This is how you ask taxi drivers to turn on the meter.
Pura vida Literally, "pure life"; translates as "everything's great."
Si Dios quiere God willing. You'll hear Ticos say this at nearly every opportunity.
Tuanis Means the same as *pura vida* above, but is used by a younger crowd.
Un rojo One thousand colónes.
Un tucan Five thousand colónes.
Un zarpe The last drink of the evening. A nightcap.
Una teja One hundred colónes.
Upe This is what Ticos shout to find out if anybody is home.

C Menu Terms

Soups

olla de carne clear broth with meat and vegetables
sopa de cebolla onion soup
sopa clara consommé
sopa de fideos noodle soup
sopa de lentejas lentil soup
sopa de mondongo tripe soup
sopa negra black bean soup
sopa de pescado fish soup
sopa de pollo chicken soup
sopa de tomate tomato soup
sopa de verduras vegetable soup

Fish

almejas clams
anchoas anchovies
atún tuna
bacalao cod
calamares squid
camarones shrimp
cangrejo crab
ceviche marinated seafood salad
corvina sea bass
dorado dolphin, or mahimahi
langosta lobster
langostinos prawns
lenguado sole
mejillones mussels
ostras oysters
pargo snapper
pulpo octopus
sardinas sardines
tiburon shark
trucha trout

Meats

albondigas meatballs
bistec beefsteak
cerdo pork
chicharrones fried pork rinds
chuleta cutlet
conejo rabbit
cordero lamb
costillas ribs
ganso goose
higado liver
jamón ham
lengua tongue
mondongo tripe
pato duck
pavo turkey
pollo chicken

Vegetables

aceitunas olives
alcachofa artichoke
arroz rice
berenjena eggplant
cebolla onion
coliflor cauliflower
elote corn on the cob
ensalada salad
esparragos asparagus
espinacas spinach
hongos mushrooms
palmito heart of palm
papa potato
pepino cucumber
remolacha beet
repollo cabbage
tomate tomato
vainica string beans
yuca yucca, or manioc
zanahoria carrot

Fruits

aguacate avocado
banano banana
carambola star fruit
cerezas cherries
ciruela plum
fresa strawberry
granadilla passion fruit
higo fig
limón lemon or lime
mango mango
manzana apple
maracuyá passion fruit
melocoton peach
melón cantelope
mora raspberry
naranja orange
pera pear
piña pineapple
plátano plantain
sandía watermelon
toronja grapefruit
uvas grapes

Desserts

flan caramel custard
fruta fruit
galletas cookies
helado ice cream
pasteles pastries
torta chilena layered sweet cake
tres leches moist sweet cake
queque seco pound cake

Beverages

agua water
agua mineral mineral water
birra slang for beer
café coffee
café con leche coffee with warm milk

cerveza beer
coca Coca-Cola
ginebra gin
guaro cane liquor
jerez sherry
jugo de naranja orange juice
jugo de tomate tomato juice
leche milk
naturales natural fruit drinks
refresco soft drink or natural fruit drink
soda club soda
té tea
vino blanco white wine
vo tinto red wine

Basics

aceite oil
ajo garlic
arreglado small meat sandwich
azucar sugar
bocas appetizers
casado plate of the day
frito fried
gallo corn tortilla topped with meat or chicken
gallo pinto rice and beans
hielo ice
mantequilla butter
miel honey
mostaza mustard
natilla sour cream
pan bread
patacones fried plantain chips
picadillo chopped vegetable side dish
pimienta pepper
queso cheese
sal salt
tamale filled corn meal pastry
tortilla flat corn pancake
vinagre vinegar

Index

Page numbers in italics refer to maps.

Accommodations, 49–51. *See also* Ecolodges and wilderness resorts
- best, 11–12
- family-friendly, 96
- price categories, 51

Active vacations (adventure tours), 4–5, 57–77. *See also* Ecolodges and wilderness resorts; Tours, organized; *and specific activities*
- adventure tours, 58–60
- health, safety & etiquette tips, 76
- near San José, 132, 134, 135
- volcano, 134–135

Addresses, locating, 48–49, 83
Adventure tours. *See* Active vacations
Aerial Tram, 134, 199
Aguas Calientes, 135
Aguila De Osa Inn (Drake Bay), 278
Air travel
- to Costa Rica, 43–44
- within Costa Rica, 46

Airlines, 43
Airport
- Pavas, 46, 82
- San José, 43, 79
  - accommodations near, 101–105

Alajuela, 40, 101–105, 137–138
Albergue de Montaña Tapantí, 272
Albergue Mirador de Quetzales, 7, 272
All Soul's Day, 41
American Express, 53, 86
Annexation of Guanacaste Day (Liberia), 40
Apartotels, 50, 90
Arenal Botanical Gardens, 212–213
Arenal Lake, 5, 10, 69, 196, 211–215
Arenal Lodge, 207
Arenal National Park, *70,* 72
Arenal Observatory Lodge, 9, 207–208
Arenal Vista Lodge, 208
Arenal Volcano, 2, 10, 19, 72, 196, 202–205, 205
Arias Sánchez, Oscar, 23, 26
Art galleries, San José, 124
Aserri, restaurants, 109
Asociación Talamanqueña de Ecoturismo y Conservacion (ATEC), 320, 322
Atlantida Lodge (Cahuita), 315
Atmosfera (San José), 11
ATMs, 35
Avenida Central (San José), 85
Aviarios del Caribe (Cahuita), 8, 61, 314, 315

Bajo del Tigre Trail, *217,* 219
Ballena Maritime National Park, 4, *70,* 262
Barra del Colorado, 300–303
Barra del Colorado National Wildlife Refuge, 198, 298
Barra Honda National Park, *70,* 72, 178
Barrio Amón (San José), 50, 83
- accommodations, 90–97

Barrio Otoya (San José), 83
Basilica de Nuestra Señora de Los Angeles (Cartago), 135
Beaches. *See also entries beginning with* "Playa"
- best, 3–4
- Corcovado National Park, 283
- riptides, 36
- Santa Rosa National Park, 149

Bebedero River, 143
Bed-and-breakfasts (B&Bs), 50
Beer, wine & liquor, 29
Bees, 36–37
Beverages, 28–29, 126
Biesanz, Barry, 123
Biking/mountain biking
- Arenal Lake, 5
- Manuel Antonio National Park, 250
- Playa de Jacó, 235
- Playa Flamingo and environs, 160
- Playa Tamarindo, 166
- San José, 121
- near San José, 132
- tour operators & outfitters, 60–61

Biological reserves. *See* National parks and biological reserves
Birds and bird watching, 19, 20. *See also* Quetzals
- Bajo del Tigre Trail, 219
- best, 7
- books on, 30
- Caño Negro, 72
- Dominical, 263
- Estrella Estuary, 314
- lodges, 61
- Monteverde cloud forest, 118, 219, 220
- Palo Verde National Park, 73, 75
- parks and preserves, 61–62
- Playa Nosara area, 182
- Santa Elena Cloud Forest Reserve, 219
- tour operators, 62

Blue Lake, 5, 144
Bolaños Bay, 69
Books, recommended, 29–30
Bookstores, San José, 86
Boruca, 41
Bosque del Cabo, 61
Bosque del Cabo Wilderness Lodge (Osa Peninsula), 286
Botanical gardens
- Casa Orchideas (near Golfito), 289–290
- Lankester Gardens (Paraíso de Cartago), 117
- Puerto Viejo, 320
- Wilson Botanical Gardens (near San Vito), 290

Braulio Carrillo National Park, 2, 9, *70,* 72
- Aerial Tram near, 134, 199

Bribri, 314, 319
Bribri Indians, 320, 322, 323
Bugs. *See* Insects
Bullfighting, 122
Bungee jumping, 62, 132
Bus travel, 44, 46
- in San José, 84
- to San José, 82

Business hours, 53
Butterflies, 30, 116–117, 220
Butterfly Farm, The (La Guácima de Alajuela), 117
Butterfly Garden (Monteverde), *217,* 220

Cabinas, 50
Cabo Blanco Absolute Nature Reserve, 190
Cabuya, 190
Café Britt, 123
- Farm (north of Heredia), 117

Cahuita, 72, 311–318
Cahuita National Park, 6–7, *70,* 72, 312, 313–314
Cameras/film, 53, 86

Camping, 62–63
  Playa de Jacó, 240
  Playa Potrero and Playa Brasilito, 164
  Santa Rosa National Park, 148
Cangrejo Falls, 5
Caño Island Biological Reserve, 277–278
Caño Negro National Wildlife Refuge, 7, 62, *70,* 72, 205
Canoeing
  Estrella Estuary, 314
  Tortuguero village area, 306
Canopy tours, 63–64, *217,* 220
Capuchin monkeys, 74
Carara Biological Reserve, 7, *70,* 227, 236
Caribbean coast, 20, *21,* 22, 39, 298–328
Carrera de San Juan, 40
Cars and driving
  best drives, 9–10
  documents and insurance, 45
  driving rules, 48
  emergency services, 48
  ferries, 48
  gasoline, 47
  maps, 47
  rentals, 46–47, 85–86
  road conditions, 47
  in San José, 85
  to San José, 82
Cartago, 10, 135
  special events, 40, 41
Casa Amarilla (San José), *119,* 120
Casa Corcovado Jungle Lodge (near Corcovado National Park), 278–279
Casa Orchideas (near Golfito), 289
Cash and currency. *See* Money
Caves
  Barra Honda National Park, 72, 178
  Venado Caverns, 204
Center for Agronomy Research and Development (CATIE), 139
Central Market (San José), 11
Central Valley, 20, *21*
Centro Nacional de Arte y Cultura (San José), *81,* 114, *119,* 120
Centro Panamericano de Idiomas (C. P. I.), 38, *217,* 221
Cerro de la Muerte, 7, 61, 271
Cerro de Tortuguero, 304
Charrarra, 136
Children's Museum (San José), 115
Chirripó National Park, 61, *70,* 73, 227, 268–270
Chirripó, Mount, 5, 9, 22, 73, 268–270
Cigars, Cuban, 52
Climate, 39
Cloud forests, 18
  Los Angeles, 61, 132
  Monteverde, 2, 6, 10, 18, 61–63, 216, 218–219
  Santa Elena, 218, 219
Coco Island, 65
Coco Island National Park, 73
Coffee, 29, 52, 78–79
  buying, 123
  farm (north of Heredia), 117
Columbus, Christopher, 24, 41, 308
Copa del Café (Coffee Cup) (San José), 40, 122
Coral reefs
  Cahuita National Park, 72, 312, 313
  Manzanillo-Gandoca Wildlife Refuge, 321
Corcovado Lodge Tent Camp, 286–287
Corcovado National Park, 6, 62, *70,* 73, 274, 276, 282–284
Corobici River, 8, 166
Corridas a la Tica, Las, 122
Coter Lake, 212
Courier services, 87
Crafts. *See* Handcrafts
Credit cards, 35
  lost or stolen, 54
Crime. *See* Safety
Crocodiles, 236
Cruises, 45, 64
  from Puntarenas, 230
  Tortuga Island, 132
Currency exchange, 86
Curú Wildlife Refuge, 186
Customs, 53

Dengue fever, 36
Dentists, 86–87
Departure tax, 55
Día de la Polvora, 41
Día de la Raza, 300
Día de los Muertos, 41
Día de San Ramon, 41
Día del Boyero (San Antonio de Escazú), 40
Diarrhea, 36
Dining customs, 27
Disabilities, travelers with, 43
Diving. *See* Scuba diving/snorkeling
Dominical, 10, 261–267
Dominicalito, 262
Drake Bay, 273–281
Drake Bay Wilderness Resort, 279
Driving. *See* Cars and driving
Drug laws, 53
Drugstores, 87
Earthquakes, 19
Ecolodges and wilderness resorts, 50, 57, 308
  Aguila De Osa Inn (Drake Bay), 278
  Albergue de Montaña Tapantí, 272
  Albergue Mirador de Quetzales (Cartago), 272
  Arenal Lodge, 207
  Arenal Observatory Lodge, 207–208
  Arenal Vista Lodge, 208
  Atlantida Lodge (Cahuita), 315
  Aviarios del Caribe (Cahuita), 315
  Aviarios de Caribe (near Cahuita), 314
  best, 13–14
  Bosque del Cabo Wilderness Lodge (Osa Peninsula), 286
  Casa Corcovado Jungle Lodge (near Corcovado National Park), 278–279
  Corcovado Lodge Tent Camp, 286–287
  Drake Bay Wilderness Resort, 279
  El Gavilán Lodge (near Puerto Viejo de Sarapiquí), 199–200
  El Tucano Resort and Spa (near San Carlos), 208–209
  Genesis II Cloudforest Preserve (near Cartago), 271
  Hotel La Garza (near Muelle), 209
  Hotel Villas Gaia (Playa Tortuga), 267
  La Paloma Lodge (Drake Bay), 279–280
  La Selva Biological Station (near Puerto Viejo de Sarapiquí), 200
  Laguna Lodge (Tortuguero), 307
  Lake Coter Eco-Lodge, 213–214
  Lapa Rios (Puerto Jiménez), 285–286
  Mawamba Lodge (Tortuguero) and, 307–308
  Montaña De Fuego Inn (near La Fortuna), 208
  Pachira Lodge (Tortuguero), 308
  Playa Chiquita Lodge (Puerto Viejo), 325
  Rainbow Adventures (Golfito), 292

Rara Avis (near Braulio Carrillo National Park), 200
Rio Chirripó Pacifico Mountain Lodge (San Gerardo de Rivas), 271
Rio Colorado Lodge (Barra del Colorado), 301–302
Río Sierpe Lodge, 280–281
Rock River Lodge (Tilarán), 214
Roy's Zancudo Lodge, 295
Samay Lagoon Lodge (Barra del Colorado), 302–303
Savegre Mountain Lodge, 272
Selva Bananito Lodge (near Limón), 311
Selva Verde Lodge (near Puerto Viejo de Sarapiquí), 201–202
Shawandha Lodge (Puerto Viejo), 325–326
Silver King Lodge (Barra del Colorado), 302
Star Mountain Eco Resort (Malpais), 195
Tabacón Hot Springs Resort, 2, 204
Tabacón Lodge, 207
Termales del Bosque (Ciudad Quesada), 210
Tierra de Milagros (Osa Peninsula), 287
Tilajari Hotel Resort (near Muelle), 209–210
Tilari Mountain Lodge (San Isidro), 271
Tiskita Jungle Lodge (Playa Pavones), 297
Tortuga Lodge (Tortuguero), 306–307
Valle Escondido Lodge (near La Fortuna), 210
Villablanca Hotel (near San Ramón), 211
Ecologically oriented volunteer & study programs, 76–77
Economy, 23–24
Ecotourism. *See* Active vacations; Ecolodges and wilderness resorts; Tours, organized
El Cangrejo Waterfall, 144
El Gavilán Lodge (south of Puerto Viejo de Sarapiquí), 199–200
El Manati Lodge (Tortuguero), 308
El Pueblo (San José), 128
El Tigre, 283
El Trapiche, 221
El Tucano Resort and Spa (near San Carlos), 208–209
Electricity, 53
Embassies/consulates, 53
Costa Rican, 32
Emergencies, 53, 87
road, 48
Entry into Costa Rica, requirements for, 32
Escazú (San José), 84
accommodations, 90, 100–101
restaurants, 112
Escuela Metálica (San José), *119,* 120
Etiquette, in the wilderness, 76
Express mail services, 87
Eyeglasses, 87

Families, 42
best vacations for, 8
Farm stay, 263
Faxes, 55, 56, 87
Ferries, 48
Festejos Populares (San José), 41
Festival Internacional de las Artes, El (San José), 127
Festival Nacional de las Artes, El (San José), 127
Fiesta de la Yeguita, 41
Fiesta de los Negritos, 41
Fiesta del Maiz (Upala), 41
Fiesta of Santa Cruz, 40
Fiesta of the Diablitos (Rey Curré), 40, 267
Fiesta of the Virgin of Los Angeles (Cartago), 41
Fiesta of the Virgin of the Sea (Puntarenas), 40
Fishing (sportfishing), 4, 160
Arenal Lake, 211, 212
Barra del Colorado, 300, 301
Golfito, 288, 289
lodges and tour operators, 65–66
Playa de Jacó, 235
Playa del Coco, 155
Playa Flamingo and environs, 160
Playa Nosara area, 182
Playa Tamarindo area, 167
Playa Zancudo, 295
near Puerto Jiménez, 284
Quepos, 250–251
Tortuguero area, 306
Food & drink, 27–29, 51, 52
street, 112–113
Four-wheeling, 5

Gasoline, 47
Gays and lesbians, 42, 130–131
Genesis II Cloudforest Preserve, 271–272
Gold Museum (San José), 115, 118, *119*
Golden toad, 219
Golf, 66, 121, 166
Golfito, 11, 288–293
Golfo Dulce, 5, 291–293
Grecia, 138
Guanacaste National Park, *70*
Guanacaste province, 5, 18, 20, *21,* 22, 39, 140–195
Guayabo, 10
Guayabo Island Biological Reserve, 62
Guayabo National Monument, *70,* 73, 134, 138
Gulf of Nicoya, 19, 48, 62, 114, 230
Gulfo Dulce Lodge (Golfito), 291–292

Hacienda Baru, 263
Hacienda Lodge Guachipelin (near Liberia), 146–147
Hammocks, 52
Handcrafts
San José, 124–126
Sarchí, 52, 138
Health concerns, in the wilderness, 76
Health information, 35–37
Health insurance, 37
Heredia, 101–105, 137
High season for tourism, 38–39
Hiking & nature walks
best, 5–7
Cerro de Tortuguero, 304
Corcovado National Park, 283–284
Dominical, 263
Mount Chirripó, 5, 268–269
Rincón De La Vieja National Park, 143–144
near San José, 132
History, 24–26
Hitchhiking, 48
Holidays, 39–40
Holy Week, 40
Horseback riding, 66–67
Arenal Lake area, 212
Arenal Volcano area, 204
Cahuita, 314
Dominical, 263
Manuel Antonio National Park, 250
Monteverde and environs, 220
outfitters & tour operators, 67
Playa Flamingo and environs, 160
Playa Montezuma, 4–5, 189–190
Playa Tamarindo, 166
near San José, 132
Hospitals, 87
Hostels, 42
Hot-air ballooning, 62
near San José, 132, 134

Hotel Club del Mar, 8
Hotel Hacienda La Pacifica, 8
Hotel La Garza (near Muelle), 209
Hotel Villas Gaia (Playa Tortuga), 267
Hotels. *See* Accommodations
Howler monkeys, 74
Hummingbird Gallery, *217*, 220

Iguana Park, 235
Iguanazul Hotel, 9
Independence Day, 41
Insects
  health concerns, 76
  Jewels of the Rain Forest Museum (Grecia), 118
  Museo de Entomología (San José), 116
Insurance, 37
Interamerican Highway, 45, 82
International Beach Clean-Up Day, 41
Intestinal diseases, 36
Irazú, 20
Irazú Volcano, 8–9, 9, 73, 134, 135–136
Irazú Volcano National Park, *70*, 73
Isla del Coco, 4. *See also* Coco Island National Park
Isla Tortuga. *See* Tortuga Island
Itineraries, 49

Jabiru storks, 7, 62, 205
Jade Museum (San José), *81*, 114–115, *119*, 120
Jaguars, 2, 73, 219, 276, 305
Jardin Gaia (Quepos), 250
Jesus Maria de San Mateo, 41
Jewelry, 52, 126
Jewels of the Rain Forest (Grecia), 117–118
Joyas del Tropico Humedo (Grecia), 117–118
Juan Santamaría Day (Alajuela), 40
Juan Santamaría International Airport, 43, 79
Jungla y Senderos Los Lagos, 205, 206

Kayaking and sea kayaking
  Golfito, 289
  Golfo Dulce, 5
  Manzanillo, 321
  Playa Tamarindo, 167
  near Puerto Jiménez, 284
  near San José, 134
  outfitters, 68–69
  Sarapiquí River, 198–199
KéköLdi Reserve, 29, 320, 323

La Casona (near La Cruz), 148
La Casona monument, 75
La Cruz, 148–150
La Fortuna, 6, 202, 203, 204, 205, 206, 207, 208, 209, 210
La Mariposa, 9
La Paloma Lodge (Drake Bay), 9, 61, 279–280
La Sabana Park (San José), 83, 121
  accommodations near, 97–99
  restaurants near, 109–111
La Selva Biological Station (near Puerto Viejo de Sarapiquí), 6, 7, 61, 200
La Virgen de Sarapiquí, 198
Lacsa, 43, 44, 46, 142
Laguna Lodge (Tortuguero), 307
Lake Coter Eco-Lodge, 213–214
Language. *See* Spanish language
Lankester Botanical Garden (Paraíso de Cartago), 5, 117
Lapa Rios (Puerto Jiménez), 61, 285–286
Las Baulas National Marine Park, 68, *70*
Las Cruces Biological Station, 62
Las Pailas Loop, 6, 143
Las Posadas, 41
Las Quebradas Biological Center, 268
Laundry, 54, 87
Leatherback turtles, 165
Leptospirosis, 36
Liberia, 10, 40, 142–147
Limón, 41, 298, 300, 308–311
  Carnival/Día de la Raza, 41, 298, 300, 309
Liquor laws, 54
Lodges. *See also* Ecolodges and wilderness resorts
  fishing, 65, 66
Los Angeles Cloud Forest Reserve, 61, 132
Los Patos, 283
Los Yoses (San José), 84
  accommodations, 99–100
  restaurants, 111–112
Lost documents, 32
Luggage storage/lockers, 87

Macaws, scarlet, 236
Malaria, 35–36
Malls, suburban, 123–124
Malpais, 194
Manatees, 75, 321
Mangoes, 113
Mangrove swamps, 18–19, 182, 186, 263, 274, 284
Manuel Antonio National Park, 2, 3–4, 22, *70*, 73, 227, 244–261
  accommodations, 251–258
  beaches, 244
  exploring, 249–250
  language school near, 251
  nightlife, 260–261
  outdoor activities and tours, 250
  restaurants, 258–260
  shopping near, 251
  traveling to, 245, 248
Manzanillo, 4, 321
Manzanillo-Gandoca Wildlife Refuge, 321
Maps, 54, 87
  road, 47
Markets, San José, 124
Mawamba Lodge (Tortuguero), 307–308
Meals, 27
Melico Salazar Theater (San José), 118, *119*
Mercado Central (San José), 118, *119*, 124
Moín, 304
Money, 33–35
  ATMs, 35
  exchanging, 34, 86
  wiring, 35, 55
Monkeys, 74
Montaña De Fuego Inn (near La Fortuna), 208
Monteverde, 8, 215–226
  accommodations, 221–226
  language school, 221
  restaurants, 226
  shopping, 221
  sights & activities, 219–221
  traveling to, 216, 218
Monteverde Biological Cloud Forest Preserve, 2, 6, 10, 18, 61–63, 216, 218–219
  canopy tour, 63
Monteverde Eco-Farm, 220
Montezuma, 188–194
Motorcycles, in San José, 85
Mountain biking. *See* Biking/mountain biking
Muelle, 209
Museo de Arte Costarricense (San José), *81*, 114
Museo de Entomología (San José), 116
Museo de Jade Marco Fidel Tristan (Jade Museum) (San José), *81*, 114–115, 120
Museo de Los Niños (San José), *81*, 115
Museo de Oro Banco Central (San José), *81*, 115
Museo Nacional de Ciencias Naturales "La Salle" (San José), 116
Museo Nacional de Costa Rica (San José), *81*, 115–116, *119*, 120
Music, San José, 127–128

Nahomi Lagoon, 251
National Arts Center (Centro Nacional de Arte y Cultura) (San José), 114, 120
National Cathedral (San José), 118, *119*
National Orchid Show (San José), 40
National parks and biological reserves, 69, *70–71,* 72–73, 75. *See also specific parks and bioreserves*
 Arenal National Park, *70,* 72
 Barra Honda National Park, *70,* 72, 178
 Braulio Carrillo National Park, 2, 9, *70,* 72
  Aerial Tram near, 134, 199
 Cahuita National Park, 6–7, *70,* 72, 312, 313–314
 Caño Island Biological Reserve, 277–278
 Carara Biological Reserve, 7, *70,* 227, 236
 Chirripó National Park, 61, *70,* 73, 227, 268–270
 Coco Island National Park, 73
 Corcovado National Park, 283–284
 Guayabo National Monument, *70,* 73, 134, 138
 information sources, 69
 Irazú Volcano National Park, *70,* 73
 Las Quebradas Biological Center, 268
 Manuel Antonio National Park. *See* Manuel Antonio National Park
 Monteverde Biological Cloud Forest Preserve. *See* Monteverde Biological Cloud Forest Preserve
 Palo Verde National Park, 62, *70,* 73, 75
 Poás Volcano National Park, *70,* 75
 Rincón de la Vieja National Park, 2, 5–6, 19, 62, *70,* 75, 142, 143–144
 Santa Rosa National Park, 3, *70,* 75, 148–149
 Tortuguero National Park, 11, 62, *70,* 75, 134, 198, 298, 303–308
National Symphony Orchestra, 127
National Theater Company, 127
Natural environment, 18–20
 books on, 30
Nauyaca Waterfalls, 263
Negritos biological reserve, 62
Newspapers/magazines, 54, 87
Nicoya, 41, 178, 182
Nicoya Peninsula, 20, *21,* 22, 140
Nicoya, Gulf of, 48, 62, 114, 230
Nightlife. *See also specific cities and towns*
 best, 16
Northern Zone, *21,* 22, 196–226

Ojo de Agua, 121
Orchid Garden, The (Monteverde), *217,* 221
Orchids, 40, 117, 221
Orosi Valley, 9, 136
Osa Peninsula, 2, 274, 276–277
 accommodations & dining around, 285–287
Ostional National Wildlife Refuge, 68
Our Lady of the Angels, Basilica of (Cartago), 135
Outfitters. *See* tour agencies, operators, and outfitters

Pachira Lodge (Tortuguero), 308
Pacific coast, 20, *21*
Package tours, 45. *See also* tours, organized
 golf, 66
Pacuare River, 4, 68
Pájaros biological reserve, 62
Palmar Sur, 274
Palo Verde National Park, 62, *70,* 73, 75
Pan American Highway. *See* Interamerican Highway
Páramos, 5, 18, 268, 269
Parque del Este (near San José), 121
Parque del Este (San José), 7
Parque La Sabana (San José), 83, 121
 accommodations near, 97–99
 restaurants near, 109–111
Parque Morazán (San José), *119,* 120
Parque Nacional (San José), *119,* 120
Parque Zoológico Simon Bolívar (San José), *81,* 116
Paseo Colón (San José), 83
 accommodations near, 97–99
 restaurants, 109–111
Passport requirements, 32
Peñas Blancas River, 205
Performing arts
 San José, 127
Photographic needs, 88
Playa Avellanas, 173
Playa Blanca, 149
Playa Bonita, 310
Playa Brasilito, 158, 159–164
Playa Cacao, 289
Playa Chiquita Lodge (Puerto Viejo), 325
Playa Conchal, 3, 158–159, 160, 161, 163
Playa de Jacó, 8, 22, 233–243
 accommodations in and near, 236–241
 beaches, 235
 nightlife, 242–243
 restaurants, 241–242
 traveling to, 234
Playa del Coco, 154–158
Playa Escondida, 235
Playa Esterillos, 235
Playa Flamingo, 158, 159, 160–164
Playa Grande, 164, 165, 166, 167, 168, 171
Playa Guiones, 182, 183
Playa Hermosa, 150, 235, 243, 262
Playa Hermosa (Guanacaste), 8
Playa Herradura, 235
Playa Junquillal, 174–177
Playa La Penca, 159, 160
Playa Matapalo, 261
Playa Montezuma, 3, 4–5, 188–194
Playa Nancite, 149
Playa Naranjo, 149
Playa Negra, 173, 174
Playa Negra (Cahuita), 314
Playa Negra (Puerto Viejo), 320
Playa Nosara, 181–184
Playa Ocotal, 154–157
Playa Ostional, 182
Playa Panamá, 150
Playa Pavones, 67, 296–297
Playa Pelada, 182
Playa Potrero, 159, 160, 162, 163, 164
Playa Sámara, 177–181
Playa Tamarindo, 3, 164–173
Playa Tambor, 184–187
Playa Zancudo, 293–296
Poás Volcano, 20, 75, 134, 136–137
Poás Volcano National Park, *70,* 75
Police, 54
 automobile accidents and, 48
Population, 22–23
Post office
 San José, 88
Pre-Columbian jewelry and artifacts, 114, 115, 116, 118, 120, 126
Pre-Columbian ruins, Guayabo National Monument, 134

Puerto Jiménez, 281–282, 283
accommodations, 284–285
restaurants, 287
Puerto Vargas, 313, 314
Puerto Viejo, 318–328
accommodations, 322–326
nightlife, 322
restaurants, 326–328
shopping, 321–322
sights & activities, 319–321
traveling to, 319
Puerto Viejo de Sarapiquí, 196–202
Punta Uva, 4, 321, 326, 328
Punta Uvita, 4
Puntarenas, 40, 227–233

Quepos, 244–245, 248. *See also* Manuel Antonio National Park
sights & activities, 250–251
Quetzals, 7, 61, 216, 219, 271

Radio and television, 88
Rafting. *See also* white-water rafting
Arenal Volcano area, 205
near Liberia, 143
Quepos area, 250
Rain forests, 18. *See also* National parks and biological reserves
Aerial Tram, 134, 199
canopy tours, 63–64, *217*, 220
safety, 76
Rainbow Adventures (Golfito), 61, 292
Rainfall, average monthly, 39
Rainmaker (Quepos), 250
Rainy season, 39
Rara Avis (near Braulio Carrillo National Park), 200
Regions of Costa Rica, 20, *21*, 22
Religion, 23
Religious holidays and festivals, 39–40
Religious services, San José, 88
Reserva Sendero Tranquilo, 219–220
Rest rooms, 54–55, 88
Restaurants, 51–52
Reventazon River
Upper, 4
Reventazón River, 134, 136
Rey Curré, 40
Rincón de la Vieja Mountain Lodge, 146
Rincón de la Vieja National Park, 2, 5–6, 19, 62, *70*, 75, 142, 143–144
Río Agujitas, 274
Rio Chirripó Pacifico Mountain Lodge (San Gerardo de Rivas), 271
Rio Colorado Lodge (Barra del Colorado), 301–302
Río Fortuna waterfall, 6, 204
Rio Sarapiquí Region, 2
Río Sierpe Lodge, 280–281
Rio Tempisque Basin, 7
Riptides, 36
River rafting. *See* rafting; white-water rafting
Road conditions, 47
Rock River Lodge (Tilarán), 214
Roy's Zancudo Lodge, 295

Safety, 45, 55
in San José, 88–89
in the wilderness, 76
Sailboat charters, 64, 155
Playa Tamarindo, 167
Salsa Brava, 67
Samay Lagoon Lodge (Barra del Colorado), 302
San Antonio de Belen, 41
San Antonio de Escazú, 40
San Isidro de El General, 267–272
San José, 8, 78–139
accommodations, 89–105
arriving in, 79, 82
bars, 129–130
gay & lesbian scene, 130
layout of, 82–83
movies, 131
neighborhoods, 83–84
nightlife, 16, 126–131
outdoor activities, 120–121
restaurants, 105–113
late-night, 113
shopping, 122–126
side trips from, 131–139
sights & attractions, 113–120
special events, 40, 41
spectator sports, 121–122
transportation, 84–86
visitor information, 82
walking tour, 118–120
San Pedrillo, 283
San Pedro (San José), 84, 111–112
accommodations, 99
hanging out in, 130
San Ramon, 41
Santa Ana (San José), 84
Santa Clara Lodge (Guanacaste), 146
Santa Cruz, 40
Santa Elena, 216, 218
Santa Elena Cloud Forest Reserve, 218, 219
Santa Rosa National Park, 3, *70*, 75, 148–149
Santa Teresa, 194
Santo Cristo Waterfalls, 263
Sarapiquí region, 196–202
Sarapiquí River, 134, 198, 205
Sarchí, 11, 52, 138
Savegre Mountain Lodge, 61, 272
Scarlet macaws, 236
Scuba diving/snorkeling, 4, 64–65
Caño Island, 277–278
Isla del Coco, 4
Manzanillo, 321
outfitters & operators, 65
Playa del Coco, 155
Playa Flamingo and environs, 160
Playa Hermosa/Playa Panamá, 151
Playa Junquillal, 175
Playa Tamarindo, 167
Sea kayaking. *See* Kayaking and sea kayaking
Sea turtles, 67–68, 75
leatherback, 165
Manzanillo-Gandoca Wildlife Refuge, 321
Playa Grande, 167–168
Playa Ostional, 182
Tortuguero National Park, 303, 304–305
Selva Bananito Lodge (near Limón), 311
Selva Verde Lodge (west of Puerto Viejo de Sarapiquí), 201–202
Seniors, 41–42
Serpentarium (San José), *81*, 116, *119*, 120
Shawandha Lodge (Puerto Viejo), 325–326
Shopping, 52
best, 11
San José, 122–126
Sierpe, 274, 276, 278
Silver King Lodge (Barra del Colorado), 302
Single travelers, 42
Sirena, 283, 284
Skywalk, 220
Snakes, 36–37, 116, 221
Snakes and snakebites, 76
Snorkeling. *See* scuba diving/snorkeling
Sodas (diners), 27, 51
South Pacific Coast, *21*, 22
Southern Zone, 273–297
Spanish language, 54
classes and schools, 37–38
near Manuel Antonio National Park, 251
Monteverde, 221
Nosara, 183
San Isidro, 268
menu terms, 330–332
phrases & vocabulary, 329–332

Special events and festivals, 40–41
 San José, 127
Spheres, stone, 277
Spider monkeys, 74
Sportfishing. *See* fishing
Spyrogyra Butterfly Garden (San José), *81,* 116–117
Squirrel monkeys, 73, 74
Storks, Jabiru, 7, 62, 205
Student travelers, 42
Study programs
 ecologically oriented, 76
 Spanish language. *See* Spanish language
Sugar Beach, 159, 160, 162
Suraska (San José), *119,* 120
Surfing, 5, 67
 Pavones, 5
 Playa Pavones, 296
 Playa Tamarindo, 167
Swimming
 Coter Lake, 212
 San José, 121

Tabacón Hot Springs Resort, 2, 204
Tabacón Lodge, 207
Talamanca region, 14, 29, 314, 320, 322
Tapantí National Wildlife Refuge, 61, *70*
Taxes, 55
 departure, 55
 room, 50
Taxis, 55
 in San José, 84
Teatro Nacional, 16
Teatro Nacional (San José), 118, *119,* 127
Telegrams, 55
Telephone country code, 86
Telephone numbers, useful, 56
Telephones, 55–56
 international calls, 89
 in San José, 89
Television, 88
Temperatures, average daytime, 39
Tennis, 121
Terciopelo Cave, 72
Terciopelo Waterfalls, 263
Termales del Bosque (Ciudad Quesada), 210
Terraba River, 277
Theater
 San José, 127
Tierra de Milagros (Osa Peninsula), 287
Tilajari Hotel Resort (near Muelle), 7, 209–210
Tilarán, 211–215
Tilari Mountain Lodge (San Isidro), 271
Tipping, 56
Tiskita Jungle Lodge (Playa Pavones), 297
Toad, golden, 219
Tobías Bolaños International Airport, 79, 82
Tobís Bolaños International Airport, 46, 79, 82
Tortuga Island, 132, 190, 230
Tortuga Lodge (Tortuguero), 306–307
Tortuguero National Park, 11, 62, *70,* 75, 134, 198, 298, 303–308
Tortuguero Village, 3, 304, 306
 canals near, 3, 75, 301, 303–307
Tours, organized. *See also* Active vacations (adventure tours); Cruises; Travel agents and agencies
 biking, 60–61
 bird watching, 62
 Cahuita, 314
 camping, 63
 canopy, 63–64, 220
 Costa Rican, 59–60
 day, from San José, 131–132
 diving/snorkeling, 65
 fishing, 65–66
 Guanacaste, 143
 horseback riding, 67
 Manuel Antonio National Park, 250
 package, 45
 Playa de Jacó area, 236
 from Puerto Viejo, 320–321
 San José, 113
 Sarapiquí region, 199
 surfing, 67
 Tortuguero National Park, 305–306
 U.S.-based, 58–59
 white-water rafting & kayaking, 68–69
Travel agents and agencies. *See also* tour agencies, operators, and outfitters
 handicapped-accessible travel, 43
 passport or visa problems and, 32
 student, 42
Travel insurance, 37
Traveler's checks, 34
Traveling to Costa Rica, 43–45
Tropical diseases, 35
Turrialba, 138–139
Turtles, sea. *See* Sea turtles

Upala, 41
Uvita, 262

Vaccinations, 35
Valle Escondido Lodge (near La Fortuna), 210
Venado Caverns, 204–205
Villa Blanca, 61
Villa Caletas, 9
Villablanca Hotel (near San Ramón), 210–211
Visitor information, 31–32
 San José, 82
Volcanoes and volcanic activity, 19. *See also specific volcanoes*
 Rincón de la Vieja National Park, 75
 tours, 134–135
Volunteer programs, ecologically oriented, 76–77
Vuelta de Costa Rica, 121

Walking tour, San José, 118–120
Walking, in San José, 84–85
Water, drinking, 29, 56, 89
Weather, in San José, 89
Web sites, 31–32
Western Union, 35, 55, 235
White-water rafting
 Arenal Volcano area, 205
 outfitters, 68–69
 near San José, 134
 Sarapiquí River, 198, 205
 Upper Reventazon River, 4
Wildlife, 19–20. *See also* Bird watching; National parks and biological reserves; Wildlife refuges; Zoo; *and specific animals*
 books on, 30
 health and safety tips, 76
 laws against trading in, 122
 Osa Peninsula, 276–277
Wildlife refuges
 Barra del Colorado, 198, 298
 Caño Negro National Wildlife Refuge, 7, 62, *70,* 72, 205
 Curú Wildlife Refuge, 186
 Manzanillo-Gandoca Wildlife Refuge, 321
Wildlife rescue center, Quepos, 250
Wilson Botanical Gardens (near San Vito), 62, 290
Windsurfing, 69
 Arenal Lake, 212
 Lake Arenal, 5
Wiring money, 55

Yoga retreat, Nosara, 183
Youth hostels, 42–43

Zarcero, 138
Zoo
 Alajuela, 118
 San José, 116
Zoo Ave. La Garita (Alajuela), 118

FROMMER'S® COMPLETE TRAVEL GUIDES

(Comprehensive guides with selections in all price ranges—from deluxe to budget)

Alaska
Amsterdam
Arizona
Atlanta
Australia
Austria
Bahamas
Barcelona, Madrid & Seville
Belgium, Holland & Luxembourg
Bermuda
Boston
Budapest & the Best of Hungary
California
Canada
Cancún, Cozumel & the Yucatán
Cape Cod, Nantucket & Martha's Vineyard
Caribbean
Caribbean Cruises & Ports of Call
Caribbean Ports of Call
Carolinas & Georgia
Chicago
China
Colorado
Costa Rica
Denver, Boulder & Colorado Springs
England
Europe
Florida
France
Germany
Greece
Hawaii
Hong Kong
Honolulu, Waikiki & Oahu
Ireland
Israel
Italy
Jamaica & Barbados
Japan
Las Vegas
London
Los Angeles
Maryland & Delaware
Maui
Mexico
Miami & the Keys
Montana & Wyoming
Montréal & Québec City
Munich & the Bavarian Alps
Nashville & Memphis
Nepal
New England
New Mexico
New Orleans
New York City
Nova Scotia, New Brunswick & Prince Edward Island
Oregon
Paris
Philadelphia & the Amish Country
Portugal
Prague & the Best of the Czech Republic
Provence & the Riviera
Puerto Rico
Rome
San Antonio & Austin
San Diego
San Francisco
Santa Fe, Taos & Albuquerque
Scandinavia
Scotland
Seattle & Portland
Singapore & Malaysia
South Pacific
Spain
Switzerland
Thailand
Tokyo
Toronto
Tuscany & Umbria
USA
Utah
Vancouver & Victoria
Vermont, New Hampshire & Maine
Vienna & the Danube Valley
Virgin Islands
Virginia
Walt Disney World & Orlando
Washington, D.C.
Washington State

FROMMER'S® DOLLAR-A-DAY GUIDES

(The ultimate guides to comfortable low-cost travel)

Australia from $50 a Day
California from $60 a Day
Caribbean from $60 a Day
England from $60 a Day
Europe from $50 a Day
Florida from $60 a Day
Greece from $50 a Day
Hawaii from $60 a Day
Ireland from $50 a Day
Israel from $45 a Day
Italy from $50 a Day
London from $70 a Day
New York from $75 a Day
New Zealand from $50 a Day
Paris from $70 a Day
San Francisco from $60 a Day
Washington, D.C., from $60 a Day

FROMMER'S® MEMORABLE WALKS

Chicago
London
New York
Paris
San Francisco

FROMMER'S® PORTABLE GUIDES

Acapulco, Ixtapa/Zihuatenejo
Bahamas
California Wine Country
Charleston & Savannah
Chicago
Dublin
Las Vegas
London
Maine Coast
New Orleans
New York City
Paris
Puerto Vallarta, Manzanillo & Guadalajara
San Francisco
Sydney
Tampa Bay & St. Petersburg
Venice
Washington, D.C.

FROMMER'S® NATIONAL PARK GUIDES

Grand Canyon
National Parks of the American West
Yellowstone & Grand Teton
Yosemite & Sequoia/Kings Canyon
Zion & Bryce Canyon

THE COMPLETE IDIOT'S TRAVEL GUIDES

(The ultimate user-friendly trip planners)

Cruise Vacations
Planning Your Trip to Europe
Hawaii
Las Vegas
Mexico's Beach Resorts
New Orleans
New York City
San Francisco
Walt Disney World

SPECIAL-INTEREST TITLES

The Civil War Trust's Official Guide to the Civil War Discovery Trail
Frommer's Caribbean Hideaways
Israel Past & Present
New York City with Kids
New York Times Weekends
Outside Magazine's Adventure Guide to New England
Outside Magazine's Adventure Guide to Northern California
Outside Magazine's Adventure Guide to the Pacific Northwest
Outside Magazine's Guide to Family Vacations
Places Rated Almanac
Retirement Places Rated
Washington, D.C., with Kids
Wonderful Weekends from Boston
Wonderful Weekends from New York City
Wonderful Weekends from San Francisco
Wonderful Weekends from Los Angeles

THE UNOFFICIAL GUIDES®

(Get the unbiased truth from these candid, value-conscious guides)

Atlanta
Branson, Missouri
Chicago
Cruises
Disneyland
Florida with Kids
The Great Smoky & Blue Ridge Mountains
Las Vegas
Miami & the Keys
Mini-Mickey
New Orleans
New York City
San Francisco
Skiing in the West
Walt Disney World
Walt Disney World Companion
Washington, D.C.

FROMMER'S® IRREVERENT GUIDES

(Wickedly honest guides for sophisticated travelers)

Amsterdam
Boston
Chicago
London
Manhattan
New Orleans
Paris
San Francisco
Walt Disney World
Washington, D.C.

FROMMER'S® DRIVING TOURS

America
Britain
California
Florida
France
Germany
Ireland
Italy
New England
Scotland
Spain
Western Europe